mylabschool™
Where the classroom comes to life!

From watching actual classroom video footage of teachers and students interacting to building standards-based lessons and web-based portfolios . . . from a robust resource library of the "What Every Teacher Should Know About" series to complete instruction on writing an effective research paper . . . **MyLabSchool** brings together an amazing collection of resources for future teachers. This website gives you a wealth of videos, print and simulated cases, career advice, and much more.

Use **MyLabSchool** with this Allyn and Bacon Education text, and you will have everything you need to succeed in your course. Assignment IDs have also been incorporated into many Allyn and Bacon Education texts to link to the online material in **MyLabSchool** . . . connecting the teachers of tomorrow to the information they need today.

VISIT www.mylabschool.com to learn more about this invaluable resource and Take a Tour!

Here's what you'll find in mylabschool™
Where the classroom comes to life!

VideoLab ▶

Access hundreds of video clips of actual classroom situations from a variety of grade levels and school settings. These 3- to 5-minute closed-captioned video clips illustrate real teacher–student interaction, and are organized both topically *and* by discipline. Students can test their knowledge of classroom concepts with integrated observation questions.

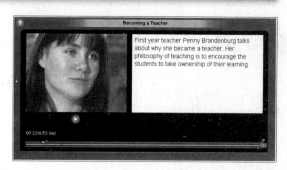

Becoming a Teacher

First year teacher Penny Brandenburg talks about why she became a teacher. Her philosophy of teaching is to encourage the students to take ownership of their learning.

00:22/4:53 sec

◀ Lesson & Portfolio Builder

This feature enables students to create, maintain, update, and share online portfolios and standards-based lesson plans. The Lesson Planner walks students, step-by-step, through the process of creating a complete lesson plan, including verifiable objectives, assessments, and related state standards. Upon completion, the lesson plan can b[...]
to a v[...]

Lesson & Portfolio Builder

New Lesson Plan | New Portfolio | Copy Open Print Delete

Type ▾	Name	modified ▾
	New Lesson Plan	11/20/06
	social studies	
	MCC	
	UNM Lesson	
	The legend	
	reading	
	New Lesson	
	The Cat in th	
	Counting	

Lesson & Portfolio Builder

New Lesson Plan (Basic Info)

- Basic Info
- Objective
- Academic Standards
- Rationale Statement
- Materials and Resources
- Procedures
- Assessment
- Style and Export
- Export Instructions

Lesson Title: What do you call this lesson?
New Lesson Plan

Area of study: What is the subject area? (e.g. Social Studies, English, Math)

Teacher Name: Enter your professional name here

Grade Level: For what grade levels is this lesson plan designed (e.g. 6th)

Duration of Instruction: How long will it take to conduct this lesson?

D1364211

Here's what you'll find in (mylabschool™)

Simulations ▶

This area of MyLabSchool contains interactive tools designed to better prepare future teachers to provide an appropriate education to students with special needs. To achieve this goal, the IRIS (IDEA and Research for Inclusive Settings) Center at Vanderbilt University has created course enhancement materials. These resources include online interactive modules, case study units, information briefs, student activities, an online dictionary, and a searchable directory of disability-related web sites.

◀ Resource Library

MyLabSchool includes a collection of PDF files on crucial and timely topics within education. Each topic is applicable to any education class, and these documents are ideal resources to prepare students for the challenges they will face in the classroom. This resource can be used to reinforce a central topic of the course, or to enhance coverage of a topic you need to explore in more depth.

Research Navigator ▶

This comprehensive research tool gives users access to four exclusive databases of authoritative and reliable source material. It offers a comprehensive, step-by-step walk-through of the research process. In addition, students can view sample research papers and consult guidelines on how to prepare endnotes and bibliographies. The latest release also features a new bibliography-maker program—AutoCite.

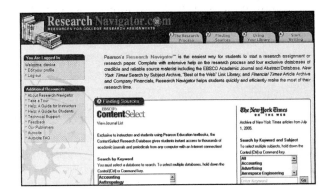

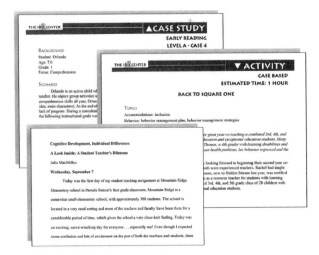

◀ Case Archive

This collection of print and simulated cases can be easily accessed by topic and subject area, and can be integrated into your course. The cases are drawn from Allyn & Bacon's best-selling books, and represent the complete range of disciplines and student ages. It's an ideal way to consider and react to real classroom scenarios. The possibilities for using these high-quality cases within the course are endless.

Literacy's Beginnings

Supporting Young Readers and Writers

FIFTH EDITION

LEA M. MCGEE
The Ohio State University

DONALD J. RICHGELS
Northern Illinois University

Boston   New York   San Francisco
Mexico City   Montreal   Toronto   London   Madrid   Munich   Paris
Hong Kong   Singapore   Tokyo   Cape Town   Sydney

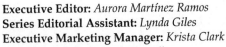

Executive Editor: *Aurora Martínez Ramos*
Series Editorial Assistant: *Lynda Giles*
Executive Marketing Manager: *Krista Clark*
Production Editor: *Paula Carroll*
Editorial Production Service: *Publishers' Design and Production Services, Inc.*
Composition Buyer: *Linda Cox*
Manufacturing Buyer: *Linda Morris*
Electronic Composition: *Publishers' Design and Production Services, Inc.*
Interior Design: *Mark Bergeron*
Cover Administrator: *Linda Knowles*
Cover Designer:

For related titles and support materials, visit our online catalog at www.ablongman.com.

Between the time website information is gathered and then published, it is not unusual for some sites to have closed. Also, the transcription of URLs can result in typographical errors. The publisher would appreciate notification where these errors occur so that they may be corrected in subsequent editions.

Library of Congress Cataloging-in-Publication Data

McGee, Lea M.
    Literacy's beginnings : supporting young readers and writers / Lea M. McGee, Donald J. Richgels. — 5th ed.
        p. cm.
    Includes bibliographical references and index.
    ISBN 0-205-53336-1
1. Reading (Early childhood)—United States. 2. Language arts (Early childhood)—United States. 3. Literacy—United States. I. Richgels, Donald J. II. Title.
    LB1139.5.R43M33 2007
    372.60973—dc22
                                                                        2007060012

Printed in the United States of America

10 9 8 7 6 5 4 3 2 1 RRD-VA 11 10 09 08 07

Contents

CHAPTER 4 From Five to Seven Years: Experimenting Readers and Writers   87

CHAPTER 5 From Six to Eight Years: Conventional Readers and Writers in Early, Transitional, and Self-Generative Phases   118

PART 2 CLASSROOMS

CHAPTER *8* Supporting Literacy Learning in Kindergarten   212

CHAPTER 9 Supporting Literacy Learning in First Grade   245

CHAPTER 10 Supporting Literacy Learning in Second through Fourth Grades   281

CHAPTER 12 Putting It All Together: Using Assessment to Guide Instruction   344

APPENDIX **A** Children's Literature   **367**

APPENDIX **B** Preschool and Kindergarten Monitoring Assessments   **372**

APPENDIX **C** Preschool and Kindergarten Monitoring Assessments: Advanced Assessments   **379**

Preface

POINT OF VIEW

Literacy's Beginnings: Supporting Young Readers and Writers is intended to help preservice and inservice teachers and other caregivers of young children to be aware of and supportive of children's literacy knowledge as it grows and changes from birth through nine years of age. Our purpose is to provide readers with a thorough understanding of the long continuum of literacy growth and of how sensitive teachers can guide children as they move along this continuum. We wish to show teachers how to be watchful of children, yet provide learning opportunities and instruction that meet children where they are and take them to the next steps. All instruction that helps children learn to do something new in a joyful way is developmentally appropriate. Teachers who are effective know when to step in and provide more support—even explicit instruction—and when to step back and let children gain independence in accomplishing a task.

We believe that literacy learning is developmental, but not in the sense of proceeding in an irreversible, step-by-step progression. No child's path to conventional reading and writing is exactly the same as another child's. However, literacy learning is developmental in a way that is very commonsensical to anyone who has spent time with children. What a child knows about reading and writing changes dramatically over time.

We also believe that teachers have a critical role to play in young children's literacy learning. Failure to learn to read and write has long-term academic, social, and emotional effects on the lives of children, their families, and society. Teachers make the difference in whether some children, especially children most vulnerable in our society, learn to become effective and motivated readers and writers. We believe that the descriptions of literacy events and instructional practices we describe in this book will help teachers be more careful observers of children so they will be more aware of what children are capable of learning. We hope our instructional suggestions help teachers deliver instruction that has a powerful impact on the learning of their children.

ORGANIZATION OF THE TEXT

Literacy's Beginnings is grouped in two parts. The theme of Part One (Chapters 1 through 5) is *learners*. The first five chapters in the book describe children and how they change as readers and writers. Each of these chapters ends with suggestions for assessing children so that readers of the book can more carefully observe children.

The word *literacy* has many connotations in everyday life. To us, being *literate* means being able to find meaning in written symbols. This definition includes much territory left out by everyday definitions of literacy; for example, a pretend reading of a favorite storybook qualifies as a literate act by our definition, but it does not usually qualify under the everyday definition. Still, our definition does not include everything that very young children do with books and writing materials.

The terms *beginner, novice, experimenter,* and *conventional (early, transitional,* and *self-generating) reader and writer* also demand clarification. We use them as convenient shorthand for the developments described in Chapters 2 through 5, but we do not mean for them to define rigid, irreversible stages. Indeed, we do not call them stages. A child may exhibit many of the knowledges in the cluster of knowledges that we associate with one of those four terms. Furthermore, a child who usually reads or writes like a novice in some situations and with some tasks will also read or write like an experimenter in other situations and with other tasks. The important point is that, over time, children will more often resemble conventional readers and writers.

Part Two of *Literacy's Beginnings* concerns *classrooms* and characteristics of school environments and teacher roles that promote children's development from beginners to conventional readers and writers. Chapter 6 is an overview of the elements included in a literacy-rich classroom. Chapter 7 focuses on preschool, Chapter 8 on kindergarten, Chapter 9 on first grade, and Chapter 10 on second, third, and fourth grades. Chapter 11 describes the literacy needs of diverse learners, and Chapter 12 addresses assessment issues and methods.

The fifth edition of *Literacy's Beginnings* has several **new features**. This edition:

- Describes embedded instruction; compares it to explicit, systematic instruction; and explains how each type of instruction is valuable in children's literacy learning.
- Describes effective instruction in phonemic awareness, phonics, fluency, vocabulary, and comprehension, all of which the National Reading Panel identifies as essential to maintaining literacy instruction standards. Describes effective instruction in alphabet recognition, concepts about print, the alphabetic principle, and phonemic awareness for preschool and kindergarten children as essential to maintaining early literacy standards.
- Provides assessments that allow teachers to determine the level of knowledge young children have in alphabet recognition, phonemic awareness, phonics, and text reading. The assessments provide valuable information about children's vocabulary and comprehension development, their use of decoding strategies and spelling strategies, and their understanding of letter-sound relationships.
- Offers new and research-based information about the importance of guided reading instruction using either basal materials or children's books. Using these ap-

proaches, teachers learn how to provide explicit instruction in the five key areas of reading identified by the National Reading Panel and how to put them to work in an integrated reading and writing program.

- Includes a discussion of English language learners in every chapter. Some chapters describe their unique literacy development, some chapters provide suggestions for assessment, and some chapters discuss modifying instruction to meet their needs. This information is further supplemented with an updated chapter on diverse learners.
- Describes how to modify instruction to meet the needs of struggling readers and writers by suggesting new research-based methods of teaching these learners.
- Details a view of new literacies which takes advantage of today's multimodal methods of communication.
- Provides updated case studies at the end of the chapters that allow students to apply the text information in real-life situations
- Provides additional practice activities at the end of the chapters that allow students to apply the text information in practice formats useful for acquiring a deeper understanding of the material.
- Includes a glossary of key terms.

Each chapter of *Literacy's Beginnings* again has four sections designed to help readers consolidate and apply what they have learned. First, we list the **Key Concepts** used in the chapter. **Applying the Information** presents a case study on children's interactions with written language similar to the many examples given in the chapter. The reader is asked to apply the chapter's concepts to this example. **Going Beyond the Text** suggests ways for readers to seek out real-life experiences that will test both the chapter's ideas and the readers' understandings. We ask questions and make suggestions to guide readers' planning and reflecting on those experiences. Finally, **References** provides a list of all publications cited in the chapter.

 # The Children and Teachers in This Book

*L*iteracy's Beginnings* is based in part on a growing body of research about emerging literacy and in part on our experiences with young children, including our own children. We incorporate many descriptions of those experiences. We wish to add here two important cautions that we will repeat throughout the text. The first is about children's ages. We usually give the age of the children in our examples in order to fully represent the facts. However, we do not intend for those ages to serve as norms against which to compare other children.

Our second caution is about backgrounds. Many, but not all, of the children in our examples have had numerous and varied home experiences with books and writing materials. Their meaningful interactions with written language are often what one would expect of children from such environments. Children with different backgrounds may exhibit different initial orientations toward written language. However, our involvement with teachers whose children come to preschool or elementary school with different backgrounds has shown us that nearly all children can benefit from the informed observation and child-centered, meaning-oriented support described in this book.

The classroom support chapters of this book are based on our own teaching experiences and on our observations of teachers. Just as we have known and observed many literate young children, so also have we known and observed many very sensitive, intelligent, and effective teachers of young children. All the samples of children's reading and writing in this book are authentic cases from our own teaching and research and the research of others cited in the text.

ACKNOWLEDGMENTS

WE OWE A GREAT DEAL to the many children whose experiences with written language were the basis for much of this book. We thank them and their parents for cooperating so generously with us—for supporting *us* in the extended "literacy event" of writing this book. We thank the teachers who shared their classroom experiences with us: Mary Jane Everett, Candice Jones, Karen Kurr, Roberta McHardy, Nancy Miller, Terry Morel, Kathy Walker, Leigh Courtney, Karen King, Jackie Zickuhr, Carolyn Vaughn, Monette Reyes, Karla Poremba, Diane Roloff, Cindi Chandler, Laurie Coleman, Richard Lomax, Michelle Tran, Michelle Bellamy, Margaret Medders, Linda Rodgers, Kay Armstrong, Litta Norris, Tomasine Lewis, Jade Turk, Ede Wortham, Anna Carlin, Joseph Warren, Andrea Schlomer, Carolyn Palmer, Jan Leopard, and Juliet Prowell.

We owe much to the editors and their assistants at Allyn and Bacon, including Aurora Martínez Ramos, Lynda Giles, and Paula Carroll. We are also grateful to Holly Crawford and Gail Farrar for their careful handling of the manuscript during editing and production. We thank reviewers Lisa Boeglin of Cape Evansville; Sheila G. Cohen, SUNY Cortland; Teunis (Tony) Donk, Hope College; Ann Porter Gifford, Southeast Missouri State University; Margaret Hagod, College of Charleston; and Melissa Stinnett, University of Wisconsin, Oshkosh for helpful comments and suggestions.

We acknowledge the contributions of our many students. We learned from our discussions with them about literacy's beginnings and from the examples they shared of their interactions with young readers and writers.

CHAPTER

1

Understanding Children's Literacy Development

KEY CONCEPTS

Schema
Feature
Thinking
Learning
Tabula Rasa
Zone of Proximal
    Development
Scaffolding
Pragmatics
Semantics
Syntax
Phonology
Morpheme
Telegraphic Speech
Phonemes

Phonological
    Awareness
Phonemic Awareness
Functions of Written
    Language
Written Language
    Meanings
Contextualization Cues
Literary Language
Written Language Forms
Letter Features
Mock Letters
Metalinguistic
    Awareness
Meaning-Form Links

Sound-Letter
    Relationships
Alphabetic Principle
Orthography
Phonograms
Rhyming Words
Beginners
Novices
Experimenters
Conventional Readers
    and Writers
Conventions of Written
    Language
Written Language
    Assessment

LANGUAGE, THINKING, AND LEARNING

OW DO CHILDREN BEGIN THE PROCESS of becoming successful lifelong readers and writers? We begin to answer that question by looking at theories of language development. Piaget (1955) and Vygotsky (1978) examined how children acquire language and the relationship of language to thinking. Both of their theories make unique contributions to what we understand about young children's literacy development.

Schemas and Learning

An important idea from both Piaget's and Vygotsky's theories is that learning occurs as children acquire new concepts, or **schemas.** A concept or schema is a mental structure in which we store all the information we know about people, places, objects, or activities.

Schemas. We will use the concept *football* as an example to explain the nature of schemas. If asked to tell everything that comes to mind when they hear the word *football,* many people in the United States will think of the game that is played with a two-pointed, nonspherical ball by two teams on a 100-yard field, with the object of accumulating points by moving the ball into the other team's end zone or kicking it through the goalposts in that end zone. All schemas, such as the schema for football, are collections of information called **features**. Because football is a game, its features include *whos, whats, hows,* and *whys,* in this case, who the players are (quarterback, tight end, halfback, tackle, etc.), what equipment they use (ball, goalpost, shoulder pad, helmet, etc.), how they perform actions and plays (pass, tackle, touchdown, field goal, etc.), and why they do so (to score touchdowns, field goals, extra point conversions, and touchbacks and to prevent the other team from scoring). If enough features are listed, the concept is adequately defined; that is, those features characterize that concept or schema and no other.

All concepts are related to other concepts. Whether they hear the word *football* or the phrase *a football,* many people in the United States will think of such related concepts as autumn, high school, college, professional, Friday night, Saturday afternoon, Sunday afternoon, Monday night, cheerleaders, mascots, marching bands, Green Bay Packers, Brett Favre, other teams, other famous players, pep rally bonfires, stadium parking lot picnics, Superbowl, Superbowl parties, television advertizing during the Superbowl, and so on.

Any concept or schema, its related concepts or schemas, and their features arise from experience, including the experience of growing up in a certain context, including within a certain culture. People in the United States often share the earlier mentioned football concepts because football as played in high school, college, and the National Football League (NFL) is a pervasive part of U.S. culture. Football in other cultures means different things; it may be played with a different-sized field, as in Canadian football; or be a different ball and a different game altogether, as in England and much of the rest of the world where football is known as soccer.

However, concept or schema formation is also influenced by our unique personal experiences. For example, individuals will have some football-related concepts not shared by all other football fans because of their personal football experiences. When they hear the word *football*, they might think of or feel pride (having scored the winning touchdown in an important game), a letter jacket (having earned a high school or college letter playing football), frostbite (having attended a football game in below-zero weather in Green Bay in January), or a hangover (having celebrated too many football victories).

We have schemas for many things, including objects such as a *computer* or *fire truck*; people, such as a *teacher* or *rock star*; places such as *home* or *restaurant*; and activities, such as *making a sandwich* or *writing a persuasive essay*. Thinking and learning depend on these many schemas and concepts. **Thinking** involves calling to mind information from schemas and using that information to perform mental actions such as making inferences, predictions, or generalizations, or drawing conclusions. Suppose, for example, that in early August we see someone at an empty high school football field kicking footballs over and over again from different distances, toward a goalpost, sometimes putting the ball through the uprights, sometimes not. We might make the inference that this person is practicing for tryouts to be that high school team's field goal kicker.

Similarly, **learning** involves adding to or changing schemas. Suppose we see for the first time, a group playing a game that looks like football. The players are divided into two teams, each trying to move a football, by carrying or passing it, across the line defended by the other team. But each player is wearing two strips of cloth, one on each side, attached at the waist. When someone carries the football, members of the opposing team do not stop play by tackling the ball carrier, but instead they steal a cloth strip from his or her waist. We might modify our football schema to include a form of the game called flag football.

Infants and Schemas.

Children begin life with few concepts—or even none. A child's mind may be thought of as a **tabula rasa**, or an empty schema. This is the tabula rasa, or blank slate, notion of the young child's mind. One of Piaget's greatest insights was a suggestion of how children acquire the knowledge to begin filling in schemas. He suggested that the infant's mind is actually far from a blank slate. Children seem to know how to go about acquiring content knowledge, or knowledge of things.

Piaget's idea was that young humans learn through action. They are born with special schemas for how to act and how to respond to their world. These action schemas bring children in contact with reality (things) in ways that produce knowledge of the world. More action produces more knowledge. As children acquire knowledge and continue to act, changes happen to the things they are in contact with (e.g., milk gets spilled) and changes happen to previous knowledge (e.g., the schema for milk changes to include the idea that milk does not behave like a cracker—it doesn't keep a shape). The action schemas themselves change as active, problem-solving children evolve more effective strategies for making their way in the world.

Two very important conclusions can be drawn from Piaget's theory of how children learn. One is that children create their own knowledge by forming and reforming concepts in their minds. The second conclusion is that children's state of knowledge— or view of the world—can be very different from one time to the next, and especially different from an adult's.

The point we wish to emphasize is that, because children construct their own knowledge, this knowledge does not come fully developed and is often quite different from that of an adult. Thus, there are differences between how an adult understands concepts and how a child understands concepts.

The Relation between Language and Learning

We have already discussed the importance of action to Piaget's idea of learning. Children's actions may physically change objects in the world. While helping to wash the family car, a child may immerse a light, dry, stiff sponge into a bucket of water, changing its appearance and texture as it gets wet. That same action may change the child's concept or schema of a sponge, introducing the features *heavy, wet,* and *squishy,* and it may allow the child to see a connection between the schemas *water* and *sponge.*

But can children change their schema for *sponge* to include the notion that it can be heavy, wet, and squishy without hearing or using those words? How important is it for the child to have the words *sponge, water, heavy, wet,* and *squishy* available as labels for what is experienced in such a situation? Vygotsky stressed the importance of having someone with the child who can supply such language. According to Vygotsky, a parent who says to the child, "Boy that's a wet sponge!" or "The water sure made that sponge heavy!" or "Now that sponge is squishy!" plays a vital role in the child's learning about sponges and water. Vygotsky placed a strong emphasis on the social component of cognitive and language development.

Social Basis for Learning. Vygotsky argued that all learning first takes place in a social context. In order to build a new concept, children interact with others who provide feedback for their hypotheses or who help them accomplish a task they could not do on their own. Children's or adults' language is an important part of the social context of learning. Suppose that a child's concept of the letter *W* does not include its conventional orientation (upright). This child may write $\bigwedge$ and call it *W*. Another child who observes this writing may say, "That's not a *W*, that's an *M*." This feedback provides the child with a label for the new concept, *M*, and prompts the child to reconsider the concept of *W* by adding an orientation (upright).

Vygotsky believed that children need to be able to talk about a new problem or a new concept in order to understand it and use it. Adults supply language that fits children's needs at a particular stage or in response to a particular problem. Language can be part of a routinized situation. It can label the situation or parts of the situation, or it can help pose a problem or structure a problem-solving task. As the child gradually internalizes the language that was first supplied by an adult, the language and a routine task that helps in solving the problem become the child's own.

An example of a child's internalizing the language of a routine is how the child learns to use the words *all gone.* The parents of a child might repeatedly hide a favorite toy and then say, "All gone!" Then they reveal the toy and say, "Here it is!" This becomes a game for the child. Eventually, the child may play the game without the adult, using the same language, "All gone" and "Here it is" (Gopnick & Meltzoff, 1986).

We can draw an important conclusion from the "all gone" example. It suggests that learning is partly a matter of internalizing the language and actions of others. A young child's ability to play the game of "all gone" alone means that he or she has internalized the actions and language of his or her mother or father. For Vygotsky, all learning involves a movement from doing activities in a social situation with the support of a more knowledgeable other to internalizing the language and actions of the more knowledgeable other and being able to use this knowledge alone.

Zone of Proximal Development. Vygotsky spoke of a **zone of proximal development,** which is an opportune area for growth, but one in which children are dependent on help from others. An adult, or perhaps an older child, must give young children advice if they are to succeed within this zone and if eventually, by internalizing that advice, they are to perform independently.

When children are working in their zone of proximal development, they complete some parts of a task, and adults or older children perform the parts of the task that the younger children cannot yet do alone. In this way, young children can accomplish tasks that are too difficult for them to complete on their own. Adults' or older children's talk is an important part of helping young children—it scaffolds the task. **Scaffolding** is what an adult or an older child does to help a child to do what he or she can do with help but could not do alone. For example, an adult may talk, give advice, direct children's attention, alert them to the sequence of activities, and provide information for completing the task successfully. Gradually, children internalize this talk and use it to direct their own attention, plan, and control their activities.

Figure 1.1 presents a letter that five-year-old Kristen and her mother wrote together. After Kristen's second day in kindergarten, she announced, "I'm not going to school tomorrow. I don't like being last in line." Apparently, Kristen rode a different bus from any of the other children in her classroom and the teacher called her last to line up for the buses. When Kristen's mother reminded her of all the things she liked to do in school, Kristen replied, "Okay, I'll go [to school], but you tell Mrs. Peters [the teacher] I don't want to be last all the time." Kristen's mother said, "We'll write her a note. You write it and I'll help." Kristen agreed and wrote Mrs. Peter's name as her mother spelled it. Then Kristen said the message she wanted to write ("I always don't want to be the last person in the line"). Her mother said, "The first word is *I*. You can

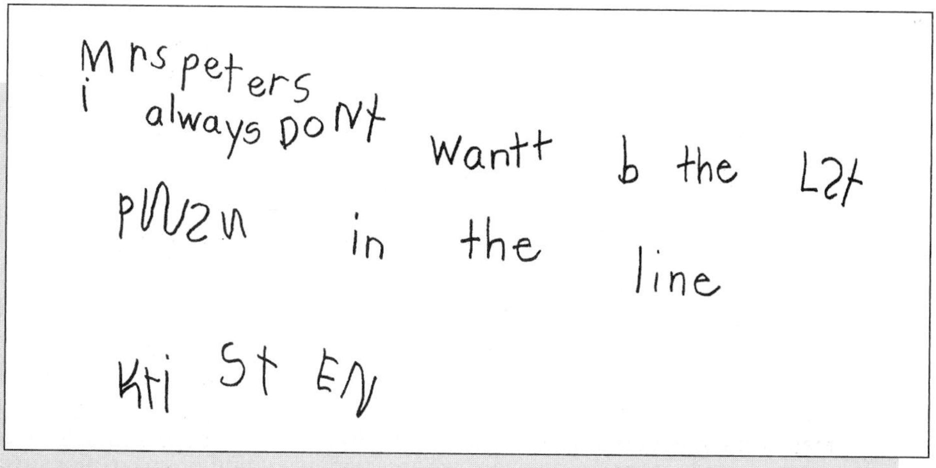

FIGURE 1.1   Kristen's Letter to Her Teacher

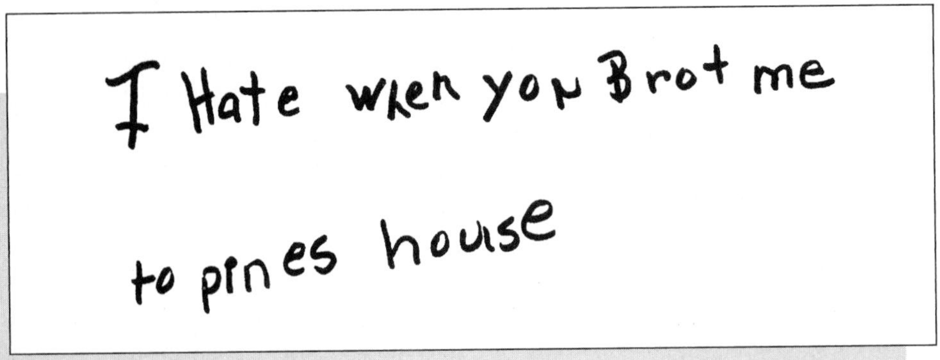

I Hate when you Brot me

to pines house

FIGURE 1.2   Kristen's Letter to Her Mother

spell that. What letter do you hear?" Kristen wrote the letter *i*, but when her mother began saying the word *always* slowly for Kristen to spell, she refused to spell any more words. So Kristen's mother wrote *always* and then spelled the word *don't* for Kristen to write. She suggested that she write one word and Kristen write one word. As shown in Figure 1.1, the final letter is a combination of Kristen's writing, with invented or incomplete spellings (*t* for *to*, *b* for *be*, *Lst* for *last*, and *pwsn* for *person*) as she listened to her mother say each sound in a word, and her mother's writing. Kristen could not have accomplished the task of writing this letter without her mother's scaffolding.

A year and a half later, Kristen ran into the kitchen where her mother was preparing dinner and handed her the note shown in Figure 1.2. This note reads, "I hate when you brought me to Penny's house" (Penny is Kristen's baby-sitter). Kristen had written the note in her room by herself after her mother was late picking her up. This note illustrates the results of scaffolding and working within the zone of proximal development. In kindergarten, Kristen needed her mother's scaffolding to write a letter of protest to her teacher. She needed her mother's support to hear sounds in words, to keep track of what she had written, and to sustain the effort of writing. At the end of first grade, she could write a letter of protest on her own, inventing spellings and reading to keep track of her message as she wrote.

FOUR SYSTEMS OF SPOKEN LANGUAGE

CHILDREN LEARN FROM THE LANGUAGE OF OTHERS. Not only do they learn about the topics of others' talk, but they also learn about language itself. At first they learn about spoken language, but even before they are fully competent speakers and listeners, they also learn about written language—how to read and write.

Spoken language allows speakers to communicate ideas to one another. We communicate and understand through sounds that make up words, through the meaning of words and sentences, and through our understanding of conventions required in conversation (for example, how to take turns so that only one person is talking at a time). Spoken language actually involves four different linguistic systems: pragmatics, semantics, syntax, and phonology (Richgels, 2004).

Pragmatics deals with social and cultural contexts of speaking and conveys the function or purpose of speech. **Semantics** is related to the system of meaning, including the meaning of words and their combinations. **Syntax** is related to the order and organization of words in sentences. **Phonology** is the system of speech sounds that make up the words of a language.

Pragmatics

An important system of language involves the functions or purposes that written language serves. Children, like the adults around them, use their spoken language in functional ways. Halliday (1975) identified seven functions of spoken language. These functions represent different ways in which we use language. Table 1.1 summarizes Halliday's seven functions of language, using examples from children's spoken language as illustrations of each (Halliday, 1975).

Semantics

Meaning is at the heart of spoken language (Halliday, 1975). The human experience demands that we communicate messages to one another, and humans are constantly engaged in meaning-making activities through face-to-face conversations. However, meaning is slippery; we must work hard to get and convey it in everyday conversations. Messages we construct from conversations are never exact; they always differ in some degree from what was actually spoken. All of us have experienced not being understood; we say, "But, that's not what I meant!" Meaning involves more than just capturing the words others say. It involves interpreting messages. One aspect of semantics, or the system of meaning, is knowing units of meaning. We usually consider the smallest unit of meaning a word; but units of meaning can actually be smaller than a word. Linguists call the smallest unit of meaning a **morpheme.** The word *start* consists of one morpheme, while the word *restart* has two morphemes: *re* and *start. Re* is considered a morpheme because it alters the meaning of the word *start* when it is added to the word. Other morphemes can be added to *start* that will alter meaning by changing the verb tense, such as adding *ed* or *s.* Morphemes can also alter meaning by changing the part of speech, such as when adding *able* to *drink.*

The meaning of words is an important part of the semantic system. We have already discussed how young children begin acquiring word meanings by developing schema or concepts related to words. For example, the meaning of the word *pineapple* may include knowing *spiky, sweet, fruit, yellow, juicy,* and *buy it at the grocery.* We have also stressed that because people have different experiences related to words, they have different meanings associated with them.

Syntax

Syntax is the set of rules for how to produce and comprehend sentences in a language and draws on order and organization. In some languages, including English, the order of words in sentences is crucial (consider, for example, *The boy kicked the goat* versus *The*

TABLE 1.1 Halliday's Language Functions

Language	Function	Spoken Language Examples	Written Language Examples
Instrumental	Satisfies needs and wants	"Gimme that!" "I want pizza!"	Birthday present wish list, sign-up sheet, grant proposal, petition
Regulatory	Controls others	"Stop that!" "Don't spill!"	List of classroom rules, traffic sign, No Smoking sign, policy handbook
Interactional	Creates interaction with others	"Let's play with the blocks" "Anybody want to paint?"	Party invitation, e-mail to a friend, membership card, "Hello, I'm _____" name tag
Personal	Expresses personal thoughts and opinions	"I like red." "I'm bored."	Letter to the editor, Valentine, journal entry, campaign button
Heuristic	Seeks information	"Are we there yet?" "Why?"	Questionnaire, survey, Internet search entry, insurance claim form, letter of inquiry
Imaginative	Creates imaginary worlds	"This can be our airplane." "You be the robber and I'm the police."	Movie script, short story, novel, poem, label on a play center prop, readers' theater script
Informative	Communicates information	"This is a rectangle." "Today is Wednesday."	Questionnaire results, survey results, Internet site, completed insurance claim form, social studies report, nutrition facts on food package, encyclopedia entry, dictionary entry, class birthday list, school–home newsletter, attendance report, drivers' manual

Source: Adapted from Halliday, 1975.

goat kicked the boy). In other languages, word order is not important. Instead, word endings are critical for understanding who did what to whom (for example, in Latin *Lupus agnum portat*, which means, "The wolf carries the lamb," versus *Lupum agnus portat*, which means, "The lamb carries the wolf").

Changes in syntax are among the hallmarks of language development (Berko-Gleason, 2005). Between the ages of 14 and 18 months, children begin putting two and then three words together to communicate what grown-ups would say with a whole sentence. This is called **telegraphic speech.** They use subject-verb "sentences" such as *Daddy come* to mean *Daddy came* or *Daddy is coming* or *I want Daddy to come home.* They use subject-object "sentences" such as *Daddy sock* to mean *Daddy got my sock* or *Daddy dropped his sock*, and verb-object sentences such as *put cookie* to mean *Put the cookie here on my plate.* Their questions have the same form as declarative sentences but with rising intonation, such as *We go now?* (with rising tone).

By the time children enter school, they typically use sentences six to eight words in length, and sometimes even longer, complex sentences with dependent and independent clauses such as *When we get to Grandma's, I'm going to play on the swing.* At school entry, children's language is so well developed that they can complete sentences by anticipating what words would both be meaningful and fit the grammatical class indicated in the sentence patterns. For example, when they hear the sentence, *I took a long ride in my mother's* _____, children readily supply the meaningful noun *car* or *truck* to complete the sentence.

When children begin reading in elementary school, their understanding of syntax helps them to read by allowing them to anticipate words before reading (Clay, 1993). In fact, children often make mistakes when reading (called miscues) that reveal that they are anticipating words that would make sense and fit the structural or grammatical pattern of the sentence. For example, one first grader when faced with the story about a mother pig and her piglets, made several miscues:

Child: Once upon a time there was a mother pig.

Text: Once there was a mother pig.

Child: She had some little pigs.

Text: She had six little piglets.

Notice that the child added the phrase *upon a time*, which would make sense in the first sentence. In the second sentence, the child substituted the word *some* for the word *six* and *pigs* for the word *piglets.* These substitutions make sense and fit the grammatical class of words expected in the sentence.

Phonology

The phonological system refers to the system of spoken sounds in a language. Each language uses some of the few hundreds of possible speech sounds of human languages. English, for example, uses approximately 44 speech sounds, or **phonemes** (see Table 1.2). Phonemes are the smallest units of sound that are combined and contrasted in a language's words.

Phonemes are the building blocks of words. Consider, for example, the four phonemes /b/, /p/, /i/, and /l/. The last three can be combined to make the word *pill*, and the first two are contrasted when distinguishing the words in the minimal pair *pill* and *bill.* The difference in the pronunciations of /p/ and /b/ is slight. It is only that for /p/ we do not use our voices and for /b/ we do; everything else—how we use our tongues and throats, how we shape our lips, how we part our teeth—is identical. Yet speakers and listeners rely on that very small difference, that contrast; it is all that signals two very different English meanings, a dose of medicine versus a duck's mouth.

TABLE 1.2 Common English Phonemes

/a/ cat	/g/ got	/O/ coat	/th/ thing
/A/ Kate	/h/ hot	/oi/ boy	/TH/ this
/ah/ cot	/i/ hit	/oo/ look	/uh/ cut, about
/aw/ caught, fought	/I/ height	/OO/ flute, shoot	/U/ cute
/b/ bought	/j/ Jake	/ow/ shout	/v/ vine
/ch/ chug	/k/ cake	/p/ pat	/w/ wine
/d/ dug	/l/ lake	/r/ rat	/y/ yes
/e/ bed	/m/ make	/s/ sat, city	/z/ zoo
/E/ bead	/n/ win	/sh/ ship	/zh/ treasure
/f/ feed	/ng/ wing	/t/ tip	

Notes:
- Any phoneme list is dialect-sensitive. That is, pronunciations differ from one dialect to another. For example, in some U.S. English dialects, *cot* and *caught* are pronounced the same, both with the middle phoneme /ah/; there is no separate /aw/ phoneme in those dialects.
- There is no "C sound"; C usually spells /k/ (cat) or /s/ (city).
- There is no "Q sound" QU usually spells the two sounds /k/ + /w/ (quick), but sometimes the one sound /k/ (plaque).
- Some phonemes are really combinations of others. The /I/ phoneme is really /ah/ + /E/. The /oi/ phoneme is really /O/ + /E/. The /U/ phoneme is really /y/ + /OO/; notice the difference between the /OO/ in flute and the /y/ + /OO/ in cute. The /ch/ phoneme is really /t/ + /sh/.
- There is no "X sound"; X usually spells the two sounds /k/ + /s/ (box) or the one sound /z/ (xylophone).
- Our list has only thirty-nine phonemes. Many sources give forty-four as the number of English phonemes, so why do we not list forty-four? We could add /hw/ for those whose dialect of English includes an additional /h/-like sound at the beginning of words spelled with *WH* (those speakers' pronunciation of the beginning of *when* is breathier than their pronunciation of the beginning of *wet*). In addition, some lists of English phonemes include additional sounds for some vowels before /r/. The R sound after a vowel often slightly changes the way the vowel is pronounced, but we do not think the difference is enough for nonlinguists to be concerned with. Finally, some lists of English phonemes include the schwa sound (/ə/) for the vowel sound in many unaccented syllables (about, basket, rapid, cotton), but the schwa sound is the same as the short *U* sound (/uh/); compare about and cut.

Phonemes are also abstractions. For example, when we say "the *p* sound," we reference a set of sounds, slightly different in pronunciation from one another, usually depending on the context in which they are pronounced (i.e., what other phonemes precede and follow them). These differences within a phoneme category do not matter. Language users can ignore them. To appreciate the breadth of phoneme categories, notice the difference between /p/ pronunciations in *span* and *pan* (most people do not at first notice this difference, but dangling a piece of paper before their mouths when they say the two words reveals the difference; one word's pronunciation is breathy enough to move the paper, the other's is not).

Phonological awareness requires the ability to think and talk about differences in speech sounds. Children who have phonological awareness notice and identify different sound units. For example, they can decide if two words rhyme and can clap out syllables in words.

An even more sophisticated level of phonological awareness is called **phonemic awareness.** This is the ability to hear phonemes—for example, to detect if two words begin or end with the same sound. Because English is an alphabetic language in which alphabet letters correspond to phonemes, acquiring phonemic awareness is important for literacy development (Stahl, Duffy-Hester, & Stahl, 1998; Nation & Hulme, 1997). As we will see later in this book, the ability to segment words into their individual phonemes comes gradually, but it is a crucial part of becoming a reader and writer (National Reading Panel, 2000).

FOUR SYSTEMS OF WRITTEN LANGUAGE

BY THE TIME CHILDREN ENTER SCHOOL, they are able unconsciously to control the four language systems—pragmatics, semantics, syntax, and phonology—to communicate with their peers and adults. Children's learning to read and write depends on a solid foundation of spoken language competence, upon which is added knowledge about and skillful use of written language forms and functions (Freeman & Freeman, 2004). Table 1.3 provides information about each of the four language systems in both spoken language and written language.

Written language is similar to, but not exactly the same, as spoken language. In this part of the chapter, we examine the four systems of written language. Notice in Table 1.3, that the system that corresponds with pragmatics is called functions, the system that corresponds to semantics is called meaning, the system related to syntax is called form, and the system corresponding to phonology is called meaning-form links. We selected these labels for describing children's concepts about written language to reflect that children are developing writing-specific concepts about language but that those concepts are related to what children know and are learning about the four systems of spoken language.

Functions of Written Language

Since children are acquainted with using spoken language for several purposes, it is not surprising that they learn how to use written language to accomplish a variety of goals as well. In fact, many of the **functions of written language** are the same as those of spoken language. Table 1.1 also presents several examples of written language that serve each of Halliday's seven functions (1975).

However, written language also serves unique purposes. It is used to establish ownership or identity and to convey authority, often legal authority. For example, two groups of preschoolers were arguing about the use of a large refrigerator box.

TABLE 1.3 Systems of Spoken and Written Language

Spoken Language	*Written Language*
Pragmatics System for using language in everyday life, including knowledge of purposes that language serves knowledge	***Functions*** The purposes written language serves, including establishing identity, recording information, and accumulating
Semantics System of meaning, including word meanings and morphology	***Meaning*** System of meaning, including word meanings, literary language, unusual words; morphology
Syntax System for structuring sentences (English syntax depends heavily on word order)	***Form*** The order of words within sentences; upper- and lowercase alphabet letters (graphemes); spatial directional principles, including left to right, top to bottom; word spaces; text formats
Phonology System for using sounds, including the combining and contrasting of phonemes in words and the use of intonation (patterns of pause, pitch, and stress) in sentences	***Meaning-Form Link*** Phoneme (sound)— grapheme (letter) relationships, including orthographic spelling patterns and phonograms

One group insisted that the box should be a dollhouse. The other group wanted it to be a fire station. Two boys in the fire station group went to a mother helper and asked her to write the words *fire station*. They copied her writing on a large sheet of paper and taped it to the box. One child pointed to the sign and said, "This is not a house. This is a fire station" (Cochran-Smith, 1984, p. 90). Thus, they established identity and authority.

Written language also has the unique power to make language and thinking permanent and transportable (Stubbs, 1980). We can communicate with others over long distances and share information with people we have never met face-to-face. Because information can be recorded and reread, facts can be accumulated and studied critically. New knowledge is built from a critical analysis of accumulated past knowledge.

Meanings in Written Language

Young children come to realize that the written symbols they see around them mean something: Print "says" messages. The printed word *McDonald's* found on the sign outside the familiar fast food restaurant says "McDonald's" and means a place to get a "Happy Meal." Nearly all young preschoolers recognize the *McDonald's* logo and find it highly meaningful. That is, children have an awareness—even before they are actually reading or writing—that printed words convey messages.

Young children's concepts about **written language meanings** are related to their experiences. For example, if children often grocery shop with their parents, when asked what a grocery list might say, they reply "bread, coke, and candy." Children who have had experiences getting birthday cards, when asked to read one, will reply, "Happy Birthday." Thus, young children's understandings of the meanings of various written texts are related to experiences in which those texts have been used by others but in the children's presence.

Reading and writing, of course, are only a few of the ways in which we can communicate meanings. We also communicate meanings through facial expression, gesture, dance, art, conversation, and music. For young children, communicating in spoken language and play are very closely related to communicating in written language (Rowe, 1998).

However, strategies that are needed to construct meaning in written language are not always needed for spoken language. One difference, paradoxically, is that written language is not exactly talk written down (Cook-Gumperz, 1986). Meaning in spoken language is often conveyed through gestures, facial expressions, and voice intonation, which provide **contextualization clues** to meaning. Contextualization clues include anything in a specific context that contributes to understanding a message. Much spoken language takes place in a context in which the actual objects discussed can be seen, or between people who know a great deal about each other.

Another difference between spoken and written language is that written language makes more frequent use of unusual words, words that are rarely used in everyday conversation. Words such as *display, exposure, equate, infinite, invariably, literal, luxury, maneuver, participation, provoke,* or *reluctantly* (Cunningham & Stanovich, 1998, p. 10) are found in written stories, newspapers, or textbooks. However, these words are rarely used in daily conversation. Similarly, written language includes **literary language** phrases that are found in literature, such as "once upon a time" and "in the previous section," but which usually are not found in everyday spoken language.

Written Language Forms

Written language forms are the visual and spatial aspects of written language such as letters, words, and texts. Written language form knowledge includes awareness of visual properties, spatial directional properties, and organizational formats. It is easy to see that words are composed of alphabet letters, sometimes called graphemes. Most accomplished readers and writers take for granted a related fact, that alphabet letters are composed of lines and curves, sometimes called **letter features** (Gibson, Gibson, Pick, & Osser, 1962). When learning to read and write, however, children cannot take letter

FIGURE 1.3 A Preschooler's Printed Letters

features for granted. Their writing often demonstrates their careful attention to letter features. Figure 1.3 presents one preschooler's printed letters. This writing does include some conventional or nearly conventional alphabet letter forms (*t*, *r*, and *M*) as well as many letter-like but unconventional symbols. These symbols look like alphabet letters because they include many letter features, such as vertical, diagonal, and curved lines (Lavine, 1977). Clay (1975) called letters like these **mock letters.**

Children all over the world construct mock letters, letters that look like the written language children will soon read and write. The features they use in order to write mock letters reveal the unique visual features found in the variety of our world's written languages. In Figure 1.4, a five-year-old Chinese girl has labeled her picture by writing two symbols that resemble Chinese characters, although neither is a real Chinese character.

FIGURE 1.4 A Five-Year-Old's Drawing with Mock Chinese Characters

Words and Sentences. Children also learn about the features of words (Pick, Unze, Brownell, Drozdal, & Hopmann, 1978) and demonstrate this knowledge in their writing (Clay, 1975; Sulzby, 1986). Figure 1.5 presents a letter that five-year-old Zachery wrote to his Aunt Carol. His writing indicates an awareness of words; he separated each word with a dash. Many young children are unsure that a space is enough to mark a word boundary. Instead, they make word spaces very obvious, using dots or dashes or circling words to indicate word boundaries to readers. Zachery's writing also demonstrates his strong grasp of the directional principles of written English: he uses left-to-right and top-to-bottom organization.

This letter also demonstrates Zachery's knowledge of the visual features of two other units of written language: sentences and text format. Zachery circled each thought unit, which we call a sentence, even though he signaled one sentence boundary with the conventional punctuation mark, a period. His writing also shows a sophisticated awareness of how the text of a letter is organized. He begins with a greeting ("Hi Aunt Carol") and ends with a closing ("from Zachery").

Text Formats. There are many kinds of texts, including poems, recipes, maps, newspapers, dictionaries, books, magazine articles, *TV Guides,* and directions. One thing young children learn about these different text forms is how they look.

Figure 1.6 presents a nine-year-old's letter to her principal. The form of the letter reflects Andrea's concepts about letter form, including a greeting, body, and signature. The content is also organized, with a statement of a problem and solution and with arguments for why the principal should consider the solution.

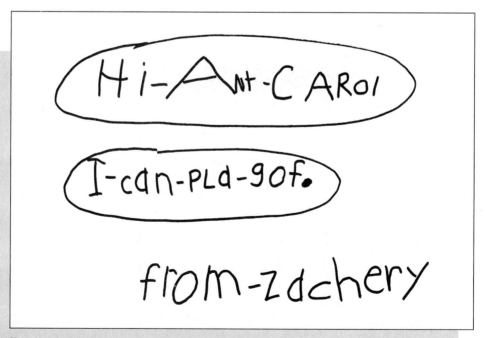

FIGURE 1.5 Zachery's Letter to His Aunt Carol

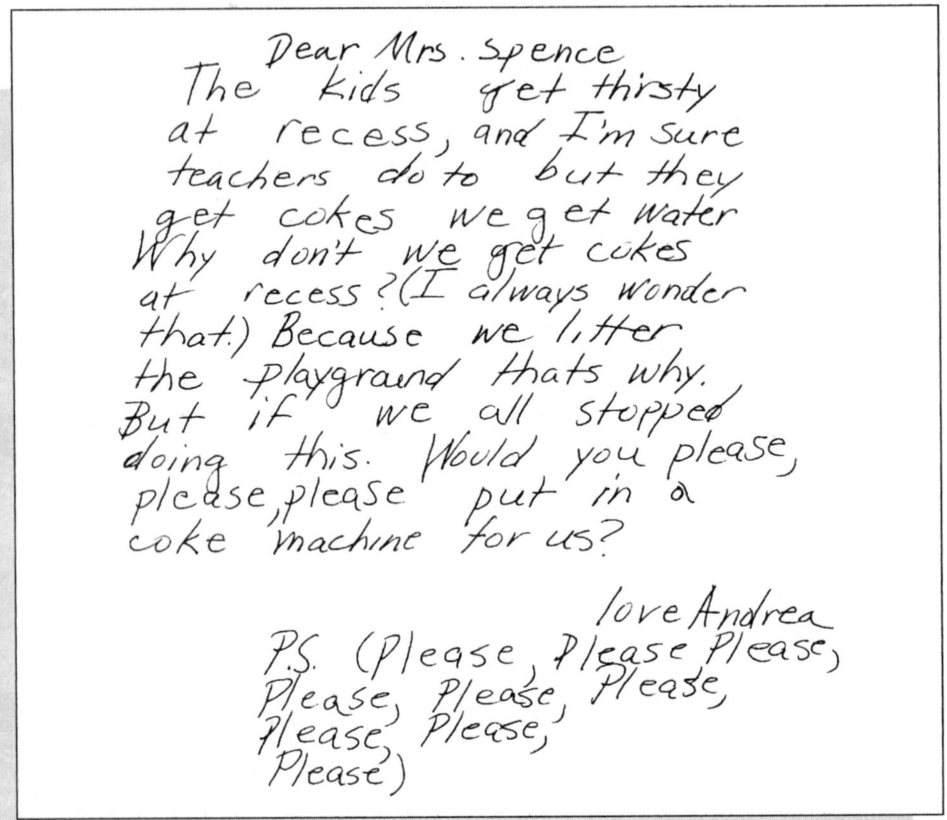

Dear Mrs. Spence
The kids get thirsty
at recess, and I'm sure
teachers do to but they
get cokes we get water
Why don't we get cokes
at recess? (I always wonder
that.) Because we litter
the playgraund thats why.
But if we all stopped
doing this. Would you please,
please, please put in a
coke machine for us?

love Andrea

P.S. (Please, Please Please,)
Please, Please, Please,
Please, Please,
Please)

FIGURE 1.6   A Persuasion Letter

We have been using words such as *letter, word, sentence,* and *story,* which make it easy to describe written language. They constitute *language about language.* Children's understanding of and ability to use language about language is a particular kind of knowledge called **metalinguistic awareness** (Yaden & Templeton, 1986). They will learn what a word is, what a sentence is, and what a story is. Experiences in school make these linguistic concepts explicit.

Meaning-Form Links

We use the term **meaning-form links** to refer to the way in which meaning is connected to written forms. The conventional meaning-form link in English is achieved through **sound-letter relationships**. Sound-letter relationships are the ways in which particular letters are associated with particular speech sounds. For example, the letter *b* is related to the sound /b/. When we see the printed word *bat,* we know that the three letters correspond to the three sounds /b/, /a/, and /t/, which blended together produce the spoken word *bat*. However, sound-letter correspondences are complex: A single letter is not always associated with just one speech sound. Some letters are associated with many speech sounds (e.g., the letter *a* with /A/ in *able*, but also with /a/ in *cat*, /ah/ in *car*, and /uh/ in *about*), and some speech sounds are associated with combinations of letters (e.g., the sound /aw/ with *augh* in *caught*, the sound /A/ with *a_e* in *make* and *ai* in *rain*, and the sound /sh/ with *sh* in *shine*).

Despite these complexities, the **alphabetic principle** does apply to written English and to other alphabetic languages. That is, spoken sounds are systematically associated with written letters. Thus, the most noticeable meaning-form link in English is spelling. For example, words with the same letters such as *slip* and *lips* are distinguished by their spellings—the order in which the letters occur and the sounds are spoken. Fortunately, certain spellings are nearly always associated with certain pronunciations. **Orthography** is the system in an alphabetic language whereby word parts (individual sounds or larger chunks of spoken words) are associated with individual letters or combinations of letters. **Phonograms** are combinations of letters that are reliably associated with particular pronunciations, especially in the middle and final positions of a word. For example, in all of the **rhyming words** *ban, can, fan, tan,* and *plan*, the phonogram *-an* is pronounced /an/.

In addition to sound-letter relationships, orthographies also use some meaning-letter relationships, where direct connections between particular combinations of letters and particular meanings are more important than maintaining sound-letter relationships. For example, in English, *-tion*, pronounced /shuhn/, often is used to mark the transformation of a verb to a noun when the noun names the process of doing the action of the verb (*combine/combination, hesitate/hesitation, inflate/inflation*). The efficiency gained from having *-tion* as a unique marker of the meaning "process of doing _____" more than makes up for the failure of *-tion* to employ the usual sound-letter correspondences of the letters *sh* with the sound /sh/ and the letter *u* with the sound /uh/. (Notice that this is true even though those correspondences are used in the totally unrelated word *shun*, meaning to avoid.)

The conventional spelling, or orthography, of a written language embodies the ways that accomplished writers in that language use sound-letter correspondences and meaning-letter correspondences to compose words. Young children take a long time—usually many years—to learn these conventional ways. In the meantime, they have many occasions to attempt to link meaning to their writing. We will describe two of their unconventional attempts: telling about drawing and scribbles and matching units of print with units of memorized speech. A third way, invented spelling, is closer to conventional spelling than these two ways; it will be described in a later chapter.

Meaning-Form Links through Letter and Scribble Strings.   Figure 1.7 presents Johanna's picture and story writing. She read her story, pointing to the print from left to right and then down the side and from right to left across the bottom: "Miss Sharon and Mr. K have a new baby, Emily. I hope we will baby-sit Emily. I love Emily Grace." Johanna's text consists of a string of conventional and mock letters wrapped around the edges of the paper framing her illustration. She does not use sound-letter relationships to connect meaning and form. Instead, Johanna's meaning—her story about a beloved new

FIGURE 1.7   Johanna's Story

baby and her desire to be with the baby—is told both through the illustration and by her spoken story. The meaning-form link for Johanna was to write and then compose a related story.

Meaning-Form Links by Matching Print with Spoken Units.   Another way that children attempt to link meaning with written language is to match a unit of written language to a unit of memorized spoken language. For example, Heather memorized the poem "Twinkle, Twinkle Little Star." Her kindergarten teacher wrote the poem on a chart and asked Heather to pretend to read it and "point to each word." Heather performed the task by reading and pointing as follows.

Text:	Twinkle	Twinkle	Little	Star		
Heather:	Twin	kle	Twin	kle		

Text:	How	I	Wonder	What	You	Are
Heather:	Lit	tle	Star	How	I	Won

Heather hesitated and then pointed back at the beginning of the poem:

Text:	Twinkle	Twinkle	Little	Star		
Heather:	Won	der	What	You		

Text:	How	I	Wonder	What	You	Are
Heather:	Are					

Then Heather stopped, pointed to the remainder of the text, and said, "I don't know what the rest says." Heather used a strategy of linking each written word to a spoken syllable that she had memorized.

CHILDREN'S CONCEPTS ABOUT WRITTEN LANGUAGE

CHILDREN LEARN WRITTEN LANGUAGE in much the same way that they learn anything else, including spoken language. They acquire and modify schemas or concepts for various aspects of written language knowledge. In this part of the chapter, we describe children's concepts about written language.

Ted's Delight: A Case Study of Two Children's Reading and Writing

Ted, who was eight years old, and his sister Carrie, who was three years old, were playing in the corner of the living room. They had set up their card table playhouse. Taped on the playhouse was the sign shown in Figure 1.8.

Ted and Carrie had collected Carrie's plastic play food and doll dishes and put them behind the playhouse. When their father entered the room, he looked at the sign and said, "Oh, I think I need some lunch." The children asked him to visit their restaurant. He entered the playhouse, and Carrie presented him with a menu (see Figure 1.9).

Carrie asked, "May I take your order?" Her father read the menu and said, "I'll take pancakes and coffee." Carrie checked off two items on the menu and took it out to Ted, who was behind the playhouse. He pretended to fix pancakes and pour coffee. Ted brought the dishes into the playhouse to his father, who pretended to eat with much relish. When he had finished he asked, "May I have my check, please?" Carrie picked up a pad of paper and a pencil and wrote a check (see Figure 1.10). Her father pretended to pay the check and left the playhouse.

Later that evening, the family discussed the restaurant play. Ted said he had made the sign so that the playhouse could be a restaurant. He had asked Carrie if he could use her toy food and dishes. She had wanted to play, too. Ted said that he and Carrie decided to write on the menu the names of the play food they had. In the middle of his writing the menu, Carrie insisted on helping him. "She wrote the letter that looks like a backwards *J* in the middle of the menu," Ted reported. "I had to turn it into the word *Enjoy* to make sense."

Ted's and Carrie's Concepts about Written Language

What do Ted's and Carrie's reading and writing reveal about their concepts of written language? First, both Ted's and Carrie's behaviors indicate that they understand many ways in which written language is used. Carrie knows that a waitperson writes something when a customer orders and when the customer asks for the check. She seems to be learning, just as Ted is, that writing and reading are functional. Ted and Carrie used written language to get their customer into their restaurant (they made a sign), to let

TED'S

DELIGHT

FIGURE 1.8   "Ted's Delight" Sign

☐ Fruit Dish ☐ Fried Banana
              ☐ Not Cooked

☐ Cooked   Curits
☐ Cooked   Pees
☐ Fried egg
☐ Pan cakes

ENJOY

DRINKS
☐ Tea ☐ Water ☐ Coffie
☐ Bananu Smuthes
☐ Orange Smuthes
☐ lemen Smuthes
☐ Grape Smuthes

FIGURE 1.9   "Ted's Delight" Menu

FIGURE 1.10 Carrie's Check

their customer know what was available to eat (they made a menu), and to let their customer know how much the meal cost (they wrote a check). They demonstrated written language functions.

Second, the sign and menu Ted wrote suggest that he is learning about written language meanings. His sign communicated a message to his father: a restaurant is open for business. Ted also knows that the messages communicated in written language should be meaningful given the written language context. Ted knew that the "backwards J" that Carrie wrote somehow had to be incorporated into a message that could be communicated on a menu. Random letters on menus do not communicate meaningful messages. Ted made the random letter meaningful by incorporating it into the word *Enjoy*. Carrie also showed that she knows that written language communicates meaning. Even though we cannot read her check, her behavior as she gave it to her father (and her father's reactions to the written check) suggests that her writing communicates a message something like "pay some money for your food."

Third, the sign and menu indicate that Ted is learning about written language forms—what written language looks like. These two writing samples certainly look like a sign and a menu. His menu is written in the form of a list. The content of his menu is organized as a menu is usually organized—drinks and food are grouped and listed separately. Carrie is also learning what at least a few written language forms look like. The writing on her check looks something like the letters *E* and *J*. Even though Carrie's letters are not yet conventional, they signal that she is paying attention to what letters look like. Although Carrie's *E*'s sometimes have too many horizontal lines, she has obviously noticed that horizontal lines are letter features. And, even though Carrie's *J*'s seem to be backwards, she does include the curve feature expected at the end of this letter. There is one exception. Carrie put a circle on her letter *E*; most letter *E*'s do not include circles. Figure 1.11 (Carrie's name written as her preschool teacher wrote it) suggests why Carrie may have included the circle on her *E*. Her preschool teacher often used what she called "bubble writing," putting small decorative bubbles on each alphabet letter. Carrie noticed that her preschool teacher wrote circles on her letters, so Carrie may have decided to put the same circles on her own letters.

Finally, Ted's and Carrie's writing demonstrates that they are learning a unique system of written language: the manner in which written language conveys meaning.

CARRIE

FIGURE 1.11 "Carrie" as Written by Her Preschool Teacher

In English, the way written language conveys meaning is that written words map onto spoken words. Letters in written words relate to sounds in speech. Therefore, English is considered an alphabetic language, and learning about sound-letter relationships is an important part of reading and writing. Ted demonstrated his understanding of the relationship between letters and sounds in his spelling errors. Ted's spelling of *pees* for *peas* shows that he knows that the letters *ee* often take the sound of long *e*.

Carrie's writing demonstrates that she does not yet know sound-letter relationships. However, she does write letters and assumes that a reader, her father, will be able to read her message. She knows that the form of her writing is related to its meaning.

DEVELOPMENTAL CHANGES IN CHILDREN'S READING AND WRITING

WE HAVE SHOWN THAT CHILDREN have many unconventional concepts about words, alphabet letters, and meaning-form links. Yet all children's concepts become increasingly more conventional. Although the journey to becoming a mature reader and writer is long, what happens during the journey is as valid as the end point. Knowing how children's concepts about written language develop is critical for understanding children's reading and writing.

Since the first edition of this book (McGee & Richgels, 1990), we have described four stages of young readers and writers: **beginners, novices, experimenters,** and **conventional readers and writers**. In the intervening years, others have documented similar stages in children's literacy development and have used their own labels for them.

Awareness and Exploration

Even very young children have meaningful experiences with books and writing materials, and these experiences lay the necessary foundations for later literacy development. The children we have called beginners are not, of course, readers and writers in the sense of being able to comprehend and create texts on their own. They are dependent on their parents or other readers and writers for their experiences. Other than when sharing books with others, beginners merely observe others as they engage in literacy activities.

In contrast, novice readers and writers are aware of print and know that printed text communicates messages. They sometimes write with the intention to communicate their own messages. Novice readers and writers still do not read and write as adults do; their attempts to read and write occur primarily during pretend play. However, they do learn some conventions. **Conventions of written language** are the characteristics of texts and the practices and processes for understanding and producing it that are accepted, expected, and used by accomplished readers and writers in a written language community. For example, one convention that novice readers and writers learn is to recognize and write some alphabet letters. Carrie is an example of a novice reader and writer. She uses what she knows about alphabet letters to write messages.

Most novice readers and writers are three to five years old. Others have characterized reading and writing during this time as the phase of awareness and exploration (IRA/NAEYC, 1998) because children become aware of print and explore its properties.

Experimenting Reading and Writing

Children eventually come to recognize that meaning is mapped onto print in a systematic way. The conventional way that meaning is mapped onto printed text is through sound-letter correspondences. Sounds in spoken words correspond to letters in printed words. Children's first attempts to use this correspondence have been characterized as alphabetic reading and writing (Ehri, 1991; Juel, 1991); they know some alphabet letters and realize that alphabet letters are associated with certain sounds. At this time, their knowledge about letters and sounds is not complete. They cannot completely sound out an unknown word or completely spell a word. Frequently they recognize a printed word's beginning sound or spell a word with only a few letters for just a few of its sounds. We call these children experimenters. They are experimenting with what they can do using the alphabetic principle.

Experimenters use more conventions than novice readers and writers: They learn most of the alphabet letters, and they attempt to spell words using their knowledge of letters and sounds. They memorize short texts and attempt to read by remembering the text and pointing to words as Heather did. Although they too are not yet conventional readers and writers, they are "almost" to that point. These accomplishments typically emerge in kindergarten and early first grade.

Conventional Reading and Writing

The final phase of learning to read and write is conventional reading and writing. Children we call conventional readers and writers have already mastered alphabet recognition and know most letter-sound associations. They now learn strategies for decoding words, meanings of new vocabulary words, and strategies for comprehending what they read. They compose texts using spelling strategies and known spellings.

One feature that distinguishes conventional readers and writers from experimenters is their attention to larger parts of words than single letters. They do not merely sound out spellings or attempt to spell using single sound-letter relationships. Rather, they come to recognize phonograms and begin to rely on using those patterns of letters to arrive at pronunciations or spellings. For example, even if the word *brand* is unfamiliar to them, they will find in it the phonogram *-and*, which they already know from the words *band, hand, land, sand,* and *stand.* This knowledge equips them to bypass decoding *brand* as five letters with five corresponding sounds that must be blended together and instead to begin with the pronunciation /and/. Then they must only determine how to pronounce the consonant blend *bl* before that familiar /and/.

As they gain experience and through instruction, children learn to understand and compose increasingly complex texts. Eventually conventional readers and writers know thousands of sight words (words they can read automatically), read a great variety of different kinds of texts, are aware of audience when they write, and monitor their own performances when they read and write. This phase of reading and writing typically emerges in first grade but continues to develop throughout the elementary, middle, and high school years.

ASSESSMENT AND PHASES OF READING AND WRITING DEVELOPMENT

WE HAVE SHOWN THAT CHILDREN generally progress through four broad phases of literacy development. We characterize children according to these phases as beginners, novices, experimenters, and conventional readers and writers. In the next four chapters, we provide more detail about each of these phases of reading and writing. In chapter two we describe what beginners learn, in chapter three we discuss the developmental milestones of novices, in chapter four we describe the new developmental achievements of experimenters, and in chapter five we describe what conventional readers and writers learn.

In order for teachers to help children pass through these phases efficiently and effectively, they need to know each child's level of development and how to provide instruction that will encourage that child's growth toward a more advanced phase (Bowman, Donovan, & Burns, 2000). The way that teachers find out about each individual child is through assessment. **Written language assessment** is any activity of teachers to determine students' literacy knowledge, abilities, and understandings (Epstein, Schweinhart, DeBruin-Parecki & Robin, 2004). Assessment can be as simple as observing what a child does, reflecting on the behaviors and talk observed, and making judgments about what this means the child knows and does not know. Assessment also may involve giving children simple tasks to perform, such as asking them to write their names or to identify alphabet letters printed on cards. Assessment may involve a paper-and-pencil test for which children are asked to read paragraphs and to circle answers to multiple choice questions about the paragraphs.

We have found that assessment is critical when making instructional decisions for children from diverse backgrounds. Children from diverse family, SES, ethnic, language, and racial backgrounds will bring to school diverse understandings about the nature of print and its uses. These concepts, like the concepts of all young children, are not likely to be conventional. For example, a preschool teacher observed as Tatie, a bilingual, two-year-old, Haitian child, made the shape of the letter *T* by crossing two fingers. When the teacher asked her what she was doing, Tatie replied, "That's me" (Ballenger, 1999, p. 45). Tatie seemed to recognize the shape of the letter, *T,* and while she did not name it, she realized that it represented her name.

Despite the importance of assessment for making instructional decisions for young children, assessing young children is challenging (Bredekamp & Rosegrant, 1992). Young children are at early stages of language development and may have difficulty focusing on a task, maintaining attention, or using language to express what they know (Epstein et al., 2004). Thus, assessments of young children may not be highly reliable; the results may not reflect what the children actually know. Therefore, effective and appropriate literacy assessment must be carefully planned, keeping in mind the possible misinterpretations that might arise because of issues of appropriateness, validity, and reliability. Appropriate assessments are consistent with a child's age and developmental level. Valid assessments are those that actually measure the concept intended to be measured. Reliable assessments are those that give consistent results. Appropriate tests for preschoolers would not involve them in answering questions using a multiple choice format. Valid assessments of reading would not have children writing. A reliable assessment of name writing would yield the same signature on one day as on the next.

We will end each of the next four chapters with information about how to assess children as they move through the phases of beginning, novice, experimenting, and conventional reading and writing. In each chapter we will identify specific assessment tools appropriate for the age and literacy development of children described in that chapter. In addition, we will identify key foundational concepts that teachers will be expected to assess in preschool and in grades K–3.

Chapter Summary

CHILDREN'S LEARNING IS DEPENDENT on having experiences that lead to the formation of concepts or schemas. Concepts are mental constructions about objects, people, events or activities, and places. Learning is a matter of acquiring new concepts or adding to and changing old concepts. Language is critical for learning when it provides labels for new concepts and when it is used to scaffold children's attempts at difficult tasks.

Children develop special concepts about written language that they use in reading and writing. They develop concepts about the functions of written language, including using reading and writing to label and record.

Their concepts about written language meanings reflect their experiences with different kinds of texts, such as stories, grocery lists, and traffic signs. They create concepts about written language forms, including learning about letter features, words, sentences, texts, and left-to-right organization. They develop understandings about meaning-form links, including unconventional concepts such as using letter strings and matching spoken units with written units.

Children's concepts about written language change and grow with their reading and writing experiences. Children begin with unconventional concepts and gradually acquire conventional concepts. Before reading and writing conventionally, they may proceed through phases of awareness and exploration and experimental reading and writing. Teachers use assessment to discover children's unique understandings about reading and writing.

USING THE INFORMATION

A list of written words follows; however, the purpose of this exercise is to listen to the words spoken aloud and to segment each word by individual phonemes. This activity is designed to help you learn to hear and say each of the phonemes found in Table 1.2. With three pennies or other coins, move a coin into a box as you say a phoneme in a word. For example, as you segment the word *bat*, you will move a coin into the left hand box as you say /b/, a second coin into the middle box as you say /a/, and a third coin into the right hand box as you say /t/. Make a list of those words for which the three boxes are insufficient because the words are composed of more than three phonemes. Which words required only two of the three boxes?

cat	Kate	cot	caught	bought
chug	dug	bed	bead	feed
got	hot	hit	height	Jake
make	win	wing	coat	boy
look	shoot	shout	pat	rat
city	ship	tip	thing	this
cut	cute	vine	wine	yes
zoo	azure	shoe	weigh	

APPLYING THE INFORMATION

A case study of a literacy event follows. Read this case study carefully and think about the four domains of written language knowledge. Discuss what each of the children in the case study is learning about written language (1) meanings, (2) forms, (3) meaning-form links, and (4) functions. Figure 1.12 presents a drawing and writing composition jointly produced by Kristen and Carrie.

Kristen, a three-year-old preschooler, and Carrie, a six-year-old kindergartner, were playing school together. Carrie began by demonstrating how to draw. She said, "This is me," as she drew the person (1) in the upper right corner of Figure 1.12. Kristen replied, "I can draw you," and she drew the figure (2) at the middle left of Figure 1.12. Carrie pointed out that the person has no hair, so Kristen drew the figure (3) in the upper left corner. Carrie decided to teach Kristen how to write. She said, "We'll write. Here is a *C.*" She wrote the capital *C* (4) on the right side of the figure. Kristen wrote the letter (5) in the top middle of the page and said "I can write *C*, too." Then Carrie wrote the remaining letters in her name, saying the name of each letter as she wrote (6). Kristen wrote similar letters, including an *A*, several *E*s, and *R*s scattered around the page. The children finished as Carrie drew a tree and Kristen added dots to the picture.

FIGURE 1.12 Kristen's and Carrie's Drawing and Writing

Going Beyond the Text

O BSERVE A LITERACY EVENT with at least two children. One way to initiate a literacy event is to prepare for some dramatic play with children. Plan a dramatic play activity that could include reading and writing. For example, plan a restaurant play activity. Bring dramatic props, such as an apron, dishes, and a tablecloth, as well as reading and writing materials, such as large sheets of paper, small pads of paper, crayons or markers, placemats with puzzles, and menus. Suggest to two or three children that they might want to play restaurant and propose that they use the paper and crayons in their play. Observe their actions and talk. Use your observations to find out what the children know about written language meanings, forms, meaning-form links, and functions.

References

Ballenger, C. (1999). *Teaching other people's children: Literacy and learning in a bilingual classroom.* New York: Teachers College Press.

Berko Gleason, J. (2005). *The development of language* (6th ed.). Boston: Allyn & Bacon.

Bowman, B. T., Donovan, S., & Burns, M. S. (Eds.). (2000). *Eager to Learn: Educating our Preschoolers.* Washington, DC: National Academies Press.

Bredekamp, S., & Rosegrant, T. (Eds.). (1992). *Reaching Potentials: Appropriate Curriculum and Assessment for Young People, Volume 1.* Washington, DC: National Association of Education for Young People.

Clay, M. (1993). *An observation survey of early literacy achievement.* Portsmouth, NH: Heinemann.

Clay, M. M. (1975). *What did I write?* Aukland: Heinemann Educational Books.

Cochran-Smith, M. (1984). *The making of a reader.* Norwood, NJ: Ablex.

Cook-Gumperz, J. (Ed.). (1986). *The social construction of literacy.* Cambridge: Cambridge University Press.

Cunningham, A., & Stanovich, K. (1998). What reading does for the mind. *American Educator, 22,* 8–15.

Ehri, L. (1991). Development of the ability to read words. In R. Barr, M. Kamil, P. Mosenthal, & P. Pearson (Eds.), *Handbook of reading research* (2nd ed., pp. 395–419). New York: Longman.

Epstein, A. S., Schweinhart, L. J., DeBruin-Parecki, A., & Robin, K. B. (2004). *Preschool Assessment: A Guide to Developing a Balanced Approach.* New Brunswick, NJ: National Institute for Early Education Research.

Freeman, D. E., & Freeman, Y. S. (2004). *Essential linguistics: What you need to know to teach reading, ESL, spelling, phonics, grammar.* Portsmouth, NH: Heinemann.

Gibson, E. J., Gibson, J. J., Pick, A. D., & Osser, H. (1962). A developmental study of discrimination of letter-like forms. *Journal of Comparative Physiological Psychology, 55,* 897–906.

Gopnick, A., & Meltzoff, A. Z. (1986). Relations between semantic and cognitive development in the one-word stage: The specificity hypothesis. *Child Development, 57,* 1040–1053.

Halliday, M. A. K. (1975). *Learning how to mean.* New York: Elsevier.

International Reading Association & National Association for the Education of Young Children. (1998). Learning to read and write: Developmentally appropriate practices for young children. *The Reading Teacher, 52,* 193–216.

Juel, C. (1991). Beginning reading. In R. Barr, M. Kamil, P. Mosenthal, & P. Pearson (Eds.), *Handbook of reading research* (2nd ed., pp. 759–788). New York: Longman.

Lavine, L. O. (1977). Differentiation of letter-like forms in prereading children. *Developmental Psychology, 13,* 89–94.

McGee, L. M., & Richgels, D. J. (1990). *Literacy's beginnings: Supporting young readers and writers.* Boston: Allyn & Bacon.

Nation, K., & Hulme, C. (1997). Phonemic segmentation, not onset-rime segmentation, predicts early reading and spelling skills. *Reading Research Quarterly, 32,* 154–167.

National Reading Panel. (2000). *Report of the National Reading Panel.* Washington, DC: National Institutes of Health.

Piaget, J. (1955). *The language and thought of the child.* Cleveland, OH: World.

Pick, A. D., Unze, M. G., Brownell, C. A., Drozdal, J. G., Jr., & Hopmann, M. R. (1978). Young children's knowledge of word structure. *Child Development, 49,* 669–680.

Richgels, D. J. (2004). Theory and research into practice: Paying attention to language. *Reading Research Quarterly, 39,* 470–477.

Rowe, D. (1998). The literate potentials of book-related dramatic play. *Reading Research Quarterly, 33,* 10–35.

Stahl, S., Duffy-Hester, A., & Stahl, A. (1998). Theory and research into practice: Everything you wanted to know about phonics (but were afraid to ask). *Reading Research Quarterly, 33,* 338–355.

Stubbs, M. (1980). *The sociolinguistics of reading and writing: Language and literacy.* London: Routledge & Kegan Paul.

Sulzby, E. (1986). Children's elicitation and use of metalinguistic knowledge about word during literacy interactions. In D. B. Yaden, Jr., & S. Templeton (Eds.), *Metalinguistic awareness and beginning literacy* (pp. 219–233). Portsmouth, NH: Heinemann.

Vygotsky, L. S. (1978). *Mind in society. The development of higher psychological processes* (Michael Cole, Trans.). Cambridge: Harvard University Press.

Yaden, D. B., Jr., & Templeton, S. (1986). Introduction: Metalinguistic awareness—an etymology. In D. B. Yaden, Jr., & S. Templeton (Eds.), *Metalinguistic awareness and beginning literacy* (pp. 3–10). Portsmouth, NH: Heinemann.

CHAPTER 2

Birth to Three Years

THE FOUNDATIONS OF LITERACY DEVELOPMENT

KEY CONCEPTS

Booksharing Routines
Bookhandling Skills
Motor Schemes
Scribbling
Romance
    Representations
Interactive Bookreading
Story Grammar

Concept of Story
Environmental Print
Caregiver Interactive
    Responsiveness
Speech Density
Contextualized
    Language

Decontextualized
    Language
Telegraphic Speech
Formulaic Speech
Systematic Observations
Anecdotal Notes
Reflections on Anecdotal
    Notes

THE BEGINNINGS OF LITERACY

MANY CHILDREN, but not all, have literacy experiences with their families as infants and toddlers, and by three years of age, most children have participated in many literacy experiences. They may share books with parents and other caregivers, they may be invited to use markers and crayons, and they are likely to notice the print found in their environment. These early experiences with books and print allow children to acquire concepts that form the foundation for later reading and writing.

Kristen's Early Literacy Experiences

As an example of the rich literacy experiences that are available to some children, we present a case study of Kristen from her birth until she turned three years old. During this time she was primarily in the stage of beginning reading and writing. She observed literacy, for example, as her mother and father read books aloud to her. She practiced drawing, but did not intend for her drawing to be considered "writing."

Literacy Experiences from Birth to One. Early in the first few months of her life, Kristen's mother and father would actively engage her in language activities especially during daily routines. For example, her father would talk with Kristen when he changed her diaper. As Kristen lay on the changing table, her father would say, "I am going to put on a nice dry diaper." Kristen would coo and gurgle, and her father would reply, "I know you like that, don't you?" Kristen would wiggle, and her father would continue, "I agree. Dry diapers are the best."

Kristen received her first books when she was just a few months old. Many of these were sturdy cardboard books such as *A Goodnight Hug* (Roth, 1986). They were kept in her toy basket along with her rattles. Her mother and father read to her while she sat in their laps. When Kristen could sit up, she began grabbing her books, picking them up, and holding them. She did not look at the pictures in her books; instead, she made insistent attempts to turn the pages. Her books were some of her favorite toys. She would pull books out of a basket and dump them on her blanket, grab for books, turn pages, and try to chew on the pages. Her mother and father engaged her in active games with books. When they read a book with nursery rhymes, they would hold Kristen and use actions to engage her attention. As they recited a nursery rhyme, they would hold her close and rock her back and forth. They would hold her arms and hands and help her clap or take her body and gently pretend to fall.

Some months before her first birthday, Kristen could recognize books by their names. Her father would say, "Let's read the Humpty Dumpty book." Kristen would crawl to the book basket and select her "Humpty Dumpty book" (*The Real Mother Goose*, Wright, 1916). She would turn to the page that had the Humpty Dumpty rhyme and sway her body as her father recited the rhyme.

Literacy Experiences from One to Two. By her first birthday, Kristen would hold a book right-side-up and turn the pages from front to back. Sometimes she smiled and patted the pictures or turned pages over from one side to the next, intently checking the pictures on each side of the page.

A few months after her first birthday, Kristen began to point to things around her, saying "dat?" with a rising intonation. She would also point to and ask "dat?" about animals and people pictured in her books. Her mother or father would obligingly name the animals and people. Kristen's mother often requested that she locate animals or people in her books. She would ask, "Where's the kitten?" and Kristen would point to it.

Kristen received crayons as a Christmas present when she was fifteen months old. Her first attempts at drawing were rapid back-and-forth swipes at paper (see Figure 2.1). She would quickly make a few marks and push the paper on the floor, indicating that she wanted another sheet of paper.

When Kristen was about sixteen months old, she began interrupting bookreading by jumping off her father's lap to seek a toy or object in the house. She did this only when she saw certain pictures in her books. Each time Kristen saw a picture of crayons, for example, she would get up and find *her* crayons.

When she was twenty-one months old, Kristen began making round-and-round lines and dots. Her mother and father began drawing to entertain her. They drew people, houses, flowers, cats, dogs, and other familiar objects.

Literacy Experiences from Two to Three.

As Kristen turned two years old, she could recite some of the text in her books. In *Hop on Pop* (Seuss, 1963b), Kristen said, "No. No. No sit" after her mother read, "No, Pat, No. Don't sit on that." As her father read the text of *Goodnight Moon* (Brown, 1947), he would pause for Kristen to fill in part of the rhyme. Kristen began recognizing McDonald's and Burger King signs. She would say "DeDonald's" or "Bugar King" each time she saw the signs. Kristen also pointed to her favorite cereals and cookies in the grocery store, saying "Aisin Ban" and "Oeos."

Drawing continued to be a favorite activity. She began to control her drawing and could make jagged lines, straight lines, and dots. When asked to tell about her drawing, she often replied, "dots." She frequently initiated drawing activities with her parents.

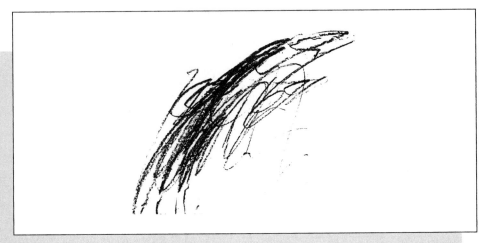

FIGURE 2.1   Back-and-Forth Lines

She would take paper and crayons to her mother and command, "Draw. Draw little girl." or "Draw little boy." After drawing a little girl, her mother would say, "That's Kristen. Now I'll write Kristen" and she would write her name next to the picture. After drawing a little boy, her mother would say, "That's daddy. I'll write daddy, too."

At twenty-seven months of age, Kristen made concentrated efforts to control her marks. She would slowly draw a continuous line all around the edges of her paper. It seemed as if she were pushing the crayon around the paper and watching its progress. She began making circular shapes of just a single line or a few lines (see Figure 2.2).

Although Kristen continued to thoroughly enjoy drawing, she resisted her mother's attempts to invite her to label her drawings. When asked to tell about her drawings, she would often shrug. However, just before Kristen turned three years old, her mother noticed a change in Kristen's drawings. Now Kristen seemed more intentional about her drawings. She made round shapes and carefully added some straight lines and dots. While her drawings still looked like scribbles, her mother could tell she was trying to draw something, rather than just make marks. One day her mother drew a round shape and asked Kristen to point to where the eyes, nose, mouth, and hair should go. Kristen pointed to where each feature belonged. Her mother coaxed her to draw some eyes. Kristen tried to put eyes on the face, but she became frustrated. She announced, "I can't draw that." Another day, Kristen's mother convinced her to draw by saying, "Just do some lines and dots and circles." Kristen selected a blue marker and made several quick line strokes down her page. After making several of these marks, she cried, "Look at the rain." She made several more marks, saying, "More rain. Look at the rain, Mommy." Then she began making dots, saying, "Look at all these raindrops (see Figure 2.3).

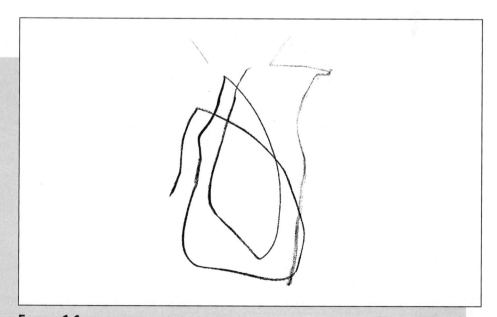

FIGURE 2.2   Circular Shapes

FIGURE 2.3 *"Rain" and "Raindrops"*

By the time Kristen was three years old, she was drawing people (see Figure 2.4). She would draw a circle, add two lines for arms, two lines for legs, and some dots for eyes. After drawing the person in Figure 2.4, Kristen said, "This is a picture of Daddy."

At three years of age, Kristen participated in book and familiar print reading in many ways. She made comments about characters and actions depicted in her books. Pointing to the picture of the wolf in *Walt Disney's Peter and the Wolf* (Disney Productions, 1974), she said, "He needs to be good." She commented about the predicament of

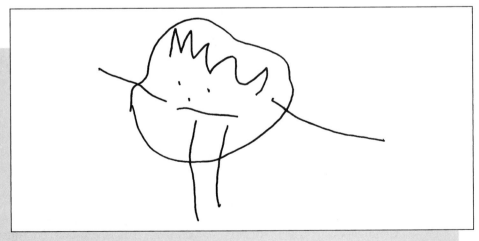

FIGURE 2.4 *"This is a picture of Daddy"*

Wully-Wully in *Babar and the Wully-Wully* (de Brunhoff, 1975), saying "He's in the cage" and "He got out" as she pointed to the pictures of Wully-Wully captured and rescued.

Concepts about Literacy Acquired from Early Book and Drawing Experiences

As part of these experiences interacting with her parents as they read books with her and using crayons and markers, Kristen acquired seven foundational concepts about literacy.

1. *Literacy activities are pleasurable.* Perhaps one of the most important concepts that children can learn at the beginning of their literacy experiences is that reading is a pleasurable activity. When children are read to beginning early in their lives, they play with books as a preferred and frequent activity (Bus, 2001). Bookreading is one of the closest activities parents and children share.

Children also enjoy drawing and writing. Adult observers sense children's intense concentration as they hold tightly to both markers and paper and watch intently the shapes they create (Taylor & Dorsey-Gaines, 1988).

2. *Literacy activities occur in predictable routines.* Toddlers and their parents learn ways of interacting with each other while reading books. They develop **booksharing routines,** that is, familiar, expected actions and language that accompanied their book reading. Kristen learned how to initiate and participate in bookreading sessions. She frequently selected a book and backed into a lap. She clearly signaled that she wanted to share a book. Once her mother or father began sharing a book, Kristen located characters when asked to do so and solicited comments from her mother or father by pointing to something in the picture or making comments and asking questions. She learned to answer questions. Gradually, she learned to listen to more of the story her mother or father was reading.

Booksharing routines make it possible for children to show parents what they are learning. Parents respond by giving children opportunities to use their new abilities and expecting children to use them. Kristen and her parents demonstrated this in their playing of a routine known as the naming game (Ninio & Bruner, 1978). It begins with an adult's pointing to and naming pictured animals, people, and objects; it progresses as adults ask questions; and it ends with children's pointing to and labeling pictures on their own.

3. *Language is an important part of reading and drawing.* Language is an important part of the routine activities of reading books together or drawing. As Kristen's language developed, so did the nature of her reading and drawing. At first, Kristen participated in reading and drawing by actively moving her body. Later, she was expected to use language to participate in these activities.

4. *Literacy materials are handled in special ways.* In this beginning period, children also learn **bookhandling skills,** ways of handling and looking at books. Kristen learned how to hold books right-side-up and how to turn pages. She also discovered that books are for viewing and reading and not just for turning pages (Snow & Ninio, 1986).

Children learn motor "schemes" for drawing shapes and lines (Gardner, 1980). **Motor schemes** are children's control of their movements so they can make intentional shapes and lines. In order to be able to put circles and dots on a page where they intend them to go, children must learn how to control their movements. As with Kristen, most children first develop motor schemes for making back-and-forth marks, round-and-round lines, dots, and jagged lines. Later, they make circlelike shapes and single lines (Gardner, 1980). Eventually, children learn to make as many as twenty basic scribbles, which become the building blocks of art and writing (Kellogg, 1969).

5. *Literacy involves the use of symbols.* Illustrations in books are symbols—they represent or symbolize real objects or people. At first, children treat books as objects. They consider books as interesting objects to manipulate and explore with all their senses. Only gradually do children learn to look at the pictures in books as representations rather than interesting colors, shapes, and lines. Kristen demonstrated her awareness that book illustrations were symbols, or representations, when she sought out her box of crayons after she saw a picture of crayons in a favorite book.

Kristen took longer to understand that her drawings could also be symbols. At first, her drawing consisted of **scribbling**—uncontrolled marks made on a page without any intention of drawing a particular object or person. Then she recognized her mother's and father's drawing as symbols for people. It was not until she was nearly three years old that Kristen created her first representational drawing—a symbol for her father. Representational drawings are intentionally constructed and look something like the object or person the child-drawer intends to create. Kristen's drawing of her father is called a tadpole. Tadpole "people" have arms and legs emerging from an oversized head. Dots serve as eyes and nose with single lines serving as mouth, arms, and legs. Gradually children add hair, feet, and other details. Bodies do not appear in children's people drawing until much later.

Some children create **romance representations** before they can produce an actual representational drawing. A romance representation is unintentional marks that a child later names. For example, a child might draw round-and-round lines as he imitates the sound of a car motor. After drawing, the child might call his picture "race car." The marks he made (round-and-round scribbles) do not resemble a car; however, after drawing, the child labeled his drawing as if it were a symbol (Gardner, 1980). True representational drawings are planned—children intend to draw a person often announcing their intentions as they draw, "I am drawing a picture of my daddy."

6. *Literacy involves communicating meanings.* A crucial outcome of children's early experiences with books and other kinds of print is that they learn that books and other print materials communicate meaning—they tell a message. Learning to "mean" (Halliday, 2002), to understand what others say and do, is involved in nearly every activity, not only in literacy activities. It is the great undertaking of life—we constantly try to understand the messages that bombard us and to send messages to others. We use many cues to help us understand others and to help others understand us. We use the situation we are in and its clues to meaning (characteristics of the location or people's clothing), as well as spoken language and its clues to meaning (words, stress, and intonation). These are called contextualization clues.

7. *Literacy arises from social interactions embedded in cultural practices.* Kristen's case study necessarily leaves out much that she experienced from birth until she turned three years old (and stops just short of the two preschool years in which she made the most literacy gains as a three- and four-year-old). What is left out of Kristen's case study is as important for understanding her literacy development as is what is told. For example, we did not include any of her experiences with the computer, the comic page of the newspaper, and toy brochures, nor even her experiences viewing television, singing, and dancing. In fact, a careful reading of Kristen's case study—of what we tell about Kristen, the print she was exposed to, and the encouragement she received from both of her parents—reveals parents carefully pushing their daughter toward school-like literacy.

What is priviledged in this case study are the acts of understanding children's books and making representational drawings. Kristen's case study illustrates how she is developing concepts about reading and writing as she participates in the particular culture of literacy in her home. It includes two dimensions: the individual dimension and the social dimension (Green & Dixon, 1996; Perez, 2004). From the individual perspective, literacy is seen as belonging to a person: what skills she controls. Kristen could handle books and knew how to draw people. From the social perspective, literacy is seen as the ability to use literacy to achieve the goals determined by a particular social context. She was able to participate in bookreading events in ways that her parents expected, by answering questions and recalling words of the text.

From a sociocultural view of literacy (Hammerberg, 2004), perceiving how children are enculturated into particular literacy practices requires examining three factors: the act of reading, the identities of participants, and the text. For Kristen, the act of reading consisted of drawing on personal experiences in order to understand a text's meaning, where that meaning was assumed to be "in" the text's words. Kristen's parents took pride in her remembering words from the text. In other homes, reading might consist of deciding the meaning of a Bible passage, problem solving how to come up with the money to pay a bill, or playing a video game.

The second factor in a sociocultural view of literacy is the identities of the participants. Children and parents take on particular identities in literacy events. Clearly, Kristen's parents expected her to take on the identity of "a reader" rather than "a listener," and "a drawer" rather than "a scribbler." In other homes, preschool children are expected to "listen and not be heard."

The third factor is the text. Kristen's experiences of texts were of personally owned quality pieces of literature. Literacy in her home included print literacy of high academic value. In other homes, a greater proportion of printed texts might be *TV Guides* and printed advertising flyers, but those homes might also provide numerous experiences with such oral and visual texts as spoken stories and television daytime talk shows, or the discussion of family finances and the video game we mentioned in connection with different acts of reading. These are the texts of multimodal literacies, that is, literacies that involve reading not just print, but also nonprint sources of meaning.

This book is primarily about how children achieve literacy in the sense of reading and writing printed texts. Nonetheless, the notion of reading nonprinted texts is not as unusual as it may at first seem. Most people are familiar with the terms *reading someone's expression*, for the act of determining someone's emotional state from the look on his or her face, or *reading the sky*, for the act of predicting the weather based on how the sky looks. The same notion of *to read* applies when someone in a highly oral culture is adept at making meaning not only from what storytellers say, but also from how they move, how they use their voices, and how they manipulate elements of their culture's story structures for didactic and entertainment value. Such a person is a good reader of the text of a spoken story. Similarly, someone who knows well the art and craft of movie making is adept at reading a movie, that is, getting meanings from what is shown on the screen. Such a person notices a director's choices of camera angles, a film editor's style of cutting, and set builders' and costumers' choices of production values. That more informed movie viewing results in a better "read" of a movie than what the average movie viewer gets.

Children grow up in many different contexts, with different effects on their reading and writing. Some children, like Kristen, have experiences with home literacies that are very much like the literacies they will experience in school (Heath, 1983; Lesman & van Tuijl, 2004). In other communities, home literacy experiences are not school-like; instead they are about getting the daily business of life accomplished (Perez, 2004). This means that nearly all children grow up experiencing many kinds of language in their home communities, especially instrumental and social language (see Halliday's instrumental and interactional uses of language in Table 1.1), but some children have far fewer experiences than other children with academic forms of spoken and written language like those they will experience in school.

Effective teachers recognize that all children come to school with rich language experiences. For example, African American children are likely to grow up in homes that value oral storytelling sometimes communicated through music (Dyson, 2003; Smith, 2004). These children are likely to have advanced abilities to entertain their peers with lively stories. However, for teachers who are only used to middle-class and school-like literacies, such as those that Kristen, Ted, and Carrie (see Chapter 1) experienced in their homes, other linguistic strengths, such as oral storytelling, might be missed. Teachers should be open to all the variteties of home language that children bring to school. For example, they may want to step back as African American children share information in oral reports or show-and-tell situations. As teachers notice the different ways children convey main points and make connections in those oral language contexts, they will come to expect and appreciate children's different styles of engagement in reading and writing (Michaels, 1981).

Observant teachers recognize that children come to school with multiple literacies (Gee, 1999) including abilities to communicate through speaking, listening, viewing, drawing, and clicking (navigating through the internet and computer games). While children have varied concepts about literacy acquired in their particular home and community cultures, sensitive teachers use these concepts to build bridges between home literacy practices and school practices. For example, after a mother brags to a preschool teacher that her child can write his name on the computer, a sensitive teacher will recognize this literacy accomplishment as a strength rather than discounting this skill by immediately insisting this child write his name the "correct way" using paper and pencil (Arthur, Beecher, & Jones Diaz, 2001; Turbill & Murray, 2006).

HOME INFLUENCES ON LITERACY LEARNING: LEARNING IN SOCIAL AND CULTURAL CONTEXTS

AS WE HAVE SHOWN, literacy learning begins in the home. Children's first experiences with literacy are mediated by the ways in which parents and other caregivers use reading and writing in their lives (Purcell-Gates, 1996). One way in which mainstream parents invite very young children to participate in literacy activities is to read storybooks aloud. In fact, one predictor of children's reading achievement in school is the number of hours they were read to as preschoolers (Wells, 1986). We also know that preschoolers who interacted more with their parents as they read aloud have larger vocabularies and better story understanding as five-year-olds than do children who contributed less during storybook readings (Leseman & de Jong, 1998). Clearly, reading aloud with young children is an important vehicle through which they acquire literacy concepts.

It is not surprising that children who have home experiences with books are more likely to have larger vocabularies and better understanding of stories than children who have few home book experiences. Reading storybooks aloud to preschoolers gives them practice in the very activity they will be expected to master in kindergarten: listening to the teacher read storybooks aloud.

Parent-Child Interactive Bookreading

We describe the interactions between two children and their parents as they shared books together. These interactions demonstrate the strategies used by parents and other caregivers to support young children's interest in and construction of meaning. They also show how children's abilities to understand books expand as a result of participating in **interactive bookreading.**

Interactive bookreading is a book sharing experience by a child and a more knowledgeable other person, usually an adult, to which both contribute. Parents read, comment, ask questions, and point to the illustrations. Children point, make comments, and answer questions. We share these examples of interactive bookreading to highlight what children can learn to do and how adults can support that learning.

Elizabeth and Her Mother Share Where's Spot?   A portion of the interaction between Elizabeth (twenty-six months) and her mother as they shared *Where's Spot?* (Hill, 1980) is presented in Figure 2.5. Elizabeth took charge of the interaction by turning the pages and making comments. She labeled objects in the pictures ("There's a doggy there") and answered her mother's questions.

Elizabeth's mother used many strategies for expanding and supporting Elizabeth's participation in this booksharing event. First, she featured an important narrative element (action and character motivation) by telling Elizabeth that the mother dog was looking for her puppy. She continually used this as a context for helping Elizabeth understand why the dog was looking behind doors and under beds. She matched her reading style to Elizabeth's ability to participate in the bookreading by interweaving her talk with reading the text (Martin, 1998). She helped Elizabeth find meaning from the words of the text by using her explanations and expansions of the story as a support for meaning construction. In addition, she asked Elizabeth questions that called for labeling ("What's inside the clock?") and provided feedback to her daughter's answers (correcting Elizabeth when she mistook the mother dog for the puppy).

Jon-Marc and His Father Share The Story of Ferdinand.   Figure 2.6 presents part of a booksharing interaction between Jon-Marc, a three-year-old, and his father. Jon-Marc listened carefully and looked intently at each illustration as his father read *The Story of*

FIGURE 2.5 Elizabeth and Her Mother Share *Where's Spot?* (Hill, 1980)

Paraphrased text is underlined. Brackets indicate portions of the dialogue that occurred simultaneously.

⎡ Mother: We are looking for Spot. Let's turn the page. He's a little tiny puppy. Can
⎢   you see if you can find him <u>behind the door.</u> Is he there?
⎣ E: (turns to next page)

M: No?—What's inside the clock? Is he in there?

E: He's in there.

M: That's a snake. That's not a little dog.

E: Let me read it.

M: Okay.

E: It's a snake.

⎡ M: Turn the page. Where's Spot? Let's see if we can find the puppy. Is he—
⎣ E: (turns back to look at snake again)

M: Let's see what's behind the next page. We need to find Spot. Is he in there?
     (points to piano)

E: There's a doggy there. (points to Mother Dog, Sally)

M: He's looking for another doggy. Spot's not there.

E: There? (points to Sally on next page)

M: Yes. That's a doggy. He's looking for another doggy, a puppy. Is there a
     puppy <u>in the piano</u>?

E: No.

Ferdinand (Leaf, 1936). One strategy Jon-Marc used to make meaning was to apply his understanding of events in the real world to make inferences about story events. Jon-Marc asked if Ferdinand would (go home) "And . . . and . . . and love her mother cow?" This question reveals that Jon-Marc used inferences to predict story events (after going home, Ferdinand would love his mother). It also illustrates that he used his own life as a frame of reference for understanding the story. Jon-Marc probably went home to love his mother, so he inferred that Ferdinand would be going home to love his mother.

Jon-Marc's father was skillful at adapting the booksharing event to his child's abilities. He expanded on information from the text and related to Jon-Marc's concerns (he explained that Madrid is a city), and he provided more adult models of language ("And love his mother"). He repeated information from the story text to answer Jon-Marc's question and, therefore, made explicit the causal relations among events in the

FIGURE 2.6   Jon-Marc and His Father Share *The Story of Ferdinand* (Leaf, 1936)

Text is presented in all capital letters.

Illustration:	Ferdinand in a small cart going over the mountain. A bull ring is the background.
Father:	SO THEY HAD TO TAKE FERDINAND HOME.
Jon-Marc:	Why?
Father:	Because he wouldn't fight. He just wouldn't fight. He didn't like to fight. He just wanted to smell the flowers. (Note, this is a paraphrase of the text that had just been read on the previous pages.)
Jon-Marc:	Is that why they wanted to . . . to . . . to fight in the drid?
Father:	In Madrid? Yeah, they wanted . . . they wanted him to fight in Madrid. Madrid's the name of a city. They wanted him to fight the matador. But he didn't. He just wanted to go home and smell the flowers.
Jon-Marc:	And . . . and . . . and love her mother cow?
Father:	Yeah, and . . . and love his mother.
Jon-Marc:	Where's her mother cow?
Father:	Well, she's back in the book a little bit.

story ("They wanted him to fight the matador. But he didn't. He just wanted to go home and smell the flowers."). All of his talk was contingent on Jon-Marc's talk; that is, it was in response to Jon-Marc's questions and comments.

Participation in Interactive Bookreading

The interactions we presented of Elizabeth and her mother and Jon-Marc and his father were carefully selected to illustrate how children's participation in and parents' support during interactive read-alouds shift as children gain more language and literacy experience. At first, parents seem to focus on gaining their children's attention and getting them actively involved. During these interactions parents are not concerned about the story (Martin, 1998); books most parents read at this age are merely a series of interesting pictures (for example, of babies eating, playing, or sleeping) rather than stories. At this age, parents cuddle children closely on their laps, let children hold the book and turn pages, and use motivating and attention getting strategies such as pointing and saying, "Look here at this baby." They encourage their children to point and label pictures by asking, "Look, what's that?" as they point to details in an illustration (Bus, 2001). They make comments that connect book ideas to their children by saying, "Look. That blanket is yellow just like yours." Parents follow children's leads by letting them turn the book's pages or close the book, signaling this book is finished.

As children develop a deep sense of enjoyment about books and gain confidence in their role as participants, parents begin taking a more active role in directing children's attention to story characters and events or ideas in an informational book (Martin, 1998). Now parents seem more concerned with helping children understand the basic sequence of events in a story although they still expect their children to be actively involved answering questions, commenting, and labeling pictures. These strategies actively engage children and call for them to use thinking at relatively low levels of cognitive demand. Activities that call on low levels of cognitive demand focus on word-level recall of ideas, mostly on the *what* of a message.

As children get older, parents intuitively select books with more complex stories or information. These books will trigger opportunities for talking about challenging vocabulary and clarifying character traits and motivations. Now parents shift from using strategies that focus on lower cognitive demand related to understanding the *what* of stories and information books to using strategies that call on high levels of cognitive demand related to understanding the *why* and *how* of stories (Dickinson & Smith, 1994). Figure 2.7 presents a summary of the range of attention getting, low cognitive demand,

FIGURE 2.7   Strategies Parents Use to Support Children's Active Engagement during Interactive Bookreading

Attention Getting and Sustaining Strategies

allowing child to hold book and turn pages

pointing to and labeling or commenting on details in illustrations

helping child imitate or asking child to make gestures or sounds

asking for child to point out details in illustrations

asking for child to label details in illustrations

adjusting language of text for child (may not read text, but talk about illustrations)

answering and responding to child's questions and comments

Low Cognitive Demand Strategies

reading text and pausing for child to supply word

asking child who, what, and where questions calling for recall of information in text

High Cognitive Demand Strategies

asking child why questions calling for inferences (I wonder why . . .?)

asking child questions calling for making connections between ideas in text and child's personal experience (What does this remind you of . . .?)

prompting child to predict (What do you think will happen next?)

prompting child to clarify or elaborate

elaborating on child's comments or text

explaining vocabulary word or connections between ideas

commenting on character traits or motivations

and high cognitive demand strategies that parents use to elicit their children's participation in interactive bookreading experiences (adapted from Dickinson & Smith, 1994 and Martin, 1998).

Concept of Story

As parents begin reading stories to their children and directing their attention to characters and story events, children develop an awareness of the elements found in typical literary stories. Most stories have a main character and several supporting characters. The events of the story are set in motion when the main character recognizes a problem or decides to achieve a goal. The plot of the story consists of a series of events in which the main character actively tries to solve the problem or achieve the goal. The story ends as the character solves the problem or achieves the goal (the happily ever after of most fairytales). A **story grammar** describes all the components that are included in an ideal story (Mandler & Johnson, 1977). Table 2.1 presents the narrative elements of a story grammar and an example of an ideal story (based on Stein & Glenn, 1979). Most adults are at least intuitively aware of the elements included in this story grammar.

TABLE 2.1　Story Grammar

Narrative Elements	Story Example A Smart Dog
Main characters (animals or people)	An old man, his grandson Jim, and their sheepdog Shep lived on a mountain side.
Setting (description of location)	
Action or event (introduction of problem)	One dewy morning, while Jim was watching the sheep, Grandpa took Shep and set out to look for wild berries. Grandpa slipped on the wet grass and broke his leg.
Goal (formulation of a goal)	He decided to send Shep for help.
Attempt (actions to solve the problem)	Grandpa tied his scarf around Shep's neck and sent him to find the sheep.
Resolution (outcome of actions)	When Jim saw the scarf around Shep's neck, he knew that Grandpa was in trouble. He left Shep to watch the sheep and followed Shep's tracks in the dewy grass toward where Grandpa lay. Soon he heard Grandpa's calling. Jim helped his grandfather back to their house where they could call a doctor.
Reaction (character's feelings about outcome)	Grandpa and Jim were glad that they had such a smart sheep dog.

Children's awareness of the story elements included in a story grammar is called their **concept of story** (Applebee, 1978). Most preschoolers have undeveloped concepts of stories. When asked to tell stories, they may list the names of their friends or describe the actions of a favorite pet. Some children have better developed concepts of stories; they may tell stories with imaginary characters but rely on their knowledge of everyday actions to invent story events. They are not likely to include problems or goals.

Environmental Print

While sharing books may not occur in every family, nearly all children have experiences with print in their environment. In fact, research has shown that especially for African American children, experiences with **environmental print** (print found on signs and in logos) often are the first and most important form of early literacy experience (Craig & Washington, 2004). As children eat breakfast, they see a box of Rice Krispies and they hear talk about eating the Rice Krispies. They observe and listen in the grocery store as their parents look for Rice Krispies. As children acquire language, they learn to talk about "Rice Krispies."

Many toddlers and two-year-olds do not notice or pay much attention to the print on their cereal boxes or cookie packages; nonetheless, the print is there. The print on the packages becomes part of what children know about those objects. Later, children will recognize just the print and stylized picture or logo without the object's being there.

Children learn about other print in their environment as they participate in a variety of everyday literacy events. They are included in shopping trips for which parents read lists, clip coupons, or write checks. They observe as parents write reminder notes or help older children with homework. Children whose homes include more frequent literacy events (such as parents' reading of magazines and books and writing letters or lists) know more about how reading and writing are used (Burns & Casbergue, 1992; Purcell-Gates, 1996).

Spoken Language Development and Its relationship to Literacy Development

AS WE HAVE SEEN in the examples of Elizabeth and Jon-Marc, children's spoken language provides a pathway into literacy. Spoken language development supports and provides a foundation for written language development.

Spoken Language Development

Two factors that are related to children's later language development are caregiver interactive responsiveness and speech density (Schickedanz, Schickedanz, Forsyth, & Forsyth, 2001). **Caregiver interactive responsiveness** refers to how effectively a parent or caregiver engages infants and later toddlers and two-year-olds in communicative interactions. Kristen's father demonstrated a high level of caregiver interactive responsiveness when he talked with Kristen as he changed her diaper. He talked and Kristen wiggled in an interaction similar to the give-and-take of a real conversation. From interactions such as these, babies learn how to take turns in conversations, how to focus their gaze on a parent, and later how to follow a gaze (turn to look at an object or person a parent is looking at). Before acquiring their first words, babies use reaching, gazing, pointing, and giving to take a turn in a conversation; responsive caregivers supply the words and keep the conversation flowing.

Speech density refers to the number of words that infants hear in a given period of time. The more that parents talk to an infant, the higher the speech density. The more words children hear, the more words they learn. Parents and caregivers who establish interactive responsiveness and produce high levels of speech density are more likely to have children with larger vocabularies and more complex syntax.

Children's vocabularies grow slowly at first, then rapidly increase. Children need responsive conversational partners to accelerate spoken vocabulary development. Adults naturally seem to repeat and expand on what children say, providing them with a more mature model of their own language. When a toddler comments about a string of lights, "Yights!", a parent may respond "You see those little lights." The toddler may continue the conversation by adding, "Yots." A parent can respond, "There are lots of lights. They are twinkling" (adapted from Post & Hohmann, 2000, p. 78). Effective parents and caregivers encourage conversation by commenting, observing, and acknowledging rather than by asking questions (Post & Hohmann, 2000). They describe what children are seeing and doing: "You see your Mom, Jamal" or "You are sucking your fingers!" Or they describe what they are seeing and doing: "I'm going to put you in this chair for a snack."

Nonimmediate and Decontextualized Spoken Language: Spoken Equivalents to Written Language

Written language used in reading and writing is similar to, but not exactly the same as, spoken language used in conversations. Conversations involve turn-taking, thoughts are not completely organized, and ideas are developed jointly through asking questions for clarification, using facial expressions and gestures, and referencing previously shared experiences. On the other hand, readers are constrained by using the words, and only the words, in order to form personal interpretations of a novel. They cannot seek clarification from the author or seek clues by looking around the setting in which they are reading.

Spoken conversations usually center on recent events and familiar people, while novels are about imaginary people in settings never before experienced. That is, spoken conversations usually focus on immediate events (events that occur in the actual world of here and now) and involve the use of **contextualized language.** Contexualized language draws on sources of meaning outside of words. It involves pointing to and looking at people, objects, and activities in a shared context. It uses facial expressions, body language, intonation, and gestures. Written language, in contrast, usually focuses on nonimmediate events (events that have occurred in the past or imagination) and draws on the use of **decontextualized language** (language that draws only on words to communicate meaning and not on real-world context) (Beals, 2001).

An example of a conversation focused on immediate events and using contextualized language and contextualized cues follows. Imagine a mother and a college-aged daughter standing in the kitchen talking as the mother makes dinner:

Daughter: I got it.

Mother: Um hm. I like it.

Daughter: See, it has five different styles. Just what I wanted, and it was only four dollars.

Mother: So, did you measure?

Daughter: Yes. I'm closest to the eight.

Mother: Okay, so you're ready to go.

There are a few clues embedded in the conversation about its actual meaning, but most of what is said is not understood without knowing a great deal about the situation, including the objects in the actual setting, and the background experiences of the participants. Here is part of the same conversation, now with the contextualization clues used by the mother and daughter made explicit in brackets.

Daughter: I got it. [Earlier in the day the daughter had called the mother to tell her she wanted to sew some dresses while she was visiting her grandmother. The last time she had sewn with her grandmother, she had made a formal gown that she wore to a party at college. However, that gown had been stored in New Orleans and was ruined during hurricane Katrina. Now, the daughter seems to want to recreate a closeness with her grandmother by sewing again.]

Mother: um hm. [She looks over the dress pattern the daughter is holding in her hand. She nods her head and smiles as she acknowledges that the style of dress is exactly what the daughter often searches for and has a hard time finding in stores.]

Daughter: See, it has five different styles. Just want I wanted, and it was only four dollars. [The daughter is feeling the pinch of having to come up with her own spending money at college and having new clothes for the fall.]

Given these contextualization clues, it is much easier for us to understand what was going on in this conversation. We are now on a more equal footing with the mother and daughter. With those clues made explicit, we have now experienced the conversation more as they did, with more of the information that was in the context but not in their spoken words. Furthermore, it is easier now to determine the meaning of the remainder of the conversation (about measuring and being "closest to the eight"): The daughter has measured herself to determine which size on the pattern she should cut.

If we were writing a story about the mother and daughter, we would have to create the context of the conversation by including in our text most of the information in the brackets. Our written words would have to make up for the text's being decontextualized. Unlike the mother and daughter in their highly contextualized—that is, context-rich but word-poor—conversation, our readers will not have the mother's and daughter's memories of past experiences with the grandmother and of losses caused by Katrina. Our readers will not have the mother's and daughter's shared understanding of the daughter's financial situation and impending return to college. They will not have the actual dress pattern to look at.

English Language Learners

The examples that we have just given are of English language speakers and their emergence as language users in English-speaking communities. The principles of language learning, developmental sequences, and components of language that must be acquired, apply across all languages. So, children learning Spanish, Dutch, Korean, or any other language must all gradually acquire the ability to form sounds, words, and sentences in ways that are culturally acceptable in their language communities.

However, when young children whose home language is not English enter English-speaking day cares or preschools, they begin a different language-learning pathway than what they had begun at home as first language learners (Tabors, 1997). Not all English Language Learners (ELLs) learn English as a second language in precisely the same way; however, four phases of language learning can be expected:

1. Children may continue to use their home language in the English-speaking setting.
2. When children discover their language is not working, they begin a nonverbal period in which they communicate without words.
3. During the nonverbal period, children pick up information about English sounds, words, and phrases.
4. Children emerge into English speech at first using single words and short phrases and only gradually acquiring productive use of English with grammatically appropriate speech (adapted from Tabors, 1997, p. 39).

During the nonverbal period, children use gestures, facial expressions, giving and taking objects, and other physical movements to gain attention, to request help or actions, to protest the actions of others, and to have fun with others. The limitations of nonverbal communications are great; without a sympathetic and perceptive listener, children often fail to communicate. Thus, the teacher's most important role is to become that sympathetic and perceptive listener.

Children use two strategies to begin to learn to communicate in English: they watch and listen intently while involved in group activities and they privately rehearse. As ELLs watch and listen, for example, in the block area, they overhear what English language speakers say. As part of watching and listening, ELLs may rehearse; they quietly repeat sounds, words, and phrases. Eventually, as they become more confident, they begin talking with other children in English. At first, children use telegraphic and formulaic speech. **Telegraphic speech** is the use of just a few words to communicate meanings that an adult would say with complete sentences. **Formulaic speech** is words or phrases that occur repeatedly and predictably in routine social situations. Children use the phrases of formulaic speech as single meaning units rather than as syntactic structures that build meaning by combining individually meaningful words. For example, a child may use *Me first* as a formula for getting ahead of his or her classmates without knowing the individual meanings of *me* and *first* or being able to use those separate words meaningfully in other contexts. Other examples of formulaic speech are *Okay?, Uh oh, Look, What's that?, Bye bye,* and *Wanna play?*

Assessing Literacy Beginners

TEACHERS OF INFANTS, TODDLERS, AND TWO-YEAR-OLDS do seek assessment information. However, they are generally more interested in children's typical performance in the areas of language, cognitive, social, emotional, and physical development than in the more specific area of literacy development. However, many three-year-olds are included in publicly funded preschool programs that require more assessments. Head Start, for example, requires that children be assessed in language and literacy as well as in all other areas of development (U.S. Department of Health and Human Services, 2003). With very young children, the most important assessment is observation and reflection.

Teachers engage in observation nearly all the time. They carefully watch their children and gauge by children's actions whether activities are going smoothly and how to interact next. However, in order to serve assessment needs, observations must be systematic. **Systematic observations** are planned and result in written notes. In this chapter we have shown that beginners participate with adults in bookreading events by attending to the illustrations, pointing to objects in illustrations upon request, naming objects in illustrations, and answering questions at both low and high cognitive levels. Beginners also pay attention to environmental print in familiar contexts and can name it. They begin to tell stories that have some of the components of ideal story grammars. Thus, teachers' planned, systematic literacy observations of beginners can include watching for these behaviors.

As children participate in bookreading and environmental print reading events and tell stories, teachers write what they observe children do and say. Teachers capture as much information about the events as they can in their written notes, which are called **anecdotal notes** (Rhodes & Nathenson-Mejia, 1992). Anecdotal notes do not include judgments of how well children are performing. Instead they are mere descriptions of actions and talk. Later, teachers will reflect on the actions and talk and write statements about what the child knows and can do. These statements are added to anecdotal notes as written **reflections**. Figure 2.8 presents an anecdotal note and reflection about four-year-old Danielle, a developmentally delayed child, as she worked in her preschool art center. The figure also includes two samples of drawings that Danielle made as the teacher observed. Notice that the anecdotal note carefully describes Danielle's actions and her words while the reflection is the teacher's judgment about what Danielle has learned to do in this activity.

Naturally, teachers will also make inferences about what children cannot yet do and do not yet know. However, these need not be included in reflections on anecdotal notes. Anecdotal notes and reflections that are stated in positive language about what children are currently capable of doing and their current level of knowledge can guide decisions about what instruction will best guide children in their next developmental steps. Children who are provided with guidance informed by observation and reflection will take those steps. In this way, anecdotal notes taken across time will reflect children's growing literacy knowledge. Of course, this depends on taking anecdotal notes and writing reflections frequently—at least once a month.

FIGURE 2.8a   Danielle's Round and Round Drawing

Anecdotal Note: Danielle was drawing at the art center. When asked what she was doing said, "I make round and round." I said it looked like a head with lots of curly hair. I asked where the eyes would be and she pointed inside her drawing. I suggested she put dots in to make a face. She made two scribble marks. I said I would add legs and I drew two lines down. Danielle got out another paper and said: "I make a head, too." Her drawing included head, eyes, legs, and maybe a mouth.

FIGURE 2.8b   Danielle's Person

Reflection: This is the first time Danielle has made a representational drawing. 4/23/05

CHAPTER SUMMARY

THIS CHAPTER DESCRIBES THE FIRST PHASE OF LITERACY DEVELOPMENT: the beginnings of reading and writing. Very young children begin their literacy learning when they interact with their parents and other caring adults as they share books or other kinds of print items. Young children who have opportunities to draw and to talk about their drawing are also on their way to knowing about literacy. Infants, toddlers, and two- and three-year-olds typically are not yet literate (as we describe *literate* in the preface of this book), but they do have many literacy behaviors and they do know something about literacy. They find reading and writing activities pleasurable, and they have bookhandling skills and participate in booksharing routines. Young children gain control over their arms, hands, and fingers as they develop motor schemes for creating shapes they have in mind. They know that the shapes they draw and the pictures they view can be named, are symbols or representations of reality, and communicate meaning.

Young children's home experiences have a powerful influence on their literacy learning. Children acquire literacy concepts through booksharing, through other literacy activities (including interactions with environmental print and drawing), and in decontextualized oral language routines.

As children share books with their parents and other caregivers, they acquire meaning-making strategies and a concept of story. Parents support children's meaning-making through storybook reading that is responsive and interactive. They also support children as they interact with environmental print. Finally, they invite children to participate in decontextualized oral language experiences, including giving explanations and telling stories.

Teachers can play an important role in very young children's literacy learning. They can make literacy materials available, offer literacy experiences, and respond to children's literacy attempts. They use careful observation and reflection as assessment. Figure 2.9 presents a summary of what literacy beginners know about written language meanings, forms, meaning-form links, and functions.

 # FIGURE 2.9   Summary: What Literacy Beginners Know about Written Language

Meaning

know booksharing routines
learn meaning-making strategies
use decontextualized language
develop concepts about stories

Forms

develop motor schemes
recognize the alphabet as a special set of
    written signs

Meaning-Form Links

make symbols

Functions

draw and share books as pleasurable
    activities
use books and drawing to gain the
    attention of others
observe family and community literacy
    activities

Using the Information

When visiting a Head Start classroom of three-year-olds, we invited several children to "tell us a story." Some of the stories the children told us are repeated here. Consider each story and compare its elements to the elements included in the story grammar presented in Table 2.1. Discuss which elements are included in the children's stories and which are omitted.

De'Brean: Me and my sister and my mother and my mother's boyfriend and my grandma and my little brother.

Keveon: Bunny seen a grandmother and gived her a flower. The grandmother dancing.

Rayshawn: There once was a little boy. He walk to the store and buy some potato chips. He walk to the store and buy milk. He walk to the store and buy some junk food.

Stanika: Girl goin home. Boy goin to sleep. The sister eatin. The mama takin a bath. The daddy washing the car.

Amber: Once upon a time there was a little girl. Her mama spank her, and then she cry.

Tyreke: Once there was a little boy. He lives in a tent. Then the little boy go up a beanstalk. There was a big giant. He ate the little boy. Then the boy go down the beanstalk and go home. The giant go down and was dead.

Figure 2.10   Steven Retells *Bears in the Night* (Berenstain & Berenstain, 1971)

Story: Bears investigate a sound in the night by creeping out of bed, down a tree, and up a hill.

Steven:	
(points to moon) moon (points to lantern) i-eet (light)	TEXT: IN BED Illustration: Seven bears in bed. Open window with a crescent moon. A lantern hangs on the wall.
(turns page, points to moon) moon (points to lantern) i-eet	TEXT: OUT OF BED Illustration: One bear out of bed, otherwise similar to previous page.
(turns several pages rapidly, gazes at picture for several seconds)(turns page)	TEXT: UP SPOOK HILL Illustration: Bear going up hill lantern in hand. Moon in sky. Owl at the top of hill.
shakes head, points at owl OOOOOOOOOOO	Illustration: The word "WHOOOOO," an owl, and four frightened bears jumping up.

APPLYING THE INFORMATION

Complete the following case study. Discuss Steven's literacy knowledge and behaviors. Also discuss the role Steven's babysitter plays in Steven's learning.

When Steven was nineteen months old, he retold *Bears in the Night* (Berenstain & Berenstain, 1971). He turned the book so that the cover faced him right-side-up. He turned past the first page (title page) quickly. Figure 2.10 presents Steven's retelling. Write a reflection that describes what elements of the illustration Steven notices. What does he know about story grammar and about bookhandling?

When Steven was twenty-five months old, he enjoyed drawing with his babysitter. She would encourage him to get his crayons, and he would color while she folded clothes or cleaned. He often made nonsense sounds as he colored. His sitter would talk to him as she worked. She would imitate his sounds and he would imitate hers. Sometimes Steven would sing songs he knew as he colored. Figure 2.11 presents one of Steven's pictures. He said, "This is a car." What does Steven know about the basic shapes of drawing? How would you describe his motor schemes? Is he a representational drawer? Write your answers as a reflection that can be included with an anecdotal note.

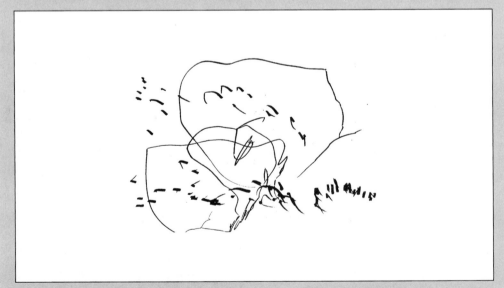

FIGURE 2.11   Steven's Drawing

GOING BEYOND THE TEXT

VISIT A CHILD CARE, Even Start, or Head Start center and take note of the literacy materials and activities in the classrooms. What books are available? How often and how do caregivers read with children? How frequently do children draw? Take at least three books to share with a small group of children. Describe their booksharing strategies. Join the children as they draw. Describe their drawing behaviors and make inferences about their literacy knowledge. Interview at least one caregiver. What does he or she believe about reading and writing for infants, toddlers, and two-year-olds? Write at least one anecdotal note and reflection.

REFERENCES

Applebee, A. N. (1978). *The child's concept of story.* Chicago: University of Chicago Press.

Arthur, L., Beecher, B., & Jones Diaz, C. (2001). Early literacy: Congruence and incongruence between home and early childhood settings. In M. Kalantzis (Ed.). *Languages of learning: Changing communication and changing literacy teaching.* Melborne: Common Ground.

Beals, D. (2001). Eating and reading: Links between family conversations with preschoolers and later language and literacy. In D. Dickson & P. Tabors (Eds.), *Beginning literacy with language: Young children learning at home and school* (pp. 75–92). Baltimore, MD: Paul H. Brookes.

Berenstain, S., & Berenstain, J. (1971). *Bears in the night.* New York: Random House.

Brown, M. W. (1947). *Goodnight moon.* New York: Harper and Row.

de Brunhoff, L. (1975). *Babar and the Wully-Wully.* New York: Random House.

Burns, M., & Casbergue, R. (1992). Parent-child interaction in a letter-writing context. *Journal of Reading Behavior, 24,* 289–312.

Bus, A. (2001). Joint caregiver-child storybook reading: A route to literacy development. In S. Neuman & D. Dickinson (Eds), *Handbook of early literacy research* (pp. 179–191).

Craig, H., & Washington, J. (2004). Language variation and literacy learning. In C. Stone, E. Silliman, B. Ehren, & K. Apel (Eds.). *Handbook of language and literacy: Development and disorders* (pp. 228–247). New York: Guilford.

Dickinson, D., & Smith, M. (1994). Long-term effects of preschool teachers' book readings on low-income children's vocabulary and story comprehension. *Reading Research Quarterly, 29,* 105–122.

Disney (Walt) Productions. (1974). *Walt Disney's Peter and the wolf.* New York: Random House.

Dyson, A. H. (2003). *The brothers and sisters learn to write: Popular literacies in childhood and school cultures.* New York: Teachers College Press.

Gardner, H. (1980). *Artful scribbles.* New York: Basic Books.

Gee, J. (1999). Critical issues: Reading and the new literacy studies: Reframing the National Academy of Sciences Report on Reading. *Journal of Literacy Research, 31,* 355–374.

Green, J., & Dixon, C. (1996). Language of literacy dialogues: Facing the future or reproducing the past. *Journal of Literacy Research, 28,* 290–301.

Halliday, M. A. K. (2002). Relevant models of language. In B. M. Power & R. S. Hubbard (Eds.), *Language development: A reader for teachers,* 2nd ed. (pp. 49–53). Upper Saddle River, NJ: Merrill.

Hammerberg, D. (2004). Comprehension instruction for socioculturally diverse classrooms: A review of what we know. *The Reading Teacher, 57,* 648–658.

Heath, S. B. (1983). *Ways with words: Language, life, and work in communities and classrooms.* New York: Cambridge University Press.

Hill, E. (1980). *Where's Spot?* New York: Putnam.

Kellogg, R. (1969). *Analyzing children's art.* Palo Alto, CA: National Press Books.

Leaf, M. (1936). *The story of Ferdinand.* New York: Viking.

Leseman, P., & de Jong, P. (1998). Home literacy: Opportunity, instruction, cooperation and social-emotional quality predicting early reading achievement. *Reading Research Quarterly, 33,* 3:294–318.

Lesman, P., & van Tuijl, C. (2005). Cultural diversity in early literacy: Findings in Dutch studies. In D. K. Dickinson and S. B. Neuman (Eds.), *Handbook of early literacy research, Vol. 2* (pp. 211–228). New York: Guilford.

Mandler, L., & Johnson, N. (1977). Remembrance of things parsed: Story structure and recall. *Cognitive Psychology, 9,* 11–51.

Martin, L. (1998). Early book reading: How mothers deviate from printed text for young children. *Reading Research and Instruction, 37,* 137–160.

Michaels, S. (1981). "Sharing time": Children's narrative styles and differential access to literacy. *Language in Society, 10,* 423–442.

Ninio, A., & Bruner, J. (1978). Antecedents of the achievements of labeling. *Journal of Child Language, 5,* 1–15.

Perez, B. (2004). Language, literacy, and biliteracy. In B. Perez (Ed.), *Sociocultural contexts of language and literacy*, 2nd ed. (pp. 25–56). Mahwah, NJ: Lawrence Erlbaum.

Post, J., & Hohmann, M. (2000). *Tender care and early learning: Supporting infants and toddlers in child care settings.* Ypsilanti, MI: High/Scope.

Purcell-Gates, V. (1996). Stories, coupons, and the "TV Guide": Relationships between home literacy experiences and emergent literacy knowledge. *Reading Research Quarterly, 31,* 406–428.

Rhodes, L., & Nathenson-Mejia, S. (1992). Anecdotal-records: A powerful tool for ongoing literacy assessment. *The Reading Teacher, 45,* 502–509.

Roth, H. (1986). *A goodnight hug.* New York: Grosset & Dunlap.

Schickedanz, J. A., Schickedanz, D., Forsyth, P., & Forsyth, G. (2001). *Understanding children and adolescents* (4th ed.). Boston: Allyn & Bacon.

Seuss, Dr. (Theodore Geisel) (1963). *Hop on pop.* New York: Random House.

Smith, H. (2004). Literacy and instruction in African American communities: Shall we overcome? In B. Perez (Ed.), *Sociocultural contexts of language and literacy*, 2nd ed. (pp. 207–245). Mahway, NJ: Lawrence Erlbaum.

Snow, C. E., & Ninio, A. (1986). The contracts of literacy: What children learn from learning to read books. In W. H. Teale & E. Sulzby (Eds.), *Emergent literacy: Writing and reading* (pp. 116–138). Exeter, NH: Heinemann.

Stein, N., & Glenn, C. (1979). An analysis of story comprehension in elementary children. In R. Freedle (Ed.), *Advances in discourse processes: (Vol 2). New directions in discourse processing* (pp. 53–120). Norwood, NJ: Ablex.

Tabors, P. (1997). *One child, two languages: A guide for preschool educators of children learning English as a second language.* Baltimore, MD: Paul H. Brookes.

Taylor, D., & Dorsey-Gaines, C. (1988). *Growing up literate: Learning from inner-city families.* Portsmouth, NH: Heinemann.

Turbill, J., & Murray, J. (2006). Early literacy and new technologies in Australian schools: Policy, research, and practice. In M. McKenna, L. Labbo, R. Kieffer, & D. Reinking (Eds.), *International handbook of literacy and technology, Volume two.* (pp. 93–108). Mahwah, NJ: Lawrence Erlbaum.

U.S. Department of Health and Human Services. (2003). The national reporting system: What is it and how will it work? *Head Start Bulletin, 76.*

Wells, G. (1986). *The meaning makers.* Portsmouth, NH: Heinemann.

Wright, B. F. (illustrator) (1916). *The real Mother Goose.* New York: Rand McNally.

CHAPTER 3

Three to Five Years
NOVICE READERS AND WRITERS IN THE PHASE OF AWARENESS AND EXPLORATION

KEY CONCEPTS

Repertoire of Literacy
    Knowledge
Literal Meaning
Implied Meaning
Level of Cognitive
    Engagement
Analytic Talk
Literary Language
Pretend Reading
Timeless Present Tense
Concepts about Print
    (CAP)
Book Orientation
    Concepts
Directionality Concepts
Letter-Like Forms

Linear Scribble Writing
Mock Cursive
Symbol Salad
Letter Features
Mock Letters
Text Formats
Alphabetic Principle
Contextual Dependency
Sign Concept
Phonological
    Awareness
Phonemic Awareness
Alliteration
Basic Interpersonal
    Communication
    Skills (BICS)

Cognitive Academic
    Language
    Proficiency (CALP)
Word Profiles
Phoneme Repertoires
Onset
Rime
Transitive Verb
Alphabet Recognition
Vocabulary
Oral Comprehension
Retelling Checklist

WHO ARE NOVICE READERS AND WRITERS?

IN THIS CHAPTER, we examine the literacy learning of many preschoolers and kindergartners who are in the phase of Awareness and Exploration (IRA/NAEYC, 1998). We draw on examples from children in a variety of preschool and kindergarten settings. We intentionally include children from diverse SES, ethnic, and language backgrounds. We call the children who are discussed in this chapter novice readers and writers while we called the children we described in Chapter 2 beginners. Our decision to use the word *novice* to describe children's interactions with literacy events in this chapter and the word *beginner* to describe children's interactions with literacy events in Chapter 2 is intentional and we believe important in differentiating what young children discover in the phase of awareness and exploration. At first, when young children are beginners, they are included in literacy events and their parents or caregivers help them participate at their level of development. Babies and toddlers learn to point to pictures in books. Two-year-olds learn to control crayons and markers and engage in simple symbolic play (e.g., by pretending to feed a baby doll). They discover how to use drawing to construct symbols—usually making representational drawings of familiar people. However, novice readers and writers demonstrate several new competencies as literacy users.

Written Language Communicates Messages: Novice Readers' and Writers' New Insights

The first new competency that novice readers and writers demonstrate is what we call intentionality. Around the age of three or four, preschoolers are not yet able to read and write in a conventional way, but they demonstrate an intention to communicate a message with their marks rather than merely to draw. Figure 3.1 presents scribble-like writing that four-year-old Javaris made as he played in the housekeeping center. At first glance, we would assume this writing was merely a scribble drawing. However, when asked what he had written, Javaris replied, "This is my grocery list. It says here bread, lettuce, tomatoes, eggs, and cheese." While Javaris's writing looks like a scribble, *he acted and talked as if the scribble were actually a written message*—he even called it a grocery list. His teacher responded to the scribble *as if it were actually writing*—she asked him what it said. When asked what his writing said, Javaris was able to construct a plausible list of food that could be expected on a grocery list. He acted as a novice writer because he intentionally created a written symbol, his scribble, with the purpose of communicating a message, the food on a grocery list. He did not intend to draw a picture, nor did he treat his written marking as a picture. He intended his mark to be writing and treated it as if it said something.

A second new competency that novice readers and writers demonstrate is awareness of print. Children demonstrate this new awareness as they explore environmental print's role in communicating messages. Novice readers may recognize "Raisin Bran," "McDonald's," and "Coca-Cola" on the familiar cereal box, fast-food restaurant sign, and drink can. However, they go beyond simple recognition of meaning in familiar items or contexts that happen to include printed symbols and words. *Novices react to the meaning communicated in printed signs and labels even when they are not located on the items*

FIGURE 3.1 Javaris's Grocery List: Bread, Lettuce, Tomatoes, Eggs, and Cheese

they represent or in the context in which they are usually found. They recognize the Raisin Bran and McDonald's logos even when the actual object (the box of cereal) is not present or when the familiar context (the restaurant building) is not available. When they see an unfamiliar environmental print sign, novice readers are likely to ask, "What does that say?" signaling their awareness that print in the environment is intended to communicate messages.

These new insights about literacy allow children sometimes to engage with literacy in new ways. However, it is important to keep in mind that novice readers and writers do not always use their new insights. Children often draw, scribble, and even write whole pages of letter-like forms without intending to do anything other than "draw" or "write." Being willing *sometimes* to use scribbles or letter-like forms to construct a message and at other times unwilling to do so is to be expected. Depending on the task or activity in which they are engaged, children display a **repertoire of literacy knowledge** (Schickedanz, 1999). This means that sometimes—for example, when pretending to be a waitress in a preschool restaurant dramatic play center—children will write with the intention of communicating a message. At other times—for example, when drawing at a preschool art center—children will create marks just for the experience of seeing what they can create.

Examples of Novices

Two literacy events involving Quadaravious and Jamyia are described next. These children have had many experiences sharing books with their preschool teachers.

Quadaravious is four years old, and he enjoys drawing and writing with his Head Start classmates. One day, his teacher invited a small group of children to draw pictures of themselves. As the children finished their drawings, the teacher reminded them to write their names on their pictures. Quadaravious immediately wrote four mock letters (see Figure 3.2). Three of the letters were circles with a long vertical line that began inside the circle and extended down from it. The fourth letter consisted of a vertical line. When he was finished writing, he said to his teacher, "I wrote my name." His teacher noticed that Quadaravious used several mock letter Qs to write his name.

Jamyia is three years old and is playing in the Beauty Shop center in her Head Start classroom. As she steps into the center, she immediately takes on the role of hairdresser and invites another child to sit down for a relaxer. She searches through the many boxes of beauty products available and selects a box of conditioner and relaxer. She opens the box, removes an empty plastic bottle, and pretends to squirt material from the bottle. She says to her friend, "Lean back now and I'll put this relaxer on now."

Both Quadaravious and Jaymia are novice readers and writers. Their behaviors and talk indicate that they find written symbols meaningful. Jamyia correctly selected the box of relaxer from six boxes of other kinds of beauty products; Quadaravious wrote his name using his special symbol, a mock letter Q. What is significant about these activities is that the children constructed meaning from written symbols that they

FIGURE 3.2 Quadaravious's signature and self-portrait

created or noticed on their own. Quadaravious was willing to write his name, and Jamyia could locate the box of relaxer from other similar printed items. It is important to note that these two children pretended to read and write within supportive activities. Quadaravious wrote his name to signal ownership or identity of his self-portrait when his teacher invited him to write his name; Jamyia recognized the box of relaxer as she pretended to be a beautician.

Would we really call these behaviors reading and writing? This is an important question, one that has created controversy. Traditionalists define reading as the ability to identify words printed in isolation or in simple stories. Similarly, they define writing as the ability to write identifiable words in isolation or in simple stories. After careful observation of children, some educators have argued that we need a new definition of reading and writing (Baghban, 1984; Goodman, 1980; Harste, Woodward, & Burke, 1984). Anytime children produce print or look at print with the intention that it be meaningful, with awareness that print "says" messages, we say that they are novice readers and writers.

MEANING

WHILE THEY DO NOT READ AND WRITE CONVENTIONALLY, novice readers and writers attend to an ever-increasing variety of texts, including menus, *TV Guides*, telephone books, grocery lists, coupons, and, especially, stories. Novice writers make meaning by creating an increasing variety of written symbols.

Constructing the Meaning of Environmental Print

By the age of two-and-a-half or three, many young children find some environmental print symbols meaningful (Hiebert, 1978). Novice readers do not really read the words on environmental print. Unlike beginners, however, they do pay attention to the print on environmental print objects. While beginners respond to such objects as wholes, which include print, novices focus on the print; they point to it. They know that the print is an important part of the object, that somehow it conveys meanings appropriate to the object.

Children expect many kinds of print items to be meaningful. For example, four-year-old Takesha was asked to read a handwritten grocery list. She said, "Green beans, coffee, and bread." She also offered to read a telephone book and said, "Takesha, 75983." Although Takesha did not really read the grocery list or the telephone book, she knew the kinds of messages associated with these kinds of print and used this knowledge to pretend to read.

Constructing Meaning While Listening to Story and Information Book Read-Alouds

In order to understand a story being read to them, children must listen to the words of the story. Of course, most books for children include pictures that provide salient contextual cues for understanding the stories. Eventually, however, children must learn to rely only on the text and not on picture context to understand stories that they read (Dickinson, 2001).

Most children's early experiences with constructing story meanings are highly personalized; they capitalize on the children's experiences with particular stories. However, as children approach school age—preschool or kindergarten—their storybook experiences will be in many-to-one situations. In group story-sharing situations, children are not as close to the pictures as they are in one-to-one story-sharing situations. Thus they have to rely more on the teacher's reading of the words of the text to construct story meaning than on extensive viewing of pictures (Cochran-Smith, 1984).

Children's Meaning-Making Strategies.

Mrs. Jones is a preschool teacher who is skilled at sharing books with her class of low-income four-year-olds. Figure 3.3 presents a portion of the interaction among nine four-year-olds and Mrs. Jones as she shared *There's a Nightmare in My Closet* (Mayer, 1968).

The children's comments and questions demonstrate that they understood much of the **literal meaning** of the story, facts stated in the text or shown in the illustrations. Obviously, the children understood that there was a nightmare in the closet; they knew that the character needed protection. Their comments and questions demonstrate that they also made many inferences about implied meanings in the story. They made inferences about motivations for the character's actions (he shut the door "Cause he doesn't want the nightmare to come out"); about the character's traits ("He's a scaredy cat"); and about reasons for the character's feelings (he was afraid "cause the wind blow"). Inferences are children's deductions of information not stated. The children also made predictions; they made guesses about upcoming story events. Just before Mrs. Jones turned to the last page of the story, which contains an illustration of a second nightmare peeking out of the closet, one child predicted, "There's gonna be another one."

In addition, the children paid attention to each other's comments. When one child commented about an action of the character ("Cause he's scared"), another one agreed ("He's a scaredy cat"). Similarly, when one child noted that "the wind blow," another child added, "Yeah, the curtain's out."

This brief story interaction illustrates that four-year-olds in group story-sharing can construct many kinds of meanings (Martinez, 1983). They understand what the author says—the literal meaning. They also understand what the author implies—**implied meaning.**

Preschoolers and kindergarteners also listen as their teachers read nonfiction or informational books aloud and participate actively in trying to understand the ideas presented in these kinds of texts. Novice readers use many of the same strategies to understand informational texts as they do story texts (Shine & Roser, 1999). For example, they may predict and speculate on behavior of animals or people in the book based on their own experiences. They also ask questions and make inferences (Tower, 2002). For example, as a teacher was reading *Let's Find Out about Ice Cream* (Reid, 1996), a book about the process of making ice cream, a teacher and three children had this discussion about an illustration of a man working in an ice cream freezer:

Teacher: He has a freezer suit on.
Kenny: Why?

FIGURE 3.3   A Portion of the Interaction as Mrs. Jones and Her Pre-kindergartners Share *There's a Nightmare in My Closet* (Mayer, 1968)

Brackets indicate portions of the dialogue that occurred simultaneously.

Mrs. J:	(shows cover of book, invites children to talk about nightmares, reads title and author, and reads first page of text stating the character's belief that a nightmare once lived inside his bedroom closet)
Child 1:	He got toys and a gun on his bed.
Mrs. J:	Umm, I wonder why?
Child 2:	So he can protect him.
Mrs. J:	Protect him. Umm. (reads text about closing the door to the closet)
Child 1:	Cause he's scared.
Child 3:	He's a scaredy cat.
Child 1:	My momma take the light off, I'm not scared.
Child 4:	He might lock it.
Mrs. J:	Why would he lock it?
Child 4:	Cause he doesn't want the nightmare to come out.
Mrs. J:	(reads text about character being afraid to even look in the closet)
Child 1:	Cause the wind blow.
Mrs. J:	The wind blows?
Child 3:	Yeah, the curtain's out.
Child 2:	It's blowing.
Mrs. J:	It must have been a dark, windy night. (continues reading text, making comments, and asking questions)
Children:	(continue making comments and asking questions)
Mrs. J:	(reads text about character deciding to get rid of the nightmare)
Child 1:	I guess he ain't cause that's not a real gun.
Mrs. J:	(turns page to illustration of the nightmare coming out of the closet and walking toward the boy in the bed)
Child 1:	There he is.
Child 5:	Why he's awake?
Mrs. J:	Well what did it say? He was going to try to get rid of his nightmare, so he stayed awake waiting for his nightmare.

Althea: Cause he won't, cause he can't get cold.

Kenny: Cause he won't catch a cold.

Jason: Yeah, and not get a cough. (Tower, 2002, p. 72)

Teachers' Roles in Helping Children Understand Interactive Read-Alouds. Figure 3.2 presented only a small portion of the interactive read-aloud of *There's a Nightmare in My Closet.* In this read-aloud, Mrs. Jones read with expression and used three different voices: one for the narrator, one for the little boy, and one for the monster. She was so familiar with this story that she frequently turned to look at the children as she read portions of the story so they could see her facial expressions. She pointed to specific places in the pictures as she read, and she paused for dramatic effect.

Mrs. Jones's reading invites a great deal of participation from the children (Martinez & Teale, 1993; Smolkin & Donovan, 2002). She reads the story, but she also encourages the children to comment and ask questions. She demands a high **level of cognitive engagement.** That is, she helps children use higher level thinking by making inferences about character traits and their motives. She helps children make connections between events in the story so that they can understand what causes characters to act as they do. She helps children understand the meaning of words and connects events in books to children's experiences. This style of reading helps children engage in **analytic talk** (Dickinson, 2001) in which they are analyzing characters and events rather than merely recalling what happened.

Teachers play many of the same roles as they share informational books with young children. Teachers connect children's comments and questions to the technical vocabulary used in the book and describe the actions and objects in the illustrations (Smolkin & Donovan, 2002). For example, while discussing the book about making ice cream, one four-year-old pointed to a picture of sugar cane stalks and asked, "And what are—snakes?" Her teacher clarified, "These are called sugar cane plants" (Tower, 2002, p. 67).

Children's Developing Concept of Story

One of the strategies that children use as they listen to stories is to pay attention to story elements. We have called children's awareness of elements of story their concept of story, or story schema (see Chapter 2). Novice readers' and writers' concepts about stories grow as they gain experience with more complex stories. One of the most important ways in which novices' concepts of stories change is that they begin to understand story-as-a-whole. Novices learn two important organizational structures that can be used to link events in stories: sequence and causal relationships. Novices learn that events in stories occur in sequence and that some events in stories cause other events to occur. They discover that the event of a character's falling down while skating is related to the event of scraping a knee—falling down caused the character's knee to become scraped.

Children's concept of story also influences their creation of text in imaginary play (Wolf & Heath, 1992). They demonstrate their awareness of **literary language,** language found in literature, rather than everyday conversational language. Three-year-old Nat did this when he called his cereal "porridge" and said, "We are the three bears. My chair's broken" (Voss, 1988, p. 275).

Constructing Meaning in Pretend Reading and Retelling

Novices also use their concept of story when they attempt to retell stories. A special kind of retelling is when children look at favorite picture books—ones they have shared many times with their parents or teacher—and attempt to reread them on their own. These retellings or rereadings are called **pretend readings** (Pappas, 1993).

However during the preschool and kindergarten years, children listen to more than just stories. They enjoy poems, songs, and information books. Just as they gain a growing awareness of the characteristics of storybooks and the organizational patterns in stories, children learn the organization of information books (Duke, 2004; Duke & Hays, 1998; Pappas, 2006), that is, the particular components that make up informational accounts. Table 3.1 presents the components that preschoolers usually include in their pretend readings of stories and information books (Pappas, 1991, 1993).

Children as young as four differentiate between retelling or pretending to read a story and an information book (Cox, Fang, & Otto, 1997). They are more likely to identify a specific character and use past tense when pretending to read a storybook. They are more likely to use **timeless present tense** and a generic group of animals or people when pretending to read an information book. Children's pretend readings begin to sound like the language of books.

TABLE 3.1   Components of stories and information books children typically include in their pretend readings

Story	Information Book
Past Tense:	*Timeless Present Tense:*
"Once there was a woodpecker."	"Squirrels have furry bodies."
Particular Character:	*General Class of Things:*
"The woodpecker"	"Squirrels"
Sequence of Events:	*Defining Characteristics of the Class:*
"The woodpecker flew to a tree and began pecking at the tree."	"Squirrels have nice furry ears. Squirrels put up their ears to keep them warm."
Problems:	*Typical Activities:*
"The tree was so hard, the woodpecker couldn't make a hole."	"Squirrels search for nuts and dig in the ground."

Writing Meaningful Messages

Novices have a new interest in participating in writing messages. Much of novice writers' message making is a part of playful activity. They pretend to read and write in their dramatic play as Javaris did when he pretended to write and read a grocery list (Figure 3.1) and Jamyia did when she pretended to read a box of relaxer.

In order to prompt this kind of reading and writing, Vang's kindergarten teacher provides many real-life experiences, such as flying kites, finding caterpillars, and visiting the zoo (Abramson, Seda, & Johnson, 1990), as well as opportunities for dramatic play. She believes that these experiences are particularly important for the learning of her children, whose first languages include Hmong, Spanish, Laotian, and Cambodian. Several days after visiting the zoo, Vang drew a picture of an elephant and wrote what appears in Figure 3.4a, saying "elephant." Then he drew a picture of a second, smaller elephant and discussed it with his teacher (Abramson, Seda, & Johnson, 1990, p. 69)

> **Vang:** Teacher, look it. I made baby. Baby el-fant.
>
> **Teacher:** A baby elephant. Oh, that's great. Can you write "baby elephant"?
>
> **Vang:** Sure!

Vang wrote what appears in Figure 3.4b. Vang knows that writing can be used to label drawings. The meaning he constructed ("elephant" and "baby elephant") is highly dependent both on his picture and on the teacher's suggestion.

Much of children's meaning making in writing depends on their experiences with meaningful uses of reading and writing. Javaris would not have used writing to create a grocery list if he had not observed grocery lists being written. Quadaravious would not have taken up name writing if he had not associated writing at school with classmates' names. Vang would not have created a message in his journal if he had not had a highly meaningful trip to the zoo or observed his classmates' daily journal writing and his teacher's responses to those written messages.

FIGURE 3.4a "Elephant"    **FIGURE 3.4b** "Baby Elephant"

Source: Abramson, S., Seda, I., & Johnson, C. (1990). Literacy development in a multilingual kindergarten classroom. *Childhood Education, 67,* 68–72. Reprinted by permission of the authors and the Association for Childhood Education International, 11501 Georgia Ave., Ste. 315, Wheaton, MD. Copyright © 1991 by the Association.

WRITTEN LANGUAGE FORMS

WHILE THEY ARE DEVELOPING NEW INSIGHTS about written language meanings, novices also demonstrate new awarenesses about written language forms. They notice the print on environmental print items and in books, they acquire notions of how print looks and how it is organized, and they begin to display those notions in their own writing.

Concepts about Print

Children's **concepts about print** (CAP) are understandings that they have about how print is visually organized and read. They learn that alphabet letters are a special category of visual symbols, that print "says," and that print is read rather than the pictures. In Chapter 2, we described several concepts about print called book handling skills that very young children learn; books are held right-side-up (children know which is the top and bottom of a book) and their pages are turned one-by-one from the front of the book to the back. These **book orientation concepts** form the foundation for later discovering **directionality concepts.** Directionality concepts involve children's awareness that print is written and read from left-to-right, line-by-line. Later we will show that novice writers display awareness of directionality in their writing. Novice readers begin this process when they pretend to read a favorite book. They may point to the print as they read, sweeping their hands across the print. Novice readers are not able to point to each word of a book one-by-one (this will come later), but they do display awareness that books are read in a systematic fashion.

From Scribbles to Alphabet Letters

Children's awareness of print and their developing concepts about print influence the kinds of marks they make in their writing. Novice writers attempt to create marks that look like print and are organized on a page like writing. However, children's early writing attempts, called scribble writing (Schickedanz, 1999), have virtually none of the features we would expect of alphabet writing. They do not include alphabet letters or even forms that somewhat resemble letters. Earlier we presented Javaris's grocery list (see Figure 3.1), and his writing as an example of scribble writing. Most of the marks he made were uncontrolled, round-and-round scribbles. A more sophisticated form of writing is called **linear scribble writing** (Bloodgood, 1999; Hildreth, 1936) and consists of horizontally arranged, wavy lines. Linear scribble writing is sometimes called **mock cursive,** because the continuous lines of up-and-down scribbling resemble cursive writing. Javaris's grocery list includes the beginnings of mock cursive where he has written two lines of up-and-down marks. Figure 3.5 presents another example of mock cursive. Three-year-old Kendrel wrote this at his Head Start writing center and announced to his teacher that he had written his name. Notice his writing's linearity.

Eventually, children's writing begins to include separate units or symbols although the units may not look very much like alphabet letters. For example, many children's writing attempts consist of a series of circles resembling the letter *O*. Other children may compose symbols using lines and curves along with circle shapes.

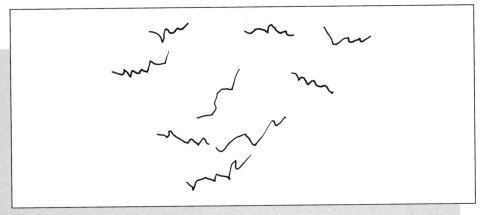

FIGURE 3.5   Kendrel Writes His Name

Figure 3.6 presents an example of writing that consists of separate units presented in a nonlinear arrangement.

As children gain awareness of alphabet letters, their writing includes a mixture of **letter-like forms,** symbols, numbers, and even conventionally formed alphabet letters. Children seem to enjoy both writing the same form repeatedly in their writing and changing forms to see what new forms they can create (Clay, 1975). Writing with a mixture of letters, numbers, other symbols, and letter-like shapes is sometimes called **symbol salad** (Bear, Invernizzi, Templeton, & Johnston, 2000). Figure 3.7 presents an example of symbol salad writing in which the writer drew on his awareness of both linearity and directionality; he wrote from left to right.

Of course, children frequently draw and write on a single sheet of paper. However, even when they draw and write, children as young as three demonstrate that they differentiate between drawing and writing. Figure 3.2 presented a picture Quadaravious drew of himself and his signature. Although his name consists only of four letter-like forms, three of which resemble the alphabet letter Q, his writing is clearly differentiated from his drawing. Often the first letter in a child's name is the first letter he or she can recognize and write (Schickedanz, 1999).

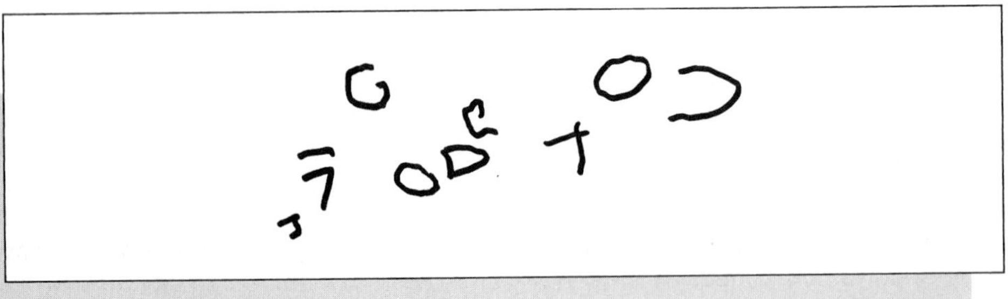

FIGURE 3.6   Writing with Separate Units

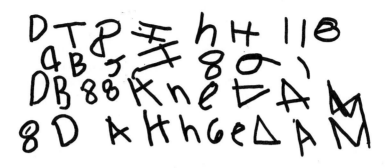

FIGURE 3.7   Symbol Salad

Alphabet Letters

Novices demonstrate in many ways their understanding of the importance of letters of the alphabet. They do not yet know what the role of alphabet letters is (to represent the fundamental units of spoken language, sounds called phonemes). However, before they learn to name any alphabet letters or to write recognizable letter formations, children discover a great deal about alphabet letters (McGee & Richgels, 1989). One thing they learn is to call this special category of written symbols *the alphabet* or *letters*. They learn that alphabet letters are related to or associated with important people, places, or objects. Kristen thought that *Special K* cereal and *K-Mart* were *her* cereal and *her* store. In one preschool classroom, Jean-Marc always wrote his name with *J* for *Jean-Marc*, *E* for *Emmanuel*, *A* for *Andre*, *N* for *Natalie*—and then he stopped writing because he did not know anyone whose name began with *M* (Ballenger, 1999, p. 45).

Eventually, preschoolers learn the names of the alphabet letters and how to write them. In order to do this, they need a clear visual image of the letter and control over motor schemes to make the lines that they visualize (Schickedanz, 1999). Children build up strong visual images of letters as they experiment with the **letter features,** the special lines and shapes that make up letters.

The letter *T* is made up of a horizontal and a vertical line; the letter *O* is made up of an enclosed, continuous curved line; and the letter *N* is made up of two vertical lines and a diagonal line. Children must learn to pay attention to letter features in order to distinguish between letters (for example, between the letters *w* and *v* or *l* and *i*).

Children show that they pay attention to letter features in their writing through their mock letters. As we described in Chapter 1, **mock letters** are letter-like shapes with many of the same features of conventional alphabet letters. There are several examples of mock letters found in Figure 3.7. This writer seems to be exploring when the letter *H* can become the letter *I* or *A*. Mock letters are often constructed as children play with letter orientation. That is, they rotate letters so they seem to lay sideways or upside down. Letters are frequently written in mirror-image form. It is not surprising that young children are slow to grasp the correct orientation of alphabet letters. For example, a chair is a chair whether it faces left or right. But lower case *b* and *d* are different letters because one faces left and one faces right.

Many three-year-olds know a few letters and some four-year-olds know nearly all the alphabet letters. Large studies of young children show that on average a four-year-old knows nine to fourteen alphabet letters (Bloodgood, 1999; Smith & Dixon, 1995). Such studies show that children from low-income families know fewer alphabet letters, but learn quickly when they are provided alphabet learning activities in preschool (Roberts & Neal, 2004).

Signatures

Just as children learn to name and write alphabet letters and acquire concepts about what alphabet letters are, they also learn to write their names and acquire concepts about what written names are. Children's ability to write recognizable signatures develops in an identifiable pattern (Hildreth, 1936). Their ability depends on their growing motor control, awareness of letter features, and knowledge of letters as discrete

FIGURE 3.8 Nah'Kiyah's Signatures: August, October, November, February, and April.

units. Figure 3.8 presents Nah'Kiyah's name-writing attempts over a nine-month period while she was in a prekindergarten program for low-income four-year-olds. The first example of her signature, produced in early August, consisted of some recognizable letters (*N, H, K,* and *Y*) and some mock letters (that also look like *N, H, K,* and *Y*). The letters are all in upper case form, although she was being taught to write her name in upper and lower case letters in her preschool. In October, Nah'Kiyah's signature still has mostly upper case letters; however, a lower case *h* and the special printed form of the lower case *a* have appeared. In November, Nah'Kiyah would only write part of her name, but notice how the letters are smaller and look more like conventional letters showing her growing motor control over writing. In February, Nah'Kiyah's signature includes every letter except the final *a* (with a little bit of ordering difficulty). By April, she has achieved a conventional signature although the apostrophe is still omitted.

As children learn to recognize and write their names, their concepts about signatures are quite different from those of adults. Ferreiro (1986) described Mariana, who claimed that she could write her name. She wrote five capital letters (*PSQIA*) as she said "Mariana" several times. When asked, "What does it say here?" about the letters *PS,* she replied, "Two Mariana." When asked, "What does it say here?" about the letters *QIA,* she replied, "Three Mariana" (Ferreiro, 1986, p. 37). Her answers reflect that Mariana believed each letter she wrote would say her name. Mariana's comments about her name illustrate that some children do not conceive of signatures as words composed of letters that represent sounds.

Texts

Novice readers and writers learn a great deal about different kinds of writing, and they use this knowledge to create a variety of texts, especially story texts. Novices come to know a variety of text formats that are used in special contexts and for particular functions. They become aware of and use text features (such as "Dear _____" at the beginning of a letter). And their concept of story and concept of information book organization develop (Duke & Hays, 1998).

Novice writers produce many different **text formats.** For example, Javaris wrote a grocery list (Figure 3.1). Later in this chapter, we will describe Johanna's birthday list (see Figure 3.11) and Jeremy's "Book of Poems." Much of these texts was included in their talk as they wrote and in the contexts in which the texts were produced. When we look only at Javaris's writing, it does not appear to be a text. It is only apparent that it is a text when we pay attention to his talk, to his actions, and to the context.

Sometimes the forms found in children's writing signal their growing awareness of the different features of texts. Figure 3.9 presents two pieces of Christopher's writing. Although Christopher composed both of his pieces using a combination of mock letters and conventional alphabet letters, the two compositions look quite different. One composition was written in the home center when Christopher decided to go grocery shopping with two friends. Christopher said, "I need candy, milk, bread, and cereal." The other composition was written at the writing center. Christopher later read this story to the teacher: "My dad went fishing but he didn't catch any fish. I caught a big fish." Each of these compositions has unique text features that make it easy to distinguish the grocery list from the story.

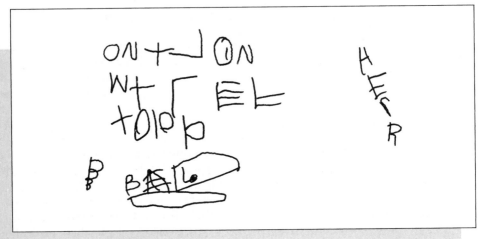

FIGURE 3.9   A Story and a Grocery List

MEANING-FORM LINKS

THE CONVENTIONAL WAY THAT MEANING (the message writers intend) is linked to form (words that writers use) is through the **alphabetic principle.** That is, words are comprised of alphabet letters and alphabet letters are related to phonemes in spoken words. As fluent readers, we are not often consciously aware of the alphabetic principle because we do not draw on it very often. Instead, we immediately recognize most of the words we read (these are called sight words because we recognize them by sight) without having to look at their letters and "sound out" words letter-by-letter. Novice readers and writers may recognize letters, and as we will see, may actually be able to isolate and say a phoneme, but they do not understand the relationship between letters and sounds. Instead, they use another method for making their writing meaningful—contextual dependency.

Contextual Dependency

Contextual dependency means that written forms convey meaning only through children's talk about their writing. All of the examples given so far in this chapter have a common characteristic: the use of contextual dependency to link written form to meaning. If we did not know what the children said about their writing, we would not be able to determine the messages that the child writers intended to communicate. We can only know the messages that novice writers convey when we listen to what they say about their writing. Clay (1975) called children's dependency on context to link meaning and form the **sign concept.** The sign concept is evident when children use the context of play to construct meaning in their writing and reading.

Matching Print to Spoken Language: More Than Contextual Dependency

Although novice readers and writers depend primarily on the context in which their writing is produced to link meaning and form, many researchers (Dyson, 1982; Ferreiro & Teberosky, 1982) have found that children's concepts about the relations between meaning and form change as they gain experience using written language. Children's knowledge of meaning-form links is very complex.

Figure 3.10 presents John's writing and story ("I have a dog. He is big. He is my best friend."). As John read the story, he swept his finger from left to right across each line of text as he said each sentence. He demonstrated contextual dependency in making meaning from his own writing. But, in addition, John noticed that printed text must be matched somehow to the oral message; he matched a line of text with a spoken sentence. Although not yet conventional, this matching of the text with the oral message is a precursor to a later, more-developed kind of meaning-form linking, that is, matching one spoken sound (or phoneme) with one letter (or grapheme).

Figure 3.11 presents Johanna's writing and story. She did not write an actual story, but instead wrote a list of things she wanted for her birthday. Although her list is composed entirely of jagged lines, correlating what Johanna said with her jagged lines reveals that Johanna often matched one continuous jagged line with one spoken word. Johanna realized that the written forms she wrote should correspond with the spoken meaning she intended.

Phonological Awareness

As novice readers and writers, young children have many experiences that allow them to develop phonological awareness. For example, the rhythm created in nursery rhymes highlights and segments speech sounds in a way that conversation does not. The syllables *PE ter PE ter PUMP kin EAT er* are naturally separated by the stress in the rhyme. This natural play with language sounds invites children to enjoy the music of language. Children who have listened to nursery rhymes and other writing that uses language play soon begin to play with speech sounds themselves. While four-year-old James was playing with a toy typewriter in his preschool room, he muttered "James, Fames, Wames" to himself. James was demonstrating phonological awareness.

Much language play that occurs during preschool and early kindergarten is relatively unconscious. Many children may not realize that they are making up rhyming

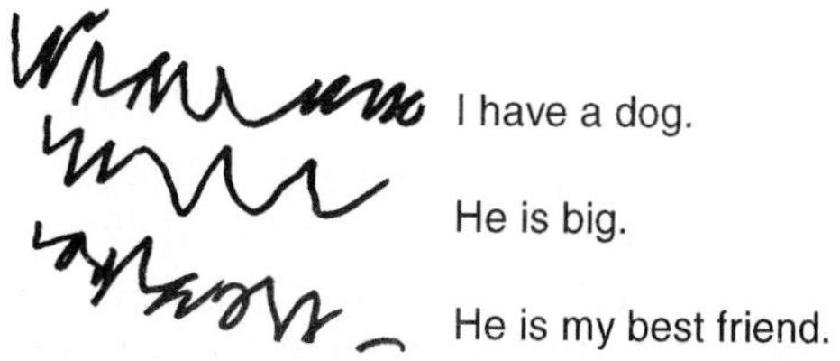

I have a dog.

He is big.

He is my best friend.

FIGURE 3.10   John's Story

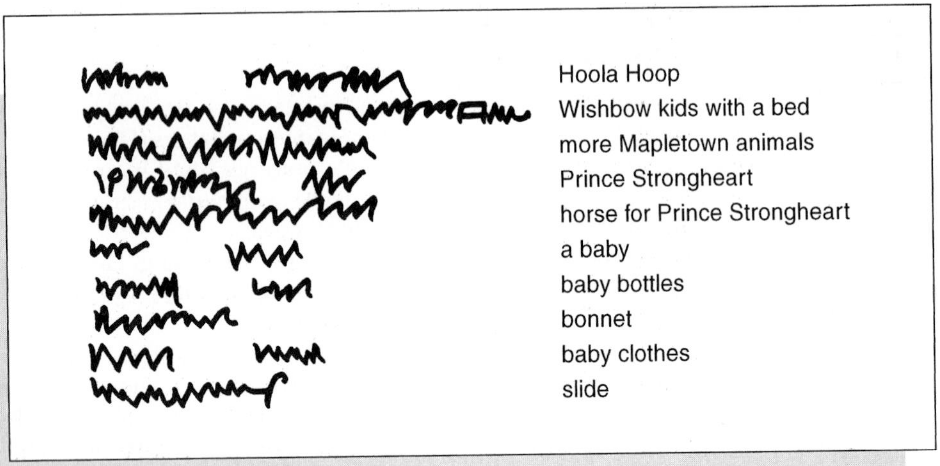

Hoola Hoop
Wishbow kids with a bed
more Mapletown animals
Prince Strongheart
horse for Prince Strongheart
a baby
baby bottles
bonnet
baby clothes
slide

FIGURE 3.11 Johanna's Birthday List

words. However, being able to consciously attend to sounds in words apart from words' meanings is a critical component of **phonological awareness.**

A special kind of phonological awareness, known as **phonemic awareness,** requires children consciously to attend to single phonemes in words. Some novice readers and writers, for example, intentionally create rhyming words by isolating beginning phonemes (beginning sounds) and substituting other phonemes for them, especially when their parents, caregivers, or teachers share books that contain many words with **alliteration.** Alliterative words begin with the same beginning sounds such as in the book *Some Smug Slug* (Duncan, 1996).

Using Symbols: The Connections among Dramatic Play, Writing, and Computer Use

Play is a critical component of the preschool years. Children's approach to writing during these years is closely connected to their play. Careful observers will notice that preschoolers most often write during dramatic play. They will take a phone message when they are pretending to be a mother with a sick baby or take notes on a patient chart when they are pretending to be a doctor. Children's pretend writing is very much like their symbolic use of objects in imaginary play. For example, they may create a symbol of a thermometer as they pretend to take a baby's temperature using a spoon to be the thermometer. Children's activities on the computer are also playful and involve the use of symbols (Labbo, 1996; Turbill & Murray, 2006). They create symbols using drawing and stamping tools and then transform them into pictures. For example, one child created a picture of his sister using a stamp of an ice cream cone to represent or symbolize her nose.

Children's ability to use complex and abstract symbols in dramatic play seems to precede their acquisition of more conventional literacy skills. Perhaps such experiences with abstract symbols during play and exploration on the computer provide a foundation for later being able to use the even more abstract symbols of letters and phonemes.

WRITTEN LANGUAGE FUNCTIONS

URING THE PRESCHOOL AND KINDERGARTEN YEARS, young children still are social-ized into their families' ways of using literacy although they will also be socialized into their school literacy culture (Dyson, 2003; Gee, 2001; Purcell-Gates, 1996). Many families use literacy in a variety of ways, such as for entertainment (reading novels), for information (surfing the Web for deals on cheap airline tickets), and for accomplishing family tasks (paying bills and filling out forms to apply for loans). Children observe the ways that family members use literacy and want to be included as they do in all fam-ily activities (Gee, 2001; Taylor & Dorsey-Gaines, 1988).

Many children from literacy-rich homes go beyond merely using literacy in their play. They use literacy as themes for play. One day Jeremy announced that he was going to make a book (Gundlach, McLane, Scott, & McNamee, 1985, p. 13). His father suggested that he use some index cards and write his book on the typewriter. After Je-remy had finished typing his cards, he and his father stapled the cards together to make the book. When his father asked him what was in his book, Jeremy replied, "A surprise" (p. 13). The next day, Jeremy's father invited him to listen to a radio program of children reading their poetry. After the program, Jeremy asked his mother and fa-ther to come into the living room to listen to him read his "Book of Poems." He opened the book he had made the previous day and said, "Page 1." Then he recited a poem that he knew. As he read "Page 2," he could not seem to remember any more poems, so he made up rhyming words and used singsong intonation. His mother and father ap-plauded his reading.

Unlike Jeremy, who uses literacy as a way of playing and gaining the attention of his parents, Tom uses literacy in more functional ways. When Tom was four, he be-came angry because his mother would not buy him a new toy. His mother said that she would be paid in three weeks and that Tom could have a toy then. Tom asked how many days were in three weeks and went to his room. He made the calendar (a portion of which is presented in Figure 3.12) with a number for each of the twenty-one days re-

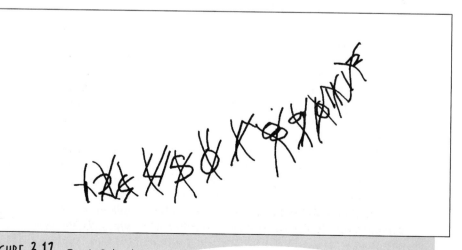

FIGURE 3.12   Tom's Calendar

maining until he could get a new toy. Every day as his father read him a story at bedtime, Tom crossed off a day on his calendar, and on the twenty-first day, his mother bought him his new toy.

ENGLISH LANGUAGE LEARNERS AS NOVICE READERS AND WRITERS

AS WE DISCUSSED IN CHAPTER 2, when children whose home language is not English enter a preschool or kindergarten in which the language of instruction is English, they face special challenges not faced by English-speaking children. Learning English is only one of these challenges. Others include learning how to fit in socially with children from different cultural backgrounds and learning the special ways of "doing school" that may be radically different from any experience these children have had previously. In English-dominant preschool and kindergarten classrooms, children will be expected not only to acquire English quickly, but also to begin learning foundational literacy concepts in English.

Although many preschool and kindergarten children may enter native language or bilingual programs in which other children and the teacher and assistant speak their home language, many children enter classrooms where teachers, even when they can speak the children's native language, are expected to teach in English. In this situation, children will be expected to learn not only basic interpersonal communication skills, but also cognitive academic language proficiency (Cummins, 1986). **Basic interpersonal communication skills (BICS)** are the skills needed to interact with and communicate with friends and others in social and play situations. On the other hand, **cognitive academic language proficiency (CALP)** is the language competence needed to learn science, social studies, mathematics, and other school subjects. This language generally includes many words that refer to abstract concepts rather than the concrete words in everyday conversation. In preschool and kindergarten, children will be expected to learn to use the academic vocabulary of reading and writing instruction, including the terms *alphabet letter, sound, word, upper case, lower case, spell, write,* and *read.*

As preschoolers and kindergartners, most English language learners will have been exposed to the written forms of their home language. They may have been taught to recognize alphabet letters or write their names in their home language. They may find to be meaningful many environmental print signs and logos in their home language and may have experiences listening to stories read from home-language picture books. Thus, children will already be learning about the unique features that make up alphabet letters in their home language as well as the concepts about print that govern reading and writing of that language.

The greater the similarty of a child's home written language to written English, the easier it will be for that child to learn to read and write in English (Cummins, 1989). For example, it is easier for Spanish-speaking children than for Chinese-speaking children to learn concepts about print in English (Barone, Mallette, & Xu, 2005). Written Spanish is an alphabetic language like written English (alphabet letters correspond to spoken phonemes), and it uses the same left-to-right and top-to-bottom directional scheme. In contrast, Chinese writing uses characters that represent whole syllables. Although some modern Chinese writing arranges these characters like English, from left-to-right and top-to-bottom of a page, traditional Chinese writing uses vertical columns starting at the right side of a page and proceeding to the left.

There are four possible areas of written language that may cause confusion for ELL children who are learning to read and write English:

- Alphabet letters (or individual symbols) differ across languages.
- Concepts about print in the home language and English may be different.
- Some aspects of phonemic awareness in English may not exist or be important in the home language because of different phoneme repertoires.
- Grammatical patterns or word order in English may differ from those in the home language.

Of course, many written languages use an alphabet that is the same as or very similar to the alphabet used to write English. Even when the letters of some alphabetic languages (Hebrew, for example) do not use the very same arrays of letter features (straight lines and curves, horizontals, verticals, and diagonals) as English alphabet letters do, these languages nonetheless depend, as English does, on the systematic use of letter-sound correspondences. That is what makes them alphabetic languages.

A more radical difference from English is found in non-alphabetic writing systems, such as Chinese, that use characters rather than alphabet letters. Each character stands for a syllable rather than an individual speech sound. Whatever the nature of their home language's writing system, children who share reading and writing experiences with other people in their homes and communities begin to learn about written language forms. Some will learn letter features; other will learn features of characters (see Figure 1.4 in Chapter 1 for an example of a Chinese girl's learning features of Chinese characters).

Concepts about print vary across languages. Some languages are not written from left-to-right and top-to-bottom. Therefore, these critical directional concepts in English may be more difficult for some children to develop than for others. Letter and word concepts may also cause confusion. For example, all Chinese characters are the same size and have the same block-like shape, whereas English words can vary from long (many letters) to short (few letters). Even when words are the same length, the different shapes of the letters from which the words are composed can result in very different **word profiles** (compare *slipped* and *sooner*) (Barone, Mallette, & Xu, 2005).

Languages also differ in their **phoneme repertoires.** Some languages have phonemes not found in English (e.g., the trilled *r* sound in Spanish that is absent in English), and English has phonemes not found in other languages (e.g., the /ng/ sound in English that is absent in Spanish). Not surprisingly, an English-language-learning child experiences difficulty detecting and producing English phonemes absent in his or her native language.

Not all languages are alphabetic, where letters stand for phonemes. Non-alphabetic languages cannot display the structure of rhyming words in their writing. In Chinese, for example, each written character represents a whole syllable. Thus the beginning consonant sound of that syllable (the **onset**) cannot be distinguished visually from the rest of the syllable (the **rime**) (of course, it can still be distinguished auditorily—

Chinese, like any language, has syllables that can be heard to rhyme). Children who are acquainted with non-alphabetic writing in their home communities will not be used to looking for onsets and rimes in writing and thus may have difficulty making use of phonograms in learning to read and write in English.

Finally, languages use different sentence structures, or syntax. The syntax of some languages depends more on word order than does the syntax of other languages. English uses subject-verb-object word order. For example, in the sentence *The goat kicked the boy*, English speakers and readers know *the boy* is the direct object of the **transitive verb** *kicked* because of its position after *kicked*. Not all languages treat transitive verbs in this way. For example, Korean sentences typically end with a verb. This means that both the subjects and the direct objects of transitive verbs appear before the verbs. It does not matter in which order one says or writes those nouns so long as neither of them takes the final position in the sentence (that is reserved for the verb). To let listeners and readers know which of the nouns appearing before that final verb is the direct object, Korean speakers and writers label it with an extra syllable. Children whose home language is Korean will be used to looking for that extra syllable and not accustomed to paying attention to word order. When confronted with the written sentences *The goat kicked the boy* and *The boy kicked the goat*, what they may notice is that *boy* looks the same in both sentences. They may wonder, "Where is the direct object label?" What they have to learn is that word order matters, that *boy* is the direct object (receiver of the kicking) in the first sentence and the subject (doer of the kicking) in the second sentence by virtue of its positions in those sentences.

In English, adjectives usually appear before nouns (*the blue house*), but in many languages, an adjective usually follows the noun, as for example, in Spanish where *the blue house* is *la casa azur*. Children whose home language is Spanish may have difficulty reading *the blue house* with appropriate intonation and comprehension because the word *blue* seems to disrupt the flow of words. They expect a noun after an article (as when *casa* comes after *la*), and instead they see an adjective; they do not expect that adjective until after the noun (as when *azur* comes after *casa*). For these children, learning to read and write English will require something that native English speakers do not have to learn, that is, a new habit about where to look for adjectives.

Assessing Novice Readers and Writers

MANY CHILDREN IN PRESCHOOL AND KINDERGARTEN are novice readers and writers. Because their literacy behaviors and knowledge are still unconventional, teachers will want to continue to document their development through systematic observation accompanied by written anecdotes and reflection. Observing children as they attempt to read and write is a critical component of a systematic approach to assessment for all young children.

Novice readers and writers do make progress in learning some conventions including alphabet knowledge, concepts about print, phonological and phonemic awareness, vocabulary, and oral comprehension. Because these concepts are critical to children's success in later becoming effective readers and writers, teachers monitor children's progress in acquiring them. In fact, in more and more preschools, teachers are required to screen children when they first enter in order to determine what they already know, and to administer frequent assessments to monitor children's progress. Early Reading First, a portion of recent legislation in the United States, the No Child Left Behind Act of 2001 (U.S. Congress, 2001), provides grants for preschools to create "centers of preschool excellence" where teachers are required to screen and monitor children's language and literacy development. Similarly, Head Start teachers are required to assess children's language and literacy development as well as their development in other domains.

In this part of the chapter, we describe preschool and kindergarten monitoring assessment tasks that teachers can use to screen and monitor children's development in four areas of foundational concepts: alphabet recognition, concepts about print, phonological and phonemic awareness, and vocabulary and oral comprehension. At the beginnings of the phase of awareness and exploration, typical novice readers and writers demonstrate few, if any, conventional concepts on these more formal assessment tasks. However, as children move through preschool and kindergarten, they make progress in acquiring many of these foundational concepts and are able to show their competence on some assessment tasks. If teachers administer these assessment tasks two or three times a year and regularly gather anecdotal notes and write reflections based on careful observations, then across the preschool and kindergarten years, they can create an evolving picture of children's emergence into more conventional reading and writing.

Appendix B presents directions and a score sheet for the preschool and kindergarten assessment tasks that we recommend that teachers use to monitor children's progress through the phase of novice reading and writing. This appendix also presents information on how teachers can prepare a class profile sheet for summarizing the information across groups of children.

Assessing Alphabet Knowledge and Signature Writing

Alphabet knowledge involves several different skills. **Alphabet recognition** is the ability to look at an alphabet letter and immediately say its name. Appendix B presents an upper and lower case alphabet recognition task score sheet and directions for making an administration sheet to use with children. To prepare the upper case alphabet administration sheet, teachers type, in a large font, five rows of six upper case letters in the order presented on the score sheet. For younger preschool children, teachers may make individual letter cards or type letters in a single row on an index card (using 26 cards in the case of one letter per card, or 5 cards in the case of typing 6 letters in a row on each card). Kindergarten children may be shown all 26 letters typed on one sheet of paper. Each child is shown the upper case administration cards or sheet, and the teacher points to each letter for the child to name. Teachers copy the score sheet found in Appendix B for each child and circle the letters each child correctly names. For children who know several upper case letters, teachers can also assess children's recognition of lower case letters. Again, teachers would construct an administration sheet with the lower case letters typed in the order presented on the score sheet.

To assess how many letters children know how to write, teachers can give children paper and ask them to write particular letters. Teachers we know ask children to write upper case letters in the order they are presented on the upper case alphabet recognition score sheet. (Children are not shown this list of letters, but rather write letters from memory.) After children write, teachers can score the alphabet writing task sheet by marking which letters children have written in recognizable form, keeping in mind that it is acceptable for preschoolers to have orientation difficulties (e.g., backwards letters) and that they are not likely to use the "correct" formation that is expected in later elementary grades.

All children should also be asked to write their names. Teachers can expect preschool and kindergarten children's signature writing to progress from level 0 to level 6 (based on Bloodgood, 1999) as follows: (0) uncontrolled scribbling, (1) controlled scribbles, such as mock cursive, (2) separate marks that do not resemble letters, (3) a signature with several marks but only one or two recognizable letters, (4) a signature with nearly all letters in recognizable form but possibly having orientation difficulties, (5) a recognizable and correct signature with few orientation difficulties, (6) a first and last name signature with mostly correct letter formation.

Assessing Concepts about Print

Novice readers and writers also begin acquiring concepts about print. **Concepts about print (CAP)** are understandings about how texts work, how they are configured, and how a reader approaches them. Children learn bookhandling skills, such as the knowledge that books have a top and bottom, and a front and back. They learn directionality concepts—that left-hand pages are read before right-hand pages, that a line of text is read from left to right, and that lines of text are read from the top line on a page to the bottom line. Children also develop concepts about words and letters—that the set of letters is limited (although they usually will not know that the number of letters is 26, they will know that the set of numbers is limited to those in the *ABC*s); that letters are combined to make words, in fact, to make a very large number of words, possibly even to make any word they want to write; that words can be long or short depending on the number of letters of which they are composed; and that spaces separate words. Appendix B presents directions for administering and scoring a concepts about print task that assesses children's bookhanding skills, knowledge about directionality, and concepts about letters and words.

Assessing Phonological and Phonemic Awareness

Novice readers and writers may acquire phonological and phonemic awareness; these concepts are an important part of a kindergarten literacy program. **Phonological awareness** is conscious attention to the sounds of spoken language. This includes **phonemic awareness,** or awareness of phonemes, but it also includes awareness of other units of language, such as syllables, onsets, and rimes, and other aspects of the sounds of a language, such as intonation patterns. For example, children show that they are aware of syllables when they can clap once for each syllable while saying a word. Teachers can assess children's awareness of rhyming by asking children to generate rhyming words. The teacher says a word and has children say other words that rhyme with it. Appendix B presents directions for administering and scoring a rhyming word assessment.

Phonemic awareness is children's conscious attention to phonemes, such as when they can say just the beginning sound of a word or match two words with the same beginning sound. Teachers can assess novice readers' and writers' phonemic awareness by asking them to say the beginning sounds of words. The Isolating Beginning Phoneme task in Appendix B includes ten words that teachers pronounce and then ask children to say the beginning sounds. The directions for administering and scoring this task are presented in the appendix.

Assessing Vocabulary and Oral Comprehension

Children expand their vocabularies and oral comprehension. **Vocabulary** refers to children's understandings about the meanings of words and their ability to use words effectively in speech. **Oral comprehension** is their ability to understand books and other texts read aloud to them (that is, they can answer literal and inferential questions or retell the story). We recommend that teachers assess children's oral comprehension and their use of sophisticated vocabulary using a retelling checklist. A **retelling checklist** is a list of the important events in a story and its important and sophisticated vocabulary. Appendix B presents directions for administering and scoring a retelling checklist for the book *Laney's Lost Momma* (Hamm, 1991). Teachers read the book aloud to a group of children for three days, and then on the fourth day ask children individually to retell what they remember. As a child retells the book, the teacher makes a check mark on the checklist for any event the child tells about and circles any listed vocabulary the child uses.

Analyzing Assessment Data

The preschool and kindergarten assessment tasks that we have described in this chapter are useful for monitoring what individual children know and can do. In Table 3.2, we present three children's scores on these tasks. All three children attended Head Start and are entering kindergarten in a school that primarily serves low-income children (98 percent of the children qualify for free or reduced lunch). Two children know most alphabet letters, but one of these children is still more advanced and has begun to develop phonemic awareness. Imani can isolate beginning sounds in spoken words, whereas Zyderrious cannot. Zyderrious also lacks any concepts about print except for basic bookhandling; he recalls few ideas from books read aloud to him; and he does not yet include sophisticated vocabulary from books in his meager retellings. In contrast, Imani knows book handling, has most directionality concepts in place, and is developing letter and word concepts. She has a strong recall of books and even incorporates a good deal of the sophisticated language from books in her retellings. The third child, Kambrisha, has very little conventional knowledge at the beginning of kindergarten although she is beginning to learn the alphabet. She was served in Head Start by the language specialist for language delays and still struggles to recall ideas from books read aloud.

These children are typical of entering kindergarten children in most locations. Some children, like Imani, have a great deal of conventional knowledge; some children, like Zyderrious, have knowledge in some areas but not in others; and other children, like Kambrisha, have very little conventional knowledge. Effective teachers will carefully observe children in classroom activities in order to acquire further information about their language and literacy development.

It is important to keep in mind that two of the children in Table 3.2 are at the end of the phase of novice reading and writing. Therefore, they have acquired many conventional concepts. If we had assessed them as three-year-olds when they began Head Start, we likely would have found them unable to do any of the conventional tasks we describe in this chapter. Instead, we likely would have seen them engaging in many pretend reading and writing activities, such as pretending to read environmental print and pretending to write telephone messages. These pretend behaviors, while unconventional, are just as much a part of literacy as being able to correctly identify alphabet letters. All children begin with unconventional notions about print, reading, and writing and gradually acquire the conventional understandings that are displayed in Table 3.2. That is why it is critical that teachers combine careful observation with preschool and kindergarten monitoring tasks.

TABLE 3.2   Beginning of the Year Kindergarten Scores on Monitoring Assessment Tasks

	Zyderrious	Imani	Kambrisha
Upper alphabet recognition (26)	25	25	1
Lower alphabet recognition (26)	24	21	5
Writing alphabet letters (15)	14	14	1
Level of name writing (6)	4	5	3
Concepts about print (15)	5	10	3
Generating rhyming words	3	0	0
Isolating beginning sounds (10)	0	10	0
Oral retelling, ideas (44)	7	17	4
Oral retelling, vocabulary (12)	0	4	0

Chapter Summary

NOVICE READERS AND WRITERS approach reading and writing in unconventional but systematic ways. They expect written language to be meaningful, and the meanings they associate with particular kinds of texts (such as environmental print, grocery lists, and stories) reflect their growing awareness of the language associated with these texts. Novice readers and writers find environmental print meaningful. The contextualized nature of this type of print initially supports children's meaning-making efforts, but novice readers respond to environmental print even when it is not in contexts that clue its meaning. Novice readers make strides in understanding the decontextualized print in stories that are read aloud to them. They learn to construct stories-as-wholes. They learn that stories are more than individual pictures, that stories are formed by a causally related series of events. They learn to make inferences and evaluations about characters and events.

Novice writers often intend to communicate a meaning in their writing, and the meaning they communicate reflects how they expect to use their written products (as a grocery list or a story). Novice readers and writers gradually begin to learn names for alphabet letters and to form conventional letters and signatures. Their concepts of letters and signatures differ from those of adults. Their learning to write many kinds of texts reflects knowledge of text features, and their talk about texts reveals an awareness of the content associated with different kinds of texts. In particular, novice readers and writers develop more complex understandings of the content, language, and organization of stories and information books.

Novices rely on stylized print and pictures to read the logos in environmental print, and they depend on the context of their writing and talk to assign meanings to their writing. They use reading and writing for a variety of purposes, including playing, interacting with others, and conducting the business of daily living in their families and communities. The kinds of reading and writing activities in which children participate may vary, and what children learn about written language functions may differ accordingly. English language learners also learn about the alphabet and concepts about print of their home language. They may also begin to acquire these concepts in English. Teachers can best capture all children's development, including that of ELLs, by combining observation and assessment tasks.

Figure 3.13 provides a summary of the concepts presented in this chapter. It is important to keep in mind that a concept may appear in more than one section of the figure. For example, children's concept of story is an important part of their knowledge of written language forms. However, concept of story is also an important part of novice readers' and writers' knowledge about written language meanings. They use their concept of story as they construct meanings of the stories read aloud to them and as they compose the content of their own stories. Children's reading and writing ultimately reflect the interdependence of meaning, form, and function.

FIGURE 3.13 Summary: What Novice Readers and Writers Know about Written Language

Meaning Making

intend to communicate meaning in writing

assign meaning to environmental print

assign meaning to a variety of texts, pretend to read, by applying knowledge of the content and language used in those texts

apply concept of story in constructing the meaning of stories read aloud, retelling stories, and pretend reading of stories especially using sequence and causality

construct literal meaning

construct inferential meaning

use some literary language in retelling and pretend reading

Forms

recognize alphabet letters as a special set of graphic symbols

learn alphabet letter names and formations

learn letter features (and may write mock letters)

write own signature

use a variety of text features to construct different kinds of texts

Meaning-Form Links

use contextual dependency

differentiate pictures from print (but sometimes think pictures are read)

pay attention to print (and sometimes know that print is read)

go beyond contextual dependency by matching segments of the printed text with segments of the spoken text (sometimes matching lines to spoken sentences, segments of text to spoken words, or letters to syllables)

develop the beginnings of phonological awareness (by constructing rhyming words and identifying beginning phonemes)

Functions

use reading and writing in play

use reading and writing across time to regulate the behavior of self and others

use reading and writing as part of family and community activities (such as to complete daily-living routines)

USING THE INFORMATION

The following is a list of some of the concepts that novice readers and writers gain during this phase of reading and writing. This listing has been taken from Figure 3.13, which summarizes what novice readers and writers are learning about written language. Go through the chapter and find a figure or a vignette that demonstrates each of these concepts about Novice readers and writers and tell why.

1. Intend to communicate meaning in their writing (for example, Figure 3.1 demonstrates that Javaris intended to communicate "bread, lettuce, tomatoes, eggs, and cheese" in his scribble—be sure to find at least one more example).

2. Assign meaning (read) environmental print (for example, Kristen recognized the KMart sign and believed it was her special place—be sure to find at least one more example).

3. Assign meaning (pretend to read) a variety of texts such as grocery lists, telephone books, and familiar stories.

4. Construct literal and inferential meaning.

5. Learn alphabet letter names and formations.

6. Write signatures.

7. Write different texts with distinctive features (such as writing grocery lists in a vertical list format and stories using horizontal lines of writing).

8. Use contextual dependency to convey meaning in writing by telling a teacher, friend, or parent the message.

9. Go beyond contextual dependency to try to match up what is written with the spoken message by reading one word for each line of text.

10. Develop phonological awareness by making up rhyming words.

11. Use reading and writing in dramatic pretend play.

APPLYING THE INFORMATION

The following vignette took place in the housekeeping area and the post office dramatic play center found in a Head Start classroom serving four-year-olds. Discuss what this event reveals about Nah'Kiyah's understandings about written language meanings, forms, functions, and meaning-form links. Use the concepts listed on Figure 3.13 to guide your discussion.

Nah'Kiyah was playing with three other children in the housekeeping center. They were planning a party that they wanted to have and discussing people to invite. The teacher casually dropped in the center and suggested that the children might want to write invitations. She went to the writing center and returned with several envelopes for the children to use. The children found markers in a special basket that is used to keep different kinds of writing implements and notepads. They sat at the kitchen table and began writing. Nah'Kiyah said, "I'm going to invite my mother, and I know how to write her name. Teresa. Yes, and we live in Greenville, Alabama." She finished her envelope quickly and said, "Now I'm fixing to go on over to that post office and mail this off." She grabbed a purse and a baby and headed over to the other center where children were pretending to be postal workers, mail carriers, and customers. Nah'Kiyah stepped up to the counter and asked for a stamp. The worker took out a date stamp (that has no ink) and stamped the envelope. He threw it in a special crate used to keep mail and said, "It'll be delivered tomorrow." Nah'Kiyah left the post office, returned to the housekeeping area, and wrote five more envelopes and mailed each one before it was time for clean up. Figure 3.14 presents the envelope Nah'Kiyah addressed to her mother.

FIGURE 3.14   Nah'Kiyah's envelope: "Teresa Greenville, AL."

GOING BEYOND THE TEXT

ARRANGE TO VISIT WITH A FAMILY that has a preschooler, or visit a preschool or kindergarten. Take a children's story book and be prepared to tape-record your interaction as you share the story with the preschooler or kindergartner. Take some paper and markers or crayons and invite the child to draw and write about the story. Record what the child says while drawing and writing. Ask the child to write his or her name. Administer the alphabet recognition task, concepts about print task, phonemic awareness task, or retelling checklist. Describe the child's knowledge of written language meanings, forms, meaning-form links, and functions.

REFERENCES

Abramson, S., Seda, I., & Johnson, C. (1990). Literacy development in a multilingual kindergarten classroom. *Childhood Education, 67*, 68–72.

Baghban, M. (1984). *Our daughter learns to read and write.* Newark, DE: International Reading Association.

Ballenger, C. (1999). *Teaching other people's children: Literacy and learning in a bilingual classroom.* New York: Teachers College Press.

Barone, D., Mallette, M., & Xu, S. (2005). *Teaching early literacy: Development, assessment, and instruction.* New York: Guilford.

Bear, D., Invernizzi, M., Templeton, S., & Johnston, F. (2000). *Words their way: Word study for phonics, vocabulary, and spelling instruction,* 2nd ed. Upper Saddle River, NJ: Prentice-Hall.

Bloodgood, J. (1999). What's in a name? Children's name writing and name acquisition. *Reading Research Quarterly, 34*, 342–367.

Clay, M. M. (1975). *What did I write?* Auckland: Heinemann.

Cochran-Smith, M. (1984). *The making of a reader.* Norwood, NJ: Ablex.

Cox, B., Fang, Z. & Otto, B. (1997). Preschoolers' developing ownership of the literate register. *Reading Research Quarterly, 32*, 34–53.

Cummins, J. (1986). Empowering minority students: A framework for intervention. *Harvard Educational Review, 56*, 18–36.

Cummins, J. (1989). *Empowering minority students.* Sacramento, CA: California Association for Bilingual Education.

Dickinson, D. (2001). Book reading in preschool classrooms: Is recommended practice common? In D. Dickinson & P. Tabors (Eds.), *Beginning literacy with language: Young children learning at home and school* (pp. 149–174). Baltimore, MD: Paul H. Brookes.

Duke, N. (2004). The case for information text. *Education Leadership, 61 (6)*, 40.

Duke, N. K., & Hays, J. (1998). "Can I say 'Once upon a time'?": Kindergarten children developing knowledge of informational book language. *Early Childhood Research Quarterly, 13*, 295–318.

Duncan, P. (1996). *Some smug slug.* New York: HarperTrophy.

Dyson, A. H. (1982). The emergence of visible language: Interrelationships between drawing and early writing. *Visible Language, 16*, 360–381.

Dyson, A. H. (2003). *The brothers and sisters learn to write: Popular literacies in childhood and school cultures.* New York: Teachers College Press.

Ferreiro, E. (1986). The interplay between information and assimilation in beginning literacy. In W. H. Teale & E. Sulzby (Eds.), *Emergent literacy: Writing and reading* (pp. 15–49). Norwood, NJ: Ablex.

Ferreiro, E., & Teberosky, A. (1982). *Literacy before schooling.* Exeter, NH: Heinemann.

Gee, J. (2001). A sociocultural perspective on early literacy development. In S. Neuman & D. Dickinson (Eds.), *Handbook of early literacy research* (pp. 30–42). New York: Guilford.

Goodman, Y. (1980). The roots of literacy. In M. Douglass (Ed.), *Claremont reading conference, 44th Yearbook* (pp. 1–32). Claremont, CA: Claremont Graduate School.

Gundlach, R., McLane, J. B., Scott, F. M., & Mc-Namee, G. D. (1985). The social foundations of children's early writing development. In M. Farr (Ed.), *Advances in writing research: Vol. 1. Children's early writing development* (pp. 1–58). Norwood, NJ: Ablex.

Hamm, D. (1991). *Laney's lost momma.* Morton Grove, IL: Albert Whitman.

Harste, J. C., Woodward, V. A., & Burke, C. L. (1984). *Language stories and literacy lessons.* Portsmouth, NH: Heinemann.

Hiebert, E. H. (1978). Preschool children's understanding of written language. *Child Development, 49,* 1231–1234.

Hildreth, G. (1936). Developmental sequences in name writing. *Child Development, 7,* 291–302.

International Reading Association & National Association for the Education of Young Children. (1998). Learning to read and write: Developmentally appropriate practices for young children. *The Reading Teacher, 53,* 193–216.

Labbo, L. (1996). A semiotic analysis of young children's symbol making in a classroom computer center. *Reading Research Quarterly, 31,* 353–385.

Martinez, M. (1983). Exploring young children's comprehension during story time talk. *Language Arts, 60,* 202–209.

Martinez, M., & Teale, W. (1993). Teacher storybook reading style: A comparison of six teachers. *Research in the Teaching of English, 27,* 175–199.

Mayer, M. (1968). *There's a nightmare in my closet.* New York: Dial.

McGee, L., & Richgels, D. (1989). "K is Kristen's": Learning the alphabet from a child's perspective. *The Reading Teacher, 43,* 216–225.

Pappas, C. C. (1991). Fostering full access to literacy by including informational books. *Language Arts, 68,* 449–462.

Pappas, C. (1993). Is narrative "primary"? Some insights from kindergartners' pretend readings of stories and information books. *Journal of Reading Behavior, 25,* 97–129.

Pappas, C. C. (2006). The information book genre: Its role in integrated science literacy research and practice. *Reading Research Quarterly, 41,* 226–250.

Purcell-Gates, V. (1996). Stories, coupons, and the "TV Guide": Relationships between home literacy experiences and emergent literacy

knowledge. *Reading Research Quarterly, 31,* 406–428.

Reid, M. (1996). *Let's find out about ice cream.* New York: Scholastic.

Roberts, T. & Neal H. (2004). Relationships among preschool English language learner's oral proficiency in English, instructional experience and literacy development. *Contemporary Educational Psychology, 29,* 283–311.

Schickedanz, J. (1999). *Much more than the ABCs: The early stages of reading and writing.* Washington, DC: National Association for the Education of Young Children.

Shine, S., & Roser, N. (1999). The role of genre in preschoolers' response to picture books. *Research in the Teaching of English, 34,* 197–251.

Smith, S., & Dixon, R. (1995). Literacy concepts of low- and middle-class four-year-olds entering preschool. *Journal of Educational Research, 88,* 243–253.

Smolkin, L., & Donovan, C. (2002). "Oh excellent, excellent question!": Developmental differences and comprehension acquisition. In C. Block & M. Pressley (Eds.), *Comprehension instruction: Research-based best practices* (pp. 140–157). New York: Guilford.

Taylor, D., & Dorsey-Gaines, C. (1988). *Growing up literate: Learning from inner-city families.* Portsmouth, NH: Heinemann.

Tower, C. (2002). "It's a snake, you guys!": The power of text characteristics on children's responses to informational books. *Research in the Teaching of English, 37,* 55–88.

Turbill, J., & Murray, J. (2006). Early literacy and new technologies in Australian schools: Policy, research, and practice. In M. C. McKenna, L. D. Labbo, R. D. Kieffer, & D. Reinking (Eds.), *International handbook of literacy and technology, Vol. II* (pp. 93–108). Mahwah, NJ: Lawrence Erlbaum.

Ungerer, T. (1958). *Crictor.* New York: HarperCollins.

U.S. Congress (2001). *No child left behind act of 2001. Public Law 107-110. 107th Congress.* Washington, DC: Government Printing Office.

Voss, M. M. (1988). "Make way for applesauce": The literate world of a three year old. *Language Arts, 65,* 272–278.

Wolf, S. A., & Heath, S. B. (1992). *The braid of literature: Children's worlds of reading.* Cambridge, MA: Harvard University Press.

From Five to Seven Years

EXPERIMENTING READERS AND WRITERS

KEY CONCEPTS

Experimenters

Alphabetic Reading and
  Writing

Phonemes

Phonics

Grapho-Syntax

Grapho-Semantics

Invented Spelling

Literary Language

Metalinguistic
  Awareness

Concept of Written Word

Concept of Word
  Boundaries

Mock Cursive

Letter Strings

Dictation

Alliteration

Sounding Literate

Being Precise

Finger-Point Reading

Phonemic Awareness

Rhyming Word Families

Onset

Rime

Phonograms

Phoneme Repertoires

Multiple Literacies

Message Concept

School Literacy
  Perspective

Situated Literacy
  Perspective

WHO ARE EXPERIMENTERS?

EXPERIMENTERS ARE CHILDREN MAKING THE TRANSITION from what we described as novice reading and writing to conventional reading and writing. They are at a unique place in their literacy development when they will make, on their own and through the careful instruction of teachers, many critical discoveries about print, written language, letters, words, stories, phonemes, and the functions of reading and writing. We call this unique phase of literacy development Experimenting Reading and Writing. We call it this because children are experimenting with what they know about print as they try to make sense of it. Throughout this chapter, we will demonstrate how children experiment with many components of literacy.

Many children's home and community experiences of literacy propel them into experimenting reading and writing. These children are usually in homes in which mothers and fathers own books, read to their children frequently, and invite them to write and participate in events that include reading and writing (such as writing postcards, thank you notes, and grocery lists and reading favorite books). Through these activities, children actually receive as many as one thousand hours of personalized guidance in reading and writing.

Other children begin to gain insights about the conventions of reading and writing because their preschool and kindergarten teachers surround them with reading and writing that is meaningful to them. Most children enter and move through the period we call experimenting reading and writing through a combination of their experiences in homes and communities and in classrooms. Teachers can expect many preschoolers and most kindergartners to begin the experimenting phase of reading and writing.

All children who eventually will become conventional readers and writers must first navigate this critical experimenting period of literacy development. They must move from the pretend reading and writing of novices to realizing that print is read in a particular way. Most children take time to acquire this understanding. They must become aware of words and how letters in written words relate to sounds in spoken words, part of what we have described as the alphabetic principle. As simple as this sounds, children approach it in different and unconventional ways.

The New Understandings and Awareness of Experimenting Readers and Writers

Four new understandings and behaviors mark experimenting readers and writers:

- thoughtful attitude toward and awareness of print
- discovery of words
- discovery of the alphabetic principle
- ability to focus on only one or a few aspects of conventional reading and writing at a time

While novices are aware of print, look at it, and attempt to write it and read it, experimenters demonstrate an awareness that print works in a special way. Unlike novice readers and writers, who are sure they can read and write and do so in their pretend play, experimenters often are convinced they cannot. One of the first indications that children have entered this new print-focused phase of awareness is their suddenly refusing to read and write when before, as novice readers and writers, they had been eager to join in these activities. Now, however, children are aware that pretending to read and write is not "really" reading and writing as adults or older children do. It takes a sensitive adult to help children get past their feelings of *I can't* in order to use what they do know. For example, children can be helped to read environmental print and copy words from this print as a way to demonstrate to them they can read and can write. Throughout this chapter (and in Chapter 8), we describe other ways to overcome children's reluctance to read and write that is to be expected in this phase.

Another shift that occurs during experimenting reading and writing is that children shift their attention from alphabet letters to words. That is, as novice readers and writers, they had learned a great deal about recognizing and writing alphabet letters. Because they come to experimenting knowing most letters, they begin to discover a new form of written language: a word. They realize that readers read words, that writers write words, and that words are composed of letters. Gradually they come to accept that words are separated by spaces.

A third shift is when experimenting readers and writers notice that the letters in written words have a relationship with the sounds in spoken words, what is called the alphabetic principle. That is, experimenters eventually discover that the English written language system is an alphabetic writing system. **Alphabetic reading and writing** uses signs (letters) in a systematic relationship to individual speech sounds (**phonemes**). Many languages are alphabetic, but not all. Some languages use written signs that stand for syllables rather than individual speech sounds, and other language have signs that stand for complete words. One of three systems for linking written forms with meanings that children learn in order to read and write English is **phonics,** the linking of letters and combinations of letters with sounds and combinations of sounds. Even though experimenters are especially focused on phonics, and even though phonics is a very important part of learning to read and write English, it is not by itself enough. Effective readers also the use two other systems, **grapho-syntax** and **grapho-semantics,** along with phonics. One reason experimenters do not yet read like adults is that they often neglect to use all three of these systems simultaneously. Such coordination is more typical of conventional readers and writers (see Chapter 5) than of experimenting readers and writers.

Examples of Experimenters

Here are two examples of experimenters:

> Three-year-old Sophie listens to her uncle read a storybook. She directs his reading, "Read that. . . . Read that." She always points first to the left-hand page and then to the right-hand page. When they finish the book, Sophie begins pointing to individual words on a page and again says, "Read that. . . . Read that," this time for each word she points to. This pointing proceeds right to left, word by word, until Sophie's uncle has identified every word in a line.

> Five-year-old Ted has been sent to his room for misbehaving. He either does not remember or does not understand why he was sent there. With pencil and paper, he writes the message shown in Figure 4.1. He dashes out of his room, tosses this

FIGURE 4.1   Ted's Protest: "Mom, why are you punishing me? Ted"

written query or protest on the floor before his mother, and runs back into his room.

Sophie knows left-to-right directionality for pages. More important, although she does not know left-to-right directionality for word reading, her careful pointing to words shows that she is able to identify word boundaries. She has a concept of written word. She explores the power of written words, the combinations of letters bordered by spaces, to evoke particular spoken words from a reader. Compared with novices, who may point to whole lines of text as representations of anything from a sentence to a word, Sophie has a much more precise understanding of word-by-word speech-to-print matching.

Ted's writing shows that he knows something about letter names and sounds in words. Compared with novices, who do not know about phonics, Ted has a very mature understanding of how writing works. Although his spelling is not conventional, he systematically pairs letters with sounds. His invented spellings show his knowledge of the alphabetic principle. **Invented spelling** is children's systematic but not conventional matching of sounds in words with letters.

Ted's message contains other examples of experimenter traits. He has learned in school how to read and spell the word *you* conventionally. Unlike novices, experimenters often have school-gained literacy knowledge. They must integrate this with literacy knowledge that they are gaining concurrently from home literacy experiences and that they gained earlier in their lives as preschoolers and literacy novices.

Ted's message shows an intensity that is often characteristic of experimenters. He sometimes worked intensely, especially when a message was as important to him as this one was. Ted's query appears unfinished; he wrote nothing for the word *me*. It is unlikely that he knowingly wrote an incomplete message; perhaps the effort required for this writing task distracted him so much that he did not realize he had omitted a word.

Experimenting with Meaning

THE MEANING MAKING OF EXPERIMENTERS is only slightly more complex than that of novices. Novices and experimenters share a basic understanding of the power and meaning found in written language. Both write in order to communicate a message, and both engage in interactive storybook reading using sophisticated strategies for constructing meaning. Experimenters continue to use the meaning-making strategies they devised as novices (see Chapter 3).

For example, experimenters are likely to have a fully developed concept of story or story schema (see Chapter 2). They are more likely to attend to problems in stories. Later in this chapter we will describe experimenters' new attention to the literary properties of informational texts. They have learned that written stories and informational books have certain language forms and word orders not found in spoken language. Experimenters are likely to use **literary language,** when composing and recalling stories, for example, "Away we went to grandmother's house."

Experimenting with Forms

EXPERIMENTERS HAVE CONSIDERABLE KNOWLEDGE about letters; they can recognize most letters, write most letters with conventional formations, and recite the alphabet. Experimenters also have **metalinguistic awareness** of letters; that is, they can talk and think about the names and properties of letters. Sarah, a kindergartner, wanted to write the *M* in *snowman.* Her classmate Jason told her, "*M.*" She asked, "Is that the up-down, up-down one?" Experimenters also show their concept of word in their reading and writing. They create a variety of texts using a variety of writing strategies.

Concept of Word

A fully developed **concept of written word** includes knowledge that words are composed of combinations of letters, that words are bounded by the spaces between them, and that the sounds within them are related to alphabet letters (Roberts, 1992). Experimenters acquire bits and pieces of this concept as they move forward in learning to read and write.

One way children show their interest in words is by attempting to write words. Figure 4.2 shows some writing that Kathy produced one day as she sat by herself in her room. When her mother asked her to read her writing, she replied, "It's just words." Notice that Kathy's writing is much like a novice's—we could not know the meaning Kathy intended to communicate unless we listened to Kathy read her writing (and, in this case, Kathy did not seem to intend to communicate a message).

However, three aspects of Kathy's attempts to write words are typical of experimenters. First, she is experimenting with letter combinations to produce writing that she calls words. Second, she is experimenting with using spaces between letter combinations to signal boundaries between her words (we will discuss more about children's concepts of word boundaries later in this chapter). Third, Kathy seems to be paying attention to only one aspect of written language—words and how they look—and ignoring other aspects of written language, such as meaning.

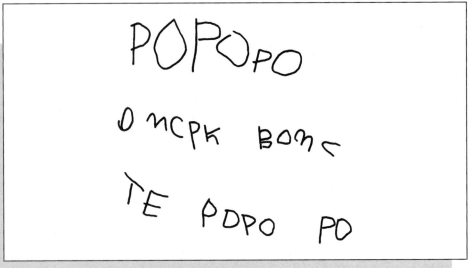

FIGURE 4.2   Kathy's Invented Words

Another way experimenters signal their interest in words is by asking questions about words. One day, Carrie's father was silently reading a typewritten letter. Carrie climbed onto his lap, pointed to a word in the letter that began with the letter *C*, and asked what it was. When told that the word was *concern*, she replied, "Oh. It has a *C* like my name." Carrie had noted that the word *concern* was something like her name. Both were composites of letters and both began with a C. Carrie then asked, "What's that word?" about several other words in the letter.

Children also signal their attention to words by attempting to write words in which some of the letters in the word capture some of the sounds in spoken words. This process is known as invented spelling (Read, 1971) (we will devote considerable attention to this topic later in the chapter). For example, in a story about dinosaurs, Meagan, a kindergartner, wrote the invented spelling *Vknl* for *volcano.*

Concept of Word Boundaries

As children become aware that words in spoken and written language can be segmented, they develop a **concept of word boundaries.** In conventional writing, we use spaces to show boundaries between individually printed words. Experimenters begin to respond to individual words in environmental print and in books, and they experiment with ways to show the boundaries between words in their own writing. Children show their awareness of word boundaries in many ways. Paul used dots between words, for example: PAULZ • HOS • PLANF • ELD • VRMAT (Paul's house, Plainfield, Vermont) (Bissex, 1980, p. 22).

Other children circle words, put them in vertical arrangements, or even separate them with carefully drawn and blackened squares (Harste, Burke, & Woodward, 1983; Temple, Nathan, Temple, & Burris, 1993).

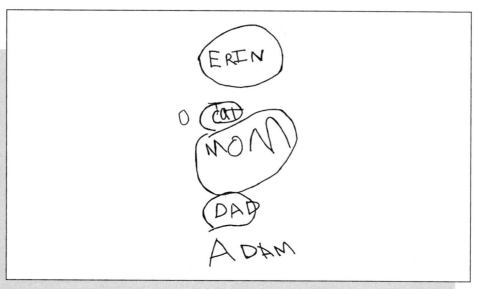

FIGURE 4.3   Erin's Dramatic Play Writing with Circles around Words

Figure 4.3 presents a list Erin composed while playing in her kindergarten house-keeping center. She wrote her name and other words she knows how to spell: *cat, MOM, DAD,* and *ADAM* (her brother's name). She emphasized her words by circling all but her brother's name.

Texts

In Chapter 3, we showed that novices are aware of several text formats when they play with writing in different contexts for various purposes. Chapter 3 included examples of novices' lists and stories. Experimenters continue to be interested in a variety of text forms, but they use more strategies to produce sophisticated texts.

The texts that experimenters create usually look more conventional than those produced by novices. Experimenters generate a greater variety of texts as well. There are several reasons for the differences between these two types of writers. Experimenters are more likely to ask for an adult's assistance in constructing their messages because they are aware that they cannot yet produce a readable message on their own. Therefore, it is not unusual for experimenters to refuse initially to write. Those who refuse are comparing easy writing tasks that they can do well, such as writing their names, with the more difficult task of writing a text, and they are saying in effect, "I can't do *that!*" This kind of refusal implies some knowledge of what *that* entails. They know that stories have many more words than they could hope to write on their own.

Eventually, most experimenters can be encouraged to try writing a story or other type of text, especially if they know that teachers will be satisfied even with their un-conventional attempts. Two composing strategies of experimenters are making **mock cursive** and writing **letter strings.** They tell a story as they write or when they are in-

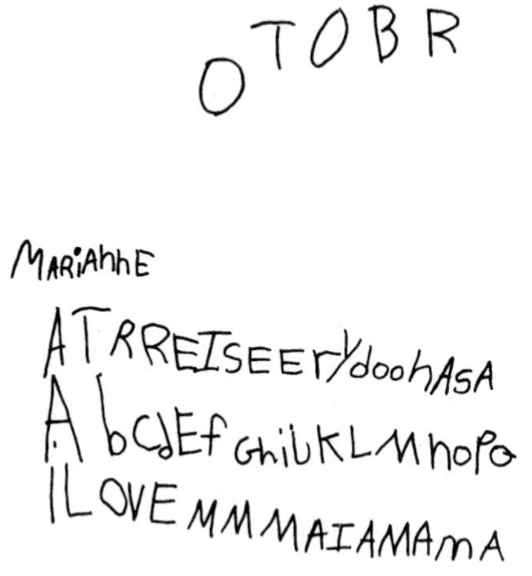

OTOBR

MARiAhhE

ATRREISEErYdoohASA
AbCJEf GhiUKLMhoPa
ILOVEMMMAIAMAmA

Once upon a time I went to the zoo and saw a zebra. Then I yelled, "Yeah," because I never saw a zebra before. He licked me on the hand. Then I said, "Mom and Dad, look. Sister, look" Then we went home. The end.

FIGURE 4.4 Mariann

vited to tell about their writing. Mock cursive is wavy lines that look like cursive writing. Letter strings are lines of letters that do not seem to include words and certainly are not attempts to invent spellings. Figure 4.4 presents a story Marianne wrote about seeing a zebra at the zoo. Marianne attended a preschool for low-income four-year-olds in which the teacher modeled writing for children daily on large charts. Figure 4.4 also includes the story Marianne told when she was invited to tell about her writing. While we would expect novices also to write using mock cursive or letter strings, the story that Marianne told is the product of an experimenter. With its consistent use of past tense, its literary language (*Once upon a time* and *the end*), and its coherent characters, events, and dialogue, it is more sophisticated than we might expect of novices.

Figure 4.5 shows another way that experimenters compose, by dictation. **Dictation** is a child's slowly speaking a message or telling a story as a teacher or other adult writes it, usually for later reading by the adult and child. The text in Figure 4.5 is a story that Muffin, a four-year-old, told her day care teacher. The language of the story reflects her home dialect. The elements that mark this as the work of an experimenter are the same as in Marianne's story: its unity (it is about events in a special day of a main character, George), its consistent use of past tense (for those events, beginning with *She saw*), and its use of the literary closing *The End*.

Children sometimes dictate literary texts other than stories. Jeffrey dictated a poem to his mother as he ran back and forth across his patio.

The Running Poem
Bubble gun boppers,
Candy heart sneakers,
Sparky love.
Buster slimers,

Booger man,
Barbecue pit.
Blue ribbons win.
The end.

While the content of Jeffrey's poem relates to what he was doing (running) and seeing (his sneakers, the barbecue pit, and the family dog, Sparky), it also shows Jeffrey's understandings of the conventions of poetry forms. His poem consisted of phrases rather than sentences, and he used **alliteration**—five lines of his poem start with words beginning with the sound /b/. Alliteration is the use of the same sound at the beginning of two or more words. It is interesting that Jeffrey ended his poem with "The end," which is the formulaic ending for a story rather than a poem. Still, his poem demonstrates Jeffrey's experimentation with language forms associated with poetry.

The third way experimenters compose is by copying. Figure 4.6 shows a journal entry that Eric composed on the day that chicks hatched in his kindergarten class's incubator. He copied words from *Inside an Egg* (Johnson, 1982), one of the information

FIGURE 4.5 "George" by Muffin

This is a story about George. She is a girl. She got a father, but her mom died. She still miss her. She saw one snowflake and soon it would be Christmas. Her father and her went and got a Christmas tree. Then they decorated the tree. They went to bed, and Santa Claus came that night. When she woke up, she saw a lot of stuff. She asked her daddy if she could go out and play and he said, "Yes." When she got outside she made a beautify heart snowman for her mama. The End.

Finally the shell breaks in two pieces, and the chick hatches.

FIGURE 4.6 Eric's Copied Journal Entry

books his teacher had collected for the chick hatching unit. It was an exciting day in Eric's classroom. His careful, time-consuming copying demonstrates the willingness of experimenters to concentrate on literacy tasks and devote considerable energy to their constructions.

The fourth way experimenters compose is shown in Figure 4.7. Experimenters eventually write words by inventing spellings. Invented spelling is the process of listening carefully to the sounds (phonemes) in words and selecting and sequencing letters to spell those sounds, often letters whose names are the same as those sounds (for example, the name of the letter *A* is *aye,* which is the same as the sound /A/) or contain those sounds (for example, the name of the letter *B* is *bee,* which begins with the sound /b/). Invented spelling is not misspelling. It is not that experimenting writers have learned but choose to disregard conventional spellings. Rather, by systematically using sound-letter correspondences, they are creating genuine, though nonconventional, spellings. Often they cannot read their invented spellings a short time after writing them. With more experience of text and with instruction, their spellings become more conventional. Composing with nearly complete and more conventional spellings and being able later to read those spellings is a sign that children are leaving experimenting reading and writing behind and entering the phase of conventional reading and writing.

Kendarick, a kindergartner, wrote the words *Super Hero* at his classroom writing center. His teacher introduced a routine for using the center in which children were asked to draw a picture and then write about it. Later as the teacher collected all the children's papers, she invited several children to tell about their writing. The teacher often wrote the words the children said on a sticky note on the back of the paper to remind her of the words in the invented spellings. Notice that Kendarick was able to spell three phonemes in the word *Super,* spelling it *SPR.* He also captured three phonemes in the word *heroes,* spelling it *H r (backwards) 0.* Notice that Kendarick worked so hard at hearing and writing sounds in his spellings that he did not put his letters down in

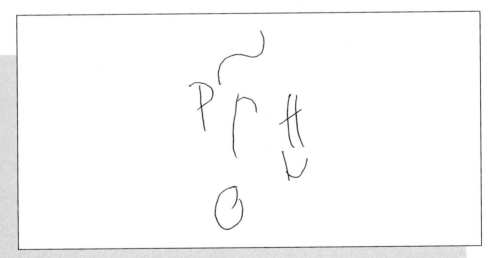

FIGURE 4.7   Super Heroes

perfect left-to-right lines. This is an example of experimenters' inability to control all aspects of written language as they experiment with a particular piece of the written language puzzle.

It is important to keep in mind that experimenters use some of the same conventions as more conventional readers and writers. We tend to think of children at this stage as not yet being very knowledgeable about written language. Even when we are accepting and supportive, what usually catches our attention in children's experimental products are their mistakes. However, there is much that is correct in their products, even by conventional standards.

Experimenting with Meaning–Form Links

DISCOVERING THE ESSENTIALS of how meanings and forms are linked in an alphabetic writing system is the main work of experimenters. It is the achievement that most clearly sets them apart from novices and puts them on the path to conventional reading and writing. In Chapter 3, we saw that novices' ways of linking form and meaning often are limited by their dependence on context, and that novices lack understanding of sound-letter relations. Experimenters' attention to print is much more purposeful than is novices'. Not only do they know that print is important, but they begin to discover how it works—that the alphabetic principle is at the core of the relation between print and meaning.

In their writing, experimenters develop two important kinds of awareness: awareness that their written messages are permanent and stable (they and others can return to them to retrieve their meanings) and awareness of phonemes, the units of sound from which words are built and to which letters are systematically matched. They move from writing by dictating stories, using booklike language, to writing with invented spelling.

Experimenters' writing and reading discoveries interact. For example, phonemic awareness practiced and enhanced during invented spelling is put to use in alphabetic reading.

Sounding Literate

A new accomplishment of experimenters is to sound literate when they pretend to read and write. **Sounding literate** means that as children look at books and retell a book's story to themselves or friends, they know to use literary language like *once upon a time* or *the end*. They use sophisticated words and word order such as *up the hill they went, leading the lovely princess.* They even use intonation that sounds like reading a text rather than conversation. Experimenters sound literate especially when pretending to read a favorite storybook they have heard read aloud many times (Sulzby, 1985; Cox, Fang, & Otto, 1997).

In contrast, novices' pretend readings of books are very simple: They label parts of illustrations or tell a story to match the illustrations. When experimenters pretend to read a favorite storybook, the words they use often quite closely resemble the actual words of the book. Eventually, experimenters can retell a favorite book word for word.

Developmental Changes in Pretend Reading. Research has documented that children go through various phases in pretend reading that show they are getting closer and closer to conventional reading (Sulzby, 1995). Table 4.1 presents three major phases of pretend storybook reading. Actually, the first phase is what novices do; they label pictures or tell stories. Their pretend readings do not sound literate and therefore are called oral-language-like because they sound more like conversation about a story than reading of a text.

The second phase of pretend reading is written language-like; children in this phase sound literate. At first, they tell a story that is only similar to what is in the book, then they begin to include words from the actual text, and finally they tell the text word-for-word. The third phase of pretend reading is more sophisticated because children are really attempting to read conventionally. It begins with refusing to attempt to read. That is, even children who have literally memorized the texts of dozens of favorite storybooks eventually say "I can't read" when invited to read one of those books. They now realize that they are not really reading. Gradually, however, as they move out of the phase of experimenting reading, they attempt to read a few words they know and can pick out from the many words in the text. Finally, they read the text as grown-ups do.

Figure 4.8 presents Carrie's pretend reading of *The Three Bears* (1952). Text from the book is presented on the left and Carrie's pretend reading on the right. Her reading is an example of what we can expect experimenters to do when asked to read a favorite

TABLE 4.1 Types of Storybook Reading

Influenced by Illustrations
- Oral Language-Like (Beginners and Novices)
  - Collections of labels and comments (e.g., "House. Flowers. He's the baby.")
  - Everyday Storytelling (e.g., "There was three bears and . . . and . . . and . . .")
- Written Language-Like (but not paying attention to the print)
  - Mixed Storyreading and Storytelling (Novices) (e.g., "There was three bears . . . and . . . and . . . tiniest voice of all.")
  - Reading in a Manner Similar to the Original Story (Experimenters) (see Figure 4.8)
  - Verbatim Recreation of the Text (Experimenters) (e.g., "Papa bear pounded nails in the roof.")

Influenced by Text (all are written language-like and come from paying attention to the print)
- Refusing (Experimenters) ("I don't know how to read.")
- Selective Reading (Experimenters) ("In. The. The. Baby. Did. On. The.")
- Connected-text Reading (Experimenters and Conventional Readers) ("Papa Bear, put n-n-n-ah-eye-lz, in the rrr-oh-ff, the roaf?" or "Papa bear pounded nails in the roof.")

Adapted from Sulzby (1985).

FIGURE 4.8   Carrie's Emergent Reading

Text	Reading
(From second and third pages. The illustration shows Mama Bear and Baby Bear in the foreground. She is watering tulips. He and a rabbit are doing handstands while a little bird watches. In the background Papa Bear is on a ladder repairing the roof of their house.)	(In an even voice, at a steady pace, until the end, when her voice rises.)
Papa Bear pounded nails in the roof. Mama Bear watered the flowers. Baby Bear did tricks on the lawn.	And Papa nailed the roof. Mama—Mama watered the flowers. And Baby Bear did tricks on the lawn."
	(Short pause. Laughter. Then in higher pitch, with rising and falling intonation, and faster pace.)
	"The bird's just watching!"

storybook. Carrie's words are close to those of the text but are not yet a verbatim rendition. Notice that Carrie's voice changes as she comments about the illustration, "The bird's just watching!" When attempting to read, Carrie uses past tense that is typical of written stories, but then she easily switches to present tense when commenting on a silly part of the illustration.

Sounding Literate in Writing.   We have seen that experimenters write by making letter strings or mock cursive and telling about them during and after composing, by dictating, by copying, and by inventing spellings. The tellings, which accompany their composing and their reading what they have already composed, sound literate just as their readings of others' texts do. They use reading intonation, literary language, and characters' dialogue. Recall Marianne's story about the zoo presented in Figure 4.4 and Muffin's dictated story about Christmas day in Figure 4.5. They included the narrative closing *The End* and such dialogue markers as *I said* and *he said*.

Being Precise

Another new characteristic of experimenters is their awareness of the need to be precise when reading and writing. **Being precise** is reading a text the same way across multiple readings because of using the exact words of the author. Further, these words are spoken at just the right times (when looking at the correct page of a storybook, for example). Being precise goes even further when children begin to track print in books and say words as they point carefully but not always correctly at certain words.

Novices notice print, but experimenters are more aware that print consists of words that are actually read. Experimenters do not yet read words, but they use what skills they have, which is to remember texts of favorite stories and attempt to point to words in the text. Teachers will notice that experimenters put their fingers on the text of books as they pretend to read. At first, experimenters merely sweep their hands across lines of text without trying to match up what they are saying with the actual words. Eventually, they deliberately point to each word and try to say just a word. They make many miscalculations in their attempts—for example, saying a syllable while pointing to a whole word or saying a phrase while pointing to a single word. Finally, experimenters learn to slow down, point word-by-word, and say word-by-word favorite memorized texts (Morris, Bloodgood, Lomax, & Perney, 2003).

When experimenters put their fingers on parts of text as they pretend to read, they are **finger-point reading** (Ehri & Sweet, 1991; Morris, 1993). This is not conventional reading, but it is critical for eventually learning to read conventionally. With finger-point reading, children experiment with where words begin and end in print. For example, a child may point one-by-one, from left to right to the words of the written text *Humpty Dumpty sat on a wall* while saying "Hump -ty Dump -ty sat on" and perhaps stop there or perhaps continue with "a wall" while pointing to the first two words of the next line of text. Finger-point reading is developmental. Eventually the child will correctly match saying the six words of that line of the nursery rhyme with pointing to the six written words.

Children may also demonstrate being precise in writing. They reveal this by the way they attempt to reread their own writing. Figure 4.9 presents a Father's Day card that four-year-old Brooke composed. On the front of her card she drew a bird and some flowers. On the inside she wrote nine letters: *R, A, Y, g, P, G, O, G,* and *I*. Afterward, she read her writing to her mother, pointing to the first five letters one at a time: "I/ love/ you/ dad/ dy." Then she paused for a few moments and pointed at the remaining four letters one at a time, reading, "ver/ y/ much/ too." Brooke is being precise by carefully matching each letter of her writing with a segment of her spoken message (in this case, a syllable).

Using Sound-Letter Relationships

Experimenters can link meaning with written form through the use of sound-letter relationships in their spellings and pretend readings. For example, a child whose teacher

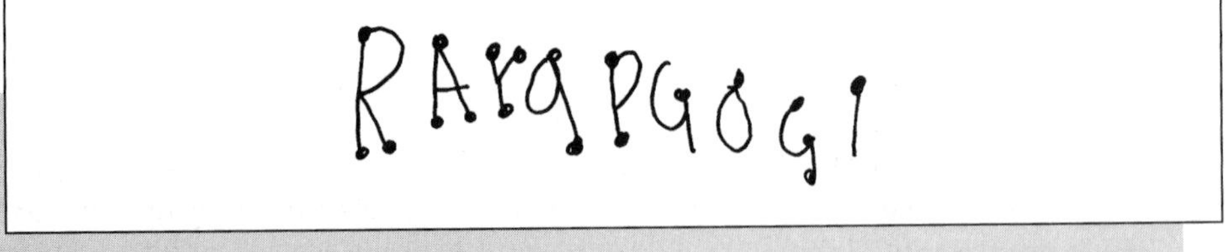

FIGURE 4.9   Brooke's Father's Day Card

frequently reads a book of nursery rhymes may notice that both *Jack* and *Jill* start with the letter *J* and that both words and the letter's name start with /j/ (see Table 1.2 for phoneme symbols). When the child comments about this and the parent acknowledges and confirms this, the child is gaining phonics knowledge. School-age experimenters may gain and consolidate such knowledge from both indirect (Dahl, Scharer, Lawson, & Grogan, 1999) and explicit (McIntyre & Freppon, 1994) phonics instruction.

A System Based on Phonemic Awareness

In order to spell, writers need a system: they need a rather precise, analytic understanding of the relationship between spoken and written language; they need the ability to examine words one sound unit at a time; and they need an awareness of some kind of relationship between spoken sounds and letters. What this means is that young writers must first be able to segment their spoken message into its component parts—words. Then spellers must further segment words into smaller parts—eventually, into phonemes. A **phoneme** is a unit of sound (e.g., /t/, /a/, /n/, /i/, /th/, and /ng/) that can contrast with another unit of sound when such units are combined to make words (e.g., *tan* vs. *tin, tin* vs. *thin, thin* vs. *thing*). In conventional spelling, phonemes are associated with single letters—such as *t, a, n*—or with letter combinations—such as *th* or *ng*. Hence teachers call /t/ the "T sound" or /th/ the "T-H sound."

Early inventive spellers do not usually separately pronounce every phoneme in a word, one at a time; this is a later-developing ability. Instead, they may pronounce only the first part, that is, the first phoneme. Then spellers must decide which letter to use to represent that phoneme. This is a long and complicated process that involves a great deal of conscious attention.

The process of attending to phonemes is part of the phonological awareness we described in Chapter 3. Phonological awareness includes attention to all aspects of the sounds of a language. One of those aspects is phonemes. Paying attention to phonemes, **phonemic awareness,** is most developed when a person can segment a word into each and every one of its phonemes, for example, segmenting the word *tan* into /t/, /a/ and /n/. This most developed kind of phonemic awareness only gradually emerges and signals that children have moved to a higher level of reading and writing than experimenting.

Invented spelling is phonemic awareness in action (Richgels, 2001). Kristen's first spellings provide a case in point. She announced that she could spell and looked around the room for things to spell. She said, "I can spell phone," and repeated the word to herself, saying it slowly, stretching out the initial /f/, "Ffffone, phone. I know—it's spelled *V*." Then she looked around again and said, "I can spell window, too." Again she slowly repeated the word, stretching out the initial /w/, "Wwwwindow. Window is *Y*."

Kristen's spellings are not conventional, but they have the characteristics of true spelling; they are systematic, and they demonstrate phonemic awareness. Using only one letter to spell each word is consistent with not pronouncing each phoneme of a word one at a time. She pronounced a whole word and paid attention to the first phoneme in that word. She was not doing the complete phoneme-by-phoneme analysis that demonstrates the most developed form of phonemic awareness, but her attention to each word was at the level of the phoneme.

Ways of Relating Sounds and Letters

While attending to the phonemes at the beginnings of *phone* and *window,* Kristen used two clues for choosing an appropriate letter for spelling: manner of articulation and identity of sound. Manner of articulation is the placement of the mouth, tongue, and teeth when speaking. Kristen noticed that her upper teeth were touching her lower lip both when she started to say the word *phone* and when she started to say the name of the letter *V.*

With *window* and *Y,* there is another possible explanation of Kristen's spelling. She may have used identity of sound. Both *window* and the name of the letter *Y* start with /w/ (the letter name *Y* is made up of two phonemes /w/ and /I/). Inventive spellers associate phonemes in letter names with phonemes in the spoken words they wish to spell.

Ted's spelling of the word *why* with a *Y* (Figure 4.1) shows use of a letter-name strategy to link letters and sounds. He used the name of the letter *Y* when choosing it to represent the word *why.*

Figure 4.10 shows the storywriting of two classmates on March 23 of their kindergarten year. They wrote in story folders, which are manila file folders that open to show a picture, and beneath it the words *Once upon a time* and a space for writing a story to go with the picture. The story folders are laminated and kindergartners write with erasable marker pens. The teacher makes photocopies of students' stories for them to keep and then wipes the folders clean so they can be reused by other kindergarten authors. The first story was written to accompany a picture of a girl hugging a woman and the second story to accompany a picture of a rabbit. Both stories are within the range of writing products we would expect of kindergartners two-thirds of the way

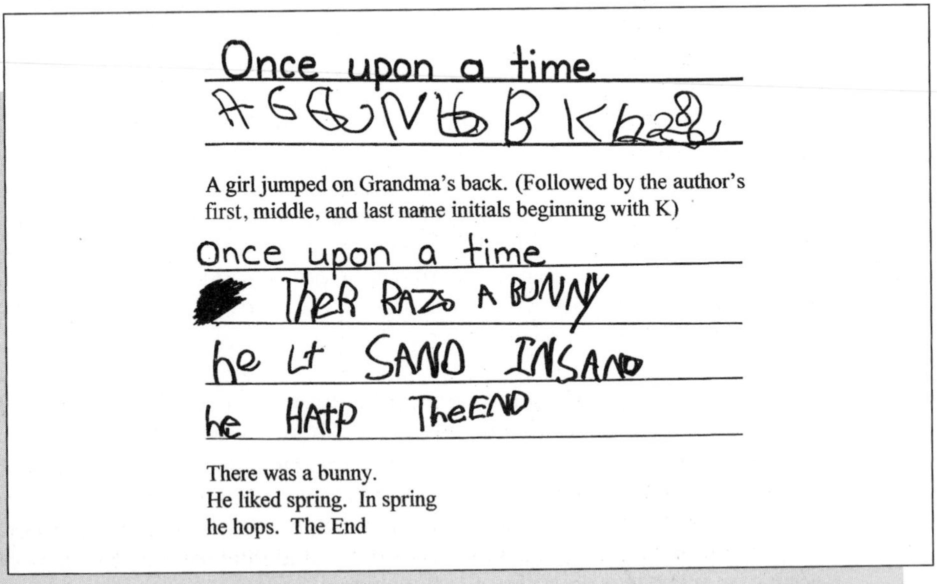

Once upon a time

A girl jumped on Grandma's back. (Followed by the author's first, middle, and last name initials beginning with K)

Once upon a time

There was a bunny.
He liked spring. In spring
he hops. The End

FIGURE 4.10   Story Folder Writing by Two Kindergartners

through the school year. Both authors used invented spelling. However, there are noticeable differences in the spelling strategies that these kindergartners employed.

The first story (A G G N G B for *A girl jumped on Grandma's back.*) is composed of one letter per word. The author's spelling choices are systematic. She uses the letter-name strategy for the first word, pronounced "aye" like the name of the letter she chooses. Many of her choices are governed by identity of the target sound and a sound in the name of a letter: a letter G for the word *jumped* (the name of the letter G and the word *jump* both start with /j/), an N for the word *in*, and a B for the word *back*. She uses G for /g/ in the words *girl* and *Grandma*, although that sound is not in that letter's name; she knows the conventional /g/-G sound-letter correspondence.

The second story (TheR RAZS A BUNNy / he Lt SAND INSAND / he HAtP TheEND for *There was a bunny. He liked spring. In spring he hops. The end.*) has discernable spaces between words, except between the two words for *in spring* and the two words for *The end*. The author uses at least two letters per word. He knows that some words require even more letters; the familiar word *and* seems to be a filler for word parts that he can not spell. The spelling for *bunny* was given to him. He routinely uses knowledge of sound-letter correspondences for many other spellings, notably the endings of *there* (TheR), *was* (RAZS), *liked* (Lt), and *hop* (HAtP) (though his spelling omits the final sound of the word as he reads it, "hops"). He uses correct vowel letters for words that are familiar to him: *he, the,* and *end*.

Stages of Spelling Development

These examples from Figure 4.10 suggest two hypotheses. First, although neither of these kindergarten authors is a conventional speller, both spell systematically. They know what spelling is supposed to accomplish, that it is an alphabetic code that matches sounds with letters with the goal of enabling readers to retrieve writers' words. Second, invented spelling seems to progress through stages, with the end point being conventional spelling.

Research supports these hypotheses, documenting stages of spelling development, from invented to conventional (Templeton & Morris, 2000; Templeton, 2003). Table 4.2 describes four stages in that progression. The progression is based on a similar scheme described by Bear, Invernizzi, Templeton, & Johnston (2000), who in turn built on the earlier work of Read (1971) and of Henderson and his students (e.g., Beers & Henderson, 1977; Gentry, 1978; Morris, 1981; Zutell, 1978). The four stages are labeled non-spelling (because it may not even involve letters and is random, not systematic), emergent spelling, early letter-name or early alphabetic spelling, and middle letter-name or middle alphabetic spelling (for later stages, beginning with late letter-name or late alphabetic spelling, see Chapter 5).

The first stage, non-spelling, is what novices do. They do not actually spell. Individual letters in their writing are not even representative of beginning sounds in the words of their intended messages.

The second, third, and fourth stages represent the kinds of spelling we expect from experimenters. In these three stages experimenters use letters to make words based on analyses of sound units in words and knowledge of sound-letter correspondences. They progress from only partial (initial or initial and final sounds) to nearly complete encoding of word sounds, and from representing only consonant sounds to representing consonants and vowels.

TABLE 4.2 Stages of Spelling Development

Non-Spelling (consistent with Bear, Invernizzi, Templeton, & Johnston's, 2000, Early Emergent Spelling and Middle Emergent Spelling) (see Figure 3.2 for an example)

- Uses drawing and writing together, at first interchangeably, later distinguishing between drawing and writing
- Arranges marks horizontally
- Uses letter-like forms

Emergent Spelling (consistent with Bear, Invernizzi, Templeton, & Johnston's, 2000, Late Emergent Spelling)

- Consistently uses left-to-right directionality
- Demonstrates concept of word, but may not always use spaces between words
- Writes some letters of the alphabet
- Occasionally uses sound-letter correspondences or memorized spellings of common words

  Example (from McGee & Richgels, 2003): MfRETfR - TZRDEfR - KHCDR for *My favorite ride is the roller coaster.*

Early Letter-Name or Early Alphabetic Spelling*

- Writes most letters of the alphabet
- Routinely uses sound-letter correspondences (e.g., MZM for *museum*, FET for *feet*)
- Routinely represents beginning consonants (e.g., T for *telephone*, L for *ladder*)

- Represents some ending consonants (e.g., n for *in*, Tr for *tiger*, SK for *sock*, BD for *bird*, Ht for *hot*)
- Only partially represents consonant blends and digraphs (e.g., BEG for *bridge*, PN for *playing*, pat for *plant*, SID for *slide*, CKS for *chicks*)
- Occasionally represents short vowel sounds using similar articulation of vowel's letter name (e.g., BEG for *bridge*)
- Occasionally represents long vowel sounds using letter whose name is the same as the vowel sound (e.g., FET for *feet*, SID for *slide*, NOZ for *nose*, Her for *here*)

Middle Letter-Name or Middle Alphabetic Spelling*

- Routinely represents both beginning and ending consonant sounds (e.g., Hct for *hatched*, WZ for *was*)
- Routinely represents long vowel sounds using the letter whose name is the same as the vowel sound (e.g., PnNO for *piano*, PePL for *people*, ONlE for *only*, AWAK for *awake*)
- Routinely represents short vowel sounds, sometimes using similar articulation of vowel's letter name (e.g., RiCS for *rocks*), sometimes using conventional spellings, especially in high-frequency words (e.g., BAtmAN for *Bat Man*, HOT for *hot*, BIG for *big*)

---

*Adapted from Bear, Invernizzi, Templeton, & Johnston's (2000) stages with the same names. Examples from research conducted by the authors.

Emergent Spelling is characterized by children's use of at least one letter to represent a phoneme in a word although the letter selected by the child may not be conventional. For example, children might spell using letters that have sounds in their names that are like sounds in the words, as Kristen did when she wrote the word *phone* with the letter *V* and the word *window* with the letter *Y*. Slightly more sophisticated is the phase of *Early Letter-Name Spelling* or *Early Alphabetic Spelling*. Children begin using the whole letter name to spell a segment of a word or a phoneme. For example, spelling the word *feet* as FET, with the name of the letter *E* as its middle sound, or the word *deep* as DP, with the name of the letter *D* as its beginning and middle sounds. In this phase, spellings routinely include sound-letter correspondences. Sometimes those include middle and ending sounds. In the *Middle Letter-Name Spelling* or *Middle Alphabetic Spelling* phase, children nearly always represent the beginning and ending sounds of words and a vowel sound in their spellings although these spellings are still not conventional.

These stages are intended to clarify the direction of change in children's spelling development. They do not represent a rigid sequence. Children may spell like emergent spellers in a particular context, including particular purposes and assistance, and spell like early or middle letter-name spellers in other contexts with other purposes and kinds of assistance.

Figure 4.11 shows Zack's writing when he was the student helper for the Words for Today routine in his kindergarten classroom (Richgels, 2003). His classmates suggested words for him to write. He wrote *windy* and *rainy* by copying them from the class's weather report chart. His teacher and classmates helped him to hear the sounds, choose the letters, and write the letters for ColD and Krme (*crummy*). For example, his teacher said, "What do you hear in the beginning of *c-c-crummy?*" and Zack answered, "K",

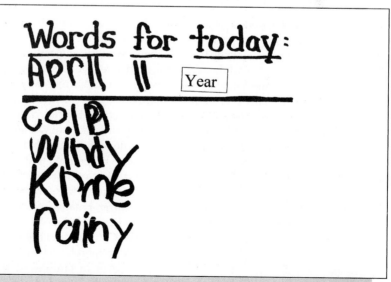

FIGURE 4.11   Zack's Words for Today

and wrote *K* without help. But when she asked, "Crrrrrrr—hear that rrrrr?" she had to prompt Zack with the letter and direct his attention to a model for writing it: "That's an *R*. An *R*. It's the first letter of *rainy*." She also had to tell Zack that *M* spells the next sound, but he decided on his own that the letter *E* spells the last sound in *crummy*.

On the very same day, Zack's teacher asked him to spell six words without help. Zack's spellings were *A* for *apple*, *D* for *ladder*, *T* for *tiger*, *P* for *porcupine*, *e* for *telephone*, and *P* for *piano*. Just a month earlier, during free play time, Zack was the clerk at a pretend pizza restaurant. With a pencil in hand and a slip of paper on a clipboard, he took a customer's order for "large, thick crust, with pepperoni and black olives." He wrote four wavy lines of mock cursive writing, one for each element of the order: *large, thick crust, pepperoni, black olives* (Richgels, 2003).

At what stage is Zack's spelling? Is he a non-speller, as his wavy-line pizza-store writing might suggest? Is he the early letter-name speller that his invented spelling assessment performance indicates? Or is he the middle letter-name speller that ColD and Krme suggest? Answers to these questions depend on the context and the level of support that is available (Richgels, in press). Zack's literacy-related pretend play does not require spelling. Independently, he seems to be an early-letter name speller. With help, he can spell like a middle letter-name speller. What is important in responding to Zack's invented spellings is not identifying his place in a scheme like the one shown in Table 4.2, but rather, supporting his continued development so that over time, his spellings resemble later stages more often than earlier stages (see Chapter 8 for extensive discussion of such support).

Children's growth in spelling does not stop at the end of the middle letter-name or middle alphabetic stage of spelling development. In Chapter 5 we will describe additional stages of invented spelling that are beyond what experimenters do.

Sound-Letter Relationships in Reading

Children's awareness of systematic (but unconventional) relations between letters and spoken language influences their reading (Richgels, 1995). Children's reading of environmental print, storybooks, and their own writing gradually reflects their awareness of written words and the relationships between letters in written words and sounds in spoken language. For example, Jeffrey, a kindergartner, looked at the *F* page in a word book (an alphabet picture book that had several pictures on a page depicting objects and actions associated with a particular letter). He called out to his mother, "Do you want to hear me read this page?" Jeffrey's mother knew that he could not really read, but she was willing to be an audience as he pretended to read this favorite book. Jeffrey pointed to the word *fence* and said "fence." He pointed to each of the words or phrases *fruit tree, flag, funny face,* and *four fish* and said the appropriate word or phrase. Then he paused as he scanned the picture of a farmer driving a tractor. The words accompanying this picture were *front wheels* and *fertilizer*. Finally Jeffrey said, "I'm looking for the word *tractor* because this is a tractor. But I can't find it. All of these words have *F*'s. But tractor shouldn't be *F*. Where is it, Mom? Can you find the word for 'tractor'?"

Another way that children use sound-letter relationships is by reading and writing new words from the patterns they discover in families of rhyming words, that is, groups of words that rhyme. Together, **rhyming word families** represent hundreds of words to which children gain access by learning a relatively small number of prototypes. As children learn only a few of the words in a rhyming word family, they notice that the rime remains the same while the onset changes. (The **onset** is the initial consonant, consonant blend, or consonant digraph of a syllable; the **rime** is the part of a syllable from its vowel though its end.) They can recognize in reading and spell in writing many new words by recognizing the rime as a written unit (a **phonogram**) and applying their sound-letter knowledge to decoding or encoding the onsets. For example, Figure 4.12 presents some word work that Ebony accomplished during small-group instruction. Her kindergarten teacher had presented the familiar words *me* and *beet*, because the sound-letter correspondences introduced in her class's instructional materials include long-vowel sounds (in this case, /E/) and consonant sounds. The teacher then demonstrated making the rhyming words *we* and *feet* and encouraged her students to write other words.

English Language Learners and Invented Spelling

Like other experimenters, those who are also English language learners listen for sounds in spoken words and associate them with letters in written words. In bilingual programs, ELLs will spell in their home language; however, in other programs they are expected to learn to spell in English. Their spelling success depends in part on how the **phoneme repertoires** of their native languages compare to those of English. They are likely to find it especially difficult to spell phonemes of English that are not phonemes of their home languages. For example, /th/ is not a phoneme of either Spanish or Chinese. The sounds /b/ and /v/ are separate phonemes in English but are only variants of a single phoneme in Spanish. That sound difference can be the sole contrast between two English words (e.g., *bat* and *vat*), but never is between two Spanish words (Barone, Mallette, & Xu, 2005). ELLs have difficulty hearing sounds that are not phonemes in their home languages and are likely to substitute sounds that resemble those in their home languages.

Because Spanish speakers are such a large proportion of ELLs, teachers must be especially informed about the similarities and differences of the sound systems of English

FIGURE 4.12   Writing Word Family Words

and Spanish (Helman, 2004). Both languages include the consonant phonemes /b/, /d/, /f/, /g/, /k/, /l/, /m/, /n/, /p/, /s/, /t/, /w/, /y/, and /ch/ (Goldstein, 2001). It is appropriate to include those in phonemic awareness and sound-letter instruction and to encourage children to use them in their invented spellings. Other English consonant phonemes are not phonemes of Spanish, and children are likely to make substitutions for them. For example, /j/ is not a phoneme of Spanish, and so Spanish-speaking experimenters are likely to substitute /ch/ for it. Similarly, /s/ will be substituted for /z/, /t/ or /d/ for /th/, and /ch/ for /sh/. Spanish-speaking children's spellings likely will be influenced by these substitutions. They might spell *them* as DEM or *shed* as CHED (Helman, 2004).

Experimenting with Functions of Written Language

Young experimenters continue what they began as novices; they continue to use written language to communicate for a variety of purposes. Experimenters do, however, cover some new ground in the domain of written language functions. They read and write with the two new purposes of learning to read and write and of preserving specific messages.

In this chapter are many examples of experimenters' devoting considerable energy to reading and writing, to *experimenting* with how written language works. Experimenters learn by doing, even when the doing is at times painstaking. Their appearing to work hard is the result of the careful analysis, the concentrated thinking, and the reasoned trying out that is the essence of experimentation and invention.

Another kind of experimenting that young experimenting readers and writers do is with **multiple literacies.** These include the ways in which children read and write and construct new meanings using new technologies such as the internet; multi-modal publication software such as *Kid Pix Delux;* text messaging, instant messaging, hypertext, and other Information and Communication Technologies (ICT) just now emerging (Karchmer, Mallette, & Leu, 2003). When considering that preschool and kindergarten age children are the fastest growing group of Internet users (a jump from 6% to 35% between 2000 and 2002; Fitzgerald, 2003), it is not surprising that many children are experimenting with new concepts about print, text formats, and methods of making meaning. Children using the internet find new ways to jump from page to page, ignore top-to-bottom orientation, and read multiple signs and symbols. Children using *Kid Pix Delux* experiment with ways to manipulate symbols in the program to extend their dramatic play (Barone, Mallette, & Xu, 2005). They also use such software to integrate digital photographs and symbols they have created with icon stamps (Labbo, Eakle, & Montero, 2004; Turbill, 2004). Children write captions for photographs and label parts of photographs. (See Labbo, Eakle, & Montero, at www.readingonline.org/electronic/labbo2/index.htlm for examples of children's experimenting with multiple literacies.)

Experimenters, unlike novices, understand that written messages, whether their own or others', are stable and permanent. Ted (see Figure 4.1), Meagan (who wrote the sentence chicks r ranein for *Chicks are running*), and two kindergarten story folder authors (see Figure 4.10) knew that by writing a protest, a journal entry, or a story, they rendered their messages readable. Ted wanted his parents to notice his protest; Meagan wanted to record the activities of the chicks that had hatched in her classroom; and the story folder authors wanted to take home photocopies of the stories they had created about the folders' pictures. All these children could achieve those goals by writing. All of them had accomplished the most significant function-related conceptual change of the experimental stage, the discovery that written language can preserve a writer's message exactly. This is known as the **message concept** (Clay, 1975).

ASSESSING EXPERIMENTING READERS AND WRITERS IN KINDERGARTEN AND FIRST GRADE

CHILDREN WHO ARE JUST SHOWING SIGNS of being experimenters are able to perform most of the preschool and kindergarten assessment tasks presented in Chapter 3. They are able to identify many alphabet letters, know several concepts about print, and have some ability to isolate beginning phonemes. Four additional assessments can be used to track children as they enter and move through experimenting reading and writing:

* sound-letter relationships
* finger-point reading and locating words
* invented spelling
* reading and writing familiar rhyming words

These assessments evaluate children's new awareness of how the alphabetic principle works. Teachers continue to assess children's vocabulary and oral comprehension development using retelling assessments such as those presented in Chapter 3.

Assessing children's knowledge of sound-letter relationships can be accomplished simply by pointing to each consonant letter on the upper-case letter recognition administration sheet and asking children to say the sound of each letter. Experimenters are not expected to know the vowel sounds; that will be assessed later in their development. Teachers can use the Upper-Case Alphabet Recognition administration sheet and score sheet presented in Appendix B.

To assess children's finger-point reading, a teacher should prepare a small booklet of a favorite nursery rhyme with four pages of text. Each page should have two lines of print. Appendix C presents the text of the rhyme "I'm a Little Teapot" with large font and extra large word spaces. To administer the assessment, the teacher first teaches all children the nursery rhyme so that each child can say it verbatim from memory. Then the teacher uses the Teapot book with individual children, saying, "Here is a book with the teapot rhyme in it. Watch as I say it and point to each word." The teacher says the rhyme and points to each word. Then the teacher invites the child to read along, "This time I'll point to the words and you say the rhyme." The teacher prompts the child so that he or she successfully says each word as the teacher points to that word. Then the teacher invites the child to practice finger-point reading, saying, "Now you can point to the words and we'll say the rhyme together." Then the child is guided by the teacher to point correctly to each word as the teacher and child together say the rhyme. Finally, the teacher assesses the child's finger-point reading, saying, "Now you point to the words and say the rhyme." The child earns a point for each line of text for which he or she correctly points to each word while saying that exact word.

The next part of the finger-point reading assessment is to locate words. The teacher says, "This poem has the word *teapot*. Can you show me which word is teapot?" The child is asked to find seven words: *teapot, short, I, up, shout, tip,* and *me*. Teachers can use the score sheet for finger-point reading and locating words presented in Appendix C.

To assess invented spelling, teachers demonstrate listening to sounds to write words. To begin, they say, "We're going to listen to sounds in words and then spell them. Like the word *tea*. I like hot tea in the winter and iced tea in the summer. I'm going to listen to the sounds in the word *tea*: /t/. I know that sound is spelled T. Let me listen again: /t/ /E/. I hear E. Now it's your turn. I'll say some words, and you spell them by listening to the sounds." Appendix C presents five words. Teachers analyze what children know by first considering whether children attempt to spell beginning consonants, beginning and ending consonants, blends, long vowels, and short vowels. At the beginning of experimenting, children likely only spell some sounds—usually beginning consonants. Even with experience, most experimenters do not spell with correct vowels or blends but eventually spell with expected beginning and ending consonants. After analyzing children's spellings, teachers can use Table 4.2 to determine the phase of spelling development of each child.

Finally, teachers want to assess whether children can use their growing awareness of letter-sound associations to read and spell new words composed from onsets and rimes of familiar rhyming words. For example, a teacher might introduce the familiar word *bat* printed on a small white board, telling a child, "This is the word *bat*. Now I am going to wipe off the letter *b* and make another word. I'll put on an *f*. Now the word is *fat*. Now let me wipe off the letter *f* and make another word. I'll put on an *r*. Now the word is *rat*. Now it's your turn. I'll put on some new letters and you read the words." The teacher creates the words *hat, mat, sat, vat,* and *cat*. Next he or she writes the word *big* and says, "This word is *big*. I want you to wipe off a letter and write the word *dig*. What would you wipe off to make *big* into *dig*?" The teacher then asks children to spell *fig, jig, mig, wig,* and *zig*. The score sheet for reading and writing new rhyming words is presented in Appendix C.

A WORD OF CAUTION

WE BEGAN THIS CHAPTER by characterizing experimenters as children who are aware that there is a system to learn, but who do not know what that system is. Throughout the chapter we have described the variety of concepts that children must grasp in order to puzzle out the system, to become what others would judge conventional readers and writers. Children gradually come to have many behaviors and understandings that we call conventional. The understandings that experimenters have about written language are unconventional in many ways (for example, their using manner of articulation to link letters and sounds in invented spelling or their counting syllables or phrases as words in finger-point reading). Yet, their reading and writing also have signs of much that is conventional (for example, their using knowledge of literary syntax to compose stories and their using sound-letter knowledge to monitor their reading).

We hope that this chapter does not lead readers to three misconceptions. The first has to do with ages. Ages are not the important part of any description of children as experimenters. We have provided children's ages only to accurately present the facts in some of our real-life examples. The ages of these children do not set norms against which to compare other children. Of much greater value than age is the behavior that can be observed in a literacy event, what the child knows or learns in the event. From this information, teachers can gain insights that will guide instruction.

The second misconception has to do with identification of children as experimenters. Identification is not important for its own sake. It does not really matter whether any child is called an experimenter. What matters is that teachers know in which literacy behaviors children are willing and able to engage. Then teachers will know how to support the children's continued development as writers and readers.

Finally, we want to caution our readers about the misconception that literacy learning is merely about the mechanics of spelling, sound-letter relationships, or concepts about print, that it can occur outside of meaningful events. We view learning to read and write more from a situated literacy perspective than from a school literacy perspective. From the **school literacy perspective,** "reading and writing are viewed as a compilation of skills that can be taught 'for school' " (Powell & Davidson, 2005, p. 249). Reading and writing are considered ends in themselves, skills to be learned, rather than tools for genuine communication. From the **situated literacy perspective,** reading and writing are activities taking place in the real world for the purpose of achieving real-life goals. Reading and writing become meaningful in the lives of young children when they serve children's need to explore the real world and their desire to connect with the power of play.

CHAPTER SUMMARY

EXPERIMENTERS ARE AWARE that there is a system of written language that they only partly understand. The meaning making that experimenters do is similar to what they did as novices. They continue writing in order to present a message, and they continue using sophisticated strategies for interacting with books.

Some of the most striking new achievements of experimenters are related to their greater control over form and meaning-form links. They acquire a concept of spoken and written words, and they devise means for showing word boundaries in their writing. In addition to knowing what physical arrangements are appropriate for different text forms, they know what special language is appropriate.

Experimenters' reading and writing are increasingly print governed. They achieve phonemic awareness and use it in alphabetic reading and invented spelling. They carefully analyze speech sounds in almost any word they want to write, and match those sounds with letters. Experimenters also show new knowledge of meaning-form links by sounding literate and being precise. Often they are aware that written language is

112

more precise than spoken language and that what readers say depends on what writers write.

As with novices, written language serves a variety of functions for experimenters. A new purpose for their reading and writing is simply to experiment. Another is to preserve readable messages. Teachers can use four additional assessments to track the growing development of experimenters: sound-letter recognition, finger-point reading and identifying words, invented spelling, and reading and writing new rhyming words.

A summary of what experimenters know about written language meanings, forms, meaning-form links, and functions is presented in Figure 4.13.

FIGURE 4.13   Summary: What Experimenting Readers and Writers Know about Written Language Meanings, Forms, Meaning-Form Links, and Functions

Meaning Making

assign meaning to text by applying knowledge of specialized literary language (such as literary syntax and alliteration)

Forms

know nearly all alphabet letter names and formations
have metalinguistic awareness of letters
develop concept of spoken words
develop concept of written words
develop concept of word boundaries
use specialized literary knowledge to construct a wide variety of texts
use a variety of strategies to produce conventional texts (including copying, asking for spellings, dictating, and spelling)

Meaning-Form Links

sound literate when assigning meaning to storybooks and compositions

are precise when assigning meaning to storybooks and compositions
develop phonemic awareness
use manner of articulation to associate sounds and letters in spellings
use letter names to associate sounds and letters in spellings
use identity of sounds to associate sounds and letters in spellings
spell at the levels of emergent, early letter-name, and middle letter-name spelling
use knowledge of sound-letter relationships to monitor emergent reading
use finger-point reading
can use familiar rhyming words to learn some sight words

Functions

read and write to experiment with written language
understand that written language is readable (develop the message concept)

USING THE INFORMATION

Go back to three figures in this chapter and describe the elements of meaning making, forms, meaning-form links, and functions (use Figure 4.13) that can be inferred from them. For example, Figure 4.1 is Ted's protest note to his mother. In the area of meaning making, Ted has expressed a powerfully felt message—a protest of his punishment. In the area of written language forms, he shows knowledge of the format of a note or letter. He begins by addressing the person he intends as the recipient of his message (Mom) and ends by identifying himself as the author with his signature (Ted). He shows control of writing alphabet letters although he still mixes upper and lower case within words. He shows an emerging concept of spoken and written words in that he listened to words and carefully selected letters to spell those words. However, he does not show clear awareness of word boundaries. In the area of meaning-form links, he used the strategy of spelling to compose his text using a letter-name strategy (the letter Y for the word *why* and the letter R for the word *are*). He also used sound-letter relationships in his spelling the word *punishing* as PNShan. His use of the vowel *a* suggests that he is in the early letter-name or early alphabetic stage of spelling. In the area of written language functions, Ted's writing clearly had the purpose of gaining the attention of his mother with a personal, precise, permanent, and readable message. At least in this event, Ted exhibits the writing of a child at the end of the experimenting phase; his writing sample demonstrates many, if not most, of the accomplishments listed in Figure 4.13.

APPLYING THE INFORMATION

Each day in Mrs. Poremba's kindergarten, children signed in on a special sign-in sheet. They routinely brought their personal sign-in sheets on clipboards with them to opening-of-the-day activities. These activities included number work (which on this day included predicting which numbers on a chart displaying numerals *1* to *110* were masked by a circle, a triangle, a square, and a rectangle), calendar work (which included adding three dates to the calendar, *9, 10,* and *11* for Saturday, Sunday, and Monday, April 9, 10, and 11), a weather report, and the Words for Today routine. Their teacher encouraged the children to use their sign-in sheets to record anything they wanted to remember from these activities. With this in mind, what can you say about Eric's writing strategies, especially his spelling as presented in Figure 4.14?

Later the same day, Eric's teacher asked him to spell six words without help. He wrote A for *apple*, L for *ladder*, T for *tiger*, P for *porcupine*, T for *telephone*, and P for *piano*. Two weeks later, Eric's class viewed the inside of a fertilized chick egg by shining a powerful light through it. Then with the help of an adult, he wrote in a journal about what he saw. His journal entry is shown in Figure 4.15. His message was *A black eye. Veins bring food.* The helper supplied the spelling for the first word, and Eric copied *black* from a black crayon. But Eric decided on the remaining spellings with help. The adult helper asked, "Do you have any ideas about how to write *eye*?" and Eric answered, "Just an *I.*" The helper asked, "What would *vvein—*" and before even hearing the end of the word, Eric answered, "*V!*" And when the helper asked, "Do you want to write any other letters for *veinzzzz*?" Eric answered, "*Z.*" With this additional information, what can you say about Eric's writing and spelling? How are his spelling attempts influenced by context? What sorts of tasks and assistance will be most helpful to Eric's continued spelling development?

FIGURE 4.14   Eric's Sign-in Writing

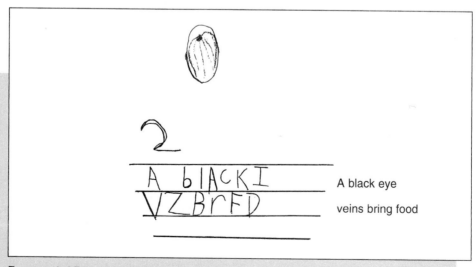

A black eye

veins bring food

FIGURE 4.15   Eric's Assisted Journal Entry

GOING BEYOND THE TEXT

VISIT A KINDERGARTEN CLASSROOM. Join the children who are writing. Notice what their writing activities are. What experimenting behaviors do you observe? What text forms are the children using? How many of them are spellers? Begin your own writing activity (writing a letter, a story, a list of some kind, a reminder to yourself, or a poem). Talk about it with the children. How many of them take up your activity and attempt similar pieces? Does the character of their writing change from what it was for their own activities? Is there more or less invented spelling, more or less word writing, more or less scribbling?

Ask the teacher if children have favorite storybooks. If so, invite children to read their favorites to you. How do they interpret that invitation? If they would rather you read to them, how willing are they to supply parts of the reading? What parts do they know best? What parts do they like best?

REFERENCES

Barone, D., Mallette, M., & Xu, S. (2005). *Teaching early literacy: Development, assessment, and instruction.* New York: Guilford.

Bear, D. R., Invernizzi, M., Templeton, S., & Johnston, F. (2000). *Words their way: Word study for phonics, vocabulary, and spelling instruction* (2nd ed.). Upper Saddle River, NJ: Merrill.

Beers, J. W., & Henderson, E. H. (1977). A study of developing orthographic concepts among first grade children. *Research in the Teaching of English, 11,* 133–148.

Bissex, G. L. (1980). *GNYS AT WRK. A child learns to write and read.* Cambridge: Harvard University Press.

Clay, M. M. (1975). *What did I write? Beginning writing behavior.* Exeter, NH: Heinemann.

Cox, B., Fang, Z., & Otto, B. (1997). Preschoolers' developing ownership of the literate register. *Reading Research Quarterly, 32,* 34–53.

Dahl, K., Scharer, P., Lawson, L., & Grogan, P. (1999). Phonics instruction and student achievement in whole language first grade classrooms. *Reading Research Quarterly, 34,* 312–341.

Ehri, L., & Sweet, J. (1991). Finger point reading of memorized text: What enables beginners to process the print? *Reading Research Quarterly, 26,* 442–462.

Fitzgerald, T. (2003). Meet the first internet babies. *Media Life Magazine.* www.meadialifemagazine. com/news2003/mar03/mar24/4_thurs/news1 thursday.hytlm.

Gentry, J. R. (1978). Early spelling strategies. *Elementary School Journal, 79,* 88–92.

Goldstein, B. (2001). Transcription of Spanish and Spanish-influenced English. *Communication Disorders Quarterly, 23,* 54–60.

Goodman, Y. M. (1980). The roots of literacy. In M. P. Douglas (Ed.), *Claremont Reading Conference, 44th Yearbook* (pp. 1–32). Claremont, CA: Claremont Reading Conference.

Harste, J. C., Burke, C. L., & Woodward, V. A. (1983). *Young child as writer-reader, and informant* (Final Report Project NIE-G-80–0121). Bloomington, IN: Language Education Departments, Indiana University.

Helman, L. (2004). Building on the sound system of Spanish: Insights from the alphabetic spellings of English-language learners. *The Reading Teacher, 57,* 452–460.

Johnson, S. A. (1982). *Inside an egg.* Minneapolis: Lerner.

Karchmer, R., Mallette, M., & Leu, D. (2003). Early literacy in a digital age: Moving from a singular book literacy to the multiple literacies of networked information and communication technologies. In D. Barone & L. Morrow (Eds.), *Literacy and young children: Research-based practices* (pp. 175–194). New York: Guilford.

Labbo, L., Eakle, A. J., & Montero, M. (2004). Digital language experience approach: Using digital photographs and software as a language experience approach innovation. *Reading Online.* www.readingonly.org/electronic/labbo2/index.html.

McIntyre, E., & Freppon, P. A. (1994). A comparison of children's development of alphabetic knowledge in a skills-based and a whole language classroom. *Research in the Teaching of English, 28,* 391–417.

Morris, D. (1981). Concept of word: A developmental phenomenon in the beginning reading and writing processes. *Language Arts, 58,* 659–668.

Morris, D. (1993). The relationship between children's concept of word in text and phoneme awareness in learning to read: A longitudinal study. *Research in the Teaching of English, 27,* 133–154.

Morris, D., Bloodgood, J. W., Lomax, R. G., & Perney, J. (2003). Developmental steps in learning to read: A longitudinal study in kindergarten and first grade. *Reading Research Quarterly, 38,* 302–328.

Powell, R., & Davidson, N. (2005). The donut house: Real world literacy in an urban kindergarten class. *Language Arts, 82,* 248–256.

Read, C. (1971). Pre-school children's knowledge of English phonology. *Harvard Educational Review, 41,* 1–34.

Richgels, D. (1995). Invented spelling ability and printed word learning in kindergarten. *Reading Research Quarterly, 30,* 96–109.

Richgels, D. J. (2001). Invented spelling, phonemic awareness, and reading and writing instruc-tion. In S. B. Neuman and D. K. Dickinson (Eds.), *Handbook of early literacy research* (pp. 142–155). New York: Guilford.

Richgels, D. J. (2003). *Going to kindergarten: A year with an outstanding teacher.* Lanham, MD: Scarecrow.

Richgels, D. J. (in press). From practice to theory: Invented spelling. In A. DeBruin-Parecki (Ed.), *Here's how, here's why: Developing early literacy skills.* Ann Arbor, MI: High/Scope Press.

Roberts, B. (1992). The evolution of the young child's concept of word as a unit of spoken and written language. *Reading Research Quarterly, 27,* 124–139.

Sulzby, E. (1985). Children's emergent reading of favorite storybooks: A developmental study. *Reading Research Quarterly, 20,* 458–481.

Temple, C., Nathan, R., Temple, F., & Burris, N. (1993). *The beginnings of writing* (3rd ed.). Boston: Allyn & Bacon.

Templeton, S. (2003). Spelling. In J. Flood, D. Lapp, J. R. Squire, & J. M. Jensen (Eds.), *Handbook of research on teaching the English language arts* (2nd ed., pp. 738–751). Mahwah, NJ: Lawrence Erlbaum.

Templeton, S., & Morris, D. (2000). Spelling. In M. L. Kamil, P. B. Mosenthal, P. D. Pearson, & R. Barr (Eds.), *Handbook of reading research, Vol. 3* (pp. 525–543). Mahwah, NJ: Lawrence Erlbaum.

The Three Bears. (1952). Racine, WI: Western.

Turbill, J. (2004). Exploring the potential of the digital language experience approach in Australian classrooms. *Reading Online.* www.readingonline.org/international/turbill7.

Zutell, J. (1978). Some psycholinguistic perspectives on children's spelling. *Language Arts, 55,* 844–850.

CHAPTER
5

From Six to Eight Years
CONVENTIONAL READERS AND WRITERS IN EARLY,
TRANSITIONAL, AND SELF-GENERATIVE PHASES

KEY CONCEPTS

Conventional Readers
    and Writers
Early Readers and
    Writers
Transitional Readers
    and Writers
Self-Generative Readers
    and Writers
High Frequency Words
Sight Words
Grapho-Semantics
Grapho-Syntax
Phonics
Orchestration
Writing Workshop
Vowel Markers

Prior Knowledge
Metacognitive
    Awareness
Interpretation
Transaction
Critical Interpretations
Referential Dimension
Exposition
Morphemes
Derivational Words
Compound Sentences
Complex Sentences
Story Grammar
Literary Elements of
    Narratives
Approximations

Elements of
    Informational Texts
Decoding
Consonant Digraphs
Fully Phonemic
    Decoding
Decoding by Analogy
Orthographic Decoding
Instructional Reading
    Level
Independent Reading
    Level
Running Record
Individualized Reading
    Inventory
Miscue Analysis

WHO ARE CONVENTIONAL READERS AND WRITERS?

LEARNING ABOUT READING AND WRITING is a gradual process. It is not possible to identify the exact moment when a child becomes a reader or writer in a conventional sense. Nonetheless, children do become **conventional readers and writers** who are able to read texts on their own and write texts that they and others can read. In this chapter, we can provide only a few of the most critical insights that children gain as they go through three phases of conventional reading and writing.

Three Phases of Conventional Literacy Development

The International Reading Association and the National Association for the Education of Young Children, two professional organizations for teachers of young children, suggest that children's conventional reading and writing emerges through three phases, which they call early, transitional, and self-generative reading and writing (NAEYC/IRA, 1998). **Early readers and writers** differ from experimenting readers in that they can read accurately both their own writing and simple texts composed by others, including simple storybooks. **Transitional readers and writers** have moved beyond the earliest forms of conventional reading and writing although they still need good teaching. **Self-generative readers and writers** are self-learners, although they still need the support of effective and caring teachers to point them in the right directions for academic success. In today's increasingly technological world, self-generative readers and writers are able to acquire new competencies through their own exploration.

Early readers are able to read simple texts on their own. This is helped by the fact that the texts contain many **high frequency words,** such as *the, is, were, she, and, of, from,* and *with.* Children with even a few years of experience seeing and being read storybooks and information books will have encountered these words many times; they appear in almost any text that is more than a few sentences in length. From instruction, experience, or both, early readers know them as **sight words,** that is, words they can read immediately upon seeing them, automatically, and without sounding them out. Early readers are also helped to read simple texts by their having learned an increasing number of strategies for identifying words that they cannot read by sight. Among these decoding strategies is the use of phonics or knowledge of sound-letter relationships to link letters or combinations of letters with pronunciations.

Transitional readers are able to read more complex text that includes longer sentences and fewer high-frequency words, and they acquire many sight words. They can read more fluently and comprehend more complicated stories and informational texts. They make the transition into reading simple chapter books during this phase, although picture books continue to be an important part of their reading diet. They use more sophisticated decoding strategies that go beyond merely blending individual letters and phonemes. These include using grapho-semantics and using grapho-syntax. **Grapho-semantics** is the application of vocabulary knowledge and knowledge of morphemes to the process of decoding. Transitional readers who know the meanings of *the, run, -er, cross, -ed,* and *finish line* and can immediately identify *the, runner,* and *finish line,* but at first are stumped by the appearance of *crossed,* can nonetheless use grapho-semantics to read the sentence *The runner crossed the finish line.* They know how words and word parts and their meanings interact. They compute that interaction something like this: What do runners do with finish lines? They *cross* them. What does *-ed* do for a verb? It makes it past tense. So the third word in that sentence must be the past tense form of *cross*, which is pronounced /krawst/. Notice that this is actually more efficient than using phonics, which likely would produce a meaningless pronunciation, /krahs-uhd/.

Grapho-syntax is the application of sentence structure knowledge to the process of decoding. In the example just given of *The runner crossed the finish line*, where a reader knows the meaning of *cross* and can use it in speech but is at first stumped by the appearance of *crossed* in print, that reader is also helped by knowledge of how English sentences work. He or she knows that a sentence needs a verb, that *The runner* and *the finish line* are not verbs, and so the unfamiliar grapheme *crossed* must be a verb. That is why the first question in the computation described above is about *doing* (What do runners *do* with finish lines?) and why the second question is about verbs (What does *-ed* do for a verb?). Thus, grapho-semantics and grapho-syntax almost always work together. Of course, they also work with **phonics.** Knowing how to pronounce the *cr* consonant blend at the beginning of *crossed* helps the reader, almost as much as do the meanings of *runner, -ed*, and *finish line*, to close in on the verb *crossed*.

Transitional readers develop more complex comprehension strategies. They recognize parts of words, make multiple predictions, monitor their understanding, and draw inferences. Transitional spellers know how to spell many words conventionally, and they learn how to use a variety of strategies for spelling words that they do not yet know how to spell conventionally. They write in several different genres including personal narratives (recounts of events in their own lives), stories, poems, and science reports (Wollman-Bonilla, 2000). Many children become transitional readers and writers sometime during second grade and continue in this phase of development through third grade.

Some third graders enter an even more sophisticated phase of literacy development. Self-generative readers are becoming highly skilled readers who can control many strategies for reading complex texts, learning from text, and acquiring new vocabulary. Self-generative writers are increasingly able to revise their own writing to communicate for a wide variety of purposes and audiences. This phase of reading and writing extends through the elementary years.

Examples of Early, Transitional, and Self-Generative Readers and Writers

Conventional readers and writers are able to orchestrate many different parts of the reading and writing process. **Orchestration** is readers' and writers' ability to do some reading processes unconsciously so they are freed up to concentrate on other processes. For example, early readers and writers are already fluent at the process of reading from left-to-right and matching one-on-one spoken words with written words. They do not have to think about these processes—they can accomplish them unconsciously. However, these early reading processes must also be orchestrated with other processes such as reading words by sight, decoding words, comprehending, and monitoring the meaning of what they read.

In order to demonstrate how readers and writers are better able to orchestrate more complex strategies and texts, we present a glimpse into one child's reading and writing as she enters the phases of early and transitional reading and writing and then begins the early steps of self-generative reading and writing. Kristen entered first grade in the experimenting phase of reading and writing. She could not read on her own yet, although she could blend many consonants into word parts such as *at* to create and read new words such as *bat, cat, fat,* and *hat*. She could invent spellings, and Figure 5.1 presents an example of a message that she wrote to her mother at the classroom writing table. Later, when asked to read her message, Kristen said, "I love you" even though her message spelling suggested that she wrote, "I like you."

Kristen entered the phase of early reading and writing mid-year in first grade. Figure 5.2 presents an example of the kinds of text she could read with support at that time. *Go, Dog. Go!* (Eastman, 1961) is considered a primer level text (text that is read during the mid part of first grade). One year later Kristen became a transitional reader; she was able to read *Frog and Toad Together* (Lobel, 1971), which is considered a second grade text and indicates the beginning of transitional reading. Mid-year in third grade Kristen could read the chapter book titled *The Chocolate Touch* (Catling, 1952), which is considered a third grade text. While she was reading on grade level at this time, Kristen had difficulty comprehending complex stories without instructional support. She would not yet be considered a self-generative reader.

The texts presented in Figure 5.2 highlight the striking differences in idea complexity, number of words, complexity of sentence structure, and level of vocabulary found in texts children read in the first, second, and third grades. As children move through the primary grades, they are expected to make rapid growth, as Kristen did, in their ability to read increasingly difficult texts with fluency and comprehension.

Kristen made similar strides in writing development during the same time period. Figure 5.3 presents three samples of Kristen's writing collected mid-year in first, second, and third grades. She wrote the first sample ("Do not come in here") on a rainy day when a classmate came to play (see grade 1). Kristen's mother found the note taped to her bedroom door. Earlier she had interrupted the girls' play twice when they were too noisy and engaged in rowdy play. Later, Kristen told her mother she had written the note so that she and her friend could "have some privacy." The writing on the note demonstrates that although Kristen did not use conventional vowels in her spellings (*iw* for *o* in *do, i* for *o* in *come,* and *i* for *e* in *here*), she does have an increasing

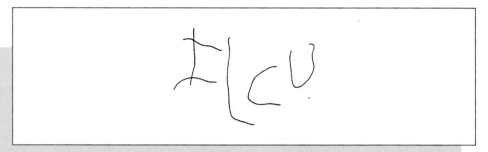

FIGURE 5.1   Kristen's Message: "I Like You"

FIGURE 5.2   Page 18 from books Kristen read with instructional support at mid-year in the first, second, and third grades

Grade	Title	Sample Text
1	*Go, Dog. Go!* (Eastman, 1961)	The green dog is up. The yellow dog is down (p. 18).
2	*Frog and Toad Together* (Lobel, 1971)	Frog was in his garden. Toad came walking by. "What a fine garden you have, Frog," he said. "Yes," said Frog. "It is very nice, but it was hard work." "I wish I had a garden," said Toad. "Here are some flower seeds. Plant them in the ground," said Frog (p. 18).
3	*The Chocolate Touch* (Catling, 1952)	A few seconds after the bedroom door had closed behind his mother, John leaped to the floor, got down on his hands and knees, and felt under the bed for the candy box. He soon had it on the pillow and set to work unfastening it. First he took off the thin outer sheet of cellophane. Then he lifted off the lid. Then he removed a sheet of cardboard. Then he pulled off a square of heavy tinfoil. Then he took out a layer of shredded paper. As the wrappings piled up around him, John became rather anxious (paragraph included on p. 18).

awareness of the need to use vowels as well as knowledge of some conventional spellings (*not* and *in*).

Kristen wrote the second sample presented in Figure 5.3 during **writing workshop** in her second grade classroom, a specific time during the day when children are expected to use the writing process of drafting, revising, and sharing (see more about the writing workshop approach in Chapter 10). This sample was a first draft (see grade 2). It demonstrates a dramatic increase in the number of words that Kristen knows how to spell conventionally, control over word spacing and handwriting, and text composition. Her spelling of vowels has shifted from the one-vowel, one-letter strategy she used in first grade to now using **vowel markers.** Vowel markers are the extra vowels that are used to indicate a long vowel or other non-short vowel phoneme. For example, some long vowels are spelled with a "silent e" at the end of the word to mark the vowel in the middle of the word as long (as in the words *cake, bike,* and *stove*) and other long vowels are spelled with two or more letters together (such as *ai* in the word *wait, eigh*

FIGURE 5.3   Writing samples composed by Kristen mid-year in the first, second, and third grades

Grade	Sample	Translation
1	Diwhorclm i h ir	do not come in here
2	my room I have a room Fild with lose of toys. I ts osem. You will not bleve Youer eiys. I have a bed and a dresr. Iv got a desch and a sefve to put all the toys in.	my room I have a room filled with lots of toys. It's awesome. You will not believe your eyes. I have a bed and a dresser. I've got a desk and a shelf to put all the toys in.
3	In the winter Caty Cot sleeps on the warm bed Pur In the spring Caty Cot sleeps on the window leg, Pur In the summer Caty Cot sleeps on tile Pur In the fall Caty Cot sleeps anywere at all	In the winter Catty Cat sleeps on the warm bed, Purr. In the spring Catty Cat sleeps on the widow ledge, Purr. In the summer Catty Cat sleeps on the tile, Purr. In the fall Catty Cat sleeps anywhere at all.

in the word *height*, and *oa* in the word *boat*). Kristen did not yet use vowel markers conventionally in second grade, but she demonstrated awareness of this spelling concept when she spelled *bleve* for the word *believe*, *eiys* for *eyes*, and *sefve* for *shelf*.

The third writing sample, collected during third grade, was also created as a part of writing workshop; however, it is a second rather than a first draft. Kristen shared her first draft with and got feedback from the other children and her teacher. Based on these comments, she produced the second draft of the poem. Nearly all words are spelled correctly, with a shift in attention from merely writing a message to writing with attention to literary qualities, such as rhythm and repetition.

MEANING CONSTRUCTION

THE CHILDREN DESCRIBED IN THIS CHAPTER are able to construct meaning from what they read by themselves and in what they write for someone else. They develop many strategies for understanding the different kinds of texts they read.

Meaning Making in Reading: Using Strategies

One of the first and most important strategies that children use to understand what they read is to monitor whether what they are reading makes sense (is meaningful), sounds like language (has acceptable syntax), and looks right (has the sequences of letters that they expect after much experience with texts). Children show that they are monitoring by rereading a portion of the text when what they have read does not make sense or by rereading to correct a word that does not fit the text.

Eventually readers are able to use several different reading strategies to help them understand or comprehend what they read (Paris, Wasik, & Turner, 1991). For example, readers pause to connect what they are reading with what they already know. If they are reading a story about a cat, readers draw on their **prior knowledge** (Pressley, 2002) of cats—what they do, what they eat, where they live, and how they interact with people. Prior knowledge is what a reader knows about a topic before reading about it. Using information from the story and their prior knowledge allows readers to predict what will happen, and as they read they look for information to confirm or disconfirm their predictions. They visualize scenes in stories and summarize to themselves what has happened so far. Sometimes readers remember events in their own lives or people they know that are like the events and characters in stories, or they think about characters from other stories.

At first, readers use simple strategies of sounding out words, skipping confusing parts of stories, and then rereading. Even these simple strategies may be used deliberately by beginning readers (Freppon, 1991). This conscious use of strategies is called **metacognitive awareness.** Later children develop fix-up strategies, that is, they correct problems they notice while reading (Sinatra, Brown, & Reynolds, 2002). Readers may reread a portion of a story when they realize that something does not make sense or that they have missed one of the elements of story form that they know to expect. They may skip a word they do not know if they are aware that they are still able to understand the story. Sophisticated readers may adjust their pace or change their level of engagement, looking for main ideas and a developing gist, or noting finer details.

Meaning Making in Reading: Constructing Literary and Critical Interpretations of Literature

An important hallmark of readers is that they go beyond understanding a story—they build literary interpretations of a story. A **literary interpretation** is an attempt to understand the story at a more abstract level, using the story to understand one's self or the world (Many, 1991; Sipe, 2000). As they read a story, readers construct their own personal understandings and, sometimes, interpretations of that text, partly based on their unique background experiences. This unique interaction between the text and the reader is called a **transaction** (Rosenblatt, 1978). Transactions also take place for children who listen to stories read aloud.

An important way in which young children build literary interpretations of literature is to participate in group discussions of books in which children share personal responses to what they read and listen to others' responses. Such experiences lead readers to insightful interpretations that they may not have had before the group discussion (McGee, 1992; 1998).

For example, a group of inner-city first graders discussed the story *Hey, Al* (Yorinks, 1986), in which Al, a janitor who is dissatisfied with his life, is enticed by a strange bird to fly to an island in the sky that the bird describes as a paradise. When he reaches the island, Al begins to turn into a bird himself, but he flies home before he completely loses his identity in this false paradise. One child interpreted the last illustration, "They [Al and his dog] painted it [his old dingy room] yellow like the place [the island]. He was happy then" (Tompkins & McGee, 1993). This child recognized that the color of the paint was a symbol for the happiness that Al and his dog were feeling after their narrow escape from the island in the sky.

Critical interpretations go beyond literary interpretations. **Critical interpretations** involve readers in asking questions such as *Whose story is this? Who benefits from this story?* and *Whose voices are not being heard?* (Leland, Harste, & Huber, 2005). Children who read from a critical perspective recognize that language is a cultural tool used to shape them as readers and to maintain systems of power and dominance (Luke & Freebody, 1997). For example, one first grade teacher had been reading aloud many picture books that focused on troubling social issues in which some characters were marginalized by past or present systems of power. The children in her class responded to *The Other Side* (Woodson, 2001), a story about a black girl and a white girl who lived on opposite sides of a fence that the black girl was not allowed to cross because it was not safe. One child commented about the events in this book, "When they knock the fence down, the black and white people can play together and their moms can meet each other and they can give their phone number and they will have a lot of fun" (Leland, Harste, & Huber, 2005, p. 266). This child clearly recognized the fence as a symbol of the power of whites compared to blacks. It stands for all obstacles to communication between races. The child's comments reflect a critical questioning of the "rightness" of the situation and provide a more equitable alternative.

Meaning Making in Writing

Conventional writers draw on many strategies for writing. Rachel wrote the story presented in Figure 5.4 when she was in second grade. Several elements of this story are noteworthy. Although Rachel uses knowledge of everyday activities (such as hide-and-go-seek) and familiar others (such as her friends) in her compositions, she clearly uses these elements to construct a believable and consistent, but imaginary, story-world. Conventional writers are able to go beyond the personal and immediate—what is happening or just recently happened—to the abstract—what has not yet happened or might never really happen. The relation of the writer with the subject matter (from immediate to abstract) is called the **referential dimension** of writing (Moffett, 1968). Rachel is in a special urban school that serves a variety of ELLs with a strong writing program.

Chester's Anfancher to Georgia Lake.

One hot sunny summer day a dog named Chester who was brown and white was playing a game with his friends. He was playing hide and go seek. Chester was it first. When he was it he looked and boked. He could not find his friends. He went to Georgia Lake because he might of found them thair. But he did not. But maybe they where deep aut in the blue lake. So he boked but he did not find them. So he gaveup and went home. He went into the house and layd down on his bed. Under his bed he herd someone say ach and he boked and he saw his friends.

FIGURE 5.4   Chester's Adventure to Georgia Lake

WRITTEN LANGUAGE FORMS

AS THEY BECOME CONVENTIONAL READERS AND WRITERS, children gain knowledge of the fine points of form at the word level in English writing. Children's writing begins to show their achievement of a fully conventional concept of word. They also start to use narrative form in their writing, and their knowledge of a different category of text form, **exposition**, grows. Expositions are nonfictional, non-narrative texts. Among these are explanatory, persuasive, and instructional pieces, and essays, how-to texts, and biographies.

Concept of Word, Morphemic Awareness, and Grammar

Conventional readers and writers know how to show word boundaries using word spaces and punctuation. Periods and even commas, question marks, and exclamation marks appear in their writing. In addition, conventional readers and writers learn how **morphemes** work in written language. A morpheme is the smallest unit of meaning in a language. Conventional readers and writers learn that morphemes may be written as individual words, such as the articles *a*, *an*, and *the*, or they may be written as word parts, such as *-ed*, *-ing*, and *-s*. Thus, the word *boys* has two morphemes, *boy* and *s*.

While conventional readers and writers already have a sense of morphemes from using them in their spoken language, they must develop a metacognitive awareness of some morphemes, especially prefixes (morphemes added before a word that change its meaning), suffixes (morphemes added after a word that change its meaning or its part of speech) and base words (words with only a single morpheme). Recall that metacognitive awareness means conscious awareness. That is, readers and writers need to know that adding the prefix *un* negates the meaning of a base word (e.g., *unhappy* means not happy*)*. Words that are created by adding prefixes or suffixes (together called affixes) are called **derivational words.** Many ELLs have difficulty developing concepts about derivational words. For example, because there are no affixes in Japanese and Chinese (Barone, Mallette, & Xu, 2005), children who speak these as their home languages find prefixes and suffixes especially difficult.

While the speech of native English speakers in the elementary school years includes simple, compound, and complex sentences, ELLs are more likely to use only phrases or simple English sentences. Simple sentences have a single subject and predicate; **compound sentences** have two or more independent clauses, each with its own subject and predicate and joined by a conjunction (*and, or, but*); **complex sentences** include at least one dependent clause and one independent clause (both dependent and independent clauses have their own subjects and predicates, but dependent clauses are not able to stand alone—they must be associated with an independent clause). *Because Clarence took an umbrella, he stayed dry* is a complex sentence, with the dependent clause *Because Clarence took an umbrella. Clarence took an umbrella and he stayed dry* is a compound sentence with two independent clauses joined by *and.* Each of those independent clauses could be a free-standing, simple sentence: *Clarence took an umbrella. He stayed dry.* With increasing experience of complex sentences, especially in written language where they occur more often than in spoken language, conventional readers and writers gain both competence with such sentences and metacognitve awareness of their syntactic knowledge. ELLs may need even more experience with complex sentences than do native English speakers.

Text Form: Story Compositions

During elementary school, children learn a great deal about how to write many different types of texts including stories, poems, and informational texts (Kamberelis, 1999), including science reports (Wollman-Bonilla, 2000). They learn about the kinds of information or elements that are included in these different text genres and also how to organize that information. In general, the number of elements children include in their compositions increases, the organization of their texts get more complex, and they demonstrate a growing awareness of audience (Wollman-Bonilla, 2001).

Literary Elements in Stories.   Before we examine children's story compositions, we review the elements identified in a **story grammar** (see Table 2.1 in Chapter 2). According to story grammar, characters are sustained throughout the story and introduced in a setting, an initiating event introduces a problem, and the main character (often intuitively) sets a goal to try to solve a problem (this is also called an internal response). The initiating event sets in place a chain of causally related attempts and outcomes in which the main character acts to achieve the goal or solve the problem. Complex stories have a series of attempts and outcomes as the main character must overcome several obstacles before achieving the goal. The story ends as the main character reacts to having achieved the goal. Well-crafted stories also include many literary elements that are similar to the elements in a basic story grammar (Lukens, 1995).

The seven major **literary elements of narratives** are setting, character, plot, point of view, style, mood, and theme. The setting introduces the location, time period, and weather in which the story takes place, and reveals mood and character. For example, characters who are put in harsh settings (such as a desert or a lonely island) are often revealed as resourceful, hardworking, and independent. The setting is sometimes used as an antagonist to introduce conflict to the story. For example, a character may have to travel through a snowstorm (an antagonistic setting) in order to get to school.

There are two kinds of characters in stories: main characters and supporting characters. The main characters are at the center of the action of the story, and supporting characters serve as helpers to the main characters. Characters are not always people (they can be animals or objects that are animated), but main characters must have human traits—we must come to know them as people. Characters are revealed through their thoughts, actions, words, and appearance. We must be able to see a character in action and hear what a character says and thinks.

The plot includes episodes, each with a problem and obstacles. The last episode in a story includes the climax and resolution of the story. The main character does not usually solve the problem simply or easily, but encounters difficulties or obstacles along the way that create conflict. A critical moment comes when the problem is solved (the climax) and the story is resolved (often happily in literature for children). Conflict is an important part of stories, because it produces tension (we do not know how the story will end, although we hope all will go well) and propels the story forward.

Point of view is the perspective from which the story is told. Point of view is particularly important because it positions the reader inside or outside the story. When point of view allows readers inside the story, they know all the characters' thoughts and feelings.

Style is the way the author uses language, including use of imagery (descriptions that appeal to the senses, such as sight, sound, or touch), word choice, and figurative language (such as the use of simile or metaphor). Each author uses language in unique ways to describe setting and character and to uncover the plot.

Mood is the emotional tone of a story (humorous, somber, lighthearted, mysterious, frightening). Theme is the abstract statement about life or humanity revealed by the story as a whole. Through theme, stories achieve a consistency at an abstract level.

Developmental Trends in Children's Narrative Writing. What kinds of literary elements might we expect to find in primary schoolchildren's compositions? Return to Rachel's story presented in Figure 5.4. It includes a main character, Chester, the brown and white dog. It also includes Chester's friends (who act as playful antagonists in the game of hide-and-seek and the story). Rachel implied one of Chester's character traits: he is persistent (he looked and looked for his hidden friends). Tension arises naturally from the conflict of searching; the friends are very difficult to find! The story is told consistently from the third-person point of view with a narrator speaking directly to the reader about how clever Chester was for searching for his friends at Georgia Lake. Rachel's literary style includes the use of repetition (looked and looked). The mood is playful, beginning with the title ("Chester's Adventure to Georgia Lake") and continuing through to the climax when "och" reveals Chester's friends hiding under his bed. This story has most of the literary elements of narratives.

Figure 5.5 presents another story written by a primary-grade student. Although the story sometimes loses sequence, it has several characters who act in a consistent manner, as we would expect (a cat chases a chick). The author tells us about the characters by revealing their feelings (the cat is hungry, and the chick is afraid) and by showing us what they say ("Peep, peep" and "Meow"). The story has a problem (the cat is trying to eat the chick) and actions to solve the problem (the mother bites the cat, and the chick hides). This story has fewer literary elements.

From the stories presented in Figures 5.4 and 5.5, we can conclude that children do use many literary elements of narratives in their stories, but not necessarily all elements, nor are the elements always well developed. We understand that primary schoolchildren's stories may lack plot complexity and descriptive detail. We might expect that young conventional writers' stories would gradually acquire overall story consistency, believability, and detail, but much of this development occurs after the primary grades.

In fact, most first graders do not write stories that include all the elements that would actually qualify their compositions to be called stories (Donovan, 2001). It is not until second and third grade that a majority of children write stories with most of the basic story grammar elements—and, therefore, would qualify to be called stories. Instead, most young children's story compositions are in emergent or approximate forms. As with their **approximations** in other areas of emergent literacy—for example, with their mock letter writing, invented spelling, and finger-point reading—children's approximations when writing a story are not as fully realized as an adult's product would be. Their attempts to write stories almost never contain all seven of the literary elements of a well-crafted story. Their stories only approximate the ideal story, with its setting, character, plot, point of view, style, mood, and theme. Figure 5.6 presents **approximate forms of children's story writing** (adapted from Donovan, 2001). When children are asked to write or dictate a story, these are the kinds of forms their stories take. We present their stories, in order from simple to more complex, without invented

FIGURE 5.5 "Peep Peep" Story

Yo tengo un pollito. El pollito hace—¡pio, pio¡—. El pollito se va a jugar y viene. Tiene hambre. El pollito hace—¡pio, pio!—. El gato lo persigue. La madre lo pica y el gato hace—¡miau!—. . . Por eso la gallina y mi pollito dice la gallina y el pollito estaba escondido. Tenía miedo que el gato lo agarrará.

(I have a chick. The chick says, "Peep, peep." The chick goes out to play and comes [back]. He's hungry. The chick says, "Peep, peep." The cat chases him. The mother bites him and the cat goes, "Meow." . . . Therefore the hen and my chick say the hen and the chick was hidden. He was afraid the cat will catch him.)

Source: Writing in a Bilingual Program, Edelsky, C., p. 91. Copyright © 1986. Reprinted with permission of Greenwood Publishing Group, Inc., Westport, CT.

spellings to emphasize their form. These narratives were collected from Pre-K through fourth-grade children in a Title I school.

Text Form: Expositions

Not all texts are stories. Some texts inform or explain, rather than relate a story; these are called expositions. Much nonfiction takes this form. Of course, readers and writers

FIGURE 5.6   Approximate Forms of Children's Story Writing

Label

present tense, word or phrase

This is David. This is Lisa. This is Casey and Wynell and Willima. This is Travis.

Statement

past tense, sentence about an event

Once upon a time there was a witch lived in the forest. (Donovan, 2001, p. 418)

No Structure

story opener, past tense, lacks sequence and sustained character

Once there was a boy and a dog. The grandmother was dancing. The bunny gave the grandmother a flower.

Action Sequence

past tense, sequence of events, sustained character, no goal

There once was a little boy. He went to the store and bought potato chips. He went to the store and bought milk. He went to the store and bought some junk food. The end.

Reactive Sequence

past tense, causally related sequence of events, no goal

There was an elephant. He climbed up and he fell and bumped his head. The gorilla kissed his head.

Simple Goal Directed

past tense, causally related sequence of events toward resolution of goal

A lady went into a castle. She saw some jewels and she took some. The giant chased her. She put it on and went home. She wore it to bed.

Complex Goal Directed

past tense, causally related sequence of events toward resolution of goal, obstacles and complications

(see Figure 5.4, Chester's Adventure to Georgia Lake)

Source: Adapted from Donovan, 2001.

in the primary grades only begin the process of learning to compose highly structured informational texts and to read and remember ideas from information books (Kamberelis, 1999).

Elements of Expository Texts.

Elements of informational texts include topic presentation in which the topic of exposition is introduced (e.g., "Zebras are intelligent animals,"; Donovan, 2001, p. 426), description of attributes in which the topic is described (e.g., "Zebras are very strong," p. 426), characteristic events in which typical activities related to the topic are described (e.g., "They eat grass and leaves. They live in packs," p. 426), category comparison in which the topic is compared to another similar topic (e.g., "Zebras are smarter than work horses," p. 426), and final summary in which all the information presented about the topic is stated in a more general way (e.g., "Zebras are wild animals and shall remain in the wild forever," p. 426). Expositions may not include all of these elements; however, all informational texts must include a topic presentation and at least one or more additional informational text elements.

Another way to examine expositions is to consider three important components found in highly organized informational material: consistency, ordered relationships, and hierarchical relationships (Newkirk, 1987). For a text to have consistency, all its ideas must be related to one another. Ordered relationships are ideas that are related in some order. For example, two ideas might be related because one idea is an example of or illustrates another idea. Causes and effects, problems and solutions, comparisons, or sequences are all ideas that are ordered—they are related to one another in specific ways.

The last component of expository text structures is hierarchical relationships. Most expository texts are complex and can be broken into one or more main topics, which, in turn, can be broken down into subtopics, forming a hierarchy. The relationships among the main topics and between the subtopics and the main topic in expositions are also ordered or related.

Developmental Trends in Children's Expositions.

Most young children attempt to write expository texts; however, it is not until second grade that many children include more than one or two elements of informational texts in their expositions (Donovan, 2001). In addition, most children do not include ordered relationships in their informational text writing. Instead, most young children's expositions, like their story compositions, are only approximations. They can be considered in emergent or intermediate forms. Figure 5.7 presents approximate forms of informational text writing (adapted from Donovan, 2001). When children are asked to write or dictate an informational text, these are the kinds of forms their expositions take. They are arranged from simple to more complex form.

Again, these samples were collected from a Title I school with a small population of ELLs and over 80 percent of children on free lunch. We have used correct spellings.

Figure 5.7 does not include the most complex forms of expository writing that children are expected to write by the end of elementary school and into the middle school years. Instead, it presents the kinds of expositions we would expect from children through third grade. Even so, most third graders and many fourth graders do not yet have control over the most complex structures presented in this figure.

FIGURE 5.7 Approximate Forms of Children's Expositions

Label
present tense, words or phrases

My dog, you, and me

Statement
present tense, sentence, may introduce topic

I know about rabbits

Simple Couplet
present tense, two related statements, second statement describes or extends first statement

The reptiles are snakes and the reptiles are in the zoo

Attribute List
present tense, random list of two or more facts related to topic

Cats get on the couch when it is tired. When it's sleepy, it goes in its bed. When it doesn't want to be by you, it would scratch. And it would hurt you if you hurt it.

Complex Couplet
present tense, attribute list in which two or more statements are related to one another

Dogs
Dogs are very furry. They are also a mammal. Most dogs bark and hear. If dogs can't bark that's because their voice box is not working very well. If dogs can't hear that's because when they were born they were born deaf or they have a real bad ear infection. Dogs can have an ear infection. Dogs are a lot like humans.

Hierarchical Attribute List
present tense, two or more basic attribute lists that introduce subtopics

Basketball
Basketball is a sport that you play with a ball and someone to play against. Usually it is played on a wooden floor or concrete. You shoot the ball into a basketball net that is held up by a long metal post. The post has a flat piece of wood with a square shape in the middle of the wood. If you take more than three steps it is called traveling and it is the other team's ball. There are four types of shooting the ball. The first one is a set shot. The second is a jump shot. Then a granny shot and lay up shot. I think there are four quarters in a game. In between each quarter is a break that is called halftime. There is an announcer that talks about the game.

Source: Adapted from Donovan, 2001.

Meaning–Form Links

EARLY, TRANSITIONAL, AND SELF-GENERATIVE READERS and writers acquire many strategies for decoding and spelling, including using alphabetic and orthographic understandings.

Decoding

Decoding is a term usually applied to what readers do when they try to figure out a word that they do not recognize by sight. In order to decode, readers must use their knowledge of the alphabetic principle—that letters represent the sounds in words and that those sounds can be blended together to pronounce words (Juel and Minden-Cupp, 2000). Early readers are alphabetic decoders, at first using only initial letters to attempt to decode a word rather than using all of the word's letters. This ability emerges from experimenters' discovery of letter-sound relationships as well as from teachers' instruction.

The trick for moving beyond this level of decoding is to know where to look beyond the first letter. For example, consonant digraphs are comprised of two letters but represent only one phoneme (e.g., *th*, *sh*, *sch* and *ng*). Similarly most long vowels (such as the sound of *ay* in the word *way*) and many other vowels (such as the sound made by *oo* in the word *foot*) are spelled with two letters. As they decode, children must quickly scan a word from left-to-right and determine which letters and letter combinations to pay attention to. The ability to sound out all of a word's letters into phonemes is called alphabetic decoding or **fully phonemic decoding.**

Transitional readers move beyond merely noticing letters or letter combinations. They use familiar word parts to pronounce unknown words. Using known word parts to decode an unfamiliar word is called **decoding by analogy** (Ehri & Robbins, 1992) or **orthographic decoding.** This is based on an awareness of spelling principles, that certain letter patterns are always associated with particular pronunciations (Pressley, 2002). For example, knowing the word *sand* allows readers to use the word part *and* along with its pronunciation to decode many words including *stand, standard,* and *stranded,* among others. As children near the end of transitional reading, they have enough sight words to use dozens and even hundreds of familiar word parts to decode, in turn, hundreds of unfamiliar and fairly rare words seemingly automatically (Share, 1995). Thus, they are on their way to becoming self-generative readers who are able to learn more about decoding merely by reading. Still, self-generative readers do benefit from instruction (especially in spelling) about prefixes, suffixes, and other advanced level word characteristics. They are orthographic decoders and intuitively decide which groups of letters should be pronounced and blended to identify an unknown word.

Spelling

Conventional writers learn new invented spelling strategies, especially visual ones, that contribute to their becoming conventional spellers. As experimenters, they may have spelled the word *weight* as *yt* or *wt*. As early writers they may spell *weight* as *wat;*

as transitional writers they may spell it *wayt* or *wate* before finally spelling the word conventionally. We have seen that experimenters' spellings are influenced merely by sound. Early readers and writers are also influenced by sound, especially as their spellings become fully phonemic (where an invented spelling includes a letter for nearly every phoneme in a word), but the hallmark of conventional writing is beginning to use new, more visual strategies for spelling.

Conventional writers' spellings are influenced by four visual factors: (1) knowledge of the standardized spellings of certain morphemes (*jumped* is spelled with an *ed* even though it sounds like *jumpt*); (2) an expectation of certain letters in certain contexts (for example, the *ight* sequence in *sight*, *might*, and *fight*)—the similar words that give rise to the expectation described in this second factor are called **word families;** (3) knowledge of spelling patterns for long vowel and other vowel pairs (*meat* is spelled with *ea*, while *meet* is spelled with *ee*), and (4) knowledge of consonant doubling (*stopping* includes the doubled *p*) and adding affixes (*restart* and place*ment*).

We now turn to three additional stages of invented spelling: later letter-name or later alphabetic spelling, within-a-word spelling, and syllables-and-affix spelling (Bear, Invernizzi, Templeton, & Johnston, 2000). These stages are presented in Table 5.1 (and follow the stages presented in Table 4.2 in Chapter 4). These stages of spelling continue considerably beyond the primary years we address in this book; however, we would expect a few second graders and some third and fourth graders to exhibit some of the characteristics of syllables-and-affix spelling.

Later Letter–Name or Later Alphabetic Spelling. Later letter-name or later alphabetic spelling marks the end of children's sole reliance on listening to sounds in words as a spelling strategy. In this stage, early writers can hear most salient phonemes in a word and assign a letter to spell that sound. Many of the spellings found in Figure 5.3 (grade 1) are representative of the later letter-name or later alphabetic spelling stage. The spelling of *come* (*cim*), for example, includes one letter for each of the three phonemes found in the word. All of the spellings include vowels, and two short vowel single-syllable words are spelled conventionally (*not* and *in*) as would also be expected at this stage. However, the spelling of the word *do* as *Diw* heralds the next spelling stage.

Within-a-Word Spelling. Within-a-word spelling is influenced by transitional writers' awareness of visual spelling patterns (how spellings look) as well as by their increasing store of known spellings. By now, nearly all single-syllable short vowel words are spelled conventionally as are consonant blends and digraphs. At this stage, children are aware that most long vowels and some other vowels require more than one vowel letter in their spelling. Thus, Kristen's spelling (in Figure 5.3) of the word *do* as *Diw* demonstrates her growing awareness of possible vowel spelling patterns. Many of Kristen's spellings in Figure 5.3 (grade 2) have characteristics representative of the within-a-word spelling stage. Her spelling of the words *eyes* (as *eiys*) and *shelf* (as *sefve*) reflect a use of a visual spelling strategy. That is, Kristen realizes that the word *eyes* has a *y* in it, so she first spells the long *i* phoneme with the letters *ei* and then adds the *y*. Similarly, Kristen is aware that the word *shelves* includes the letter *v*, so she spells the /f/ phoneme with the letter *f* and then adds the *v*. Notice her use of the final *e* visual pattern in the words *believe* (*bleve*) and *shelf* (*sefve*).

TABLE 5.1   Stages of Spelling Development (continued from Table 4.2 on page 104)

Later Letter-Name or Later Alphabetic Spelling*

* Routinely represents one-to-one all salient sounds in a word (also called fully phonemic spelling) (e.g., LadR for *ladder*)
* Occasionally to routinely spells consonant blends and digraphs conventionally (e.g., BREG for *bridge*, Thr for *there*)
* Routinely uses word spaces
* Occasionally differentiates spellings of **homophones** (words that are pronounced the same but spelled differently) (e.g., *to* and *two*, *for* and *four*)
* Routinely includes vowels

Within-a-Word Spelling*

* Routinely spells single syllable short vowel words conventionally
* Occasionally to routinely spells r-controlled vowels conventionally in common single syllable words (e.g., *star, her*)
* Routinely represents long vowel sounds and other vowel sounds using vowel markers (e.g., GRATE for *great*, TEE for *tea*, TOOB for *tube*) sometimes using conventional spellings
* Routinely spells nasals conventionally (e.g., *jump*)
* Routinely spells common morphemes (e.g., *ed, ing, s*) conventionally

Syllables-and-Affixes Spelling*

* Occasionally to routinely uses consonant doubling at syllable junctures (e.g., *battle, riddle*)
* Occasionally to routinely uses consonant doubling when adding a suffix (e.g., STOPPING for *stopping*)
* Occasionally to routinely spells common prefixes and suffixes (e.g., PICHER for *pitcher*, MOSHUN for *motion*)
* Occasionally to routinely drops e when adding suffixes (e.g., RIDDING for *riding*)

*Adapted from Bear, Invernizzi, Templeton, & Johnston's (2000) stages with the same names.

Syllable-and-Affix Spelling. Self-generative writers who use syllable-and-affix spelling learn how consonant and vowel patterns work in multisyllabic words (words with more than one syllable) and what occurs when syllables join (Bear et al., 2000). At this stage of spelling, children learn how to combine prefixes and suffixes to base words as well as spelling rules associated with adding suffixes to words (for example, when to drop an *e* or double a consonant). During the early parts of this stage, children confuse rules for adding suffixes; however, their spelling errors reveal their awareness of these spelling patterns.

FUNCTIONS

CONVENTIONAL READERS AND WRITERS have a keen awareness of audience. They have a more constant and pervasive realization that literacy involves creating meaning with someone else in mind, whether it is the author whose book they are reading, the intended reader of their writing, or the listener to whom they are reading. They understand that such meaning making is the single most important element of reading and writing.

One indication of children's increasing identification of themselves as authors who communicate with others is their willingness to use ICT technology, such as text messaging and instant messaging. They enjoy reading and writing during internet projects such as those shown on the Internet Projects Registry at http://gsh.lightspan.com/pr/_cfm/index.cfm. These projects involve hundreds of children from around the world who complete a common task and register their results on a single website so that all children who participate can see all the results. Recently, elementary students have discovered electronic magazines or e-zines (Cohen & Meyer, 2004). For example, a group of second graders each wrote a zine on a topic of his or her choice and included a cover *dear reader* letter, poem, fiction story, nonfiction piece, word search, or picture search. The zines were published on the school website.

NATIONAL READING PANEL DEFINITIONS OF READING AND WRITING

THE NATIONAL READING PANEL (NRP) was charged by Congress to evaluate research on reading instruction for elementary students and provide a synthesis of the best ways to teach children to read. Such instruction, based on research, is considered evidence-based. The NRP focused on five elements: phonemic awareness, phonics, vocabulary, comprehension, and fluency (see a summary and discussion of this report at www.gov./programs/readingfirst/guidance.doc). We began our book using the terms *form, meaning, meaning-form links,* and *functions* rather than the terms *phonemic awareness, phonics, vocabulary, comprehension,* and *fluency.* This was deliberate in that we want to highlight the beginnings of literacy (as suggested in the title of this text). By maintaining these categories throughout this book, we show the importance of respecting children's early development, their explorations, and their discoveries.

However, as we have discussed children's development toward being conventional readers and writers, we have addressed each of the five critical components of reading reviewed in the Report of the National Reading Panel (2000). We demonstrated in Chapters 1 through 5 that:

- Children acquire phonemic awareness.
- Children who have phonemic awareness learn to read, in part, due to such awareness.
- Children who have phonemic awareness learn to spell.

- Children learn phonics, a systematic method for matching phonemes (sounds in spoken language) with graphemes (letters in written language).
- Children who know and use phonics principles systematically pass through more advanced phases of reading and writing.
- Phonics is needed by all children of all social economic statuses and by English language learners.
- Phonemic awareness and phonics are critical during the experimenting, early, and transitional phases of reading and writing.
- Without phonemic awareness and phonics knowledge, children cannot enter into the experimenting phase of reading and will be hampered in rapid development as effective readers and writers.
- Phonemic awareness and phonics are not the only elements of reading and writing children need to know in order to move quickly and effectively through the phases of reading and writing development.
- Children's vocabulary increases and plays a critical role in language comprehension, both spoken and written.
- Children's oral language, especially their metacognitive understandings about morphemes and grammar, increases and plays a critical role in reading and writing.
- Children gain fluency as they learn to monitor their reading and apply fix-up strategies.
- Children gain conscious awareness of reading and writing strategies that enhance their comprehension and composition of increasingly more complex text.

That is, in Chapters 1 through 5 we have carefully focused on children and what they can learn to do when they are immersed in reading and writing in their homes and communities and when they are taught well. In the remainder of this book, we focus on the qualities of effective instruction that allow all children to develop the high levels of reading and writing described so far.

ASSESSING CHILDREN'S ABILITY TO READ TEXTS OF INCREASING DIFFICULTY

ONE OF THE MOST IMPORTANT ASSESSMENTS that teachers can make as children enter the conventional reading phase is to monitor their progress reading and writing texts at increasingly more difficult levels with sufficient fluency and comprehension. This could be considered the *real* essential component of reading and writing. The first step in monitoring whether children are able to read text of increasing levels of difficulty is to determine children's **instructional and independent reading levels.** Instructional reading level is the level of text that children can read with support from their teacher. They can read most words (90% to 95%) correctly and, when asked questions, can answer most (70% to 90%) correctly. However, these texts are still challenging enough that teachers guide children as they read. Independent reading level is the level of text that children can read on their own. They read all or nearly all of the words (96% to 100%) correctly and, when asked questions, answer nearly all correctly (91% to 100%).

Over time, children's instructional and independent reading levels should increase. Traditionally, the progression of levels of difficulty at first grade included pre-primer, primer, and then first grade, second grade, and so on. More recent concepts of levels of text difficulty have arisen from levels used in Reading Recovery instruction (Peterson, 1991). Reading Recovery includes more levels of difficulty; by the end of third grade proficient readers would have progressed from level 1 to level 38 with levels 1 through 16 to 18 considered first grade level texts. Other leveling schemes use alphabet letters to indicate increasing difficulty (Fountas & Pinnell, 1996).

Using Running Records to Determine Reading Levels

A **running record** is used to analyze children's reading; it provides information about reading level and children's use of cueing systems during reading. Making a running record involves several steps. To begin, the teacher selects texts at several levels of difficulty. For example, the teacher can select books at each of the Reading Recovery levels. One commercial assessment, *Developmental Reading Assessment* (Beaver, 1997), provides books at levels 1, 2, 3, 4, 6, 8, 10, 12, 14, 16, 18, 20, 24, 28, 30, 34, and 38. Or, teachers may select texts from a basal reading series at several levels of difficulty. Another alternative is to use texts found in an **Individualized Reading Inventory,** a commercial collection of texts written at pre-primer to middle school or even high school levels of difficulty.

Next, children read texts that have been selected to reflect their level of reading. The teacher selects a level of text that he or she believes a child can read with ease. The teacher records miscues as the child reads either by marking on a copy of the text or by using checks and other symbols on a separate sheet of paper.

Figure 5.8 presents a running record of Charlie's reading of "The Three Little Pigs." This figure indicates words that Charlie omitted—crossed out in text; words that he inserted—added above the text; words that he substituted—written over the text; and words that he self-corrected—marked with "SC." The figure also shows the teacher's running record, which captures Charlie's omissions, insertions, substitutions, and self-corrections.

Teachers then determine the child's accuracy rate, the percentage of words read correctly, by counting the total number of miscues not including miscues that were self-corrected. The total number of miscues is subtracted from the total number of words in the passage to find the number of words read correctly. Finally, the number of words read correctly is divided by the total number of words in the passage. For example, Charlie read the "The Three Little Pigs" passage with 14 miscues including 3 self-corrected miscues for a total of 11 miscues. This number (11) is subtracted from the total number of words in the passage (181) to determine the number of words read correctly (170). The number of words read correctly is divided by the total number of words to reach the percentage of words read correctly—the accuracy rate. The accuracy rate for Charlie's reading of "The Three Little Pigs" is 93 percent. The accuracy rate is used to determine whether the text is on the independent, instructional, or frustrational reading level. Charlie's accuracy rate indicates that the passage "The Three Little Pigs" is at his instructional level.

The level of the text determines children's instructional reading level. For example, the *Three Little Pigs* text is approximately a first grade level text. Thus, Charlie's in-

FIGURE 5.8   Running Record for "The Three Little Pigs"

TEXT: The Three Little Pigs

three^sc
Once upon a time there were three pigs. Mother pig| *said*^sc sent the

the   T
three little pigs ~~out~~ to make their way in the world. The first

sticks
pig made a house of straw. The second pig made a house of

sticks. The third pig made a house of bricks. A wolf came to

the first pig's house and said, "I'll huff and puff and blow your

house down." The wolf blew the house down and the little pig ran

little
away fast. The wolf came to the second ∧pig's house and said,

"I'll huff and puff and blow your house down." The wolf blew the

fast
house down but the little pig ran away faster. The wolf came to

the third pig's house and said, "I'll huff and puff and blow your

did   *down*
house down." He blew and blew but could not blow ~~down~~ the house ∧

s *T*
He tried to ˆsneak down the chimney but the pig put a big pot of

water on the fire. The wolf came down the chimney and burned his

fast^sc
tail. He ran away the fastest of all.

EXAMPLES:	
child matches text	✓
child substitutes	*child* / *text*
child omits	• / *text*
child inserts	*child* / •
child repeats	⌐ *text*
child self-corrects	sc
teacher prompts	T

RUNNING RECORD

✓ ✓ ✓✓ *three*^sc/*there* ✓ ✓ ✓ ✓ ✓| *said*^sc/*sent* ✓

✓ ✓ ✓ •/*out* ✓ ✓ *the*/*their* ✓✓✓ T ✓ ✓

✓ ✓ ✓ ✓ ✓ *sticks*/*straw* ✓ ✓ ✓ ✓✓✓✓

✓ ✓✓✓ ✓✓✓ ✓ ✓✓ ✓✓ ✓ ✓

✓✓✓ ✓ ✓ ✓✓ ✓✓✓✓✓ ✓

✓ ✓ ✓✓✓ ✓✓ ✓ ✓ ✓✓✓

✓ ✓ ✓✓✓✓ ✓ *little*/• ✓✓ ✓✓

✓✓✓✓✓ ✓✓ ✓ ✓ ✓✓

✓ ✓ ✓✓✓✓✓ *fast*/*faster* ✓✓ ✓✓

✓✓✓ ✓ ✓✓ ✓✓✓✓✓ ✓

✓ ✓ ✓✓ ✓ ✓ ✓ *did*/*could* ✓ ✓ •/*down* ✓ ✓ *down*/•

✓✓✓ *s* *T*/*sneak* ✓ ✓ ✓ ✓✓✓✓✓✓

✓ ✓✓✓ ✓ ✓ ✓ ✓ ✓ ✓ ✓ ✓

✓ ✓✓✓ *fast*^sc/*the* ✓ ✓✓

structional reading level is first grade. The teacher would need to have Charlie read even easier text to determine his independent reading level.

Miscue Analysis

A **miscue analysis** provides information about children's use of the semantic cuing system (grapho-semantics), the syntactic cuing system (grapho-syntax), and the grapho-phonic cuing system (grapho-phonics, usually called phonics) (Goodman & Burke, 1972). To assist in a miscue analysis, teachers construct a miscue analysis chart. Figure 5.9 displays the miscue analysis for Charlie's reading of "The Three Little Pigs." First, the teacher analyzes only substitutions to determine whether they are semantically acceptable (miscue has a meaning similar to that of the text word), syntactically acceptable (miscue is syntactically acceptable in the sentence), or graphophonically acceptable (miscue matches the text word at the beginning, middle, or end). The teacher also records whether the miscue was self-corrected.

According to the miscue analysis presented in Figure 5.9, none of Charlie's miscues was semantically acceptable, but Charlie self-corrected three miscues. Over half of his miscues were syntactically acceptable. All the miscues except two had the same beginning letters as the text word. According to this analysis, Charlie attends especially to beginning letters, but also to word order.

FIGURE 5.9   Miscue Analysis Chart for "The Three Little Pigs"

Child/Text	Semantically Acceptable	Syntactically Acceptable	Graphophonically same as B	M	E	Self-Corrects	Comments
three/there			✔			✔	*
said/sent			✔			✔	*
the/their		✔	✔				
sticks/straw		✔	✔				
fast/faster	✔		✔	✔			
did/could	✔	✔			✔		
fast/the						✔	*
s/sneak			✔				
	2/8	3/8	6/8	1/8	1/8	3/8	

* sentence makes sense up to point of miscue

Using Running Records to Analyze Fluency and Decoding

Running records and miscue analyses can also be used to assess children's strategy use (whether they are paying attention to meaning along with monitoring the letters in words, for example), their fluency, and their use of alphabetic or orthographic decoding skills. Slow, word-by-word reading indicates children are paying too much attention to individual words rather than focusing on the meaning of what they are reading. Fluent reading emerges when children know most of the words they are reading by sight, when they can rapidly employ orthographic decoding strategies to identify unknown words quickly, and when their understanding is sufficient to allow them to read with intonation and phrasing that expresses the meaning of the text.

Using Questions to Analyze Comprehension and Vocabulary

Teachers need to assess children's comprehension and their understanding of vocabulary as a part of their determining a child's instructional or independent reading level. To assess a child's comprehension of a particular text, a teacher could ask questions. The questions can probe children's literal, inferential, and evaluative understanding of the text as well as their understanding of vocabulary meanings within the context of the text. Teachers can construct their own questions being sure to include those that can be answered with information directly stated in the text (literal) and those that require inferences (inferential).

When children can answer 70 to 90 percent of questions, the passage is at their instructional level. When they can answer 90 percent or more of the questions, the passage is at their independent level.

CHAPTER SUMMARY

THERE ARE THREE PHASES of conventional reading and writing: early, transitional, and self-generative. Conventional readers and writers are able to orchestrate several processes and to control several strategies in extended episodes of writing or reading. They are aware of how well or how poorly their reading is going; they monitor their reading and use fix-up strategies when it goes poorly. Conventional readers' meaning making extends to being able to make interpretations and understand abstract literary elements, including point of view, symbol, and theme. They know the fine points of form at the word level in English; they have a conventional concept of word. They acquire sophisticated awareness of story form that comprises knowledge about setting, characters, plot, point of view, style, mood, and theme.

These children also gain a greater knowledge of text structure than they had as experimenters, especially knowledge of expository text. However, before writing fully developed stories or expositions, they produce approximations.

Conventional readers and writers have many new spelling strategies. They build on their previous understandings of what spelling is all about by adding multiple strategies for representing words in print, some using their earlier knowledge of sound-letter correspondences, and some using visual information in new ways.

Conventional writers move through three stages of spelling: later letter-name or later alphabetic spelling, within-a-word spelling, and syllable-and-affix spelling.

It is critical that teachers monitor conventional readers' ability to read text of increasing difficulty. Teachers use grade-leveled tests selected from leveled text sets, tests, or basal readers. Children read these aloud as teachers take running records and ask questions about the texts. Later teachers do miscue analyses and determine word-reading accuracy rates and levels of comprehension to know which texts are on children's independent and instructional reading levels.

Figure 5.10 summarizes what conventional readers and writers know about written language meanings, forms, meaning-form links, and functions.

FIGURE 5.10 Summary: What Conventional Readers and Writers Know about Written Language Meanings, Forms, Meaning-Form Links, and Functions

Meaning Making

use metacognitive strategies to focus on meaning while reading, including monitoring that reading makes sense

use strategies for generating ideas during composing, including knowing the expectations of their audience

interpret literature and move toward interpretations at the abstract level, including point of view, theme, and symbol

use knowledge of abstract literary elements and style to compose stories and other literary texts

Forms

have fully developed concept of word

understand morphemes

develop an ever-increasing stock of sight words

know conventional spellings of an ever-increasing stock of words

use knowledge of literary elements in narratives to compose stories that include settings, characters, and some

plot elements and that signal growing control over point of view, mood, and style

develop knowledge of how exposition is organized, using consistency, ordered relationships, and hierarchical relationships to produce gradually more organized expository text compositions

Meaning-Form Links

develop conventional spelling ability, including learning alternative spelling patterns, phonograms, and morphemes

use orthographic concepts to spell and to decode words in reading (decoding by analogy)

Functions

read and write to meet a variety of personal needs

read and write to join the classroom literate community

USING THE INFORMATION

Figure 5.11 presents a graphic organizer prepared to summarize the accomplishments of children in the conventional phases of early, transitional, and self-generative reading and writing. Here is a set of terms that can be used to fill in this organizer. Place the terms on the graphic organizer under the appropriate phases of conventional reading and writing.

Uses alphabetic decoding

Monitors, summarizes, and interprets

Predicts, confirms, and recalls literal ideas

Knows 300-400 high frequency sight words

Makes high-level text approximations

Knows 400-2,000 sight words

Reads second-to-third-grade level texts

Knows thousands of sight words

Makes low-level text approximations

Reads preprimer-to-end-of-first-grade level texts

Uses orthographic decoding (syllables, affixes)

Reads third-grade level texts or higher

Is a later letter-name or later alphabetic speller

Is a syllable-and-affix speller

Uses beginning orthographic decoding (word parts)

Infers abstract themes and uses strategies for fix-ups

Writes with within-a-word spelling

Makes moderate-level text approximations

FIGURE 5.11   Graphic Organizer for Conventional Reading and Writing

	Early Readers and Writers	Transitional Readers and Writers	Self-Generative Readers and Writers
Level of Text Read			
Sight Words			
Level of Decoding			
Comprehension Strategies			
Level of Narrative and Exposition Compositions			
Level of Spelling			

APPLYING THE INFORMATION

In the following literacy event, a first grader writes a story and shares it with his classmates. Discuss what this event shows about understandings of written language meanings, forms, meaning-form links, and functions.

Figure 5.12 displays Zachary's "whale story." He wrote this as a first draft on six sheets of paper. Later, he read his story aloud to his classmates as part of an author's circle (a gathering of students who listen to others read their compositions, give compliments, and ask questions): "Made and illustrated by Zachary. To my mom and dad. Once upon a time there were two whales. They liked to play. One day when the whales were playing, a hammerhead came along. They fought for a time. Finally it was finished and the whales won. And they lived happily ever after."

After Zachary read his composition, his classmates asked him several questions, including "What kind of whales are they?" "Where do they live—what ocean?" and "How did they win the fight?" After listening to his classmates' questions, Zachary announced, "I am going to change my story by saying they lived in the Atlantic Ocean and they won the fight because they were bigger than the hammerhead and used their tails to defeat him."

GOING BEYOND THE TEXT

VISIT A THIRD GRADE CLASSROOM. Observe the class during a time devoted to reading or writing. Try to identify two children whose behaviors suggest conventional reading or writing. Interview them. Ask them what they do when they begin a new writing piece. What do they do to make a piece better? Ask how they choose a book to read for enjoyment. How do they begin a reading assignment for social studies or science class? Ask them if they would be willing to show you something they have written lately. Ask if they would read part of a book or tell about part of a book they are reading. Make a running record of the children's reading and analyze their writing samples.

FIGURE 5.12   Zachary's "Whale Story"

REFERENCES

Barone, D., Mallette, M., & Xu, S. (2005). *Teaching early literacy: Development, assessment and instruction.* New York: Guilford Press.

Bear, D. R., Invernizzi, M., Templeton, S., & Johnston, F. (2000). *Words their way: Word study for phonics, vocabulary, and spelling instruction,* (2nd ed.). Upper Saddle River, NJ: Prentice-Hall.

Beaver, J. (1997). *Developmental reading assessment.* Parsippany, NJ: Celebration Press.

Catling, P. (1952). *The chocolate touch.* New York: William Morrow.

Cohen, B., & Meyer, R. (2004). The zine project: Writing with a personal perspective. *Language Arts, 82,* 129–138.

Donovan, C. (2001). Children's development and control of written story and informational genres: Insights from one elementary school. *Research in the Teaching of English, 35,* 394–447.

Eastman, P. (1961). *Go, dog. Go!* New York: Random House.

Edelsky, C. (1986). *Writing in a bilingual program: Habia una vez.* Norwood, NJ: Ablex.

Ehri, L., & Robbins, C. (1992). Beginners need some decoding skills to read words by analogy. *Reading Research Quarterly, 27,* 12–26.

Fountas, I. C., & Pinnell, G. S. (1996). *Guided reading: Good first teaching for all children.* Portsmouth, NH: Heinemann.

Freppon, P. (1991). Children's concepts of the nature and purpose of reading in different instructional settings. *Journal of Reading Behavior, 23,* 139–163.

Goodman, Y., & Burke, C. (1972). *The reading miscue inventory.* New York: Macmillan.

Juel, C., & Minden-Cupp, C. (2000). Learning to read words: Linguistic units and instructional strategies. *Reading Research Quarterly, 35,* 458–492.

Kamberelis, G. (1999). Genre development and learning: Children writing stories, science reports, and poems. *Research in the Teaching of English, 33,* 403–463.

Leland, C., Harste, J., & Huber, K. (2005). Out of the box: Critical literacy in a first-grade classroom. *Language Arts, 82,* 257–268.

Lobel, A. (1971). *Frog and Toad together.* New York: HarperCollins.

Luke, A., & Freebody, P. (1997). Shaping the social practices of reading. In S. Muspratt, A. Luke, & P. Freebody. (Eds.) *Constructing critical literacies* (pp. 185–225). Cresskill, NJ: Hampton.

Lukens, R. (1995). *A critical handbook of children's literature* (5th ed.). Glenview, IL: Scott, Foresman/Little, Brown.

Many, J. (1991). The effects of stance and age level on children's literary responses. *Journal of Reading Behavior, 23,* 61–85.

McGee, L. (1992). An exploration of meaning construction in first graders' grand conversations. In C. Kinzer & D. Leu (Eds.), *Literacy research, theory, and practice: Views from many perspectives* (pp. 177–186). Chicago: National Reading Conference.

McGee, L. (1998). How do we teach literature to young children? In S. B. Neuman & K. A. Roskos (Eds.), *Children achieving: Best practices in early literacy* (pp. 172–179). Newark, DE: International Reading Association.

Moffett, J. (1968). *Teaching the universe of discourse.* Boston: Houghton Mifflin.

National Association for the Education of Young Children (NAEYC) and International Reading Association (IRA). (1998). Learning to read and write: Developmentally appropriate practices for young children. *Young Children, 53,* 30–46.

National Reading Panel. (2000). *Teaching children to read: An evidence-based assessment of the scientific research literature on reading and its implications for reading instruction. Reports of the subgroups.* Washington, DC. National Institute of Child Health and Human Development.

Newkirk, T. (1987). The non-narrative writing of young children. *Research in the Teaching of English, 21,* 121–144.

Paris, S., Wasik, B., & Turner, J. (1991). The development of strategic readers. In R. Barr, M. Kamil, P. Mosenthal, & P. Pearson (Eds.), *Handbook of reading research* (2nd ed., pp. 609–640). New York: Longman.

Peterson, B. (1991). Selecting books for beginning readers. In D. DeFord, C. Lyons, & G. Pinnell (Eds.), *Bridges to literacy: Learning from Reading Recovery* (pp. 119–147). Portsmouth, NH: Heinemann.

Pressley, M. (2002). Comprehension strategies instruction: A turn-of-the-century status report. In C. Block & M. Pressley (Eds.), *Comprehension instruction: Research-based best practices* (pp. 11–27). New York: Guilford.

Rosenblatt, L. (1978). *The reader, the text, the poem: The transactional theory of the literary work.* Carbondale: Southern Illinois University Press.

Share, D. (1995). Phonological recoding and self-teaching: Sine qua non of reading acquisition. *Cognition, 55,* 151–218.

Sinatra, G., Brown, K., & Reynolds, R. (2002). Implications of cognitive resource allocation for comprehension strategies instruction. In C. Block & M. Pressley (Eds.), *Comprehension instruction: Research-based best practices* (pp. 62–76). New York: Guilford.

Sipe, L. (2000). The construction of literacy understanding by first and second graders in oral response to picture storybook read-alouds. *Reading Research Quarterly, 35,* 252–275.

Tompkins, G., & McGee, L. M. (1993). *Teaching reading with literature: Case studies to action plans.* New York: Merrill/Macmillan.

Wollman-Bonilla, J. (2000). Teaching science writing to first graders: Genre learning and recontextualization. *Research in the Teaching of English, 35,* 35–65.

Wollman-Bonilla, J. (2001). Can first-grade writers demonstrate audience awareness? *Reading Research Quarterly, 36,* 184–201.

Woodson, J. (2001). *The other side.* New York: Putnam.

Yorinks, A. (1986). *Hey, Al.* New York: Farrar, Straus and Giroux.

CHAPTER

6

Literacy-Rich Classrooms

KEY CONCEPTS

Classroom Environment
Language- and Print-
  Rich Classrooms
Centers
Literacy Workstation
Dramatic-Play-with-Print
  Centers
Classroom Displays
Shared Writing
Interactive Writing
Interactive Pocket Chart
  Activities
Write-On Chart
Authentic Materials

Leveled Books
Guided Reading
Analytic Talk
Shared Reading
Big Book
Modeled Writing
Volume of Reading and
  Writing
Assessment
Monitoring
  Assessments
Screening Assessments
Kid Watching
Curriculum

Curriculum Integration
Integrated Language
  Arts Activity
Multicultural Literature
Culturally Authentic
  Literature
Literature Theme Unit
Integrated Content Units
Indirect Instruction
Direct Instruction
Explicit Instruction
Gradual Release of
  Responsibility
Embedded Instruction

COMPONENTS OF LANGUAGE- AND LITERACY-RICH CLASSROOMS

CHILDREN AND TEACHERS interact for many hours everyday in their classrooms. The classroom setting includes a physical component (the arrangement of furniture, displays, and materials); a temporal component (the routine scheduling of various activities); and a social-interactive component (patterns of teacher-student and student-student interaction) (Hoffman et al., 2004). Taken together, these components constitute a **classroom environment.** In this chapter, we describe classroom environments that research suggests accelerate children's language and literacy development. We call these environments **language- and print-rich classrooms** (Wolfersberger et al., 2004).

One way to consider classroom environments is to describe the learners they produce. We ask what sorts of learners would emerge from an ideal classroom environment. We argue that language- and literacy-rich classrooms will produce children who are reflective and motivated readers and writers who use literacy to learn more about themselves and the world in which they live. For example, four-year-olds who listen to their teacher read about the differences between tortoises and turtles to help identify the animal that one of them brought to school are reflective, motivated readers who use reading to find out more about their world.

Being reflective means that children are thinkers; they construct meanings for themselves and can use the thinking of others to modify those meanings. Reflective readers construct personal understandings from information books, poems, and stories. Their initial understandings are usually tentative and unfocused. Sharing such undeveloped understandings requires great risk taking. Reflective thinkers often modify their understandings given additional information from other books or from talking with their friends or teachers. Similarly, reflective writers compose personally meaningful stories, expositions, and poems, but they also take into account the needs and interests of their audience. Constructing and sharing personal meanings with others both honors the voice of children and creates a "rich broth of meaning" (Oldfather, 1993, p. 676). This concept of literacy emphasizes the social nature of learning.

Being motivated means that children are self-directed and self-motivated (Guthrie, Wigfield, & Von Secker, 2000). Many children, especially in the primary grades, are expected to participate in reading and writing activities because the teacher tells them to, but motived learners also participate in many activities because they choose to. Motivating activities have three characteristics: they allow children some choices in materials and experiences, provide challenges but call on strategies previously modeled by the teacher, and require social collaboration (Morrow & Gambrell, 1998).

The goal of all literacy instruction is not merely to produce children who are capable readers and writers (although that is certainly an admirable goal), but also to encourage and support children as they use reading and writing to achieve their own worthwhile personal and social goals. To achieve this aim, teachers must make careful decisions about the physical layout of the classroom, classroom routines, and interaction patterns. Seven conditions are characteristic of language- and literacy-rich classrooms:

- Physical arrangements of furniture and displays facilitate the variety of reading and writing activities called for in daily routines.

- Materials are abundant, varied, authentic, accessible, and placed where they are most likely to serve the needs of readers and writers.
- Daily schedules maximize instructional time and include a variety of reading and writing routines.
- Assessment is routine and informs instruction.
- The literacy curriculum supports positive teacher-student and student-student interactions by being culturally sensitive and integrated with content studies.
- A variety of grouping patterns facilitate whole-class, small-group, and individual teacher-student and student-student interactions.
- A variety of instructional practices facilitate teacher-student and student-student interactions for optimal learning by all.

PHYSICAL ARRANGEMENT OF CLASSROOMS

THE PHYSICAL ENVIRONMENT OF A CLASSROOM matters and sets the stage for all learning that will occur in that space (Fraser, 1991). Classrooms that are cluttered and dirty suggest that no one cares about what happens in them. Children and teachers are not likely to be motivated or energized in such settings. Classrooms arranged with desks in straight lines facing the front, with commercial materials on bulletin boards, and with displays of routine, fill-in the blank work by children are likely to be places where children have little choice, where all children are treated the same, and where teaching is viewed as merely telling children what to do. Students may be well managed in such classrooms, but neither they nor their teachers are likely to be reflective decision-makers.

Language- and literacy-rich classrooms have a variety of seating arrangements, including spaces for small groups and pairs of children to work cooperatively, spaces for small groups and whole-class groups of children to work with the teacher, and spaces for individual children to work and store materials. They include at least one large carpeted area for whole-class activities. The carpet is large enough so that all the children can be seated comfortably on it, and it accommodates a seat for the teacher, a pocket chart and stand, and an easel that holds large chart paper. Language- and literacy-rich classrooms have at least one table big enough to accommodate as many as eight children for small-group instruction. This small-group instruction area should be near an easel with chart paper, a pocket chart, and shelves that hold teaching materials. Preschool classrooms have table seating to accommodate all the children working at the same time at centers (for example, tables in the art or writing center, the housekeeping area, and the small manipulatives area). Primary grade classrooms may have tables or clusters of desks in a central location that can serve as a second whole-class area and general work area.

Centers or Workstations

All language- and literacy-rich early childhood classrooms include small partitioned spaces called **centers** created by an arrangement of bookshelves and other dividers (Dorn, French, & Jones, 1998). Typically, preschools have a library center, a computer center, an art center, a writing center, a center for housekeeping and other dramatic play, a block center, and a center for puzzles and other maniuplatives (Smith & Dickinson, 2002). They may have a work bench and sand or water table. In order to prompt children to engage in reading and writing and extend children's opportunities for literacy learning, many centers besides the library, computer, and writing centers are stocked with materials that prompt children to engage in reading and writing (Roskos & Neuman, 2001; Vukelich, 1994). For every center, teachers supply not just materials typical of that center, but also reading and writing props that are related to those typical materials, and related storybooks and information books.

For example, if children were studying light and shadow, then the science center might include a collection of flashlights that children can take apart and reassemble and use in shadow experiments. It might include objects such as stuffed animals and kitchen utensils to use in shadow experiments. This center might include a display of a labeled drawing of the parts of a flashlight created by the teacher and a poster that challenges children to identify the animal or object that created variously shaped shadows. Also displayed might be a chart giving directions on how to make two hand shadows. The teacher might provide several clipboards and booklets made of blank paper stapled together, with a typed title page saying *Scientist's Journal*. Other sheets with the title *Labeled Drawings of a Flashlight* and *Shadow Shapes I Made* might be provided in trays along with a can of pens, pencils, and markers. The center might also include books about shadows such as *Nothing Sticks Like a Shadow* (Tompert, 1988) and *What Makes a Shadow?* (Bulla, 1994). Figure 6.1 presents a list of traditional preschool and kindergarten centers and suggestions of reading and writing materials that might be provided in each center. The teacher uses the time when some children are in centers to teach small groups of other children.

Another designation of space in primary grade classrooms is the **literacy workstation** (Diller, 2003), a classroom space—often an already existing center—designated for children's individual use of materials previously used for group instruction. These materials serve children's meaningful practice of reading and writing independent of the teacher. For example, the listening center might be designated a literacy workstation after a reading of the storybook *Blueberries for Sal* (McCloskey, 1976). As a literacy workstation, the center would be stocked with two copies of the book and blank sheets of paper with directions for folding a sheet into four parts, drawing in one part a picture of the book's main character, writing in a second part a sentence about the character's problem, and writing in the remaining two parts two ways that the character tried to solve the problem.

In this case, the teacher's reading of *Blueberries for Sal* aloud to the whole class as a prelude to the workstation activity might proceed as follows: He or she tells the children the two main characters' names and asks them to be thinking about these characters' problems as they listen. While reading, he or she makes comments about what each main character is thinking and pauses to say, "You know I think I just read a hint about one of the problems. Did anybody else get an idea about what the problem might be?" After discussing the problem, the teacher says, "Now that we know the problem that both Sal and the little bear had, we have to listen to find out how each of them solves that problem." After reading, the teacher has children recall several ways the characters attempted to solve the problem. Next, he or she demonstrates on a large sheet of chart paper hung on the easel how to divide the paper into four parts. He or she draws a quick

FIGURE 6.1 Traditional Preschool and Kindergarten Centers and Related Literacy Materials

Blocks Center

Lumber order forms

Work order forms

Measuring tapes and clipboards with paper and with pencil attached by string

Building supply catalogs

Schematic drawings of "block buildings"

Plumbing supply catalogs

Housekeeping Center

Telephone message pad

Grocery list pad

Checkbooks

Envelopes and stationary

Blank invitation cards and birthday cards

Coupons

Telephone book

Calendar

Take-out menus

Bills

Sand Table

Recipe card for making "sand pie"

Blank recipe cards

Treasure map showing buried plastic toys

Blank "Treasure map" paper on clip boards

Firehouse Dramatic Play

Telephone and Fire report form

Equipment checklist

Sign-in-and-out sheet for all firemen

Directions for putting out fires

Labeled drawing of a fire truck

Blank "Labeled Drawing of a Fire Truck" paper on clipboards

---

sketch of two of the main characters in the first portion of the paper and then invites children to compose a sentence telling the problem. Next the teacher elicits from the children their recollections of at least two ways the main characters tried to solve the problem and writes these on the remaining portions of the chart. After the four-part chart is completed, the teacher announces, "Now I am going to hang this chart in the listening center to remind you what you will be doing there this week. In the listening center, you will listen to the story again, and then, as workstation work, you will make your own four-part story chart." Later, the teacher might stock the listening center with an incomplete version of the same four-part chart and an unfamiliar storybook in order to see how well children can infer problems and solutions on their own and to determine who needs small-group instruction in this comprehension strategy.

Workstations should be large enough for two children to work together, and some stations may be large enough for up to four children. When there are many workstations in a classroom, and only two children in each station, teachers have found children are more on task and speak in quieter tones of voices, which is important as teachers are conducting small group lessons (Diller, 2003). Figure 6.2 presents a list of possible literacy workstations that can be included in primary grade classrooms. This

FIGURE 6.2 Literacy Workstations and Suggested Materials

Listening

Book, audiocassette, and paper labeled "beginning" on the front and "end" on the back

Overhead

Overhead projector, transparent film with the letters *at,* transparent film with the letters *b, c, f, h, m, p, r, s, v , br, f',* and *spl*

Writing

Red and yellow paper to cut in the shape of an apple for writing apple shape poems, collection of books about apples

Library

Books in tubs with colors indicating levels, book summary forms (which include a blank space for the title of the book, a place to circle if it is a story or information book, and a box titled *What I liked about this book*)

Retelling

Three books and three sets of props to retell each book

Word-Letter-Sound

Words written on cards for sorting into *ow like snow* and *ow like owl*

Pocket Chart

Favorite poem about snow cut up into words, a copy of the poem in an envelope for checking

Big Book

Collection of big books and a *Big Book Summary Form* (same as in library center)

Computer

Directions for how to get to a particular website for gathering information about acorns

Discovery

Directions for how to make a Halloween snack in the shape of a witch's hat, a digital camera for taking pictures of each step, including eating and enjoying the snack

list includes an example of one activity that might be placed in each of the centers. However, it is critical to keep in mind that all materials placed in literacy workstations are first used in small or whole-class activities to teach children concepts or strategies that they need. Workstations provide an important opportunity for children to practice and gain fluency in reading and writing activities introduced by the teacher.

Of particular importance in language- and literacy-rich classrooms are the spaces that house the library center, writing center, computer center, and preschool/kindergarten dramatic play centers. Research has demonstrated that if these centers are well designed, they are more likely to attract children, and children are more likely to stay on task for longer periods of time. That is, in addition to materials placed in these centers when they serve as literacy workstations, these centers have literacy materials for children to use during free-choice times.

Library Center

Children spend more time reading when their classrooms libraries are well designed and stocked with an abundance and variety of reading materials than when their classroom libraries are cramped and poorly stocked (Morrow, 1997; Morrow & Weinstein, 1986; Neuman, 1999). All classrooms need a well-designed and well-stocked library. There are seven requirements of well-designed library centers and four additional, optional characteristics. Well-designed classroom libraries:

- Are large enough for as many as six children and the teacher.
- Are partitioned off from the rest of the classroom with book shelves or other dividers.
- Have an abundance and variety of books (the number of books should at least be five times the number of children in the classroom).
- Have at least one book shelf on which book covers can be displayed facing outward.
- Have additional shelving for other books.
- Use a method of organization, such as using baskets or crates to separate books by theme or content, by level of difficulty, by author, or by whether the books are fiction or nonfiction.
- Have soft seating.
- May include storytelling props, such as cutout pictures of characters stapled on straws or small objects related to events in a particular book.
- May include a listening center with books, audiocassettes or CDs of the books, tape players or CD players, and headphones.
- May include a special basket for the "read aloud of the day."
- May include displays of books and related objects for children to play with as they look at those books. (Adapted from Fractor, Woodruff, Martinez, & Teale, 1993; Morrow & Weinstein, 1986.)

Writing Center

All classrooms need a well-designed writing center. This center serves as a place for children to practice writing strategies learned during instruction and to test out personal hypotheses (Rowe, 1994). Well-designed writing centers:

- Are spaces devoted only to writing, not, for example, serving also as an art center.
- Include a table and chairs that can accommodate comfortably up to four children and the teacher.
- Have ample storage space, for example, a shelf or a rolling cart, for writing tools and other materials such as clipboards.
- Include a variety of writing tools and writing surfaces and book-binding materials.
- Display models of the teacher's writing, such as, restaurant menus, thank you letters, or story compositions.
- Display children's writing.
- Have writing reference materials, such as charts showing alphabet letters, letter-sound association charts with pictures for each letter sound, word cards related to content areas of study, and picture dictionaries.

- May include picture cards to prompt writing ideas and to give directions for writing particular genres or for completing other activities teachers assign for the writing center.

Computer Centers

All classrooms need a computer center with one or more computers, a printer, and a scanner. Digital cameras may also be housed in this center. Even young children develop unique concepts related to the multiple ways in which literacy is used and created digitally (Labbo, 1996). The computer center also fosters children's social interactions as they learn from one another. Well-designed computer centers:

- Are placed in a central space to encourage movement to and from other centers.
- Are large enough for at least three children to work at a single computer.
- Have sufficient space around the computers so that children can bring stuffed animals or other props to use in computer play. For example, children might bring a stuffed character related to a CD-ROM book they are viewing.
- Display computer-generated work by the teacher and by children—for example, checks created for pretend shopping in a housekeeping play center or menus created for a restaurant dramatic play area.
- Have a *Helpful Hints* poster that explains computer operations with easily interpreted icons—for example, how to use the paint brush or pencil (adapted from Labbo & Ash, 1998) and how to download digital photographs.
- Use a variety of software programs, including a word-processing program, such as *Word* (produced by Microsoft), a graphics program such as *KidPix* (produced by Broderbund), CD-ROM books (e.g., *Arthur's Adventures with DW* produced by The Learning Company), and games (e.g., *Alphabet Express* produced by School Zone).

Preschool/Kindergarten Dramatic-Play-with-Print Centers

Dramatic play is a critical vehicle for young children's learning (Snow, Burns, & Griffin, 1998). Children take on new roles and try out using language in ways that are different from their everyday talk. They become police captains, superheroes, and fairy princesses. Teachers can support children's dramatic play at the same time as encouraging pretend reading and writing. Police captains write reports, superheroes read messages, and fairy princesses get invitations to balls.

Dramatic-play-with-print centers are specially planned dramatic play centers that encourage children to engage in themed play that offers potential for pretend reading and writing (Neuman & Roskos, 1997). Teachers can plan dramatic-play-with-print centers around themes and activities that are familiar to children and that have the potential for pretend reading and writing (Neuman & Roskos, 1997). For example, children are familiar with having their hair cut. From their experience visiting hair salons or barbershops, children are likely to have seen customers reading magazines in the waiting area and stylists writing bills and appointments. Therefore, teachers can easily capitalize on children's knowledge by setting up a hair salon-barbershop dramatic-play center enriched with literacy materials such as magazines, pads of paper, small cards, and a large appointment book. To arrange dramatic-play centers enriched with print, teachers

- Select play themes that are familiar to children and have literacy potential.
- Separate the center from the classroom with movable furniture, such as bookcases, screens, or tables.
- Label the center with a sign posted prominently at children's eye level.
- Select dramatic-play props related to play themes, for example, empty food boxes, a toy cash register, and plastic bags for a grocery store or plastic food, trays, and wrapping paper for a fast-food restaurant.
- Select literacy props related to play themes, for example, coupons and pads of paper for the grocery store and an appointment book, appointment cards, patient's chart, and prescription slips for the doctor's office.
- Arrange the materials within the space to suggest a realistic setting related to the play theme. (Neuman & Roskos, 1990)

Teachers sometimes play with children in dramatic-play-with-print centers and model new and more complex ways in which reading and writing can be used (Morrow & Rand, 1991). For example, a teacher in a hair-salon play center may comment, "I'll write you a card so that you can remember your next appointment," as she writes a child's name and date on a small card.

Teachers can make a variety of dramatic-play-with-print centers. Figure 6.3 describes dramatic-play-with-print props that can be used in a shopping mall, a drugstore, and a beauty and barbershop center. Reading books can support and expand children's play in such centers. For example, *Uncle Jed's Barbershop* (Mitchell, 1993) describes not only what happens in a barbershop, but also one man's sacrifice for his family. This book will provide children with many ideas for dramatic play beyond merely pretending to cut hair.

Children's play in dramatic-play-with-print centers is enhanced when teachers introduce children to the materials included in the center and model how to play with these materials. For example, Mrs. Miller carefully prepares her children for centers. On the day that she introduces a center, she uses whole-class time to orient the children to the center. They discuss what happens, for example, at McDonald's. She shows the children the dramatic-play-with-print props, and they discuss how the props might be used. Mrs. Miller and two or three children role-play with the center props. Several children have opportunities to play with Mrs. Miller. Later, while the children play in the center during center time, Mrs. Miller occasionally joins in. She realizes that children will think of many ingenious ways to use props in their dramatic play and that they should have plenty of opportunities to create their own unique imaginary worlds. However, she also knows that she can help expand the children's language and increase the complexity of their play by playing along with them (Neuman & Roskos, 1993).

Displays in Language- and Literacy-Rich Classrooms

Classroom displays are the materials placed on walls, shelves, or bulletin boards (Taylor, Blum, & Logsdon, 1986). Many displays result from shared and interactive writing

FIGURE 6.3   Dramatic-Play-with-Print Centers

	Dramatic Props	*Print Props*
Shopping Mall Center	1. standing racks for drying clothes 2. hangers and play clothes (hang on racks) 3. cash registers 4. hats, purses, wallets 5. play baby strollers 6. dolls	1. checkbooks and play money 2. signs, such as names of departments, and sale signs 3. sales slips 4. pads to write shopping lists 5. tags to make price tags 6. paper bags with store logos 7. credit cards 8. credit application forms
Drugstore Center	1. boxes for counters 2. cash register 3. empty bottles, boxes of various sizes for medicine 4. play shopping carts	1. magazines and books 2. checkbooks and play money 3. prescriptions 4. paper bags for prescriptions 5. labels for prescription bottles
Beauty and Barbershop Center	1. chairs 2. towels 3. play barber kit with non-cutting scissors, combs 4. telephone 5. hair clips, curlers 6. empty bottles of cologne	1. appointment book 2. checkbooks and play money 3. magazines for waiting area 4. bills

activities. With **shared writing,** the teacher writes on chart paper so that the children can see, and they contribute ideas for the content of the piece. **Interactive writing** is also on chart paper, but the children have a more active role. The teacher helps the children to determine what will be written and then selects children to step up to the chart and write words or parts of words. During shared and interactive writing, teachers model for children how to write texts that serve a variety of purposes. For example, teachers model using writing to keep records by writing a list of predictions that children make about an experiment mixing different colors of paint. Later, children return to the record of their predictions and compare them with the actual results of the experiment.

Directions for completing tasks play a prominent role in language- and literacy-rich classrooms. Teachers may prepare the directions before a lesson, or they can share direction writing with the children as part of the lesson. Directions, composed with print and pictures, are an important reading resource for children and help to keep them on task in workstations.

Interactive pocket chart activities and write-on charts are another kind of display. **Interactive pocket chart activities** are game-like activities placed in a pocket chart. In preschool, for example, teachers may display cards with alphabet letters for children to use in spelling their own names and names of classmates. In kindergarten, cards with pictures of objects may be displayed for sorting by the beginning sounds of the objects' names. In third grade, phrases that are subjects and predicates may be displayed for children to use to build sentences.

Write-on charts are shared or interactive writing charts that are hung low on a wall or placed on an easel for individual children to write on (McGee & Richgels, 2003). In preschool, for example, after composing on chart paper, in a shared writing activity, a graph showing children's favorite colors, the teacher may invite the children at center time to copy the names of their favorite colors by writing directly on the chart paper. Or a kindergarten teacher might use interactive writing to create a large birthday card to the principal and then invite children to sign their names on the card.

Displays should highlight the reading and writing accomplishments of all children, whatever their writing abilities. In preschool and kindergarten, some children use scribble writing and others copy words. In kindergarten and the primary grades, children write at different stages of spelling development. Teachers should change displays frequently in order to maintain children's motivation to write and to acknowledge continually developing writing behaviors. As teachers coordinate displays of shared writing, interactive pocket charts, and directions with changing science, social studies, art, music, and mathematics content, they keep the classroom environment fresh and interesting for their students.

MATERIALS

MATERIALS IN A LANGUAGE- AND LITERACY-RICH CLASSROOM are abundant, varied, authentic, accessible, and located near where they are most likely to be used (Roskos & Neuman, 2001). Children need enough books and other reading materials, writing tools and surfaces, and reference materials to meet their various developmental levels, interests, and instructional needs. Because children will not all be reading and writing at the same level, teachers need a variety of materials to meet these needs. In addition to textbooks, the primary purpose of which is instruction, children also need access to materials the primary purposes of which are other than for instruction. We call these **authentic materials** because, although they are used for instruction purposes in language- and literacy-rich classrooms, they also serve real-world purposes outside of school. These are books, such as reference books (dictionaries, thesauruses, encyclopedias), telephone books, catalogs, and children's information books and storybooks, and such other traditional reading materials as newspapers and magazines. Environmental print items, such as maps, calendars, video tapes, and DVDs, are also authentic materials.

Children should know where to locate materials and be responsible for returning them when finished. The most efficient storage places are near where children are likely to use the materials. Preschool children are more likely to write when pencils and markers are stored in the block center near catalogs of building supplies and clipboards with lumber orders than when pencils and markers are kept only in one central location. In primary grades, children need erasable markers in the overhead-projector workstation and crayons and pencils in the listening workstation.

Children's Literature

Research confirms that the amount of experience children have with literature correlates with their language development (Chomsky, 1972), reading achievement (Feitelson, Kita, & Goldstein, 1986), and quality of writing (Dressel, 1990). Children who are exposed to quality literature are more likely to learn to love literature and to include reading quality books as an important part of their lives (Hickman, 1979). They are more willing to sustain their involvement with a book through writing, doing projects, and participating in discussions (Eeds & Wells, 1989). Research has also shown that children whose classrooms have a large number of books in a high-quality library center choose to read more often (Morrow & Weinstein, 1982, 1986) and have higher reading achievement (Morrow, 1992).

The process of locating a sufficient number of quality books can be daunting. Experts recommend that the number of books in a high-quality classroom collection should be eight to ten times the number of children (Fractor, Woodruff, Martinez, & Teale, 1993). Teachers can borrow books from local and school libraries, use bonus points from book clubs to obtain free books, and collect inexpensive books from book clubs and bookstores that offer educational discounts.

The classroom literature collection should include books from a variety of genres. Figure 6.4 presents genres of literature, their defining characteristics, and an example book for each. Figure 6.4 also includes three special kinds of picture books: wordless picture books, predicable books, and alphabet books. These books are especially enjoyable for young children from preschool through the elementary grades. They play critical roles in teaching children comprehension strategies, phonemic awareness, letter-sound knowledge, and sight words (Bridge, 1986; Murray, Stahl, & Ivey, 1996). Also included in Figure 6.4 are various reference materials.

In addition to providing books from a wide variety of genres, teachers must make sure that children have access to texts of various difficulty levels. Each page in some books will have only one or two words or a simple sentence. Other books' pages will have several lines of text and be considered easy-reading books. Finally, some books will have text that is organized in paragraphs and uses sophisticated vocabulary.

Teachers will also need sets of **leveled books.** These are calibrated and labeled by level of difficulty, from very easy, beginning-level books to middle-school-level texts. Many commercial companies sell sets of storybooks and nonfiction books at identified levels (Fountas & Pinnell, 2005). These texts are usually used in reading instruction and for reading practice during workstation activities.

DVDs and videos also present valuable information to children. Teachers can collect videos of children's stories and information books or informational television programs. Finally, language- and literacy-rich classrooms are stocked with children's magazines. Many magazines extend children's interest in science and social studies and provide examples of published writing by children.

Materials for Writing

Writing materials are located throughout the classroom, in centers and workstations, in whole-class and small-group instruction areas, and especially in the writing center. Materials are abundant, varied, accessible, and fresh (new materials are added frequently

FIGURE 6.4   Genres of Literature Included in Literacy- and Language-Rich Classrooms

Type of Literature Definition	Example Books
Traditional Literature Tales once told by storytellers but now published in picture book or chapter book format	Zelinsky, P. (1986). *Rumpelstiltskin: From the German of the Brothers Grimm*. New York: Dutton.
Fables Traditional stories with animal characters and explicitly stated morals	Young, E. (1992). *Seven blind mice*. New York: Philomel.
Folktales Traditional stories with flat characters (good, bad, tricky) with happy endings	Pinkney, J. (2006). *The little red hen*. New York: Dial Press.
Myths and Legends Traditional stories that explain natural occurrences often including heroes or heroines with superhuman or magical abilities	Lindbergh, R. (1990). *Johnny Appleseed*. New York: Little, Brown and Company.
Fantasy Narratives that include elements that can never occur in the real world	Long, M. (2003). *How I became a pirate*. New York: Harcourt, Inc.
Realistic Fiction Narratives about things that could plausibly happen in the real world	Booth, D. (1997). *The dust bowl*. Tona wanda, NY: Kids Can Press.
Historical Fiction Realistic fiction set in the past	Hest, A. (1997). *When Jesse came across the sea*. Cambridge, MA: Candlewick Press.
Biography and Autobiography True stories about the lives of everyday or famous people	Giovanni, N. (2005). *Rosa*. New York: Henry Holt and Company.
Information Books Nonfiction that presents realistic, accurate, and authentic information	DK Eye Wonder. (2004). *Weather*. New York: DK Publishing.
Poetry Text with condensed language that may include special lining, imagery, and elements of rhythm and rhyme	Myers, W. (1993). *Brown Angels*. New York: HarperCollins.
Wordless Picture Books Books without texts in which the story is told or information conveyed only through illustrations	Wiesner, D. (1991). *Tuesday*. New York: Houghtin Mifflin.
Predicable Books Text with repeated dialogue or events or patterns of occurrences and text	Ho, M. (1996). *Hush! A Thai lullaby*. New York: Orchard.
Alphabet Books Books using the sequence of the alphabet to present information	Pallotta, J. (1986). *The Yucky reptile alphabet book*. Watertown, MA: Ivory Tower Press.
Reference Materials Dictionaries, atlases, and encyclopedias	Scholastic (2005). *Scholastic pocket dictionary*. New York: Scholastic.

FIGURE 6.5 Writing Materials

A variety of writing tools, including

  pencils and pens with interesting shapes or fancy toppers such as feathers or objects
  markers such as highlighters, smelly markers, markers that change colors, and fat and
    thin markers
  alphabet stamps, tiles, cookie cutters, sponge letters, magnetic letters, felt letters
  crayons, chalk, and mechanical pencils

A variety of writing surfaces, including

  clipboards, small white boards, chalkboards, and lined and unlined paper in a variety
    of shapes and colors
  a variety of writing pads, including sticky notes, spiral notebooks, to-do lists
  sand tray

A variety of bookbinding materials, including

  a digital camera to take photos for "all about the author" pages
  stapled books of four to eight pages
  construction paper and other materials for making book covers

A variety of reference materials, including

  a photo book of all the children with their first and last names
  special words on index cards (such as seasonal or theme vocabulary)
  pictionaries, dictionaries, visual dictionaries
  alphabet charts and letter-sound association charts

to keep children's interest high). Figure 6.5 presents a list of writing materials that might be found in language- and literacy-rich classrooms

DAILY SCHEDULE AND ROUTINE LITERACY ACTIVITIES

THE DAILY SCHEDULE in language- and literacy-rich classrooms includes extended times for reading and writing instruction in whole-class and small groups (Morris & Slavin, 2003). It also includes sufficient time for individual practice in workstations or centers. Routine reading and writing activities are embedded in the daily schedule to maximize learning time for all children. Many schools have adopted policies that children will have at least 90 minutes daily of uninterrupted time for reading instruction. During this block of time, no announcements are allowed, and no specials (physical education, art, music, library) are scheduled. Additional time is devoted to writing and to content studies that integrate reading and writing. In preschool, children have at least one hour of time in self-selected centers that offer opportunities for reading and writing.

Small-Group Literacy Instruction

One of the most important daily literacy routines is small-group instruction in literacy (Pinnell & Fountas, 1996). All children need daily small-group literacy instruction tailored to their levels of development. Children are grouped—and regrouped as the pace of their growth demands—with other children who are at similar points in their literacy development. All children will pass through novice reading and writing, experimenting reading and writing, early reading and writing, and transitional reading and writing before becoming self-generative readers and writers, and they learn much within each of these broad phases of literacy development. However, the pace of their progress through these phases is variable and unpredictable. Some children move quite quickly through a phase that others take much time in. Likewise a child may move quickly through one phase and then spend many months in the next phase.

In elementary school, small-group instruction often includes guided reading. **Guided reading** occurs when teachers select a particular text for children to read and then direct and support children as they read that text (Fountas & Pinnell, 1996; Schulman & Payne, 2000). The teacher provides an introduction to the text and then directs children to read on their own. As they do so, the teacher observes the group but also focuses on individual children in order to coach them when they encounter difficulty. After all the children finish reading the text, the teacher asks questions to help them more fully comprehend what they have read. Or teachers may guide children's reexamination of the text, for example, to locate a main idea and its supporting details. A few children may read selected portions aloud to the other children. After or before guided reading, the teacher may teach a targeted lesson on using a particular decoding or comprehension strategy or on a particular spelling pattern found in some words in the text.

The goal of guided reading is to maximize the volume of children's engaged reading of text (Allington, 2005). Engagement in reading is readers' active seeking of meaning from text using their most sophisticated strategies. It occurs with a moderately challenging text under the guidance of a teacher who has carefully prepared children to read that particular text. New learning occurs as readers consciously attempt to use new strategies in the context of a new text.

Whole-Class Literacy Routines

While small-group instruction is designed to match instruction with children's literacy development, whole-class instruction is more open-ended so that all children can participate at their own levels. At least five instructional activities occur routinely during whole-class instruction in language- and literacy-rich classrooms. These are reading aloud, shared reading, modeled writing, shared and interactive writing, and letter-sound-word workshop. While teachers in preschool through the primary grades use these literacy routines, they are used in different ways with different-aged students. Here we present overviews of the activities, which we also discuss in greater detail in Chapters 7 through 10. Of course, these literacy routines may also be used effectively in small-group instruction.

Reading Aloud. Reading aloud daily to children accelerates their literacy development (Reese & Cox, 1999; Wasik & Bond, 2001). Children are more motivated to read on their own and have better vocabularies and comprehension when they are in classrooms where teachers frequently read aloud, modeling good comprehension strategies and drawing attention to sophisticated vocabulary (Dickinson, 2001). The most effective read alouds are those that prompt children to engage in analytic talk (Dickinson & Smith, 1994; Sipe, 2002). **Analytic talk** is going beyond the literal meaning presented in the text or illustrations; children infer character traits and motivations, infer problems, connect events across parts of a book, infer cause-and-effect relationships, and construct explanations for why characters act as they do. Children can engage in analytic talk during read alouds or after the entire book is read.

Six characteristics of effective read alouds maximize children's analytic talk:

- Before reading, teachers provide short introductions that either identify a storybook's main character and hint about the problem that character will encounter or introduce an information book's topic and organizational scheme. These introductions allow children to call to mind prior knowledge related to the book they will listen to.
- As they read, teachers make comments that model analytic thinking.
- During reading, teachers ask a few questions that help children to recall what has happened so far and then to think analytically. These questions promote discussion that includes analytic talk.
- During reading, teachers highlight the meaning of a few sophisticated vocabulary words by slipping in short defining phrases. These definitions help children comprehend the story more fully.
- After reading, teachers lead their students in a brief recall of the main events in a story or the main ideas in informational text and then ask one question that requires analytic thinking. This question again promotes analytic talk by requiring children to explain events and to connect characters' motivations to their actions.
- Teachers read some books at least three times. As a book becomes more familiar, even shy children are more willing to make comments, and other children notice details they missed during a first read. (Adapted from McGee & Schickedanz, in press).

Teachers can also tell stories and help children to dramatize and tell stories using storytelling props (McGee, 2003).

Frequently, teachers tell stories using special storytelling props (McGee, 2003; Ross, 1980). Among the many kinds of literature props that teachers can use to tell a story are objects, clothesline props, flannel board props, puppets, and masks. *Object props* are objects that represent certain characters and actions. Object props for the story *Where the Wild Things Are* (Sendak, 1963) might include a teddy bear (to represent Max sent to bed with no supper), an oar (to represent his travels to the land where the Wild Things Are), and a crown (to represent Max's becoming King of the Wild Things).

Clothesline props include pictures drawn to represent important events in the story. These pictures are clothespinned to a clothesline stretched across the classroom as a story is read or told. *Stick puppets* can be made by coloring characters on stiff paper, cutting them out, and attaching them to soda straws. *Flannel board props* can be made from Velcro, felt, yarn, lace, or other sewing notions.

Children have many creative ideas for constructing their own story-retelling props. First graders used a green pipe-cleaner for a caterpillar and punched holes in construction paper food cutouts to retell *The Very Hungry Caterpillar* (Carle, 1979). As they retold the story, they slipped each food cutout onto the green pipe-cleaner caterpillar. Third graders worked together to decide the number and content of pictures needed to retell *Nine-in-One. Grr! Grr!* (Xiong, 1989) on a story clothesline. They retold the story collaboratively—each illustrator hung his or her picture on the clothesline and retold that portion of the story.

It is important that teachers select information books for reading aloud to children (Richgels, 2002). Many teachers do not choose information books, and they are not as plentiful in most classrooms (Duke, 2000). However, many children prefer information books over storybooks (Duke & Kays, 1998), and discussions of information books can be especially lively and thought provoking (Smolkin & Donovan, 2002).

Shared Reading.

Shared reading is a form of reading aloud to children with a dual focus. In addition to reading a good book for enjoyment and understanding, the teacher and children can read for teaching and learning literacy concepts and strategies (Parkes, 2000). This process is called shared reading because the text is large enough so that the children can read the text along with the teacher. Teachers read from **big books,** which are large, display versions of published children's books or from texts written on chart paper or projected onto a screen. Shared reading is especially beneficial for developing children's concepts about print (Clay, 1979). To teach concepts about print during shared reading, teachers point to the text as they read. Later, and more importantly, children attempt to point to print as they remember language patterns found in the text (Clay, 1993). Recall that pointing to print while saying a memorized text is called fingerpoint reading.

Books, poems, and texts used in shared reading in preschool and kindergarten are usually very easy to understand and frequently use repetition. Children naturally catch on to the repeated language and spontaneously begin reading along with teachers. These texts are especially popular; children are attentive and engaged when teachers read big books, pocket-chart displays, or poems on chart paper.

As teachers read from the enlarged print of a big book or a chart paper text during shared reading, they teach concepts about print or reading strategies that they have chosen based both on what their students already know and what they are prepared to learn. A teacher who focuses, for example, on book orientation concepts will demonstrate how to open a book to the title page and then to locate the first page of the story. He or she will teach directionality concepts by pointing and saying, for example, "Let me point out exactly where I am going to start reading. Put your eyes right up here. Now I am going to read across the line like this." In order for this instruction to be effective, the printed words and word spaces must be large enough for children to see easily.

For older children, teachers may share a portion of a longer, more complex text, using an overhead projector. They might help children to make inferences about character motivation and character traits by stopping and asking, "What do you think this character is thinking right now? What gives us a clue?"

Modeled Writing, Shared Writing, and Interactive Writing.

Modeled writing occurs when teachers compose a text as children watch. The teacher first thinks aloud about what he or she might write, then talks through the composition process. The teacher then thinks aloud while rereading and revising the text. Thus, modeled writing demonstrates for children the processes writers use before, during, and after writing. Teachers also use modeled writing to introduce children to the characteristics of text genres. For example, they might demonstrate writing a shape poem, that is, a poem whose shape is a critical feature, for example, a poem about birds whose words are arranged in the shape of a bird. Teachers first use shared reading to present an example of a shape poem. Then they talk about the special way the poet has placed words on a page to create a shape. Then they begin thinking aloud about a topic for an original shape poem, how to express the desired ideas, and, where on a piece of chart paper to start writing and continue writing in order for the printed words to make the desired outline, for example, a leaf-shaped poem about leaves.

Shared writing occurs when the teacher invites children to contribute to the ideas to be written. For example, after reading many versions of *Henny Penny*, a group of children compose their own version. The teacher asks children to contribute their ideas for the text as the teacher writes. Later, this text can be reread and revised, and finally typed so each child can make an illustration for it. The children's work can be bound as a book for the classroom library. Shared writing teaches concepts about print, reinforces alphabet knowledge and letter-sound knowledge, and demonstrates composing in various genres.

Interactive writing occurs when the teacher goes beyond shared writing by inviting children not only to contribute ideas, but also to take the pen or marker and form letters, words, phrases, or sentences. Interactive writing provides practice deciding which words to use while composing, applying letter-sound knowledge, and using spelling patterns.

Letter–Sound–Word Workshop. Preschoolers receive instruction in recognizing the alphabet and developing phonemic awareness. Kindergarten and primary grade students receive daily instruction that focuses on decoding and spelling words. All these activities occur during small-group instruction targeted at specific needs of children. However, teachers can also provide a daily letter-sound-word workshop as part of whole-class instruction (Cunningham, 2004). This is the setting for quick, game-like activities that reinforce and provide daily practice in basic concepts. For example, in preschool children might play the Mystery Letter game with their teacher (Schickedanz, 1998; 2003). The teacher writes the first stroke of a particular alphabet letter, such as the vertical line used to write the capital letter L. The children take turns guessing which letter it could be until someone guesses the correct letter. In kindergarten, the teacher might use magnetic letters to spell a familiar rhyming word on a magnetic board. Children are invited to step up to the board and select letters to spell a new word. In second grade, children might be asked to step up to an overhead projector that displays words with the letters *ea*, some with a short *e* sound (e.g., *instead*) and some with a long *e* sound (e.g., *team*); they are asked to circle the long *e* words. Chapters 7 through 10 will provide more detailed examples of activities for letter-sound-word workshop.

Independent Practice

A critical goal of scheduling is to provide daily time for each child to have extended practice reading and writing (Allington, 2005). The materials placed in centers and workstations are not merely to keep children busy so that the teacher can meet with small groups for instruction. Rather, they are carefully considered to provide children with extensive opportunities to consolidate strategies and skills and to develop fluency. Independent practice is for exercising concepts, skills, and strategies already taught in instruction; for reading texts previously used in instruction and writing texts previously modeled during instruction; and for reading self-selected books and engaging in self-selected writing. Effective practice activities blend the exercise of what students have been taught with trying out new texts.

Daily routines should include much time for students' independent practice in order to maximize the volume of their reading and writing (Allington, 2005). **Volume of reading and writing** can be determined either by the amount of text read or written in a day or by the number of minutes in a day spent reading and writing continuous texts (not working with words, filling in work sheets, or answering questions). In elementary school, good readers spend more than an hour reading at home daily. Poor readers spend less than 10 minutes a day reading at home and probably no more than that amount in school (Taylor, Frye, & Maruyama, 1990). It is clear that teachers can contribute to children's developing reading and writing prowess by ensuring that they read and write daily in school for extended periods of time.

CONTINUOUS ASSESSMENT TO INFORM INSTRUCTION

ASSESSMENT INCLUDES ALL THE ACTIVITIES that a teacher does in order to determine what an individual child knows. Assessments can be informal, as when a teacher observes a child completing a task to determine what the child knows and can do, or when a teacher develops and assigns a task (such as having children attempt to spell a few words) and then analyzes children's performance of that task. Or assessments can be formal, as when teachers administer standardized tests. In Chapters 2 through 5, we described several assessments that are appropriate for tracking children's progress in literacy development.

It is critical that teachers assess children frequently throughout the school year. Routine assessment allows teachers to identify children who need to be regrouped for instruction, either because they have accelerated into the next phase of development or because they are not responding to current instruction. Such assessments can monitor children's progress and identify children who may need more intensive teaching; thus they are called **monitoring assessments.** We recommend that teachers perform initial, **screening assessments** at the beginning of the year and then monitoring assessments three or four times during the remainder of the school year. Continuously and routinely assessing children bridges the gap between the specific concepts that an individual child currently uses in reading and writing and instruction that is aimed at enhancing that child's current level of knowledge. In order to know what to teach next, teachers carefully watch what children do as they are reading and writing. **Kid watching** involves informal observation of children as they are using reading and writing in play, reading or writing independently, or working in a cooperative group to accomplish an assigned task (Goodman, 1978).

Good assessment cannot be separated from teaching. While teachers are teaching, they are also assessing. Research confirms that children's literacy learning is enhanced when teachers draw from informed observation during teaching to provide feedback on children's reading and writing (DeFord, Pinnell, Lyons, & Place, 1990) and to plan instruction (McCormick, 1994). A critical component of assessment is determining not just what kind of feedback and instruction individual children need, but also how to deliver instruction and provide opportunities for practice.

CULTURALLY SENSITIVE AND INTEGRATED CURRICULUM

CURRICULUM IS WHAT CHILDREN LEARN related to the disciplines of language arts and literature, social studies, science, mathematics, art, music, health, and physical education. Recent research and theory regarding the literacy curriculum (language arts and literature, which includes reading, writing, and spelling) suggest that children learn better when the curriculum is integrated across the language arts and across disciplines and when it is culturally sensitive.

The Case for Culturally Sensitive and Integrated Curriculum

All children belong to cultural groups that in some way shape their attitudes, beliefs, and ways of making meaning with written language (Heath, 1983). When children perceive of a writing task or a text as having content that reaffirms their cultural identities, they are more likely to become engaged in the task and to construct personal meaning (Meier, 2000). Culturally relevant topics, topics that children perceive as culturally affirming, are an important avenue to learning and literacy development (Au, 2000).

Curriculum integration—teaching broad topics that cover areas in more than one discipline—improves teaching and learning (Dewey, 1933; Vars, 1991). One way of integrating the curriculum is to capitalize on the "interrelationships of the language processes—reading, writing, speaking, and listening" (Routman, 1991, p. 272). An **integrated language arts activity** is one in which children talk, listen, read, and write. For example, writing a poem often includes talking to others about possible topics for writing, listening to others as they talk about topics or read their poems, and reading one's own composition.

Recent recommendations for curriculum development strongly support curriculum integration across content topics (Hughes, 1991). Children learn concepts and ideas related to a topic that cuts across more than one content area, for example, incorporating earth science, geography, and math. This kind of instruction allows children to see connections among facts and theories, provides a focus for selecting instructional activities, provides for coherence of activities, allows children to study topics in depth, and promotes positive attitudes (Lipson, Valencia, Wixson, & Peters, 1993).

Culturally Sensitive Curriculum

The curriculum in literacy-rich classrooms reflects sensitivity for children's cultures in both its content (what is taught and what children are expected to read and write) and its instruction (how concepts are taught). In most classrooms, one or more students have recently arrived in the United States and speak a language other than English at home. Many classrooms include children from a variety of cultural and language backgrounds. Regardless of the mixture of children in a particular classroom, all children need exposure to literature that presents nonstereotyped information about a wide variety of cultural groups.

A culturally sensitive curriculum eliminates the artificial dichotomies created when studying "other" cultures; it includes examples from many cultures as a part of all learning experiences. That is, the content that children study and the material they read naturally present many different cultures. Teachers are careful to include many examples of multicultural literature in all their literature theme units and content units. **Multicultural literature** consists of

> fiction with characters who are from cultural groups that have been underrepresented in children's books: African Americans, Asian Americans, Hispanic Americans, Native Americans, and Americans from religious minorities;

> fiction that takes us to other nations and introduces readers to the cultures of people residing outside of the United States; and

> information books, including biographies, that focus on African Americans, Asian Americans, Hispanic Americans, Native Americans, Americans from religious minorities, and people living outside the United States. (Zarrillo, 1994, pp. 2–3)

The best in multicultural literature presents culturally authentic information (Bishop, 1992). **Culturally authentic literature** portrays people and the values, customs, and beliefs of a cultural group in ways recognized by members of that group as valid and authentic. Most culturally authentic literature is written or illustrated by members of the cultural group. Appendix A provides a list of multicultural literature including culturally authentic literature.

An important part of a culturally sensitive curriculum is consideration of the language of instruction. Children learn best in their home language. However, many teachers are unable to provide instruction in children's home languages. They may not be qualified speakers of the language, or there may be children with several different home languages in one classroom. Teachers should always be sensitive to children's natural tendency to use home language to communicate complex ideas. Chapter 11 provides more information about teaching children whose home language is not English.

Literature Theme Units

Teachers can integrate activities across the language arts by using literature themes as a focus for curriculum development. **Literature theme units** are units of instruction focused on learning about authors or illustrators, genres, themes, or a single book.

As a part of literature theme units, children engage in activities that include talking, listening, reading, and writing. For example, in a kindergarten literature theme unit comparing versions of "The Gingerbread Boy" story (Tompkins & McGee, 1993), the teacher could read five versions of the story aloud to the class, including

> Arno, E. (1985). *The Gingerbread Man*. New York: Scholastic (this book is also available in big book format).

Brown, M. (1972). *The Bun: A Tale from Russia.* New York: Harcourt Brace Jovanovich.

Cauley, L. (1988). *The Pancake Boy.* New York: Putnam.

Galdone, P. (1975). *The Gingerbread Boy.* New York: Seabury.

Sawyer, R. (1953). *Journey Cake, Ho!* New York: Viking.

Figure 6.6 presents a web of talking, listening, reading, and writing activities that could be included in this literature theme unit.

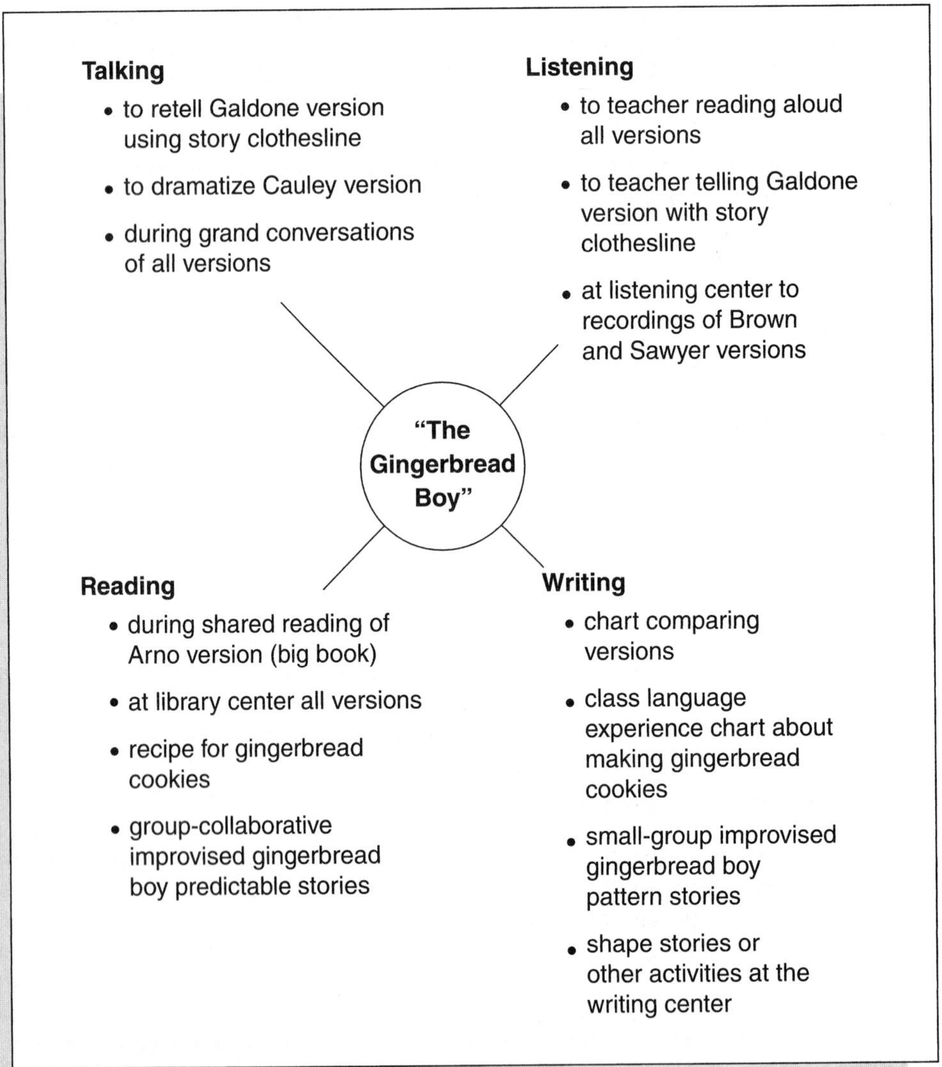

Talking
- to retell Galdone version using story clothesline
- to dramatize Cauley version
- during grand conversations of all versions

Listening
- to teacher reading aloud all versions
- to teacher telling Galdone version with story clothesline
- at listening center to recordings of Brown and Sawyer versions

"The Gingerbread Boy"

Reading
- during shared reading of Arno version (big book)
- at library center all versions
- recipe for gingerbread cookies
- group-collaborative improvised gingerbread boy predictable stories

Writing
- chart comparing versions
- class language experience chart about making gingerbread cookies
- small-group improvised gingerbread boy pattern stories
- shape stories or other activities at the writing center

FIGURE 6.6   Integrated Language Arts Activities for "The Gingerbread Boy" Literature Theme

Integrated Content Units

Integrated content units use themes to plan instruction. Units of instruction are organized around a broad theme that includes learning concepts across more than one content area, active inquiry activities, and activities incorporating all the language arts.

For example, a teacher may use the theme of "growing" as a focus for learning experiences for a group of first graders. This theme explores physical changes that occur as a part of growth in plants, animals, and humans; measurement; and the literary theme "growing up." As a part of the activities included in the theme, the teacher may read aloud folktales in which plants grow to enormous sizes (such as *The Enormous Turnip,* retold by Kathy Parkinson, 1986), stories that contrast children at different ages (such as *Stevie,* by John Steptoe, 1969), poems about childhood activities at different ages (*I Want to Be,* by Thylias Moss, 1993), and information books about growing up (such as *Pueblo Boy: Growing Up in Two Worlds,* by Marcia Keegan, 1991). The teacher may guide the children in dramatizing the stories, and children may create storytelling props to use in retelling the folktales.

The teacher may also read information books about the growth of plants and animals (such as *How a Seed Grows,* by Helen Jordan, 1992, and several books from the *See How They Grow* series published by Dorling Kindersley, 1992, including *See How They Grow: Butterfly, See How They Grow: Frog,* and *See How They Grow: Mouse*).

GROUPING

CHILDREN LEARN IN WHOLE-CLASS GROUPS, small groups, partner groups, cooperative groups, and as individuals (Dickinson & Sprague, 2001; Hiebert & Colt, 1989). Whole-class groups foster a sense of community; small groups provide more mature language interactions, and independent work allows children to learn at their own pace while engaged in personal pursuits (Berghoff & Egawa, 1991). Because children will be grouped for reading instruction according to their level of literacy development, it is important that they be included in other kinds of small groups at other times during the day. For example, they may be grouped with others at a variety of reading and writing levels to complete a science experiment, to conduct inquiry as part of a social studies project, or to complete an art activity.

Because of the importance of small-group literacy instruction that is carefully tailored to meet the needs of children, we wish to discuss historic and current conceptions of levels of reading. Historically, reading level was believed to be related to ability: the higher a child's ability, the higher his or her reading level. Ability was thought to be an inherent trait—something children were born with, but which might be influenced by experience. So children considered to have high reading ability were placed in high reading groups, and children considered to have low reading ability were placed in low reading groups.

The type of reading instruction children received and its pace were determined by their reading group placements and by teachers' perceptions of children's abilities. In kindergarten and first grade, children in the high-ability group were provided conventional reading instruction, and the pace of instruction was fast. Children in the low-ability group received a great amount of reading readiness training, and instruction in conventional reading was considerably delayed. Once it began, it moved at a slow pace. Therefore, it is not surprising that children who started elementary school in the low group remained there (Juel, 1988).

Our current thinking about reading level has changed drastically. We know that most—though not all—children who have had many rich early home and community experiences with reading and writing have higher reading and writing achievement scores at the time of school entry than children who have relatively few literacy experiences. Instead of attributing experience-rich children's high achievement to high inherent ability, we now recognize it as a product of their experiences. They simply have had many opportunities to learn. The advantage enjoyed by many middle-class children often reflects an opportunity gap compared to their less experienced classmates, not an ability gap. However, this advantage, associated with early and intensive literacy experiences, is not necessarily an emblem of socioeconomic class or ethnicity. Children from low-income families and from diverse cultural backgrounds who have had high levels of literacy support in the home or in preschool have, as a result, the same literacy learning opportunities as most middle-class children. There is no opportunity gap for them, and so they are able to display levels of reading and writing knowledge at school entry as high as those of most of their middle-class classmates (Barone, 1999; Taylor & Dorsey-Gaines, 1988).

From this perspective, all children, though at different ages, need instruction aimed at helping them to move from current to more developed understandings of and abilities with reading and writing. Some children in a given age cohort, for example, require instructional support to move from novice reading and writing to experimenting reading and writing, while others in that age cohort need support to progress from the experimenting phase to the early reading and writing phase. Though instruction must always be tailored to the interests, prior knowledge, and learning styles of individual learners, there will be basic similarities in all children's instruction at any phase of reading and writing. For example, teachers will not slow the pace of instruction nor change the basic literacy content (e.g., the concepts about meaning making, forms, meaning-form links, and functions of reading and writing listed at the ends of Chapters 2 through 5) for children merely because they are making a transition from one phase to another later in the school year than some of their classmates.

DEVELOPMENTALLY APPROPRIATE INSTRUCTION

THIS BOOK DESCRIBES the literacy development of and appropriate instructional practices for children from preschool through grade four, the period often called the early childhood years. Professional organizations concerned with education during those years have taken an active role in defining *appropriate practices.* In a joint position statement, the National Association for the Education of Young Children (NAEYC) and the International Reading Association (IRA) (1998) define appropriate instruction from a developmental perspective (see http://www.reading.org/resources/issues/positions_appropriate.html). During the early childhood years, children experience significant development emotionally, physically, socially, cognitively, and linguistically. Developmentally appropriate practices in literacy instruction take into account interactions among those areas of development, including the ways that literacy development is influenced by linguistic, cognitive, emotional, and social development (Cunningham & Stanovich, 1997). Only recently, for example, have we begun to appreciate how critical children's emotions are to their engagement in cognitive activities and how children's literacy learning in school is influenced by the social and cultural knowledge they acquire in their homes and communities (Dyson, 2006).

The NAEYC/IRA (1998) statement presents a continuum of goals for young children's literacy development. The statement indicates that our goals for individual children must be challenging, but achievable with the support of well-qualified teachers. In order to set such goals, teachers must know what to expect in children's literacy acquisition; that is, they must understand the continuum of development in language and literacy. In this book, we characterize that development in terms of literacy beginners, literacy novices, experimenting readers and writers, and conventional readers and writers; we have presented milestones of those phases of development at the ends of Chapters 2 through 5 (see Figures 2.9, 3.13, 4.13, and 5.10).

The NAEYC/IRA statement about developmentally appropriate instruction also indicates that children will follow their own unique paths to reach conventional literacy. Children have individual patterns of development, grow up in different home and community environments, and have different educational experiences. Therefore, a wide range of individual variation in literacy learning is expected each year in preschool and through the elementary grades. In order to meet the needs of individual children, teachers must be able to assess each child's progress toward conventional reading and writing. We have described some simple assessment procedures at the ends of Chapters 2 through 5 in order to help teachers evaluate each child's progress on the language and literacy continuum.

Teachers have three critical roles in helping children achieve challenging goals. They must be knowledgeable about the continuum of language and literacy development, able to assess individual children and determine their placement on that continuum, and able to formulate goals and plan instruction that will help children reach those goals. Effective teachers carefully consider all methods of instruction in order to select those most likely to reach a particular child at a particular point in his or her literacy development.

One way to view instructional methods is in terms of directness; methods range from indirect to direct. With **indirect instruction,** teachers provide materials, but children learn from doing and from watching others. Indirect teaching methods easily meet children's individual needs; each child interacts with materials at his or her own level of development and at his or her own pace. Indirect instruction is considered child-centered because activities are planned to allow children to respond in their own ways, with multiple acceptable responses. For example, teachers may place writing materials in a writing center, and children in kindergarten might copy, write a string of random letters to which they tell a story, attempt to use invented spellings, or merely draw a picture. Indirect methods of teaching do not mean that teachers ignore children. Rather they require that teachers interact with individual children as they participate in planned activities. Teachers let children take the lead (for example, teachers say, "Tell me about your writing"), but they provide children with feedback and support when invited. These interactions provide teachers with opportunities to see how children put information gained through instruction into independent action. Teachers may want to use these activities in order to collect samples of children's work and take anecdotal notes.

Other methods of instruction are more direct and more teacher-directed. With **direct instruction,** teachers more directly determine outcomes—that is, what children show they know and can do by participating in a planned activity. Teachers model how to perform tasks and talk aloud as they perform tasks in order to provide explanations of their mental activities. Such specifying of learning outcomes, modeling of processes, thinking aloud, and explaining are also characteristics of **explicit instruction.** Explicit instruction is usually part of an instructional sequence called **gradual release of responsibility** (Pearson & Gallager, 1983).

Gradual release of responsibility begins with explicit teaching of a single concept or strategy, one that can be expressed in the performance of a discrete task. (Of course, not all literacy work is expressible in this way, and so not all literacy teaching and learning are amenable to this method.) For example, awareness of the concept we call the phoneme /b/ can be expressed in the performance of a phoneme segmentation task (saying a word such as *bug* and then saying only its initial /b/). Similarly, mastery of the comprehension strategy of activating prior knowledge of an essay's topic can be expressed in the performance of a think-aloud task (saying, "I see from the title and the photographs that this essay is about elephants. What do I know about elephants? I know they are very large animals, that they have tusks and trunks. And I think they are vegetarians.").

First, teachers provide explicit instruction about the target literacy concept or strategy. This includes a demonstration of the task that expresses knowledge of that concept or mastery of that strategy, with accompanying think-alouds and explanations. Then teachers release some responsibility for performing that task. They might repeat their demonstration of the task, but with pauses for asking children to recall next steps or to participate in the demonstration. Next, teachers reduce their responsibility further, by having one child demonstrate while other children help by providing some of the thinking aloud and explaining. Now, the teacher's role is to provide feedback about the accuracy or effectiveness of the children's demonstrations, think-alouds, and explanations. After several children have demonstrated, the teacher may pair children up or assign small groups. Children in the pairs or small groups perform the task together, helping each other as the teacher circulates to give feedback. Only after all of these steps (sometimes called *I do it, We all do it,* and *You all do it*) are children asked to perform the task independently. Now the entire responsibility for knowing a concept or strategy and being able to express it in performance of a relevant task is the child's.

Direct instruction, explicit teaching, and gradual release of responsibility can meet the needs of individual children. Instruction is developmentally appropriate when it is based on teachers' having assessed children and determined that they have the necessary background experiences and concepts to learn a new strategy or concept. This can be the case even for whole-class groups, especially when teachers take a playful stance and provide positive feedback to children. However, providing explicit instruction to whole-class groups of children all the time without regard to individual children's levels of achievement is never developmentally appropriate.

Instruction that includes elements of both direct and indirect teaching is called embedded instruction. **Embedded instruction** occurs when teachers provide a meaningful reading and writing experience for a whole class or small group of children and embed opportunities within that experience for individual children to participate at levels appropriate to their unique needs and phases of development. For example, teachers might prepare a shared writing activity for a whole class after reading aloud several information books about birds. All children can contribute ideas for the final composition. In interactive writing, teachers may ask one child to come up and write the beginning letter of a word and another child to spell an entire word. All children can benefit from read-alouds and can provide input in discussions.

Language- and literacy-rich classrooms are the venue for all three types of instruction: embedded, direct, and indirect. Embedded instruction not only allows individual children to interact with reading and writing at their own levels, but also involves children in whole acts of reading or writing: the setting of purposes, the creation of or interacting with forms, and the construction of meaning. Activities that provide embedded instruction benefit all children, but especially those whose homes and communities seldom provide school-like literacy activities. However, all children also must receive direct, explicit instruction in specific literacy skills and strategies that assessment shows they lack but are prepared to learn. Finally, all children need opportunities to put into practice what they have learned in embedded and direct instruction. This they do with indirect instructional activities. Teachers must find the balance of embedded, direct, and indirect instructional methods that will best meet the needs of their students.

CHAPTER SUMMARY

EARLY CHILDHOOD PROFESSIONAL ORGANIZATIONS stress the importance of all aspects of children's development. Children's literacy learning should be embedded within child-centered early-childhood programs with developmentally appropriate practices. Exemplary early-childhood programs are found in language- and literacy-rich classrooms where children are reflective, motivated readers and writers who use literacy to learn about their world.

To create language- and literacy-rich classrooms, teachers select quality classroom literature collections that include traditional literature, fantasy, realistic fiction, historical fiction, biography, information books, poetry, wordless picture books, predictable books, and alphabet books. They select reference materials, audiovisual materials, children's magazines, and writing materials.

Teachers infuse reading and writing materials throughout the room to encourage functional use of literacy. They set up a classroom library center, a writing center, and a computer center.

Teachers establish daily routines using reading and writing. Teachers read or tell stories, poems, or information books daily; they set aside time for children to read and write independently; and they plan small-group activities.

The curriculum is organized around literature content units that include talking, listening, reading, and writing activities. All units include multicultural literature.

Teachers provide instruction in a variety of settings as they demonstrate reading and writing, guide interactive discussions, and provide direct teaching through modeling. They form a variety of groups, including whole-class gatherings, small groups, and pairs, and they set aside time for children to work alone. Teachers assess children's literacy learning and use results of assessment to guide instruction.

USING THE INFORMATION

Use the information presented in this chapter to make a classroom environment checklist. For example, such a checklist might include the following:

LITERACY ENVIRONMENT CHECKLIST

Physical Layout of Classroom

_____ sectioned into centers
_____ carpeted whole-class area large enough for all children
_____ small-group instructional area
_____ easel for chart paper
_____ pocket chart
_____

Library Center

_____ includes number of books equal to 5 times the number of children
_____

Writing Center

_____

Computer Center

_____

APPLYING THE INFORMATION

A description of Mrs. E's kindergarten classroom and literacy activities follows. Use the seven characteristics of a literacy-rich classroom to think about the literacy environment in Mrs. E's classroom. Discuss how Mrs. E's classroom illustrates each of the seven characteristics. What suggestions might you make about room arrangement and instruction?

Mrs. E has twenty-two kindergartners in a relatively small room. Nearly all of the children who attend this school receive free lunch (their families fall below the poverty limit established by the federal government). A map of the classroom is presented in Figure 6.7. This map illustrates that Mrs. E's room is equipped with twenty-four desks and two tables. The entire room is carpeted.

Each morning Mrs. E reads at least one selection of children's literature to the entire class. The children gather around her on the rug in the large-group area. Next, Mrs. E has experience time. During this time, she might demonstrate a science experiment, have a guest speaker, or read nonfiction. Each of these daily experiences is related to a topic of study. For example, one unit of study focused on insects. A man who keeps bees visited the classroom and brought his equipment to the class. The children kept ants in an ant farm. Mrs. E read many books that had insects as characters as well as informational books about insects.

After experience time, Mrs. E usually leads children in a shared writing activity about what they learned that day or a retelling of a favorite story. Sometimes she prepares her own accounts of the previous day's experience for shared reading.

Next, Mrs. E holds a five- to ten-minute lesson or discussion designed to motivate the children to write. During the insect unit, children were encouraged to write poems, stories, and predictable stories about insects. In one lesson, Mrs. E showed the children a poster she had made about the letters *b* and *c*. On the poster were several pictures of objects with names beginning with these letters (*boat, bat, beaver, cat, candy, cookie*). Mrs. E reminded the children that as they listened to words they wanted to write, they might hear some sounds like those in the words *boat* or *cat*. They could use the letters *b* and *c*.

After the lesson, the children write at their desks. Mrs. E circulates around the room, asking questions, making comments, and answering children's questions. As the children finish their writing, they read their writing to each other, select books from the library center, or read child-authored poems, stories, and books that are kept on the authors' tables.

Last, Mrs. E holds "author's chair." (A special chair is placed in the group area on the rug for a child to sit in as he or she reads his or her writing.) Many children have opportunities to read their writing. The children know that they may choose to "talk about their writing" or "read what they wrote." They feel very comfortable as the other children make comments and offer praise. Mrs. E always comments on some aspect of the content of the writing, "I didn't know there were ants called carpenters. We will need to read more about them. Will you help me find out about them?"

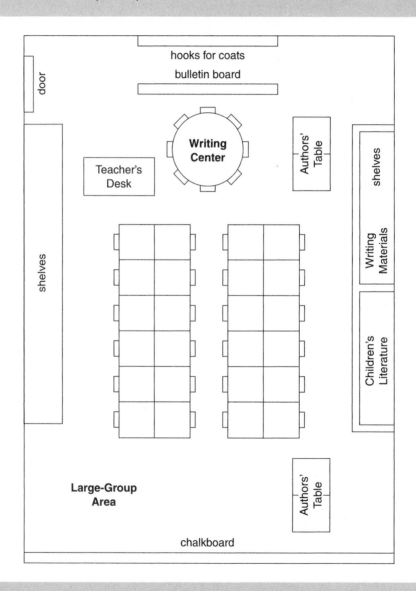

FIGURE 6.7   Mrs. E's Classroom

GOING BEYOND THE TEXT

V ISIT A PRESCHOOL OR ELEMENTARY SCHOOL CLASSROOM and observe literacy instruction and activities. Look carefully at the literacy materials that are available in the room. Note how often children interact with these literacy materials. Observe the children and their teacher as they interact during literacy instruction and as the children work on literacy projects. Use the Literacy Environment Checklist you made to guide your observations.

 # REFERENCES

Adams, M. (1990). *Beginning to read: Thinking and learning about print.* Cambridge: MIT Press.

Allington, R. (1983). The reading instruction provided readers of differing ability. *Elementary School Journal, 83,* 255–265.

Allington, R. (2005). *What really matters for struggling readers: Designing research-based programs* (2nd ed.). Boston: Allyn & Bacon.

Au, K. H. (2000). Multicultural factors and the effective instruction of students of diverse backgrounds. In A. E. Farstrup & S. J. Samuels (Eds.), *What research has to say about reading instruction* (3rd ed.) (pp. 392–413). Newark, DE: International Reading Association.

Barone, D. (1999). *Resilient children: Stories of poverty, drug exposure, and literacy development.* Newark, DE: International Reading Association.

Barr, R., & Dreeben, R. (1991). Grouping students for reading instruction. In R. Barr, M. Kamil, P. Mosenthal, & P. Pearson (Eds.), *Handbook of reading research, vol. 2* (pp. 885–910). White Plains, NY: Longman.

Berghoff, B., & Egawa, K. (1991). No more "rocks": Grouping to give students control of their learning. *The Reading Teacher, 44,* 536–541.

Bishop, R. (1992). Multicultural literature for children: Making informed choices. In V. Harris (Ed.), *Teaching multicultural literature in grades K–8* (pp. 37–53). Norwood, MA: Christopher-Gordon.

Bridge, C. (1986). Predictable books for beginning readers and writers. In M. R. Sampson (Ed.), *The pursuit of literacy: Early reading and writing* (pp. 81–96). Dubuque, IA: Kendall/Hunt.

Bulla, C. (1994). *What makes a shadow? Let's read and find out science 1.* New York: HarperCollins.

Carle, E. (1979). *The very hungry caterpillar.* New York: Collins.

Chomsky, C. (1972). Stages in language development and reading exposure. *Harvard Educational Review, 42,* 1–33.

Clay, M. M. (1979). *The early detection of reading difficulties* (2nd ed.). Auckland, New Zealand: Heinemann.

Clay, M. M. (1993). *An observation survey of early literacy achievement.* Auckland, New Zealand: Heinemann.

Cunningham, P. (2004). *Phonics they use: words for reading and writing* (4th ed.). Boston: Allyn & Bacon.

Cunninghham, A. E., & Stanovich, K. E. (1997). Early reading acquisition and its relation to reading experience and ability 10 years later. *Developmental Psychology, 33,* 934–945.

DeFord, D., Pinnell, G., Lyons, C., & Place, Q. (1990). *Report of the follow-up study, Columbus Reading Recovery program 1988–1989* (Report Vol. 11). Columbus: The Ohio State University.

Dewey, J. (1933). *How we think* (rev. ed.). Boston: Heath.

Dickinson, D. (2001). Book reading in preschool classrooms: Is recommended practice common? In D. Dickinson & P. Tabors, *Beginning literacy with language* (pp. 175–203). Baltimore, MD: Paul H. Brookes.

Dickinson, D. K., & Smith, M. W. (1994). Long-term effects of preschool teachers' book readings on low-income children's vocabulary and story comprehension. *Reading Research Quarterly, 29,* 104–122.

Dickinson, D. K., & Sprague, K. E. (2001). The nature and impact of early childhood care environments on the language and early literacy development of children from low-income families. In S. B. Neuman & D. K. Dickinson (Eds.), *Handbook of early literacy research* (pp. 263–280). New York: Guilford.

Diller, D. (2003). *Literacy workstations: Making centers work.* Portland, ME: Stenhouse.

Dorn, L., French, C., & Jones, T. (1998). *Apprenticeship in literacy: Transitions across reading and writing.* Portland, ME: Stenhouse.

Dressel, J. (1990). The effects of listening to and discussing different qualities of children's literature on the narrative writing of fifth graders. *Research in the Teaching of English, 24,* 397–414.

Duke, N. (2000). Print environments and experiences offered to first-grade students in very low- and very high-SES school districts. *Reading Research Quarterly, 35,* 456–457.

Duke, N. K., & Kays, J. (1998). "Can I say 'once upon a time'?": Kindergarten children developing knowledge of information book language. *Early Childhood Research Quarterly, 13,* 295–318.

Duke, N., & Purcell-Gates, V. (2003). Genres at home and at school: Bridging the known to the new. *The Reading Teacher, 57,* 30–37.

Dyson, A. (2006). On saying it right (write): "Fit-its" in the foundations of learning to write. *Research in the Teaching of English, 41,* 8–42.

Eeds, M., & Wells, D. (1989). Grand conversations: An exploration of meaning construction in literature study groups. *Research in the Teaching of English, 23,* 4–29.

Feitelson, D., Kita, B., & Goldstein, Z. (1986). The effects of listening to series stories on first graders' comprehension and use of language. *Research in the Teaching of English, 20,* 336–356.

Ferdman, B. (1990). Literacy and cultural identity. *Harvard Educational Review, 60,* 181–204.

Fountas, I. C., & Pinnell, G. S. (1996). *Guided reading: Good first teaching for all children.* Portsmouth, NH: Heinemann.

Fountas, I., & Pinnell, G. (2005). *The Fountas and Pinnell leveled book list K–8, 2006–2008 edition.* Portsmouth, NH: Heinemann.

Fractor, J., Woodruff, M., Martinez, M., & Teale, W. (1993). Let's not miss opportunities to promote voluntary reading: Classroom libraries in elementary school. *The Reading Teacher, 46,* 476–484.

Fraser, B. J. (1991). Two decades of classroom environment research. In B. J. Fraser & H. J. Walberg (Eds.), *Educational environments: Evaluation, antecedents and consequences* (pp. 3–27). New York: Pergamon.

Goodman, Y. M. (1978). Kid watching: An alternative to testing. *National Elementary Principals Journals, 57,* 41–45.

Guthrie, J., Wigfield, A., & Von Secker, C. (2000). Effects of integrated instruction on motivation and strategy use in reading. *Journal of Educational Psychology, 93,* 211–225.

Heath, S. B. (1983). *Ways with words: Language, life, and work in communities and classrooms.* New York: Cambridge University Press.

Hickman, J. (1979). *Response to literature in a school environment. Doctoral dissertation,* The Ohio State University, Columbus, OH.

Hiebert, E., & Colt, J. (1989). Patterns of literature-based reading instruction. *The Reading Teacher, 43,* 14–20.

Hoffman, J., Sailors, M., Duffy, G., & Beretvas, S. (2004). The effective elementary classroom literacy environment: Examining the validity of TEX-IN3 observation system. *Journal of Literacy Research, 36,* 303–334.

Hughes, M. (1991). *Curriculum integration in the primary grades: A framework for excellence.* Alexandria, VA: Association of Supervision and Curriculum Development.

Jordan, H. (1992). *How a seed grows.* New York: HarperCollins.

Juel, C. (1988). Learning to read and write: A longitudinal study of 54 children from first through fourth grades. *Journal of Educational Psychology, 80,* 437–447.

Keegan, M. (1991). *Pueblo boy: Growing up in two worlds.* New York: Dutton.

Labbo, L. D. (1996). A semiotic analysis of young children's symbol making in a classroom computer center. *Reading Research Quarterly, 31,* 356–382.

Labbo, L. D., & Ash, G. E. (1998). What is the role of computer-related technology in early literacy? In S. Neuman & K. Roskos (Eds.), *Children achieving: Best practices in beginning literacy* (pp. 180–197). Newark, DE: International Reading Association.

Lipson, M., Valencia, S., Wixson, K., & Peters, C. (1993). Integration and thematic teaching: Integration to improve teaching and learning. *Language Arts, 70,* 252–263.

McCloskey, R. (1976). *Blueberries for Sal.* New York: Puffin.

McCormick, S. (1994). A nonreader becomes a reader: A case study of literacy acquisition by a severely disabled reader. *Reading Research Quarterly, 29,* 156–176.

McGee, L. M. (2003). Book acting: Storytelling and drama in the early childhood classroom. In D. M. Barone & L. M. Morrow (Eds.). *Literacy and young children: Research-based practices* (pp. 157–172). New York: Guilford.

McGee, L. M., & Schickedanz, J. (in press). Reading books aloud in preschool and kindergarten: Accelerating language and oral comprehension. *The Reading Teacher.*

McGee, L., & Richgels, D. (2003). *Designing early literacy programs for at-risk preschoolers and kindergartners.* New York: Guilford.

Meier, D. R. (2000). *Scribble scrabble, learning to read and write: Success with diverse teachers, children, and families.* New York: Teachers College Press.

Mitchell, M. (1993). *Uncle Jed's barbershop.* New York: Scholastic.

Morris, D., & Slavin, R. E. (2003). *Every child reading.* Boston: Allyn & Bacon.

Morrow, L. (1992). The impact of a literature-based program on literacy achievement, use of literature, and attitudes of children from minority backgrounds. *Reading Research Quarterly, 27,* 250–275.

Morrow, L. (1997). *The literacy center: Contexts for reading and writing.* York, ME: Stenhouse.

Morrow, L. M., & Rand, M. (1991). Promoting literacy during play by designing early childhood classroom environments. *The Reading Teacher, 44,* 396–402.

Morrow, L. M., & Weinstein, C. S. (1982). Increasing children's use of literature through program and physical design changes. *The Elementary School Journal, 83,* 131–137.

Morrow, L. M., & Weinstein, C. S. (1986). Encouraging voluntary reading: The impact of a literature program on children's use of library centers. *Reading Research Quarterly, 21,* 330–346.

Morrow, L., & Gambrell, L. B. (1998). How do we motivate children toward independent reading and writing? In S. Neuman & K. Roskos (Eds.), *Children achieving: Best practices in beginning literacy* (pp. 144–161). Newark, DE: International Reading Association.

Moss, T. (1993). *I want to be.* New York: Dial.

Murray, B. A., Stahl, S. A., & Ivey, M. G. (1996) Developing phoneme awareness through alphabet books. *Reading and Writing: An Interdisciplinary Journal, 8,* 306–322.

National Association for the Education of Young Children (NAEYC) and International Reading Association (IRA). (1998). Learning to read and write: Developmentally appropriate practices for young children. *Young Children, 53,* 30–46.

Neuman, S. B. (1999). Books make a difference: A study of access to literacy. *Reading Research Quarterly, 34,* 286–311.

Neuman, S. B., & Roskos, K. (1990). Play, print, and purpose: Enriching play environments for literacy development. *The Reading Teacher, 44,* 214–221.

Neuman, S. B., & Roskos, K. (1993). Access to print for children of poverty: Differential effects of adult mediation and literacy-enriched play settings on environmental and functional print tasks. *American Educational Research Journal, 30,* 95–122.

Neuman, S. B., & Roskos, K. (1997). Literacy knowledge in practice: Contexts of participation for young writers and readers. *Reading Research Quarterly, 32,* 10–32.

Oldfather, P. (1993). What students say about motivating experiences in a whole language classroom. *The Reading Teacher, 46,* 672–681.

Pappas, C., & Barry, A. (1997). Scaffolding urban students' initiations: Transactions in reading information books in the read-aloud curriculum. In N. J. Karolides (Eds.), *Reader response in elementary classrooms: Quest and discovery* (pp. 215–236). Mahwah, NJ: Erlbaum.

Parkes, B. (2000). *Read it again! Revisiting the shared reading.* Portland, ME: Stenhouse.

Parkinson, K. (1986). *The enormous turnip.* Niles, IL: Albert Whitman.

Pearson, P. D., & Gallager, M. C. (1983). The instruction of reading comprehension. *Contemporary Educational Psychology, 8,* 317–344.

Pinnell, G., & Fountas, I. (1996). *Guided Reading: Good first teaching for all children.* Portsmouth, NH: Heinemann.

Reese, E., & Cox, A. (1999). Quality of adult book reading affects children's emergent literacy. *Developmental Psychology, 35*(1), 20–28.

Richgels, D. J. (2002). Informational texts in kindergarten. *The Reading Teacher, 55,* 586–595.

Roskos, K., & Neuman, S. B. (2001). Environment and its influences for early literacy teaching and learning. In S. B. Neuman & D. K. Dickinson (Eds.), *Handbook of early literacy research* (pp. 281–292). New York: Guildford.

Ross, R. R. (1980). *Storyteller* (2nd ed.). Columbus, OH: Merrill.

Routman, R. (1991). *Invitations: Changing as teachers and learners K–12.* Portsmouth, NH: Heinemann.

Rowe, D. (1994). *Preschoolers as authors: Literacy learning in the social world.* Cresskill, NJ: Hampton Press.

Schickedanz, J. A. (1998). What is developmentally appropriate practice in early literacy?: Considering the alphabet. In S. B. Neuman & K. A. Roskos (Eds.), *Children achieving: Best practices in early literacy.* Newark, DE: International Reading Association.

Schickedanz, J. A. (2003). Engaging preschoolers in code learning: Some thoughts about preschool teachers' concerns. In D. M. Barone & L. M. Morrow (Eds.), *Literacy and young children: Research-based practices.* New York: Guilford.

Schulman, M. B., & Payne, C. (2000). *Guided reading: Making it work.* New York: Scholastic Professional Books.

Sendak, M. (1963). *Where the wild things are.* New York: Harper and Row.

Sipe, L. (2002). Talking back and taking over: young children's expressive engagement during storybook read-alouds. *The Reading Teacher, 55,* 476–483.

Smith, M. W., & Dickinson, D. K. (2002). *User's Guide to the early language and literacy classroom observation (ELLCO) toolkit.* Baltimore, MD: Paul H. Brookes.

Smolkin, L. B., & Donovan, C. A. (2002). "Oh excellent, excellent question!": Developmental differences and comprehension acquisition. In C. Block & M. Pressley (Eds.), *Comprehension instruction: Research-based best practices* (pp. 140–157). New York: Guilford.

Snow, C. E., Burns, M. S., & Griffin, P. (Eds.). (1998). *Preventing reading difficulties in young children.* Washington, DC: National Academy Press.

Steptoe, J. (1969). *Stevie.* New York: Harper and Row.

Taylor, B. M., & Dorsey-Gaines, C. (1988). *Growing up literate: Learning from inner-city families.* Portsmouth, NH: Heinemann.

Taylor, B. M., Frye, B. J., & Maruyama, G. (1990). Time spent reading and reading growth. *American Educational Research Journal, 27,* 351–362.

Taylor, N. E., Blum, I. H. & Logsdon, D. M. (1986). The development of written language awareness: Environmental aspects and program characteristics. *Reading Research Quarterly, 21*(2), 132–149.

Tompert, A. (1988). *Nothing sticks like a shadow.* New York: Houghton Mifflin.

Tompkins, G., & McGee, L. (1993). *Teaching reading with literature: Case studies to action plans.* New York: Merrill/Macmillan.

Vars, G. (1991). Integrated curriculum in historical perspective. *Educational Leadership, 49,* 14–15.

Vukelich, C. (1994). Effects of play intervention on young children's reading of environmental print. *Early Childhood Research Quarterly, 9,* 153–170.

Wasik, B. A., & Bond, M. A. (2001). Beyond the pages of a book: Interactive book reading and language development in preschool classrooms. *Journal of Educational Psychology, 93*(2), 243–250.

Wolfersberger, M., Reutzel, D., Dudweeks, R., & Fawson, P. (2004). Developing and validating the literacy profile (CLEP): A tool for examining the "print richness" of early childhood and elementary classrooms. *Journal of Literacy Research, 36,* 211–272.

Xiong, B. (1989). *Nine-in-one. Grr! Grr!* San Francisco: Children's Book Press.

Zarrillo, J. (1994). *Multicultural literature, multicultural teaching: Units for the elementary grades.* New York: Harcourt Brace Jovanovich.

CHAPTER 7

Supporting Language and Literacy Learning in Preschools

KEY CONCEPTS

Sounding Literate
Block Center
Home Center
"I Can Read" Bag
Environmental Print Puzzle
Letter Game
Written Language Talk
Interactive Read-Aloud

Vocabulary Prop Box
Shared Writing with Write On
Guided Drawing
Confusable Letters
Continuants
Text and Toy Sets
Sit and Stay
Pattern Innovation

Sign-In Procedure
"I Can Hear" Talk
Language Play Books
Consonant Phonemes
Consonant Digraph
Vowel Phonemes
Language Scaffolds

THE PRESCHOOL CONTEXT

IN THIS CHAPTER, we describe exemplary preschool practices that foster high levels of language and literacy development for all children including children in day care, Head Start or Even Start, public or private preschools, and pre-kindergarten programs. Exemplary preschool programs foster parent involvement and attend to children's safety and aesthetic, physical, emotional, social, and cognitive development. They also provide developmentally appropriate instruction in math, language, literacy, and science.

The Critical Role of Preschool

Many preschoolers develop language and literacy concepts as a result of participating in routine activities that occur in their families and communities. Through these activities children gain an awareness of how to use language and literacy in particular literacy events, the way that literacy operates, and how literacy use empowers family members (Gee, 2001).

In many preschools, children continue to be involved in literacy activities that are remarkably similar to those they have already experienced in their homes and communities (McGill-Franzen, Lanford, & Adams, 2002). These children have a double dose of highly effective language and literacy learning opportunities. They have supportive parents or caregivers who provide materials, opportunities, and informal teaching about how to interact with books and pretend to read, and how to draw and pretend to write. Further, they have highly skilled preschool teachers who provide additional reading and writing opportunities within a high-quality early-childhood program. As a result, they acquire high levels of literacy development.

However, some children get very few opportunities to engage in sustained language and literacy activities either in home or at preschool (Dickinson, 2001). For a variety of reasons, many parents do not read books aloud to their young children or encourage their children to pretend to write. Children growing up in poverty are more likely to attend preschools that have low-quality programs and ineffective preschool teachers (McGill-Franzen, Lanford, & Adams, 2002). Children from low literacy preschools and homes enter kindergarten with extremely low levels of literacy development.

However, high-quality preschool experiences do make a difference in young children's lives. Effective preschool teachers can accelerate the learning of children whose parents or caregivers provide low levels of home support for literacy learning (Tabors, Snow, & Dickinson, 2001). Using the activities we describe in this chapter, preschool teachers can create opportunities that will accelerate the language and literacy learning of all children.

Most children who attend high quality preschools can be expected to enter kindergarten with high levels of language and literacy development. At the beginning of their kindergarten year, they will be able to:

* Retell a favorite story using some language of the story, past tense verbs, and other features of **sounding literate** (see Chapter 4).

- Retell a familiar information book, using some information from the text, timeless present tense verbs, and other features of sounding literate.
- Explain events in a familiar text using analytic talk.
- Use complex sentence structures in everyday conversation.
- Use increasingly complex vocabulary learned from preschool experiences.
- Recognize as many as 40 of the 52 upper and lower case alphabet letters, including most upper and some lower case letters.
- Write a recognizable first-name signature.
- Say the beginning sound of a spoken word or identify two rhyming words.
- During shared reading, demonstrate understanding of book-orientation concepts and beginning directionality concepts. (McGee, 2005)

Learning in the Preschool Classroom

Most preschool programs are founded on common principles of learning. First, is that three- and four-year-olds learn best when they are actively engaged in manipulating materials. Preschoolers do not learn effectively when they must sit for long periods of time and merely listen to the teacher. Young children can participate actively in whole-class activities when teachers intersperse reading aloud with more active singing, movement activities, and recitation of finger plays. However, they need extended opportunities to manipulate the variety of learning materials usually found in preschool classrooms. Further, teachers need to be mindful that small-group instruction will be more successful when each child has materials than when children must wait long periods of time to have a turn.

Second, preschoolers learn from play. For example, over time as children play in the block center, their block constructions and their play with the constructions become more complex. Through the explorations and trial and error that are part of playing with blocks, they discover more complex concepts about balance, size, and spatial relationships. Third, preschoolers need some times in which they select their own activities. When young children must select their own activities, they use cognitive processes that are not required when they merely are told what to do and how to do it. When children self-select, they must consciously plan, thinking ahead about what they want to do. Then they further plan how they will accomplish those goals. Then, as they carry out their play, they monitor their progress toward completing their plans. When good teachers notice children roaming the room without finding an activity that attracts their attention or sustains their interest, those teachers realize they must not make play decisions for the children but instead must help the children plan and monitor their own play.

The Preschool Classroom

Figure 7.1 presents a design for a well-appointed and arranged preschool classroom that includes many traditional centers. The **block center** has bin and shelf storage spaces for large cardboard blocks, large wooden blocks, smaller wooden blocks, and durable model cars and trucks. It includes a workbench for play with pegs and ham-

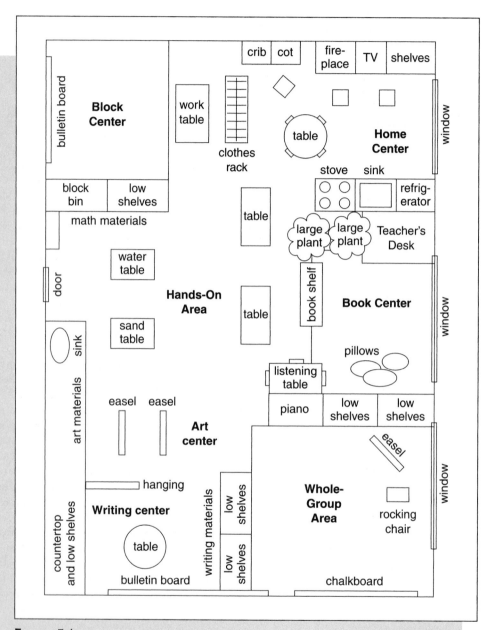

FIGURE 7.1   A Preschool Classroom

mer and wrench. On the bulletin board are posters of city skylines and their distinctive buildings (e.g., the Chicago lakefront with the skyscrapers of The Loop in the background), other distinctive buildings (e.g., Frank Lloyd Wright's Falling Water, a cantilever-constructed house over a waterfall, and the Eiffel Tower), and vehicles (e.g., ocean liners on a travel-agency poster and truck and car posters from a car dealership). These posters contain the print that is part of the poster (e.g., "Chicago," "Cruise the Caribbean") as well as taped-on labels (e.g., "skyscraper," "ship"). On the workbench are hardware-store advertising flyers and a do-it-yourself carpentry book. There are two large, empty pasteboard boxes. There is a large area for playing with blocks.

The **home center** includes a cardboard fireplace with chairs around it, a cardboard television (such as furniture stores use in their entertainment-center displays), shelves, a kitchen set with a small table and four chairs, a small cot, a doll crib, and a doll high chair. The shelves are stocked with magazines, including *TV Guide,* newspapers, a phone book, a few adult books, and a few children's picture books. The kitchen is stocked with plastic food, empty food containers (e.g., cereal boxes, a plastic ketchup bottle, a cottage cheese container), and several illustrated cookbooks, including *My First Cookbook* (Wilkes, 1989). Over the crib is a *Sesame Street* poster picturing Bert and Ernie and displaying their names.

Between the home and block centers is a clothing rack to serve dramatic play in the home and block centers. In both play centers, there are several small, spiral-bound, vertical-flip notebooks, small clipboards with paper, and pencils. In the home center, a waiter or waitress may use these props during restaurant play to take an order, or a mommy or a daddy may use them to take a telephone message or to make a grocery list; in the block center, astronauts may use these items for a countdown checklist.

In the hands-on area are a sand table, a water table, and the art center. There are a sink and storage for supplies, including water toys and plastic aprons, and storage for and places to use children's individual collections of environmental print items, math manipulatives (e.g., Unifix cubes), musical instruments, puzzles, Legos, clay, and science manipulatives (e.g., magnets). There is display space for content centers. All items and storage places are labeled. There is a travel poster of a beach near the sand table and one of Niagara Falls near the water table. The musical instruments are stored near the piano and an easel; sometimes the easel displays the lyrics to a song the children are learning, written on a large piece of posterboard. There are small easels for painting near the art supplies, tables for using many of the manipulatives, and a large, open area for group singing activities and for other large-group activities, such as story performances.

The library and writing centers are on the opposite side of the room from the play centers. These contain writing materials, a computer, books (including pattern books, movable books, alphabet books, and big books), and space to use them, as described in Chapter 6. A large, round table at the edge of the writing center is the location for children's signing in at the beginning of their day and for checking out and checking in books from the classroom library.

These spaces and materials set the stage for children's learning. As children interact with the materials, each other, and their teacher, they act as novice readers and writers. They are invited to read from familiar big books and pretend to read favorite information books. They dictate messages that their teacher writes for them and pretend to write messages as they play.

READING AND WRITING IN EXEMPLARY PRESCHOOL CLASSROOMS

THERE ARE THREE WAYS that exemplary preschool teachers help children develop language and literacy concepts. The first way is to infuse literacy materials throughout the classroom in nearly every center. The second way is to talk with children and model how to use literacy materials as children are playing in these centers. The third way that exemplary preschool teachers help children develop language and literacy concepts is to frequently and routinely include literacy experiences during whole-class and small-group activities. In exemplary preschools, literacy activities that occur in small-groups and whole-class settings form a foundation for children's later playful literacy interactions in centers. For example, after a teacher reads aloud a story and helps children dramatize the story using simple props, children enjoy dramatizing the story with a friend later in the library center. After a teacher writes a thank-you note to a classroom visitor as a shared writing activity, several children pretend to write thank-you notes in the writing center.

Literacy in an Exemplary Language- and Print-Rich Environment

We describe one morning in Mrs. Miller's pre-kindergarten classroom for at-risk four-year-olds. She is an exemplary teacher who arranges her classroom so that print is included in every center, and she provides large blocks of time for children to play in the centers. First we describe the children as they play in Mrs. Miller's centers, and then we describe how Mrs. Miller interacts with the children as they play. Finally, we describe some of her whole-class and small-group activities that provide a strong foundation for many of the activities in which the children were engaged.

Children at Play. Mrs. Miller's classroom has many centers, including book, McDonald's, writing, games, art, science and math discovery, and home centers. By mid-morning, children are working and playing at nearly every center. Two children are on the rug in the library center. They are looking at several books together, commenting about the pictures and talking about the stories. Then they take paper bags labeled with their names and "I can read" from a storage shelf for manipulatives. They look at the coupons, food wrappers, and fronts cut from food boxes that they have taken from their **"I can read" bags.** One child gets a doll from the home center, puts it in her lap, and points to each of the items. She reads to her doll by saying a word or two for each item.

Four children are at a McDonald's center. The center is made from a puppet theater to which Mrs. Miller has attached a sign and menu. Inside the theater are empty containers for hamburgers and French fries. Two children are behind the counter in the center. Both have on hats worn by employees at McDonald's. One child is writing on an order pad, and the other is pretending to put a McDLT in a container. Two children are standing in front of the counter. One is dressed in a hat and heels from the home center. She is "Mama." She asks "Baby" what he wants to eat and then orders. The child taking orders writes an order and announces, "That will be ten dollars." "Mama" looks in her purse for money and pays her bill. Figure 7.2 presents the McDonald's order.

Two children are at the writing center. A number of menus and placemats from local restaurants are displayed at the center. Also displayed are several menus composed by children. Some menus have pictures cut from magazines; some have children's mock letters or mock cursive writing; some have words children have copied from menus or newspapers; and others were written and drawn by parent volunteers. One of the menus on display was composed by Mrs. Miller. It is titled "Miller's Meals" and consists of a drawing of people eating, cutout pictures of food from the food section of the newspaper, and words. One of the children at the center is drawing and writing a menu. She announces, "I'm going to have ice cream," and draws a picture of a double dip cone. The other child comments, "I like ice cream, too. Maybe I'd better write *ice cream*." She writes a scribble on her menu.

Two children are in the games center. They play for several minutes with Legos and other small manipulative toys in the center. Then they remove two **environmental print puzzles** from the game shelf. The puzzles consist of boxes of brownie and cake mixes. Inside each box are pieces cut from the front of an identical box. The children spread the cut-up puzzle pieces on the table. They put the puzzles together by looking at the pieces and then placing them on top of the boxes where they match. They talk together as they complete the puzzles, "I like chocolate. I could eat a whole box of these."

Two other children come to the games center and sit on the floor to play the **letter game**. A large *L* is painted on the front of a pasteboard box and a *K* on another. Attached to one of the boxes is a plastic bag containing several *L*'s and *K*'s that have been cut from construction paper and laminated. The two children play the letter game by sorting the letters and placing them inside the large pasteboard boxes. As they sort the letters, they say, "I'll be the *L* and you be the *K*. I know whose letter *K* is—Kelita's."

One child is in the science and math discovery center. Included in this center is a graph divided into two segments, "No TV Last Night" and "TV Last Night." The first title is accompanied by a picture of a TV with a big *X* over it. The second title is accompanied by a picture of a TV. Under each title some squares of paper have been pasted. Many squares have children's names written on them. Most of the squares are pasted under the "TV Last Night" title. Jermain writes his name on a square of paper and pastes it under the "TV Last Night" title. Displayed on the bulletin board in the center is a graph that the children completed the day before. Under this chart are two sentences: "Two children saw no TV Monday night. Ten children saw TV Monday night."

Three children are in the home center. Two children decide to cook a meal for their babies, using empty food containers and plastic food in the center. One child says, "I think I'll cook some chicken. Let me look up a good recipe." She opens a cookbook on one of the shelves in the center and begins looking through the pages. Another child is sitting in a rocking chair, looking at magazines. Nearby, Mrs. Miller steps into a telephone booth made from a large box. She looks up a number in the telephone book (class telephone book with each child's name and telephone number). She says, "Ring. Ring. Is Melody home?" The child in the rocking chair says, "I'll get that," and answers a toy phone in the center. She says, "Melody is not here. Can I take a message?" She writes on a tablet near the phone and then says, "I'll give her the message. Bye-bye." Figure 7.3 shows the phone message.

FIGURE 7.2 McDonald's Orders

FIGURE 7.3 Telephone Message

The Teacher at Work: Mrs. Miller Teaches Literacy All Day. While most of the children in Mrs. Miller's classroom do not come from homes with rich literacy experiences, they demonstrate a willingness and eagerness to play with literacy materials in the classroom. This is a result of Mrs. Miller's deliberately infusing in classroom spaces and activities the authentic literacy materials she has previously used in instruction (Casbergue, McGee, & Bedford, in press). For example, all children, from the beginning of the school year, are encouraged to bring in a box or package of a favorite food. Mrs. Miller talks about the items first thing in the morning during whole-class time. Children say what they know about the items, and then Mrs. Miller points to a word on the print and also talks about the first letter in that word. For example, Lorenzo brought in a licorice candy wrapper and Mrs. Miller found the word *licorice* and pointed out the letter *L* and further commented that the word *licorice* started with the same sound as Lorenzo's name. Lorenzo put the candy wrapper in his "I can read" bag. Later, Mrs. Miller brought in two more of these same candy wrappers. She placed one of the candy wrappers in the home center and the second she kept to use later when she and the children would make an alphabet book out of familiar print. In other words, Mrs. Miller knows that children will bring in different kinds of print from their homes, and she uses these print items to introduce children to notions that print "says" a message and is composed of letters. Later, she will use that same print to teach alphabet recognition more explicitly.

Each of the literacy activities in her classroom was first introduced to a whole-class group, then used for a small-group lesson, and finally placed in the centers. For example, the McDonald's center materials were demonstrated to the whole class. Then, during a small-group activity, the children played with Mrs. Miller in the center. Then the center was officially open as a choice for all children's play. The letter game with the two large boxes was used for several days in small-group instruction to teach recognition of *K* and *L*.

Mrs. Miller frequently comments, "I teach literacy all day, everyday. I teach all the letters all the time. There isn't a day in which I don't segment a phoneme, identify two rhyming words, or clap out syllables. Some of my children catch on with this 'all day' teaching approach. However, some children need more. So I deliberately plan language and literacy activities each day for the whole class and teach a small-group lesson every day for all my children."

Planned Lessons

Mrs. Miller uses modeled and shared writing during whole-class and small-group instruction. One activity she planned was to model how to write a letter to Santa Claus. This lesson emerged from her children's interest in the upcoming holiday. She placed a large sheet of paper on an easel near a table so a small group of children could interact with her as she modeled writing the letter. As she wrote her letter to Santa, she used **written language talk** to make explicit many of the concepts she was demonstrating. Written language talk is teachers' explanations of the conventions of writing.

She told the children that she would begin the letter by writing "Dear Santa Claus." At the end of her letter, she wrote, "Love, Mrs. Miller." She explained that letters always begin with the word *Dear* and often end with the word *Love.* From this written language talk, the children learned about the language of a letter.

As Mrs. Miller wrote her Santa letter, she explained that the letter would start with a sentence about her good behavior in the last year. She reminded the children that Santa would want to know that in order to bring what she wanted for Christmas.

As Mrs. Miller wrote, she said each word as she wrote it. As she read her letter, she underlined the text with her hands. The children had many opportunities to connect what they heard Mrs. Miller read with the print she was highlighting. Mrs. Miller's talk about letters provided children with information for discovering sound-letter relationships. Some of the children in her class had begun making some of these discoveries. When Mrs. Miller was writing that she wanted a new sewing machine, Serita commented, "I know what letter sewing has, an *S.*" Mrs. Miller knew that Serita only made these sound-letter comments about *S* words. Still, Serita was beginning to display some sound-letter relationship awareness.

As Mrs. Miller talked about taking the letter to the post office and mailing it, her written language talk helped the children learn about function. She commented that it was a good thing that Santa would have her letter because he would be getting many, many requests for gifts. She did not want him to forget what she wanted.

Interactive Read-Alouds in Exemplary Preschools

Miss Leslie teaches in a private preschool with an emphasis on academic learning. She is an exemplary teacher who is careful to meet those expectations while maintaining a child-centered approach. One way in which she balances these two needs is through **interactive read-alouds** (see Chapter 6). The interaction comes from children's being expected to answer questions, make comments, and predict outcomes. Miss Leslie plans questions that help children use analytic talk and call for high levels of cognition. She also plans response-to-literature activities to extend the read-aloud experience.

Children Talk about Books and Respond to Literature.   Miss Leslie and six three-year-olds are gathered for storytime on the rug in their classroom. The children are sitting in a square area bordered by tape on the rug. As she announces storytime, Miss Leslie points to a sign entitled "Storytime" that has a picture of a mother reading to two children. On the sign are clothespinned cards with the names of the children who are to come to story-time: Cory, Echo, Leah, Paul, Laura, and Evan. Miss Leslie points to the name on the chart as she calls each child and reminds the child to come to the rug for storytime. As the children approach the rug, she begins to sing one of the children's favorite songs, "Twinkle, Twinkle Little Star."

After she and the children are settled on the rug, Miss Leslie holds up the book *The Little Rabbit Who Wanted Red Wings* (Bailey, 1987). She reads the title, pointing to each word. She reminds the children that she has read this book to them before. The book is about a little rabbit who is not happy with himself and wishes he had what other animals have. The children ask questions and make comments during the booksharing. Miss Leslie reads the text, talks about the illustrations, and asks questions. Figure 7.4 presents a segment of their interactive read-aloud.

Then Miss Leslie takes a paper bag from beneath her chair. She tells the children that it contains pictures of each of the animals Little Rabbit met in the story. She asks the children to guess what they are. As the children guess, she pulls out a construction-paper picture of the animal and asks, "What did Little Rabbit like about this animal?" She clothespins each animal picture to a clothesline hung a few feet off the floor behind her chair. She tells the children they might want to use the clothesline props to retell the story to a friend during center time. She also suggests that they might want to draw pictures and write about the animals or Little Rabbit in the writing center. All the children are then free to select center activities.

Miss Leslie's Role in Interactive Read-Alouds: More than Reading.   Miss Leslie was a master of interactive read-alouds. She prompted discussion before she began to read a book, paused while she read to make comments and ask questions, and continued the discussion after reading. The four purposes of talking about the book before, during, and after interactive reading are to:

- prompt children's active participation in constructing the meaning of the book
- extend and clarify children's language, understanding of, and thinking about the book
- explain some vocabulary
- prompt children to use vocabulary as they talk about the book (McGee & Richgels, 2003)

In order to achieve these goals, teachers like Miss Leslie carefully plan interactive read-alouds. They preview the book to consider what concepts children may not understand and how to connect what children do know with these unfamiliar concepts. They also select eight to ten vocabulary words that are important for the story and that may be unfamiliar to children to explain during the read-aloud. Exemplary teachers plan questions they might ask children to prompt discussion about critical events in a story or information book. However, they are careful during reading not to make interactive read-alouds like an oral quiz. Chapter 2 (Figure 2.7) presents several high-cognitive demand comments and questions that teachers can use during interactive read-alouds.

Text is presented in all capital letters. Brackets indicate portions of the dialogue that occurred simultaneously.

The illustration depicts a porcupine who is wearing glasses standing under a tree. Little Rabbit is sitting in a large hole in the tree looking at the porcupine.

Miss L:	Now who does Little Rabbit see? (points to porcupine)
Child 1:	um um its . . .
Child 2:	Mr. Beaver.
Child 3:	Mr. Porcupine.
Miss L:	It does look a little like a beaver. This is Mr. Porcupine.
Child 2:	(reaches up and touches the picture of the porcupine) Ouch.
Miss L:	Ooh, I wouldn't want to touch that.
Child 1:	Me either.
Child 4:	Oh, oh.
Miss L:	His bristles would stick me. They would stick like a needle.
Child 3:	Not me.
Child 2:	He sticks you? If you touch him like this? (puts her finger on the picture of the porcupine and pulls it off as if she were stuck)
Miss L:	Yes, he might. Those bristles are special. Now I wonder what Little Rabbit likes about Mr. Porcupine?
Child 5:	Glasses. (porcupine has on glasses)
Child 1:	Needles.
Child 2:	I wouldn't want to touch Porcupine.
Miss L:	I wouldn't want to touch him either. But what about Little Rabbit? What do you think *he* thinks about those bristles? What do you think Little Rabbit likes?
Child 3:	um, um.
Child 4:	Glasses.
Child 1:	Needles.
Miss L:	Do you think *he* wants those bristles? Or maybe those glasses? (laughs, and smiles at Child 1)
Child 1:	Yeah.
Miss L:	What would *you* like to have like Mr. Porcupine?
Child 2:	I want glasses.
Child 5:	Bristles.
Child 1:	I want needles.
Miss L:	Let's see. (looks at book) WHEN MR. PORCUPINE PASSED BY, THE LITTLE RABBIT WOULD SAY TO HIS MOMMY (looks at children as if inviting them to join in), "MOMMY, I WISH I HAD (looks back at print) A BACK FULL OF BRISTLES LIKE MR. PORCUPINE'S."
Child 1:	Mommy, I want those needles.
Child 5:	I wish I had those bristles.
Child 4:	I want some bristles.
Child 2:	Mommy, . . .

Interactive read-alouds are more powerful when the books are related—for example, related to a theme the class is exploring. Reading related books provides more opportunities for children to hear vocabulary words in different contexts and to expand concepts. **Vocabulary prop boxes** can be used to further enhance vocabulary and concept development for related books. For example, the books *The Carrot Seed* (Krauss, 1945) and *Jack's Garden* (Cole, 1997) are about gardening. A vocabulary prop box for these two books might include seeds, a trowel, a small rake, a portion of a garden hose, a watering can, plastic insects, a variety of plastic flowers, and a plastic carrot (Wasik & Bond, 2001). As teachers share these props, they can invite children to "tell me what you know about this" or "tell me how you would use this." As they read aloud, teachers can remind children of the objects in their prop box. For example, when reading *The Carrot Seed*, a teacher paused to ask a question:

> Teacher: How did the little boy plant the seed?
>
> Child 1: He dug a hole.
>
> Techer (to same child): Tell me more.
>
> Child 1: He dug a hole in the ground and he put the seed in.
>
> Teacher: How did he dig the hole?
>
> Child 2: With a shovel like this. [The child demonstrates the action of digging.]
>
> Teacher: Kind of like the [trowel] that I showed you." (Wasik & Bond, 2001, p. 249)

This teacher used a clarifying and extending prompt ("Tell me more") to encourage the children to expand their sentence (Child 1 responded to the teacher's questions with "he dug a hole" and expanded this sentence to "he dug a hole in the ground and he put the seed in" after the prompt).

Information books sometimes prompt more conversation and questions than do simple stories (Smolkin & Donovan, 2002). When reading information books, teachers want to make explicit the connections among ideas. Books dealing with science concepts often include, for example, cause-and-effect relationships—how animals catch their prey or why animals hibernate in the winter. Teachers can make these connections explicit by helping children understand that a spider can catch an insect *because* its web is sticky.

After reading books aloud, effective teachers make sure they make those books available in the classroom book center. Children are especially interested in browsing through a book immediately after it has been read aloud. Children develop stronger literacy skills when they have access to and engage with books on their own (Neuman, 1999) and are supported in this activity by frequent teacher read-alouds.

Teaching Concepts about Print, Alphabet Recognition, and Phonemic Awareness in Exemplary Preschools

Ms. Rodgers teaches Head Start in a rural community center. At the beginning of the school year, almost none of her children could write their names, and most children's grips on markers suggested they had had few experiences drawing, coloring, or pretending to write. Almost none of the children could recognize any alphabet letters although two children did know the first letters in their names. When assessed for concepts about print, most children knew front, back, top, and bottom, but very few realized that the left page was read before the right page or anything about directionality of print, and none could point at words one-to-one.

Even with these low-level skills at entry to Head Start, these children would be expected to have high levels of skills at kindergarten entry. The elementary school the children would attend is a Reading First school; that is, it receives funds through the No Child Left Behind legislation. It uses *DIBELS* (Dynamic Indicators of Basic Early Literacy Skills, http://dibels.uoregon) to assess kindergartners' literacy progress in the early fall, winter, and spring. By the time of the winter *DIBELS* assessment, kindergartners are expected to identify 40 alphabet letters in less than a minute and to segment beginning phonemes from spoken words. In the spring they are expected to be able to identify some sounds in nonsense words.

In order to prepare her Head Start students for these kindergarten expectations, Ms. Rodgers and her colleagues decided to increase the intensity with which they taught concepts about print, alphabet recognition, and phonemic awareness while still meeting Head Start guidelines for balancing child-initiated activities with teacher-directed activities. They did so using **shared writing with write on** (see Chapter 6 for a discussion of shared writing and write-on charts), guided drawing, and daily literacy lessons, at first in alphabet recognition and later in phonemic awareness.

Shared Writing with Write On. Ms. Rodgers used shared writing nearly every day to demonstrate directionality concepts and to contextualize alphabet instruction. For example, after reading *The Three Billy Goats Gruff* (Stevens, 1995), she drew children's attention to the picnic the goats enjoyed after getting across the bridge. She talked about the tablecloth spread on the ground, the picnic basket, and the food the goats ate. She talked about going on a picnic in the park with her grandchildren. She had brought to class a picnic basket in which she packed sandwiches, apples, potato chips, juice boxes, and cookies along with paper plates and napkins. The children talked about why these were good foods for packing in a basket and which foods might not be good. Finally, she said, "Now we will write a list for packing a picnic basket. Let me read the title of our list. It is right up here." She points to the first word. "I'll read each word and point to it. 'List, of, Picnic, Food.'"

Ms. Rodgers had written the title on chart paper in preparation for this lesson. She said, "I want someone to come up here and point to the words of the title as I read it and then count the number of words." A child quickly came forward and pointed as everyone read the title again. Now Ms. Rodgers says, "I'll say the first sound of something I packed in my basket, and you see if you know what it is. I packed something that starts /s/." There are many guesses from the children, so Ms. Rodgers says, "Yes, "Quadaravious, it is ssssandwich. And it starts with the letter *S*." She writes the word and then says, "Here is something else I packed, see if you can guess: /p/, /p/, /p/."

Ms. Rodgers continues saying the first sound for the words *juice* and *cookie*. After the list is complete (*sandwich, potato chips, juice, cookies*), Ms. Rodgers says, "I am going to let three people step up to the chart and find a letter they want to write. Then I am going to leave this picnic list on the easel during center time. All of you can step up and write letters or draw pictures." Three children step up, and Ms. Rodgers lets them write a letter. If they need help, she writes the letter first, reminding the class about the lines they will need to make the letter. Later that day, eight other children step up to the chart during center time and write on the chart. Ms. Rodgers invites five other children—ones she knows need more practice writing letters—to write with her.

Guided Drawing. Ms. Rodgers realized that her four-year-olds had had few experiences drawing and writing before coming to Head Start. The children's motor control was below age expectations because of their lack of opportunity to practice. She needed a way to make sure children drew every day. Unfortunately, just putting materials in a writing center and art center did not seem to promote practicing as often as the children needed. Therefore, she decided to include a teacher-directed guided drawing activity every day as a part of morning entry activities, a small-group activity, or center activities.

Guided drawing is an activity in which the teacher demonstrates basic strokes used in drawing and writing (such as vertical, horizontal, diagonal, and curving lines, circles, ovals, squares, triangles, and dots). As the teacher demonstrates making the marks, she tells a story such as going on a car trip to grandma's that would go through tall trees (long vertical lines), past a cow pasture (short vertical lines), crossing a bridge (long horizontal line), over some bumps (curved lines), and through mountains (diagonal lines in a V). Ms. Rodgers took one or two minutes to do one guided drawing and then invited children to draw on their own. Gradually as most children gained better motor control, Ms. Rodgers no longer guided drawing activities.

Small-Group Lessons in Alphabet Recognition and Phonemic Awareness. Ms. Rodgers presented information about alphabet letters and phonemic awareness all day, every day in just the same way as Mrs. Miller. However, she also took a more systematic approach during daily small-group lessons. In the fall, she focused on alphabet recognition. In the winter, she interspersed phonemic awareness activities with alphabet activities. In the spring, she introduced sound-letter correspondences. Ms. Rodgers taught four letters each week, two of which were confusable letters. **Confusable letters** are letters that share many of the same letter features, often causing children to confuse them. Pairs of letters such as *I* and *H*, *N* and *Z*, and *C* and *U* differ only in their orientation. So, Ms. Rodgers taught letters such as *A, C, U,* and *T* together in one week. Children sorted letter tiles, practiced writing the letters, fished for letters (letters were paper-clipped to paper fish and "fished" with a magnet tied to a pole), fed letters to a puppet (Roberts & Neal, 2004), and played letter concentration.

When Ms. Rodgers began teaching phonemic awareness, she selected the phonemes /s/ and /m/. She chose these because of the contrasting mouth shapes involved in their pronunciation and because they are **continuants;** that is, their pronunciations can be prolonged. In contrast to /s/, which is pronounced with the lips apart, /m/ is pronounced with the lips together. Children can easily see this difference as Ms. Rodgers shows them how the two phonemes are spoken. Because /s/ and /m/ are continuants, Ms. Rodgers can stretch out their pronunciation while children listen to the sounds and observe the different mouth shapes. Later in her teaching phonemic awareness, Ms. Rodgers will demonstrate phonemes whose distinctive features are more difficult to see (such as /t/ with its distinctive tongue tap on the roof of the mouth) and whose pronunciations cannot be prolonged (such as /b/, which is "popped," that is, it can be spoken only in an instant).

In her phonemic awareness lessons, Ms. Rodgers pronounced words with stress on individual phonemes. She directed her students to watch her mouth as she said the sounds and words. She helped them to say phonemes in isolation, to emphasize the sounds in words, and to feel what their mouths, tongues, teeth, and vocal chords were doing. Children can feel their vocal chords vibrate by placing their hands lightly on their throats. They will feel the vibrations of voiced sounds and feel no vibration for unvoiced sounds (for example, compare /b/ and /p/, /d/ and /t/, /g/ and /k/, /v/ and /f/, /z/ and /s/, /j/ and /ch/, and /zh/ and /sh/). Later, the children sorted pictures with two different initial phonemes, fished for pictures and isolated the phonemes in the pictured words, and played sound concentration, matching two pictures with the same initial phoneme.

WHAT ARE THE CHARACTERISTICS OF AN EXEMPLARY PRESCHOOL LITERACY PROGRAM?

EXEMPLARY LITERACY PROGRAMS, such as those we observed in Mrs. Miller's, Miss Leslie's, and Ms. Rodgers's classrooms, include frequent and routine literacy activities that are geared to the developmental levels of children (Neuman, Copple, & Bredekamp, 2000). Much of what preschoolers can do is not conventional—many preschoolers do not yet write alphabet letters conventionally and even their signatures are not fully developed. They ask many questions about books read aloud to them that reveal they often do not understand some vocabulary words or sequences of events. Therefore, exemplary literacy programs for preschoolers are not the same as those found in kindergartens or first grades.

Exemplary preschool literacy programs have as their desired outcomes that children learn many conventional literacy skills that we described earlier. However, in exemplary literacy programs, young children are provided many playful opportunities to achieve these expected conventional literacy outcomes through discovery and experimentation. Mrs. Miller encouraged her children to write orders in the McDonald's center—and most of the children's writing in the activities was unconventional. Yet, Mrs. Miller provided frequent demonstrations of how to write conventional alphabet letters. Miss Leslie encouraged her children to talk about the stories she read aloud and was tolerant of their diverse comments. However, she skillfully guided children to attend to more salient story elements even when their interest focused on personally interesting story details. Ms. Rodgers knew that her children needed daily experiences with print.

Exemplary preschool literacy programs help teachers find a balance between instruction geared toward helping children develop conventional literacy concepts and activities in which children are allowed and encouraged to explore literacy on their own terms. These programs are systematic—they present experiences that are compatible with children's current level of literacy knowledge yet at the same time provide opportunities for children to develop more complex concepts. In the remainder of the chapter, we describe instructional activities that strike this balance around five major areas of literacy development in preschool:

- Vocabulary
- Oral comprehension

- Concepts about print
- Alphabet knowledge
- Phonemic awareness

Supporting Vocabulary and Oral Comprehension

READING AND WRITING ARE ULTIMATELY ABOUT MEANING—readers must construct meaning as they read, and writers must convey meaning through their writing. Vocabulary and oral comprehension in preschool play a key role in children's later being able to comprehend highly complex books and write detailed and persuasive compositions (Wells, 1986; Senechal et al., 1996). Therefore, vocabulary and concept development, experience and knowledge of books, and extended conversations form a strong foundation for children's literacy success (Hargrave & Senechal, 2000; Schickedanz et al., 2001).

Storytelling and Drama

Storytelling and dramatizing are favorite preschool activities. Young children's play often includes extended episodes of fantasy play in which they become their favorite characters in stories or movies (Wolfe & Heath, 1992). **Text and toy sets** can also be used to stimulate dramatic play about books (Rowe, 1998). Text and toy sets are realistic, small-scale toys and other props that are placed in a special box or basket in the book center along with related books. First, teachers read aloud several books on a related topic. Then, children help find the toys in the classroom to place in the book's box or basket. These toys prompt children to enact scenes from books they have read or to create new related events in fantasy play.

Teachers also can extend children's vocabulary and language by modeling storytelling, retelling, and drama by using props. Folktales and fairytales are particularly effective for storytelling activities. Instead of reading a book, teachers share props with the children to involve them in the telling. For example, props that children can use in retelling the *Three Little Pigs* story might be as simple as laminated pictures of three pigs, a wolf, a bundle of straw, a bundle of sticks, a pile of bricks, and a big black pot gathered together in a zip-lock bag. Each child can manipulate these props and join in saying the repetitive phrases ("not by the hair of my chinny chin chin" and "I'll huff, and I'll puff, and I'll blow your house down"). After several days of retelling with the teacher, children enjoy retelling the story to each other when the props are placed in the book center.

Another kind of storytelling is when the teacher offers to write a story dictated by a child in the room. Later, that child invites others to join in as he or she acts out the story earlier dictated (Paley, 1990). The teacher invites children to dictate their stories as they arrive for their school day. She sits where she is accessible to all the children. As children tell their stories, the teacher repeats each dictated sentence as she writes it down. She wants the storyteller to be able to correct her if she makes a mistake or to revise if a new idea comes to mind. She questions any part of the story that she is not certain she has gotten correctly. "The child knows the story will soon be acted out and the actors will need clear directions. The story must make sense to everyone: actors, audience, and narrator" (Paley, 1990, p. 22). During the day the teacher talks about the stories, always looking for and voicing connections.

Acting out the stories at the end of the school day is equally social and open to change (Paley, 1990). To play out the story, the teacher reads the dictation, and the storyteller and selected classmates dramatize it. Children are free to comment on the dramatizing, and their comments often result in revision in the dramatization. "Intuitively the children perceive that stories belong in the category of play, freewheeling scripts that always benefit from spontaneous improvisations" (1990, p. 25).

Taking Time to Talk

As surprising as it sounds, many preschoolers have few opportunities to have a one-on-one conversation with their teachers (Dickinson, 2001). Teachers are often busy with the whole class of children so that taking a few minutes each day to talk with each child seems impossible. However, when teachers **sit and stay** in centers for extended periods of time, they can capitalize on numerous opportunities for conversations with children. Effective conversations begin with children's interests and their actions. The best conversations are extended over several turns (where each person takes a turn to talk) and where a topic is explored in depth. Children who are learning English and children with low levels of vocabulary development need more frequent conversations to extend their language skills.

The focus of conversations with children should be on genuine communication rather than on correcting children's language errors. Young children are still acquiring proficiency in language, and attempting to be understood through rephrasing and clarifying are more effective for their language development than repeating a correct sentence. Teachers should include some sophisticated vocabulary in their conversations. One-on-one conversations provide many opportunities to explain words and to use both rare words and everyday words for the same concepts—for example, using the word *infant* as well as *baby*.

As teachers talk with children, they may engage children in conversations about past events or planning for the future. Such conversations require children to use decontextualized language that describes events, objects, and people not present in the here and now of the classroom. Teachers can prompt such conversations by talking about familiar events they have engaged in—going to the dentist, shopping at the mall, or visiting a relative.

SUPPORTING CONCEPTS ABOUT PRINT AND ALPHABET LETTER LEARNING

TO BECOME SUCCESSFUL READERS AND WRITERS, children need experiences with print. Teachers can make these concepts more explicit by using written language talk, as Mrs. Miller did in her modeled and shared writing lessons. Shared writing also provides an authentic context for teaching alphabet recognition and concepts about print.

Shared Reading

Shared reading is a form of interactive read-aloud using big books or enlarged charts of poems or songs (Parkes, 2000). The text selected for shared reading often includes rhyming words, words with alliteration, or repeated words or phrases that make the text highly memorable. After teachers introduce the text to children, the children naturally join in saying the text—thus it is called shared reading because the children share reading with the teacher. Effective books for shared reading have a limited amount of text and the print is large enough for children to see when they are seated near, but not next to, the book. Word spaces should also be large enough so that words are easy to isolate. For reading, teachers will need a sturdy easel large enough to support the big book or enlarged chart.

As they read, teachers can pause to allow children to chime in and say parts of the text. Teachers may want to point out words that rhyme or begin with the same sound (alliteration). As teachers read, they use a pointer to point to each word from left to right across the page of text. Eventually children can take turns pointing to the words (with a teacher's guidance) as the teacher and children chant the story or poem. As children point, teachers can make explicit pointing to the top of the page and the exact place to begin reading. They can make explicit their one-on-one matching and the return sweep each time they read.

Shared reading can be used to teach alphabet recognition (Justice & Ezell, 2002). After reading a big book or a poem written large on chart paper, teachers can ask children to step up to the book or chart paper and find particular letters. This is very effective when a letter appears frequently on a single page of text or in the text of a poem displayed on chart paper. Teachers can have children step up and find a letter that also occurs in their name or find two letters that are the same. Teachers can write a letter on a dry erase board, have children name that letter, and then step up to the displayed text and find it there.

Because of their familiarity with shared reading texts, children enjoy pretending to reread these books and poems on their own. Small copies of big books or poems should be included in the book center to encourage children's pretend reading.

Shared Writing

We have found that shared writing with preschoolers is easier when children dictate words or phrases to add to a list. Lists can be made quickly, since it only takes a few seconds to write a word in the list. Like Ms. Rodgers, Miss Leslie wrote several lists with her children related to the book *The Little Rabbit Who Wanted Red Wings*. The children dictated a list of animals included in the book, a list of animal features they would like to have, and a list of wishes.

Another activity calling for shared writing is to compose a **pattern innovation.** Pattern innovations begin as the teacher reads a predictable poem or story. Once the children are familiar with the pattern created by the repeated phrases in the book, they can construct their own innovation on the pattern. For example, *A Dark, Dark Tale* (Brown, 1981) tells the story of entering a scary house, going slowly up the stairs, and looking inside a shadowy cupboard only to find a mouse. It includes the repetitive pattern, "In the dark, dark _____, there was a dark, dark _____."

A group of four-year-olds retold the story using their school as the setting:

Once there was a dark, dark school.
In the dark, dark school there was a dark, dark hall.
Down the dark, dark hall was a dark, dark classroom.
In the dark, dark classroom there was a dark, dark cubbie.
In the dark, dark cubbie there was a SPIDER!

Pattern innovations that are carefully copied on large charts become favorite reading materials for shared reading and pretend reading. Teachers can make these texts into books by typing the text on several pages and illustrating the text with magazine pictures or clip art. These books can be bound and placed in the book center; they often become children's favorites.

The Sign-in Procedure and Other Name Activities

Novice readers and writers who realize that written marks can communicate messages are ready for the **sign-in procedure.** In this procedure, each child writes his or her name each day on an attendance sign-in sheet (Richgels, 2003). This procedure is functional; it should actually serve as the attendance record of the classroom. With young three-year-olds, the procedure may consist of having children place a card with their name on it in a box or on a chart. Later, they may place their name card and a slip of paper (the same size as the name card) on which they have written their names in the attendance box. Eventually, children will sign in by writing their signatures on an attendance sheet. Naturally, three- and four-year-olds' signatures will not be conventional when they first begin the sign-in procedure. However, by signing in daily, children gradually refine their signatures into readable names.

Ms. Rodgers uses the sign-in procedure because many of the children who come to her classroom have had few writing experiences prior to beginning preschool. Many children do not have crayons and paper in their homes. Before she began the sign-in procedure, few children voluntarily visited the writing center. The sign-in procedure gave the children an opportunity to write each day. As they became comfortable with that very brief writing experience, they gained confidence and began visiting the writing center for more lengthy writing experiences. The children also observed that their writing was useful; Ms. Rodgers used the sign-in list to comment on children's absences. Figure 7.5 presents an example of Ms. Rodgers's sign-in sheets.

Activities to Promote Alphabet Letter Learning

Shared reading, shared writing, and the sign-in procedure provide many opportunities for teachers to talk about alphabet letters and demonstrate their conventional formation. Through "all day, all the time activities" evident in Mrs. Miller's classroom, many children will learn to recognize many alphabet letters. They will hear about letters during

FIGURE 7.5 A Sign-in Sheet from Ms. Rodgers's Classroom

shared reading and shared writing; they will locate and write letters in step-up and write-on activities. Teachers often use letters as transition activities. For example, they may call children to line up to go to the playground by saying, "If your name begins with the letter *K*, you may line up now." We do not recommend that preschool teachers engage children in handwriting practice or require children to copy alphabet letters merely for the purpose of learning a letter's correct formation (Schickedanz & Casbergue, 2004). However, we do recommend that teachers frequently model for children how to write letters, and as they model, that they talk about the strokes they are making (Schickedanz, 1999). This naturally occurs during shared writing as teachers spell words as they write them. However, teachers can also capitalize on other opportunities to introduce and reinforce alphabet letters. For example, one preschool teacher noticed that one child was writing a letter *S* in nearly conventional form in his sign-in signature while most of the other children had not yet mastered this difficult letter. During whole-group, the teacher complimented the writer, "I noticed that Sakeil wrote a very nice *S* today at sign-in." Then she quickly demonstrated how to write the letter on a large chart and invited Sakeil to step up to the chart and also write the letter. Later, the chart was hung in the writing center and all the children were invited to practice writing *S*s. This is an example of a letter write on in which children are invited to write on the chart.

Another activity that directs attention to alphabet letters is teaching children to write everyone's name (Cunningham, 2000). Every day the teacher demonstrates how to write one child's name on a large chart paper. Children practice writing the name on small wipe-off boards or on paper attached to a clipboard. As they write, the teacher and children talk about the alphabet letters they are writing. One preschool teacher also reads a special alphabet book coordinated with the name being introduced. For example, on the day that the children wrote Eldric's name, she read *Ellen's Book* (Brown & Ruttle, 1999). This small alphabet book includes pictures of an egg, an elephant, and an elf. In this way, the teacher introduced children to still another literacy concept—listening to the beginning sounds in the words *Eldric, Ellen, egg, elephant,* and *elf.* The next section of this chapter provides more activities that direct children's attention to the sounds in language.

SUPPORTING CHILDREN'S DEVELOPMENT OF PHONEMIC AWARENESS

PHONEMIC AWARENESS, that is, conscious attention to individual sounds (phonemes) in words, is essential to learning to read and write (Adams, 1990; Goswami, 2004). Fully developed phonemic awareness, the sort of awareness that allows children to use the alphabetic principle in reading and writing, entails phoneme-by-phoneme segmentation of words. Most preschoolers do not achieve this level of awareness. However, preschoolers can develop other sorts of phonological awareness that are first steps toward this fully developed phonemic awareness.

With experience, preschoolers can learn to detect syllables, recognize and produce rhyming words, and recognize words with the same beginning sounds by segmenting first sounds in words. This will occur as teachers read nursery rhymes and other texts with many examples of rhyme and alliteration. In the last part of this chapter we describe many activities that allow preschoolers to develop the beginnings of phonemic awareness, including playful lessons with a systematic approach to phonemic awareness.

Attending to Syllable and Rhyme

Nursery rhymes and other rhyming jingles can be found in literature from around the world. They provide a perfect starting point for drawing children's attention to the sounds of language. In fact, three-year-olds who have had so many experiences with nursery rhymes that they have memorized some of them are far more likely to have high levels of phonemic awareness as five-year-olds than children who have not had many experiences with nursery rhymes (MacLean, Bryant, & Bradley, 1987). Children naturally learn nursery rhymes when they are repeated again and again as a part of whole-group activities in preschool. Many nursery rhymes and jump rope jingles can be quickly recited emphasizing the rhythm created by accented syllables. Using the word *syllables* as children chant the rhyme raises their awareness of this unit of sound in language. Teachers can make syllables even more explicit by chanting and emphasizing the syllables in children's names.

When teachers turn to rhyme, attending to syllables should be eliminated so that children can concentrate on this new unit of sound. Teachers can draw children's attention to the rhymes included in nursery rhymes with **"I can hear" talk.** For example, when listening to the nursery rhyme *Hickory Dickory Dock,* teachers can say, "I can hear 'clock' and 'dock'; they rhyme." Or, with another rhyming book, teachers can say, "I hear *mouse, house*—those two words rhyme *mmmm ouse* and *hhh ouse*." Simply pausing to notice a few rhyming words during shared or interactive read-alouds is enough to capture some children's attention (Cunningham, 1998). Soon a few children will be noticing rhyming words themselves. Once children begin to notice rhymes, teachers can prepare pictures of rhyming words found in favorite books for small-group or center activities. Children can match pictures of rhyming words in pocket charts. As they do so, teachers can model how to segment the words into their onsets and rimes using more "I can hear" talk: "I hear /k/ /an/ and I can hear /p/ /an/." Preschoolers usually will not be able to segment the words, but teacher modeling helps draw attention to these salient sound units.

A next step, following teachers' "I can hear" talk about rhyming words, is to invite children to make rhymes, to involve them in rhyming games. From "I can hear rhymes," teachers can proceed to "Let's make rhymes."

Rhyming games include inviting children to repeat rhymes the teacher has made and to make their own rhymes. However, because of the difficulty of making rhymes, preschool teachers can expect students to give responses that involve sound similarities but are not rhymes.

Attending to Beginning Phonemes

Drawing attention to both the rime and the onset is the bridge from rhyming words to words with alliteration. Many **language play books** contain both rhyme and alliteration as well as other sounds of language. These books are specially designed to highlight sounds in words. *Charlie Parker Played Be Bop* (Raschka, 1992), for example, is a picture book that contains a bit of a story line—about Charlie Parker's cat waiting for him to come home. But its power to captivate listeners is in its rhythm and rhyme, its made-up words, and its imaginative illustrations. Readers and listeners of any age can enjoy its use of the sounds and accents in the made-up words to re-create the feel of be bop music. Preschool teachers can also use it (after more than one reading just for fun) to heighten awareness of sounds in words. After reading the single line of text displayed across two facing pages, "Boppitty, bibbitty, **bop. BANG!**", a preschool teacher might say, "I can hear /b/ in those words!" and repeat all four words, emphasizing their initial *b* sound.

Teachers can continue making "I can hear" statements about beginning sounds when talking about children's names. If Miguel is chosen as helper for the day, the teacher can say, "I can hear Miguel's /mmmm/." Or she may say, "I can hear /mmmm/ at the beginning of *Miguel*." In a later instance of Miguel's being helper, the teacher might ask, "What sound do you hear at the beginning of *Miguel*?" Still later, the teacher might withhold display of Miguel's name card until she gets a response to "The name of today's helper starts with /mmm/. Who could it be?" Teachers can use the beginning phonemes of children's names in transition activities. For example, when calling children to line up for lunch, teachers might say, "If your name begins with /m/, you may get in our line now."

Preschoolers need frequent opportunities to practice hearing and articulating the **consonant phonemes.** These can be spelled with single letters (e.g., /b/ spelled with *b*) or with pairs of letters (e.g., /f/ spelled with *ph* or /sh/ spelled with *sh*). A two-letter spelling of a consonant sound is called a **consonant digraph.** Preschoolers need to attend to **vowel phonemes** only when their names begin with them (e.g., Emily or Avery).

Reading and Constructing Alphabet Books

Reading many kinds of alphabet books extends children's awareness of letters and alliteration. The best alphabet books for helping children listen to beginning sounds are books with large alphabet letters and pictures of a few items that are familiar to children. A picture of a walrus on the *W* page is not helpful when children call it a seal ("W is for seal!"). As teachers select alphabet books for reading aloud with preschoolers, they should carefully consider whether the illustrations and words used in the book help children's understanding of beginning sounds (Murray, Stahl, & Ivey, 1996). For example, alphabet books with illustrations of a ship on the *S* page are not useful in helping children hear the /s/ phoneme or later in making the connection between the phoneme /s/ and the letter *S*. Making an alphabet wall or book together is one way to call attention to beginning sounds. Children can bring in environmental print or cut pictures from magazines to contribute to this activity.

The Internet includes many websites featuring alphabet letters (Duffelmeyer, 2002). At www.learningplanet.com/act/abcorder/htm, the alphabet letters are spoken aloud and children are invited to click on alphabet letters to indicate which letter comes next in a sequence. All of the alphabet letters are displayed in order so the child does not need to remember letters to play the game. An alphabet chart is presented at www.literacyhour.co.uk/kids/alph_char2.html. Children can click on the letters and a page of an alphabet book is displayed. The alphabet letters are animated at www.enfagrow.com/language008.html. Letters are presented in both upper- and lower-case letters along with an animal whose name begins with that letter. The animal moves across the screen. The alphabet game presented at http://funschool.com is more challenging. Here children must locate alphabet letters hidden in a scary Halloween picture. The sound effects add to the pleasure of this activity. However, children need to already know the alphabet letters in order to play the game. A similar game is found at http://sesameworkshop.org/sesamestreet.

MODIFYING INSTRUCTION TO MEET THE NEEDS OF DIVERSE LEARNERS

IN PRESCHOOL the first place to meet the needs of individual learners is in interacting with children as they select and play with center materials. Teachers can engage a child in conversation and provide informal instruction while still honoring and respecting the child's lead. Teachers use systematic observation and careful documentation in anecdotal notes to make decisions on when to intervene with children in a more targeted way.

Targeted Classroom Interventions

When teachers notice, for example, that children are not catching on to letter names during "all day, all the time activities" or as a result of using the name game for each child's name, or even after a class experience writing an alphabet book, then they will use more explicit and systematic approaches during targeted classroom interventions. Ms. Rodgers's systematic approach was to teach four letters each week, targeting two confusable letters and two other letters. Each Friday, she observed her students in a small-group activity in order to assess their ability to name each of the four letters and to write them from memory. Most of her children knew fewer than ten letters when she began this targeted approach, and many recognized half or more of the letters at the end of eight weeks of instruction. It is important to note that the activities used in this intervention were playful (for example, feeding alphabet letters to a puppet), and most of them included games that are engaging to young children (for example, playing concentration by matching two of the same letters). Figure 7.6 presents the four letters Ms. Rogers selected for instruction in each of ten weeks of targeted intervention.

Meeting the Needs of Preschool ELLs

At the age of three, middle-class children's spoken language includes about 2,000 words, and they learn nearly 2,000 more each year (Roskos, Tabors, & Lenhart, 2004). So by the time they enter kindergarten, middle-class children, regardless of their home language, know about 5,000 words. Despite their acquisition of a home language, English language learners may have very little English vocabulary. Because of the critical role that vocabulary plays in learning to read and write, preschool teachers need to plan intentionally for ELLs' language and vocabulary growth. First, teachers need to learn to use language scaffolding strategies to help preschoolers to expand their English vocabularies and their sentence structure knowledge.

Language Scaffolding Strategies. **Language scaffolds** are the teacher's intentional attempts to sustain conversation and provide children with models of new vocabulary and slightly more complex sentence structures. The following effective language strategies are adapted from Roskos, Tabors, and Lenhart (2004, p. 40–41):

- The teacher repeats a few of the child's words from a child's comment and inserts additional words using slightly more complex sentence structure. For example, at breakfast a child holds his milk carton out expecting the teacher to open it for him.

FIGURE 7.6 Letters for Targeted Intervention Lessons

Week	Letters
1.	A, C, U, T
2.	E, F, I, O
3.	H, L, B, I
4.	D, P, R, B
5.	G, J, L, E
6.	K, R, X, M
7.	M, W, V, S
8.	N, Q, Y, Z
9.	V, W, A, M
10.	E, F, T, L

The teacher says, "Should I open it? Open it?" After the child nods or says "yes," the teacher says, "I will open your milk. You watch."

- As teachers perform an action, they talk about their action. For example, at the writing center when making birthday cards, the teacher says, "I will fold my paper. Now I will write *Happy Birthday.* Now you fold."
- As a child performs an action, the teacher explains what the child is doing. For example, at the home center, the teacher says, "You got a cup. A cup. Will you drink?"
- Before children are to perform an action, teachers demonstrate the action and describe in detail what they are doing. Teachers repeat the most critical vocabulary for actions and objects. For example, as children pretend to make cookies using sand for flour, the teacher says, "This is flour. We scoop up the flour. We scoop up more flour. Now it is full."
- Before children are to perform an action, teachers ask children to tell what they will do first. For example, after a child empties a cup of flour (sand), the teacher says, "Now we are scooping flour. Scooping flour. What will you do first?"

These scaffolds wrap English around the child while the child is actively partici-pating in an activity. The actions support children's understanding even when they know very little of the vocabulary. However, the term *scaffolding* implies not just sup-port, but also that the support is removable. As children show greater competence, they need less support. As teachers provide daily language scaffolding, children gradually begin using the modeled English vocabulary and sentence structures, eventually in non-scaffolded situations (Richgels, 1995).

Shared Reading with Planned Language Activities.   One kind of planned language activity is to read aloud carefully selected books and scaffold children's attention to verbs, adjec-tives, and adverbs (Justice et al., 2005). For example, action verbs are a critical compo-nent of the book *Mr. Gumpy's Outing* (Burningham, 1970). The animals *flap, trample, muck,* and *bleat.* Teachers act out these as they read the story aloud (for example, by flapping their arms up and down), and then ask children to apply their new knowledge (for example, by naming other animals that can flap) (Justice et al., 2005). Other books can be used to introduce adjectives, opposites, and time-related adverbs. For example, *The Napping House* (Wood & Wood, 1984) includes repeated adjective-noun phrases (such as *cozy bed, snoring granny, dreaming child*). Teachers can ask questions such as "Who is cozy? How do you get cozy?" Then teachers can help children form their own phrases, such as *the cozy chair, the cozy couch, the cozy blanket.*

Talking about Objects Related to a Book or Theme.   Another appropriate language activity for ELLs is to guide their talk about objects related to a book or a theme. For example, after reading aloud *The Little Red Hen (Makes a Pizza)* (Sturges, 1999), teachers can bring in a variety of baking dishes, including glass and aluminum baking dishes in a variety of shapes, such as round cake and pie pans and rectangular bread and muffin pans. Teachers might also bring in pizza pans and cookie sheets. Each child is given a baking dish. Children match these with pictures of foods that might be baked in them. The teacher talks about and names the dishes, tells what they are made of, and names their shapes. If the children's language about these shapes is already fairly sophisticated, teachers might provide additional information using such words as *slanted* and *straight* (comparing the sides of a pie pan with those of a cake pan) or *shallow* and *deep* (com-paring the muffin pan or pizza pan with the bread pan). Teachers can also bring in cooking utensils such as bowls, measuring cups, and spoons, so that children can pre-tend to use them with their baking dishes.

CHAPTER SUMMARY

PRESCHOOLERS CAN BE EXPECTED to achieve much written language competence. They enjoy storybook read-alouds and discussions, identify signs and labels, play rhyming games, have partial alphabet and sound-letter knowledge, and use some al-phabet letters or mock letters to write meaningful words and phrases, including their names. They retell favorite storybooks and information books and write pretend mes-sages as part of dramatic play. Although most preschoolers do not develop full phonemic awareness, teachers help them to take first steps through enjoyable, informal phonological awareness activities, such as "I can hear" and rhyming games.

Preschoolers acquire concepts about written language when their classrooms are filled with print and when teachers model how to use that print in play. Mrs. Miller's classroom included many games and dramatic-play opportunities in which children used print in entertaining and functional ways.

Well-planned interactive read-alouds and response-to-literature activities support preschoolers' developing literary awareness, story concepts, and concepts of print. Miss Leslie demonstrated effective interactive reading techniques, including making comments and using gestures and voice to interpret stories as she read aloud. She was especially skillful at getting children to participate in interactive reading. She provided story concept activities and literary prop boxes.

Effective preschool teachers use written language talk to demonstrate how to use print and to encourage children's own writing attempts. In shared writing activities, including pattern innovations and list writing, preschoolers learn from their teachers' modeling about written language meanings, forms, meaning-form links, and functions. Finally, preschoolers learn much from play, including play in dramatic-play-with-print centers and in storytelling and playing activities.

Together all the literacy activities in preschool support children's learning in three major areas of literacy development: language and concept development, concepts about print and alphabet letter recognition and writing, and phonemic awareness.

Using and Applying the Information

We suggest two activities for applying the information presented in this chapter. First, make a list of the seven characteristics of literacy-rich classrooms presented in Chapter 6. Then reread this chapter and locate classroom activities from Miss Leslie's and Mrs. Miller's classrooms that are examples of these characteristics. Discuss these examples with your classmates.

Second, make a list of all the literacy learning activities mentioned in this chapter, including interactive reading books, shared writing, writing lists, story concept activities, response-to-literature activities, sign-in procedure, dramatic-play-with-print centers, print puzzles, letter games, "I can read" bags, and storytelling and drama. For each of these activities, describe what children learn. For example, as children participated in interactive read-alouds with Miss Leslie, they had opportunities for meaning making by answering questions and retelling the story with storytelling props.

GOING BEYOND THE TEXT

VISIT A PRESCHOOL CLASSROOM and observe several literacy activities. Take note of the interactions among children as they participate in literacy experiences. Also note the teacher's talk with children in those experiences. Make a list of the kinds of literacy materials available in the classroom. Talk with the teacher about the kinds of literacy activities he or she plans. Compare these materials, interactions, and activities with those found in Miss Leslie's, Ms. Rodgers's, and Mrs. Miller's preschool classrooms.

REFERENCES

Adams, M. J. (1990). *Beginning to read.* Cambridge: M.I.T. Press.

Bailey, C. (1987). *The little rabbit who wanted red wings.* New York: Platt and Munk.

Brown, R. (1981). *A dark, dark tale.* New York: Dial.

Brown, R., & Ruttle, K. (Eds.). (1999). *Ellen's book.* Cambridge, UK: Cambridge University Press.

Burningham, J. (1970). *Mr. Gumpy's outing.* New York: Holt, Rinehart and Winston.

Casbergue, R., McGee, L., & Bedford, A. (in press). Characteristics of classroom environments associated with accelerated literacy development. In L. Justice & C. Vukelich (Eds.), *Creating preschool centers of excellence in language and literacy.* New York: Guilford.

Cole, H. (1997). *Jack's garden.* New York: Mulberry.

Cunningham, P. (1998). Looking for patterns: Phonics activities that help children notice how words work. In C. Weaver (Ed.), *Practicing what we know: Informed reading instruction* (pp. 87–110). Urbana, IL: National Council of Teachers of English.

Cunningham, P. (2000). *Phonics they use: Words for reading and writing.* New York: Longman.

Dickinson, D. (2001). Large-group and free-play times: Conversational settings supporting language and literacy development. In D. Dickinson & P. Tabor (Eds.), *Beginning literacy with language: Young children learning at home and school* (pp. 223–255). Baltimore, MD: Paul H. Brookes.

Duffelmeyer, F. (2002). Alphabet activities on the Internet. *The Reading Teacher, 55,* 631–635.

Gee, J. (2001). A sociocultural perspective on early literacy development. In S. Neuman & D. Dickinson (Eds.), *Handbook of early literacy research* (pp. 30–42). New York: Guilford.

Goswami, U. (2001). Early phonological development and the acquisition of literacy. In S. Neuman & D. Dickinson (Eds.), *Handbook of early literacy research* (pp. 111–125). New York: Guilford.

Goswami, U., 2004. *Linguistic factors, phonological and orthographic processing in dyslexia.* Swindon, Great Britain: Economic and Social Research Council.

Hargrave, A., & Senechal, M. (2000). A book reading intervention with preschool children who have limited vocabularies: The benefits of regular reading and dialogic reading. *Early Childhood Research Quarterly, 15,* 75–90.

Justice, L. M., & Ezell, H. K. (2002). Use of storybook reading to increase print awareness in at-risk children. *American Journal of Speech-Language Pathology, 11,* 17–29.

Justice, L. M., Pence, K. L., Beckman, A. R., Skibbe, L. E., & Wiggins, A. K. (2005). *Scaffolding with storybooks: A guide for enhancing young children's language and literacy development.* Newark, DE: The International Reading Association.

Krauss, R. (1945). *The carrot seed.* New York: Harper Trophy.

MacLean, M., Bryant, P., & Bradley, L. (1987). Rhymes, nursery rhymes, and reading in early childhood. *Merrill-Palmer Quarterly, 33,* 255–281.

McGee, L. M. (2005). The role of wisdom in evidence-based preschool literacy programs. In B. Maloch, J. V. Hoffman, D. L. Schallert, C. M. Fairbanks, & J. Worthy (Eds.) *54th Yearbook of the National Reading Conference* (pp. 1–21). National Reading Conference, Oak Creek, WI.

McGee, L., & Richgels, D. (2003). *Designing early literacy programs for at-risk preschoolers and kindergartners.* New York: Guilford.

McGill-Franzen, A., Lanford, C., & Adams, E. (2002). Learning to be literate: A comparison of five urban early childhood programs. *Journal of Educational Psychology, 94,* 443–464.

Murray, B., Stahl, S., & Ivey, G. (1996). Developing phoneme awareness through alphabet books. *Reading and Writing: An Interdisciplinary Journal, 8,* 306–322.

Neuman, S. (1999). Books make a difference: A study of access to literacy. *Reading Research Quarterly, 34,* 286–311.

Neuman, S., Copple, C., & Bredekamp. S. (2000). *Learning to read and write: Developmentally appropriate practices for young children.* Washington, DC: National Association for the Education of Young Children.

Paley, V. G. (1990). *The boy who would be a helicopter: The uses of storytelling in the classroom.* Cambridge: Harvard University Press.

Parkes, B. (2000). *Read it again! Revisiting shared reading.* Portland, ME: Stenhouse.

Raschka, C. (1992). *Charlie Parker played be bop.* New York: Orchard.

Richgels, D. J. (1995). A kindergarten sign-in procedure: A routine in support of written language learning. In K. A. Hinchman, D. J. Leu, & C. K. Kinzer (Eds.), *Perspectives on literacy research and practice, Forty-fourth yearbook of the National Reading Conference* (pp. 243–254). Chicago: The National Reading Conference.

Richgels, D. J. (2003). *Going to kindergarten: A year with an outstanding teacher.* Lanham, MD: Scarecrow Education Press.

Roberts, T., & Neal, H. (2004). Relationships among preschool English language learner's oral proficiency in English, instructional experience and literacy development. *Contemporary Educational Psychology, 29,* 283–311.

Roskos, K. A., Tabors, P. O., & Lenhart, L. A. (2004). *Oral language and early literacy in preschool: Talking, reading, and writing.* Newark, DE: The International Reading Association.

Rowe, D. W. (1998). The literate potentials of book-related dramatic play. *Reading Research Quarterly, 33,* 10–35.

Schickedanz, J. (1999). *Much more than the ABCs.* Washington, DC: National Association for the Education of Young Children.

Schickedanz, J. A., & Casbergue, R. M. (2004). *Writing in preschool: Learning to orchestrate meaning and marks.* Newark, DE: The International Reading Association.

Schickedanz, J., Schickedanz, D., Forsyth, P., & Forsyth, G. (2001). *Understanding children and adolescents.* Boston: Allyn & Bacon.

Senechal, M., LeFevre, J., Hudson, E., & Lawson, E. (1996). Knowledge of storybook as a predictor of young children's vocabulary. *Journal of Educational Psychology, 88,* 520–536.

Smolkin, L., & Donovan, C. (2002). "Oh, excellent, excellent question!": Developmental differences and comprehension acquisition. In C. Block & M. Pressley (Eds.), *Comprehension instruction: Research-based best practices* (pp. 140–157). New York: Guilford.

Stevens, J. (1995). *The three billy goats gruff.* New York: Harcourt.

Sturges, P. (1999). *The little red hen (makes a pizza).* New York: Dutton Children's Books.

Tabors, P., Snow, C., & Dickinson, D. (2001). Homes and schools together: Supporting language and literacy development. In D. Dickinson & P. Tabor (Eds.), *Beginning literacy with language: Young children learning at home and school* (pp. 313–334). Baltimore, MD: Paul H. Brookes.

Wasik, B., & Bond, M. (2001). Beyond the pages of a book: Interactive book reading and language development in preschool children. *Journal of Educational Psychology, 93,* 243–250.

Wells, G. (1986). *The meaning makers: Children learning language and using language to learn.* Portsmouth, NH: Heinemann.

Whitehurst, G., & Lonigan, C. (2001). *Emergent literacy: Development from prereaders to readers handbook of early literacy research* (pp. 11–29). New York: Guilford.

Wilkes, A. (1989). *My first cookbook.* New York: Alfred A. Knopf.

Wolf, S., & Heath, S. (1992). *The braid of literature: Children's worlds of reading.* Cambridge: Harvard University Press.

Wood, A., & Wood, D. (1984). *The napping house.* San Diego: Harcourt, Brace, Jovanovich.

CHAPTER 8

Supporting Literacy Learning in Kindergarten

KEY CONCEPTS

Continuous Text
Authentic Text
Functional Text
Open-Ended Activities
Choral Reading
Text Reconstruction
Finger-Point Reading
"What Can You Show Us?" Activity

Writing the Room
Morning Message
Consonant Cluster
Decodable Word
Guided Reading
Decoding an Unfamiliar Word
Kid Writing
Journal Writing

Interactive Writing
High Frequency Words
Say-It and Move-It Activity
Elkonin Boxes
Dramatic-Play-with-Print Center
Project Approach
Environmental Print

THE KINDERGARTEN CONTEXT: WHAT'S NEW HERE?

IN THE LAST TWENTY-FIVE YEARS, there has been a shift toward a more academic kindergarten experience. No longer is kindergarten viewed as merely a socialization for school, a year to get used to how to behave for teachers and with other children. Kindergarteners are expected to recognize and write numerals, count, and understand the number line. The academic agenda also includes knowledge in a variety of mandated social studies and science curriculum units (e.g., the neighborhood or the life cycle). Expectations about literacy learning in kindergarten also have changed.

What Kindergartners Learn about Literacy

The greatest change from preschool to kindergarten is that kindergartners approach written language with an explicit focus on print. Kindergartners can recognize and write alphabet letters, match spoken and written words, know rhyming words and beginning sounds in words, know sound–letter correspondences, understand concepts of print, and begin to write some high-frequency words. All of these expectations involve a mastery of knowledge that is not expected of preschoolers. We would add that kindergartners learn to write their first and last names; identify initial and final sounds in spoken words; know sounds associated with many letters, especially consonants; use sound-letter correspondences in invented spellings; and participate in read-alouds with increasingly complex comments and answers to teachers' questions.

The Teacher's Role

We feel that it is possible for kindergarten teachers who are knowledgeable about the characteristics of young children as they emerge into literacy to turn this academic expectation to their advantage. Furthermore, we believe that it is possible and desirable for kindergarten teachers to maintain the child-centered approach that has always been part of their outlook, even while addressing the new academic agenda. Kindergarten teachers can still be attentive to and responsive to individual children's interests and abilities; they can still be flexible.

Teachers can be flexible by presenting models of conventional reading and writing, but expecting kindergartners to respond in unique ways. For example, a teacher may model a handwriting method and give children many opportunities to write (in a sign-in routine, at a dramatic-play-with-print center, or at a writing center), but not require drill and practice in hand writing. A kindergarten teacher may offer shared reading experiences with big book stories or chart-paper poems, opportunities for individual children to tell the class what they know on a big book page or on a poster at the easel, and follow-up experiences with little books in guided reading and individual reading and writing activities, but not require learning all the words in the big book or poem as sight words.

Most important of all is for kindergarten teachers to provide models (theirs and children's) and to provide children with opportunities for the unique kind of exploration that we have argued is characteristic of experimenters (see Chapter 4). Then children will show what they know, what they are working on, and what scaffolding they can benefit from. When teachers let the children shape the task, children can achieve goals that will surprise even the most academically oriented parents and administrators.

The Kindergarten Setting: Space and Materials

As with all teachers, an important part of being a kindergarten teacher is arranging the classroom and gathering materials. Figure 8.1 presents our design for a well-appointed and well-arranged kindergarten classroom. One whole-class area in this classroom is the large, open, carpeted area in front of a bulletin board. Teachers often use an area like this when they conduct opening-of-the-day activities, such as their calendar activity.

In our exemplary classroom, the bulletin board holds a Helpers' Tree on which the names of each day's two helpers are displayed (on apple-shaped cutouts taken from an apple basket containing every child's name); a tooth graph (on which the names of children who lose teeth are written); a calendar; a specials schedule and hook for displaying a sign that tells each day's special class (gym, music, art, or library story); and a weather chart with yes and no options for reporting whether it is sunny, cloudy, windy, rainy, or snowy.

A pocket chart hangs from a nearby stand. This large vinyl chart has several horizontal pockets running the width of it in which words on cards can be placed to make sentences or lines from poems. Also near to the carpeted whole-class area is an easel used for displaying big books, chart paper, and an erasable marker board.

This classroom has a second whole-class area where children can sit at tables near a chalkboard. There are five centers in the classroom: blocks and make-believe play, home and restaurant, computing, writing, and reading. In addition to the centers, this classroom has five workstations. The workstation materials are located in centers or are stored in bins and low cupboards. During center time, children place the materials either on the tables in the whole-class area or in other designated locations in the classroom. For example, an overhead projector on a low rolling stand is located in the whole-class table area. Children pull out the projector and take materials out of a small plastic tub placed on top of the projector to complete work in the overhead projector workstation. Children play in the whole-class centers when they are not being used for group activities. Play props are stored in bins and low cupboards in these centers and in the home center's kitchen furniture.

The writing center has a large, round table where children are able to see others' work and to share their own work. On low shelves, there are many kinds of writing tools and paper; picture dictionaries; several letter-stamp sets and ink pads; several laminated cards, each showing the alphabet in uppercase and lowercase letters; and a file box filled with cards on which children have written words for future reference, some of which are illustrated. On the countertop above the shelves are pigeonhole mailboxes, one for each child. They hold unfinished writing and letters to kindergartners from classmates or the teacher. The computer center is next to the writing center and provides space for two children. It includes a computer, printer, and scanner. The classroom digital camera is located in a special tub in that center. Directions for downloading pictures from the camera are on a laminated card in the center.

In the reading center, children's books stand on low, deep shelves and lie on low cupboard tops, where they are easily accessible. These include story and informational

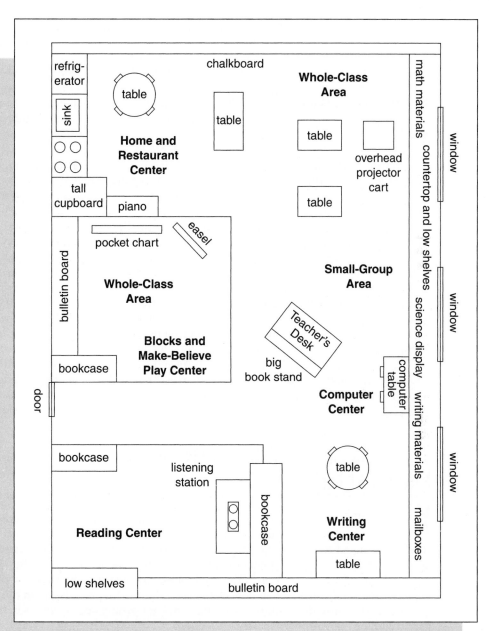

FIGURE 8.1   A Kindergarten Classroom

picture books, often chosen to complement a unit of study; class-made books (such as a book of bear stories written from children's dictation on bear-shaped pages during a bear unit); big books that the class has read; and multiple standard-sized copies of some of the big books. There are soft cushions on which the children can make themselves comfortable when they read. The cushions can be stacked out of the way when the reading center is used for a small-group area. The listening station is set up on a small table near the reading center, with chairs for four children to use a tape player with headsets.

Materials for a letter-and-word workstation are located in a small tub in the low shelves near the windows. Children place the tub on one of the tables to work at this workstation. The retelling workstation materials are kept in a tub in the reading center. Children take the retelling materials to the whole-class area rug. Pocket chart materials are located in a tub next to the pocket chart.

Together this combination of larger centers and smaller workstations creates space for kindergarten children to work on assignments and to choose locations to play when given free-choice time. This combination of self-selected activities and assigned activities supports the wide range of knowledge, abilities, interests, and learning styles that can be expected in kindergarten. Some children will be like those we described in Chapter 3 with very little conventional literacy knowledge. Other children will be like those we described in Chapter 4 who know quite a bit about the alphabet, are discovering the alphabetic principle, and are beginning to fingerpoint read and invent spellings. At the end of kindergarten, some children will read and write like those we described in Chapter 5. They will read easy-to-read books and spell many words conventionally. The challenge for kindergarten teachers is to expect this wide range of knowledge and competence and to plan activities that support all children's moving forward.

THREE MAJOR LEARNING OPPORTUNITIES IN KINDERGARTEN

KINDERGARTEN TEACHERS use many of the same teaching procedures that preschool teachers use. They use daily routines in which they read aloud to children, engage children in shared reading and writing, and provide opportunities for children to practice reading and writing independently. In this chapter, we describe how these teaching strategies, and other more advanced ones, are adapted to fit the needs of kindergartners. However, all of these classroom activities that we discuss in this chapter are aimed at providing children with three major learning opportunities in kindergarten and the early primary grades.

One critical learning opportunity occurs when teachers demonstrate reading and writing continuous, authentic, functional texts. **Continuous texts** build meaning across a number of words—often very many words, as in a poem, a storybook, or an information book. Words do not stand in isolation, but instead work together, as in a line or a stanza of a poem or a sentence or paragraph of a story or an essay.

Continuous texts are also **authentic texts** when they are composed and read to serve readers' and writers' own communication needs rather than only as vehicles for instruction. For example, a thank you letter lets the giver of a gift know that the recipient received and appreciated it, or a novel allows a reader to share in an author's imaginary world, perhaps for enjoyment, perhaps in order to learn from the experiences and dilemmas of the novel's characters. Merely instructional texts, that is, texts created only to teach about reading and writing, such as a list of spelling words or a letter-sound worksheet, do not communicate in these ways.

Another way to think about authentic texts is that they are functional in ways that merely instructional texts are not. **Functional texts** serve authentic purposes in people's everyday home and classroom lives. A merely instructional text has an instructional function, as when a beginning-sound-letter worksheet teaches or reinforces correspondences between initial phonemes and the letters that represent those phonemes. Functional texts can be used for instruction, but their primary function is to help people get things done in their everyday lives that they would not as easily accomplish without the texts. For example, a telephone book helps people to locate telephone numbers, a grocery list helps them to remember what foods to purchase, and a graph helps them to convey and remember numerical information.

Children, like adults, learn best when instruction is relevant to their lives. Thus the best instructional texts are also authentic, functional texts. When a teacher and students create a classroom telephone book for the housekeeping center, they are composing a text that serves their dramatic play. Arranging classmates' names alphabetically in the telephone book can be an opportunity for instruction about initial phoneme-letter correspondences.

Children need many opportunities to see their teachers demonstrate reading and writing continuous, authentic, and functional texts. Research has shown that children attend to such texts in their homes and learn from them about how print works and what it can do for them (Purcell-Gates, 1996).

A second critical learning opportunity occurs when teachers emphasize the conventions of reading and writing, such as phoneme-letter correspondences. Kindergartners will learn to recognize and write letters, hear and segment phonemes from spoken words, and attempt spellings by matching letters with what they hear. They will recognize letters within the context of written words and use what they know about phoneme-letter correspondences when attempting to read easy, predictable texts. Kindergartners do learn such conventions during reading and writing activities that use continuous, authentic, and functional texts. However, some kindergartners require that the instruction taking place with such texts be more explicit about literacy conventions than the instruction that other kindergartners receive, that it be more focused on their current level of knowledge and on next steps that can be achieved with appropriate scaffolding. Effective teachers know which children need more focused and intensive instruction *at a particular point in time* in order to catch on to the conventions. We have found that all five-year-olds at some points in their literacy and language development benefit from small-group instruction focused on the conventions.

A third critical learning opportunity occurs when teachers provide time and resources for kindergartners' independent practice. All children need to try out what they have been learning. As they work on materials that are familiar to them, they will make new discoveries. This requires that children's practice be with materials they can use successfully. Independent practice and self-selected exploration of appropriate materials are critical to kindergartners' developing fluency and confidence.

In the next sections of this chapter, we describe exemplary teachers and their approaches to kindergarten instruction. We show how they offer daily whole-class activities that are open-ended so that all children can participate. **Open-ended activities** are those in which there is no one right answer. Children at all levels of development can participate successfully in these activities. For example, after a read-aloud, all kindergartners can share their favorite part, recall a character, or talk about a related experience. During shared writing of a graph presenting information about children's ice cream flavor preferences, all children can participate in counting. We have found that all children, but especially the children who struggle the most, are more successful when their whole-class instruction is with open-ended, authentic reading and writing activities. Exemplary teachers provide instruction about literacy conventions to small groups of learners who will be successful because instruction is based on what they know and focused on needed next steps in their literacy development.

CONTINUOUS TEXT READING AND WRITING IN EXEMPLARY CLASSROOMS

MRS. POREMBA is an exemplary kindergarten teacher who uses shared reading very effectively. She uses follow-up activities to reinforce the concepts she taught during shared reading such as left-right directionality, matching words letter-by-letter, and using letter-sound knowledge to check word predictions.

Shared Reading in Mrs. Poremba's Classroom

Mrs. Poremba teaches a mixture of middle-class and working-class children. She has only one English language learner. Many of her children come to school with a wealth of reading and writing experiences in preschool, but some children do not. Mrs. Poremba frequently reads poetry charts and big books using typical shared reading procedures. She introduces the children to the text before reading by talking about what the children already know about the topic, discussing the author and illustrator, and reading the title and counting words in the title. For example, early in the year Mrs. Poremba read the big book *Bears, Bears Everywhere* (Connelly, undated). This is a book with a repeated pattern on each page. The kindergartners are in the middle of studying bears and learning facts from information books as well as enjoying books with bear characters. Mrs. Poremba orients the children to the title of the story. She helps the children to concentrate on where to begin reading, how to spell the first sound in *bears,* and how a written word looks (by counting words in the title).

Mrs. Poremba: Where could I look to find the name of the story?

Children: B! B!

Mrs. Poremba: What do you mean *B*?

Child: The title page.

Mrs. Poremba: Well that's one place to look.

Child: The cover.

Mrs. Poremba: The cover? Okay . . . and I noticed that some of you said the letter *B* because that's the very first letter in the word (pointing) *Bears*. Here's another one (pointing to the *B* at the beginning of the second word *Bears*). This story is called (pointing) *Bears, Bears Everywhere!*

Child: Bears, bears everywhere?

Mrs. Poremba: I'll read it again—first of all, how about if we count the words in the title, so we know how many words there are. (With some children reading and counting along) "Bears"—one. "Bears"—there's two. "Everywhere"—three words in the title.

As she reads, she invites children's comments and questions and models using meaning-making strategies. She stops to comment about character or plot, to invite predictions, to remark about illustrations, and to accept and acknowledge students' comments and questions. Sometimes she points out a familiar or an unusual word or comments about punctuation, especially a question mark or an exclamation point.

For example, during reading of *Bears, Bears Everywhere,* one of the children had a question about a word in the text.

Child: Pairs?

Mrs. Poremba: I wonder what it means—bears in pairs?

Jason: Two together make a pair.

Mrs. Poremba: Oh, there are two together. So this isn't the kind of *pear* that you buy at the store and eat, like a fruit. This is a different way to use the word *pair*. Jason said that a pair is when two things are together. Look at your shoes. Like a pair of socks.

Children: Pair of earrings. . .pair of shoelaces. . .eyes. . .ears. . .arms. . .pair of legs. . . pair of elbows!

Mrs. Poremba: So things that come in twos are pairs.

Here Mrs. Poremba took just a minute to digress from reading aloud to address a vocabulary word and develop children's comprehension. Still later, another opportunity arose for her to focus on the spelling of the familiar words *on* and *no*.

Mrs. Poremba: What's this word (pointing to the word *on*)?

Several children respond at once with their guesses, including "Sitting in chairs," "Zero," and "No."

Mrs. Poremba: Does anyone know what O-N spells?. . .Let me show you.

Child: (still working on her own) On chairs.

Mrs. Poremba: (writing on the erasable board) Here is how you spell *no*. How do you spell it?—with *N* first and then—

Eric: Oh, I get it! I get it. The *O* has to be on that side and the *N*'s on that side.

Mrs. Poremba: Yes, when the *O* is on this side and the *N* is second, that's the word *on.*

Tara: It's like a pattern! (The children are used to finding patterns in the shapes on which the numbers of the calendar are written.)

Mrs. Poremba: It *is* kind of.

Children: (reading) On. On. On. On chairs! It's "On chairs"!

When a poem has become familiar enough, Mrs. Poremba's class reads it aloud together while she directs with a pointer on the chart-paper text. She knows that it is important for children to look at the print during such a **choral reading.** Before reading, she asks, "Where will you look to find the first word of the poem?" and makes sure that children are looking there.

Response Activities after Shared Writing

The final step of Mrs. Poremba's shared reading involves response activities with the text. The purpose of these activities is for children to attend to print on their own without the support of a teacher. In kindergarten, many of these activities take place in pairs or small groups; some are done by individuals.

A pocket chart provides opportunities for response activities that focus on print. After reading a poem about November, Mrs. Poremba wrote the poem on long strips of posterboard, one strip for each line of the poem. She placed these strips in the pocket chart, one strip per pocket, and the class read the poem one line at a time. Then she invited students to step up to the pocket chart, choose a line of the poem, read it, and remove that strip from the chart. When all the strips were removed, Mrs. Poremba returned them to the pocket chart and repeated the activity until every student had had a turn choosing and reading a line of the poem.

On another day, this opportunity to attend to print with a now familiar poem was extended through a **text reconstruction** activity. Text reconstruction is putting the words of a cut-apart sentence back together. Mrs. Poremba assigned students to small groups. Each group had all the words of the poem on separate word cards and a large piece of lined posterboard. Their job was to work together to reconstruct the poem by placing the word cards onto the lines on the posterboard.

The pocket chart with the poem displayed on strips was still available as a model for students who wanted one during their text reconstruction. As some children worked in their small groups to reproduce the poem, they used the model from the pocket chart to match words. Some children were able to locate words using picture clues, such as a drawing of blades of grass on the word card for *grass* in the line "No green grass."

As an individual activity with the November poem, Mrs. Poremba's students made their own books, each page of which contained a line from the poem and a pop-up illustration. Because they had listened to Mrs. Poremba read the poem, had read the poem together, and had done a small-group activity with the poem, all the children could read their November poem books when they took them home.

Another individual response activity, **finger-point reading,** provides opportunities for a student to focus on print and for the teacher to assess the student's print-related knowledge. An example of **finger-point** reading occurred in May after Mrs.

Poremba's class had observed the three-week-long process of chicken eggs' incubating and hatching in their room. A chart-paper poem/song used during this unit began, "Cluck Cluck Red Hen" and followed the pattern of "Baa Baa Black Sheep." During free-choice time, Zack was singing this song while visiting the brooder box that contained the class's newly hatched chicks. Mrs. Poremba noticed this and invited Zack to the easel. She pointed out that he was singing what was written on the chart paper, which the class had read together many times. She invited him to point with a pointer as he read the text. She watched and listened, nodding as he read.

The "What Can You Show Us?" Activity

Mrs. Poremba has developed a unique step in shared reading called the **"What can you show us?" activity.** She uses this step *before* she reads a chart or big book. During this step, children step up to the chart or big book, point to something in the print they notice, and talk about it. Figure 8.2 presents a letter Mrs. Poremba intends to read as a shared reading activity. She wrote the letter as a pretend message from Uncle Wally. He and Aunt Edith are large, floppy stuffed dolls who reside in the reading center.

The following example is from a "What Can You Show Us?" lesson in Mrs. Poremba's class, using Uncle Wally's letter (see Figure 8.2). In October, Erin is at the easel doing a student demonstration with Uncle Wally's letter. She points to the word *is*.

Mrs. Poremba: You're pointing to that *i-s*, Erin. Tell us about it.

Erin: It's *is!*

Dear Kindergarteners,
It is fall!
Fall is apple time.
We picked an apple
on a tree.
Yum! Yum!
Love,
Uncle Wally

FIGURE 8.2 A Letter from Uncle Wally

Mrs. Poremba: That's the word *is?* (Erin nods, and Mrs. Poremba points to the word and reads.) "Is."

Mrs. Poremba calls on Eric to come to the easel. Unlike Erin's focus on the whole word *is,* Eric's focus is on a letter that he recognizes.

Mrs. Poremba: (to the class) Watch Eric.

Eric: There's a *Y* for Freddy (pointing to the first letter in *Yum*).

Mrs. Poremba: Oooh. There's a *Y* for Freddy. What do you mean "a *Y* for Freddy"? Does Freddy have a *Y* somewhere in his name?

Eric: Yeah, and he has an *F* (pointing to the first letter in *Fall*).

Ten days later, the class reads another letter, this time from imaginary Aunt Edith. Now Mayra, who speaks almost no English at this point in the school year (Spanish is her first language), shares what she knows about letters.

Mrs. Poremba: Mayra has something she would like to teach you. . . .

Mayra: A *W* (pointing).

Mrs. Poremba: A *W!* (pointing to the same *W* that Mayra had pointed to).

Mayra: *W.*

Mrs. Poremba: That's a *W.* Thank you, Mayra, for showing us the *W.* Thank you.

In February, children show advanced knowledge about words. When Mrs. Poremba invites her kindergartners to show what they know about a new poem, Freddy makes a connection with a familiar word. He uses one of Mrs. Poremba's word frames (window-shaped cutouts with handles that can be placed around a word to isolate it from the other words in a text) to show the word *Little* on the poem displayed for reading.

Freddy: It starts like— (He goes to the wall and points to the word *Library* in the "Library Story" sign posted there for that day's special class.)

Jason: *Library* has the same two letters.

Another Child: And *Lisa* (his sister's name).

Mrs. Poremba: Okay now, Freddy, you touch the *L* and the *i* right there and I'll get the *L* and the *i* right here. Freddy, that's very interesting. What about the rest of the word, Freddy?

Freddy: No.

Mrs. Poremba: . . . Freddy noticed the *L* and the *i* at the beginning of that word—the same thing as in *Library.* Freddy, that was important.

Freddy's and his classmate's recognition of the beginning similarities in *Little, Library,* and *Lisa* is indeed important. Mrs. Poremba's affirmation of student demonstrations includes explicit talk about letters and sounds. Reinforcing their focus on print results in their associating letters with sounds and doing the sort of phoneme segmentation and phoneme deletion required for explicit work with onsets and rimes.

Capitalizing on Opportunities to Create Authentic Shared Writing

Mrs. Poremba is a master at seizing opportunities to demonstrate reading and writing for authentic purposes. For example, at the beginning of every school day, children do calendar work in which they say the days of the week, write in the number of the date, and count how many days of school have passed. They have a number line stretched across the bulletin board on which Mrs. Poremba writes the number of days in school. One day one of the children asks, "When will we get to 100?" Mrs. Poremba tells everyone that the 100th day will be in February, and that every year she plans special activities to celebrate that day. Another child, Eric, is upset at this news because he will be moving after the winter holidays.

Ms. Poremba takes advantage of this event and turns it into a literacy learning activity. She asks, "You know what I could do right now? I'm going to write it down right now to remind myself." She says, "I'm going to remember the 100th day by writing *100*," and she does so on a slip of paper displayed for the whole class to see (see Figure 8.3). Then she says, "I'm going to write a word next to it."

"*Day*," predicts a kindergartner.

The kindergartners know this word from their 70 days of calendar work so far in kindergarten. Several of them read as Mrs. Poremba writes: " 'Day.' "

Mrs. Poremba reads the whole message so far: " '100 day.' " She asks, "What else could I write down to remember?"

"Party!" say several kindergartners. "Eric," suggest others.

"Write down *party?*" asks Mrs. Poremba. "The word *party?*"

One kindergartner already knows how to begin: "*P! P!*"

Mrs. Poremba echoes this, "*P?*", and she writes *p*. Then she cues the kindergartners for another letter by saying "*Parrrrr—*"

"*R*," say several kindergartners.

100 day

prty

Eric D.

Invtsn

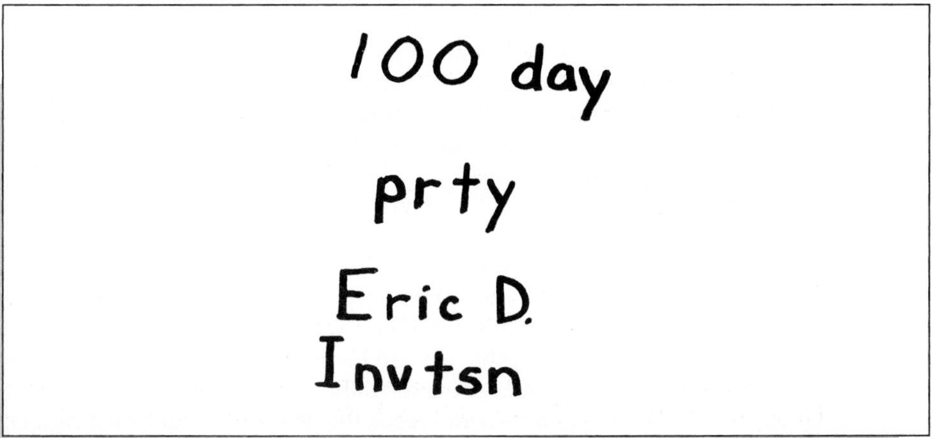

FIGURE 8.3 Shared Writing: A Reminding Note

"Is there an *R* in it?" Mrs. Poremba responds as she writes *r*.

A kindergartner suggests the next letter: "*D*." And this kindergartner is right. It is difficulty to enunciate the /t/ in *party*. Often the word ends up sounding more like "pardee." One kindergartner even isolates a /d/ phoneme; he says, "Duh."

Mrs. Poremba emphasizes the /t/: "*Par-tee*."

Now several kindergartners say, "*T!*", and Mrs. Poremba writes *t*.

Now a kindergartner suggests the last letter: "*Y*."

"You think we need a *Y* in it?" responds Mrs. Poremba. The kindergartners have seen *Y* for /E/ all year, in words on their weather chart (*windy, snowy, sunny, cloudy, rainy*) and in other words (e.g., *muddy, frosty*) they have written together on a Words for Today sheet posted next to the weather chart.

But this is a difficult concept. One kindergartner says, "No—*E!*"

But Mrs. Poremba is writing *y* and reading, " 'Par-ty.' "

Now Eric suggests, "You should write my name on there, 'cause—"

"We need your name on there also?" responds Mrs. Poremba. The kindergartners are very familiar with one another's names by December 13, and they quickly lead Mrs. Poremba through the writing of *Eric D.* "Why do we need the *D*?" asks Mrs. Poremba. The kindergartners explain that it distinguishes this Eric from another Eric in their class.

"Anything else we need to write down to remind us about inviting Eric to our 100 day party?" asks Mrs. Poremba. "Do you think this will remind us?"

"Write *invitation*," suggests a kindergartner. And others take this up: "*Invitation!*" "*Invitation!*"

Mrs. Poremba responds, "Write *invitation*? That's a big word. How would I write that?"

A kindergartner says, "*I*."

Eric is thinking about his invitation. He suggests, "Everybody can sign that card if they want."

Mrs. Poremba says, "And we can all sign it when we send it to you? That's good." She writes *In* and reads, " 'In—' "

A kindergartner says the next syllable, "Vuh."

And Mrs. Poremba repeats it: "Vuh."

Several kindergartners provide the next letter: "*V!*" "*V!*" And another notices something about *In*: "Hey, that's part of Ian's name!"

Mrs. Poremba writes *v* and reads, " 'In-vuh,' " and says the next syllable: "Tay."

"*T!*" "*T!*" "*T!*" several kindergartners say.

Mrs. Poremba writes *t* and continues, "-tay-shhhhun."

Several kindergartners suggest, "*S!*" "*S!*" "*S!*"

Mrs. Poremba responds, "*S*?" and writes *s*. Then she asks, "What would be on the end? *-shunnn?*"

"*N!*" "*N!*" "*N!*" several kindergartners say.

"Do you hear an *N* on the end?" Mrs. Poremba writes *n* and reads, " 'In-vi-ta-tion.'"

When Tara contends, "That's not a long word," Mrs. Poremba repeats a spelling strategy that the kindergartners have heard before and that accounts for this shortened spelling: "We wrote down the big sounds in the word. We wrote down the big sounds that we hear." Then she points to and reads the whole message (see again, Figure 8.3), pointing to each word as she reads it: "So we have, '100 day party. Eric D. Invitation.' "

This writing activity was unplanned, but it shows that Mrs. Poremba is prepared for it by being on the lookout for opportunities to demonstrate meaningful uses of writing and to involve her students in writing processes. This episode began in a routine number activity, counting and recording the days spent so far in kindergarten. It turned into a writing activity that had the authentic purpose of reminding. The words (meanings) came from the students; Mrs. Poremba asked, "What else could I write down to remember?" and "Anything else we need to write down to remind us about inviting Eric to our 100 day party?" With this real-life writing piece, Mrs. Poremba demonstrated two kinds of form. By frequently directing her students' attention to the print as she created it, she modeled letter formation. By accepting a list of key ideas (*100 day party—Eric D.—invitation*) rather than a complete sentence (*Remember to send Eric D. an invitation to the 100 Day party),* she demonstrated an acceptable, workable format for a reminder. Finally, the spellings came from the students, demonstrating that Mrs. Poremba knew that in December of their kindergarten year, they had several strategies for spelling.

When she responded to Tara's observation about the length of *Invtsn*—that it does not look so long for a word that Mrs. Poremba had introduced as a big word—Mrs. Poremba made explicit an invented spelling strategy the students had used before ("We wrote down the big sounds that we hear"). She also knew what her kindergartners could not do at this time in the school year; she did not expect fully conventional spellings for all the words in this reminder. She knew that her kindergartners were not able yet to produce letter matches for all the sounds in *party; prty* is a more conventional spelling than *prde* would have been, but it is not as conventional as *party.* More important, the product of this writing episode was readable; it would be able to serve its purpose when the time for the 100th day celebration drew closer.

Writing the Room: Extended Sign-In

Mrs. Poremba uses the sign-in procedure, but she searches for ways to make this simple procedure more complex as her children mature as readers and writers. One way she does this is to put each child's sign-in sheet on a clipboard and invite them to **write the room,** that is, to walk around the classroom in search of print and then to copy words that interest them.

One day there was a new Halloween bulletin board above the writing center table. Several children wanted to sit at the writing center table and copy onto their sign-in sheets the words labeling the Halloween pictures on the bulletin board, more children than could sit at the writing center table. Several children pulled chairs up to make a second row of writers at the table. Mrs. Poremba gave these children clipboards for their sign-in sheets so that they, too, could write. Then everyone wanted a clipboard, and soon the entire class had clipboards and pencils and sign-in sheets, freeing them to wander around the room copying whatever print they found, not just the print on the new Halloween bulletin board. Figure 8.4 shows Meagan's sign-in sheet. She copied "Color Cats" and color words from a color-word bulletin board; "big blocks" from a label in the block center; "bat," "pumpkin," and "witch" from the Halloween bulletin board; and "Please," "Thank you!" and a smiley face from the sign-in sheet itself! She used dashes to mark spaces between some of the words she copied.

F IGURE 8.4   Meagan's Writing the Room Sign-in Sheet

By midyear, Mrs. Poremba had added to the sign-in sheet the sentence "Today is
_____." Children were free to complete the "Today is" sentence as they wished. For ex-
ample, on March 15, Ian noted that "Today is 120," that is, it was the 120th day of
school. The next day, Tara noted that "Today is Gym."

Another year Mrs. Poremba used her classroom computer, connected to a large
overhead monitor, to post sign-in questions. Each day the kindergartners saw a question on the monitor as they entered the classroom. This allowed them to begin talking
together about the question and how they would answer it even before they saw the
same question on their sign-in sheets and wrote their individual answers there. This
also motivated them to think of their own questions, which might appear on the screen
the next day or the day after. One kindergartner's question, for example, was "Do you
like salami?" (Richgels, 2003).

Dramatizing Information Books

Dramatizing books is a playful and powerful way to develop kindergartners' comprehension and vocabulary. Teachers frequently dramatize stories, but children can use
drama to explore information books as well. Mrs. Poremba included drama as a part of
her chick-hatching unit. Her students had read many information books and posters
about chick development and hatching. As the children anticipated their first chick's
hatching, they applied what they had learned from their reading.

Mrs. Poremba: Let's pretend that we are a chick that's been in the egg twenty-one days. You are SO crowded, your legs and your wings and your head and your back and your beak are ALL crunched together. . . . Okay, the first thing you do is you SLOOOOOWLY move your head up and you're going to poke your air sack on the top of your egg to take that breath of your first air. Poke your air sack. Okay. Take your breath. Do you like that air?

Children: Yes. Uh huh.

Mrs. Poremba: But you know what? That took a lot of work. So now you're tired again. . . . Ohhhh. Now a little bit of a rest. Now we're going to take our head and get your egg tooth up, part of the end of your beak. And we're going to make our very first pip in the shell—and that's very hard work. Find your place to pip.

Children: Pip, pip, pip. Peep, peep, peep.

Mrs. Poremba: Did you get a pip in your shell?

Children: Yeah. Yes.

Mrs. Poremba: Go back to sleep. You are so tired. This is HARD work hatching. Okay, now let's look at our picture to see what we need to do next.

In this classroom, dramatic play provided a rich context for extending children's understandings of the world (Putnam, 1991). As students dramatized information from books, they showed their understandings of the meanings of words such as *air sack, pip,* and *egg tooth.*

Reading the Morning Message

Mrs. Palmer teaches in an elementary school with a mixture of children from low-income families and middle-class families. Approximately 50 percent of the children qualify for free or reduced lunch. She has 90 minutes of uninterrupted time each day for reading instruction with additional time for opening activities and writing activities. She integrates reading and writing instruction in the afternoon with social studies and science topics.

Each morning the children read a **morning message** (presented in Figure 8.5). A morning message is a short message written by the teacher on chart paper and hung on an easel for reading (Labbo, 2005; Mariage, 2001). Teachers use morning messages to teach alphabet recognition and concepts about print early in the year, and sight word recognition later. Mrs. Palmer uses the same pattern to write each day's morning message. It always begins "Good Morning" followed by the sentence "Today is _____." She always writes something that will happen that day and ends with a question about the activity.

The kindergartners look at the morning message as they come in each day, and by mid-year most children can read the familiar words *Good Morning* and *Today is* on their own. They puzzle out the other words by talking among themselves. During opening activities, Mrs. Palmer reads the morning message using a pointer. Her voice is quiet as she reads familiar words and louder for new words. She knows many children know the words *We* and *will,* so she is quiet to let children take the lead. When she gets to the word *bugs,* she stops and says, "I think we can figure out this word. What sound will it

Dear boys and girls,
Good morning. Today is Friday
April 24, 2006. We will read a book
about bugs. Do you like bug
hunting?

Mrs. Palmer

FIGURE 8.5 Mrs. Palmer's Morning Message

start with? Does anyone see anything else to help us?" Many children talk about the letter *b* and the sound /b/, and someone recognizes the whole word *bug* in *bugs*. Then Mrs. Palmer points across the letters, slowly saying, "/b-uh-g-z/. I noticed it ended with the letter *s*, so it is *bugs*." Again Mrs. Palmer knows many children know the words *Do you like* and so she is quiet to let them read. She pauses to see which children will recognize the word *bug* in the last sentence, and many children do.

After reading the message, Mrs. Palmer leads the children in familiar work with the message. Some children come up to the chart and find a period. Some find capital letters. Others count words in the first sentence. Still others come up to use a word frame to find familiar words such as *Today, We, Do, you,* and *like.* Mrs. Palmer always leaves the morning message hanging on the easel so that during choice time, children can copy words that interest them. Sometimes she makes a small copy of the morning message cut into words to use in a special morning message workstation.

Teaching Small Group: Word Work That Starts with Book Reading

After opening activities (and after special classes such as library, music, physical education, or art), children are sent to workstations while a small group of children work with Mrs. Palmer. Five children sit on the carpet with Mrs. Palmer while other children consult the chart for their workstation assignments. Mrs. Palmer gives a small white board and a marker to each of the five children. She tells the children they are going to build new words. She begins with a continuous text: she reads the book *Spring in the Kingdom of Ying* (Charlesworth, 2002), which includes many examples of words with the rime *-ing.* Then she invites children to recall a word, say it slowly, isolate the onset and spell it, then add the *-ing* rime. The children segment and spell *king, wing, sing,* and *ding* before moving to harder words with **consonant cluster** onsets such as *fling, swing, sting, string,* and *spring.* As the children write each word and wipe it off their boards, Mrs. Palmer writes it on a list on a chart hung on the easel. At the end of the lesson, the children read from this list the words they had earlier spelled. Mrs. Palmer ends the lessons by showing children cards printed with *ing, k, w, s, d, fl, sw, st, str,* and *spr.* Mrs. Palmer makes a word using a letter card and the *ing* card, and children read the word. Then she tells children that these word-building cards and writing paper and pencils will be in the letter and word center, and that the next time they go there, they should write a list of as many words as they can make and read using those cards.

Mrs. Palmer dismisses the small group and signals that all children should go to their second workstations. Then she calls together a second small group of children to read a continuous text from their Open Court basal materials. These children are reading small books using decodable words. **Decodable words** are consistent with phonics generalizations; for example, the vowel in a CVC (consonant-vowel-consonant) word is short or the first vowel in a CVCe (consonant-vowel-consonant-silent *e*) word is long. The children in this group are familiar with today's book, which has many short-0 (/ah/) words.

Mrs. Palmer uses a form of guided reading to read this little book. For **guided reading** in kindergarten, the teacher introduces very-easy-to-read books and then guides children's independent reading of the books. Mrs. Palmer introduces today's book by having children look through the pictures and talk about what is happening. She writes on the white board many of the familiar words the children will be reading. Then she reads aloud the first page of the book, followed by her listening to one child read it to her while the others read it quietly to themselves. The children then talk about the story before Mrs. Palmer reads the second page as a model for their later reading on their own. In this stage of early guided reading, children use the pictures, their memory of the text read by the teacher, their store of known words (many learned in the morning message), and some simple decoding skills that they have already learned (for example, to try a short vowel sound for a CVC word).

Mrs. Palmer teaches children to decode unfamiliar words after they can successfully build and read familiar rhyming words (as they did with *-ing* words). **Decoding unfamiliar words** requires more than building and reading words from a familiar rime; for example, if a word's rime is unfamiliar, the reader must look at each letter in the word in sequence from left to right and blend the sounds associated with those letters. The decodable book Mrs. Palmer and her students are reading has the words *mop* and *job.* The class has not learned the *-op* or the *-ob* phonograms needed to decode these words from familiar rhyming words. That is, the children have not worked with families of words that rhyme with *mop* (*bop, cop, chop, flop, hop, lop, pop, sop, shop, stop, top*) or with *job* (*Bob, cob, gob, job, lob, mob, rob, sob, snob*). However, the day before, Mrs. Palmer had used magnetic letters on the white board to help children decode these words. She had put the letters *m, o,* and *p* together on the board and said, "Let's say I don't know this word and I have to figure it out. I look at the first letter and say its sound, then I look at the second letter and say its sound, and I look at the last letter and say its sound. Watch me keep my sounds going all the way through the word, mmmmaaaahp."

On this second day with the decodable book, Mrs. Palmer listens to each child read a page to see which children can use the decoding strategy of matching the correct sounds to the three letters of a CVC word (including the short vowel) and keeping those sounds going all the way through the word. If she finds someone who can do that, then before moving to the next page, she invites that child to demonstrate for the group. For example, she says, "Camille used our strategy of keeping the sounds going." She points to the word *job* and says, "Camille, show us how you did that on this word."

Two considerations guide such teaching of decoding strategies in kindergarten. The first is that teachers must not expect that all kindergartners will learn to decode unfamiliar words. Mrs. Palmer has only a few children who are ready for the strategy of applying the CVC generalization and keeping the sounds going all the way through a word; many children will learn it as first graders. The second consideration is that not all words are amenable to such strategies. Teachers must be careful to demonstrate decoding strategies and invite children to apply them only with words that are decodable, that is, consistent with phonics generalizations. For example, pronouncing a vowel as short in a CVC word works for many CVC words (e.g., *cat, dot, pug*); it does not work for all CVC words (e.g., *car, dog, put*). Once children are very familiar with a generalization, teachers can point out its exceptions. Non-decodable words must be learned as sight words. Phonics generalizations that have too many exceptions (e.g., that when two vowels are together, the first vowel is long and the second is silent) are not really generalizations and should not be taught.

Finger-Point Reading and Kid Writing

Mrs. Trimble teaches in a rural school with many children on free and reduced lunch. Many of her kindergartners attended a very effective Head Start center in a local community center and entered kindergarten with high levels of literacy skill. Other children have very few conventions in place when they enter kindergarten. Mrs. Trimble begins using finger-point reading with children with few experiences and introduces kid writing to children who have more conventional concepts in place.

Finger-point Reading Nursery Rhymes.   Mrs. Trimble teaches children many nursery rhymes at the beginning of kindergarten during a nursery rhyme theme unit. She teaches most nursery rhymes orally using dramatic games such as jumping over a candlestick or using finger plays. A favorite of most children is "Jack Be Nimble" because they enjoy jumping over a candlestick. They are intrigued with the new word *nimble*, which they know means being able to do something quickly without falling or spilling.

When the kindergartners are familiar with several rhymes, Mrs. Trimble introduces a rhyme written on sentence strips in the pocket chart. Children chant the rhyme while she points. Later, for the finger-point reading, children attempt to point as she guides them. Children match word cards to words on the chart, count the number of letters in words, find words that are the same, and find words that begin with a particular letter. Mrs. Trimble has found that repeatedly engaging children in simple finger-point reading and word-matching activities and in counting letters in words helps children develop strong concepts about letters, words, and "first letter in a word."

Kid Writing and Journal Writing.   Mrs. Trimble uses a combination of journal writing and kid writing during morning opening activities. **Kid writing** is a teacher-supported activity in which children decide on a short message, write lines to indicate each word that will be needed to write that message, listen to the sounds in each word, and write the sounds they hear (Feldgus & Cardonik, 1999). **Journal writing** is children's daily independent writing about personal topics. For kindergartners, this writing combines drawing a picture with writing a message by using what they know about letters and sounds. In Mrs. Trimble's classroom, journal writing is the first activity of the day. As the children enter the classroom, they locate their journals, which are kept in color-coded plastic tubs, stamp the day's date using a date stamp, and begin drawing and writing.

Once the children are settled, Mrs. Trimble calls a small group of four or five children to the small-group table to work with her on kid writing. While kid writing is often described as an activity for a whole-class group, Mrs. Trimble finds that it works better in a small group. She works with a different group each day of the week so that all the children experience this supported writing activity weekly.

To begin kid writing, children are asked to draw a picture of something of personal interest. The teacher selects one student, and they compose a sentence together. They count the number of words, and make a word line for each word. The teacher helps the child recall the first word. If it is a word on the classroom word wall (a place on the classroom wall where words are posted under alphabet letters), the teacher reminds the child to look at it and spell it quickly. If not, the teacher asks the child to say the word slowly and listen to its sounds. Mrs. Trimble has found that children have difficulty saying words slowly and segmenting all the individual sounds. She models listening for the beginning and ending sounds. When children are consistently successful with those, she asks them to attend to middle sounds as well. The children write letters that they think go with the sounds. In kid writing, the teacher does not expect perfect spelling, but she makes notes of what sound-letter correspondences might be expedient to teach. The teacher helps all children compose and read their sentences in their *kid writing*. Quickly the teacher records each child's sentence in conventional spelling on a post-it note and places it at the bottom of the child's writing. This *teacher writing* is also read by the child.

When each child is finished writing, the teacher make a decision on the spot each day to highlight something one child has done that all the children might learn from. For example, someone might have spelled the /sh/ sound with the correct digraph letters SH or someone might have used a word family to spell a word. The teacher would point out these good strategies.

At the end of journal time and kid writing, all the journals are collected and put away in their tubs for the next day's writing. At the end of each month, Mrs. Trimble reviews her students' journal writing for progress. Figure 8.6 presents Addie's kid writing in November and in January and one of her January journal entries. In November with support Addie could spell some sounds in the word *scared* (SCD), but she also included many letters that have no relationship to the sounds in *of thunder*. In contrast, in January Addie heard and spelled the beginning and ending sounds of *got* and *haircut* and some middle sounds of *haircut*. Addie's journal entry is equally sophisticated with spellings of many sounds in the middles of words. Her journal writing, however, without the lines on which to place words, sometimes lacks spaces between words.

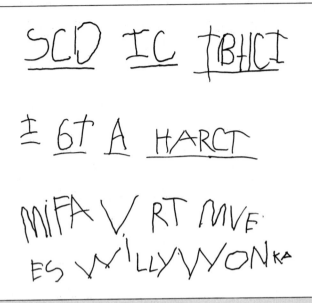

FIGURE 8.6 Addie's Kid Writing and Journal Writing

Interactive Writing

With **interactive writing,** teachers let children write some of the letters or words on a shared writing chart; thus, it is also called "sharing the pen" (Tompkins & Collom, 2004,). Effective teachers know which child to invite to step up to the chart and write the next letter and which child to invite to write a high frequency word. **High frequency words** are those that appear often in just about any text that is longer than a few sentences, for example, *the, is, me, am, can, is,* and *in.* These are words that teachers place on word walls (usually introducing five new words each week). By the end of kindergarten, with daily journal writing, kid writing, morning messages, shared reading, shared writing, and interactive writing, most children learn to read and spell twenty-five or more high frequency words (McGill-Franzen, 2006).

Interactive writing proceeds in a very similar manner as kid writing. However, unlike kid writing, where each child writes his or her own sentence, with interactive writing, a group of children decide on one sentence before writing. Then a line is written on the chart paper for each word in the sentence. The teacher helps children locate high frequency words on the word wall and writes these words herself. For other words, the teacher demonstrates saying the word slowly and segmenting the beginning sounds. Words in interactive writing are spelled conventionally, so the teacher spells difficult middle parts of words and has children spell beginnings and endings.

Figure 8.7 presents a page of a book composed with interactive writing. Each of four days after reading a little book about go-carts during guided reading, the teacher

FIGURE 8.7 A Page of a Book Composed with Interactive Writing

helped a small group of four children compose a new page for their *Go-Cart Book*. For the page shown in Figure 8.7, one child wrote *The* from memory. A second child listened to the beginning sound of *blue* and wrote the letter b, and the teacher completed the spelling of that word. The teacher also wrote the letter *g* for *go-cart,* and then invited a child to hear the /O/ sound and to write it. After writing *cart,* the teacher invited another child to write the period. Each of the four children drew and colored a picture of a go-cart, and then the teacher assembled the papers into a book.

Some teachers use texts composed with interactive writing for later shared reading activities. After the messages are written, they are read and reread for many successive days of instruction.

Summing It Up: Reading and Writing Continuous, Authentic, Functional Texts

We have described three exemplary teachers and their daily use of reading and writing continuous, authentic, functional texts. While we did not present an example of reading aloud to kindergartners, all effective kindergarten teachers daily read aloud books in addition to those they read in shared reading and guided reading. They read sophisticated storybooks and information books and engage children in thoughtful discussions about what they read. They draw attention to vocabulary and help children to learn new concepts.

TEACHING CHILDREN THE CONVENTIONS

W E HAVE ALREADY SHOWN that kindergarten teachers are teaching the conventions of reading and writing during their daily activities using continuous, authentic, and functional texts. Children's attention is drawn to alphabet letters, sound-letter associations, concepts about print, and high-frequency words. They see demonstrations of and apply phonemic awareness and decoding. They make sense of books read aloud to them by recalling information and making inferences. Kindergartners are introduced to most conventions in reading and writing. Many children acquire these without further guidance by the teacher, but nearly all kindergartners need focused attention to some aspects of the conventions during the year. Some children need small-group lessons daily to accelerate their learning to reach the average level of the class.

Experienced kindergarten teachers and professionals recognize several profiles of knowledge and need, each requiring its own kind of responsive teaching in order to guide students to next steps in literacy development. Some children might be called "letter and sound kids" (McGill-Franzen, 2006). They know that print is the vehicle for reading and writing, but they need instruction noticing letter features, learning to identify letters, and attaching sounds to those letters. Other kids might be called "sounds kids." They know letter features and names and some sounds associated with those letters, but they need instruction in stretching out the sounds in spoken words and attaching letters to those sounds in print. With instruction, they can apply skills and strategies to inventing spellings and building and reading new words from word families. Other children might be called "finger-point readers and inventive spellers." They know a large number of sound-letter associations and some word families, but they need guided reading activities—with predictable or decodable little books, using finger-point reading and writing activities, using guided dictation and invented spelling. These children are on the verge of conventional reading and writing, and they need support in using their insights about the alphabetic principle in both reading and writing tasks. A few kindergartners, especially at the end of the school year, will read many high-frequency words and be able to decode most decodable words. They will spell many high-frequency words conventionally and spell other words inventively without a teacher's help. They will need guided reading in leveled books, that is, books identified by their increasing level of difficulty, with increasing numbers of new words, greater length of text, and greater dependence on that text for successful, full understanding of the book's content. They will need opportunities and support for composing longer-than-sentence texts, for example, in their journals or in writing center activities. Kindergarten teachers need to give small-group instruction planned for these different knowledge and need profiles, so that children can make use of what they know and be guided to appropriate next steps.

Alphabet Instruction Including Letter-Sound Knowledge

By the end of kindergarten, children must quickly and accurately recognize all the upper and lower case letters by name, be able to write recognizable letters, and know the sounds associated with a majority of the consonant letters. Kindergarten teachers are better able to meet the needs of children when they know what children already know through systematic assessment and observation (see Chapters 3 and 4). Many kindergartners still confuse similar looking letters and reverse letters when writing. Teachers need to confront the issue of confusable letters (such as *M* and *W* and *b, p, d,* and *q*). Teachers can select one of the confusable letters and teach children to recognize this letter using a set of letters the children already recognize. For example, if children already know *A, C, F,* and *T,* then teachers use that set of letters in games to teach an unknown but confusable letter such as *M*. Writing should accompany letter recognition. Although teachers will not want to require perfect conformity to any handwriting system, they should demonstrate and talk through the strokes they use for making letters. When one confusable letter is well known, teachers add another.

When teaching lower case letters, teachers should begin with letters that have the same shape in both upper and lower case form. These will be learned quickly. Then teachers can add lower case letters with different shapes than their upper case partners.

Teachers should begin teaching a letter's sound or sounds only after children can identify the letter without hesitation. If teachers are careful to teach sound-letter associations only of those letters that children can name, then sound-letter instruction need not await children's being able to identify all the letters. In addition to choosing letters that children can name, teachers begin sound-letter instruction with sounds that children have already used in phonemic awareness activities, whose manners of articulation are quite different from one another, and whose names contain that sound. For example, if children have already learned to hear /f/, /v/, and /s/ in spoken words, as demonstrated, for example, by their being able to say words beginning with those sounds and then separately say the onset and rimes of those words (*"fan, /f/-/an/; vine, /v/-/In/; soon, /s/-/OOn/"*), then they are ready to learn which letters are associated with those three consonant sounds. However, they will find activities contrasting /v/ and /s/ to be easier than activities contrasting /v/ and /f/ because the latter pair are so similar in manner of articulation. All three consonant sounds, /f/, /v/, and /s/, are good candidates for the teacher's demonstrating the similarity of a chosen sound to a sound found in its letter's name. For example, the sound associated with the letter *V* is /v/ (see Table 1.2 in Chapter 1), and that sound can be heard as the first phoneme in the letter name "vee" (/vE/). On the other hand, the /g/-G sound-letter association does not benefit from such instruction; the letter name "gee" (/jE/) does not contain the sound /g/. Teachers should teach both sound-to-letter associations (listening to the sounds in spoken words and associating letters with them) and letter-to-sound associations (looking at letters in written words and identifying sounds with them).

Alphabet recognition and sound-letter associations can be taught in small groups, first using explicit instruction and then providing practice with engaging and motivating games. With explicit instruction in letter recognition and formation, for example, the teacher talks explicitly about a letter's features. While writing an *H*, the teacher says, "This is an *H*. I make two up-and-down lines, side by side, and then I connect them in the middle with an across line." Then the children are given several opportunities to make, name, and describe the letter on a chalkboard or in a sand table, repeating the teacher's naming and describing language. Or the children may close their eyes and visualize the letter while the teacher repeats the naming and describing language. Motivating games to practice letter naming include fishing for letters, feeding letters to a puppet, playing concentration and other letter-matching games, and going on letter searches in the classroom.

Letter instruction about specific letters should be followed by opportunities for children to locate, identify, and write those letters during reading and writing of continuous, authentic, and functional text. Teachers, for example, follow small-group instruction in naming and forming the letter *W* with shared writing that includes inviting children in that group to locate *W* on the writing chart during step-up activities. Similarly, after teaching the /w/-*W* sound-letter association to a small group, a teacher invites a child from that group to listen to a word beginning with *w* that occurs in the shared writing message, isolate the phoneme /w/, and talk about the sound-letter match.

Phonemic Awareness Instruction Including Decoding

"Rounding up Rhymes" (Cunningham, 1998) is an activity in which children must identify rhyming words, listen to and segment beginning phonemes or onsets as well as rimes, analyze spelling patterns including vowels, and build new rhyming words. It includes many different levels of phonemic awareness and involves decoding and spelling new decodable words. Figure 8.8 presents an appropriate poem for this activity. First, children listen to a poem and chime in with the rhyming words. Then they say all the words that rhyme.

The next day, the children reread the poem and again identify the rhyming words. As the children identify each word, the teacher helps children segment it orally into its onset and rhyme (e.g., the word *cold* is segmented into the onset /k/ and rime /Old/). After the children orally segment the word, the teacher places a card with the written word in a pocket chart. With all the rhyming words in the chart, the teacher says, "Now we know that all these words rhyme. Our job today is to look very closely and see which ones have the same spelling pattern" (Cunningham, 1998, p. 91). Part of using

FIGURE 8.8   "I Don't Like the Cold"

I Don't Like the **Cold**

I *told* you I don't like the *cold!*

I'm not *sold* on *cold*—

I *told* you **so!**

Take this **snow** and **go!**

I *told* you **so!**

I'll *hold* out for sun and hot—not *cold* and **snow!**

I *told* you **so!**

Copyright by Don Richgels.

this step of "Rounding Up the Rhymes" is helping children to understand words such as *spelling pattern* and *vowel*. With frequent use of "Rounding Up the Rhymes," children begin to remember that the vowels are *a, e, i, o,* and *u,* and that the spelling pattern is the part of the word from the first vowel to the end.

The teacher picks up a pair of rhyming word cards from the pocket chart, explains or reminds the children what *spelling pattern* and *vowel* mean, and invites children to identify the letters in the spelling pattern in the rhyming words, for example, *o-l-d* in *gold* and *told*. Then the teacher underlines the *-old* part of each word, and the teacher and children decide that *gold* and *told* have the same spelling pattern, and they rhyme. "We emphasize that we can *hear* the rhyme and *see* the spelling pattern" (p. 91). Then the teacher replaces those word cards and moves on to another pair of rhyming words from the pocket chart. If some rhyming pairs have different spelling patterns (e.g., *snow* and *go*), they are discarded. Finally, when the teacher and students have underlined spelling patterns in several pairs of rhyming words, they move to an application activity that involves using the word card words to read and write additional words. For the reading-new-words activity, the teacher writes words that rhyme with and have the same spelling pattern as the words of an already displayed pair (e.g., *sold* and *fold* to go with *gold* and *told*), elicits the children's telling what letters to underline in the new words, displays them in the pocket chart under the original pair of words, and helps the children to read the new words using the spelling pattern. In this part of the lesson, they are decoding.

For the writing-new-words activity, the teacher mentions a word the children might want to write and gives an example of a sentence in which it might be needed. For example, if one of the already displayed rhyme pairs is *dog* and *log*, the teacher might say, "What if you wanted to write *fog*, like in 'I saw *fog* on the way to school today'?" Then the teacher leads the children through a reading of all the rhyme pairs in the pocket chart, adding *fog* after each, until they find the pair that rhymes with *fog*: "*gold, told, fog; man, can, fog; dog, log, fog!*" When they notice that *fog* rhymes with *dog* and *log*, the children can use the underlined spelling pattern in the two displayed words to help the teacher to spell the new word on a word card for display. Later, children can read and write words in the letter-and-word workstation.

Some children may benefit from additional more direct instruction. Many phonemic awareness training methods are adopted from research tasks. Some involve children's clapping or other rhythmic activity to coincide with spoken words or syllables (e.g., Lundberg, Frost, & Petersen, 1988). Some involve **say-it-and-move-it activities,** in which children move poker chips or other such tokens as they pronounce syllables or individual phonemes in words (Elkonin, 1973).

Yopp (1992) describes several singing activities, performed to the tunes of traditional children's songs, that help children to isolate, blend, or substitute sounds in words. She suggests first using these as strictly oral activities, especially with preschoolers or beginning kindergartners, who may lack alphabet knowledge and for whom the use of written letters may be a distraction from the intended work with sounds. Then, as children learn alphabet letters—often during the kindergarten year—written words or letters may be used.

Ball and Blachman (1991) concluded that their study of phonemic awareness training in kindergarten "supports the notion that phoneme segmentation training that closely resembles the task of early reading may have more immediate effects on reading . . . than instruction that does not make this connection explicit. . . . It may be . . . that the most pedagogically sound method of phoneme awareness training is one that eventually makes explicit the complete letter-to-sound mappings in segmented words" (p. 64). They suggest using blank tokens for say-it-and-move-it phoneme awareness activities and then introducing tokens with letters written on them as children learn to identify the letters.

Griffith and Olson (1992) describe a say-it-and-move-it activity borrowed from Clay (1985) that can be changed in a similar way as children learn the alphabet. Students are given a picture, below which are **Elkonin boxes,** that is, boxes arranged in a horizontal matrix, one box for each phoneme in the pictured word. As the teacher slowly pronounces the word, the children move tokens into the boxes. She says "mm-mmmmmaaaaaaannnnnn" for *man,* for example. The children move a token into the first box while she is pronouncing the phoneme /m/, move another token into the second box while she is pronouncing the phoneme /a/, and, finally, move a third token into the third box while she is pronouncing the phoneme /n/. As children learn the alphabet, rather than moving tokens into boxes, they can write letters in the boxes. We present additional activities with Elkonin boxes in Chapter 9.

We suggest that whenever teachers use these direct-instruction activities, which use isolated words and rather prescribed sequences of teacher talk and student behavior, they keep in mind ways to reestablish connections to children's classroom and home lives and to continuous texts—in other words, ways to make them more functional and contextualized. The words used for Elkonin box work, for example, can come from a displayed big book text or chart-paper poem, and after doing the Elkonin box work, the teacher and students can return to that text and highlight the words there. Or the Elkonin box words may be used in a subsequent piece of writing that is meaningful to the children, such as a class letter to parents that tells about a current unit of study. The letter is composed on chart paper, reproduced by word processor on the classroom computer, and taken home the same day.

Independent Literacy Experiences

CHILDREN NEED MANY OPPORTUNITIES to explore literacy on their own, for their own purposes and to practice with materials and activities introduced by their teachers. Kindergarten teachers will use a combination of traditional centers and workstations to provide those experiences.

Dramatic-Play-with-Print Centers

One particularly effective center in kindergarten is called a **dramatic-play-with-print center.** This is a center in which children pretend around a theme that includes much real-world reading and writing. Mrs. Poremba used several of these centers in her classroom. A popular dramatic-play-with-print center was the classroom pizza parlor. One day Deborah was taking orders at the "pizza parlor." She had chosen this play center for at least a small part of the free-choice time several times a week. Like most of her classmates, when taking a customer's order, she always wrote a line of mock cursive for each

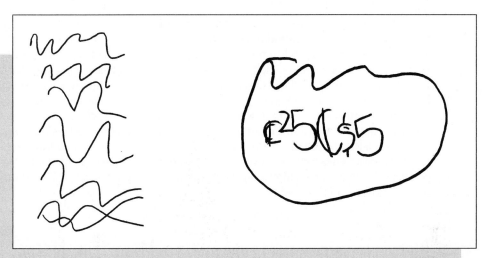

FIGURE **8.9** Deborah's Pizza Parlor Writing ("Extra Large," "Thin and Crispy," "Green Olives," "Sausage," "Extra Cheese," "Root Beer," "Large") and a Receipt

item in the customer's order. She took a pizza order from one of the authors of this book: seven lines of mock cursive for "extra large . . . thin and crispy . . . green olives . . . sausage . . . extra cheese . . . root beer . . . large." Later, however, when delivering the order, Deborah used a different writing strategy, one she had never before used during pizza parlor play. "Wait—you need your receipt," she said, and she used the numerals and symbols on the toy cash register to copy "¢ 25¢" and "$5" on the back of the paper she had used for writing the order (see Figure 8.9).

Sign making was another use of written language during play times in Mrs. Poremba's class. In December, Mrs. Poremba turned the block center into a shoe store. In response to a letter asking for help stocking the store, parents sent old shoes, slippers, and boots; shoehorns; and foot sizers. The children arranged the footwear on shelves and set up a checkout counter. They also wrote signs and their own paper money.

Frequently, children in Mrs. Poremba's room wanted to continue a play project from one free-choice time to another. At the beginning of the day, on April 20, Eric, Zack, Jeff, Jason, and Ian were playing at a table with dominoes and little plastic, brightly colored bears and bunnies. They made towers or enclosures with the dominoes and arranged the animals on the towers and in the enclosed spaces. They wrote *No* on slips of paper next to their materials so that no one would remove their constructions.

Using the Project Approach

The **project approach,** like dramatic-play-with-print centers, emphasizes real-world literacy experiences. In dramatic-play-with-print centers, children pretend to play in real-world settings such as pizza parlors and shoe stores. They pretend to be customers, waiters and waitresses, and shoe store employees. In these roles, they pretend to read store advertisements and menus and to write receipts and order forms. The project approach involves children in constructing simulations of real-world settings for literacy activity; once established, these function like dramatic-play-with-print centers. Powell and Davidson (2005) described how their urban kindergartners decided to build a donut shop in their classroom. They invited bankers to their classroom to tell them how to get a loan and find potential stockholders to buy stock. They wrote to staff members in the school and a nearby college to invite them to become stockholders and thank you letters when they received money for shares. They invited building inspectors to come and describe how to get building permits. Children wrote labels for the ingredients in their donut store, a big book about their experience, and invitations to the grand opening of the store.

DIFFERENTIATED INSTRUCTION TO MEET THE NEEDS OF DIVERSE STUDENTS

SMALL-GROUP INSTRUCTION in kindergarten should meet the needs of nearly all children by providing them with instruction appropriate to their knowledge and need profiles. Some children may need more frequent small-group instruction in even smaller groups than other children. When children are not making progress in small groups of four to seven children, then teachers should consider providing instruction in groups of two or three. Instruction needs to include what children know and build bridges to what they do not know. When children are not succeeding, teachers might consider whether instruction provided enough known items to provide success and build confidence before moving to new items. English language learners may need special attention to insure they understand instructions, have adequate vocabulary and concepts, and can connect their background experiences with the materials to be learned.

Using Environmental Print

Environmental print is the print found in our homes and communities. It is found on packages, plastic bags, billboards, junk mail, signs, and television. It is usually the first print that children find meaningful as they learn to associate favorite toys with logos on toy packaging or favorite fast food restaurants with logos found on signs. Environmental print is found in every home and community and is the most familiar print for all children. Kindergarten teachers can use this print to teach alphabet letters, phonemic awareness, sound-letter relationships, and decoding.

One way to find out more about the environmental print familiar to English language learners is to take a walk through neighborhoods in which they live (Orellana & Hernadez, 1999) with older children (if parents give their permission) or with someone familiar with the community. Teachers can take digital photographs of the logos and signs located in neighborhood groceries, video stores, and restaurants. Teachers can use the photographs in lessons and in classroom displays. They invite children to tell about their experiences in these locations. Children can bring in empty packages from their homes to use in show and tell and for small-group skill instruction in alphabet recognition and sound-letter associations (Xu & Rutledge, 2003). These materials can be used to make books by pasting familiar environmental print into pages stapled together. These familiar books can be displayed in the library center.

Using Similarities between Spanish and English

Spanish-speaking children make up nearly 80 percent of the ELL population in the United States (Harris, 2006). Understanding the similarities and differences between Spanish and English can provide teachers with a useful starting point for teaching phonemic awareness, phonics, and spelling. Figure 8.10 compares consonants and consonant digraphs in English and Spanish. Phonemic awareness and phonics lessons should begin with the sounds that are found in both languages (Helman, 2004). The sounds that are *only* found in English will require explicit, systematic lessons in which teachers show children how to attend to manner of articulation and compare and contrast with sounds in Spanish.

FIGURE 8.10   Phonemes in *Both* English and Spanish and *Only* in English.

Both in English and Spanish	Only in English
/b/	/d/
/f/	/j/
/g/	/r/
/h/	/v/
/k/	/sh/
/l/	/th/
/m/	/zh/
/n/	
/p/	
/s/	
/t/	
/w/	
/y/	
/ch/	

Source: Adapted from Helman, 2004.

Using Finger-Point Reading

Many ELL children have experiences with printed language that do not involve left-to-right and top-to-bottom directionality (Barrone, Mallete, & Xu, 2005). Some languages use a different word order, such as adjectives following verbs rather than preceding them. Thus, the activity of finger-point reading to accompany memorized text is critically important to establish directionality and letter/word concepts in English. While English-speaking children may quickly establish these concepts, English language learners may need extra practice with texts with just a few lines, very exaggerated word spaces, and few words per line. Because it is critical that all children before the end of kindergarten establish one-to-one matching left-to-right with a return sweep, teachers must be especially concerned to observe ELLs' acquisition of these concepts.

Chapter Summary

KINDERGARTNERS ARE EXPECTED to recognize and begin to write alphabet letters, match spoken and written words, know rhyming words and beginning sounds in words, know sound-letter correspondences and use them in invented spellings, understand concepts of print, write their first and last names, begin to write some high-frequency words, and enjoy and participate in read-alouds. Many of these expectations are in the area of meaning-form links, and their achievement depends on a related achievement—fully developed phonemic awareness. Kindergartners meet these expectations and continue to develop in all areas of written language acquisition when classrooms are filled with print, when teachers and children model reading and writing, and when children participate in functional and contextualized written language experiences.

Kindergartners' literacy learning is supported through classroom routines using print. Routines such as journal writing, "What Can You Show Us?," and the extended sign-in procedure encourage children's reading and writing and provide opportunities for teachers and children to talk about written language. Shared reading is a rich context for literacy learning; teachers orient children to print, read with children, and plan response activities. Shared reading is used with poems, songs, letters, stories, and informational texts presented on charts and in big books.

Shared writing is another context for language and literacy development in kindergarten. Teachers and students compose texts together. Students suggest ideas, teachers model writing processes, and the students participate in both the writing and the subsequent reading and rereading of the text. Finally, play is a critical component of the kindergarten curriculum. Children learn about written language in dramatic-play-with-print centers and during computer play.

Applying the Information

We suggest two activities for applying the information. First, make a list of the characteristics of literacy-rich classrooms from Chapter 6. Then reread this chapter and identify classroom activities appropriate for kindergartners that are examples of each of these characteristics. Discuss with your classmates why these activities fit the characteristics.

Second, make a list of all the literacy-learning activities described in this chapter, including group and individual activities. For each activity, describe what children learn about written language meanings, forms, meaning-form links, or functions. For example, children who participate in text reconstruction activities with a pocket-chart text as a model are learning about written language forms as they match words and letters. Children who finger-point read a familiar poem are learning about meaning-form links as they adjust their pointing using what they know about sounds and letters.

Going Beyond the Text

VISIT A KINDERGARTEN and observe several literacy activities. Take note of the interactions among the children and between the teacher and the children as they participate in literacy experiences. Make a list of the kinds of literacy materials and describe the classroom routines in which children read and write. Talk with the teacher about the school's academic expectations for kindergarten. Find out how the teacher meets those expectations. Compare these materials, interactions, and activities with those found in Mrs. Poremba's classroom.

References

Ball, E. W., & Blachman, B. A. (1991). Does phoneme segmentation training in kindergarten make a difference in early word recognition and developmental spelling? *Reading Research Quarterly, 26,* 46–66.

Barone, D. M., Mallete, S. H., & Xu, M. H. (2005). *Teaching early literacy: Development, assessment, and instruction.* New York: Guilford.

Charlesworth, L. (2002). *Spring in the kingdom of Ying.* New York: Scholastic.

Cunningham, P. (1998). Looking for patterns: Phonics activities that help children notice how words work. In C. Weaver (Ed.), *Practicing what we know: Informed reading instruction.* (pp. 87–110). Urbana, IL: National Council of Teachers of English.

Elkonin, D. B. (1973). Reading in the U.S.S.R. In J. Downing (Ed.), *Comparative reading* (pp. 551–579). New York: Macmillan.

Feldgus, E. G., & Cardonick, I. (1999). *Kid writing: A systematic approach to phonics, journals, and writing workshop.* Bothell, WA: The Wright Group.

Griffith, P. L., & Olson, M. W. (1992). Phonemic awareness helps beginning readers break the code. *The Reading Teacher, 45,* 516–523.

Harris, P. (2006). Teaching English language learners: NCTE guideline offers help for English teachers working with ELLs. *The Council Chronicle of the National Council of Teachers of English, 16,* p. 1, 5–6.

Helman, L. (2004); Building on the sound system of Spanish: Insights from the alphabetic spellings of English-language learners. *The Reading Teacher, 57,* 452–460.

Labbo, L. D. (2005). From morning message to digital morning message: Moving from the tried and true to the new. *The Reading Teacher, 58,* 782–785.

Lundberg, I., Frost, J., & Petersen, O. (1988). Effects of an extensive program for stimulating phonological awareness in preschool children. *Reading Research Quarterly, 23,* 263–284.

Mariage, T. V. (2001). Features of an interactive writing discourse: Conversational involvement, conventional knowledge, and internalization in "Morning Message." *Journal of Learning Disabilities, 34,* 172–196.

McGill-Franzen, A. (2006). *Kindergarten literacy: Matching assessment and instruction in kindergarten.* New York: Scholastic.

Orellana, M. F., & Hernadez, A. (1999). Talking the walk: Children reading urban environmental print. *The Reading Teacher, 52,* 612–619.

Powell, R., & Davidson, N. (2005). The donut house: Real world literacy in an urban kindergarten classroom. *Language Arts, 82,* 248–256.

Purcell-Gates, V. (1996). Stories, coupons, and the *TV Guide:* Relationships between home literacy experiences and emergent literacy knowledge. *Reading Research Quarterly, 31,* 406–428.

Putnam, L. (1991). Dramatizing nonfiction with emerging readers. *Language Arts, 68,* 463–469.

Richgels, D. J. (2003). *Going to kindergarten: A year with an outstanding teacher.* Lanham, MD: Scarecrow.

Tompkins, G., & Collom, S. (2004). *Sharing the pen: Interactive writing with young children.* New York: Prentice Hall.

Xu, S. H. & Rutledge, A. L. (2003). Chicken starts with ch! Kindergartners learn through environmental print. *Young Children, 58,* 44–51.

Yopp, H. K. (1992). Developing phonemic awareness in young children. *The Reading Teacher, 45,* 696–703.

CHAPTER

9

Supporting Literacy Learning in First Grade

KEY CONCEPTS

Sight Words
Decoding
Spelling
Phonics
Systematic Phonics
    Instruction
Explicit Instruction
Sound Boxes
Embedded Phonics
    Instruction
Decoding Coaching

Making Words
Daily Oral Language
Word Wall
Automatic Sight
    Vocabulary
High Frequency Words
Guided Reading
    Approach
Strategic Readers
Leveled Texts

Dynamic Ability
    Grouping
Grand Conversations
Phonogram
Word Sort Activity
Mini-Lesson
Scope and Sequence
Comprehensive
    Reading Program
Core Reading Programs

WHAT'S NEW HERE?

THE "WHAT'S NEW" in first grade is the expectation that by the end of the year all children will be reading and writing conventionally. They are expected to comprehend stories and informational texts, learn the meanings of new words, learn several hundred sight words, and use strategies to decode unknown words, including using sound-letter relationships. They are expected to use sound-letter relationships and other strategies to spell words. They are expected to write a variety of kinds of compositions for a variety of purposes (to inform, to interact with others, to entertain).

But how do children get to these end points? Many children begin first grade already reading and writing conventionally. The print-rich environment and literacy instruction provided for them in preschool and kindergarten were sufficient for them to make the transition from experimenters to conventional readers and writers. Children who begin first grade already reading and writing often make tremendous gains in reading during first grade. They often end their first grade year reading on a third grade level or above (Dahl et al., 1999).

Other children enter first grade as experimenters. They have sufficient knowledge about and experience with written language to make the transition to conventional reading and writing during first grade. For them, beginning to read and write conventionally will be relatively easy as they participate in instructional activities such as those we describe in this chapter (Snow, Burns, & Griffin, 1998). For other children, this transition requires careful attention from a highly knowledgeable teacher (Clay, 2001). Children who begin first grade with knowledge and experiences of written language like those of novice readers and writers need carefully planned instruction in order to become conventional readers and writers by the time they are seven years old. We expect that most children will become early conventional readers and writers by age seven (IRA/NAEYC, 1998).

We know a great deal about what children need to learn in order to begin reading conventionally (Adams, 1990; Juel, 1991). The hallmark of conventional reading is orchestrating all sources of information so attention is free to focus on meaning. Experienced conventional readers pay attention to print; they look at and read every word in a text. However, the print seems transparent; readers' attention is on the meaning they are constructing rather than on the print. Attention can be focused on a text's meaning when readers automatically and fluently recognize words, know their meanings, and parse those meanings into phrases, sentences, and larger chunks. That is, readers recognize and access the meanings of words quickly (in a fraction of a second) "by sight" and chunk them together into phrases without consciously having to decode words or "sound them out." **Sight words** are words that readers recognize instantly. Learning words and hooking words together in reading and writing is critical.

As most children acquire sight words, an amazing thing happens quite unconsciously. As they read more and more text, they go beyond just learning specific words. They automatically relate letter sequences in frequently encountered words to spoken word parts. Knowing the pronunciations of word parts allows them to decode very complicated words they have never before encountered. They can do so very quickly, seemingly without stopping to "sound out." For example, for older readers, the letters *con, tempt,* and *ible* in the word *contemptible* automatically trigger pronunciation of

/kuhn/, /tempt/, and /ibl/ even when they have never encountered the word *contemptible* in their reading before. This seemingly automatic decoding of an unfamiliar word marks the beginning of a phase of reading usually not achieved until the end of first grade or even into second grade.

In this chapter, we will focus much of our attention on words and decoding. However, it is critical to keep in mind that reading continuous texts necessarily takes readers beyond the level of the individual word. Reading continuous texts is more than automatically identifying sight words and using word recognition strategies with words that students cannot read automatically, as significant as those achievements are. It also involves combining words into phrases, sentences, and larger sequences that make sense. This combining process uses but supersedes word identification; it involves always looking at next words and identifying them, but also connecting them meaningfully to the current context. In other words, readers must always attend to the ways that word meanings interact in the sentence they are reading and to the still larger, unfolding meaning of an entire text. This entails understanding the workings of sentence structures often more complex than those they use and encounter in their everyday conversations and relating what they are reading to what they already know about the world. Table 9.1 summarizes the wide variety of strategies and understandings that we expect children at the end of first grade to have acquired.

TABLE 9.1   Reading and Writing Outcomes for First Grade

By the end of first grade, children

Read and retell familiar narrative and informational text

Use strategies (predicting, rereading, imagining, questioning, commenting) for comprehension

Choose to read and write for a variety of purposes

Have an awareness of a wide variety of literary elements found in narratives, informational texts, and poetry (character, setting, problem, event, sequence, lining, rhyming, repetition)

Write personal, narrative, informational, and poetic text

Have an interest in and strategies for learning meanings of vocabulary

Acquire many sight words in reading and correctly spell many words in writing

Use a variety of strategies for decoding and spelling (including strategies that build from phonemic awareness, maintain fluency, detect and correct errors, solve problems with words using multiple sources of information, and link to current knowledge, including the use of consonants, short vowels, long vowels, and high-frequency phonograms)

Use punctuation and capitalization

Engage in independent reading and writing

Source: Based on IRA/NAEYC, 1998; Fountas & Pinnell, 1996; and Bear, Invernizzi, Templeton, & Johnston, 2000.

WORD STUDY: DECODING PRINT AND SPELLING WORDS

EFFECTIVE READERS AND WRITERS have many flexible strategies that allow them to be successful decoders and spellers. **Decoding** is the ability to look at an unknown word—that is, a word that is not a sight word, that the reader cannot identify automatically, on sight—and to produce a pronunciation that is accurate—that is, a pronunciation that identifies the word as one that the reader knows from his or her spoken vocabulary. Notice that decoding presumes preexisting knowledge of the decoded word; the reader already has a concept for that word, usually from experience of it in speech. That is why vocabulary development is so important to children's reading and writing development.

One can use decoding strategies to arrive at pronunciations of nonsense words. For example, knowledge of the d-/d/ and j-/j/ letter-sound correspondences and of the CVC–short vowel generalization can produce a correct pronunciation (/duhj/) of the nonsense word *duj*. But that is not reading. Reading occurs when decoding causes a connection with a known vocabulary concept, a click of recognition. Imagine a reader who is unfamiliar with the letter string *fez*, but knows the f-/f/ and z-/z/ letter-sound correspondences, knows the CVC–short vowel generalization, and also knows the word *fez* to be the name for a rimless, cone-shaped, flat-crowned, usually tasseled cap. Application of the letter-sound correspondences and CVC generalization can lead that reader not only to the correct pronunciation /fez/, but also to the realization that that sequence of letters, *fez,* is the written form of the name for that cap. He or she pronounces and understands *fez.* That is reading. Then with some repetition of that decoding experience, *fez* can become a sight word, connected automatically with the cap concept, without any further need for decoding. That is why extensive reading experience is so important to children's reading and writing development. With greater numbers of sight words, children need to decode fewer of the words they encounter in continuous texts and can devote more attention to comprehending.

Spelling is a system for associating word parts (individual sounds or larger chunks of spoken words) with individual letters or combinations of letters. Both spelling and decoding are inexact processes. First pronunciations in decoding often are merely "close approximations" of the target word. A close approximation is enough to cause the click of recognition, and, if pronunciation is important, it is then adjusted to match what the reader knows—from having the word in his or her spoken vocabulary—about how to say the recognized word. Similarly, first spellings often are not perfect. When writing a word whose spelling they are not sure of, children may use knowledge of letter-sound associations to produce a close approximation. Then they can compare that approximation with what authorities (books, more knowledgeable classmates, a teacher) tell them about correct spelling. In first grade, teachers help children learn a variety of strategies first to arrive at close approximations during decoding and spelling and then to check for accuracy.

Early Decoding Strategies

In early decoding, we teach children to apply phonics, to commit words to "automatic sight vocabularies," and to use context as a cross-check.

Phonics.   **Phonics** is the more or less regular linking of letters and combinations of letters with sounds and combinations of sounds. We say *more or less regular* because a letter or combination of letters can have a very high frequency of association with a sound or combination of sounds but not always be so associated. For example, the letter combination *st* is very frequently linked to the consonant blend /st/ (as in *step, faster,* and *list*), but not always (consider, for example, *fasten* and *listen*). When particular letters and combinations of letters (phonograms) frequently—even if not always—stand for particular sounds (phonemes) or combinations of sounds, then those relationships merit teaching as one part of the decoding process. Children must have sufficient levels of phonemic awareness, an understanding of the alphabetic principle, and a knowledge of consonant and vowel patterns that goes beyond knowing only single letter–single phoneme relationships.

In kindergarten (or preschool), children build a foundation for decoding strategies. They learn to recognize the alphabet letters and begin phonemic awareness by being able to identify the beginning sounds of spoken words. They learn sound-letter associations for most consonants. Most children discover the alphabetic principle as they realize that the sounds they hear in words are spelled by letters.

We teach consonant sound-letter relationships first because they are fairly regular. Children can learn to expect a particular consonant letter to represent a particular consonant sound, even though the full range of phonics generalizations is more complex than that. For example, children may come fairly quickly to associate the letter *f* with the sound /f/. That is a good beginning point; it is an association that "works" a high percentage of times. Such an understanding helps to consolidate the alphabetic principle in the mind of the young reader and writer. With more experience and instruction, however, that reader and writer will learn about the greater range and complexity of phonics generalizations, for example, that sometimes other letters and combinations of letters represent the sound /f/ (as with *ph* in *phone* and *graph, ff* in *cuff,* and *gh* in *laugh*).

Phonics Generalizations.   In first grade, children must begin to grapple with such complexity. Not only can a sound have more than one spelling, as in our /f/-*f-ph-ff-gh* examples above, but a letter can represent more than one sound. Consider, for example, the letter *s,* which represents both /s/ (as in *sit*) and /z/ (as in *his*), or the letter *g,* which represents both /g/ (as in *go*) and /j/ (as in *gem*). Most importantly, first graders learn about vowels, which are the most variable of all letters. For example the letter *o* can represent the sound /O/ as in *go* or the sound /ah/ as in *got*. Figure 9.1 presents some phonics and spelling generalizations to be introduced in first grade. As shown in this figure, children will need to learn the letters or combinations of letters associated with these English sounds and sound combinations:

- *Initial consonants*—consonants at the beginning of a word
- *Final consonants*—consonants at the end of a word
- *Initial and final consonant blends*—two or three consonants spoken together at the beginning or ending of a word. Initial consonant blends include *r* family blends (*br, dr, gr, cr, fr, pr, tr*), *l* family blends (*bl, cl, gl, gl, pl*), *s* family blends (*sc, sk, sl, sm, sn, sp, st, sw, scr, spl, spr, squ, str*), and the *w* family blends (*dw, sw, tw*). Final blends include *l* family blends (*lb, ld, lf, lk, lt*), *n* family blends (*nd, nk, nt*), *s* family blends (*sk, sp, st*), and *mp* final consonant blends.

FIGURE 9.1 Some Phonics and Spelling Generalizations

1. Many consonant letters regularly correspond to one consonant sound:

bag	jar	nest	violin
dog	kite	pie	wig
fan	lamp	rug	zebra
hair	milk	toe	

2. Consonant clusters or blends are two or more consonant sounds blended together (e.g., *bl, cr, dr, fl, gl, pr, sm, st, scr, str, thr, nt*).

3. Consonant digraphs are two consonant letters that correspond to a single consonant sound:

   church *shoe* *phone* *thumb* *there* *whistle* *puff* *toss*

4. Each of the vowel letters *a, e, i, o,* and *u,* corresponds to more than one vowel sound:

long	short	r-controlled	other	diphthong
ape	apple		awful	
eagle	estimate	her		
ice	igloo	sir		
only	octopus	word	boot foot	oil cow
unicorn	under	fur		

5. Some consonant letters are associated with more than one consonant sound:

   When the letter *c* is followed by the letters *e, i,* or *y,* it usually has a soft sound, that is, it has the sound of the letter *s,* as in *center, city,* and *cyst.* Otherwise it usually has a hard sound, that is, it has the sound of the letter *k,* as in *car, cot,* and *cube.*

   When the letter *g* is followed by the letter *e* or *y,* it usually has a soft sound, that is, it has the sound of the letter *j,* as in *gem* and *gym.* Before the letter *i, g* is sometimes soft, as in *gist* and *gin,* and sometimes hard (/g/), as in *give* and *girl.* Otherwise, *g* usually is hard, as in *gas* and *gum.*

   The letter *s* sometimes has the sound /s/, as in *ask, east, fist, hostage,* and *us,* and sometimes has the sound /z/, as in *as, easy, is, hose,* and *use.*

6. Vowel letters in unaccented syllables often correspond with the short-*u* (/uh/) sound, sometimes called the *schwa sound,* regardless of the letter used to spell that sound:

   *a*bout basket pencil cotton

FIGURE 9.1 (Continued)

7. When a word is spelled with a consonant-vowel-consonant (CVC) pattern or a consonant-vowel-consonant-consonant (CVCC) pattern, the vowel sound is usually short (/a/, /e/, /i/, /ah/, /uh/):

lap	bed	his	pod	cup
lamp	bend	hiss	pond	cusp

   However, when *o* is the vowel letter in a CVC word or CVCC word, it often corresponds not to the short-*o* (/ah/) sound, but to the sound /aw/: *dog, moss, cost.*

8. When a word is spelled with a consonant-vowel-consonant-*e* (CVCe) pattern, the first vowel is usually long (/A/, /E/, /I/, /O/, /U/), and the final *e* is silent:

wave	Pete	time	bone	mute

   However, when *u* is the first vowel letter in a CVCe word, it often corresponds not to the long-*u* sound (/U/), but to the sound /OO/: *tube, tune, duke, jute, rude.*

9. Knowing phonograms that have CVC, CVCC, and CVCe patterns enables one to spell and write families of words—that is, words that share a phonogram:

cat	camp	cake
fat	damp	lake
hat	lamp	make
sat	ramp	take

10. Vowel sounds vary from dialect to dialect. For example, the *however* statement about short-*o* in number 7 above is not as widely applicable to some dialects as to others. For example, speakers of some dialects do pronounce *dog* as /d-aw-g/, but they use a vowel sound that is much closer to a short-*o* in *cost* (/k-ah-s-t/).

- *Consonant digraphs*—consonant phonemes that are spelled with two letters (for example, /th/ spelled *th* as in *thin,* /TH/ spelled *th* as in *that,* /ch/ spelled *ch* as in *chin,* /sh/ spelled *sh* as in *sheet,* and /s/ spelled *ss* as in *toss*)
- *Long vowels*—/A/ as in *ate,* /E/ as in *east,* /I/ as in *ice,* /O/ as in *oat,* and /U/ as in *use*
- *Short vowels*—/a/ as in *ask,* /e/ as in *ebb,* /i/ as in *it,* /ah/ in *odd,* /uh/ as in *up*
- *R-controlled vowels*—vowels whose distinctiveness is diminished by their being followed by /r/. This does not happen to all vowels followed by /r/; for example, /I/ followed by /r/ retains its usual "long I" sound (as in *fire*) and the /ah/ in *-ar* words (e.g., *bar, car, far, tar*) remains distinctive, even though it is not the short *a* (/a/) sound that one expects in a CVC word. Still, *r* has a diminishing effect often enough to warrant this category; for example, /uh/ almost disappears in *first, fern, turtle, word,* and *waiter.*

- *Other vowels*—the remaining American English vowels: /aw/ as in *fawn*, /oi/ as in *boy*, /oo/ as in *book*, /OO/ as in *boot*, and /ow/ as in *town*.

Children must learn more than the association of single phonemes with single letters. They must understand that:

- Order matters in writing as it does in speech, and in English writing we represent the first-to-last sequencing of speech sounds by left-to-right sequencing of letters. Readers must see *pit* and *tip* as two different words.
- Each sound in a word can be presented by a letter or combination of letters. So children need to learn which letters work in combination. For example, more important than the fact that *ship* has four letters and *sip* has three letters is the fact that both *ship* and *sip* have only three phonemes. A reader who knows this will see the letter *s* as a representation of the phoneme /s/ in *sip* but as only half of the two-letter (diagraph) representation (*sh*) of the phoneme /sh/ in *ship*.
- Some letters are silent, for example, *w* and *e* in *write* and *h* in *ghost*.
- The patterning of consonants and vowels influences the sounds of vowels; for example, the vowel in CVC, CCVC, and CVCC words is usually short (as in *bed*, *bled*, and *best*), and the first vowel in CVCe words is usually long and the final *e* silent (as in *cake*, *pine*, and *tone*).
- Some patterns of letters are associated with two or more different sounds—for example *ea* with /e/ in *bread* and /E/ in *bead*, and *ow* with /O/ in *snow* and /ow/ in *cow*.

Systematic, Explicit Instruction in Phonics. Children will have multiple opportunities to learn phonics generalizations and apply them in their reading and writing. To make sure that all children have the strong decoding skills of good readers and writers, teachers provide **systematic phonics instruction;** that is, they teach with a sequence of phonics skills in mind. When children find in their homes and classrooms real-life opportunities and support from adults, they will be engaged and interested in unstructured literacy activities that will result in their acquiring some literacy knowledge, including some phonics knowledge, outside of any planned sequence. And even with structured classroom instruction, not all literacy instructional materials use the same sequence. Nonetheless, in general, phonemes are addressed in decoding instruction in this order:

- Consistent initial consonants (those for which there is a consistent single-phoneme-to-single-letter correspondence)
- Consistent final consonants
- A few short vowels (/a/ and /ah/)
- Consonant digraphs
- The remainder of the short vowels (/e/, /i/, and /uh/)
- *L, r,* and *s* consonant blend families
- Long vowels (/A/, /E/, /I/, /O/, and /U/)

Not all reading programs use this sequence of instruction, but all programs use a systematic approach to phonics instruction. Systematic phonics can also be developmentally appropriate when teachers first assess what children know and are now ready to learn, and then teach from a sequence like the one just listed only those phoneme-letter associations that children have not yet learned.

With **explicit instruction,** teachers deliberately and clearly put into words what students are to learn from a particular lesson. If the instruction is about phonics, then teachers' talk explicitly states the target sound-letter correspondences or other phonics generalizations around which the lesson is planned. For example, if teachers present a list of words to illustrate a sound-sound letter correspondence (such as *bed, boat, bike, bell, bear, bake, bee* for the /b/-*b* correspondence) or present contrasting pairs of words to highlight the quality of a vowel sound (such as *pat-pot, cat-cot, pad-pod* for the differences in sound and spelling between /a/ and /ah/), then they do not leave it for students to guess what those lists or pairings are about. They tell the students. If teachers demonstrate a decoding skill (for example, recognizing a CVC pattern and using a short vowel sound), they do not just do it (for example, read the CVC word *bed* correctly), they also talk through what they are doing (for example, say, "I see that this word has a consonant, then a vowel, then a consonant. That means the vowel will probably be /e/ not /E/. Let's see if I'm right. 'Goldilocks lay in the *bed*'—that makes sense.").

Generally, with explicit phonics instruction, teachers deliberately and clearly direct children's attention to a target sound in isolation ("*S* stands for the sound /s/"), to that sound spoken within words ("I hear /s/ in *sat* and *fast* and *moss*"), to that sound segmented from words ("I can tell that /s/ is the first sound in *sat* because I can say /s/ first and then say the rest of the word: /s/-/at/"), and to the sound-letter association applied to new words ("There's another *s* word: 'Goldilocks opened her eyes and *saw* Father Bear'—Can you hear the /s/ in *saw?*"). In other words, teachers ensure that their explicit instruction about sound-letter associations includes stating the association ("The letter *b* stands for the sound /b/ as in the word *bear*") and then telling how the target sound is blended ("Listen while I blend the /b/ sound in *bear*: /b/-/A/-/r/, /bAr/"), how it is segmented ("Now I'm just going to start to say *bear* and then say the rest: /b/-/Ar/"), and how it applies during decoding and spelling of unfamiliar words ("Well, let's listen to the start of that word. I see that it begins with the letter *b,* so that means it's going to start with /b/").

Teachers may use **sound boxes** in explicit instruction, such as those shown in Figure 9.2. Using sound boxes, one for each phoneme in a target word, a teacher might say, "Today we are going to listen to the /a/ vowel sound. Listen for the /a/ sound in this word as I say it slowly: mmmaaap. That is the word *map* and it has the /a/ sound right in the middle. Let me show you on our sound boxes." The teacher points one-by-one, left-to-right to the empty sound boxes as she pronounces the three phonemes in *map*. She says, "I'll push up the letters as I say the sounds." The teacher says the word slowly again and pushes up the letters *m, a,* and *p* (on alphabet tiles) as she says each of the sounds /m/, /a/, and /p/. She can stretch out /m/ and /a/ because they are continuants; she must say /p/ quickly, trying not to say /puh/. Now the children attempt to say the sounds and move their letters into their sound boxes. Then the teacher introduces several more words with /a/ (*pan, fat, gas*), demonstrating how to say the words slowly in order to isolate their component phonemes and showing children how to construct the words with letter tiles pushed into sound boxes.

Embedded Phonics Instruction during Decoding Coaching. **Embedded phonics instruction** occurs while children are reading continuous, authentic, and functional texts, such as in guided reading instruction or writing in journals. As children read and write,

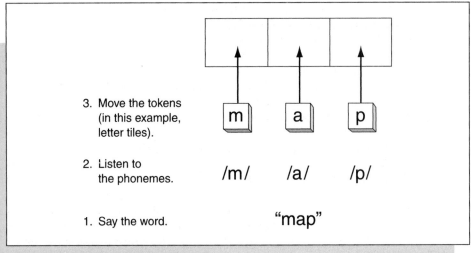

3. Move the tokens (in this example, letter tiles).

2. Listen to the phonemes.   /m/   /a/   /p/

1. Say the word.   "map"

FIGURE 9.2   Sound Boxes

they encounter words they cannot yet read or spell and must apply phonics generalizations. Teachers use these opportunities to teach such applications. As shown in the Goldilocks examples, some embedded instruction can also be explicit instruction. **Decoding coaching** is a broader term than explicit instruction; it includes all that a teacher might do or say during embedded instruction to support a child in successfully applying phonics generalizations (Clark, 2004). Research has shown that the most effective first grade teachers are those who both provide explicit instruction in phonics generalizations and coach children to apply those generalizations during their reading and writing of continuous, authentic, and functional texts (Taylor, Pearson, Clark, & Walpole, 2002). Highly effective teachers can deliver explicit, systematic phonics instruction and extend the power of that instruction by skillfully coaching children's applications of what they have learned.

During decoding coaching, teachers may ask a question, prompt a child to take a specific action, or provide specific information. Some coaching is very general in nature, consisting of questions and statements intended to prompt the child to think about what he or she already knows and can do. These are teachers' first responses to a child's reaching the point of difficulty in reading. For example, a coach might say the following:

- What could you do?
- Look for something you know.
- Think of all the things you can do.
- Use your strategies. (based on Clark, 2004)

When children continue to have difficulty, coaches ask a question, prompt the child to take an action, or provide information that could be useful (Clark, 2004):

- Cover up the *e-d* and see what the word is.
- Is it *grund* or *grunt?*
- Look for a chunk in there.
- What is this chunk? (p. 443)
- Please touch the letters and say those sounds for me. (p. 445)
- It's a vowel team (oa, ea, oi, ay, ou, ai, ee).
- It's an *r*-controlled vowel.
- What do you think that *e* sounds like?
- It's a blend. (p. 443)
- What sound does *y* make at the end of words?
- The *gh* is silent.
- It begins like *return.* (p. 446)

Whole-Class Word Study. Word study is careful examination of how words are put together and how sound-letter associations work in reading and writing words. Because children begin first grade with different levels of phonemic awareness, alphabet knowledge, and knowledge of sound-letter associations, their teachers must plan whole-class word study that allows children with little word knowledge to participate while also challenging children who have considerable word knowledge (Bear, Invernizzi, Templeton, & Johnson, 2004; Pinnell & Fountas, 1998). Making Words (Cunningham & Hall, 1994), Daily Oral Language (Vail & Papenfuss, 1982), and Word Walls (Cunningham, 1995; Wagstaff 1997–1998) offer structures within which to provide such flexiblity.

Making Words (Cunningham, 2005) is an activity in which children change or add just one letter at a time within words to construct new words. For example, children are given a set of six to ten letters such as *a, b, c, f, g, h, n, r, s,* and *t*. Teachers might help children form the word *can* and then challenge children to change just one letter to make the word *tan*. Then children would be challenged again to change just one letter to make the word *tag*. Children can continue, making *bag, bat, fat, fan, ran, rat,* and *hat*. Later teachers add more letters so that children can make words with digraphs and blends such as *bath, black, stamp,* and *crash* (Combs, 2006). Teachers help children develop skill with vowels by including sorts in which children change both consonant and vowel sounds. For example, teachers can give children the letters *a, b, e, h, i, l, m, p, s,* and *t* and they can make *bat, bit, hit, hat, sat, sit, set, met, mat, map, math, mash, lash, slash,* and *splash.*

The first steps in implementing Making Words are to prepare materials and to demonstrate with large letters and a pocket chart. Each child has a notebook with plastic sleeves (like those in a baseball card collection notebook) in which to store his or her set of alphabet letters. The letters are printed on cards and placed in the notebooks in alphabetical order. The teacher has a similar set of much larger letters. The teacher tells children which letters will be needed for a lesson and assists them in removing those letters from their notebooks. The teacher forms the first word placing his larger, easy-to-see letter cards in a pocket chart. He names the word ("We will begin with the word *bat*"), uses it in a sentence ("A baseball player uses a *bat* to hit the baseball"), and divides it into its phonemes while pointing from left to right across the word ("I hear three sounds in *bat*, /b/-/a/-/t/"). Next, he announces the new word to be made, giving a meaning clue ("It's what Snow White did to the poison apple: She *bit* the apple."). Then he gives a hint about the new sound ("Change only one letter and make *bat* into *bit*. It's a vowel letter."). He guides children's discovery of how the word in the pocket chart differs from the word to be spelled ("Now let's listen while I slowly say the old word and the new word: *baaaat, biiiit*. What is the different vowel in *biiiit?* Can you hear the /i/ sound in *bit?*), and he helps children find the correct letter to make the new word. A child is selected to come to the pocket chart to demonstrate the correct new spelling. Then the teacher confirms: "*Bat* has /a/ and *bit* has /i/. We know the letter that makes /i/. It's *i*. So we replaced the letter *a* with the letter *i*."

Daily Oral Language (Vail & Papenfuss, 1982) involves using a text that has many errors for children to notice and fix up. In first grade, children are shown a few sentences such as the following:

> jimmy he CAN wach
>
> the car jast lik his dad
>
> what can you do

The teacher first asks children to read the text; then they determine whether the information in the text is true. Then the children offer suggestions about how to correct the text.

Child: (about CAN) You put all capitals. . . .

Teacher: There's no real reason to have all capitals here, although I'm still seeing a lot of capital letters in some of [your] journals. . . .

Another Child: We don't need the *he*.

Teacher: Okay, when we have that *he*, it's just like we said "Jimmy Jimmy," isn't it?

Another child suggests a period after *do*.

Teacher: Think about this—"What can *you* do?" (with question intonation and emphasis on *you*).

Child: It's a question!

Teacher: I'm asking you something, aren't I? I'm asking you what you can do. So does it need a period? What does it need?

Eventually they find all the errors and the text is now written correctly on the chalkboard.

A **Word Wall** is a wall in the classroom on which teachers place word cards grouped by initial letter. Figure 9.3 presents a portion of a first-grade Word Wall. It contains important words such as the children's names and high-frequency words children are learning to read and spell. These words are in the texts children are reading during instruction and are words that children frequently use in their daily writing. Many teachers add five or six new words each week to their Word Walls.

During the week, the children practice reading and writing the words. Teachers use the Word Wall daily for a variety of activities as part of their phonics and spelling instruction. For example, the children might use the words on the wall to find words with short-*a* and short-*i* sounds. Other times, teachers might add words to the wall when an occasion arises, such as when several children need the same high-frequency words (e.g.,

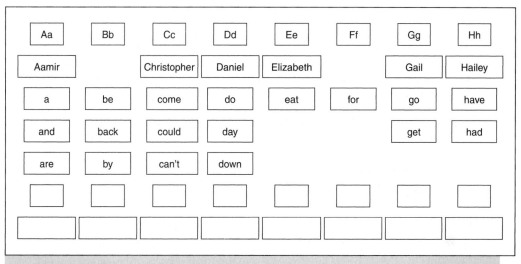

Aa	Bb	Cc	Dd	Ee	Ff	Gg	Hh
Aamir		Christopher	Daniel	Elizabeth		Gail	Hailey
a	be	come	do	eat	for	go	have
and	back	could	day			get	had
are	by	can't	down				

FIGURE 9.3 Portion of a Word Wall

they, where, or *this*) in their writing. They may add words from social studies and science units, and later in the year, they may add words with suffixes such as *s, es,* and *ing.*

Teachers frequently lead children in activities using the words on the Word Wall. For example, they may give children a "spelling test." Teachers call out five or six words on the wall, have children quickly locate the words with their eyes and then write the words. After the "test" teachers and children check the spellings. Later, teachers can urge children to see the words in their minds and then check the spelling by looking at the Word Wall. These short "spelling tests" and checks provide many opportunities to discuss first letter and sound, last letter and sound, vowels, and unusual spellings.

Teachers may limit play to just part of the Word Wall; they call out words for children to find and spell under a single letter or two or three letters and thus promote fast recognition and spelling of words. Effective teachers make this activity playful and help all children locate the correct words. Practice using the Word Wall during whole-class activities like these increases the likelihood that children will use it successfully during their independent writing and reading. For example, children who have practiced using the search strategy of first identifying a word's initial letter will not make the mistake while writing in their journals of looking on the Word Wall for *was,* but instead copying *saw.*

Building Automatic Sight Vocabularies

Automatic sight vocabularies are all the words that can be read immediately, on sight, without having to use decoding strategies; a reader looks at a sight word and recognizes it in less than one-tenth of a second. It is fortunate for children beginning the conventional phase of reading, that on a list of a few hundred **high-frequency words,** they can find over 70 percent of the words in almost any continuous text. An example of such a list is Fry's Instant Words (Fry & Kress, 2006). Many high-frequency words are not decodable words; their pronunciations cannot be derived from phonics generalizations. For example, the CVCe generalization does not produce the correct pronunciation of the word *come;* although that generalization calls for a long vowel sound, *come* is pronounced /kuhm/ not /kOm/. Children must learn to read undecodable words "by sight." With words like *come,* phonics generalizations will not help them and, in fact, will mislead them. When an undecodable word is also a high-frequency word, readers cannot afford to be bogged down by frequently and pointlessly sounding it out.

Readers acquire sight words from repeated exposure to them both in isolation and in continuous, authentic, and functional texts. For example, assembling a word letter-by-letter on a magnetic board, writing it during writing center and workstation activities, seeing it in poems written on chart paper and in directions written for centers, and reading it in familiar, easy-to-read books are just a few of the ways children get the multiple exposures needed to make a word a sight word. Other ways include seeing the word on a Word Wall and playing search games (such as "spelling tests") with it. Word Walls in first grade should display many of the words found in a high-frequency word list, such as Fry's Instant Words (see the words *a, and, are, be, by, come, could, can't, do, day, down, go, get, have* and *had* on Figure 9.3).

Using Context

Using context usually refers to readers' use of world knowledge, picture clues, understanding of the parts of a text they have already read, and oral language knowledge (especially knowledge of vocabulary and syntax) to anticipate upcoming words in the text of storybooks. Early in their literacy development, readers often make word reading errors due to overreliance on such input. Beginning conventional readers, however, learn to check what they have anticipated by looking carefully at the print, at first comparing the overall size and configuration of the word in print to the appearance of the word they anticipated and later looking carefully at letters, especially initial and final letters, and at known chunks of letters (phonograms). To progress beyond the beginning phases of conventional reading, children must acquire a habit of looking carefully at words that they must decode (that they cannot read automatically as sight words) and then using other input—especially their sense of language and their evolving construction of a story's meaning—to check the result of their decoding. This approach helps children read words with an appreciation for the importance of making sense consistent with context (Combs, 2006).

READING AND WRITING INSTRUCTION IN EXEMPLARY FIRST-GRADE CLASSROOMS

WE SHOW HOW EXEMPLARY TEACHERS guide reading and writing in first grade. Mrs. Tran uses the guided reading approach to first grade reading instruction. Mr. Schultheis exemplifies good first grade writing instruction. Mrs. Duthie's and Mrs. Zickuhr's teaching includes examples of mini-lessons to support first graders' informational text writing and poetry writing.

Guided Reading Instruction in Mrs. Tran's First Grade

Mrs. Tran teaches twenty first-grade children in a large urban district. The majority of the children in her classroom have home languages that are not English; the classroom includes six different home languages. We describe six components of Mrs. Tran's instruction: literacy centers, talk-through as an introduction to children's guided reading, teaching for strategies while children are reading, interactive writing, teaching for comprehension, and word study. Mrs. Tran's literacy program also includes multiple daily read-alouds, shared reading, independent reading, and writing workshop.

The **guided reading approach** (Fountas & Pinnell, 1996) to reading and writing instruction has three critical components. The first is the development of **strategic readers** as active problem solvers who are expected to take initiative in solving their own reading difficulties. Important teaching occurs at the point of difficulty (Askew & Fountas, 1998) while children are reading. Children are expected to work at difficult points in reading by monitoring and discovering new information for themselves. Children make new discoveries as they search for and use information in the text, check one source of information with another, and link to what they already know. Teaching for strategies is helping children develop strategies to use during reading and writing.

A second critical component of the guided reading approach is using sets of **leveled texts** that begin with easy texts that are highly repetitive with few words. Gradually children read more difficult texts that include more words and more complex, literary and informational language. Reading Recovery uses over a dozen levels of text difficulty in the first grade. Fountas and Pinnell (1996) recommend using sixteen levels of text difficulty in first through third grade, and Gunning (1998) has identified thirteen levels of text difficulty from first through early second grade. Lists of texts at several levels of difficulty can be found in Fountas and Pinnell (2005) or Gunning (1998), and many school districts have developed their own lists of leveled texts. Many texts at the easiest levels of difficulty can be purchased through publishers such as Wright Group, Rigby, Sundance, or Scholastic. Table 9.2 presents a description of eight levels of text difficulty and example books for each level (based on Peterson, 1991; Gunning, 1998).

A final component of the guided reading program is small dynamic ability groups (Fountas & Pinnell, 1996). In **dynamic ability grouping,** a small number of children who have similar reading abilities are selected to read together. Texts are carefully selected to match the needs of the small group of readers. Teachers read twenty to thirty minutes with the small group of readers at least four times per week. However, many teachers meet twice daily with some small groups of children who are struggling to make progress. In the following section, we describe Mrs. Tran's first-grade classroom and her use of the guided reading approach.

Literacy Centers. In order to provide time for instruction of small guided reading groups, Mrs. Tran prepares several activities for children to work on independently, which she places in seven centers in her classroom. Mrs. Tran plans these activities carefully so they present a range of challenges to the variety of learners she has in her classroom. Mrs. Tran expects that the children will work together without teacher support in the centers, capitalizing on peer support for learning (MacGillivray, 1994; Sipe,

TABLE 9.2   Levels of Text Difficulty

Level	Description	Example
1. Picture or Phrase Text	Each page includes a single word or phrase with close relationship to illustrations.	*Colors* (Birningham) Crown *1 Hunter* (Hutchins) Greenwillow *Count and See* (Hoban) Macmillan *Have You Seen My Cat?* (Carle) Scholastic
2. Sentence Pattern Text	Each page includes a repetitive sentence with some new content. From close to some relationship with illustration as difficulty increases. Number of different words in pattern increases with difficulty.	*I Went Walking* (Williams) Harcourt *Spots, Feathers, and Curly Tails* (Tafuri) Greenwillow *Things I Like* (Browne) Knopf *Five Little Ducks* (Raffi) Crown *Bears on Wheels* (Berenstain) Random House *It Looked Like Spilt Milk* (Shaw) HarperCollins
3. Sight Word Text	Includes one sentence per page; most words are high-frequency, but a few content words. Most words strongly related to illustrations. Up to thirty-five different words and may have one hundred words in text.	*Blue Bug Goes to School* (Poulet) Children's Press *All By Myself* (Mayer) Golden Books *Go Dog Go* (Eastman) Random House *Just Like Daddy* (Asch) Simon and Schuster *Pardon? Said the Giraffe* (West) HarperCollins *A Dark, Dark Tale* (Brown) Dial *Cookie's Week* (Ward) Putnam *Marmalade's Nap* (Wheeler) Knopf
4. Easy Beginning Text	Text of 100 to 150 words, with many high-frequency words and some content words. Less repetition and more words per page. Up to fifty different words.	*The Carrot Seed* (Kraus) HarperCollins *One Monday Morning* (Shulevitz) Scribner *Peanut Butter and Jelly* (Wescott) Dutton *Sheep in a Jeep* (Shaw) Houghton Mifflin *Titch* (Hutchins) Macmillan *More Spaghetti I Say* (Gelman) Scholastic

TABLE 9.2   (Continued)

Level	Description	Example
5. Moderate Beginning Text	Text of 150 to 200 words, with more content words, but the majority are still high-frequency words.	*Are You My Mother?* (Eastman) Random House *Hattie and the Fox* (Fox) Harcourt *Henny Penny* (Galdone) Clarion *George Shrinks* (Joyce) HarperCollins *Where Are You Going Little Mouse?* (Kraus) Greenwillow *Hop on Pop* (Seuss) Random House
6. Difficult Beginning Text	Varied vocabulary, longer text, more detailed information and complex plots. Most vocabulary in reader's listening vocabulary.	*Mouse Soup* (Lobel) HarperCollins *Do Like Kyla* (Johnson) Orchard *Kiss for Little Bear* (Minarik) HarperCollins *More Tales of Amanda Pig* (Van Leeuwen) Dial *Elephant and the Bad Baby* (Vipont) Putnam *Clifford, the Big Red Dog* (Bridwell) Scholastic
7. Early Transitional Text	Some vocabulary not in reader's listening vocabulary. May have short chapters and some unfamiliar concepts.	*Henry and Mudge* (Rylant) Simon and Schuster *Frog and Toad Together* (Lobel) HarperCollins *Fox in Love* (Marshall) Dial *Three Little Pigs* (Galdone) Clarion *The Art Lesson* (de Paola) Putnam *Bear's Picnic* (Berenstain) Random House
8. Later Transitional Text	Vocabulary beyond reader's listening vocabulary, complex plots and unfamiliar concepts.	*Nate the Great* (Sharmat) Dell *Cam Jan and the Mystery of the Dinosaur* (Adler) Dell *The Chalk Box Kid* (Bulla) Random House

Source: Based on B. Peterson, 1991; and T. Gunning, 1998.

1998). Figure 9.4 lists the materials found in Mrs. Tran's seven literacy centers and describes activities that are typical for each center. Mrs. Tran changes the materials and activities included in the centers weekly or bi-weekly. During September and early October, she demonstrates how to work in the centers, showing children how to find and

FIGURE 9.4 Mrs. Tran's Literacy Centers

Listening Center. Tape recorder, multiple headphones, and approximately one hundred audiotapes of children's literature, including commercially available tapes as well as tape recordings of parents of present and past students, the principal and other teachers, and other guests reading books aloud. Sentences from the information book or storybook that is read aloud are placed on sentence strips. Children select a sentence after listening to the book and illustrate it. Children later write their own sentences.

Big and Little Book Center. Small easel with four or five recently read big books, small children's chair, pointer, and small tubs of books for each child in the classroom, with copies of five or six books or poems read during shared or guided reading. Children take turns being the teacher and pretending to direct a shared reading experience. They also reread poems and books from their book tubs.

Library Center. Cozy corner created by shelves with nearly 300 books, including books Mrs. Tran has recently read aloud, books included in a social studies or science unit, and books by favorite authors and illustrators. Children browse through books and use props to retell stories (during this week, the retelling props are spoon puppets for versions of *The Three Billy Goats Gruff* and transparency props for retelling *Where's Spot?* on an overhead projector, which sometimes is located in this center).

Writing Center. A large, round table with shelves stocked with a variety of writing tools and materials. This week, Mrs. Tran has included letter writing as a part of the writing center. She has posted several examples of letters children may use.

Letter and Word Center. An easel, a small table for writing, and shelves to hold letter and word games and puzzles. Mrs. Tran writes words on chart paper each day and places the paper on the easel for children to copy if they wish. This week, Mrs. Tran has written her name and invited children to write her name several times on the chart paper. This week, small clipboards are available for children to copy the names of other children in the class (located on sentences strips and clipped on a ring in the center). Children are also challenged to write ten words included on the word wall, using letter tiles.

Computer Center. A large table with two computers, word-processing packages, reading and other games, and Internet access. This week, children are challenged to write a grocery list. Food ads from the newspaper and alphabet books with food are located at the computer center.

Specials Center. This center is for special activities that occur in the classroom. This week, three parents have volunteered to read aloud with children. Other specials include art projects, cooking activities, and science experiments.

replace materials and sustain their activity in a center for twenty minutes. She shares a classroom aide, who assists in supervising the children as they work in the centers for an hour three mornings a week, with three other first grade teachers in her building.

Mrs. Tran assigns four or five children with mixed abilities to a center group; each center group is assigned to three centers a day. The membership of the groups changes every month so that children work with a variety of others throughout the school year. Mrs. Tran's schedule includes a large block of uninterrupted time for reading instruction, during which the children spend one hour and twenty minutes in centers while Mrs. Tran teaches three guided reading groups. In early November, the children are divided into five groups, and Mrs. Tran reads with each group four or five times a week. A reading specialist works in Mrs. Tran's classroom four mornings a week, and she works with another guided reading group. The reading specialist returns to the class in the afternoon to conduct a final guided reading group lesson. Altogether, most children read with a teacher in a guided reading group once a day, but some children work with a teacher twice a day for three days a week.

Talk-Through to Introduce Guided Reading.

The guided reading approach uses the talk-through activity to prepare children to read a particular text (Clay, 1991b; Fountas & Pinnell, 1996). Keep in mind that guided reading prepares children to read text on their own without teacher support during reading. Talk-through is intended to orient children to the text: to text meaning, repetitive patterns, particular words that might not be decodable, or phonics and other strategies for identifying unknown words and monitoring meaning prior to reading. Talk-through can provide much support for children's reading or minimal support. Teachers carefully gauge how much support to provide in talk-through, given their awareness of the reading abilities of particular children and the level of challenge presented in a particular text.

In this lesson in early November, Mrs. Tran is working with six children who are struggling to read conventionally. Mrs. Tran carefully selects an instructional level text to use with this group and decides how much support to provide during talk-through. She considers what the children already can do. She knows that these children have acquired a few sight words and can track print at the word-by-word level in pattern sentence books by using some initial consonant sounds to monitor their finger-pointing. They know many consonant sound–letter associations, are beginning to learn vowel associations, use initial and sometimes final consonants in their invented spelling, and are developing a strong concept of written words. Mrs. Tran's goals for this group are to develop a larger store of high-frequency sight words, practice monitoring reading by using initial and final consonant cues to cross-check, and practice using the strategy of linking new with known.

After careful consideration, Mrs. Tran decides to use *Where's Spot?* (Hill, 1980) as an introduction to the guided reading text *Where's Tim?* (Cutting, 1996). *Where's Spot?* is familiar to the children, employs the same repetitive language pattern found in *Where's Tim?*, and includes many of the same positional words she intends children to learn (for example, the words *under* and *behind*). Further, Mrs. Tran plans to use the pattern in *Where's Spot?* during a writing process lesson within the next few weeks. Before teaching, Mrs. Tran reads through both books in order to make decisions about what to include in her talk-through activity.

Mrs. Tran knows that the words *no, he, the, is,* and *in,* which are found in the text of *Where's Tim?,* are familiar to these children. These words along with left-to-right pointing should anchor their reading. She will introduce the linking to the known strategy by having children try to figure out the word *Tim* in the title by using what they already know about short vowels. Later, she will work with the short-*i* vowel in further word study.

Before the talk-through, Mrs. Tran reads *Where's Spot?* to the children, asking questions and inviting children to make comments. She quickly rereads the story a second time. Then she introduces the guided reading book *Where's Tim?*, using the talk-through. Figure 9.5 presents her talk-through introduction to this text. Notice how she calls attention to the connection to the earlier book she read aloud; establishes the repetitive pattern; focuses on locating the words *under, bathroom,* and *behind;* has children figure out the surprise ending; and models the linking with the known strategy as they read the title. Following the talk-through, the six children read the book independently. They read quietly, but aloud, and Mrs. Tran listens to all the children as they read, noting children's tracking of print, cross-checking, and linking to the known.

As children are reading aloud, Mrs. Tran observes and notes one or two teaching points she will make with the children during the next part of the lesson. She decides to refocus on the vowel sound in the word *Tim* and use a small, dry erase board to have children use the phonogram *im* to build more words such as *dim, him, rim,* and *slim.* Mrs. Tran has children reread portions of the entire text several times; she integrates teaching during the rereading. She prepares a printed version of the text without the picture cues which goes in a special binder and is available in each child's independent reading tub. After rereading the illustrated text once or twice and participating in the instructional activity focusing on reading and spelling words with the *im* phonogram, the children read the print-only version. Finally, children choose one or two stories from the binder that they have recently read during guided reading to reread.

Teaching for Strategies during Guided Reading.

Keep in mind that a critical component of the guided reading approach is to foster active readers who solve by themselves the problems they encounter while reading. Teachers are aiming for readers who have self-extending reading strategies (Clay, 2001). That is, eventually readers acquire a sufficient number of strategies that enable them to actually get better at reading with minimal teacher support. Rather than solve reading problems before reading by providing children with all the sight words they will need, teachers in the guided reading approach intentionally leave problems for children to solve on their own during the very first reading of a text. In this way, children must use strategies to solve their own reading difficulties (Askew & Fountas, 1998; Schwartz, 1997).

Mrs. Tran has already taught several strategies to this particular group of children and uses prompts to encourage children to employ these strategies while they are reading. Mrs. Tran demonstrates a strategy several times during talk-throughs and then uses prompts and comments to encourage and reinforce strategy use when children are at a point of difficulty in their reading. This group of children has some strategies firmly under control, such as moving left to right and matching word-for-word while reading. Mrs. Tran demonstrated "reading with her finger" and often praises children for carefully reading with their fingers during guided reading (Fountas & Pinnell, 1996). When children have difficulty, she prompts for this strategy by asking, "Are there enough words? Were there too many words? Try rereading it again."

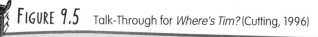

FIGURE 9.5   Talk-Through for *Where's Tim?* (Cutting, 1996)

T: We're going to start today by reading this book. (Several children make overlapping comments: "Where's Spot?" "I know that book." "I like that book.")

T: How many words are in the title?

C: Two.

T: Yes (points), one, two (reads and points to the words) *Where's Spot?*

(Mrs. Tran and children discuss the author and read the book together, stopping frequently to talk about the story. She reads the story twice and stresses the positional words, such as *under* and *behind*.)

T: Now, today for guided reading we are going to read this book (passes out copies of book for each child), and it is also a book about someone searching. This man is searching. He can't find someone. I wonder who he is searching for?

(Mrs. Tran and children make guesses about who the man might be searching for.)

T: How many words in the title? Let's count them together. One, two. The title is *Where's* (pauses). Um, who are they searching for? Does anybody know anything that will help me figure out the name of the person this man is searching for?

C: It starts like Tamika.

T: Yes, it starts with the sound (Mrs. Tran pauses and many children offer sounds, most of which are /t/. Mrs. Tran confirms the /t/ sound).

T: Anything else that could help us? What about this vowel? Does anyone know anything that might help us? (Children offer a variety of vowel sounds, and Mrs. Tran helps the children blend /t/ /i/ /m/.)

T: Now let's look through the book. Find the title page. (Mrs. Tran observes as children locate the page.) Let's look and see where the man is searching for Tim.

(Children discuss each page and where the man is looking. Mrs. Tran stresses the positional words that will be read on each page, especially *under* and *behind*.)

T: (page 5) Where is the man looking on this page? (Some children suggest the bathtub.) Yes, he is looking in the room where we find the bathtub. He is looking in the *bathroom*. Put your finger on the word *bathroom*. (Mrs. Tran makes sure everyone is on the correct word.)

T: (page 8) There's Tim! Why he's *fast asleep*, isn't he? Who can find the word *fast*. How would you check if this word was *fast*? (Children discuss cross-checking the *f* and *t* sounds.) Ok. Now use your pointing finger and read the book softly to yourself.

These children sometimes use other strategies, such as cross-checking picture and meaning cues with initial consonants and noticing mismatches between words they attempt and the way they appear in print. Mrs. Tran demonstrated the strategy by reading text that makes sense but does not match the initial consonant and talking about how to cross-check. When children have difficulty reading, she may provide several prompts for the strategy, such as asking, "Where's the tricky word? What did you notice? What letter did you expect at the beginning? Would _____ fit there?"

Children in this group are beginning to make more than one attempt at a word before asking for help. They are beginning to use the strategy of backing up and trying again. In this lesson, Mrs. Tran demonstrated a more complex strategy of linking to known information to figure out an unknown word during the talk-through. Later, she will use prompts such as, "Can you find something you know about here? Does it look like _____? Do you know a word like this? Do you know a word that starts with those letters? Do you know a word that ends with those letters? What do you know that might help?"

Other groups of children in Mrs. Tran's classroom are learning more sophisticated strategies, such as using decoding a new word by analogy (using a familiar phonogram to identify a new word, such as using *ham* to figure out *scram*) or decoding multisyllabic words by using several analogies (such as using *ex* and *fan* to figure out *Mexican*). Other strategies focus on expanding vocabulary knowledge, such as calling to mind related concepts for words that are only somewhat familiar. Still other strategies focus on meaning, such as inviting children to predict and confirm, pause and build a mental picture, assess whether a character's action is expected or unusual, and connect story events or characters to life experiences and acquaintances.

Decoding Coaching.

Mrs. Tran encourages her students to use strategies that she has already taught using decoding coaching. She observes her students so that she knows to what extent they are able to put what she has taught into practice. Some students will have internalized those strategies and will be able to use them in the self-extending reading that is the goal of guided reading. But Mrs. Tran's observations also show her which students need the sorts of prompts quoted in the previous section. This teaching of specific strategies, giving students opportunities to use them, observing who can and cannot do so, and prompting those who are not yet self-extending readers is the essence of coaching.

Interactive Writing.

Mrs. Tran uses interactive writing as part of her guided reading program. She may use it during a guided reading lesson. Or she might use it prior to or after reading a particular text. Mrs. Tran has decided to use an interactive writing activity using the pattern found in *Where's Spot?* with a small group of at-risk children. Mrs. Tran is particularly concerned about these children in her classroom because of their need to develop many foundational concepts. These children do not have a firm grasp of identifying and writing all alphabet letters and are just beginning to control the left-to-right print orientation. They need many experiences with rhyming words and words with similar beginning consonants.

This group has already heard Mrs. Tran read *Where's Spot?* several times. Mrs. Tran has made a pocket chart of the text from this book for shared reading experiences. The children have practiced using a pointer to reread the story from the pocket chart, pointing to the words from left to right. They have participated in many pocket-chart extensions, such as matching words on word cards to words on the pocket chart.

Now Mrs. Tran has decided they will use interactive writing to compose pattern writing. The children decide to compose a pattern story called *Where's Mrs. Tran?* For this lesson, the children will only write the title of the story together during the interactive lesson. Mrs. Tran guides the children by having them repeat the title (*Where's Mrs. Tran?*) and count the number of words. She writes three lines on chart paper from left to right, emphasizing that they will write the three words in the title across the paper on these lines.

Mrs. Tran reminds the children of the first word in the title that they will write. She tells the children they will use the strategy of finding the word and copying its spelling. She asks the children, "Where could we look? Where do we know to find this word?" Mrs. Tran recognizes that an important reading and writing strategy for children at this stage is to draw on resources such as familiar stories, poems, and charts to read and write words (Sipe, 1998). The children find the word *Where's* both on the book *Where's Spot?* and on their pocket chart. Then the children spell the word, saying its letters left to right. Mrs. Tran briefly discusses the apostrophe. She invites first one child and then another to come to the chart and write the first four letters in the word *Where's*. Mrs. Tran quickly writes the remaining letters on the chart as the children tell her the letters. She has children remember the second word in their title and again has children think of where they could find the word. They locate five different places in the classroom where Mrs. Tran's name is written. Again, they name the letters, and children are selected to write them on the chart. Figure 9.6 presents the interactive writing result of *Where's Mrs. Tran?*

Mrs. Tran uses interactive writing with all the groups in her classroom. Depending on what the children know, Mrs. Tran adjusts what she expects children to write, the amount of support she provides, and how much text will be written in one lesson. In some groups, children write sight words quickly and spend more time discussing how to write words with complex vowel spelling patterns or adding suffixes, such as consistent spelling of *ed* and *s*. In other groups, children focus on writing the beginning, middle, and final sounds in words.

Teaching for Comprehension.   The guided reading approach uses leveled texts, and many first graders begin reading picture and phrase- or sentence-level books, which are not difficult to understand. These books, of course, have meaning, but their meanings are obvious from the illustrations. Not much interpretation—going beyond the literal words of the text—is needed to enjoy and understand these texts. While children are

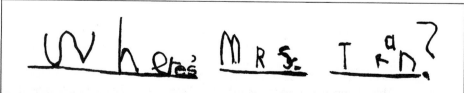

FIGURE 9.6   Interactive Writing of *Where's Mrs. Tran?*

having a heavy dose of these kinds of texts, they should also be engaged in comprehension activities from teacher read-alouds. Children should be encouraged to ask questions, make predictions, insert comments, and draw conclusions during teacher read-alouds. Children may be part of small or large groups that have **grand conversations** about a book their teacher has read aloud (McGee, 1996). Grand conversations are directed by children's comments and questions rather than by a teacher's asking of questions. Teachers begin the conversation by asking, "What did you think?" or "Who has something to say about the book?" Improved understandings result from the comprehension work that emerges during a grand conversation.

However, first graders are also expected to move beyond reading easy books. They will read sight word-level, beginning-level, and transitional-level books that have more complex story structures and detailed information with unfamiliar vocabulary. Meaning in these books goes beyond what is illustrated, and children can be encouraged to interpret them beyond the literal level. Grand conversations about these books in guided reading activities support children's deep thinking. Similarly, there are many comprehension activities that extend children's understandings of what they have read. Children can retell stories or information in journals, act out stories or draw diagrams of information, or compose new endings for old favorites.

Word Study. Mrs. Tran uses twenty minutes daily to engage in word study with the entire class. She began the year with make-a-word activities. She selected two familiar word families from **phonograms** (word families) that she knows are frequently found in words first graders encounter, such as *ack, ail, ain, ame, eat, est, ice, ide, ick, ock, oke, op, uck, ug,* and *ump.* (Figure 9.7 presents thirty-seven phonograms that are most frequently found in English spellings; Adams, 1990, pp. 321–322.) Each child is given a card with the phonogram written on it, several cards with individual consonants, and a folder that had been stapled to hold the cards. Mrs. Tran says, "I have the word *eat;* now what do we need to make the word *beat?* Who can show me?" She emphasizes the sound of the letter *b* by repeating it. The children use their letter and phonogram cards to spell words while Mrs. Tran or the other children pronounce them.

FIGURE 9.7 Thirty-Seven Phonograms That Are Most Frequently Found in English Spellings

ack	ail	ain	ake	ale	ame	an
ank	ap	ash	at	ate	aw	ay
eat	ell	est	ice	ick	ide	ight
ill	in	ine	ing	ink	ip	ir
ock	oke	op	ore	or	uck	ug
ump	unk					

Source: Adams, 1990, pp. 321–322.

Mrs. Tran places word-building activities in her letter and word center. She writes several words on a sheet of writing paper and challenges children to write additional words when they are in the center. Figure 9.8 presents a word-building activity that Sindy completed in the letter and word center. She composed the words *bat, mat, rat, sat,* and *vat* using the pattern Mrs. Tran provided in her word *cat.* Then Sindy went on to build words from another pattern, one that Mrs. Tran did not suggest. She wrote *Mom* and *Tom.*

Later in the year, Mrs. Tran will also introduce a **word sort activity** (Bear, Invernizzi, Templeton, & Johnston, 2000). Children will collect and sort words according to particular spelling patterns. For example, over several days, children may collect words that have the long-*a* sound. All the words will be collected and placed on cards. Then children can sort the words to discover all the patterns used to spell long *a,* such as in the words *fade, rage, fail, raise, pale, paste,* and *straight.*

Mrs. Tran's Balanced Reading Program. Mrs. Tran has crafted a balanced reading program that supports and extends the literacy learning of children who began first grade with a wide range of knowledge about literacy. Mrs. Tran uses multiple instructional contexts as ways to support children who might otherwise be at risk for literacy failure. For many children, she uses a mixture of shared reading and interactive writing to provide opportunities for children to gain foundational concepts about print, the alphabetic principle, and phonemic awareness. However, these children are also engaged in guided reading experiences in which they acquire sight words, develop strategies, and build vocabulary as they read texts at increasing levels of difficulty. Mrs. Tran's word study extends children's reading and writing experiences through systematic examination of words. Finally, Mrs. Tran provides many opportunities for children to gain

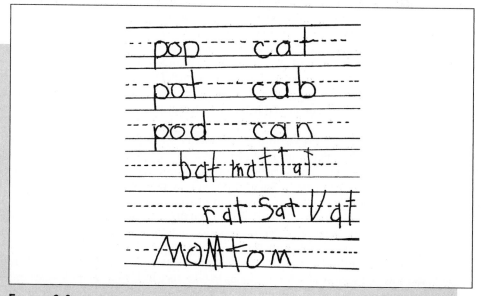

FIGURE 9.8 Sindy's Word-Building Activity

fluency by reading and rereading favorite books and poems. She carefully selects books for individual children, which she places in small tubs for each child in the room. Children read these materials at the beginning of every day and during some center activities. Mrs. Tran also provides time for children to browse through a variety of books, most of which will be beyond their reading level. She reads several books aloud daily and places these books in the library center.

Writing in Mr. Schultheis's First Grade

Mr. Schultheis is a first grade teacher who has been identified as an exemplary teacher, one whose students' literacy development far exceeds that of average teachers' students (Pressley, Allington, Wharton-McDonald, Block, & Morrow, 2001; Wharton-McDonald, 2001a, 2001b). Children in his classroom sit in clusters of desks. They begin the day with independent reading of books selected from tubs placed at each cluster of desks. Independent reading is followed by whole-class discussion in which he may discuss upcoming activities, review previous day's activities, including new vocabulary or spelling patterns, preview a new book the children will be reading, or introduce a new topic for writing. The remainder of the morning is devoted to large blocks of time for reading and writing. During the reading block, Mr. Schultheis meets with guided reading groups. Some children read copies of children's books at their level, other children may read decodable books in which the text is primarily composed of words following expected phonics patterns. Other children might read a class book composed by the children during writing block. Other children may be reading big books used in shared reading.

A three-part approach to writing provides the organization for a successful writing block. First, the teacher gives a short whole-class lesson on some aspect of writing. This may include reading a short excerpt from a text shown to the class on an overhead projector. They discuss the writing, and the teacher models writing a similar piece. Then children begin the second part of the writing approach, an extended writing period during which they are asked to write for as long as thirty minutes (but shorter in the beginning of the year). Children are expected to use the strategies and skills just taught, and the teacher circulates to work with them individually, to observe their successes, and to determine their needs. For the third part of this approach to writing instruction, some children attend small-group writing conferences where they receive instruction focused on their demonstrated needs, which they have in common with other members of the small group.

Effective teachers carefully read students' writing in order to note common needs and group students for targeted instruction in writing conferences. For example, they frequently read students' writing journals, not to correct their writing, but to notice strengths and weaknesses. Some children may need to provide more details in their writing; others may need to reread and rework drafts to vary sentence structure; others may need to be more careful about capitalization and punctuation.

During the short, whole-class lessons, sometimes called **mini-lessons,** which Mr. Schultheis teaches before his reading and writing blocks and sometimes as an interlude during reading and writing blocks, he addresses some small part of what writers need to know. This allows for these lessons to take very little time. Mini-lessons merely raise students' awareness, sometimes as a reminder of what they already know and sometimes as an introduction to a new topic. This makes them appropriate for whole-class groups, which include a wide range of writing abilities. More individualized instruction occurs when the teacher circulates during the thirty-minute extended writing period and during writing conferences. Mini-lesson topics may be about characteristics of texts:

- Beginnings that grab readers' attention, middles that keep that attention and provide much of the information, and endings that resolve conflicts, summarize, or present conclusions
- A paragraph as a set of sentences related to one another because they develop a single idea
- Indenting at the beginning of a paragraph
- The parts of a story (characters, an initiating event that sets up a problem, attempts at solving the problem, obstacles, and solutions)
- The parts of a how-to description
- The parts of a compare-and-contrast informational text
- The elements of imagery in poetry

Or mini-lessons may be about processes writers use, including the following:

- Selecting a topic
- Reworking a draft, with attention both to conventions, such as grammar, spelling, punctuation, and capitalization, and to features of story grammar or expository text structure, with the goal of making the text comprehendible to a reader who is not the author (The author has to assume the role of a reader.)
- Editing, including the use of grammar, spelling, punctuation, and capitalization to make a text that is "finished"; that is, one that meets the class's standards for publication (which depend on what students have been taught and have mastered about those conventions)

Mr. Schultheis constantly reminds children that "the first part of writing is getting your writing down. Then we go back and make sure the skills have been incorporated" (Wharton-McDonald, 2001a, p. 123).

After each whole-class lesson and during the extended writing period, children are expected to apply in their own writing what they have been taught. A teacher might, for example, observe children to see who is independently writing single-idea paragraphs with indentation and who needs to be reminded of this model.

During his writing conferences, Mr. Schultheis asks children to read what they have written. He asks, "How could we make that sound better?" (Wharton-McDonald, 2001a, p. 124). He tells children that first drafts are like skeletons; they have to add ideas to fill out the bones of the story. He always emphasizes that children's writing should be interesting and coherent (flow from one idea to the next).

As children write, Mr. Schultheis provides instruction to individual children. One way to support children's writing of first drafts is to make getting at words easy. Teachers can create an alphabetized dictionary of words children need in their writing and post word lists from theme study.

Because Mr. Schultheis has twenty-one years of experience teaching, he has internalized the first-grade scope and sequence of skills. A **scope and sequence** is usually found in a published basal reading series or in a district or state curriculum guide. It is the list of skills students in a particular grade are expected to learn and that their teachers are required to assess and teach. Mr. Schultheis does not follow a published scope and sequence, but rather teaches the skills in his internalized scope and sequence when his children demonstrate a need for them. He teaches these skills in guided reading, in whole-class discussion, in writing demonstrations, during small-group writing conferences, and during individual conferences with children. In other words, his teaching is guided by what he knows he is expected to teach and by his continuous assessment of what his students currently know and can do.

His teaching usually serves multiple purposes. Figure 9.9, for example, shows how he taught about the phonics generalization that *oa* spells /O/ while at the same time developing vocabulary. This is an example of the instructional density of Mr. Schultheis's teaching, or teaching more than one thing at a time.

Children's writing in Mr. Schulthies's classroom at the end of the year is far different from children's writing in typical teachers' classrooms. In adequate first grade classrooms, children's writing pieces usually consist of two or three sentences and rarely exceed a page. Children write mostly personal narratives, stories that describe a typical sequence of events (first this, then that), and daily journal entries that tend to be

FIGURE 9.9   Mr. Schultheis Combines Phonics and Vocabulary Instruction

Mr. Schultheis*:	How about something that Mom puts in the oven—a kind of meat?
Student 1:	Meat loaf!
Mr. Schultheis:	I was thinking of something else, but that's a good one, too.
Student 2:	Roast beef!
Mr. Schultheis:	Yes. Roast. Put that on your list. (*Students write.*) How about something that comes in a bar?
Student 3:	Soap!
Mr. Schultheis:	What happens when you put wood in water?
Students:	Float!
Mr. Schultheis:	Now, I like that word that Amy thought of—What was that?
Students:	Loaf!
Mr. Schultheis:	Put that on your lists. (*Students write.*) How about something that Charlie made in the story we read yesterday [referring to the Tomie dePaola book *Charlie Needs a Cloak*; dePaola, 1973]?
Students:	Cloak.
Mr. Schultheis:	And what's the difference between a coat and a cloak?

*Wharton-McDonald uses *Andy*, Mr. Schultheis's first name, here; we continue our usual reference to the teachers in this chapter by Mr., Miss, Mrs., or Ms. and their last names.
Source: Wharton-McDonald, 2001a, p. 121

repetitive (such as, "I like to . . . I like to . . . I like to . . ."). Their writing often lacks co-herence, that is, it is a collection of unconnected sentences. They write left to right, usu-ally with spaces at word boundaries, but they use capitals and periods intermittently. Strong first-grade writers in typical teachers' classrooms write on average three sen-tences with a total of fourteen or fifteen words. Average writers write one sentence with eight to nine words. Struggling writers write one sentence with three words. In contrast, students in exemplary classrooms usually write a page or more and in many genres. Strong first-grade writers in exemplary teachers' classrooms write up to eight sentences with over eighty words. Average writers write seven sentences with over fifty words. Struggling writers write six sentences with over forty words. These differ-ences in just the number of sentences and words between children in typical and ex-emplary classrooms are striking. The differences also exist in the number of different genres children write. In exemplary classrooms, children write personal journal entries and personal narratives; they write in science, math, and response journals. They write letters, informational texts, and stories about fictional characters. Their stories, in gen-eral, are coherent. Specifically, their plotting includes beginnings, middles, and ends; their characters are consistent; and their structures conform to story grammar. Coher-ence is demonstrated not just in stories, but in all genres. The first grade students of ex-emplary teachers can remain on topic for a page or more and write with consideration of their intended audiences. Finally, they use capitals and periods consistently and ac-curately, and they frequently use question marks and exclamation marks (Wharton-McDonald, 2001b).

Informational Writing in Mrs. Duthie's First Grade

Mrs. Duthie is a first grade teacher who has written about her experiences helping stu-dents read and write informational texts (Duthie, 1996). She knows that informational reading and writing are inspirational to all children, but especially to those children who naturally select this kind of text for their independent reading and writing (Caswell & Duke, 1998). Mrs. Duthie's classroom library has a special section for infor-mation books, and she makes a special effort to read information big books as part of shared reading experiences, as well as stories and poems. The class learns about as many information book authors and illustrators as authors and illustrators of stories and poems. Her children keep personal lists of the call numbers of books in the library for quick reference (information books about cats are found under 636.8 and dinosaurs under 567.9).

Mrs. Duthie also uses mini-lessons to teach about informational writing. First, she shares one or more information books that have a special feature. Children talk about these special features and sometimes construct a group drawing or composition that in-cludes the feature. For example, Mrs. Duthie showed *Oil Spill!* (Berger, 1994) to illus-trate labeled drawings, *Jack's Garden* (Cole, 1995) to illustrate cutaway drawings, and *Water* (Asch, 1995) to illustrate cross-sectioned drawings.

As a part of mini-lessons about informational writing, children can learn how to put information into sets or groups, write about one part at a time, or lead with a ques-tion. They may discover and use captions, headings, tables of contents, and indexes. They may experiment with many different kinds of informational writing beyond that found in information books. Figure 9.10 presents a first grader's want ad.

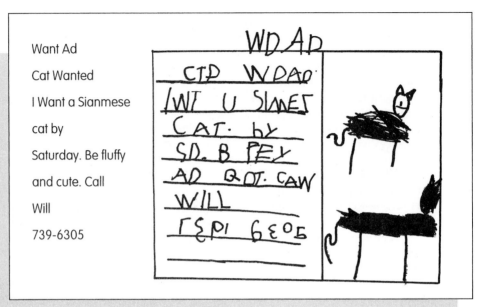

Want Ad

Cat Wanted

I Want a Sianmese

cat by

Saturday. Be fluffy

and cute. Call

Will

739-6305

FIGURE 9.10 A First Grader's Want Ad

Poetry Writing in Mrs. Zickuhr's First Grade

Poetry reading and writing is an important part of literature enjoyment and literacy instruction in another first grade teacher's room. In Mrs. Zickuhr's room, children respond to poems through choral reading, collecting poems, drama, art, music, talking, and writing. Mrs. Zickuhr teaches several mini-lessons about poetry as a part of writing instruction. With one, she stresses the importance of feelings in writing and responding to poetry.

Cullinan, Scala, and Schroder (1995) agree with Mrs. Zickuhr:

> Students need to experience enjoying poetry before they begin to look at the technical aspects of poetry forms. Children often become so caught up in the rules and regulations that they lose the pulse and emotion of what they want to say. Meaningful poetry must touch us personally. It dies when that element is missing. (p. 38)

She reads a poem about which she feels strongly, shares her feelings about it, and invites the students to respond in small groups. Another mini-lesson is about topic selection ("Poetry has to hit a person right in the heart or it won't work"). Another is about form. Mrs. Zickuhr suggests that after writing a draft, her young poets should think about structure: "Just like buildings have architecture—some are tall and thin, some are short and wide—poems also have to be built according to a design which works." She finds that first drafts often look proselike, so she has students read their poems aloud and add slashes for line breaks where they naturally pause. Another mini-lesson is about endings, that they can hold the rest of the poem together, surprise the reader, or make the reader think.

As inspiration, Mrs. Zickuhr reads poems that make use of sounds, such as the sound "vroom" found in the poem "The Go-Go Goons" from *Street Poems* (Froman, 1971). Children use these ideas in their own poetry compositions. Figure 9.11 shows a poem about motorcycles written by Mike, one of Mrs. Zickuhr's first graders. Mike's use of *vrooming* shows that he benefited from Mrs. Zickuhr's reading "The Go-Go Goons" to his class.

Summary: Effective First-Grade Literacy Instruction

Studies of exemplary first-grade literacy instruction (Morrow et al., 1999; Pressley et al., 2001) suggest the following recipe for effective teaching: knowledge, balance, expectation, opportunity, and support. Teachers must have thorough knowledge of what they will teach their students. In fact, they must know more about phonemes or punctuation or paragraphing than they will ever teach, because they always must have in mind the big picture, only parts of which are ever embodied in any student's performance or in any one of the teacher's specific mini-lessons. Teachers must have balance in order to hold many students' varying abilities and needs in mind at one time, to teach more than one thing at a time, and to use more than one approach to instruction. Teachers must expect much of their students while providing the instruction about literacy skills and strategies that will enable them to meet those expectations. They must give students opportunities to apply and practice what they have taught immediately following the teaching and frequently thereafter, and they must use those student application and practice sessions as opportunities for determining what their students can and cannot do. They determine which skills and strategies need additional emphasis in later mini-lessons.

Motorcycle	Modrigl
Fast, too loud	fast, to lode
Racing, driving, vrooming	rasing, Driveing, vroming
I like motorcycles	I like modrsigls
Bike	Bike
	By Mike

FIGURE 9.11 Mike's Poem

Modifying Instruction to Meet the Needs of Diverse Learners

WE HAVE DESCRIBED EXEMPLARY TEACHERS' instruction using guided reading of leveled books and other kinds of texts, a writing approach that includes interactive writing, and word study in focused, explicit lessons and in embedded lessons during reading and writing. These teachers were not required to use a commercial basal reading program. Their instruction was guided by district guidelines for students' reading and writing achievement rather than by a commercial program. Nonetheless, increasingly teachers are required to teach from commercial programs. Teachers working with required commercial reading programs will need a systematic approach to modifying the activities in that program to meet the needs of their diverse learners.

Modifying Commercial Reading Programs

Many schools, as part of their comprehensive reading programs, require teachers to use a core reading program. A **comprehensive reading program** is an approach to teaching all children in an elementary school. It includes a scope and sequence of skills that will be taught at each grade level, materials that are to be read at each grade level, assessments for determining what children need to learn and for checking whether they have learned what they have been taught, and materials for reteaching when children demonstrate a need for it. A comprehensive reading program also includes provisions for reading intervention. That is, when children are identified as struggling and not making grade-level progress, the school must develop a plan to intervene with extra, targeted instruction. Intervention programs are designed to bring children up to grade-level expectations.

Core reading programs are commercial products promoted as having all that teachers and students need for the students to achieve grade-level expectations through daily instruction and practice in phonics and phonemic awareness, vocabulary, comprehension, and fluency. Some core reading programs are scripted, telling teachers what to say as they teach, what to expect students to say, and how to respond to students. These programs also are sequenced; teachers are expected to teach all parts of all lessons and to teach them in the order given in the teachers' manuals.

In order to modify instruction to meet the needs of individual children, teachers need to consider where in the sequence of instruction to begin a small group of children. Because first graders are so different in their beginning competency in reading, teachers cannot expect all children to begin with lesson one and move lesson-by-lesson through the rest, sometimes as many as 160 lessons. Basal reading programs that are not scripted and strictly sequenced are more easily modified. They provide a wide variety of activities in each lesson, allowing for teachers to select those few that fit the needs of individual children with whom they are working.

As teachers know more about their students, they are better able to skip activities provided for teaching skills and strategies that their children already know. Effective instruction is based on the kind of assessments described in Chapters 2 through 5. It is focused only on what students need to know, not on what they already know. This saves time, facilitates students' progress, and spares them frustration.

Modifying Instruction for English Language Learners

Shared reading of big books is enjoyable and beneficial for all children, but especially for ELL children. Most big books have comprehensible language such as simple sentence structures, direct matches between the text and illustrations, repetitive sentence and event patterns that support prediction, and words used in everyday conversations. Before reading aloud a big book in shared reading with English language learners, teachers can use a talk-through approach, pointing to important parts of the illustrations, speaking slowly, and focusing on simple explanations of a few words. Teachers invite children to talk about what they know. During a talk-through, the teacher can begin to use some of the language patterns that are used in the book. Then teachers read the book slowly, carefully articulating the words (Barone, Mallette, & Xu, 2005).

After reading, teachers select a few of the words to highlight in oral vocabulary instruction and a few words to teach as sight words. When strengthening oral vocabulary, teachers select rich content words illustrated clearly in the book. When teaching sight vocabulary, teachers select one or two high-frequency words used in a repeated sentence pattern. They can be written on a white board using magnetic letters or in a sand tray.

Teachers can use the linguistic structure of the big book to stimulate writing (and more practice of the targeted sight words). Sentence structures in easy pattern books include the following:

- I can _____.
- Look at me _____.
- I see a _____.
- Here comes a _____.
- I am at the _____.
- We are going to the _____.
- I have a _____.
- I can put a _____ in my bag.
- This is a _____.
- Where is the _____?
- Look at the _____.
- I see a _____ looking at me.

CHAPTER SUMMARY

FIRST GRADE MARKS AN IMPORTANT TIME in children's schooling. They are expected to begin "really" reading and writing; at the end of first grade, society expects children to have made great strides toward conventional reading and writing. We have shown that there are many ways in which this journey is taken.

We have described conventional reading as reading from print, but attending to meaning. Similarly, we could describe conventional writing as writing words, but attending to message. Acquiring knowledge about the alphabet, phonemic awareness, and print concepts forms a foundation for the later acquisition of sight words and strategies for identifying unknown words and extending understanding.

First graders gain this knowledge when their teachers carefully observe their students and provide targeted instruction. We described Mrs. Tran's guided reading methods, including her use of talk-through before guided reading, guided reading lessons, teaching for strategies, teaching for comprehension, and use of interactive writing. Mr. Schultheis's literacy instruction used flexible groups and varied materials. His teaching frequently served multiple purposes, and he constantly integrated reading and writing. Mrs. Duthie and Mrs. Zickuhr used mini-lessons to teach reading and writing of informational texts and poetry. All four teachers featured in this chapter demonstrate characteristics of exemplary literacy instruction. Such instruction is balanced, there is a lot of it, and it can often be characterized as targeted coaching.

APPLYING THE INFORMATION

We suggest two applying-the-information activities. First, make a list of the characteristics of a literacy-rich classroom presented in Chapter 6. Then reread this chapter to locate an activity that is consistent with each of these characteristics. Discuss your examples with a classmate.

Make a list of all the literacy-learning activities described in this chapter. For one or two of these activities, describe what children learn about written language meanings, forms, meaning-form links, or functions.

GOING BEYOND THE TEXT

VISIT A FIRST GRADE CLASSROOM and observe several literacy activities. Make a list of all the print and literacy materials in the classroom. Take note of the interactions among the children and between the children and the teacher during literacy activities. Talk with the teacher about his or her philosophy of beginning reading and writing. Compare these materials, activities, and philosophies with those of Mr. Schultheis, Mrs. Duthie, Mrs. Zickuhr, and Mrs. Tran.

References

Adams, M. (1990). *Beginning to read: Thinking and learning about print.* Cambridge: MIT Press.

Asch, F. (1995). *Water.* New York: Harcourt Brace.

Askew, B., & Fountas, I. (1998). Building an early reading process: Active from the start! *The Reading Teacher, 52,* 126–134.

Barone, D., Mallette, M., & Xu, S. (2005). *Teaching early literacy: Development, assessment and instruction.* New York: Guilford Press.

Bear, D. R., Invernizzi, M., Templeton, S., & Johnston, F. (2000). *Words their way: Word study for phonics, vocabulary, and spelling instruction* (2nd ed.). Upper Saddle River, NJ: Merrill.

Bear, D., Invernizzi, M., Templeton, S., & Johnston, F. (2004). *Words their way: Word study for phonics, vocabulary, and spelling instruction* (3rd Ed.). Upper Saddle River, NJ: Prentice-Hall.

Berger, M. (1994). *Oil Spill!* New York: Harper-Collins.

Caswell, L., & Duke, N. (1998). Non-narrative as a catalyst for literacy development. *Language Arts, 75,* 108–117.

Clark, K. (2004). What can I say besides "sound it out"?: Coaching word recognition in beginning reading. *The Reading Teacher, 57,* 440–449.

Clay, M. (1991). Introducing a new storybook to young readers. *The Reading Teacher, 45,* 264–273.

Clay, M. (2001). *Change over time: In children's literacy development.* Portsmouth, NH: Heinemann.

Cole, H. (1995). *Jack's garden.* New York: Greenwillow.

Combs, M. (2006). *Readers and writers in primary grades: A balanced and integrated approach K–4.* Upper Saddle River, NJ: Pearson.

Cullinan, B. E., Scala, M. C., and Schroder, V. C. (1995). *Three voices: An invitation to poetry across the curriculum.* York, ME: Stenhouse.

Cunningham, P. (1995). *Phonics they use: Words for reading and writing* (2nd ed.). New York: Harper-Collins.

Cunningham, P. M. (2005). *Phonics they use: Words for reading and writing* (4th ed.). Boston: Allyn & Bacon.

Cunningham, P., & Hall, D. (1994). *Making words: Multilevel, hands-on, developmentally appropriate spelling and phonics activities.* New York: Good Apple/Frank Schaffer.

Cutting, J. (1996). *Where's Tim?* Illus. by J. van der Voo. Bothell, WA: Wright Group.

Dahl, K. L., Sharer, P. L., Lawson, L. L., & Grogan, P. R. (1999). Phonics instruction and student achievement in whole language first-grade classrooms. *Reading Research Quarterly, 34,* 312–341.

Duthie, C. (1996). *True stories: Nonfiction literacy in the primary classroom.* York, ME: Stenhouse.

Fountas, I., & Pinnell, G. (1996). *Guided reading: Good first teaching for all children.* Portsmouth, NH: Heinemann.

Fountas, I., & Pinnell, G. (2005). *The Fountas and Pinnell leveled book list K-8, 2006–2008 edition.* Portsmouth, NH: Heinemann.

Froman, R. (1971). *Street poems.* New York: McCall.

Fry, E.B., & Kress, J.E., (2006). *The reading teacher's book of lists* (5th ed.). San Francisco: Jossey-Bass.

Gunning, T. (1998). *Best books for beginning readers.* Boston: Allyn & Bacon.

Hill, E. (1980). *Where's Spot?* New York: Putnam.

International Reading Association (IRA) and the National Association for the Education of Young Children (NAEYC). (1998). Learning to read and write: Developmentally appropriate practices for young children. *The Reading Teacher, 52,* 193–216.

Juel, C. (1991). *Beginning reading.* In R. Barr, M. Kamil, P. Mosenthal, & P. Pearson (Eds.), *Handbook of reading research* (vol. 2) (pp. 759–788). New York: Longman.

MacGillivrary, L. (1994). Tacit shared understanding of a first-grade writing community. *Journal of Literacy Research, 26,* 245–266.

McGee, L. (1996). Response-centered talk: Windows on children's thinking. In L. Gambrell & J. Almasi (Eds.), *Lively discussions: Fostering engaged reading* (pp. 194–207). Newark, DE: International Reading Association.

Morrow, L. M., Tracey, D. H., Woo, D. G., & Pressley, M. (1999). Characteristics of exemplary first-grade literacy instruction. *The Reading Teacher, 52,* 462–476.

Peterson, B. (1991). Selecting books for beginning readers. In D. E. DeFord, C. Lyns, & G. Pinnell

(Eds.), *Bridges to literacy: Learning from Reading Recovery* (pp. 111–138). Portsmouth, NH: Heinemann.

Pinnell, G., & Fountas, I. (1998). *Word matters.* Portsmouth, NH: Heinemann.

Pressley, M., Allington, R. L., Wharton-McDonald, R., Block, C. C., & Morrow, L. M. (2001). *Learning to read: Lessons from exemplary first-grade classrooms.* New York: Guilford.

Schwartz, R. (1997). Self-monitoring in beginning reading. *The Reading Teacher, 51,* 40–48.

Sipe, L. (1998). Transitions to the conventional: An examination of a first grader's composing process. *Journal of Literacy Research, 30,* 357–388.

Snow, C., Burns, S., & Griffin, P. (1998). *Preventing reading difficulties in young children.* Washington, DC: National Academy Press.

Taylor, B. M., Pearson, P. D., Clark, K., & Walpole, S. (2002). Effective schools and accomplished teachers: Lessons about primary-grade reading instruction in low-income schools. In B. M. Taylor & P. D. Pearson (Eds.), *Teaching reading: Effective schools, accomplished teachers* (pp. 3–72). Mahwah, NJ: Lawrence Erlbaum.

Vail, N. J., & Papenfuss, J. F. (1982). *Daily oral language.* Racine, WI: D.O.L. Publications.

Wagstaff, J. (1997–1998). Building practical knowledge of sound–letter correspondences: A beginner's word wall and beyond. *The Reading Teacher, 51,* 298–304.

Wharton-McDonald, R. (2001a). Andy Schultheis. In M. Pressley, R. L. Allington, R. Wharton-McDonald, C. C. Block, & L. M. Morrow (Eds.), *Learning to read: Lessons from exemplary first-grade classrooms* (pp. 115–137). New York: Guilford.

Wharton-McDonald, R. (2001b). Teaching writing in first grade: Instruction, scaffolds, and expectations. In M. Pressley, R. L. Allington, R. Wharton-McDonald, C. C. Block, & L. M. Morrow (Eds.), *Learning to read: Lessons from exemplary first-grade classrooms* (pp. 70–91). New York: Guilford.

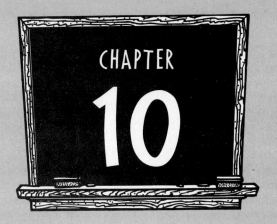

CHAPTER 10

Supporting Literacy Learning in Second through Fourth Grades

KEY CONCEPTS

Literature Text Set
Guided Reading
Guided Spelling
Book Club
Writing Workshop
Inquiry Unit
Internet Workshop
Orthography
Spelling
Orthographics
Making Big Words
Morpheme
Free Morpheme
Bound Morpheme
Affix
Prefix

Suffix
Motif
Schema
Grand Conversation
Readers' Theater
Response Journal
Instructional Reading
    Level
Independent Reading
    Level
Frustrational Reading
    Level
Listening Level
Strategy Sheet
Word Wall
Content-Specific
    Vocabulary

Homophones
Homographs
Word Sort Activities
Word Hunt
Fluent Reading
Choral Reading
Prewriting
Drafting
Revising
Editing
Publishing
Mini-Lesson
Editing Checklist
Simple Sentence
Compound Sentence
Complex Sentence

WHAT'S NEW HERE?

THIS CHAPTER DESCRIBES INSTRUCTION that moves children into and beyond transitional reading and writing described in Chapter 5. While many of the same kinds of instructional activities we described in Chapter 9 continue to be important during this phase of reading and writing, teachers can expand reading and writing activities to capitalize on children's new competencies.

Increasing Expectations for Traditional Skills, Child-Centered Classrooms, and New Competencies

In second through fourth grades, children are held accountable for mastering an ever-increasing number of academic skills in all subject areas. However, child-centeredness does not have to end in these grades. Student choice continues to be an essential component in the reading and writing program. As we will demonstrate, teachers continue to weave opportunities for children's own active exploration of reading and writing with instruction that is directed at helping children achieve the school's expectations for literacy achievement.

An important aspect of the context in second through fourth grades is that a class as a whole usually has achieved a critical mass of literacy competence. Teachers can rely on this competence to integrate learning in content areas with instruction in reading and writing. All students can work together with increasing independence on tasks that require literacy competence. All can function in heterogeneous cooperative-learning groups, using strategies for problem solving and content learning as well as reading and writing.

Activities like these have a characteristic that we can call social construction of meaning (Wells & Chang-Wells, 1992). They involve both a social component and a process of revision. In social construction of meaning, children work together to create an understanding as they interact with others. As a result, children become a community of learners (Miller, 2002).

A Balanced Reading and Writing Program

Perhaps the biggest struggle to achieve balance in the second grade and beyond is meeting the very diverse needs of children. Some children begin second grade reading and writing far above grade-level expectations. They are transitional readers capable of reading more complex picture storybooks, information books, and easy chapter books independently.

Other children begin second grade as early readers. However, these children will have in place many literacy skills and strategies. They are on their way, but need continued teacher support and extended practice to move into and beyond the transitional text levels.

Some children have not yet accomplished what we expect in first grade. They may be reading only at the beginning stage of early reading. They need considerable teacher support and extensive amounts of practice in texts at their instructional level to enhance their early literacy skills and strategies.

Teaching for strategies within the context of rich reading and writing experiences with narrative, poetic, and informational text is another component of balancing the literacy program in second and third grade. Teachers must balance the amount of time used for instruction, guided practice, and independent reading and writing. Teachers continue to provide direct instruction in reading and writing strategies during instructional lessons. They also provide children with opportunities for guided practice using strategies in reading and writing activities. However, strategy development is only a part of competent reading and writing. Competent readers and writers are motivated and knowledgeable about a variety of text genres (Dowhower, 1999; Guthrie & McCann, 1996). Therefore, strategy instruction is embedded in rich conversations about literature (Taberski, 2000).

Components of a Balanced Reading and Writing Program

We present in this chapter a balanced literacy program that has six components:

- Advanced word work in whole-class word study activities
- Literature study, vocabulary instruction, and comprehension instruction in daily, whole-class, interactive read-alouds and response activities
- Small-group instruction in daily guided reading and spelling activities
- Independent reading by individual children and in small flexible book club groups
- Guided and independent writing in daily writing workshop
- Content study in internet workshop and inquiry units

This flexible plan of whole-class, small-group, and individual activities allows teachers to meet the needs of the wide range of students found in second grade and beyond. Whole-class word study in second grade and beyond increasingly focuses on multisyllable words, such as *elephant, writing,* and *rewrite.* The texts that children read both for reading instruction and for content study increasingly have sophisticated vocabulary with more than one syllable, with specific scientific meanings, or with multiple meanings beyond children's everyday experiences. Therefore, studying words and their structures is critical for all children, but especially for children who are English language learners.

Children also need to experience, by listening to teachers read to them, literature that they cannot read, even with teacher guidance. This is especially true in second and third grade, but even in fourth grade children need to be challenged to comprehend complex chapter books. Teachers provide this challenge by systematically planning a read-aloud program in which they read to children literature from **literature text sets**— that is, selections of books with a common theme (e.g., that friends are often found in unusual places), author or illustrator (e.g., books illustrated by Jerry Pinkney), literary element (e.g., tricksters or dynamic characters), or genre (e.g., poetry or animal fantasy). Of course, children listen to read-alouds for the enjoyment of challenging, high-quality literature and for the vicarious experiences it provides, but also to stretch their vocabularies and increase their comprehension ability.

Read-aloud experiences provide children a basis for the comprehension and vocabulary work they will do in guided reading, where they read books at their instructional level. **Guided reading** occurs in small groups with children at the same reading level, reading from books that pose some challenge, but not so much as to be frustrating.

Guided spelling also occurs in small groups of children with similar abilities. Here instruction is about spelling patterns the members of a group are just beginning to recognize and use. For example, some children may be working on particular vowel spellings, others on suffixes or prefixes, and still others on dropping a final *e* or doubling a final consonant before adding *ing*.

All children must engage in a large volume of independent reading to consolidate the strategies taught in guided reading and to build fluency. Teachers guide children in selecting a large set of books for independent reading, they have children reread books first encountered in guided reading, and they help children to make book club selections. **Book clubs** are small groups of children who decide to read a particular book or set of books together. They read the books independently or with partners but discuss the books and engage in response activities as a group.

Finally, a balanced literacy program for children in second grade and beyond includes instruction in writing and content study. Instruction in writing (which includes attention to conventions such as punctuation, capitalization, and grammar) takes places during writing workshop. **Writing workshop** is a particular technique for teaching writing that includes mini-lessons taught by the teacher, concentrated writing time, sharing by student authors, and individual and small-group conferences. Study of content (social studies, science, math, or a combination) takes place in inquiry units and during internet workshops. **Inquiry units** are studies of a particular topic for which children observe, participate in experiments or other hands-on experiences, read from a variety of texts, and communicate their findings often through writing. **Internet workshops** are much like writing workshops but with a focus on children's learning to use the internet to gather information for inquiry units.

 ## ADVANCED WORD STUDY

IN THE SECOND GRADE and beyond, children must increasingly use word "chunks" in their decoding and spelling. Their word identification relies less on applying phonics generalizations that merely match one or two letters with a single phoneme (e.g., the letter *m* and the sound /m/ or the letters *oa* and the sound /O/) and more on recognizing combinations or "chunks" of sounds and letters that function predictably and reliably in many words (e.g., *-at* in *fat, flat,* and *flattered*). Many English words are constructed from such chunks. For example, among the chunks in *complete, balloon, emotion, presuppose, imaginary,* and *confident* are *com-, -oon, -tion, pre-, -up-, -pose, -ary,* and *-tent,* which are also found in *compare, spoon, election, predict, cup, impose, fragmentary,* and *competent.* Some of these chunks are merely common sound combinations, while others are meaningful root words, prefixes, or suffixes.

In the second grade and beyond, spelling work increasingly involves orthographics. **Orthography** is simply another name for **spelling.** We use the term **orthographics,** however, not for just any study of spelling, but rather for the study of complex spelling principles that go beyond simple sound-letter associations. Students come to understand that spelling is much more than matching single letters or pairs of letters with individual phonemes. It also requires attending to sound chunks within syllables (e.g., /ap/ in *cap, gap, lap, map, nap, rap, tap, zap, chap, flap, slap, snap,* and *trap*) and to the meaning chunks, or morphemes, that we call base words, prefixes, and suffixes (e.g., *happy, un-* and *-ly* in *unhappily*). Students of orthographics learn that spelling is not always about sounds. Sometimes it is about meanings. For example, the spelling of the vowel in the word *know* is based on a sound-letter association, that one of the ways of spelling /O/ is *ow*, as also in *snow, grow, low, blow, tow, flow, mow,* and *row*. However, the spelling of the first vowel in *knowledge* is not based on sound-letter associations at all. The sound /ah/ is not usually spelled *ow*, but English spelling preserves the base word *know* in *knowledge* in order to show the relation between the two words' meanings.

Learning about Sound Chunks in Making Big Words

One way to help children develop an intuitive sense of syllables and how to break words apart into familiar sounds is to use the **making big words** approach (Cunningham & Hall, 1994). Making big words begins with a big word's letters (for example, the letters in *p i c k p o c k e t s,* p. 83). Teachers help children make one syllable words that highlight a variety of familiar word parts such as the words *pet, sit, tick,* and *sock.* Then children build multisyllable words again focusing on the use of multiple familiar word parts in these words including *picket, pocket,* and *cockpit.* Finally, they build *pickpockets.* Throughout the activity, the teacher and children discuss the words' meanings. Teachers can keep a list of familiar word parts (such as *ick, ock, et,* and *it*) that can be used to decode and spell big words on a spelling word-part word wall.

Morphemes, Base Words, and Affixes

Morphemes are units of meaning. A word may be a single unit of meaning, as in *flow,* which means to move along in a stream, and as in *flower,* which means the blossom of a plant. Or a word may have more than one morpheme. For example, *flowed* has the meaning of *flow* plus the meaning of "already happened" or past tense; and *flowers* has the meaning of *flower* plus the meaning of "more than one" or plural. **Free morphemes** may stand alone; like *flow* and *flower,* they need not be attached to another morpheme. **Bound morphemes,** like *-ed* and *-s* in *flowed* and *flowers,* must be attached to another morpheme. Much depends on context; *-ed, -s,* and *-er* are not always morphemes. We have seen that *-ed* and *-s* are morphemes in *flowed* and *flowers,* but they are not in *red* and *is.* And *-er* is not a morpheme in *flower,* but it is in *flatter,* where it means "more" (if something is flatter, it is more flat than that to which it is being compared), and in *farmer,* where it means "one who" (a farmer is one who farms).

Multisyllable words often consist of base words and affixes. Good readers use their knowledge of familiar base words to infer the meaning of unfamiliar base-word-plus-affix combinations (for example, using the base word *fresh* to infer the meanings of *refresh* and *freshen.*

Affixes are bound morphemes, either at the beginning of a base word, where we call them **prefixes,** or at the end, where we call them **suffixes.** A prefix alters the meaning of a base word in a predictable way. For example, the prefix *re-* usually means "again" as in *rewrite,* while the prefix *un-* usually means "not" as in *unhappy.* Suffixes are either inflectional suffixes (e.g., *-s, -es, -ed, -ing, -'s, -s', -er,* and *-est*), which signal such meanings as number (dog/dogs, box/boxes), tense (walk/walk*ed*/walk*ing*), possessive (boy/boy*'s*/boys*'*), and degree of comparison (flat, flat*ter,* flat*test*) or derivational suffixes (e.g., *-less, -ment, -ly, -ful, -able, -ish, -ize, -ify,* and *-ion*), which change a word's part of speech, as when *-ful* changes the verb *help* to the adjective *helpful.*

When teaching about affixes, teachers may show children the base word and then carefully add suffixes and prefixes. Inflectional suffixes are easier to learn than derivational suffixes because inflectional suffixes usually do not change the part of speech of base words. Teachers demonstrate putting on and removing prefixes and suffixes, compare words' meanings with and without affixes, and help children construct sentences using various forms, such as *help, helps, helped, helping, helper, helpless, helpful, unhelpful, helpfully, helplessly.*

LITERATURE STUDY THROUGH INTERACTIVE READ-ALOUDS

READING ALOUD TO CHILDREN remains a critical component of the literacy program throughout the elementary years. The central purpose of reading is to comprehend the variety of texts that are encountered in daily life and in our multicultural literary world. One of the best ways to increase comprehension is through listening to high-quality literature as it is read by a teacher who guides children through texts much too difficult for them to read on their own. In these texts, children encounter complex ideas presented in complex literary language structures using sophisticated and relatively rare vocabulary words (Sipe, 2002). Good books read aloud by sensitive and thoughtful teachers offer children opportunities to experience good writing, gripping plots, admirable and despicable characters, and moral dilemmas. With appropriate guidance, children experience emotions, reflect on life, and engage in critical thinking.

Not all literature children encounter in school is of sufficient quality to provoke such reactions. Some children read basal reading materials whose designers' first concern is providing readable texts at levels of difficulty appropriate to children's developing reading abilities; sampling quality literary works is of secondary importance to the designers of these materials, if it is important at all. Other children read good but not very complex literature during their reading instruction; their low-reading ability limits them to only the simplest sentence structures, vocabulary, and plot structures. Finally, even when exposed to good literature during reading instruction, children rarely study it for itself; often, the primary purpose is to improve their reading ability. Teachers can make up for this in carefully planned read-alouds of high-quality literature.

During elementary school, children can learn a variety of elements of literature. They can learn about different genres (see Figure 6.4 for a description of major literary genres), popular and influential authors and illustrators, and literary elements. For example, second graders might enjoy a study of all the Junie B. Jones books. Third graders are fascinated to read several Maurice Sendak books and discover all the windows in the illustrations of his books. They engage in thoughtful discussions of how eating and food are used in many of his stories. Fourth graders can be challenged to discover character traits by collecting examples of what an author says about a character, what other characters say about the character, and what the character says and does.

As teachers read aloud from a text set of books carefully chosen to focus on a particular aspect of literature, children gain literal comprehension of what is explicitly stated in the text or illustrations, inferential comprehension of what is only implied through the text, and critical comprehension when they react to a character or event in the story.

Most children in the United States easily answer literal and inferential comprehension questions. However, very few can take a stand about a character or event and present evidence from the story to support their stand (NAEP, 2003). Interactive read-alouds can close this gap if they are structured to provide children with opportunities to respond to literature using information from what they have heard the teacher read to them.

Reading Aloud

Before reading aloud, teachers preview a book for themselves, reading through it carefully. They select vocabulary words to be discussed and places to stop and ask questions that will help children understand more clearly. They introduce the book to their students by telling a little about a character and building anticipation for the problem. They might teach a little about a literary element they want children to notice. They read with expression and frequently make eye contact with children. They adjust their pace of reading and their voice to bring the story to life in dramatic ways. Most important, they stop to ask a few questions and to answer children's questions or comments. Their read-alouds are interactive; they are active exchanges with their audience. After reading, teachers engage children in discussing the story, usually by posing a "why" question. During or after reading, they may reread a short part of the book to demonstrate a comprehension strategy.

Selecting a Text Set and a Literary Focus for Discussion

Teachers will select five to ten books related in some way. Figure 10.1 presents a list of suggested literary elements that might be studied in the elementary grades. This list suggests studying characters, types of conflict, or special genres of literature.

One third grade teacher, Mrs. Meddors, decided to study folk and fairy tales with her children. She wanted the children to learn about motifs, locate motifs in stories she read aloud, and use the motifs to write their own versions of a folk or fairy tale. A **motif** is a kind of character, event, or other story element recurring across many folk or fairy tales. Motifs include the following:

- Events or characters occur in threes.
- The weakest or smallest character usually saves the day or causes a break in a chain of events.
- Some characters are all good or all bad.
- Some characters are tricky while other characters are tricked.

FIGURE 10.1   Literary Elements to Include in Text Sets for Interactive Read-Alouds

Character Studies to Identify

Character traits (enduring qualities of a character such as brave, secretive, kind-hearted, stubborn, happy-go-lucky, thoughtful)

Well-rounded characters (characters with several different kinds of character traits)

Dynamic characters (characters who change during the story)

Conflict Studies

Conflict between two characters is the central problem

Conflict between a character and himself or herself is the central problem

Conflict between a character and nature is the central problem

Conflict between a character and society is the central problem

Study of Special Genres

Fantasy
   Animal fantasy
   Toy fantasy
   Little ones

Time slip
High fantasy
Realistic Fiction
   Friendships
   Growing up
   Family
   Facing danger
   Making a difference
Traditional Literature
   Myths and legends
   Noodlehead stories
   Trickster tales
   Talking animal tales
   Modern variants of folk and
      fairytales
Post Modern Picture Books
Wordless Picture Books
Nonfiction
   How-to books
   Graphic Illustrations in nonfiction
   Gripping writing in nonfiction
Poetry
   Shape and line in poetry
   Language in poetry
   Humor in poetry

- Some items are magical.
- Some characters must perform tasks, while other characters are helpers.
- Some characters are magical.
- Some characters are clever, while other characters are silly or stupid.
- There are many opposites (clever/stupid; good/bad; rich/poor).

In order to expose her children to these motifs, Mrs. Meddors selected high-quality versions of popular folk and fairy tales, including *Rumpelstiltskin* (Zelinsky, 1986) and *Mufaroe's Beautiful Daughters: An African Tale* (Steptoe, 1987).

Ms. Meddors read aloud a different book from her text set each day, and each day she had a different focus for reading. During the first read-aloud of the text set, she introduced the idea of motifs by listing three motifs on the chalkboard and defining them. As she read, she challenged the children to raise their hands when they thought they had recognized a motif. Mrs. Meddors read aloud *Borreguita and the Coyote* (Aardema, 1998), and the children identified the trickster, the character who was tricked, the clever character, and the stupid character. During this read-aloud, Mrs. Meddors also introduced the concept of opposites by having the children talk about how the coyote and ewe lamb were different (Temple, 1991).

The next day, she introduced three additional motifs, then she read aloud *Rumpelstiltskin* (Zelinsky, 1986). After reading, she defined opposites and asked the children which opposites could be found in the book. The children noticed that the miller and his daughter were poor, the king was rich, but the miller's daughter became rich when she was queen. They thought Rumpelstiltskin, the miller, and the king were greedy, but they thought the miller's daughter was generous and giving. They noted that the miller's daughter and the king were tall and beautiful and handsome; Rumpelstiltskin was small and ugly. They noted that, at night, the miller's daughter was with Rumpelstiltskin, and during the day, she was with the king.

After listing such opposites in *Rumpelstiltskin,* one teacher initiated a question-making activity (Commeyras & Sumner, 1995). In this activity, children construct questions that will lead to long discussions about literature. The teacher modeled asking questions that could be easily answered and did not generate much talk versus questions that generated many different ideas and opinions. Good questions are those that have no single correct answer, generate many different ideas, and take a long time to discuss. This class called these kinds of questions "long questions."

The teacher invited children to suggest long questions to use for talking about *Rumpelstiltskin.* The children posed the following questions with the teacher's guidance:

If the miller was poor, why did he give a daughter to the king?

What kind of father was he to lie to the king in a way that might harm the daughter?

Why would the daughter fall in love with a king who demanded she spin gold or be killed?

Why are the king and Rumpelstiltskin so alike in character, but not looks? Did the miller's daughter think about this?

Another approach to help children perceive multiple perspectives on a story is the multiple-character perspective approach. Here, teachers select books that have characters who are in conflict, such as Nyasha and Manyara in *Mufaro's Beautiful Daughters: An African Tale* (Steptoe, 1987). Children discuss the story from first one character's, and then the other character's perspectives, focusing especially on the characters' conflicting goals, motivations, intentions, and actions. Differing themes which emerge from discussions of the differing goals, motivations, intentions, and actions of characters can be critically compared and contrasted (Shanahan & Shanahan, 1997).

Selecting and Teaching Comprehension Strategies

In addition to having a literary focus during interactive read-alouds, teachers also model specific strategies for comprehension. Most good readers are not aware that they use any comprehension strategies because they use them automatically, without conscious attention (Sinatra, Brown, & Reynolds, 2002). Sometimes good readers do notice when they have not understood what they have just read. They may then reread, slowing down and subvocalizing in order to give more conscious attention to what they read, or they may continue reading to find additional information that will resolve their confusion. Good readers are always trying to make sense of what they read, drawing on their own experiences. For example, if good readers read about a coyote, they use what they know about similar animals such as dogs, wolves, or foxes to make inferences about what coyotes might be like (Pressley & Block, 2002). Most children need to be taught to use these strategies of rereading, slowing down, subvocalizing, and drawing on past experiences. As teachers read aloud, they can model using these strategies and explicitly draw children's attention to them.

One set of strategies that teachers might demonstrate during read-alouds is using prior knowledge to make connections with a text. Such knowledge is organized in **schemas,** or cognitive structures (Miller, 2002). Readers activate prior knowledge or search schemas when they stop during reading in order to think about how the ideas in the text are related to their own lives (text-to-self connections), to something else they read in the story or in another story (text-to-text connections), or to events in the world (text-to-world connections). Another strategy that draws on prior knowledge is to consider the relationships between characters and the events in a story (Taberski, 2000). For example, character traits, that is, the enduring qualities of a character that determine how he or she acts, often account for problems in a story. When children identify character traits and consider how these are related to a story's problem and its eventual solution, they are moving from what happened in the story (literal comprehension) to why (inferential comprehension).

Another comprehension strategy is to create mental images while reading. Good readers visualize characters in action. They use images to anticipate future actions and to fill in detail. When they stop and ask themselves why characters might have acted as they did, good readers often make images and predict what might happen next. Good readers use additional strategies when reading information books. They use special text features such as flow charts, graphs, and labeled drawings. They make note of information and make decisions about which information is most important to remember. Figure 10.2 summarizes comprehension strategies that teachers should model during read-alouds.

One way to teach comprehension strategies during read-alouds is for teachers to stop reading and to think aloud about what they are doing as they use a strategy. Then they explain why it is important to use that strategy. For example, Miller (2002) starts strategy instruction by telling what the strategy is that she will be demonstrating and why it is important: "Thinking about what you already know is called using your schema, or using your background knowledge. Schema is all the stuff that's already in your head, like places you've been, things you've done, books you've read—all the experiences you've had. . . . When you use schema, it helps you use what you know to better understand [what you read]" (p. 57). She identifies and explains the strategy she wants children to learn, "Today we are going to talk about one way [you use schema]: using schema to make connections from our reading, or the text, to ourselves. We'll call these text-to-self connections" (p. 57).

FIGURE 10.2   Reading Strategies

Using schema

Text-to-self connections
  stopping to think about big ideas and
  making connections to my life
Text-to-text connections
  comparing characters in different or
  the same texts
Text-to-world connections
  stopping to think about big ideas and
  connecting to events in life
Schema for story elements
  considering characters and their
  enduring qualities
  determining the relationship between
  character traits and problems, plot,
  and theme
  moving from what happens, to how,
  and why it happens
Activating, building, and revising
  schema

Creating mental images

Creating images from readers' schema
  and words in the text
Changing images to incorporate new
  information

Inferring

Inferring the meaning of words
Predicting
  making more than one prediction and
  using text as support

Stopping to think what happened and
  why it happened (from what to
  why)
Stopping to think why the character
  acted as he/she did (from what to
  why)
Inferring answers to questions (when
  the answers are not in the text)

Asking questions

Asking "I wonder why"
Asking questions before, during, and
  after reading
Determining whether questions can be
  answered in text, in schema, or from
  outside source

**Using special strategies for informational
text**

Noticing and remembering when we
  learn something new
Using informational text features
Distinguishing important from
  unimportant information

Synthesizing

Retelling what's important and makes
  sense, but not telling too much
Moving from literal level to inferential
  level
  I'm thinking that, now I'm thinking,
  I used to think—but now I'm
  thinking

Source: Adapted from Miller, D. (2002). *Reading with meaning: Teaching comprehension in the primary grades.*
Portland, ME: Stenhouse; Taberski, S. (2000). *On solid ground: Strategies for teaching reading K–3.*
Portsmouth, NH: Heinemann.

Next, Miller demonstrates using the strategy, "Let me show you what I mean. I'm going to read a story to you; its title is *The Relatives Came* by Cynthia Rylant. I'll read for a while, then I'll stop and think out loud to show you how I use my schema, or what I already know, to make connections from my life to the story" (pp. 57–58). She reads the book, then stops at a page and puts the book down in her lap signaling she will be talking about the book rather than reading. She says, "[T]his page made me laugh. You see right here, where I read to you 'It was different going to sleep with all that new breathing in the house'? I understood exactly what Cynthia Rylant meant. That's because at the same time I was reading I was making a connection to when I was a little girl, remembering how my family and all my cousins and aunts and uncles would visit my grandparents in their farmhouse on old Route 92 near Oskaloosa, Iowa. Sometimes it was so hot and sticky at night that we'd all pile down to the living room—just like this picture. We'd sleep together on the black carpet with the pink and red roses" (p. 58). Next Miller (2002) makes explicit that she has modeled using the strategy, "Do you see how using my schema helped me understand just how the people in the book feel?" (p. 58).

Strategy instruction helps children reflect on how and why strategies help to make them better readers. One student reflected that "If we connect to a word, like mailman or cat or soccer ball, that doesn't really help us, but if we connect to a bigger thing, like if it's on almost all the pages and it's what the book is really about, like an idea or something, then it can help you" (p. 61). Miller makes what she calls an anchor chart that summarizes children's reflections about using strategies.

Response Activities

For some but not all books, teachers may want to extend children's literary experiences through response activities. One response activity that extends children's comprehension is a **grand conversation** (McGee, 1995), that is, a book discussion prompted by a teacher's open-ended question, such as "What did you think?" but guided by children's comments and questions rather than by the teacher's continued questioning. Figure 10.3 presents a grand conversation among second graders and their teacher about the book *Hey, Al* (Yorinks, 1986). In this story, Al is dissatisfied with his life as a janitor. When a fantastic bird one day invites him to an island in the sky, he escapes his old life to what he thinks is paradise. However, he begins to turn into a bird and decides to return home with his dog. On the way home, the dog plunges into the ocean, but he later makes his way safely to Al.

During this grand conversation, children talked about events they remembered, clarified details, made inferences, and extended their own understanding of the story. Grand conversations such as these are not dominated by teacher questions (Scharer, 1996); instead they are exchanges among children. Grand conversations can be initiated by having children identify topics or "seeds" that they would like to talk about (Villaume et al., 1994), or teachers can generate a list of possible discussion questions from which children select a few (Vogt, 1996).

Story retelling is another activity that improves children's comprehension and fluency (Gambrell, Pfeiffer, & Wilson, 1985). Children should recall the main characters and critical events in a story in the order in which they appeared and with sufficient detail so that someone not familiar with the story can get the gist from the retelling. They

FIGURE 10.3 Grand Conversation about *Hey, Al* (Yorinks, 1986)

Teacher:	What did you think about the story?
Child:	I like the part when the bird stuck his head in.
Child:	It was funny when he was in his underwear in the bathroom.
Child:	He started to look like a bird, and then he got back and painted his room.
Teacher:	Why did you like that part?
Child:	It looked like he was happy and his shirt was like the island.
Child:	The dog was sad. I didn't think he was going to make it.
Child:	Al really was happy to see the dog and he gave him a big ol hug.
Teacher:	Are there any happy and sad parts in the story?
Child:	Dog was sad at the beginning but I don't think Al was so sad.
Child:	I wouldn't be happy as a janitor washing the floor.
Child:	I wouldn't want to turn into a bird.
Teacher:	Why wouldn't you want to turn into a bird?
Child:	I couldn't play baseball, but I could fly.
Teacher:	Let's look at this page here. Did you see this (teacher points to the wing of one of the birds in which it ends in a human hand)?
Child:	Look, look, it's a hand. They are people. Those birds might have been people.
Child:	Al is going to turn into a bird like those other birds.
Child:	They were all people? Those birds, they were all people?
Child:	Yes, look at that hand. Al would have stayed up there as a bird.
Teacher:	I think he is happy to be back to his old home, and he is going to fix it up like a paradise, but a safe one.

naturally use the story's rich vocabulary and complex sentence structure in their retelling, thereby expanding their own language and vocabulary.

Readers' theater is another response activity that benefits children's reading fluency. Children who have read the same book can form a readers' theater group. **Readers' theater** is a simple form of dramatization in which players read their lines rather than memorize them (Trousdale & Harris, 1993; Wolf, 1993). Players usually sit on stools but may stand in groups. There are few props and only the simplest of costumes. To begin readers' theater, teachers can write their own script from a simple story or informational text. They demonstrate how dialogue from stories is translated into dialogue in script form and how narrative in text is translated into a narrator's words in a script. Eventually, students compose their own readers' theater scripts from a picture or information book they have selected. Because children need not memorize lines, they are free to work on interpretation as they read the script aloud, they feel less anxiety, and, overall, there is less emphasis on the performance than in traditional drama.

Once children (or the teacher) have composed a readers' theater script, teachers read it aloud during rehearsal. Then players experiment with reading the script by varying their voices and rate of speaking. The teacher assists students who are having difficulty (Hoyt, 1992). Even the least able readers can participate in readers' theater. They are helped by the repeated reading of the scripts that occurs as a natural part of rehearsal. In fact, rereading is another proven comprehension booster and fluency enhancer (Stahl & Kuhn, 2002).

Readers' theater works just as well using nonfiction books as an alternative to content-area textbooks. It "gives the words on the page a voice, and the students in the classroom an active role in internalizing and interpreting new knowledge" (Young & Vardell, 1993, p. 405).

Another important response activity is writing in **response journals.** Children are encouraged to reveal parts of the book that are memorable, surprising, or unusual and to describe related personal experiences or connections they have made to another book or poem (Barone, 1990; Kelly & Farnan, 1991; Taberski, 2000). Students usually are not required to write an entry in their response journals for every book the teacher reads, but they may be expected to write responses two or three times per week.

GUIDED READING AND SPELLING

GUIDED READING occurs when groups of children, reading on similar levels, are taught reading strategies and practice reading texts under the guidance of the teacher. Teachers select books at a group's instructional level. **Instructional reading level** text is of moderate difficulty. Children can read the words with 90 to 95 percent accuracy and can answer correctly 70 to 90 percent of comprehension questions. **Independent reading level** texts are easier, read with higher word accuracy and comprehension. **Frustrational reading level** texts are more difficult; they are read with below 70 percent comprehension and below 90 percent word accuracy. Figure 10.4 presents an overview of the levels of text difficulty (also including **listening level** for which children can answer correctly at least 75 percent of questions and which teachers use to choose books for read-alouds). Teachers select books to use in guided reading from a set of books that have been leveled for difficulty or from basal reading materials (Fawson & Reutzel, 2000).

Determining Instructional Level and Selecting Children

Assigning students to small groups for guided reading requires that teachers know every child's instructional reading level. To determine this, they ask children to read aloud books that are labeled for difficulty level (Brabham & Villaume, 2002). Teachers count the number of words children read incorrectly and determine the percentage of words correctly identified (word identification accuracy percentage). For example, a

FIGURE 10.4   Levels of Text Difficulty

	Text Difficulty	Word Accuracy	Comprehension
Frustration Text	Difficult	less than 90%	less than 70%
Instructional Text	Moderate	90–95%	70–90%
Independent Text	Easy	more than 95%	more than 90%
Listening level	Moderate	N/A	75% or more

child who reads a 100-word passage with 8 errors demonstrates word identification accuracy of 92 percent. Teachers ask at least five comprehension questions and determine the percentage of correct responses. A child's instructional level is the level of the highest leveled book that he or she can read with 90 to 95 percent accuracy of word identification and 70 to 90 percent correct response to comprehension questions. Teachers can label for difficulty level books they already own by consulting published lists of titles and levels (e.g., Fountas & Pinnell, 2006), or they can purchase books already leveled (Fountas & Pinnell, 1996). Basal reading publishers level their own books, and they often provide assessments, with leveled reading passages and comprehension questions, that teachers can use to determine children's instructional reading levels.

Once each child's instructional level is determined, teachers select children with similar instructional levels to form up to four guided reading groups of four-to-six children each (Taberski, 2000). Teachers check children's instructional levels frequently so that they can regroup children to match their changing instructional levels. Teachers meet with each group of children three to five times per week for twenty to thirty minutes of instruction.

In guided reading instruction, teachers provide an introduction to a book, and children read a few pages independently. Then teachers guide discussion. They may demonstrate decoding or comprehension strategies, have children do so, or have children read portions of the text aloud. After that, teachers introduce the next portion of the text, and children read again independently. The children read silently, but teachers may at the same time listen to individual children read very quietly.

Explicit Teaching of Orthographic Decoding and Vocabulary Using Shared Reading in Guided Reading Instruction

Guided reading provides children with practice using orthographic decoding strategies learned in whole-class word work. Explicit instruction in orthographic decoding may include four steps (Pearson & Gallagher, 1983):

1. Teacher modeling and explanation of a strategy
2. Guided practice, in which the teacher participates with the children as the strategy is jointly used

3. Children's independent practice of the strategy with feedback from the teacher
4. Application of the strategy, in which children use the strategy when appropriate in their reading

Teachers in second grade and above may use explicit instruction in a shared reading approach to teach decoding and vocabulary in guided reading groups. Shared reading in second grade and above takes a different form than shared reading in kindergarten or first grade. Teachers use enlarged copies of short text (for example, using an overhead projector to show a paragraph the teacher and children will read together in guided reading).

Shared reading is especially useful in helping children learn strategies for decoding words. Although as first graders, children learned to apply phonics as a word-solving strategy, in second grade and above they need multiple strategies for both decoding and figuring out a word's meaning. For example, a third grade teacher used *Golem* (Wisniewski, 1996) to demonstrate how to decode difficult words and to infer their meanings. She borrowed copies of the book from other teachers and the library so that pairs of children had a copy of the book to examine as she read aloud. She read the first page of the story and paused at several difficult words including *Protestant, ignorant, matzoh, incited,* and *vicious.* Each time she modeled how to stop and look all the way through the word, break the word into parts, and use familiar word parts, such as *tes, tant, ig, ant, mat, in* and *ous,* to decode the word. She modeled rereading the entire sentence saying the new word. She also modeled how to read the surrounding text to look for clues that would help her infer the word's meaning.

At the end of the shared reading lesson, she guided the children in summarizing the steps in the decoding and word meaning strategy and wrote them on a chart. Over the next several days, the teacher used the chart in guided reading lessons.

Explicit Teaching of Comprehension Strategies in Guided Reading Instruction

Transitional readers in second grade and beyond need to learn how to infer character traits and be able to see how a story's problems, its plot, and possible themes are related to these traits (Taberski, 2000). *Fox and his Friends* (Marshall, 1982) is a perfect text for helping transitional readers learn how to use this strategy. First, the teacher reminds children about this strategy (usually strategies are introduced first in whole-class interactive read-alouds). In this case, the teacher has decided to use a **strategy sheet** to help children use the strategy during reading. A strategy sheet is a simple graphic that children fill in as they read. In this case, the teacher decides to use a character cluster as a strategy sheet (Taberski, 2000). The character cluster strategy sheet is a simple graphic organizer with a circle in the center of the sheet in which the children write the character's name. Around the circle they write information about the character that indentifies the character's traits.

To prepare for reading, the teacher usually decides how much text the children will read. She also plans a focus for the discussion after reading, depending on their purpose for reading. Transitional readers in second grade and beyond can read several pages of text, but in this case the teacher wants the children to decide where to stop reading when they think they have discovered information about Fox. Now the chil-

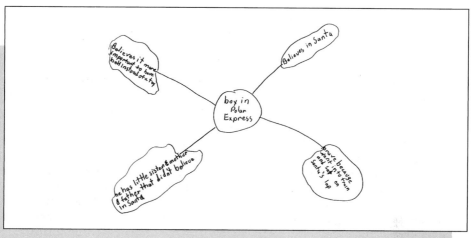

FIGURE **10.5**   Character Cluster for *The Polar Express* (Van Allsburg, 1985)

dren read, stop when they find information about Fox, and fill in a character trait on their strategy sheet. When all the children are finished, the teacher leads a discussion about the traits children have discovered. As they talk, the teacher has children reread portions of the text aloud to support their ideas.

Next the teacher asks the children to use what they have discovered about Fox to predict a problem that will occur in the story. After children predict and justify their ideas, they read further in the story looking for information about another character, Louise. The cycle of setting a purpose, reading, and discussion is repeated. As the children leave guided reading, the teacher asks them to finish reading the book on their own and to fill in the strategy sheet finding out about both Fox and Louise as they continue reading. They are to bring the book and strategy sheet to guided reading when they next meet. For example, Figure 10.5 presents a character cluster written by a third grader for the main character, the boy, in *The Polar Express* (Van Allsburg, 1985). This child noticed the boy's altruism (although she did not have the sophisticated vocabulary to label this concept) when she said, "[I]t was more important to have the bell instead of a toy." She also clearly identified the boy as a believer and as brave, two character traits strongly implied in the text. She was able to find two details from the text as support for one character trait (the boy was brave "because he went on the train" and "he sat on Santa's lap").

In second grade and beyond, children encounter an increasing number of words in their reading that are not included in their listening vocabularies. They need to learn independent strategies for learning the meanings of these new words. A group of third graders used a word cluster during guided reading to practice the strategy of noticing words and inferring their meanings from clues in the text. Figure 10.6 presents a word cluster for the word *polar* constructed by one member of the guided reading group. The teacher introduced the cluster and the children talked about what they knew about the word before reading *The Polar Express* (Van Allsburg, 1985). Then as they read the

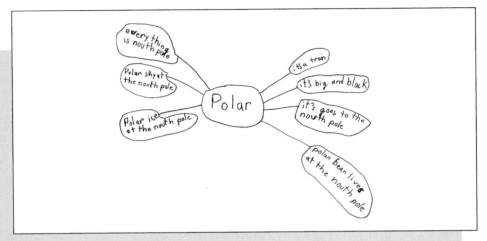

FIGURE 10.6 A Word Cluster for the Word *Polar*

story, the children added more concepts. Fran's cluster includes "it's a train" and "it's big and black" because she noticed the train on the cover of the book. These ideas reflect her understanding of the story but not the meaning of the word *polar*. After reading the story and discussing how *polar* was used in the story (to describe the polar ice cap and the polar sky), Fran became more aware of the word's meaning. When she spontaneously said, "Hey, polar bear! It's like a *polar* bear. They must live at the North Pole," she finally made the connection between the word *polar* and its referent *North Pole*.

The group discussion surrounding the construction of word clusters (and other strategy sheets) is more important to children's growth as readers than being able to complete a cluster. When we look at the content of Fran's cluster, we are not particularly impressed with her understanding of this word. However, her contributions to the discussion of the word's meaning during guided reading were important and helped the other children develop more sophisticated understandings. Effective teachers realize that having children complete strategy sheets is not the goal of instruction. Rather, these sheets are tools for coaching children to be active thinkers while they are reading.

Another way to stimulate children's active thinking about words and their meanings is to construct **word walls** for specific books. As children in a guided reading group read a book together, they can select interesting and important story words to place on a special word wall. After gathering the words on the wall, teachers can help children extend their understandings of these words using a list, group, and label activity (Tompkins & McGee, 1993).

A group of third graders reading *Keep the Lights Burning, Abbie* (Roop & Roop, 1985) gathered several vocabulary words from the story into a list and constructed a *Keep the Lights Burning, Abbie* word wall. The word wall included the words *Puffin, medicine, lighthouse, trimmed, wicks, towers, pecked, scraped, waded, henhouse, dangerous,*

weather, whitecaps, steered, ruffled, Hope, Patience, and *Charity*. Next, pairs of children selected three to five words from the word wall to form a group. Then they described
how the words were alike (the label portion of the activity). They wrote the words on
a transparency along with the label for their group of words. Then, using the overhead
projector, they shared their group of words and title with the guided reading group.
One pair of children grouped the words *scraped, waded, trimmed, pecked,* and *steered*
with the title "things you can do." Another pair of children grouped *pecked, ruffled,* and
henhouse with the title "words related to hens," while a third pair of children gathered
weather, whitecaps, and *dangerous* with the title "words related to a storm."

Reading Information Books in Guided Reading

Guided reading should include instruction in special techniques for reading information books. For example, informational texts have much **content-specific vocabulary,**
words that have specific scientific meanings and that do not appear in everyday conversation (Leu & Kinzer, 1999). Information books intentionally introduce scientific
terms that are used to explain phenomena. For example, *Bald Eagle* (Morrison, 1998)
provides definitions and illustrations of *nestling, prenatal down, natal down, egg tooth, eye
shield, fledgling, thermal soaring, kettle, eyrie,* and *embryo.* Most information books provide more than one source of information about content-specific vocabulary. Definitions are embedded in text, provided in glossaries, and illustrated in diagrams and
drawings.

Teachers can demonstrate strategies such as using multiple sources to find and
cross-check definitions of content-specific vocabulary. Children can be encouraged to
demonstrate other strategies for locating information about content-specific vocabulary. Figure 10.7 presents a third grader's labeled drawing of a spider, which demonstrates his awareness of the content-specific words *abdomen* and *spinnerets.*

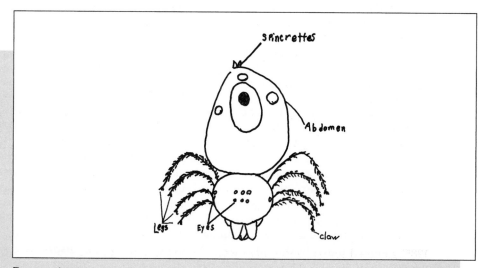

FIGURE 10.7   A Third Grader's Labeled Drawing of a Spider

Explicit Teaching of Spelling

Children who are similar in reading levels usually have similar spelling levels, although this is not always the case (Bear, Invernizzi, Templeton, & Johnston, 2004). In Chapters 4 and 5, we introduced four spelling levels:

- Emergent spelling
- Letter name or alphabetic spelling
- Within-a-word spelling
- Syllable and affix spelling

Children in second grade and beyond will be beyond emergent spelling, but will pass through the other three levels of spelling as they move through elementary school. Just as in guided reading where teachers match the level of text to children's instructional level, spelling teachers will target spelling instruction to match students' spelling levels. To determine a spelling level, the teacher may administer a spelling inventory (e.g., Bear, Invernizzi, Templeton, & Johnston, 2004), which is a list of words with increasingly more complex spelling patterns. Children's errors in spelling words from such a list determine the level of spelling instruction they need.

Most second- and third-grade spellers benefit from activities focusing on the variety of long-vowel and other-vowel spellings. Knowing how to change word spellings when adding suffixes is also a critical skill acquired at this time. For example, children learn that words having a CVC pattern require doubling the final consonant before adding the suffix, as with *hop* and *hopping.* Also important is learning to differentiate the appropriate spellings of homophones and homographs. **Homophones** are words that sound alike but are not spelled alike, as in *bear* and *bare*. **Homographs** are words that are spelled alike but do not sound alike, such in the words *bow* (weapon used to shoot arrows) and *bow* (to bend from the waist). Again **word sort activities** are appropriate. For example, children can sort words that take *s* or *es* or *ies* as their plural spellings (Fresch & Wheaton, 1997). Other activities include **word hunts,** in which children search for words with specific patterns in books, magazines, and newspapers.

Most teachers tailor spelling lists to the level of the learner and put into place a spelling routine (Wilde, 1992). We describe here a spelling program for second grade and beyond that has four features:

1. A large number of words that children are expected to learn to spell come from the children's needs, for example, from their own writing and reading, from current and upcoming content-area units, and from current events.
2. There is a balance among individual, small-group, and whole-class work. Students work with spelling lists that include personal words that only they are expected to learn, a small-group's words, and words that the whole class is expected to learn.
3. There is a balance between words that follow generalizations and high-frequency words that do not follow generalizations (e.g., *said*). The teacher may have a master list of high-frequency words and generalizations (see Bear et al., 2004).
4. Children are involved in identifying words to learn and in discovering spelling generalizations or rules.

With these features in mind, we suggest a program using a three- or four-week spelling cycle. At the start of each spelling cycle, the teacher and the children generate a word pool of seventy to eighty words from content units, high-frequency words, or words that follow spelling patterns. Children keep their own lists of words.

In some activities, the group works with words from the word pool for understanding, not for spelling. For example, children may categorize the words or make word clusters, resulting in adding related words to the word pool. In other activities, the group works together to discover spelling rules or devices to help remember spellings. Children may divide the pool into words that follow spelling generalizations, words that do not follow spelling generalizations (most high-frequency words do not), proper nouns, long words, and short words. Word groupings should highlight features of the words that will aid in learning to spell them.

Children in each guided reading group choose fifteen to twenty words from the word pool to create a list of words to study and learn to spell for the first week. Each child is expected to add one or two personal challenge words to the group list that are unique to that child.

The children learn the words from their group's list. They test each other on Friday. Then groups generate new lists for the next week, still using the pool of seventy to eighty words that began the unit. The cycle continues through several weeks. Three or four weeks seem long enough to make good use of the original pool of words, but not so long that it gets boring.

FLUENCY AND INDEPENDENT READING PRACTICE

CHILDREN NEED TO READ many more texts than the few they read during guided reading instruction. They need to read 30 minutes or more each day. This volume of reading is necessary to build stamina and fluency. **Fluent reading** involves quick and accurate word recognition and appropriate prosody (voicing and phrasing) (Kuhn, 2003). It includes a component of comprehension because readers cannot read with appropriate phrasing if they do not understand what they are reading. Fluency can be built through repeated reading of familiar text, with each reading bringing a reader to quicker, better phrased reading. Or, fluency can be built through reading many different books, some modeled by the teacher. The goal for second graders is fluent reading of 70 to 100 words per minute, for third graders 80 to 110 words per minute, and for fourth graders 100 to 140 words per minute (Rasinski, 2003).

Monitoring Independent Reading

In exemplary classrooms, while the teacher is working with a small group of children during guided reading, the other children engage in independent reading practice. The teacher carefully helps each child select eight to ten books at his or her independent reading level (Taberski, 2000). From these, each child is expected to have available two to four books for a particular day's independent reading. Many teachers have children keep these books in bags that hang on their chairs.

Before beginning a guided reading group, teachers identify small groups of children who will be reading books for independent practice (while other groups may be assigned to workstations, to complete response activities from a whole-class interactive read-aloud, or to response activities from earlier guided reading activities). The teacher very briefly does a status-of-the-group check of all children who will be engaging in independent reading during this time. On a dated list of all students' names, the teacher records the titles of the books to be read independently that day (Kelley & Clausen-Grace, 2006). Children keep track of books they have read by recording the title and author of each book in a weekly reading log.

Using Book Clubs and Choral Reading to Extend Independent Reading and Fluency

An alternative way to extend independent reading is sometimes to form book clubs (Raphael & McMahon, 1994) to read and discuss the same book and occasionally do book-related response activities together as a group. The following are activities of a book club:

- Children or teachers select a book or text set (text sets are five to ten books around a topic or theme).
- Teachers model how to talk during book discussions.
- Children read the book or text sets without teacher guidance alone or in pairs.
- Children participate in literature discussions without the teacher.
- Children sometimes participate in response activities.

The heart of the book club approach is the actual book discussions (Goatley, Brock, & Raphael, 1995). To start a book club, the teacher provides multiple copies of a book, previews it for the class, and then signs up a club of children who are interested in that book. Children read the book without teacher guidance and then have a discussion. Children can have very productive literature discussions without the involvement of the teacher (Almasi, 1995).

Book clubs focusing on poetry can be exciting additions to children's independent reading practice. Poetry is an important literary genre that all too often is neglected in elementary school. However, teachers have discovered that poetry "not only [is] accessible to primary children, [but] can be *the* genre that excites children and motivates them to read and write" (Duthie & Zimet, 1992, p. 14).

Choral reading is ideal for demonstrating the joy of poetry and providing opportunities to develop reading fluency (Trousdale & Harris, 1993). Poetry is meant to be read aloud again and again. First, teachers read a poem aloud during whole-class interactive read-aloud, perhaps displaying the poem on an overhead projector. Children are invited to respond to the poem by discussing interesting words, phrases, and events in the poem. A copy of the poem is distributed to the children, and the teacher rereads the poem again. Children are invited to reread favorite lines or phrases, using different voices, such as loud or soft, fast or slow, for effect. Finally, the teacher guides the children in a choral reading, in which the children read the poem aloud.

Choral reading uses several different reading methods that make it a unique experience (Trousdale & Harris, 1993). One method of choral reading is to use call and response. Here, a leader reads a line or two of the poem and the remainder of the group rereads the line or lines as a response. Another method of choral reading is to use a solo and chorus arrangement. One child or the teacher may read particular lines of the poem and the remainder of the children read other particular lines. This arrangement is good to use with poems with repeating refrains. Another way to arrange choral reading is to use two or more parts. Two groups of children may alternate reading every other line of the poem, or several groups of children may read specific stanzas of the poem, and all the children may read the concluding stanza. A combination of approaches is also effective. A group of children could read the first stanza, two groups of children could read the next stanza, and so on. Choral reading provides for more than enjoyment; it offers meaningful rereading opportunities that extend fluent reading (Dowhower, 1987).

After teachers have introduced poems and demonstrated and practiced choral reading of poems with children, they can establish poetry book clubs. Children can choose to join a book club for reading particular poems. The children read the poems in pairs, then aloud in unison with their book club. Finally, they plan, practice, and perform a choral reading for their classmates.

WRITING

C HILDREN IN THE SECOND GRADE and beyond know from their experiences in kindergarten and first grade the beginnings of a process approach to writing. They continue using writing processes as they develop greater writing sophistication.

Components of Writing Workshop

As we showed in Chapter 9, first graders use at least three writing processes: planning, revising, and sharing. In second grade and beyond, children are taught prewriting, drafting, revising, editing, and sharing or publishing.

One writing process is called **prewriting.** This process includes a writer's search for a topic, identification of audience and purpose, and collection of ideas about which to write. Many young children plan by talking to a friend or to their teacher, by writing a list of ideas, by role-playing an experience, by listening to or reading literature, or by simply thinking. The purpose of rehearsing and planning during prewriting is to generate ideas and formulate plans for writing.

Teachers demonstrate planning strategies in mini-lessons. One second grade teacher demonstrated how to use a cluster to plan for writing a mystery. His class brainstormed a list of all the elements found in mysteries, such as clues, scary characters, frightening events, and spooky settings. Then the teacher demonstrated using this list to write a cluster of ideas as a prewriting strategy. Figure 10.8 presents a planning cluster one second grader wrote to identify the characters, setting, and clues for her Campout Mystery.

Another writing process is called **drafting.** In this process children commit their ideas to paper. First drafts of inexperienced and writers can be short, sometimes consisting of only a few words. More accomplished writers write longer first drafts and more consciously consider the necessity of writing details.

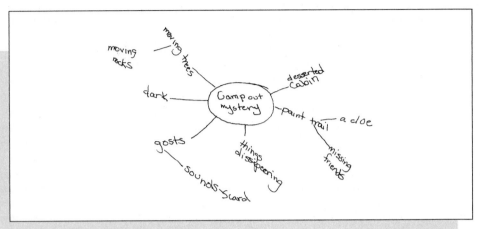

FIGURE 10.8   Cluster for Planning Campout Mystery

A third writing process is **revising;** it consists of children's rethinking what they have written. In revising, children reread their drafts; add or delete words, phrases, or sentences; and move sentences. The focus of these activities is the ideas and content of the writing. In another writing process, **editing,** children focus on misspellings and errors in capitalization, punctuation, and usage. Children gradually learn to edit their own writing. The last writing process, **publishing,** consists of sharing writing with an audience.

Many teachers use the author's chair for informal classroom sharing as one way of publishing. Other ways of sharing children's published writing include having a "Share Fair" once a month, in which child-authors read to their parents or to other classrooms of children, write letters to members of the community, construct birthday cards to authors and illustrators, publish a class newspaper or literary magazine, bind books for a nursing home or children's ward of the hospital, and send compositions to children's magazines that publish children's writing. Many sites on the Internet provide outlets for publishing student writing.

Writing Workshop Format. Most teachers use a routine format for their writing workshop that includes the following:

- (Five to ten minutes) **Mini-lesson** on a writing or illustrating technique; literary elements; features of informational text; organizational patterns such as sequence or compare and contrast; rehearsal strategies for gathering and organizing information; revision strategies; or editing strategies
- (Three to four minutes) Status of the class (Atwell, 1987), in which each child very briefly states what he or she will do during workshop
- (Twenty to thirty minutes) Writing block, in which children write while the teacher conducts large- and small-group conferences

FIGURE 10.9   An Editing Checklist

☐ I have reread my writing to a writing partner.

☐ I have listened for sentences.

☐ I have a capital letter at the beginning of each sentence.

☐ I have a period, question mark, or exclamation mark at the end of each sentence.

☐ I have a capital letter for every time I used the word *I*.

☐ I have a capital letter for every person's name.

☐ I have checked spellings of the word wall words.

- (Five to ten minutes) Whole-class share by one or two children who read their compositions and lead discussion (from Duthie, 1996, p. 56)

Mini-lessons and Conference Groups.   Mini-lessons are short whole-class lessons in which teachers demonstrate particular writing strategies, patterns that can be used in writing, or a special feature of text (Calkins, 1986). Conference groups serve as collaborative learning groups. Writers' conference groups can be used to provide additional time and support for small groups of children to try out various strategies introduced in mini-lessons. They can also be used to teach children knowledge related to literary and written language conventions, such as letter writing, using similes or metaphors, and sequencing of events, as well as proper use of capital letters, periods, commas, quotation marks, and even colons.

Figure 10.9 presents an **editing checklist** that would be useful for second graders. To develop such a list, teachers plan a mini-lesson focusing on just one editing skill, such as listening for sentences. The teacher demonstrates this strategy using her own writing. Later, in a writers' conference group, children practice the strategy using a selected piece of their own writing. Then the teacher adds the strategy to a class list of editing strategies. The list grows longer as children learn more and more strategies. Often teachers will ask children to come to a writers' conference group and bring a draft of their writing with the editing checklist completed for that composition.

Using Computers in Writing Workshop.   Second, third, and fourth grade classrooms usually include at least one computer. We suggest using computer time for word processing, exploring graphics, and conducting Internet inquiry projects.

Students can do some of their writing on computers, using a word-processing program, but it is not practical for them to do all their writing that way. Most students can do much of their planning and drafting with paper and pencil, rather than with a computer. They are adept at making revisions with cross-outs, arrows, and brackets and cut-and-paste (see Figure 10.10). Then students can sign up for computer time to do final drafts, to run spelling checks, to add graphics, and to print final copies of their pieces for publication in the classroom. They appreciate the ease of making changes with the computer and the clean look of their computer-printed final copies.

FIGURE 10.10   Carrie's Writing in Writing Workshop (A Rough Draft and One Page from the Published Story)

Writing Fluency and Handwriting.   Second graders, can write their ideas more fluently than first-graders. They are less likely to focus on spelling and more likely to focus on the ideas they want to write. Because they also know more about spelling patterns, they are able to spell unfamiliar words relatively quickly. They also have many more strategies for finding the words they want to write. By this time, their handwriting is fairly automatic and readable. Most children's letter formation, through practice, has become conventional.

Handwriting instruction is beneficial in this phase of writing, because children are more likely to expect other children to read what they have written. Instruction in handwriting should focus on legibility rather than on imitation of examples; it should provide children with language with which to talk about their handwriting and letters, and it should be connected with publishing children's writing.

There are four aspects of legibility that young writers need to learn. First, letters should conform to expected formations as defined by the writing program. Expected formations, especially of capital letters, differ from one handwriting program to another. The second aspect of legibility is that letters should be of uniform size, proportion, and alignment. Third, letters and words should be evenly spaced. Fourth, letters should have a consistent slant. The time to be concerned about legible handwriting is when writing is for an audience. Just prior to binding children's writing into a hardbound book is an opportune time for focusing on handwriting.

Poetic Elements

Writing workshop is an excellent place to begin a poetry unit or to prepare for a poetry festival in which children present to their parents or other classrooms of children their favorite poems and poems they have written (Durham, 1997). During mini-lessons in a poetry-writing workshop, children can learn that not all poems have rhyme, but many do. They can learn effective sound elements, such as repetition, alliteration (repeating beginning sounds), rhyme, and assonance (repeating vowel sounds). They can learn about using invented words, focusing on a single image, and saying common things in uncommon ways. Finally, children can learn about lining, shape, and special uses of punctuation, capitalization, and spaces (Duthie & Zimet, 1992). Together the teacher and children discuss the impact of using the poetic element in the poem. For example, children notice that indentations in the poem's lines make the shape of stair steps in the poem "Descent" (Merriam, 1989, p. 36) and different-length lines and special indenting create the shape of a wiggly snake in "The Serpent's Hiss" (Merriam, 1989, p. 48). A third grader composed the poem "Tree House," making use of line length and indenting to create a tree-shaped poem appropriate to the topic of his poem.

> Tree house
> Just you and me house
> Kick up your feet house
> Tree house
> Free
> House

Poetry and Technology

There are many online resources for teaching poetry (Roberts, 2002). Children enjoy visiting www.poetryteahers.com to read funny poetry, download a readers' theatre of a favorite poem, and even learn how to write poems. This site invites children to submit their poems to a poetry contest. At www.night.net children can listen to poetic songs and play games. At www.gigglepoetry.com children meet Bruce Lansky and can read poems, take a poetry class, and submit their own poems in another contest. An unusual site for writing poetry is http://home.freeuk.net where children can use clicking and dragging to arrange words and compose poems.

Writing Informational Texts

Information books are often neglected both in reading instruction and in writing instruction. However, many children find these texts especially engaging (Duke, 1998; Duthie, 1996). Ray (2004) recommends that teachers use mini-lessons in the writing workshop to introduce children to "Wow Nonfiction." All information books provide facts, but "Wow Nonfiction" books do so in a fashion that especially interests readers in their topics. In writers' workshop, the teacher reads aloud portions of a "Wow Nonfiction" book, and the children analyze what the writer did to capture their interest. For example, children observed that:

- *I Call it Sky* (Howell, 1999) has facts placed at the end, related to the story.
- *Atlantic* (Karas, 2002) uses first person narrative so the writer is speaking directly to the reader.
- *Tiger Trail* (Winters, 2000) uses created spellings.
- *Bat Loves the Night* (Davies, 2001) is written in present tense and makes readers believe the activities are happening right this minute.
- *Red-eyed Tree Frog* (Cowley, 1999) follows the action of one animal.

- *Gentle Giant Octopus* (Wallace, 1998) uses very short sentences with dramatic verbs. (adapted from Ray, 2004, p. 104)

The children recorded their observations on a large poster that remained in the classroom. The teacher in conferences encouraged children to think of which of these techniques would be useful in writing their own informational pieces. Children were expected to use some of the techniques and to be able to explain why they used particular ones.

Teachers can use the special features of computer word-processing and graphics programs to help children compose unique kinds of text. For example, a third grade teacher combined learning about computer graphics with newspaper writing. Children read and analyzed newspapers to discover their special features. At the same time, they explored a graphics and word-processing program on the computer. Figure 10.11 presents a page of two children's newspaper about the Oklahoma City bombing. In their multimedia composition they used a drawing to create the bomb, graphics to create a picture, and word processing to write their text.

Inquiry Units

Reading and writing informational texts is an important part of content-area learning. Children need to learn how to search for specific information, evaluate whether information is relevant for their topic or question, and integrate and summarize information across several texts (Schmidt et al., 2002). Inquiry units involving the study of particular topics in social studies and science, using hands-on experiences, a variety of informational texts, and reading and writing activities, increase children's reading and writing abilities as well as their understanding of science and social studies concepts (Morrow et al., 1997).

Observe and Personalize.   During the first phase of inquiry, the observe and personalize phase, children observe objects and events from the natural world. For example, in a unit on birds, children can observe a variety of birds in zoos or museums. They can examine different kinds of bird nests, feathers, and bird bones. They can observe and record behavior at a bird feeder. Observations are extended by browsing through information books that provide facts and present drawings related to the observations. As children gain more knowledge of birds, they generate questions that they might use for later searches. Teachers gather questions on large charts posted in the room. Questions are added, deleted, and revised as children continue observing in the natural world and in information resources.

Search and Retrieve.   In the next phase, search and retrieve, children participate in idea circles (Guthrie & McCann, 1996), in which they extend their concept knowledge. They learn and practice locating sources that will provide information on a specific topic or question. For example, children who are studying garden flowers would participate in an initial discussion about flowers. As the children share information, the teacher would write headings related to the different kinds of information that children share. For example, a teacher would write the following headings: height, spread, color, foliage, and fragrance. As a part of the discussion, the teacher would take opportunities

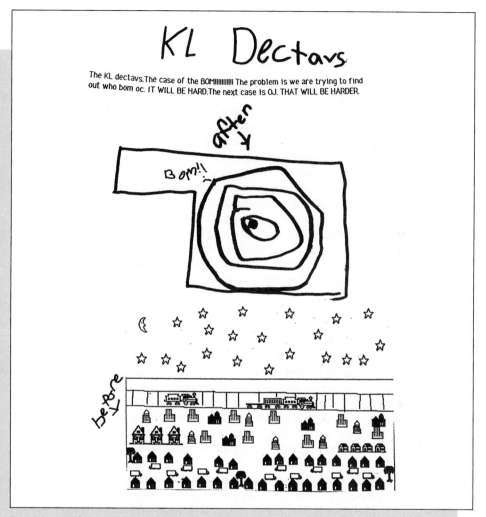

KL Dectavs

The KL dectavs. The case of the BOMIIIIIIIII The problem is we are trying to find out who bom oc. IT WILL BE HARD. The next case is OJ. THAT WILL BE HARDER.

FIGURE 10.11   A Page from Two Children's Newspaper about the Oklahoma City Bombing

to expand children's vocabulary. He might be introducing the words *fragrance* and *foliage* as children talk about a flower's smell or the different kinds of flowers and leaves (Wray & Lewis, 1996, p. 64). Later these headings would be used in an activity in which children search for and select information about flowers from informational texts.

Then the teacher and children would gather a variety of resource books, including children's information books, adult information books, and pamphlets about gardening. The teacher would prepare a recording grid with the headings he had gathered during the class discussion. Over several days, each child would fill in the recording grid with information about one or two flowers of his or her choice. To begin the work, the class would brainstorm a list of flowers, which the teacher would record on a chart. Then the teacher would demonstrate searching through informational texts to find information about a particular flower. He would show the children how to find the name of the flower in an index or table of contents.

Comprehend, Integrate, and Communicate.   In the final phase, comprehend and integrate, children work on more complex questions, often questions they generate for themselves. For example, third graders were answering the questions, "What are the body parts of your bird, and how do these body parts help this bird to survive?" (Guthrie et al., 1996, p. 326). Children selected birds of choice, located information about body parts, and wrote explanations for how the body parts allowed the bird to adapt to its environment through breeding, feeding, and protecting itself. Here, children needed to read carefully in order to detect critical information relevant to the question, integrate information across different texts, and find meanings of specialized vocabulary they were encountering. Children capitalized on knowing how to read graphs, diagrams, and other illustrations. They learned how to break up the question into parts, gather information, and then put the parts back together. In the final phase, children communicated their information in reports, group-authored books, charts, and informational stories.

Internet Workshop and Inquiry Learning

Internet workshop (Leu, 2002) consists of children's searching, reading, and using information from the internet around a topic of inquiry. It is a natural partner with reading and writing across the curriculum as a part of inquiry units. The purpose of the internet workshop is simultaneously to help children learn more about how to use the internet and develop the special reading strategies needed for this kind of text as well as to help them learn to evaluate and integrate internet information with other sources of information. Internet workshop includes five steps:

1. Teachers locate a site on the internet with content related to a unit of inquiry.
2. They design an activity to support children's search through the site to find specific information (including finding links to other sites).
3. They help children evaluate and critique the information they find at the site using what they know about who authored the site.
4. Children complete the activity.
5. Children share the results of their activity and discuss strategies they used to search, read, evaluate, and use the information they found.

There are hundreds of excellent sites that can be used for internet workshop including sites designed specifically for children. For example, students can learn more about New York City by visiting www.sdcoe.k12.ca.us/score/abuela where several links are posted for finding information about the Statue of Liberty. They can visit www.acs.ucalgary.ca/dkbrown/authors.html to find a list of authors' websites they can visit. Jan Brett's website has a wealth of information about her life, her books, and her activities as well as fun activities for children to download (Karchmer, 2000). Another enjoyable children's literature website is www.sags.k12.il.us.library/Caldecott_

Clues.htm. Here clues about Caldecott books are posted weekly and children are invited to e-mail in their guesses of the books' titles. Another site with extensive information is www.enchantedlearning.com/subjects. At this site children can explore habitats and learn facts about animals living in those habitats. The text at this site is very engaging and provides an excellent model for children's own informational writing. Another excellent site is www.kids-learn.org/stellaluna/project.htm where children are invited to search for information about bats. A similar site for finding facts about bats and their homes is http://members.aol.com/bats4kids/homes.htm.

Differentiating Instruction for Diverse Learners

THE BALANCED READING AND WRITING described in this chapter supports learners who are reading and writing at many different levels. Children are taught in small, guided reading groups in which they read text matched to their levels of reading ability. They practice spelling words matched to their level of spelling development. They read books independently that their teacher has helped them to select to meet their individual needs as readers. In their writing workshop, the teacher intentionally selects a small group of children for a writers' conference that is directed at the strategies those children are working on. For example, children needing more support for using commas correctly are provided that instruction in conference groups. Children who need help using punctuation to avoid run-on sentences are grouped together to practice that skill.

Despite the many different ways in which small-group instruction is tailored to meet individual needs, English language learners need additional and targeted support. Teachers need to pay special attention to helping children who are ELLs to read complex sentences and obtain critical information from those sentences. They need to teach explicitly the differences between narrative and expository texts, and provide additional support in learning sophisticated, academic vocabulary.

Explicit Attention to the Sentence Structures of Written Text

The more advanced the level of a text, in general the more complex are its sentence structures. Teachers can point out different kinds of sentences and help children collect examples of each sentence structure (Tompkins, 2003). A **simple sentence** is composed of a subject and its predicate (e.g., *Patrick bought groceries,* in which *Patrick* is the subject and *bought groceries* is the predicate). A **compound sentence** has two or more independent clauses, each with its own subject and predicate and joined by a conjunction (e.g., *Patrick went to town, and he bought groceries*). A **complex sentence** has at least one dependent clause and one independent clause (e.g., *Patrick bought groceries when he went to town,* in which *when he went to town* is the dependent clause because although it has a subject and predicate, it could not stand alone as a sentence). A group of third grade English language learners collected the following sentences from *Apples* (Gibbons, 2000).

- Simple: *An apple is a fruit.*
- Compound: *Some apples are grown at home, but most are grown commercially.*
- Complex: *As the colonists moved westward, they brought apple seeds and seedlings with them.*

Another way to scaffold English language learners' understanding of sentence structure is to outline (Echevarria, Vogt, & Short, 2004). The teacher composes a short paragraph that includes the major concepts from a book that the children will be reading. Sentences may be taken directly from the text or modified slightly. Figure 10.12 presents a paragraph and outline a third grade teacher prepared for the book *Apples* (Gibbons, 2000). These are not the sentences directly from the book, but each of the sentences contains phrases from sentences in the book. The sentence structure is simplified, and the concepts are defined more directly than in the book's sentences. This provides ELLs with opportunities to gain prior knowledge and learn a book's important concepts in simpler sentence structure. Children read the paragraph with the teacher's support, discuss the information using the vocabulary introduced in the text, and then together fill in the outline using words from the paragraph. Children cannot copy from the sentences, but they must read carefully to select which information to use.

Explicit Attention to Narrative and Expository Text Forms

In Chapter 5, we described elements typically found in narrative and expository texts. Elementary students demonstrate in their writing that they know some information about narrative and expository text structures. Nonetheless, during the elementary years teachers will provide direct instruction about how to notice these elements dur-

FIGURE 10.12   *Apples* (Gibbons, 2000)

In the springtime, apple blossoms begin to bloom on the apple trees. They are flowers. Each blossom has a stamen with tiny grains of pollen on it. Bees visit the blossoms and they catch pollen on their feet. When they land on another apple blossom, they put the pollen on that flower. When pollen moves from one apple blossom to another, it is pollinated. Now the blossom can get ready to turn into an apple.

Pollination:

First, _____ apple blossoms begin to bloom in _____.

Tiny grains of pollen are found in each blossom on its _____.

Bees catch _____.

When bees visit another blossom, they _____.

Pollination is when the pollen from one blossom _____

_____.

ing reading and how to incorporate them in writing. English language learners need this explicit instruction more frequently before reading and writing. Figure 10.13 presents structures characteristic of both narrative and expository texts. For example, narratives generally have only text that tells the story and illustrations that show it. Expository texts may also have specialized text, such as headings, sidebars, and endnotes or footnotes, and specialized illustrations such as graphs, charts, and illustrated drawings. The textual features of expository text provide critical information, and teachers make sure ELLs know about these features and how to read them (Barone, Mallette, & Xu, 2005).

Explicit Attention to Vocabulary

Children in second grade and beyond make a transition from using language to communicate about immediate and everyday concerns to using language to demonstrate understanding of academic topics. The vocabulary demands of this transition are especially great for English language learners (Cummins, 2003). Typically, they have smaller vocabularies for communicating about content-area topics than do their native

FIGURE 10.13   Characteristics of Narrative and Expository Text

Narrative Text	Expository Text
Specific characters	Generic character
Setting (location, weather, time)	Topic introduction
Problem/conflict/plot	Description of attributes
Obstacles/solutions/climax	Characteristic events in sequence
Endings/theme	Category comparison
Point of view	Summary
Past tense (narration)	May include problem/solution
Present tense (dialogue)	May include cause/effect
Many high-frequency words	Mixture of timeless present, present, past
Common and uncommon meanings	Many low-frequency words
Text and illustrations	Content-specific meanings
	Text and illustrations, including graphs, diagrams, figures, maps, labeled drawings, cut-away illustrations, lists
	Headings, subheadings, sidebars
	Endnotes, footnotes

English-speaking peers. Teachers must provide introductions to vocabulary before ELLs read content materials, and more extensive practice with vocabulary after reading.

One way of introducing vocabulary before reading is to capitalize on books with labeled drawings (Barone, Mallette, & Xu, 2005). Visual dictionaries such as *The Scholastic Visual Dictionary* (Corbeil & Archambault, 2000) define over 5,000 words using labeled drawings. Many nonfiction books include at least one or two labeled drawings. For example, *Apples* (Gibbons, 2000) has labeled drawings of the parts of an apple and an apple blossom that provide good introductions to the words *stem, seed chambers, skin, core, pollen, stamen,* and *stigma.*

Before reading, teachers also can help children use a reverse word cluster (Peregoy & Boyle, 2004). In word clusters, children place a vocabulary word in a central circle, and then, on rays emanating from the circle, write synonyms for the word, phrases defining the word, or sentences using the word. In a reverse word cluster, the teacher writes a sentence from the text the children will read but omits the target vocabulary word. The children use the context to make guesses about the actual word and these guesses are placed on the rays emanating from the empty central circle. Later as children read the text, they discover the actual target word and write it in the central circle.

Chapter Summary

ECOND, THIRD, AND FOURTH GRADES are an exciting time for children and their teachers. The great strides that students make as they become able to move beyond transitional reading present teachers with great challenges, opportunities, and satisfactions.

In writing workshop, children use five writing processes: prewriting, drafting, revising, editing, and sharing. Teachers model a variety of writing strategies for each of these processes in mini-lessons and provide guided practice in conference groups. Similarly, teachers demonstrate reading strategies in mini-lessons during reading workshop. Children read extensively and respond to books they have read.

The guided reading approach involves small groups of children reading and discussing a book together. Teachers extend children's understanding of narratives by inviting retellings and helping children discover literary elements by using activities such as constructing character clusters. They extend children's vocabulary knowledge with activities such as list, group, and label. Choral reading allows children to enjoy poetry and provides opportunities for the rereading that is so important for comprehension and fluency development. Teachers extend children's understanding of poems in writer's workshop by calling attention to poetic elements.

Children read and write informational texts in content units in science and social studies. They learn organizational patterns found in expository text. As part of idea circles, children locate, retrieve, and comprehend informational text. They pay particular attention to the content-specific vocabulary they encounter in information books and learn strategies for independent vocabulary learning. Word study continues in second grade and beyond, extending children's abilities to spell and decode multisyllabic words. A program for learning the spellings of words is also critical.

Applying the Information

We suggest two activities for applying the information. Make a list of the characteristics of a literacy-rich classroom presented in Chapter 6. Then reread this chapter to locate one activity from those presented that is consistent with each of these characteristics. Discuss your examples with a classmate.

Next, make a list of all the literacy learning activities described in this chapter. For each of these activities, describe what children learn about written language meanings, forms, meaning-form links, or functions.

Going Beyond the Text

VISIT A SECOND, THIRD, or fourth grade classroom and observe several literacy activities. Write a list of all the print and literacy materials in the classroom. Take note of the classroom layout and the interactions among the children and between the children and the teacher during literacy activities. Talk with the teacher about his or her philosophy of literacy instruction. Compare these materials, activities, and philosophies with those presented in this chapter.

References

Aardema, V. (1998). *Borreguita and the coyote.* New York: Alfred A. Knopf.

Almasi, J. (1995). The nature of fourth graders' sociocognitive conflicts in peer-led and teacher-led discussions of literature. *Reading Research Quarterly, 30,* 314–351.

Atwell, N. (1987). *In the middle.* Portsmouth, NH: Heinemann.

Barone, D. (1990). The written responses of young children: Beyond comprehension to story understanding. *The New Advocate, 3,* 49–56.

Barone, D., Mallette, M., & Xu, S. (2005). *Teaching early literacy development: Development, assessment, and instruction.* New York: Guilford.

Bear, D., Invernizzi, M., Templeton, S., & Johnston, F. (2004). *Words their way: Word study for phonics, vocabulary, and spelling instruction* (3rd ed.). Upper Saddle River, NJ: Prentice-Hall.

Brabham, E., & Villaume, S. (2002). Leveled texts: The good and the bad news. *The Reading Teacher, 55,* 438–441.

Calkins, L. M. (1986). *The art of teaching writing.* Portsmouth, NH: Heinemann.

Combs, M. (2006). *Readers and writers in primary grades: A balanced and integrated approach* (3rd ed.). Upper Saddle River, NJ: Pearson.

Commeyras, M., & Sumner, G. (1995). *Questions children want to discuss about literature: What teachers and students learned in a second grade classroom* (NRRC Reading Research Rep. No. 47). Athens, GA: University of Georgia and University of Maryland, National Reading Research Center.

Corbeil, J., & Archambault, A. (2000). *Scholastic visual dictionary.* New York: Scholastic.

Cowley, J. (1999). *Red-eyed tree frog.* New York: Scholastic.

Cummins, J. (2003). Reading and the bilingual student: Fact and friction. In G. Garcia (Ed.), *English learners reaching the highest level of English literacy* (pp. 2–33). Newark, DE: International Reading Association.

Cunningham, P., & Hall, D. (1994). *Making big words.* Torrance, CA: Good Apple.

Davies, N. (2001). *Bat loves the night.* Cambridge, MA: Candlewick.

Dowhower, S. (1987). Effects of repeated reading on second grade transitional readers' fluency and comprehension. *Reading Research Quarterly, 22,* 397–414.

Dowhower, S. (1999). Supporting a strategic stance in the classroom: A comprehension framework for helping teachers help students to be strategic. *The Reading Teacher, 52,* 672–688.

Duke, N. (1998, December). 3.6 minutes per day: The scarcity of informational texts in first grade. Paper presented at the annual meeting of the National Reading Conference, Austin, TX.

Durham, J. (1997). On time and poetry. *The Reading Teacher, 51,* 76–79.

Duthie, C. (1996). *True stories: Nonfiction literacy in the primary classroom.* York, ME: Stenhouse.

Duthie, C., & Zimet, E. (1992). "Poetry is like directions for your imagination!" *The Reading Teacher, 46,* 14–24.

Echevarria, J., Vogt, E., & Short, D. (2004). *Making content comprehensible for English language learners: The SIOP model* (2nd ed.). Boston: Allyn & Bacon.

Fawson, P., & Reutzel, D. (2000). But I only have a basal: Implementing guided reading in the early grades. *The Reading Teacher, 54,* 84–97.

Fountas, I., & Pinnell, C. (1996). *Guided reading: Good first teaching for all children.* Portsmouth, NH: Heinemann.

Fountas, I. C., & Pinnell, G. S. (2006). *Teaching for comprehending and fluency: Thinking, talking, and writing about reading, K-8.* Portsmouth, NH: Heinemann.

Fresch, M., & Wheaton, A. (1997). Sort, search, and discover: Spelling in the child-centered classroom. *The Reading Teacher, 51,* 20–31.

Gambrell, L., Pfeiffer, W., & Wilson, R. (1985). The effects of retelling upon reading comprehension and recall of text information. *Journal of Educational Research, 78,* 216–220.

Gibbons, G. (2000). *Apples.* New York: Scholastic.

Goatley, V. J., Brock, C. H., & Raphael, T. E. (1995). Diverse learners participating in regular education "Book Clubs." *Reading Research Quarterly, 30,* 352–380.

Guthrie, J., & McCann, N. (1996). Idea circles: Peer collaborations for conceptual learning. In L. Gambrell & J. Almasi (Eds.), *Lively discussions! Fostering engaged reading* (pp. 87–105). Newark, DE: International Reading Association.

Guthrie, J., Van Meter, P., McCann, A., Wigfield, A., Bennett, L., Poundstone, C., Rice, M., Faibisch, F., Hunt, B., & Mitchell, A. (1996). Growth of literacy engagement: Changes in motivations and strategies during concept oriented reading instruction. *Reading Research Quarterly, 31,* 306–332.

Howell, W. (1999). *I Call It sky.* New York: Walker.

Hoyt, L. (1992). Many ways of knowing: Using drama, oral interactions, and the visual arts to enhance reading comprehension. *The Reading Teacher, 45,* 580–584.

Karas, G. B., (2002). *Atlantic.* New York: Putnam's Sons.

Karchmer, R. (2000). Using the Internet and children's literature to support interdisciplinary instruction. *The Reading Teacher, 54,* 100–104.

Kelley, M., & Clausen-Grace, N. (2006). R5: The sustained silent reading makeover that transformed readers. *The Reading Teacher, 60,* 148–156. Newark, DE: International Reading Association.

Kelly, P. R., & Farnan, N. (1991). Promoting critical thinking through response logs: A reader-response approach with fourth graders. In J. Zutell & S. McCormick (Eds.), *Learner factors/teacher factors: Issues in literacy research and* instruction (pp. 227–284). Chicago: The National Reading Conference.

Kuhn, M. (2003). How can I help them pull it all together? A guide to fluent reading instruction. In D. Barone & M. Morrow (Eds.), *Literacy and young children: Research-based practices* (pp. 210–225). New York: Guilford.

Leu, D. (2002). Internet workshop: Making time for literacy. *The Reading Teacher, 55,* 466–472.

Leu, D., & Kinzer, C. (1999). *Effective literacy instruction* (4th Ed.). Columbus, OH: Merrill.

Marshall, E. (1982). *Fox and his friends.* New York: Scholastic.

McGee, L. (1995). Talking about books with young children. In N. Roser & M. Martinez (Eds.), *Book talk and beyond* (pp. 105–115). Newark, DE: International Reading Association.

Merriam, E. (1989). *Chortles.* New York: Morrow.

Miller, D. (2002). *Reading with meaning: Teaching comprehension in the primary grades.* Portland, ME: Stenhouse.

Morrison, G. (1998). *Bald eagle.* Boston: Houghton Mifflin.

Morrow, L., Pressley, M., Smith, J., & Smith, M. (1997). The effect of a literature-based program integrated into literacy and science instruction with children from diverse backgrounds. *Reading Research Quarterly, 32,* 54–76.

National Assessment of Educational Progress 2003 (2003). Washington, DC: Office of Educational Research and Improvement.

Pearson, P., & Gallaher, M. (1983). The instruction of reading comprehension. *Contemporary Educational Psychology, 8,* 317–345.

Peregoy, S., & Boyle, O. (2004). English learners reading English: What we know, what we need to know. In R. Robinson, M. McKenna, & J. Wedman (Eds.), *Issues and trends in literacy education* (3rd ed.). Boston: Allyn & Bacon.

Pressley, M., & Block, C. (2002). *Comprehension instruction: Research-based best practices.* New York: Guilford.

Raphael, T. & McMahon, S. (1994). Book club: An alternative framework for reading instruction. *The Reading Teacher, 48,* 102–116.

Raskinski, T. (2003). *The fluent reader: Oral reading strategies for building word recognition, fluency, and comprehension.* New York: Scholastic.

Ray, K. (2004). Why Cauley writes well: A close look at what a difference good teaching can make. *Language Arts, 82,* 100–109.

Roberts, S. (2002). Taking a technological path to poetry prewriting. *The Reading Teacher, 55,* 678–687.

Roop, P., & Roop, C. (1985). *Keep the lights burning, Abbie.* Minneapolis: Carolrhoda.

Scharer, P. (1996). "Are we supposed to be asking questions?": Moving from teacher-directed to student-directed book discussions. In D. Leu, C. Kinzer, & K. Hinchman (Eds.), *Literacies for the 21st century: Research and practice* (pp. 420–429). Chicago: National Reading Conference.

Schmidt, P., Gillen, S., Zollo, T., & Stone, R. (2002). Literacy learning and scientific inquiry: Children respond. *The Reading Teacher, 55,* 534–548.

Shanahan, T., & Shanahan, S. (1997). Character perspective charting: Helping children to develop a more complete conception of a story. *The Reading Teacher, 50,* 668–677.

Sinatra, G., Brown, K., & Reynolds, R. (2002). Implications of cognitive resource allocation for comprehension strategies instruction. In C. Block & M. Pressley (Eds.), *Comprehension instruction: Research-based best practices.* New York: Guilford.

Sipe, L. (2002). Talking back and taking over: Young children's expressive engagement during storybook read-alouds. *The Reading Teacher, 55,* 476–483.

Stahl, S., & Kuhn, M. (2002). Making it sound like language: Developing fluency. *The Reading Teacher, 55,* 582–584.

Steptoe, J. (1987). *Mufaro's beautiful daughters.* Boston: Houghton Mifflin.

Taberski, S. (2000). *On solid ground: Strategies for teaching reading K–3.* Portsmouth, NH: Heinemann.

Temple, C. (1991). Seven readings of a folktale: Literary theory in the classroom. *The New Advocate, 4,* 25–35.

Tompkins, G. (2003). *Literacy for the 21st century* (3rd ed.). Columbus, OH: Merrill.

Tompkins, G., & McGee, L. (1993). *Teaching reading with literature: From case studies to action plans.* Columbus, OH: Merrill.

Trousdale, A., & Harris, V. (1993). Missing links in literary response: Group interpretation of literature. *Children's Literature in Education, 24,* 195–207.

Van Allsburg, C. (1985). *The polar express.* Boston: Houghton Mifflin.

Villaume, S., Wordon, T., Williams, S., Hopkins, L., & Rosenblatt, C. (1994). Five teachers in search of a discussion. *The Reading Teacher, 47,* 480–487.

Vogt, M. (1996). Creating a response-centered curriculum with literature discussion groups. In L. Gambrell & J. Almasi (Eds.), *Lively discussions!: Fostering engaged reading* (pp. 181–193). Newark, DE: International Reading Association.

Wallace, K. (1998). *Gentle giant octopus.* Cambridge, MA: Candlewick.

Wells, G., & Chang-Wells, G. L. (1992). *Constructing knowledge together: Classrooms as centers of inquiry and literacy.* Portsmouth, NH: Heinemann.

Wilde, S. (1992). *You kan red this! Spelling and punctuation for whole language classrooms, K–6.* Portsmouth, NH: Heinemann.

Winters, K. (2000). *Tiger Trail.* New York: Simon & Schuster.

Wisniewski, D. (1996). *Golem.* New York: Clarion.

Wolf, S. A. (1993). What's in a name? Labels and literacy in readers' theatre. *The Reading Teacher, 46,* 540–545.

Wray, D., & Lewis, M. (1996). "But bonsai trees don't grow in baskets": Young children's talk during authentic inquiries. In L. Gambrell & J. Almasi (Eds.), *Lively discussions! Fostering engaged reading* (pp. 63–72). Newark, DE: International Reading Association.

Yorinks, A. (1986). *Hey, Al.* New York: Farrar, Straus, & Giroux.

Young, T., & Vardell, S. (1993). Weaving readers' theatre and nonfiction into the curriculum. *The Reading Teacher, 46,* 396–406.

Zelinsky, P. O. (1986). *Rumpelstiltskin.* New York: Dutton.

CHAPTER

11

Meeting the Needs of Diverse Learners

KEY CONCEPTS

At-Risk Learners
Utterance Length
Utterance Complexity
Vocabulary Variety
Decontextualized
   Language
Phonemic Awareness
Children with Special
   Needs
Repeated Reading

Cultural Discontinuity
Culturally Responsive
   Instruction
Participation Structures
Balance of Rights
English Language
   Learner (ELL)
Preproduction
Total Physical Response
   (TPR)
Early Production

Speech Emergence
Comprehensible Input
Intermediate Fluency
ELL Interactive Read-
   Aloud Procedure
Additive Approaches
Subtractive Approaches
Shared Language
Extended Discourse
Multiliteracy

LEARNERS AT RISK

TEACHERS ARE CONCERNED with supporting all children's literacy growth, and with thoughtful instruction, most children do succeed in becoming reflective, motivated readers and writers. Most children develop a range of expected knowledge within a reasonable time frame when they are given adequate opportunities and instruction. For young children, this time frame and range of expected knowledge is wide and allows for much individual variation. However, teachers also recognize that some children seem to struggle to acquire literacy even within literacy-rich classrooms and with a wide variety of instructional experiences. We call these children **at-risk learners.** At-risk learners need teachers who are especially observant and adept at modifying instructional techniques.

Ideally, teachers should know ahead of time which children are most likely to experience difficulty learning to read and write so that they can provide targeted intervention instruction. Unfortunately, that is not always possible. Still, with careful attention to characteristics that put children at risk of failure, we can at least reduce the likelihood of such failure for a large number of children. Visual impairments, hearing impairments, severe cognitive impairments, and extreme developmental delays are likely to result in low levels of reading and writing achievement. These risk factors are usually identified and addressed by specialists.

Early childhood and primary grade teachers should be familiar with risk factors related to language development and to early literacy experiences. That is, classroom teachers can assess children's language and early literacy development, and they can provide instruction that responds to identified needs. Fortunately, such instruction is the same sort of instruction provided for all children, the sort we have described in this book. It is targeted, child-centered, developmentally appropriate instruction.

The difference when risk of failure is present—and almost all teachers will have at least some students at risk—is that the children at the center of child-centered instruction have been identified as having gaps in their language development or early literacy experiences. Targeted instruction for these children merely means that as soon as they are found to have language development and literacy experience risk factors, their teachers make doubly sure that they receive targeted instruction (McGee & Richgels, 2003).

Risk Factors Related to Language Development

Within the wide range of normal language development, some specific accomplishments serve as guides. Steady preschool growth in utterance length, utterance complexity, and vocabulary variety prepare children for successful literacy learning; lack of accomplishment in those areas makes literacy success difficult (Walker et al., 1994; Scarborough, 1991). **Utterance length** is how many morphemes a child uses, on average, in a turn at talking. **Utterance complexity** is how many and what kinds of phrases and clauses a child uses to make a number of different kinds of sentences. **Vocabulary variety** is the number of different words, especially rare words, that a child understands and uses (Dickinson & Sprague, 2001). Teachers can take stock of children's utterance length and complexity and vocabulary variety through observation.

Two special abilities with language are involved in early reading and writing, and so lacking them almost always puts children at risk of failing to learn to read and write. One is the ability to use language without the support of immediate context. Children must be able to use **decontextualized language,** as when they talk about things not in the present time or place, if they are to be able to read text written by a non-present author where the words alone provide the only clues to the author's intended message (Dickinson & Smith, 1994). Similarly, they must be able to create texts that future, non-present readers will be able to understand with only the texts to go by. The second special language ability is being able consciously to recognize phonemes and manipulate them (**phonemic awareness**). When they are beginning to read and write in an alphabetic language such as English, children must be able to match sounds with letters. This entails being able to focus on individual phonemes in the stream of speech, a special consciousness that is required for literacy learning but is not required for speaking or for understanding speech (Adams, 1990; National Reading Panel, 2000; Snow, Burns, & Griffin, 1998). Teachers should note children's use of these language processes.

Risk Factors Related to Family and Community

Three family and community related risk factors that often overlap and interact are socioeconomic status (SES), minority status, and limited proficiency with English. Children from families with high and middle SES are usually more successful at learning to read and write than children from families with low SES (Lonigan et al., 1998). Poverty is among the factors most predictive of poor literacy achievement (Snow, Burns, & Griffin, 1998). Socioeconomic status, however, is not simply a family factor. Schools and neighborhoods whose populations are mostly low SES are associated with children's low literacy achievement. This may be due to a number of related factors that may include poor literacy resources, such as little publicly displayed print; few public spaces for reading; and poorly provided public libraries in low SES neighborhoods (Neuman et al., 2001). They also may include poor quality school libraries, low numbers of books in classrooms, and high numbers of fellow students who are also at risk in low SES schools.

Minority status is another factor related to risk for failure at learning to read and write. In particular, literacy achievement of non-white children is lower than that of white children (National Center for Educational Statistics, 1996).

Limited English proficiency is another risk factor; Spanish speakers, the largest group of English language learners, have low reading achievement. However, this factor, like SES and minority status, is not simple. Generally, Spanish-speaking children's reading scores are low even when they are taught and assessed in Spanish and when their families have high motivation for their succeeding (Goldenberg & Gallimore, 1991). All three of these factors compound: high percentages of children who are non-English speaking are also non-white and living in poverty (McGee & Richgels, 2003). When teachers are working in these situations, they will need to assess children and provide small-group instruction at children's levels.

Mismatch with School Culture as a Risk Factor

An easily overlooked risk factor is a child's having different dispositions and ways of interacting with others than are expected in school, ways that interfere with a successful transition from home life to classroom life. Schools are social settings with their own special ways for students to enter the group and be accepted and their spoken and unspoken rules about interacting with classmates and teachers. Knowing these ways and rules is sometimes referred to as knowing how to "do school." When some children do not know how to "do school" because their home ways are in conflict with these school ways (Comber, 2000; Gee, 1996), teachers may mistakenly perceive them as having behavior problems or low levels of literacy knowledge (McMillon & Edwards, 2000). Unless the mismatch between home and school ways is perceived and alleviated, this will become a self-fulfilling prophecy.

This is not the only misunderstanding to adversely affect children's prospects for success at learning to read and write. Unfortunately, the very use of the term *risk factor* implies negative consequences for characteristics that are not by themselves causes of failure. It is true that a preventative efficiency might be attained by identifying groups in which there are children who are more likely to need help than children in other groups. However, we risk harming those very children if their group membership blinds us to the benefits of the rich cultural capital and specialized funds of knowledge they bring to diverse classrooms (Neuman et al., 2001) or if it lulls us into providing fewer opportunities for their active problem-solving (McGee & Richgels, 2003).

Teachers can avoid shortchanging children considered at risk for low literacy achievement if their teaching is guided by the principle that good literacy practices are good literacy practices—regardless of the type of student. Preventative early literacy instruction, that is, early literacy instruction intended to prevent the failure that some children seem at risk of experiencing, is not qualitatively different from facilitative early literacy instruction, that is, early literacy instruction intended to support children who seem already on the way to literacy success.

Teachers who are aware of intervention programs may be able to adapt some of those programs' procedures to meet the observed needs of at-risk learners in the regular classroom. The best-known program is Reading Recovery, designed by Marie Clay in New Zealand (Clay, 1985) and implemented widely in the United States. Reading Recovery materials are organized from easier to more difficult according to repetition and language patterns. Easier texts have fewer words, more repetition, and spoken language patterns. More difficult texts have more words, less repetition, and literary language (Peterson, 1991). Children are taught to use several reading strategies, including using the meaning (does that make sense?), language patterns (does that sound right?), and orthographics (do you expect to see that letter?). Thirty-minute daily lessons have five components: reading familiar stories, taking a running record, working with letters, writing a message or story, and reading a new book (Pinnell, Fried, & Estice, 1990). Reading Recovery has survived a good deal of controversy (e.g., Barnes, 1996–1997a, 1996–1997b; Browne et al., 1996–1997) and even has inspired change in more traditional reading remediation programs (Spiegel, 1995).

SPECIAL-NEEDS LEARNERS

Children with special needs include children with challenging social and emotional behaviors, pronounced differences in learning styles or rates, or deficits in hearing, vision, or mobility (Truax & Kretschmer, 1993). Despite being singled out as having special learning difficulties, most special-needs children develop literacy knowledge in patterns that are similar to those found in all children's literacy understandings. For example, one researcher examined the literacy development of young children who were prenatally exposed to the drug crack or cocaine (Barone, 1993). The children were asked to reread a favorite storybook, write a story, and spell words once a month over a year. During this time, the children's emergent readings became more advanced and their writing evidenced more sophisticated concepts about written language. In a similar study, profoundly deaf preschoolers with delayed receptive language were found to have understandings of written language that were developmentally appropriate (Williams, 1994).

Therefore, we could conclude that the most effective way to support special-needs children's literacy learning is similar to the way in which we support all children's learning. Many special education professionals recommend the use of holistic, integrated approaches to reading and writing instruction similar to the activities and approaches proposed in the preceding chapters (Cousin, Weekley, & Gerard, 1993; Truax & Kretschmer, 1993).

Supporting Special-Needs Children's Literacy

Children with special needs "may vary from their age peers, making connections in their own time and in their own ways; but the steps in the learning process" are similar (Truax & Kretschmer, 1993, pp. 593–594). Adapting instruction to serve special-needs learners often means careful observation of children as they participate in reading and writing activities in order to make modifications that will allow all learners to take small risks and reap large rewards (Salvage & Brazee, 1991).

Children with developmental or learning differences in elementary school are placed in regular classrooms when special education teachers feel they can benefit from instruction and activities planned for non-special-needs children. With some adjustments, children with special needs can benefit from instruction along with other children in the regular classroom.

Figure 11.1 shows the writing of a mainstreamed autistic child. His teacher met with him while his classmates were at the computer lab. The writing processes that produced this piece were no different from what other students would use. The difference was the amount of one-on-one coaching the teacher needed to provide. She helped the student to compose his idea and listen for sounds in the words. When he had finished writing, she reread the piece and showed him all the sounds he had captured. The product looks no different from what we expect of most first graders.

All special-needs children from the age of three who have identified developmental or learning differences have an individualized educational plan (IEP) developed by a team of specialists and the child's parents. Teachers should ask for a copy of the plan and quickly become familiar with it so that they can prepare activities to help the child achieve the goals outlined in the IEP.

Modifying Instruction

One of the most effective techniques for supporting the literacy learning of children with developmental delays is to provide instruction that is compatible with the child's

I had Matthew chkn fegr for lUNCH.

FIGURE 11.1   Interactive Writing of "I had chicken fingers for lunch."

developmental level, rather than with the child's age. A second effective technique is to provide social experiences that involve interacting with other children on similar social developmental levels, rather than with children of similar ages. Many of the techniques that we have described for younger novice readers and writers or experimenters with reading and writing are appropriate for older children with developmental delays.

More formal techniques for teaching children with developmental delays to read and write are similar to techniques that support all children's learning to read and write (Dixon, 1987; Sindelar, 1987). There are several ways for teachers to help children read texts and give them the extra practice they need to become good readers. Teachers can read stories first as children follow the text. The method of **repeated reading** provides practice with whole texts (Dowhower, 1989; O'Shea & O'Shea, 1987). In this method, children repeatedly read stories (or parts of stories) that are fifty to one hundred words in length until they can read the selection with only three to six errors. Children begin the repeated readings only when they understand the story.

The writing process is an effective approach in helping emotionally and learning-disabled children successfully communicate their feelings (D'Alessandro, 1987). Daily writing encourages children by implying that they have something meaningful to communicate. A process approach to writing deemphasizes spelling and mechanics, which can be significant stumbling blocks for special-needs children. By focusing on ideas, the writing process supports these children's self-esteem.

As the children brainstorm ideas, teachers can record their ideas on a chart. Then teachers can help the children cluster their ideas into groups. Teachers can demonstrate how to use the cluster by writing a group-collaborated composition that in turn may also be used in reading instruction. During revision, teachers need to be especially careful, because too much revision can be frustrating, causing the child to discard a good composition. The most effective motivation for revision occurs when children discover that they have difficulty reading their own compositions as they present their work in the author's chair (D'Alessandro, 1987).

There are many ways in which teachers can help special-needs children become more actively involved in reading and writing. Two ways in which children are active during reading are by making predictions about what they are going to read and by drawing conclusions about what they have already read (Norris, 1988). Pattern books are effective for supporting active reading and writing of learning-disabled children. These books have predictable sequences that make it easier for children to draw inferences as they predict what will happen next.

LEARNERS FROM DIVERSE CULTURAL BACKGROUNDS

SOME CULTURAL GROUPS HAVE DIFFERENT ways of helping children learn. In some Native American communities, children are expected to learn by observing adults as they perform tasks; this implies that little verbal interaction takes place. Children who expect to learn from watching adults may not learn well in writing centers, in which teachers expect children to learn by talking with each other as they write. In other communities, children learn cooperatively with other children; the emphasis is on developing a group understanding and performance rather than on individual achievement. Children from these communities may have difficulty in reading groups, in which teachers expect only one child at a time to answer a question, and read aloud.

Differences between mainstream and other cultural groups in how they socialize their children into language and literacy use provide an example of **cultural discontinuity** (Au, 1993). Cultural discontinuity means that there may be a mismatch between the literacy culture of the home and that of the school (which usually represents mainstream practices and values). Children who experience a cultural discontinuity are more likely to have learning difficulties in school. This is one possible explanation for the difference in achievement between children from mainstream and from other cultural backgrounds.

If teachers are to support the literacy learning of children from diverse cultural backgrounds, they need to be sensitive to the possibilities of cultural discontinuities as well as knowledgeable of how to change the classroom to better fit the learning of all children (Gee, 1996). Instruction that supports all children's learning and capitalizes on their cultural ways of learning is called culturally responsive instruction (Au, 1993).

Culturally Responsive Instruction

Culturally responsive instruction is instruction that is "consistent with the values of students' own cultures and aimed at improving academic learning" (Au, 1993, p. 13). We describe two examples of culturally responsive instruction. In these examples, teachers develop instructional strategies that are compatible with the learning styles of their children and at the same time help their children learn to operate more successfully with the learning styles usually associated with schools. This kind of instruction is called *culturally responsive*. The first example of instruction is from Au and Kawakami's (1985) description of the Kamehameha Early Education Project (KEEP); the second presents learning in school and in the community at the Warm Springs Indian Reservation (Philips, 1972).

KEEP: The Talk Story Lesson. Teachers in a special school in Honolulu for children of Polynesian Hawaiian ancestry studied carefully the kinds of interactions or talk used by Hawaiian children. They researched talk in the community and talk in the classroom. These teachers discovered that their Hawaiian children engaged in interactions resembling "talk stories." In talk stories, many speakers participate together, jointly speaking—often at the same time—to create a narrative. There are few times in a talk story when only one child is speaking. Leaders in talk stories are skillful in involving other children, rather than in carrying the conversation alone. This way of interaction is not compatible with interaction that teachers traditionally expect during reading instruction.

Once teachers recognized that children who "spoke out" during reading group time were not being disruptive, they began to consider ways of using this type of interaction to foster reading growth. They decided that they would plan the questions they asked, but allow children freedom in the way they answered questions. They allowed more than one child to respond at a time. The teachers tape-recorded reading lessons to examine whether allowing children to talk in what seemed to be a disruptive manner helped children to learn better. They found that 80 percent of the children's responses in "talk story" reading lessons focused on the story. In contrast, only 43 percent of the children's responses in a traditional lesson focused on the story (Au & Kawakami, 1985).

Learning on the Warm Springs Reservation. The second example of culturally sensitive instruction comes from a study of Native American children's learning in school and in their community (Philips, 1972). On the Warm Springs Indian Reservation, Native American adults work together to solve problems. Leadership is assumed by many adults who have special skills or knowledge, rather than by an appointed leader, and adults choose whom they follow. Adults participate in group activities only when they feel they will be successful, and they participate at the level at which they feel comfortable. Children are observers in community meetings, but are often included in conversation.

These cultural ways of interacting are very different from the behaviors usually expected in school. In school, teachers expect children to follow their directions, to speak when asked a question, and to participate willingly in classroom activities. In contrast, Native American children expect to choose their own leader and make decisions about whether to participate in an activity. It is not surprising that Native American children do not volunteer to answer questions and often refuse to speak when called on in whole-class discussions.

One reason for the lack of participation by Native American children in whole-class recitation activities in school is that the **participation structures** in classrooms and in the community differ. Participation structures include the different rules for speaking, listening, and turn taking. Native American children are uncomfortable in the participation structures of whole-class recitations and discussions used frequently in school. They are more comfortable in the participation structures of small groups in which children initiate and direct their own activities. These participation structures have patterns of interaction more like those that the children have observed in their community.

Culturally Responsive Instruction: A Summary.   These projects demonstrate how teachers can alter their ways of instruction and help children develop new ways of interacting in the classroom. First, teachers researched not only their children's community, but also their own way of teaching. They were willing to make changes in how they conducted lessons in order to support their students' learning. Second, teachers sought methods of helping their children make the transition from community ways of learning to school ways of learning. Teachers not only helped children learn, but also helped children learn how to learn in school. Tape-recording lessons, visiting community activities, and talking to parents can provide all teachers with valuable information about developing culturally sensitive learning activities for their children.

Culturally Sensitive Instruction in Multicultural Settings

Many classes, especially in urban settings, include children from several different cultural backgrounds. For example, a classroom might include Hispanic American children from different Spanish-speaking countries, African American children, and Vietnamese children. In these situations, developing culturally sensitive instruction cannot be a matter of merely matching instruction with cultural features. Instead, teachers employ instructional approaches that are successful with most of the children, and at the same time provide extra support for those children who are struggling. They are willing to depart from familiar approaches to instruction and to experiment with different ways of learning and teaching (Au, 1993). Teachers craft culturally sensitive instruction when they invite collaboration from families and the community, use interactional styles of instruction, strive for a balance of rights, and seek culturally relevant content (Au, 1993; Cummins, 1986).

Balance of Rights.   The concept of balance is that both the children and the teacher have input into what is learned. **Balance of rights** recognizes that in a classroom there are three dimensions of interaction: who gets to speak, what topic is discussed, and with whom children speak (Au & Mason, 1981). In mainstream classrooms with conventional recitation lessons or discussion-participant structures, teachers control which children speak, what they speak about, and to whom they speak (usually the teacher). Achieving a balance of rights means allowing children choices about one or more of the three dimensions of interaction (Au & Mason, 1981).

For example, in grand conversations, teachers and children together choose topics of discussion. Children talk about events or characters of interest to them, but the teacher also poses one or two interpretive questions. Children may speak without raising their hands, but the teacher helps quiet children hold the floor or facilitates turn taking when many children want to speak at once. The children listen carefully to one another and react to each other's comments, and teachers encourage such interactions by asking such questions as, "Jane, did you want to comment on what Jeff just said?"

Culturally Relevant Content.   Children who perceive that what they are learning affirms their cultural heritage are more likely to become engaged in learning (Ferdman, 1990).

Teachers can draw especially on two sources to provide culturally relevant content in the classroom: multicultural literature that is culturally authentic and community resources.

Multicultural Literature. Multicultural literature is literature that incorporates people of diverse cultural backgrounds, including African Americans, Hispanic Americans, Asian Americans, Native Americans, and people from other cultures (see Chapter 6). Culturally authentic multicultural literature is usually written by members of a particular culture and accurately reflects the values and beliefs of that culture.

Children from diverse backgrounds need access to literature that includes characters from those backgrounds. Seeing children like themselves in literature increases children's self-esteem and enlightens others about the worth of different cultures. All children need experiences with culturally authentic literature about a variety of different cultural backgrounds.

Using multicultural literature in the classroom should entail more than merely highlighting the heroes or holidays of a culture or reading works of culturally authentic literature (Rasinski & Padak, 1990) as teachers help children see issues from multiple cultural perspectives. Appendix A presents a list of multicultural literature including folk literature, poetry, fantasy, and realistic fiction that reflects the culture of African Americans, Asian Americans, Hispanic Americans, and Native Americans.

Community Resources. The community can provide many rich resources for the classroom. Inviting local storytellers into the classroom is especially useful when teachers have difficulty locating children's literature representative of a child's cultural heritage. For example, a first grade teacher had a few children in her classroom from Cape Verde, an island off the African coast. When she failed to locate literature that included children from this cultural background, she turned to the community liaison in her school for help and learned that the neighborhood included many families from Cape Verde. The community liaison helped the teacher locate a storyteller from the neighborhood, who came to class and shared several stories from Cape Verde. After the storyteller's visit, the children retold two stories, which the teacher recorded in big book format. The children illustrated the big books, and these books became class favorites.

Culturally sensitive instruction is inclusive—it invites participation from children, parents, and the community. It recognizes the value of cultural heritage and children's experiences. It uses children's knowledge as a beginning point for instruction.

ENGLISH LANGUAGE LEARNERS AS A SPECIAL CASE OF AT-RISK LEARNERS

COMING TO SCHOOL can be challenging for all young children. However, **English language learners (ELLs)** face unique challenges. Many live in communities where only their home language is spoken; the language used in business transactions, conversations, television, and radio is not English. Going to school may be the first encounter these children have with a language different from their familiar home language. Even adults are overwhelmed when faced with such an environment in which the language to which they are accustomed is never spoken and where even street signs and other environmental print are unfamiliar.

ELLs face another challenge, called the "double bind," when they are in school situations in which they are expected to learn to speak English (Tabors, 1997, p. 35). They can only gain competence as English speakers by communicating with other English speakers (Barone, Mallette, & Xu, 2005). However, in order to play with other children, they need to be able to communicate with those other children. They are faced with needing to make friendships without the English to do so and with needing to develop English without having friends with whom to speak it. Teachers will need to support ELLs' interactions with other children so that they do have the opportunities both to learn English and to form friendships.

English language learners also need special support in school in order to make a transition into academic learning in English. The support provided for ELLs in gaining English and learning content when they come to school differs from school system to school system, and different states have different requirements about the use of English in instruction and testing. Some school systems provide bilingual programs in which children learn both English and home languages. In some school systems, specially trained teachers provide English-as-a-Second-Language (ESL) instruction. In ESL programs, children are taught English at school; teachers expect that children will continue to develop their home language through experiences at home and in the community. However, in many school systems, the regular classroom teacher provides the only instruction that ELLs receive (Au, 2000). In all cases, the classroom teacher must be aware of the special needs of ELLs in developing their English language, reading, and writing.

Second Language Acquisition

Children go through four phases of oral language development as they acquire a second language. Figure 11.2 presents an overview of these phases, which are similar to the stages of first language acquisition (Hadaway, Vardell, & Young, 2002).

Preproduction. During **preproduction,** the first phase of second language acquisition, children speak very little English, and teachers perceive them as being silent during the school day. While they do not speak, the English language learners are actively listening to the sounds of the English spoken around them and trying to connect the actions they see with the sounds they hear. They intuitively acquire information about English intonation, speed, pausing, loudness, and pitch. Children in this phase comprehend and respond to short commands, such as *Get out your math book* or *Come sit in the circle,* after teachers physically demonstrate the actions while slowly speaking the commands.

Dramatic play using realistic props is an excellent activity to build early language comprehension and use (Genishi & Dyson, 1984). The structure provided by familiar objects and activities supports children's language learning. To be effective, the objects must be real and the children must use them in real activities. Just as many toddlers first learn familiar phrases or words associated with repeated activities (called "routines"), so do English language learners first learn familiar phrases and words in English (Urzua, 1980). Many children learn to say "Night night," "go to sleep," and "read books" because these routine phrases are repeated daily as they participate in the ac-

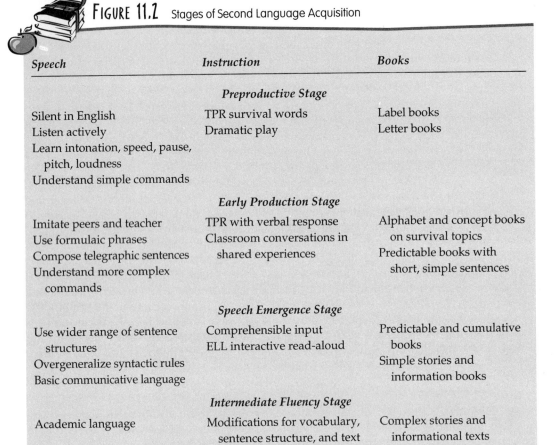

FIGURE 11.2 Stages of Second Language Acquisition

Speech	Instruction	Books
Preproductive Stage		
Silent in English	TPR survival words	Label books
Listen actively	Dramatic play	Letter books
Learn intonation, speed, pause, pitch, loudness		
Understand simple commands		
Early Production Stage		
Imitate peers and teacher	TPR with verbal response	Alphabet and concept books on survival topics
Use formulaic phrases	Classroom conversations in shared experiences	Predictable books with short, simple sentences
Compose telegraphic sentences		
Understand more complex commands		
Speech Emergence Stage		
Use wider range of sentence structures	Comprehensible input	Predictable and cumulative books
Overgeneralize syntactic rules	ELL interactive read-aloud	Simple stories and information books
Basic communicative language		
Intermediate Fluency Stage		
Academic language	Modifications for vocabulary, sentence structure, and text structure	Complex stories and informational texts

tivity of getting ready for bed. Preschool and kindergarten English language learners can learn the same phrases as they interact with their teacher and other children in their play with dolls, blankets, beds, and books in the housekeeping center. Many dramatic-play activities, such as grocery shopping, visiting the dentist, and taking a trip to McDonald's, provide rich language-learning experiences. Teachers can join in play and provide models of language. At first, many English language learners will be silent in their play as they internalize the sounds of English and discover the actions of routines. They may switch between using English and using their home language (this practice should not be forbidden; Lara, 1989).

Even in elementary school, props and dramatic play can be used as a bridge to English. All children enjoy a pretend trip to McDonald's that includes such props as bags, hamburger containers, drink cups, and hats for the employees. As part of the McDonald's play, children learn the English words *hamburgers, French fries, Coke, milk, ketchup, salt,* and *money.* They might learn routine phrases such as "Welcome to McDonald's," "May I take your order, please?" "I'd like a hamburger," or "Give me a Coke." Pictures of familiar activities can also be used to increase English language learners' oral language proficiency (Moustafa & Penrose, 1985).

During this first phase of production, teachers should plan to build children's listening comprehension of familiar words and phrases used in school. English language learners should learn to comprehend and speak such words as labels for objects used in school (*scissors, marker, glue, paper, chair, table, rug, calendar, book center, blocks, book, reading, coloring, painting, building*), colors, days of the week, shapes, body parts, food, clothing, family concepts, parts of houses or items in the home, and animals. Teachers may teach children this vocabulary using **total physical response (TPR)** (Asher, 1982; Hadaway, Vardell, & Young, 2002). Teachers hold up an object or a picture of an object and say its name. Children respond physically rather than verbally to indicate their understanding. For example, if the teacher says the correct name for the pictured object, children would stand up. This is especially fun when teachers often say the wrong name for the object. Alternatives to standing are for children to tap their feet, clap their hands, or touch their noses. Gradually teachers can ask children to repeat the name of the object in English. To collect pictures for vocabulary instruction, teachers can borrow sets of photographs from speech/language specialists, take digital photographs of objects around the classroom, or cut pictures from magazines or catalogues.

Like all children, English language learners even in the preproductive stage should be familiar with classroom routines. However, teachers must explicitly teach the words used in each routine and demonstrate the action the children should take. We recommend that teachers display a printed list of events in the daily schedule along with a photograph of children engaging in each event and a picture of a clock indicating the beginning time of the event (Barone, Mallette, & Xu, 2005). For example, to call children's attention to the transition from whole-class interactive read-aloud to guided reading groups, teachers point to the picture of the classroom in which a small group of children are sitting with the teacher and say, "It is time for guided reading (holding up the word card for guided reading). It is 10:00 (pointing to the picture of the clock). We will go to guided reading. Come with me (gesturing)."

Books to be read aloud during the preproduction stage of language acquisition are very simple, with one or two words on a page and clear illustrations. Letter books, each page of which presents photographs of four objects whose names begin with the same sound, are quite useful at this stage. Similarly, teachers can make books for children by scanning photographs and pictures used in TPR activities to create personalized concept books.

Early Production. During **early production,** the second phase of second language acquisition (Hadaway, Vardell, & Young, 2002), children attempt to speak, but they use very limited language, drawing on the words and gestures learned during vocabulary games or other interactions during the silent period. They frequently imitate formulaic phrases spoken by the teacher or their peers (e.g., *Hi, Wanna come?, Let's go*). Children also point and use other gestures and facial expressions to communicate along with their small store of English words. Children at this stage can comprehend more complicated commands than in the first stage, including ones children frequently use during play, such as *Gimme that block, You be the mama,* or *It's time to clean up.*

During the early production phase of language acquisition, children begin to generate speech rather than merely imitate what they have heard or use formulaic language. Early "sentences" are telegraphic, using only one or two words to convey the meaning of an entire sentence such as saying "Chips" when meaning *I want some chips.* Children at this stage of second language learning focus on words related to *who, what,* and *where* rather than *how* and *why* (Hadaway, Vardell, & Young, 2002).

Children in the early production stage benefit from classroom instruction that is more like conversation (Martinez-Roldan & Lopez-Robertson, 1999/2000). With such instruction, teachers demonstrate and teach, but within the back-and-forth structure of a conversation. Teachers are responsive to students' contributions; they validate and expand students' comments. They do not give up on students when their utterances seem limited. In a shared writing activity with four kindergartners, one teacher stayed with Carlos until he revealed the full meaning of a one-word comment about what the teacher had written so far.

Carlos: (pointing to a word at the end of a line) *Spot.*

Teacher: What do you mean, Carlos?

Carlos: *Spot.* (points again to the last word in a line)

Teacher: Tell me more. What do you mean?

Carlos: No room. (pointing to the end of the first line)

Teacher: (recognizing Carlos's point that there was no more room on the line to write another word) Oh, I see, Carlos. There is no more room for words on this line, so I will continue writing on the next line. (Williams, 2001, p. 753)

Alphabet and concept books make excellent read-aloud materials for English language learners at the stage of early production. These and other concept books can focus on basic survival topics and extend the vocabulary children learned earlier from simple pictures and TPR activities. As teachers read aloud, they should slow down their rate of reading so that children can pick out critical vocabulary words from the rapid flow of language (Echevarria, Vogt, & Short, 2000). Teachers should also point to the salient parts of illustrations and repeat words slowly. For after reading, teachers plan vocabulary activities reinforcing critical vocabulary introduced in the book using TPR response activities. At this stage of language acquisition, ELLs also are expected to say the vocabulary words during TPR. For example, as they read *Mouse Paint* (Walsh, 1995), teachers can have children stand up and say the color words when they hear them in the story.

Highly predictable pattern books are also excellent read-alouds for the phase of early production. These books have short, repeated, and very predictable phrases and strong picture clues to meaning. From these predictable books, children learn to use very simple English sentences such as *I am _____, I like _____, I can _____* and *I have _____.* Commercial materials intended for beginning readers are excellent for ELLs' first read-alouds. For example, *Well Done, Worm!* (Caple, 2000) includes four little books using the simple sentences: *Worm paints a_____, Worm sees a _____, Worm is a _____,* and *Worm gets a _____.*

Speech Emergence.   **Speech emergence** (Hadaway, Vardell, & Young, 2002) is the third stage of language acquisition. In this stage, children continue to acquire vocabulary, and they develop a wider range of sentence structures. As they learn more syntax during this phase of development, they may overgeneralize these syntactic rules, and so their use of grammatically incorrect sentences is to be expected and not corrected. It is important to keep in mind that in order to make gains in English competence, children still need face-to-face interactions that include visual clues to meanings.

Shared activities, in which a small group of children complete a project together, provide many opportunities for conversations. Activities such as composing a shared writing chart, writing together in journals, and retelling a pattern story facilitate conversations among children who have different home languages. During these conversations, teachers use **comprehensible input** (Krashen, 1985); that is, they reduce the number of words they use, slow down their rate of talking, and limit their words to those that are very familiar. Teachers support their simplified language by pointing and using other gestures, repetition, pictures, and dramatic movements. Comprehensible input makes it easier for English language learners to understand and participate in conversation even when they too heavily rely on pointing and other gestures, facial expressions, and dramatic movements. With comprehensible input, ELLs can engage in conversation even when they have limited understanding of the language. For example, the teacher may comment, "That building is high," emphasizing the word *high* with a dramatic gesture and repeating that word. The ELL child responds with a nod and a smile.

In this stage of learning, teachers should continue to read aloud predictable and cumulative books, but search also for books, such as *The Napping House* (Wood, 1996), that include more complex sentences. Books, such as *Where Is My Baby?* (Ziefert, 1996) or *Where's Spot?* (Hill, 1980), that ask and then answer questions are particularly useful in providing models of language use. Children at this stage of language production can begin to listen to simple stories and information books; however, they still need introduction to unfamiliar vocabulary, concepts, and sentence structures.

Intermediate Fluency.   The last stage of second language acquisition is **intermediate fluency.** This is the stage of language proficiency that native English-speaking children have when they enter kindergarten. Native English speakers at the age of five have acquired sufficient vocabulary and fluency with a variety of sentence structures that they are ready to acquire academic concepts in reading, writing, math, and science. In contrast, English language learners can spend nine months in the stage of preproduction, six months in early production, and up to one year in speech emergence, before reaching the stage of intermediate fluency (Hadaway, Vardell, & Young, 2002). Therefore, ELLs who learn English at home or in preschool have a head start over their peers who begin learning English only when they enter kindergarten.

Making Adjustments in Literacy Instruction for English Language Learners

ELLs face many obstacles in learning to read and write in English that are the result of cultural incongruities. Cultural incongruities arise when teachers are unfamiliar with the cultures or languages of their English language learners or when books present concepts that are different from children's cultural expectations.

Teachers who have little or no experience with minority cultures in the United States or other cultures abroad and do not speak another language must seek ways to become more knowledgeable. They must find out more about their students' home languages and experiences and about languages in general in order to bridge the gap between school cultures and children's home cultures. One resource for learning more about different languages is to read children's books that present familiar phrases in different languages such as *Hello World!* (Stojic, 2002), which presents greetings in forty-two languages.

Perhaps one of the most critical ways that teachers can become more familiar with the languages and cultures of their students is to conduct family interviews. Schools in which there are many ELLs have interpreters for teachers to use when conducting family interviews. Or teachers may use school or district parent liaisons as translators during parent interviews. During the interview, teachers seek out the parents' pronunciation of their children's names in the home language and gather information about the home language. Teachers should have parents write their child's name in the home language. This label can be displayed along with the child's picture and name written in English on the child's cubbie or in classroom displays (Schwarzer, Haywood, & Lorenzen, 2003). Teachers ask parents to characterize their children's home language development and to relate experiences the children have had reading everyday print items such as newspapers, magazines, catalogs, or children's books.

Teachers can gain a wealth of information about the language and culture of English language learners by taking a tour of the school's intake neighborhood (Orellana & Hernandez, 1999) with children (if parents give their permission) or with an adult who is familiar with the community. During the tour, they can take digital photographs of the environmental print and signs they see in busy markets, video stores, and restaurants frequented by the residents of the neighborhoods. They can use the photographs as writing prompts in shared writing or in writing workshop. Children may bring print from their homes that can be used for small-group instruction in alphabet recognition and sound-letter associations (Xu & Rutledge, 2003). Children can also make environmental print books to be housed in the classroom's book center.

Selecting Books for English Language Learners and Adjusting Reading-Aloud Techniques

Figure 11.2 presented suggestions for books to read aloud to English language learners at each of the first three levels of English acquisition. During early stage preproduction, teachers will read books about survival topics with few lines of text and alphabet books that have just a few words and a clear match between text and illustrations. Sets of alphabet books that include a book for each letter of the alphabet and few pages of text are appropriate at this stage (for example, the *Cambridge Alphabet Books*, published by Cambridge University Press). Teachers accompany their reading with gestures, pointing to illustrations, and dramatic movements.

At the stage of early production, teachers read aloud easy predictable books with simple language patterns and slightly more complex books on survival topics. The text and illustrations should continue to be related, and there should be only a few words of text on each page. Teachers will also read aloud very simple, short stories and information books.

As children enter the stage of speech emergence, teachers read aloud books that have varied language patterns and include an increasing number of words on each page. Wordless picture books provide excellent visual support for English language learners at this stage of language acquisition. Illustrations in these books provide direct information about actions, characters' thoughts and emotions, and the relationship between actions and characters' feelings. Children can be invited to tell stories in their home language using a parent or community volunteer when the teacher does not speak the home language (Hadaway, Vardell, & Young, 2002). Children at the stage of speech emergence can be be expected to tell their stories in English with support. At the stage of speech emergence, teachers can read slightly more complex books.

ELL Interactive Read-Aloud Procedure

The **ELL Interactive Read-Aloud Procedure** (Hickman, Pollard-Durodola, & Vaughn, 2004) is a technique that teaches vocabulary and comprehension using longer, more complex picture books, both narrative and informational. These are books that teachers would normally read aloud to native English-speaking kindergarten and first grade children. However, without modification, English language learners would not be able to understand them. The ELL Interactive Read-Aloud Procedure is designed to make these books easier for ELLs to understand and to teach them vocabulary used in the books.

The ELL Interactive Read-Aloud Procedure is similar to that used in interactive read-aloud, which we described in Chapter 10. First, teachers divide the book into three or four segments that are read on successive days. Thus, ELLs hear only a little bit of text each day. Teachers select only three or four vocabulary words to teach from each day's text, giving ELLs more opportunity to repeat and use these few words as they talk about the story. The words selected for focus in ELL interactive read-alouds should not be in children's current vocabularies, but should be likely to be encountered again in other books or in real life. Each day teachers introduce a few new vocabulary words, but they also continue to review previously introduced words.

Each day a segment of the book is read and reread, and on the final day, the entire story is reread and retold. Thus, each day ELL children review previously read text and vocabulary, and they add a new segment of text and some new vocabulary. As teachers read each day, they ask *who* and *what* questions that require recall of information from the text. They do not ask *why* questions because children's language at this level of acquisition makes these questions very difficult to answer. The steps each day of the ELL Interactive Read-Aloud Procedure are as follows:

- Introduce the text and three new vocabulary words in a book introduction, using illustrations in the book, objects, or dramatizations.
- Read a segment of the text, highlighting the three vocabulary words by providing short definitions, pointing to illustrations, or using dramatic gestures or facial expressions.
- While reading, ask three questions requiring children to use the ideas and the vocabulary from the story.

* Reread the text, drawing attention to the three vocabulary words.
* Guide recall of story events and talk about children's experiences related to the story or to the three vocabulary words.
* Close the lesson by summarizing the main events or ideas of the text using the three vocabulary words.

The second day of ELL interactive read-alouds is very similar. On each successive day until the book is completed, teachers begin by summarizing the text read on previous days. Then they give an introduction to this day's segment of text. On the final day, the teacher guides children's retelling of the entire story, using all of the target vocabulary words. To make ELL interactive read-alouds even more powerful, we recommend that teachers read two or three related books to build even stronger understandings about concepts and vocabulary. For example, teachers may read two or three versions of the stories of the "Three Billy Goats Gruff" or "Little Red Riding Hood."

Using Oral Language to Support Reading and Writing

Additive approaches build on children's home language and culture (Cummins, 1986) and are in contrast with **subtractive approaches,** which replace children's home language and culture with English and mainstream values. All teachers can take an additive approach to their literacy instruction when they allow students to use their home language in some reading and writing activities.

A third grade teacher who had several Spanish-speaking children in her class introduced the characters and events in *Mirandy and Brother Wind* (McKissack, 1988) by using simple props to act out important parts of the story. As part of her introduction, the teacher used descriptive phrases from the story and illustrated the meaning of these phrases through her dramatic portrayal of the characters in action. Then the children formed pairs to read the story. Next the children gathered to have a grand conversation about the story. As part of the conversation, the teacher shared many responses in which she used several of the vocabulary words from the story. These portions of the lesson were all conducted in English. Finally, the class broke into small groups to act out portions of the story, and several children planned their dramatic reenactments in Spanish. Although most groups presented their dramas to the class using English, one group used Spanish in its enactment.

Another way in which spoken language supports reading is through the use of shared writing. Dialogues that emerge from activities such as a pretend trip to McDonald's provide material for reading and writing (Feeley, 1983). After participating in dramatic play about a visit to McDonald's, children can learn to read and write many words found on the environmental print at McDonald's and associated with going to a McDonald's restaurant, such as *McDonald's, restrooms, men, women,* and *push* (Hudelson & Barrera, 1985). Children can dictate shared writing stories (Moustafa & Penrose, 1985). Photos of the children taken during the activity provide useful support for reading these shared writing stories or writing about the experience (Sinatra, 1981). These language stories can be used to help children develop sight words or practice decoding skills. Figure 11.3 presents a story dictated by an English language learner in second grade after he made Play Doh.

Developing Shared Language. Effective teachers of English language learners realize that students can be easily overwhelmed by too many changing instructional techniques. These children need repeated use of familiar instructional routines and activities using shared language. **Shared language** refers to vocabulary that is used repetitively when talking about a reading or writing task (Gersten & Jiménez, 1994). For instance, one teacher who taught many children with limited knowledge of English repeatedly used a few familiar words when talking about literature. She taught her children the components of a *story grammar* (see Chapter 2 for a description of a story grammar and its components), and her students understood the English words *character, goal, obstacle, outcome,* and *theme.* The students knew how to look for character clues because the teacher frequently asked questions such as, "What kind of character is he? What are the clues?" (Gersten & Jiménez, 1994) and modeled answer-finding techniques.

Another teacher taught students the vocabulary needed to conduct writers' conferences with partners. Using whole-class mini-lessons, the teacher taught children to talk about " 'favorite part,' 'part you didn't understand,' 'part you'd like to know more about,' and 'part you might like to work on' " (Blake, 1992, p. 606). Through modeling, the teacher showed children the kinds of language that he expected them to use and the kinds of information that he expected them to talk about in a writers' conference.

These teachers focused on teaching their children how to participate in highly successful activities. They did not use many different strategies, but instead used only a few strategies routinely. As children gained confidence using these strategies, these teachers gradually added other instructional strategies.

Extended Discourse. Mastering English and becoming competent readers and writers of English is possible only when students use English for a variety of purposes in situations that are not anxiety producing (Faltis, 1993). That is, children need opportunities for **extended discourse,** or talking and writing extensively in a variety of settings (with

FIGURE 11.3 An English Language Learner's Story

Lim Makes Play Doh

> I can use two cup flour.
> I put one cup salt.
> I am mix with spoon.
> I am measure with water and flour.
> I put spice in bucket.
> I put two tablespoon oil in bucket.
> We put color in bucket.

a variety of partners, including the teacher, in small groups, and in whole-class gatherings). Teachers can encourage extended discourse by acknowledging children's input to lessons and by providing models of more complete English-language structure, as in the following example (Gersten & Jiménez, 1994, p. 445).

> Teacher: What does he hope will happen when he shoots the arrow?
>
> Child: The rain (gestures like rain falling).
>
> Teacher: Right, the rain will fall down.

One kindergarten teacher provided opportunities for extended discourse that use repeated readings of a favorite book, storytelling with flannel-board props, and emergent reading of the favorite book (Carger, 1993). First, the teacher read aloud an engaging picture book that appealed to young Hispanic children. After each reading, the teacher invited individual children to reread the story using the pictures in the picture storybook as prompts (for emergent readings). The teacher accepted the children's attempts at reading using their limited English. Then the teacher reread the story and retold the story in Spanish, using flannel-board props. She invited the children to retell the story once again in English, this time using the flannel-board props.

Teaching Reading and Writing Using a Multiliteracy Approach

In this chapter, we have provided information for teaching reading and writing in English and have assumed that the teacher is English-speaking. However, we want to make clear our recognition that children's experiences reading and writing in their first language support their learning to read and write in English (Freeman & Freeman, 2001). Increasingly educators have sought ways of teaching that promote children's spoken and written language development *in their first language,* in order to prevent first-language loss and to make available those abilities as resources for second-language learning (Peyton, Ranard, & McGinnis, 2001). Educators have sought methods, usable by all teachers, even those who speak only English, that preserve **multiliteracy** (in which both the home language and English are honored and used).

As a first start, we recommend that teachers learn how to write all children's names in their home language. Parent volunteers or community liaisons can be helpful in guiding a teacher's practice. Teachers should also learn to say simple phrases in the children's home language such as *Good morning* or *How are you today?* (Schwarzer, Haywood, & Lorenzen, 2003). Teachers can also obtain posters of the alphabet in each of the children's home languages and purchase a few books in each language.

One kindergarten teacher used all five of the home languages in her classroom to conduct a special theme study of insects and spiders. Volunteers wrote the words *insects* and *spiders* in each of the five languages, and parent volunteers taught children the words to the song *Itsy Bitsy Spider* in each language. All the children attempted to sing the song and write the words in all five languages (Schwarzer, Haywood, & Lorenzen, 2003).

In another school, teachers at all primary grades decided to purchase dual-language picture books and to launch a dual-language writing project. Teachers purchased books that were available in one or more languages. Where possible, they purchased books with two languages in the same book. Later, children used writing project time to draw illustrations and to write texts in English. They took their books home, and their parents helped them to write the same text in their home language (Cummins, Chow, & Schecter, 2006).

CHAPTER SUMMARY

A T-RISK LEARNERS are children who are especially at risk for school failure. At-risk learners include children who struggle to acquire literacy concepts despite quality classroom support.

While it is helpful to be aware of language, literacy, family, and community factors that might suggest a need for preventative early literacy instruction, it is also important to be aware of the rich cultural capital inherent in diversity. Fortunately, early literacy instruction aimed at preventing the failure of at-risk children is not qualitatively different from early literacy instruction for other children. Observant teachers adapt instructional activities to meet the needs of special learners without resorting to reductionist methods of instruction.

Teachers recognize that culture influences the way in which children learn and how they interact with each other and with adults. For example, children of Hawaiian ancestry are familiar with interaction styles in which more than one speaker talks at a time and children from one Native American culture are more familiar with talking in small informal groups than in whole-class recitation. Once teachers recognize the ways in which culture affects how children learn and interact, they are on the way to crafting culturally sensitive instruction. Culturally sensitive instruction is characterized by interactive instruction, a balance of rights, and culturally relevant content. Culturally relevant content includes multicultural literature and resources from the community.

Children who speak English as a second language learn spoken English at the same time that they learn to read and write in English. Teachers support this process when they use additive approaches, shared language, and extended discourse. All teachers of diverse learners must strive for a balance between supporting children as they construct their own understandings and providing explicit instruction.

APPLYING THE INFORMATION

Julia Felix is a first-year teacher in a large urban school that serves children from a variety of cultural and language backgrounds. This year she will be teaching third grade (or, you may assume that she will be teaching kindergarten). She opens her class list and reads the following names (X = ELL Student) (Faltis, 1993, p. 5).

1. Brown, Leon
2. Cavenaugh, Kimberly
3. Cui, Xiancoung X
4. Cohen, Daniel
5. Evans, Lisa
6. Fernandez, Maria Eugenia X
7. Freeman, Jeffrey
8. Garcia, Aucencio X
9. Gomez, Concepcion X
10. Hamilton, Jessica
11. Mason, Tyrone
12. O'Leary, Sean
13. Pak, Kyung X
14. Petruzzella, Gina
15. Quinn, Frank
16. Rosen, Chatty
17. Rojas, Guadalupe X
18. Sandoval, Kathy
19. Tran, Do Thi X
20. Vasquez, Jimmy X
21. Williamson, Amy
22. York, Leonard
23. Zbikowski, Antonin

Julie thinks to herself, "I especially want the ESL students to fully join in my class" (Faltis, 1993, p. 6). How will Julie accomplish this task? What suggestions can you make about her room arrangement, the materials she will need, and the modifications she can be expected to make in instruction? Suppose that Julie decides to teach a unit about animals. Make suggestions for materials that she can include in the unit, and plan at least one lesson that will meet the needs of the English language learners in her class.

GOING BEYOND THE TEXT

VISIT A PRESCHOOL OR ELEMENTARY SCHOOL that has special-needs children. Observe the children in their classroom as they interact with the other children and during literacy activities. Take note of ways in which the special-needs children are similar to and different from the other children. If possible, talk to a teacher about supporting the literacy learning of special-needs children. Take at least one reading and one writing activity that you can share with a special-needs child. For example, take a children's book and literature props for the child to retell the story; plan a hands-on experience, such as popping corn, that will stimulate writing; or prepare a special book that you can give to the child for his or her own journal. Carefully observe the child's language and behaviors during these literacy activities. Be ready to discuss what this child knows about literacy.

REFERENCES

Adams, M. (1990). *Beginning to read.* Cambridge: MIT Press.

Asher, J. (1982). *Learning another language through actions: The complete teachers' guidebook.* Los Gatos, CA: Sky Oaks.

Au, K. (1993). *Literacy instruction in multicultural settings.* New York: Harcourt Brace Jovanovich.

Au, K. H. (2000). Multicultural factors and the effective instruction of students of diverse backgrounds. In A. E. Farstrup & S. J. Samuels (Eds.), *What research has to say about reading instruction* (3rd ed.) (pp. 392–413). Newark, DE: International Reading Association.

Au, K. H., & Kawakami, A. J. (1985). Research currents: Talk story and learning to read. *Language Arts, 62,* 406–411.

Au, K., & Mason, J. (1981). Social organizational factors in learning to read: The balance of rights hypothesis. *Reading Research Quarterly, 17,* 115–152.

Barnes, B. L. (1996–1997a). But teacher you went right on: A perspective on Reading Recovery. *The Reading Teacher, 50,* 284–292.

Barnes, B. L. (1996–1997b). Response to Browne, Fitts, McLaughlin, McNamara, and Williams. *The Reading Teacher, 50,* 302–303.

Barone, D. (1993). Wednesday's child: Literacy development of children prenatally exposed to crack or cocaine. *Research in the Teaching of English, 27,* 7–45.

Barone, D. M., Mallette, M. H., & Xu, S. H. (2005). *Teaching early literacy: Development, assessment, and instruction.* New York: Guilford.

Blake, B. (1992). Talk in non-native and native English speakers' peer writing conferences: What's the difference? *Language Arts, 69,* 604–610.

Browne, A., Fitts, M., Mclaughlin, B., McNamara, M. J., & Williams, J. (1996–1997). Teaching and learning in Reading Recovery: Response to "But teacher you went right on." *The Reading Teacher, 50,* 294–300.

Caple, K. (2000). *Well done, worm!* Cambridge, MA: Candlewick.

Carger, C. (1993). Louie comes to life: Pretend reading with second language emergent readers. *Language Arts, 70,* 542–547.

Clay, M. (1985). *The early detection of reading difficulties* (3rd ed.). Portsmouth, NH: Heinemann.

Comber, B. (2000). What *really* counts in early literacy lessons. *Language Arts, 78,* 39–49.

Cousin, P., Weekley, T., & Gerard, J. (1993). The functional uses of language and literacy by students with severe language and learning problems. *Language Arts, 70,* 548–556.

Cummins, J. (1986). Empowering minority students: A framework for intervention. *Harvard Educational Review, 56,* 18–36.

Cummins, J. , Chow, P., & Schecter, S. (2006). Community as curriculum. *Language Arts, 83,* 297–307.

D'Alessandro, M. E. (1987). "The ones who always get the blame": Emotionally handicapped children writing. *Language Arts, 64,* 516–522.

Dickinson, D. K., & Smith, M. W. (1994). Long-term effects of preschool teachers' book readings on low-income children's vocabulary and story comprehension. *Reading Research Quarterly, 29,* 104–122.

Dickinson, D. K., & Sprague, K. E. (2001). The nature and impact of early childhood care environments on the language and early literacy development of children from low-income families. In S. B. Neuman & D. K. Dickinson (Eds.), *Handbook of early literacy research* (pp. 263–280). New York: Guilford.

Dixon, R. (1987). Strategies for vocabulary instruction. *Teaching Exceptional Children, 19,* 61–63.

Dowhower, S. L. (1989). Repeated reading: Research into practice. *The Reading Teacher, 42,* 502–507.

Echevarria, J., Vogt, M., & Short, D. (2000). *Making content comprehensible for English language learners: The SIOP model.* Boston: Allyn & Bacon.

Faltis, C. (1993). *Joinfostering: Adapting teaching strategies for the multilingual classroom.* New York: Merrill/Macmillan.

Feeley, J. T. (1983). Help for the reading teacher: Dealing with the Limited English Proficient (LEP) child in the elementary classroom. *The Reading Teacher, 36,* 650–655.

Ferdman, B. (1990). Literacy and cultural identity. *Harvard Educational Review, 60,* 181–204.

Freeman, D., & Freeman, E. (2001). *Between worlds: Access to second language acquisition.* Portsmouth, NH: Heinemann.

Gee, J. P. (1996). *Social linguistics and literacies: Ideology in discourses* (2nd ed.). Bristol, PA: Taylor & Francis.

Genishi, C., & Dyson, A. H. (1984). *Language assessment in the early years.* Norwood, NJ: Ablex.

Gersten, R., & Jiménez, R. (1994). A delicate balance: Enhancing literature instruction for students of English as a second language. *The Reading Teacher, 47,* 438–449.

Goldenberg, C., & Gallimore, R. (1991). Local knowledge, research knowledge, and educational change: A case study of early Spanish reading improvement. *Educational Researcher, 20,* 2–14.

Hadaway, N. L., Vardell, S. M., & Young, T. A. (2002). *Literature-based instruction with English language learners, K–12.* Boston: Allyn & Bacon.

Hickman, P., Pollard-Durodola, S., & Vaughn, S. (2004). Storybook reading: Improving vocabulary and comprehension for English-language learners. *The Reading Teacher, 57*(8), 720–730.

Hill, E. (1980). *Where's Spot?* New York: G. P. Putnam's Sons.

Hudelson, S., & Barrera, R. (1985). Bilingual/second-language learners and reading. In L. W. Searfoss & J. E. Readence (Eds.), *Helping children learn to read* (pp. 370–392). Englewood Cliffs, NJ: Prentice-Hall.

Krashen, S. (1985). *Inquiries and insights: Second language teaching: Immersion and bilingual education, literacy.* Hayward, CA: Alemany Press.

Lara, S. G. M. (1989). Reading placement for code switchers. *The Reading Teacher, 42,* 278–282.

Lonigan, C. J., Burgess, S. R., Anthony, J. L., & Baker, T. A. (1998). Development of phonological sensitivity in 2- to 5-year-old children. *Journal of Educational Psychology, 90,* 294–311.

Martinez-Roldan, C. M., & Lopez-Robertson, J. M. (1999/2000). Initiating literature circles in a first-grade bilingual classroom. *The Reading Teacher, 53,* 270–281.

McGee, L. M., & Richgels, D. J. (2003). *Designing early literacy programs: Strategies for at-risk preschool and kindergarten children.* New York: Guilford.

McKissack, P. (1988). *Mirandy and Brother Wind.* New York: Knopf.

McMillon, G., & Edwards, P. (2000). Why does Joshua "hate" school . . . but love Sunday School? *Language Arts, 78,* 111–120.

Moustafa, M., & Penrose, J. (1985). Comprehensible input PLUS, the language experience approach: Reading instruction for limited English speaking students. *The Reading Teacher, 38,* 640–647.

National Center for Educational Statistics. (1996). *NAEP 1994 reading report card for the nation and states.* Office of Educational Research and Improvement. U.S. Department of Education.

National Reading Panel. (2000). *Report of the National Reading Panel.* Washington, DC: National Institutes of Health.

Neuman, S. B., Celano, D. C., Greco, A. N., & Shue, P. (2001). *Access for all: Closing the book gap for children in early education.* Newark, DE: International Reading Association.

Norris, J. A. (1988). Using communication strategies to enhance reading acquisition. *The Reading Teacher, 41,* 668–673.

O'Shea, L., & O'Shea, D. (1987). Using repeated reading. *Teaching Exceptional Children, 20,* 26–29.

Orellana, M.E., & Hernandez, A. (1999). Talking with the walk: Children reading urban environmental print. *The Reading Teacher, 51,* 612–619.

Peterson, B. (1991). Selecting books for beginning readers. In D. DeFord, C. Lyons, & G. Pinnell (Eds.), *Bridges to literacy: Learning from Reading Recovery* (pp. 119–147). Portsmouth, NH: Heinemann.

Peyton, J., Ranard, D., & McGinnis, S. (Eds.). (2001). *Heritage languages in America: Preserving a national resource.* McHenry, IL: Delta Systems.

Philips, S. (1972). Participant structures and communicative competence: Warm Springs children in community and classroom. In C. Cazden, V. John, & D. Hyumes (Eds.), *Functions of language in the classroom.* New York: Teachers College Press.

Pinnell, G., Fried, M., & Estice, R. (1990). Reading recovery: Learning how to make a difference. *The Reading Teacher, 43,* 282–295.

Rasinski, T., & Padak, N. (1990). Multicultural learning through children's literature. *Language Arts, 67,* 576–580.

Salvage, G., & Brazee, P. (1991). Risk taking, bit by bit. *Language Arts, 68,* 356–366.

Scarborough, H. (1991). Early syntactic development of dyslexic children. *Annals of Dyslexia, 41,* 207–220.

Schwarzer, D., Haywood, A., & Lorenzen, C. (2003). Fostering multiliteracy in a linguistically diverse classroom. *Language Arts, 80,* 453–460.

Sinatra, R. (1981). Using visuals to help the second language learner. *The Reading Teacher, 34,* 539–546.

Sindelar, P. T. (1987). Increasing reading fluency. *Teaching Exceptional Children, 19,* 59–60.

Snow, C. E., Burns, M. S., & Griffin, P. (Eds.). (1998). *Preventing reading difficulties in young children.* Washington, DC: National Academy Press.

Spiegel, D. L. (1995). A comparison of traditional remedial programs and Reading Recovery: Guidelines for success for all programs. *The Reading Teacher, 49,* 86–96.

Stojic, M. (2002). *Hello World!: Greetings in 42 languages around the globe.* New York: Scholastic.

Tabors, P. O. (1997). *One child, two languages.* Baltimore, MD: Paul Brookes.

Truax, R., & Kretschmer, R. (1993). Focus on research: Finding new voices in the process of meeting the needs of all children. *Language Arts, 70,* 592–601.

Urzua, C. (1980). A language-learning environment for all children. *Language Arts, 57,* 38–44.

Walker, D., Greenwood, C., Hart, B., & Carta, J. (1994). Prediction of school outcomes based on socioeconomic status and early language production. *Child Development, 65,* 606–621.

Walsh, E. (1995). *Mouse paint.* New York: Red Wagon Books.

Williams, C. (1994). The language and literacy worlds of three profoundly deaf preschool children. *Reading Research Quarterly, 29,* 124–155.

Williams, J. A. (2001). Classroom conversations: Opportunities to learn for ESL students in mainstream classrooms. *The Reading Teacher, 54,* 750–757.

Wood, A. (1996). *The napping house.* New York: Harcourt.

Xu, S. H., & Rutledge, A. L. (2003). Chicken starts with ch! Kindergarteners learn through environmental print. *Young Children, 58,* 44–51.

Ziefert, H. (1996). *Where is my baby?* Brooklyn, NY: Handprint Books.

CHAPTER

12

Putting It All Together
USING ASSESSMENT TO GUIDE INSTRUCTION

KEY CONCEPTS

Reliability	Portfolio	Rubric
Validity	Decoding Analysis	Portfolio Conference
Work Samples	Developmental Spelling	Portfolio Summary
Assessment Notebook	Inventory	

A MODEL OF COMPREHENSIVE ASSESSMENT AND INSTRUCTION

A SSESSMENT IS ALWAYS A PART OF TEACHING. Each time a teacher presents a lesson to a group of children, he or she considers, at least briefly, how well those children have learned and whether this particular classroom activity is having a positive influence on learning. Most teachers decide either that a lesson has been effective because children seemed to be learning or that the lesson needs to be modified before being taught again because it failed to have the desired effect on children. Most early childhood teachers, informally and perhaps intuitively, engage in the cycle of assessing children's learning and planning future instruction to keep new learning moving forward. When children are not making progress, teachers ponder changes in their instruction to meet those children's needs or consider seeking intervention services. However, fewer early childhood teachers employ a systematic and comprehensive model of assessment and instruction (Epstein, Schweinhart, DeBruin-Parecki, & Robin, 2004). Few consider the ethical and appropriate use of the various assessments they administer, some of which they are required to give (Bredekamp & Rosegrant, 1992).

Screening

A comprehensive and systematic model of assessment and instruction serves several purposes (Invernizzi, Meier, Swank, & Juel, 1999). First, it allows teachers to screen children to determine their current levels of knowledge. At the beginning of a year of instruction, teachers assess in order to determine what progress children already have made toward the mastery expected of them by the end of the school year (McGee & Morrow, 2005). We have provided at the ends of Chapters 3 through 5, lists of accomplishments typically expected of children at the ends of preschool, kindergarten, first grade, and second grade and beyond. These lists provide starting points for teachers in thinking about the new learning their children will do during the course of a school year. Also in Chapters 3, 4, and 5 (and in Appendices B and C), we provided examples of assessments that enable teachers to screen children in preschool, kindergarten, and first grade and beyond.

Not all children follow the developmental path we laid out in Chapters 3, 4, and 5 (McGee & Richgels, 2003). However, certain components of early literacy development have been shown to be highly related to later literacy achievement (National Institute of Child Health and Human Development, 2000; Snow, Burns, & Griffin, 1998). As researchers have sought to identify components of early literacy that seem to matter in preschool, kindergarten, first grade, and the remaining elementary grades, they have found that children's early development of conventional foundational skills is critical for later success (Anthony et al., 2003). They have found that before entering kindergarten, a child's levels of knowledge in five categories are directly related to later reading and writing success or failure (summarized in Snow, Burns, & Griffin, 1998):

1. Alphabet knowledge
2. Phonological and phonemic awareness

3. Phonics and the alphabetic principle
4. Concepts about print and books
5. Oral comprehension and vocabulary

In the elementary years, some of these foundational concepts continue to be critical as children apply their knowledge to the reading of texts. In those years, five factors are critical for reading success (National Institute of Child Health and Human Development, 2000):

1. Reading comprehension
2. Vocabulary
3. Fluency
4. Phonemic awareness
5. Phonics

A comprehensive model of assessment and instruction would include measures of these essential foundational concepts and reading constructs. Schools with Reading First programs (a portion of the federal government's No Child Left Behind program) are required to use reliable and valid measures of these constructs. **Reliability** refers to a test's yielding the same or similar results over several administrations. **Validity** refers to a test's measuring what it is purports to measure (e.g., that a phonemic awareness test really measures phonemic awareness and not, for example, alphabet recognition or phonics knowledge). Teachers must seek out information regarding the validity and reliability of the assessments they use (McConnell et al., 1998; Yopp, 1988)

Monitoring

The second purpose of a comprehensive model of assessment and instruction is to monitor whether on-going classroom instruction and classroom activities are effecting learning in desired ways throughout the year (Good & Kaminski, 2002). To achieve this purpose, teachers readminister some of the screening assessments or similar assessments to determine whether children have actually progressed to expected levels (Morris & Slavin, 2003). The data collected from monitoring assessments can inform adjustments in classroom routines and instructional activities for individual children or groups of children. The data might allow teachers to identify children whose progress significantly differs from what is expected of them and demonstrated by other children.

In addition to administering monitoring assessments, teachers systematically observe children as they work during classroom activities. Weekly, or at least bimonthly, teachers make anecdotal notes of what they observe children doing and saying as they read and write (see Chapter 2 for a description of anecdotal notes). Later, teachers analyze their anecdotal records and write, as captions to their records, hypotheses about what children know and can do. They reread their notes and captions periodically to determine whether children are making changes over time. Teachers also collect work samples on a systematic basis. **Work samples** are children's actual writing products. A work sample might be a picture with a label that a child wrote at the writing center, a digital photograph of a shared writing step-up chart on which the child has copied some letters, a finished draft of a composition from a science inquiry unit that compares and contrasts snakes and lizards, or a response journal entry in which a child wrote a retelling of a text she read as a part of a book club. Teachers select samples of children's writing that provide insight into their continuing literacy development.

Essential Features

A comprehensive assessment program has seven essential features (McGee, in press):

1. A description of language and literacy outcomes expected to emerge in a variety of language and literacy domains.
2. A small number of valid, reliable, and perhaps standardized measures aligned with expected outcomes, which can be adapted to meet special populations of children (for example, Spanish-speaking children) and which are administered at least twice yearly.
3. A procedure within a school to select a smaller number of these valid and reliable measures to be administered quarterly for monitoring purposes.
4. Professional development to insure teachers are trained to administer these measures in ways that insure maximum validity and reliability and to analyze the results efficiently and accurately.
5. Professional development in methods of observing, recording, and analyzing children's reading, writing, and language use and of gathering samples of writing from ongoing classroom activities on a bimonthly or monthly basis.
6. Professional development for integrating data collected from classroom activities with screening and monitoring data to make instructional decisions about individuals and groups of children.
7. Professional development for communicating assessment data to all stakeholders including parents, other teachers, school administrators, and other agencies of concern (such as Head Start or Title I).

Developing an Assessment Plan

Once teachers have selected screening and monitoring assessments, they schedule times to administer them (usually early fall for screening and then three times throughout the year for monitoring). Teachers may select all or only a subset of the screening measures to use on particular monitoring occasions. For example, assessments of alphabet knowledge are useful at the end of first and second quarter in kindergarten while assessments of phonemic awareness are useful at the end of second and third quarter.

Finally, teachers make a schedule that allows systematic observation of all children (such as observing each child closely for 10 to 15 minutes twice a month) as they participate in a variety of classroom activities. One plan is to schedule observations on Mondays and Thursdays. The first week of the month, the teacher designates three or four children for observation on Monday and three or four additional children on Thursday. During center or workstation time, outside play, and mealtimes, the teacher observes each of the designated children for a total of approximately 10 to 15 minutes and makes anecdotal notes. During the second, third, and fourth Mondays and Thursdays of the month, other children are observed. Once all the children have been observed, the cycle of observation repeats.

Keeping Records

Teachers must keep track of the results of screening and monitoring assessments as well as the work samples and records of classroom observations for each child and for the classroom as a whole. One method of keeping track of anecdotal records and their captions and work samples is to have an assessment notebook. **Assessment notebooks** are notebooks in which teachers keep all of their anecdotal notes and analyses. Teachers can use dividers to make a separate section for each child in the classroom. Teachers place their anecdotal notes in the assessment notebook immediately in order not to misplace them. Most teachers write anecdotal notes on dated sticky notes during observations and then later tape these sticky notes to pages in their assessment notebooks. Once or twice after school each week, they analyze observations taped in their notebooks since their last opportunity to analyze. They quickly read through the previous month's observations for a child and jot down a few insights about the significance of what was observed most recently.

Assessment notebooks should also have a class profile of the results of the screening and monitoring assessments for all children in the classroom (see Appendices B and C for class profiles). While analyzing anecdotal notes, teachers can see with a glance at these profiles how well individual children performed on the profiled assessments.

Using Insights to Plan Responsive Instruction

After teachers have written reflections that interpret children's literacy work, they use the reflections to make decisions about instructional activities that will nudge children forward in their literacy learning. Teachers should consider adjustments they might make in instructional activities, materials and activities planned for centers or workstations, and classroom routines that will result in all children taking their next steps in reading and writing development.

THE COMPREHENSIVE MODEL OF ASSESSMENT AND INSTRUCTION IN ACTION

IN THE FOLLOWING SECTION, we present Ms. Orlando and how she uses the comprehensive model of assessment and instruction. Ms. Orlando and her kindergarten children are studying travel. As a part of this unit, Ms. Orlando has read many stories about characters who travel away from their homes and poems about traveling (including imaginary travel of the mind). The children have learned different methods of transportation and are examining ways in which seeds travel.

A Day in Ms. Orlando's Classroom

Ms. Orlando's half-day kindergarten class is divided into four time periods: whole-class gathering, center time, snack and recess or a special class, and storytime.

Whole-Class Gathering. The children are gathered on the rug as the teacher reads Kovalski's (1987) version of *The Wheels on the Bus*. Two other versions of this story are displayed in the classroom library center. Ms. Orlando holds up the book and says, "I'm going to read a new version of *The Wheels on the Bus*. This one is written and illustrated by Maryanne Kovalski. It begins differently from the other 'Wheels on the Bus' stories that we have read before. Listen carefully to find out how this version is different. When I come to the part of the story that you know, join right in and read with me." Then she begins reading, and after several pages all the children are reciting the familiar story along with her. After reading the story, Ms. Orlando and the children talk about how this story is different from the other two versions they read.

Finally, Ms. Orlando says, "Let's sing our version of the song." She finds the chart for "The Wheels on the Bus" song which was dictated earlier in the week. Ms. Orlando says, "Husalina, you can be pointer first." Husalina comes to the front of the group and takes the pointer. The children sing the song as Husalina points across the lines of the text. Then another child is selected to be pointer, and the class sings the song again.

Next Ms. Orlando introduces a new story. She says, "Our new story today is about another character who leaves home and travels to many different places. But instead of reading the story to you, I am going to tell it. The title of the story is *The Runaway Bunny*, and it was written by Margaret Wise Brown (1942)." Ms. Orlando hangs a copy of the front cover of the book on the classroom story clothesline as she reads the title (see clothesline props in Chapter 6).

After telling the story, Ms. Orlando begins a grand conversation by saying, "What did you think about the story?" The children spend several minutes sharing their personal responses. Then Ms. Orlando says, "Little Bunny sure did become a lot of things in this. You might want to draw a picture in the art center about Little Bunny and his mother and all the different things he became. Let's write a list of all the things Little Bunny turned into, and I'll put the list in the art center to remind you what you might want to draw."

Ms. Orlando uses the interactive writing technique with the children to write the list of things Little Bunny turns into. One child offers, "Little Bunny turned into a flower." Ms. Orlando asks the children to tell her which letters she will need. She says, "Flower. FFFFFlower. Everyone say out loud what letter I need to begin spelling the word *flower*." Many of the children say "F," some children offer other letters, and a few children are silent. Ms. Orlando confirms, "Yes. *F*. FFF." She calls on Rayshawn, who comes to the chart and writes the letter *f*. Ms. Orlando writes the remainder of the word. She and the children complete the chart, with different children writing each initial letter.

Center Time: Ms. Orlando Teaches a Mini-lesson and Observes Children.

The children select centers, and Ms. Orlando circulates among the children helping them find materials and making sure that everyone has settled into an activity. (Figure 12.1 presents a description of the activities available in the centers in Ms. Orlando's classroom.) Then she calls five children to a table where she frequently conducts small-group lessons for a mini-lesson on phonemic awareness and spelling. She has a collection of environmental print objects and small toys that the children have brought to school in the past two weeks. The objects include toys or print objects that begin with the letters *T, R, V,* or *L*, including a toy rabbit, a box of Tide, a toy train, a bunch of violets, and a box of lima beans. Each of the children has a metal pizza pan and several magnetic letters.

To begin a familiar game, Ms. Orlando holds up an object and emphasizes its beginning sound. She says, "Rrrrice. Now let's listen to the first sound at the beginning

FIGURE 12.1 Ms. Orlando's Centers

Blocks: sets of large and small blocks, several toy trucks, several toy cars, road maps, toy road signs, clipboards with paper and pencils (on which children pretend to keep track of mileage)

Art: assorted art materials (including a variety of papers, crayons, markers, collage materials, scissors, and glue) and materials for making a visor, including paper plates and a pattern (for cutting the plate into a visor shape), elastic, and hole punchers (to punch a hole for the elastic)

Travel— Dramatic Play: dress-up clothes, including purses and wallets; checkbook, play credit cards, play airline and bus tickets; materials for going to the beach, such as empty bottles of suntan lotion, towels, sunglasses, sand bucket and shovel; travel brochures and other materials, such as maps, blank postcards, paper, markers; materials for an ice-cream stand, including play money, cups, spoons, order pads, and a cash register

Library: quality collection of literature; retelling props for "Henny Penny" and "The Gingerbread Man"; display of "Wheels on the Bus" books; display of books featuring ways to travel and toy boats, airplanes, trucks, motorcycles, and cars that the children collected; special tub of books, labeled "Traveling Characters," which includes four books each in a plastic bag with an audiotape for the listening center

Letter and Word: markers and two pieces of chart paper on which Ms. Orlando has printed the letters *T* and *R* in upper- and lowercase letters (children write on the charts practicing letter formations); magazines, scissors, glue, and paper (children cut letters and pictures out of magazines and glue them on the paper); a collection of environmental print items and toys with beginning sounds of /t/, /r/, /v/, and /l/, which the children have gathered, and four grocery store sacks labeled with those letters; picture dictionaries; names of all the children in the class, and other words, such as the days of the week, months of the year, colors, and numbers

Math: assorted manipulatives and math materials for sorting and counting; toy coins; directions for playing a game with the coins (money madness)

Discovery: a display of different kinds of seeds the children have collected; several books about seeds and how seeds travel; magnifying glass; directions for an experiment exploring how far a piece of paper can travel when it is shaped like an acorn and when it is shaped like a maple seed, string for measuring, and paper for drawing and writing the results

Writing: assorted writing materials and tools, blank postcards, paper, envelopes, a variety of stamps (which children use as postage stamps), picture dictionaries, photo album of children in the class with their pictures and first and last names, directory of children's addresses, telephone book, maps of rrrice." She models saying /r/ and several children select the letter *r* and put it on their pizza pans. After spelling several more words, Ms. Orlando says, "Today we are going to change this game a little bit. We are going to spell the beginning and ending of words. Like this (she holds up the toy rabbit). First I listen to the beginning of the word. Rrrrabbit. I hear an *r*." (She puts the letter *r* on her pizza pan.) "Now I have to listen for the ending. Rabbit /t/-/t/. I hear a *t*." (She puts the letter *t* after the letter *r* on her pizza pan.) "Now I've spelled *rabbit* with two letters, one for the beginning and one for the ending. Now let's try one together."

Ms. Orlando and the children spell several more words. Then Ms. Orlando says, "I want everyone to visit the writing center today or tomorrow. When you are writing, think about using beginning and ending letters." Then the five children choose centers for the remainder of center time; three of the children begin writing at the writing center.

Ms. Orlando picks up a clipboard on which she has placed six pieces of sticky notepaper with five children's names written at the top of each paper (one extra, blank notepaper is included). Ms. Orlando observes five or six children nearly every day. At the beginning of the year, she divided her twenty-two children into two groups of five and two groups of six children. Then she assigned each group of children to a day of the week. The first group of children is observed on Monday, the second group on Tuesday, and so on. One day a week she does not observe children, but uses the day for more small-group instruction, guests, films, cooking, or other special activities.

Ms. Orlando circulates among the children in the centers. She decides to watch Ishmail as he works in the letter and word center. She observes as he dumps out the bag of *R* and *T* objects that the class has gathered and separates them into two piles. He says "ro-bot," and places the toy in the *R* bag. He says "rrr-ice," and places it in the *R* bag. He says "t-t-tums," and places it in the *T* bag. He says "tr-ain," and places it in the *T* bag. Ms. Orlando writes her observations on one of the sticky notes.

In the library center, Ms. Orlando observes Husalina retell "Henny Penny" using the story clothesline. Husalina includes every event in the story, recalls the characters' names correctly, and repeats the dialogue, "Wanna come? Yes. Tell king sky's falled." Ms. Orlando then observes Cecelia playing in the travel dramatic-play center with Josephine and Barbara. All three girls pretend to write a letter home to their mothers. Ms. Orlando observes their writing and then asks Cecelia to read her letter. Cecelia reads, "Dear Mom, I'm having fun. Cecelia."

Ms. Orlando invites Rayshawn to read the "Wheels on the Bus" chart with her; she is aware that he rarely chooses to reread the classroom charts or retell stories in the library center. Rayshawn points to the text from left to right and across the lines as he recites the words to the song. Ms. Orlando notes that he has memorized the words to the song, but is not matching the words he says with the words in the text.

Storytime. As center time comes to an end, Ms. Orlando helps the children put away their center activities and get ready for snack and outdoor recess. After recess, she reads a big book version of *Rosie's Walk* (Hutchins, 1968). As she reads, she pauses to invite children to make predictions about what will happen next. She notes that Jasmine, Tuong, and Ishmail catch on to the repetitive pattern and make accurate predictions of the story. After reading, the children share responses.

Ms. Orlando Reflects and Plans

After the children are dismissed, Ms. Orlando takes time to organize her observations and make plans for instruction. First she takes the sticky notes off the clipboard and puts each note in her **assessment notebook.** This notebook is divided into sections, one for each child in the classroom. As she places the sticky notes in the notebook, she reflects on what the observations show about each child's understanding about reading or writing. She writes her analysis beside the sticky note in the observation notebook.

Her notes capture what she observed Ishmail and Husalina doing and saying. She indicates that Ishmail segmented the word *robot* into syllables (*ro*) and (*bot*), the word *rice* into its beginning phoneme (*r*) and rime (*ice*), and the word *train* into its onset (*tr*) and rime (*ain*) by segmenting these words in her notes. She indicated in her notes that he matched each of the words with its appropriate letter. Her analysis reflects these observations: "Ishmail segments words between syllables, onset and rimes, and beginning phonemes. He knows the sounds associated with *T* and *R*. He is making the transition from phonological to phonemic awareness."

Ms. Orlando decides to put Cecelia's letter, which she collected from the travel dramatic-play center, in Cecelia's **portfolio** (a large folder in which she keeps examples of that child's work). She quickly writes a caption for Cecelia's letter and clips it to the letter. The caption includes the date and Ms. Orlando's analysis of what the letter reveals about Cecelia's understanding about writing. Figure 12.2 shows Cecelia's letter and Ms. Orlando's caption.

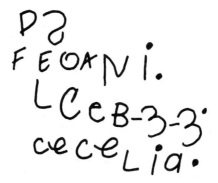

Caption: 11/2   Cecelia is using emerging letter form. Her signature is in the appropriate location for letters. She shows awareness of linearity, hyphens, and periods. Her meaning is appropriate for the situation (pretending her mother misses her) and includes language used in a letter. She uses conventional alphabet letter forms (with one reversal). She relies on contextual dependency.

Text: Dear Mom,
         I'm having fun.
         Cecelia

FIGURE 12.2   Cecelia's Letter and Caption

Then Ms. Orlando thinks back on the day's activities and her observations. She decides that she needs to teach a small-group lesson with Jasmine, Rayshawn, and a few other children on finger-point reading of memorized stories. She plans to teach a minilesson on monitoring fingerpoint reading and plans to include a pocket-chart activity for the "Wheels on the Bus" song.

PULLING IT ALL TOGETHER: USING PORTFOLIOS

MS. ORLANDO used both an assessment notebook and a portfolio for each child as part of her record keeping in assessment. A portfolio is a large envelope or folder, one for each child in the classroom, into which teachers put work samples and their captions and eventually anecdotal notes and analyses (captions). Portfolios serve several functions in the classroom. They are used to make instructional decisions, help children reflect on what they have been learning, and share with parents information about their children's literacy growth (Hansen, 1996; Porter & Cleland, 1995). For portfolios to be useful, they must be manageable and up-to-date. Most importantly, portfolios help teachers reflect on their own practice (Bergeron, Wermuth, & Hammar, 1997; Kieffer & Faust, 1994).

Before grading periods in the elementary school, teachers pull out anecdotal notes and captions taken weekly or biweekly and gather them together in each child's portfolio. In preparation for giving grades and meeting in conferences with parents, teachers look through the anecdotal notes and work samples to determine progress and areas of needed instruction. They gather any running records and miscue analyses (see Chapter 5 for a discussion of these assessment tools). They look through all of the children's samples to make an analysis of the children's decoding and spelling strategies and their growing awareness of story and expository text structures (see Chapter 5 for a discussion of the narrative and expository text structures we expect elementary students to acquire).

Analyzing Anecdotal Notes over Time

Teachers usually choose to write an anecdotal note when they observe an event that reflects a child's current level of understanding or a new level of understanding. For example, suppose that a first grade teacher is concerned about a child's inability to select and sustain interest in a book for independent reading. The teacher observes that the child selects three different books in five minutes and does no more than look quickly through the books at the illustrations. Figure 12.3 presents the teacher's anecdotal note and analysis of this behavior. Several months later, the teacher may observe the same child spending more than fifteen minutes reading *Hop on Pop* (Seuss, 1963) with a friend in the library center. The teacher writes an anecdotal note about this event because the teacher knows that it documents significant growth in the child's ability and willingness to sustain interest in reading. Figure 12.3 also shows the teacher's anecdotal note about this new behavior and analysis of the child's progress.

Teachers in kindergarten and first grade will want to use observation and analysis to supplement the assessments of children's conventional reading and writing profi-

FIGURE 12.3 Anecdotal Notes Showing Development

Note 10/15	Analysis 10/15
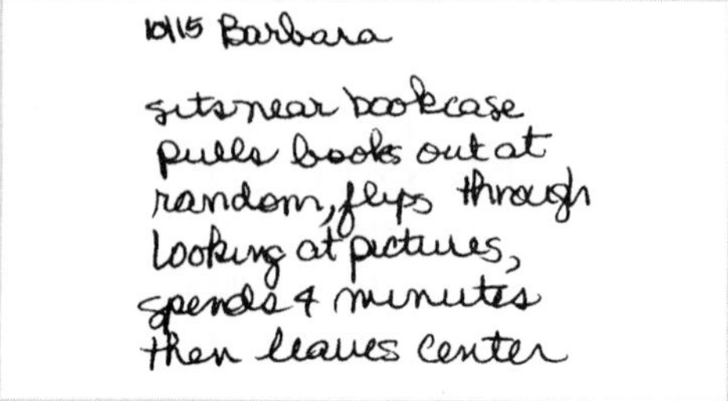 10/15 Barbara sits near bookcase pulls books out at random, flips through looking at pictures, spends 4 minutes then leaves center	Barbara willingly participates in independent reading. She browses through books looking at pictures. (needs support in selecting books and strategies for sustaining interest)
Note 2/7	Analysis 2/7
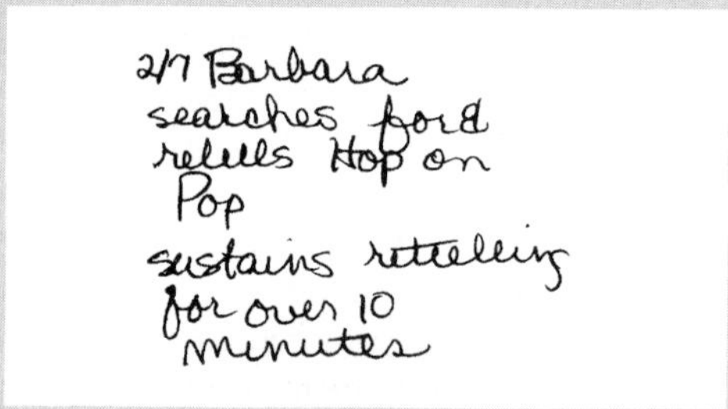 2/7 Barbara searches for d retells Hop on Pop sustains retelling for over 10 minutes	Barbara enjoys reading books to others. She is comfortable reading books she has memorized and spends long periods of time rereading these books. She selects these books for independent reading. Note progress from unable to sustain interest in books to sustains interest for prolonged periods of time from 10/15.

ciency that often are required at that level. They are often required to assess children's conventional knowledge about, for example, alphabet letter recognition, phonemic awareness, or letter-sound correspondences. During these phases of literacy development, children will display conventional knowledge, for example, of alphabet letter names, knowing the sounds or phonemes associated with some letters, and being able to name rhyming words. However, they will also display incomplete, not fully developed awareness of these concepts in their reading and writing attempts. The combination of observation, collection of work samples, and careful analyses along with more conventional assessment will provide the most powerful information to guide teachers' decision making.

Analyzing Children's Decoding Strategies

Children's miscues, or errors, in running records provide excellent resources for determining their knowledge and use of alphabetic and orthographic principles in decoding (knowledge of sound-letter relationships, prefixes, suffixes, and familiar word parts). Teachers examine children's miscues to conduct a decoding analysis. A third grade teacher recorded the following miscues in Raymond's running record.

Text	Child
street	stairs
strutting	starting
mournful	m
deserted	distant
abruptly	ab
mysterious	mysteries

In a **decoding analysis** of Raymond's miscues, conducted to determine what decoding strategies he uses, his teacher noted that Raymond consistently used beginning consonants but frequently omitted the *r* in the *str* consonant cluster and had difficulty decoding multisyllabic words (all the miscues were words of more than one syllable, except for *ceased*). However, Raymond is aware of some prefixes and familiar word parts (for example, he correctly read *ab*).

Analyzing Spelling

To assess strategies in spelling, teachers can examine children's spellings in first draft compositions looking for late emergent spellings, letter name or alphabetic spellings, within-a-word spellings, and syllable and affix spellings. A more systematic approach is to use a **developmental spelling inventory.** A developmental spelling inventory is a list of words children are asked to spell. The list is purposefully designed so that many different spelling patterns are included. For example, one list (Johnston, Invernizzi, & Juel, 1998) intended for first graders includes ten words (*van, pet, rug, sad, plum, chip, shine, skate, float,* and *treat*) that have initial and final consonants, short vowels, blends and digraphs, and long vowel markers (p. 49). We recommend using the *Elementary Spelling Inventory* (Bear et al., 2003) and its accompanying *Feature Guide*. The feature guide allows teachers to record which spelling patterns children use correctly or misspell. Teachers can determine whether children consistently use, use but sometimes confuse, or do not use particular spelling patterns including:

- Consonants
- Consonant clusters (*br, gl, st,* etc.)
- Consonant digraphs (*sh, ch, th, ph, wh,* and *ng*)
- Short vowels (*mad,* etc.)
- Silent *e* long vowels (*made,* etc.)
- Long and other vowel combinations (*mail, pay, meat, toy,* etc.)
- Prefixes
- Suffixes
- Familiar word parts (*le* in *bottle,* etc.)

Analyzing Children's Compositions

Early childhood classrooms such as Ms. Orlando's provide children with many opportunities to try their hand at telling and retelling stories and writing at the writing center. Composing activities such as these provide opportunities for teachers to gather rich assessment information about their children's literacy development.

Teachers and older children select compositions to include in portfolios. These compositions may be written during writing workshop and may be highly polished stories that have gone through several drafts, or they may be informal compositions written at a writing center. Teachers analyze compositions for children's understanding of written forms and meanings.

Analysis of Form. Young children's compositions can be examined for the following forms.

- Mock cursive (indicates awareness of linearity)
- Mock alphabet letters (indicates awareness of letter features)
- Conventional alphabet letters (indicates knowledge of alphabet formations)
- Copied words (indicates awareness of words in environment)
- Spelled words such as the child's name or other learned words such as *mom, dad,* and *love* (indicates learned spellings)
- Conventions (such as capitalization and punctuation)
- Invented spelling

In addition, teachers note whether children's writing shows awareness of linearity, for example, writing mock letters from left to right in lines, or spacing, for example, leaving spaces between strings of conventional letters as if writing words (Feldgus & Cardonick, 1999). Young children frequently circle words, place periods between words, or separate words with dashes. These unconventional strategies indicate that children are experimenting with word boundaries.

Older children's compositions can be analyzed for their knowledge of conventions, such as capital letters and punctuation. Teachers note all examples of children's use of these conventions and keep a list of all conventions the children use correctly. For example, a teacher may note that a child capitalizes the beginnings of sentences, the word *I*, the name of the local town, and the name of the school; consistently uses a period or question mark at the end of a sentence; uses apostrophes in the contractions *don't* and *I've*; and uses a comma after the greeting in a letter.

Story Form. Teachers take special note of children's control over story form which includes:

- Setting, which identifies time, place, and weather
- Characters, who are revealed through their thoughts, actions, appearance, and dialogue
- Plot, which includes a problem, episodes, climax, and resolution—episodes consist of actions toward solving the problem and outcomes
- Point of view, which reveals who tells the story
- Mood
- Theme

Figure 12.4 presents a story composition dictated by five-year-old Kristen to her kindergarten teacher. The composition contains sixteen pages and a title page. As Kristen's kindergarten teacher analyzed the form of Kristen's story, she noted that Kristen had included three characters: a little girl, a cat, and baby cats. These characters were developed through the illustrations (which showed what the characters looked like), a few revelations of the cat's thoughts (she wanted to go home and she was happy), the girl's and cat's actions, and dialogue.

Kristen's story incorporates three plot episodes (rescuing the cat, the cat's birthday, and taking the baby cats to live in the woods). The first episode, about rescuing the cat, has a fully developed plot. It includes a problem (the cat was caught in a trap), actions toward solving the problem (the girl pulled and pulled, and pushed and pushed on the trap), a climax (the cat was almost out), and an outcome (the cat was out). The other episodes are descriptions of actions, and all the episodes are loosely connected through common characters.

Kristen relied on having the cats go to sleep to resolve the story. The story is told in the third person, with the cat's thoughts revealed. The mood of the story is pleasant

FIGURE 12.4　"The Girl with the Cat and the Babies"

Title:	The Girl with the Cat and the Babies
page 1	The little girl took her cat for a walk.
page 2	She got caught in a trap.
page 3	The little girl came.
page 4	And she pulled, and she pulled, and she pushed, and she pushed on the trap.
page 5	She opened the cage and the cat was almost out.
page 6	The little cat was out. She was happy.
page 7	The cat was purring because the little girl was rubbing her.
page 8	The little girl was taking her home.
page 9	The sun was coming down.
page 10	Tomorrow was the cat's birthday. She was happy because she was going to have a party.
page 11	It was the cat's birthday and the people were fixing it up because they were awake.
page 12	One day the cat was knocking on the little girl's door because she had four babies on her birthday.
page 13	The cat asked, "Can I go out in the woods with my babies to live?"
page 14	Far, far away they went. She waved good-bye and so did the babies.
page 15	The cat built five houses.
page 16	They were all ready to go to sleep.

except for when the cat is caught in the trap. Kristen's story shows her ability to manipulate all the literary elements of a story form except for theme.

Expository Text Form.   Teachers also analyze the form of children's informational writing. At the simplest level, children's expositions consist of labels (see Chapter 5). They may be one-word, phrase, or sentence labels identifying objects, people, or events.

At the next level are couplets, two related sentences about the same topic. An attribute list includes a main idea and several supporting ideas, although the ideas are not ordered in any way. More complex expositions include complex couplets or ideas that are related to the main topic (they have consistency), but they also have ordered relationships (ideas that are presented in a sequence, explain cause and effects or problems and solutions, or compare and contrast). Usually children's first use of ordered relationships is embedded in an attribute list. Even more complex expositions include hierarchy, where a topic is introduced followed by subtopics. Teachers analyze children's expositions for their use of consistency, ordered relationships, and hierarchy. They also analyze expositions for topic presentation, description of attributes, characteristic events, category comparisons, and final summaries (Donovan, 2001).

Analyzing Meaning and Content.   In analyzing the content in children's compositions, teachers consider the characters, events, settings, or information in relation to children's own experiences and to literature. They analyze the ideas included in compositions for consistency, believability, and unity. They examine children's use of dialogue, literary word order, or literary language such as alliteration, rhyme, repetition, simile, or imagery.

In the story presented in Figure 12.4, Kristen included a familiar character (she has a cat). Many of the actions of the story are from Kristen's own life—her cat often follows her on walks, she likes to rub her cat until he purrs, her birthday was less than a month away, she often explores the woods around her house, and she wishes that her cat could have babies.

Kristen also incorporated three examples of literary language in her composition. She used repetition of words and actions, including actions similar to those in the familiar folktale *The Enormous Turnip* (Parkinson, 1986) (And she pulled, and she pulled, and she pushed, and she pushed on the trap). She also used literary word order (Far, far away they went) and dialogue (Then the cat asked, "Can I go out in the woods with my babies to live?").

Using Scoring Rubrics as Assessment Tools

Rubrics are assessment tools that show how well children have learned particular features taught in instruction. Rubrics identify key areas or elements that should be included in a high-quality work sample (Skillings & Ferrell, 2000). For example, when evaluating a child's story composition, a scoring rubric would identify the components that should be included in the story (e.g., setting, character names, and problem) as well as indications of quality (e.g., sometimes, usually, or always includes descriptive words).

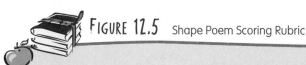

FIGURE 12.5   Shape Poem Scoring Rubric

Excellent Shape Poem	Good/Adequate Shape Poem	Poor Shape Poem
best handwriting	good handwriting	sloppy handwriting
all words spelled correctly	most words spelled correctly	many words misspelled
good title	has a title	no title
appeals to two or more senses	appeals to one sense	does not appeal to senses
words written in obvious shape of poem's topic	words written in a shape but not obvious	words written in lines
very interesting ideas	some interesting ideas	no interesting ideas

Scoring rubrics can be even more effective when children and teachers develop the rubric together. Figure 12.5 presents a scoring rubric developed by second graders and their teacher as a part of a poetry writing unit. As a part of the unit, the children learned to use words that appeal to the five senses, lining and shape, alliteration and rhyme, and other poetic elements. They wrote shape poems and developed the rubric to evaluate their poems. To develop the rubric, the teacher asked the children to describe what would be included in an excellent shape poem. The children said that these poems would have good ideas, correct spelling and punctuation, and have good handwriting. Then the teacher guided the children to also think about some of the poetic elements that she had been teaching: the poem's title, the shape of the poem, and if the poem appeals to the five senses. Then the teacher guided the children to discuss what would be included in a poor shape poem and finally an adequate one.

Figure 12.6 presents Lane's shape poem. His poem was judged to be an excellent shape poem because it had a good title, the shape was related to the poem's topic, it appealed to two senses (taste and sight), he used good handwriting, and he spelled words correctly.

Using Portfolios to Make Instructional Decisions

We have stressed that teachers' observations and analyses focus on what children *can* do. However, making instructional decisions means that teachers look beyond what children can do and consider the next steps in learning. For example, Ms. Orlando noticed that Rayshawn attempted to point to text while he recited a familiar song. She knows that eventually the children need to be able to match the text word for word. With this objective in mind, she made plans to provide instruction to nudge children in this direction. Teachers always keep in mind the next step in learning and consider whether they need to plan instruction to help children take that next step.

FIGURE 12.6   Apple Shape Poem

Using Portfolios to Support Children's Reflections

One way to encourage children to reflect on their learning is to hold portfolio confer-ences. **Portfolio conferences** provide opportunities for children to select pieces to in-clude in their portfolios and to reflect on their learning (Bauer & Garcia, 1997). Children talk about reasons for selecting samples to add to a portfolio (most interesting story, best writing, favorite poem, and so on).

After the conferences, teachers prepare **portfolio summaries** (Courtney & Abodeeb, 1999), which summarize the children's literacy growth and achievement of literacy goals. To prepare the summaries, they review all their anecdotal notes, chil-dren's work samples, and children's performances on any literacy tasks that they have administered.

Using Portfolios to Inform Parents

Portfolios provide teachers with an excellent resource for sharing information about children's learning with parents. To prepare to share with parents, teachers consider in-formation that parents will find useful and make a list of a few of each child's key new understandings. Then they select eight to ten work samples, anecdotal notes, or check-lists to illustrate each child's learning. Finally, teachers think about one or two areas in which the child needs further practice or instruction.

Children may be involved in the parent conferences. If so, teachers help children prepare for the conferences by having them identify two or three things that they have learned and find evidence of this learning in their work samples. During the confer-ences, children share what they have learned. Teachers extend the conferences by sharing their analyses with both parents and children. The conferences might end with having the children formulate one or two goals for future learning.

Making Portfolios Selective

Many teachers believe that they need to collect many work samples and anecdotal notes (Roe & Vukelich, 1998). They carefully observe each child once a week, write analyses, and collect one or two work samples for each child each week. However, collecting this much information on each child may not be productive. Portfolios are intended to document children's typical literacy performances and to show how those typical performances change over time (Gronlund, 1998). Therefore, teachers should be selective in choosing to write an anecdotal note or collect a work sample (Sarafini, 2001). Notes and samples need to be collected when teachers notice a change in children's understanding or performance. When they observe the children performing the same way with similar levels of proficiency, they may decide not to take note of this activity or collect this particular sample.

Keeping Portfolios Manageable

Teachers' time is limited, and collecting and analyzing assessment information is time-consuming. Teachers need to make manageable plans and then make a commitment to follow those plans (Gronlund, 1998). For example, Ms. Orlando takes fifteen minutes four days a week to observe her children. She writes anecdotal notes as she observes in the classroom and analyzes those notes the same day. She realizes that collecting notes on children over time is extremely valuable in helping her to know individual children. All teachers must make decisions about how much time they have to devote to assessment and which assessments will provide them with the information they need. Teachers cannot use all the assessments described in this chapter—they would do nothing but assess! Nevertheless, teachers are responsible for documenting children's growth as readers and writers. Their assessments reflect their commitment to a quality, child-centered program that supports the literacy learning of all children.

Chapter Summary

ASSESSING YOUNG CHILDREN'S language and literacy development has long been a critical component of early childhood programs. Comprehensive assessment models are planned to meet specific language and literacy goals and draw upon thoughtful observation of children. These observations are supported by teachers' analyses of work samples for evidence of spelling and decoding growth, and by rubrics. Teachers carefully consider the results gathered from monitoring assessments, which systematically sample children's development of essential literacy concepts.

Portfolio assessment is a systematic form of classroom assessment. Portfolios may include anecdotal notes, work samples, and running records. Portfolios also include children's and teachers' reflections in the form of analyses, captions, and summaries. Portfolios are used to make instructional decisions, encourage children's reflections on

362

their own learning, and share information about children's learning with parents. Assessments must be kept manageable by planning a reasonable time frame for collecting assessment information, selecting only a few most informative assessments, and collecting information on a systematic basis.

Teachers are responsible for screening children's initial levels of achievement related to essential components of reading and writing. These components are similar for experimenting, early, and transitional readers and writers; however, as children progress through these phases of reading, they are expected to master more sophisticated and complex strategies and skills. Teachers monitor children's progress in these essential components. These assessments guide teachers as they make instructional decisions about individual children.

As teachers assess individual children, the best practice is to form tentative conclusions about a child's language development and literacy knowledge. These tentative conclusions are then refined through ongoing, multiple assessments including a combination of observation, standardized or formal tests, monitoring assessments, informal teacher-developed tasks and rubrics, and samples of children's writing. Thus, a comprehensive assessment model is continuous, planned, and guided by knowledge of a broad overview of literacy development, such as we provide in Chapters 2 through 5. It provides insights into children's underlying cognitive concepts and their overt strategies, is used to make plans for future instruction, and informs decisions about program and classroom adaptations.

APPLYING THE INFORMATION

We provide samples from Katie's third grade reading and writing portfolio. Katie selected a letter that she wrote to her grandmother and included the first two drafts as well as a copy of the final draft of the letter in her portfolio. Figure 12.7 presents Katie's drafts of her letter. Write a caption for the letter, analyzing Katie's knowledge of written language meanings, forms, meaning-form links, and functions.

Jonathan is a five-year-old beginning kindergarten. His teacher has observed him four times over the first two months of school. For three of the observations, she also collected work samples of his writing. Figure 12.8 presents Jonathan's work samples and his teacher's anecdotal notes about her observations. Write an analysis for the anecdotal note and captions for the compositions. Then write a portfolio summary that describes what Jonathan knows about written language meanings, forms, meaning-form links, and functions.

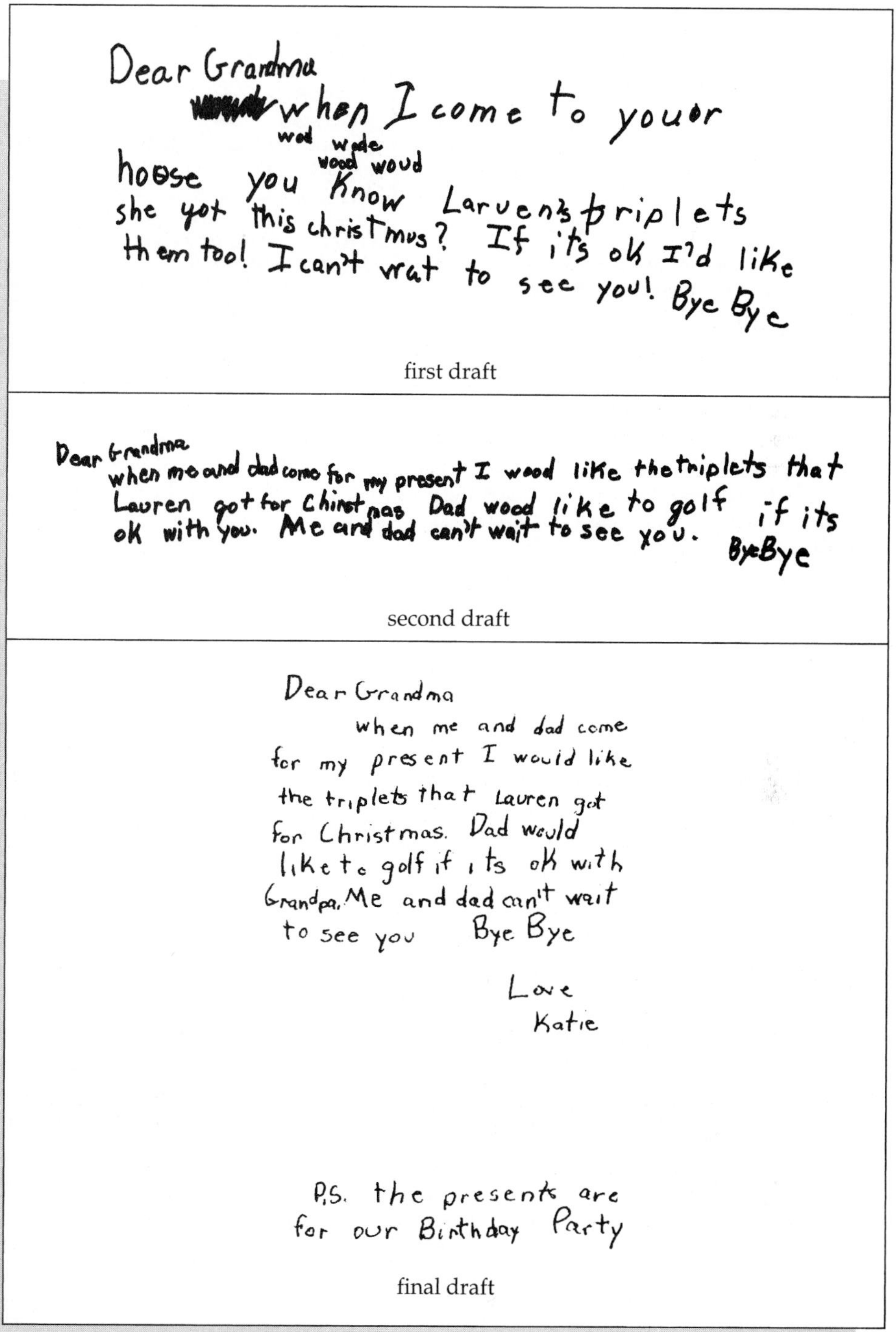

Dear Grandma
~~weneve~~ when I come to your
wod wode
wood woud
hoose you know Laurens triplets
she yot this christmus? If it's ok I'd like
them too! I can't wrat to see you! Bye Bye

first draft

Dear Grandma
when me and dad come for my present I wood like the triplets that
Lauren got for Chirstmas. Dad wood like to golf if its
ok with you. Me and dad can't wait to see you.   Bye Bye

second draft

Dear Grandma
    when me and dad come
for my present I would like
the triplets that Lauren got
for Christmas. Dad would
like to golf if its ok with
Grandpa. Me and dad can't wait
to see you   Bye Bye

            Love
            Katie

P.S. the presents are
for our Birthday Party

final draft

FIGURE 12.7   Katie's Letter

a. Notes

9/20 Johnathan
at the computer
center
Johnathan complains
his words are run
together. He is copying
words from around
the room. I show
him space bar. He
types discovery center
writing center pet mouse
with spaces

b. Notes

9/24 Johnathan
at the library center
Johnathan is looking
at the tag on the stuffed
Snoopy dog and reads
"Snoop" "Snoopy". I ask
him which part spells
snoop = he spells snoop!
Earlier we were writing
notes to parents for open
house. He copied mom and
read mommy. I said no, it
only said mom. It would
have a y at the end to
say mommy.

c. Notes

10/7 Johnathan
at writing center
Johnathan copies words
from letterhead of scrap
paper in the center. He
asks me to read what
he'd written. After he
reads he underlines
each word. He says I
can spell pub-pub. He
says I can spell comp-com!
I spell words and he writes.
I stress sounds but he wants
me to tell him letters. See sample

d. Sample

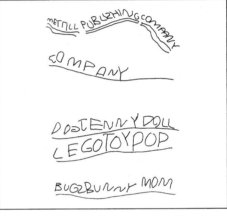

e. Notes

10/30 Johnathan
at writing center
Johnathan wants to
write about Joker and
Batman. He says Joker and
I repeat segmenting /j/.
He writes 6 he says kills
I segment /k/ = K people
/p/ = p Batman /b/ = B bat =
/t/ = t helps /h/ = H people
/p/ = P I do all segmenting
* first invented
spelling I've observed
see sample

f. Sample

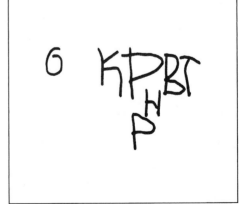

FIGURE 12.8   Jonathan's Writing and His Teacher's Observations

GOING BEYOND THE TEXT

INTERVIEW A TEACHER who uses portfolio assessment about his or her classroom assessments. Find out what the teacher expects to collect in the portfolios, how he or she analyzes the information, and how he or she shares the information with parents. Examine the contents of several of the children's portfolios. Talk with children about the contents of their portfolios. Compare the results of your interview with Ms. Orlando's portfolio assessment plans and procedures.

REFERENCES

Anthony, J. L., Lonigan, C. J., Driscoll, K., Phillips, B. M., & Burgess, S. R. (2003). Phonological sensitivity: A quasi-parallel progression of word structure units and cognitive operations. *Reading Research Quarterly, 38,* 470–487.

Bauer, E., & Garcia, G. (1997). Blurring the lines between assessment and instruction: A case study of a low-income student in the lowest reading group. In C. Kinzer, K. Hinchman, & D. Leu (Eds.), *Inquiries in literacy theory and practice* (pp. 166–176). Chicago: National Reading Conference.

Bear, D. R., Invernizzi, M., Templeton, S., & Johnston, F. (2003). *Words Their Way: Word Study for Phonics, Vocabulary, and Spelling Instruction.* Columbus, OH: Merrill.

Bergeron, B., Wermuth, S., & Hammar, R. (1997). Initiating portfolios through shared learning: Three perspectives. *The Reading Teacher, 50,* 552–561.

Bredekamp, S., & Rosegrant, T. (Eds.). (1992). *Reaching Potentials: Appropriate Curriculum and Assessment for Young People, Volume 1.* Washington, DC: National Association of Education for Young People.

Brown, M. (1942). *The runaway bunny.* New York: Harper and Row.

Clay, M. M. (1998). *By Different Paths to Common Outcomes.* Portland, ME: Stenhouse Publishers.

Courtney, A. M., & Abodeeb, T. L. (1999). Diagnostic-reflective portfolios. *The Reading Teacher, 52,* 708–714.

Donovan, C. (2001). Children's development and control of written story and informational genres: Insights from one elementary school. *Research in the Teaching of English, 35,* 394–447.

Epstein, A. S., Schweinhart, L. J., DeBruin-Parecki, A., & Robin, K. B. (2004). *Preschool Assessment: A Guide to Developing a Balanced Approach.* Rutgers, The State University of New Jersey: National Institute for Early Education Research.

Feldgus, E., & Cardonick, I. (1999). *Kid writing: A systematic approach to phonics, journals, and writing workshop.* Bothell, WA: The Wright Group.

Good III, R. H. & Kaminski, R. A. (2002). *Dynamic Indicators of Basic Early Literacy Skills, (DIBELS),* 6th ed. Eugene, OR: University of Oregon.

Gronlund, G. (1998). Portfolios as an assessment tool: Is collecting of work enough? *Young Children, 53,* 4–10.

Hansen, J. (1996). Evaluation: The center of writing instruction. *The Reading Teacher, 50,* 188–195.

Hutchins, P. (1968). *Rosie's walk.* New York: Scholastic.

Invernizzi, M., Meier, J., Swank, L., & Juel, C. (1999). *Phonological Awareness Literacy Screening (PALS).* Charlottesville, VA: University of Virginia.

Johnston, F., Invernizzi, M., & Juel, C. (1998). *Book buddies: Guidelines for volunteer tutors of emergent and early readers.* New York: Guilford.

Kieffer, R. D., & Faust, M. A. (1994). Portfolio process and teacher change: Elementary, middle, and secondary teachers reflect on their initial experiences with portfolio evaluation. In C. K. Kinzer & D. J. Leu (Eds.), *Multidimensional aspects of literacy research, theory, and practice* (pp. 82–88). Chicago: National Reading Conference.

Kovalski, M. (1987). *The wheels on the bus.* Boston: Little, Brown.

McConnell, S., McEvoy, M., Carta, J., Greenwood, C. R., Kaminski, R., Good, R. H. III, Shinn, M. (1998). *Research and Development of Individual Growth and Development Indicators for Children between Birth to Age Eight. Technical Report No. 4.* University of Minnesota, Minneapolis, MN: Early Childhood Research Institute on Measuring Growth and Development.

McGee, L. M. (in press). Language and literacy assessment in preschool. In J. Parratore & L. McCormack (Eds.), *Classroom literacy assessment.* New York: Guilford.

McGee, L. M., & Morrow, L. M. (2005). *Teaching Literacy in Kindergarten.* New York: Guilford.

McGee, L., & Richgels, D. (2003). *Designing Early Literacy Programs: Strategies for At-Risk Preschool and Kindergarten Children.* New York: Guilford.

Morris, D., & Slavin, R. (Eds.). (2003). *Every Child Reading.* Boston, MA: Allyn & Bacon.

National Institute of Child Health and Human Development. (2000, April). *Report of the National Reading Panel: Teaching children to read.* (NIH Publication No. 00-4769). Available at http://www.nichd.nig.gov/publications/nrp/smallbook.htm.

Parkinson, K. (1986). *The enormous turnip.* Niles, IL: Albert Whitman.

Porter, C., & Cleland, J. (1995). *The portfolio as a learning strategy.* Portsmouth, NH: Heinemann.

Roe, M., & Vukelich, C. (1998). Literacy portfolios: Challenges that affect change. *Childhood Education, 74,* 148–153.

Sarafini, F. (2001). Three paradigms of assessment: Measurement, procedure and inquiry. *The Reading Teacher, 54,* 384–393.

Seuss, Dr. (1963). *Hop on pop.* New York: Random House.

Skillings, M., & Ferrell, R. (2000). Student-generated rubrics: Bringing students into the assessment process. *The Reading Teacher, 53,* 452–455.

Snow, C., Burns, M., & Griffin, P. (Eds.). (1998). *Preventing reading difficulties in young children.* Washington, DC: National Academy Press.

U.S. Department of Health and Human Services. (2003). The national reporting system: What is it and how will it work? *Head Start Bulletin, 76.*

Yopp, H. K. (1988). The validity and reliability of phonemic awareness tests. *Reading Research Quarterly, 23,* 159–177.

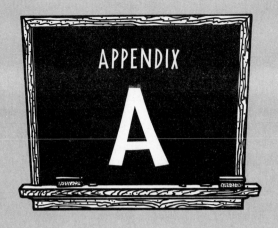

APPENDIX A

Children's Literature

Alphabet Books

Anno, M. (1976). *Anno's alphabet*. New York: Crowell.

Archambault, J., & Martin, B. (1989). *Chicka chicka boom boom*. New York: Scholastic.

Baskin, L. (1972). *Hosie's alphabet*. New York: Viking Press.

Bruna, D. (1967). *B is for bear*. New York: Macmillan.

Burningham, J. (1964). *John Burningham's ABC*. London: Johnathan Cape.

Ehlert, L. (1989). *Eating the alphabet*. New York: Harcourt Brace Jovanovich.

Eichenberg, F. (1952). *Ape in cape*. San Diego, CA: Harcourt Brace Jovanovich.

Elting, M., & Folsom, M. (1980). *Q is for duck*. New York: Clarion.

Hoban, T. (1987). *26 letters and 99 cents*. New York: Greenwillow.

Holtz, L. T. (1997). *Alphabet book*. New York: DK Publishing.

Ipcar, D. (1964). *I love an anteater with an A*. New York: Knopf.

Isadora, R. (1983). *City seen from A to Z*. New York: Greenwillow.

Johnson, S. T. (1995). *Alphabet city*. New York: Penguin.

Kellogg, S. (1987). *Aster Aardvark's alphabet adventures*. New York: Morrow.

Lionni, L. (1985). *Letters to talk about*. New York: Pantheon.

Lobel, A. (1981). *On Market Street*. New York: Greenwillow.

McCurdy, M. (1998). *The sailor's alphabet*. Boston: Houghton Mifflin.

McMillan, B. (1986). *Counting wildflowers*. New York: Lothrop.

Schnur, S. (1997). *Autumn: An alphabet acrostic*. New York: Houghton Mifflin.

Seuss, Dr. (Theodore Geisel). (1963). *Dr. Seuss's ABC*. New York: Random House.

Shannon, G. (1996). *Tomorrow's alphabet*. New York: Greenwillow.

Tudor, T. (1954). *A is for Annabelle*. New York: Walck.

Wildsmith, B. (1963). *Brian Wildsmith's ABC*. Danbury, CT: Franklin Watts.

Books for Very Young Children

Baker, K. (1994). *Big fat hen*. New York: Harcourt Brace.

Berenstain, J., & Berenstain, S. (1971). *Bears in the night*. New York: Random House.

Brown, M. (1942). *The runaway bunny*. New York: Harper.

Brown, M. (1947). *Goodnight moon*. New York: Harper.

Burningham, J. (1971). *Mr. Grumpy's outing*. New York: Holt.

*Carroll, R. (1932). *What Whiskers did*. New York: Walck.

*Carroll, R. (1970). *The Christmas kitten*. New York: Walck.

Cauley, L. (1982). *The three little kittens*. New York: Putnam.

Chorao, K. (1977). *The baby's lap book*. New York: Dutton.

Clifton, L. (1977). *Amifika*. New York: E. P. Dutton.

Crews, D. (1978). *Freight train*. New York: Greenwillow.

de Paola, T. (1985). *Tomie de Paola's Mother Goose*. New York: Putnam.

Eastman, P. D. (1960). *Are you my mother?* New York: Random House.

Freeman, D. (1968). *Corduroy*. New York: Viking.

Galdone, P. (1973). *The little red hen*. New York: Scholastic.

Galdone, P. (1973). *The three bears*. New York: Scholastic.

Galdone, P. (1985). *Cat goes fiddle-i-fee*. New York: Clarion.

Galdone, P. (1986). *Three little kittens*. New York: Clarion.

Havill, J. (1986). *Jamaica's find*. Boston: Houghton Mifflin.

Hill, E. (1982). *The nursery rhyme peek-a-book*. New York: Price/Stern/Sloan.

Hill, E. (1989). *Where's Spot?* New York: Putnam.

Hort, L. (2000). *The seals on the bus*. New York: Henry Holt and Company.

Hughes, S. (1985). *Bathwater's hot*. New York: Lothrop, Lee and Shepard.

Hutchins, P. (1971). *Rosie's walk*. New York: Macmillan.

*Keats, E. (1974). *Kitten for a day*. Danbury, CT: Franklin Watts.

Kuskin, K. (1959). *Which horse is William?* New York: Harper and Row.

Lewis, K. (1991). *Emma's lamb*. Cambridge: Candlewick.

Lewis, K. (1996). *One summer day*. Cambridge: Candlewick.

Lewis, K. (1997). *Friends*. Cambridge: Candlewick.

Marshall, J. (1979). *James Marshall's Mother Goose*. New York: Farrar.

*Ormerod, J. (1981). *Sunshine*. New York: Puffin.

*Oxenbury, H. (1982). *Good night, good morning*. New York: Dial.

Rice, E. (1981). *Benny bakes a cake*. New York: Greenwillow.

Shannon, D. (1998). *No, David!* New York: Scholastic.

Slobodkina, E. (1947). *Caps for sale*. New York: Addison.

Steen, S., & Steen, S. (2001). *Car wash*. New York: G. P. Putnam's Sons.

Tolstoy, A. (1968). *The great big enormous turnip*. Danbury, CT: Franklin Watts.

Wright, B. F. (Illustrator). (1916). *The real Mother Goose*. New York: Rand McNally.

Wordless Picture Books

Baker, J. (1991). *Window*. New York: Greenwillow.

Day, A. (1985). *Good dog, Carl*. New York: Scholastic.

de Paola, T. (1978). *Pancakes for breakfast*. San Diego: Harcourt Brace Jovanovich.

Goodall, J. (1988). *Little red riding hood*. New York: McElderry Books.

Hoban, T. (1972). *Push-pull, empty-full*. New York: Macmillan.

Hoban, T. (1980). *Take another look*. New York: Greenwillow.

Hoban, T. (1988). *Look! Look! Look!* New York: Greenwillow.

Mayer, M. (1974). *Frog goes to dinner*. New York: Dial.

Mayer, M. (1977). *Oops*. New York: Dial.

McCully, E. (1984). *Picnic*. New York: Harper and Row.

McCully, E. (1985). *First snow*. New York: Harper and Row.

McCully, E. (1987). *School*. New York: Harper and Row.

McCully, E. (1988). *New baby*. New York: Harper and Row.

Rohmann, E. (1994). *Time flies*. New York: Crown.

Spier, P. (1982). *Peter Spier's rain*. New York: Doubleday.

Turkle, B. (1976). *Deep in the forest*. New York: Dutton.

Weisner, D. (1991). *Tuesday*. New York: Clarion.

Winter, P. (1976). *The bear and the fly*. New York: Crown.

Predictable Books

Burningham, J. (1978). *Would you rather. . .?* New York: Crowell.

Carle, E. (1977). *The grouchy ladybug*. New York: Crowell.

Fleming, D. (1993). *In the small, small pond*. New York: Scholastic.

Fox, M. (1987). *Hattie and the fox*. New York: Bradbury.

Galdone, P. (1968). *Henny Penny*. New York: Scholastic.

Ho, M. (1996). *Hush! A Thai lullaby*. New York: Orchard.

Hutchins, P. (1982). *Goodnight, owl!* New York: Macmillan.

Jackson, A. (1997). *I know an old lady who swallowed a pie*. New York: Dutton.

Kavalski, M. (1987). *The wheels on the bus*. Boston: Little, Brown.

Kent, J. (1971). *The fat cat*. New York: Scholastic.

Kraus, R. (1970). *Whose mouse are you?* New York: Collier.

Lexau, J. (1969). *Crocodile and hen*. New York: Harper and Row.

Martin, B., Jr. (1983). *Brown bear, brown bear*. New York: Henry Holt.

Martin, B. (1991). *Polar bear, polar bear, what do you hear?* New York: Scholastic.

Root, P. (1998). *One duck stuck*. Cambridge: Candlewick.

Schneider, R. M. (1995). *Add it, dip it, fix it*. Boston: Houghton Mifflin.

Sendak, M. (1962). *Chicken soup with rice*. New York: Harper and Row.

Smith, M., & Ziefert, H. (1989). *In a scary old house*. New York: Penguin.

Sweet, M. (1992). *Fiddle-i-fee*. Boston: Little, Brown.

Tabak, S. (1997). *There was an old lady who swallowed a fly*. New York: Scholastic.

Tafuri, N. (1984). *Have you seen my duckling?* New York: Greenwillow.

Tresselt, A. (1964). *The mitten*. New York: Lothrop, Lee and Shepard.

Weiss, N. (1989). *Where does the brown bear go?* New York: Trumpet Club.

Westcott, N. B. (1987). *Peanut butter and jelly*. New York: Trumpet Club.

Williams, L. (1986). *The little old lady who wasnÕt afraid of anything*. New York: Harper and Row.

Wood, A. (1982). *Quick as a cricket*. Singapore: ChildÕs Play (International).

Zemach, M. (1965). *The teeny tiny woman*. New York: Scholastic.

Language Play Books

Ahlberg, J., & Ahlberg, A. (1978). *Each peach pear plum*. New York: Scholastic.

Benjamin, A. (1987). *Rat-a-tat, pitter pat*. New York: Harper.

Brown, M. (1994). *Four fur feet*. New York: Hyperion.

Carlstrom, N. W. (1987). *Wild wild sunflower child Anna*. New York: Macmillan.

Demming, A. G. (1994). *Who is tapping at my window?* Puffin.

Edwards, P. M. (1996). *Some smug slug*. New York: Harper-Collins.

Koch, M. (1991). *Hoot howl hiss*. New York: Greenwillow.

Komaiko, L. (1987). *Annie Bananie*. New York: Harper and Row.

LeCourt, N. (1991). *Abracadabra to zigzag*. New York: Lothrop, Lee and Shepard.

Melser, J. (1998). *One, one, is the sun*. Bothell, WA: Wright.

---

*Wordless books

Most, B. (1996). *Cock a doodle moo.* New York: Harcourt Brace.

Noll, S. (1987). *Jiggle wiggle prance.* New York: Greenwillow.

Paparone, P. (1995). *Five little ducks.* New York: Scholastic.

Plourde, L. (1997). *Pigs in the mud in the middle of the rud.* New York: Blue Sky.

Raschka, C. (1992). *Charlie Parker played be bop.* New York: Orchard.

Reddix, V. (1992). *Millie and the mud hole.* New York: Lothrop, Lee and Shepard.

Root, P. (1998). *One duck stuck.* Cambridge: Candlewick.

Seuss, Dr. (Theodore Geisel) (1957). *The cat in the hat.* New York: Random House.

Seuss, Dr. (Theodore Geisel) (1963). *Hop on pop.* New York: Random House.

Silverstien, S. (1964). *A giraffe and a half.* New York: Harper and Row.

Sonneborn, R. A. (1974). *Someone is eating the sun.* New York: Random House.

Thomas, P. (1990). *The one and only, super-duper, golly-whopper, Jim-dandy, really-handy, clock-tock-stopper.* New York: Lothrop, Lee and Shepard.

Watson, C. (1971). *Father FoxŌs penny-rhymes.* New York: Scholastic.

Wells, R. (1973). *Noisy Nora.* New York: Dial.

Wildsmith, B. (1986). *GoatŌs trail.* New York: Knopf.

Wood, A. (1987). *Heckedy Peg.* New York: Harcourt Brace Jovanovich.

Ziefert, H. (2002). *Who said moo?* New York: Handprint Books.

Multicultural Books

Barnwell, Y. (1998). *No mirrors in my nana's house.* New York: Harcourt Brace.

Baylor, B. (1986). *Hawk, I'm your brother.* New York: Scribner's.

Bruchac, J. (1985). *Iroquois stories: Heroes and heroines, monsters and magic.* Freedom, CA: The Crossing Press.

Bruchac, J., & Longdon, J. (1992). *Thirteen moons on turtle's back: A Native American year of moons.* New York: Philomel.

Bryan, A. (1977). *The dancing granny.* New York: Atheneum.

Bryan, A. (1986). *Lion and the ostrich chick and other African folk tales.* New York: Atheneum.

Bunting, E. (1998). *So far from the sea.* New York: Clarion.

Caines, J. (1982). *Just us women.* New York: Harper and Row.

Choi, S. (1993). *Hal Moni and the picnic.* Boston: Houghton Mifflin.

Clifton, L. (1970). *Some of the days of Everett Anderson.* New York: Holt, Rinehart and Winston.

Connolly, J. (1985). *Why the possum's tail is bare and other North American Indian nature tales.* Owings Mills, MD: Stemmer House.

Coutant, H., & Vo-Dinh. (1974). *First snow.* New York: Knopf.

Crews, D. (1991). *Big Mama's.* New York: Greenwillow.

Cruz Martinez, A. (1991). *The woman who out-shone the sun/La mujer que brillaba aun mas que el sol.* San Francisco: Children's Book Press.

Delacre, L. (1989). *Arroz con leche: Popular songs and rhymes from Latin America.* New York: Scholastic.

Delacre, L. (1990). *Las Navidades: Popular Christmas songs from Latin America.* New York: Scholastic.

Dorros, A. (1991). *Abuela.* New York: Dutton.

Garcia, R. (1987). *My Aunt Otilia's spirits.* San Francisco: Children's Book Press.

Garza, C. (1990). *Family pictures.* San Francisco: Children's Book Press.

Giovanni, N. (1985). *Spin a soft black song.* New York: HarperCollins.

Goble, P. (1989). *Iktomi and the berries.* New York: Orchard.

Goble, P. (1992). *Crow chief: A Plains Indian story.* New York: Orchard.

Greene, B. (1974). *Philip Hall likes me. I reckon maybe.* New York: Dial.

Greenfield, E. (1975). *Me and Nessie.* New York: Crowell.

Greenfield, E. (1978). *Honey, I love.* New York: Harper and Row.

Greenfield, E. (1988). *Grandpa's face.* New York: Philomel.

Greenfield, E. (1988). *Nathaniel talking.* New York: Black Butterfly Children's Books.

Hamilton, V. (1985). *The people could fly.* New York: Knopf.

Hamilton, V. (1992). *Drylongso.* New York: Harcourt Brace Jovanovich.

Havill, J. (1989). *Jamaica tag-along.* Boston: Houghton Mifflin.

Howard, E. (1991). *Aunt Flossie's hats (and crab cakes later)*. Boston: Houghton Mifflin.

Johnson, A. (1989). *Tell me a story, Mama*. New York: Orchard.

Johnson, A. (1990). *Do like Kyla*. New York: Orchard.

Martin, F. (2000). *Clever tortoise: A traditional African tale*. Cambridge: Candlewick.

Martinez, E., & Soto, G. (1993). *Too many tamales*. New York: Putnam.

Mathis, S. (1975). *The hundred penny box*. New York: Viking.

McKissack, P. (1986). *Flossie and the fox*. New York: Dial.

McKissack, P. (1989). *Nettie Jo's friends*. New York: Knopf.

Mollel, T. (1993). *The king and the tortoise*. New York: Houghton Mifflin.

Mollel, T. M. (1995). *Big boy*. New York: Clarion.

Ortiz, S. (1988). *The people shall continue*. San Francisco: Children's Book Press.

Pena, S. (1987). *Kikiriki: Stories and poems in English and Spanish for children*. Houston: Arte Publico Press.

Price, L. (1990). *Aida*. New York: Harcourt Brace Jovanovich.

Rohmer, H., & Anchondo, M. (1988). *How we came to the fifth world: Como vinimos al quinto mundo*. San Francisco: Children's Book Press.

Say, A. (1982). *The bicycle man*. Boston: Houghton Mifflin.

Say, A. (1988). *The lost lake*. Boston: Houghton Mifflin.

Say, A. (1990). *El Chino*. Boston: Houghton Mifflin.

Say, A. (1991). *Tree of cranes*. Boston: Houghton Mifflin.

Say, A. (1993). *Grandfather's journey*. Boston: Houghton Mifflin.

Say, A. (1997). *Allison*. Boston: Houghton Mifflin.

Sneeve, V. (1989). *Dancing teepees: Poems of American Indian youth*. New York: Holiday House.

Soto, G. (1993). *Too many tamales*. New York: Putnam.

Steptoe, J. (1969). *Stevie*. New York: Harper and Row.

Steptoe, J. (1987). *Mufaro's beautiful daughters*. New York: Lothrop, Lee and Shepard.

Strete, C. (1990). *Big thunder magic*. New York: Greenwillow.

Tafolla, C. (1987). *Patchwork colcha: A children's collection*. Flagstaff, AZ: Creative Educational Enterprises.

Takeshita, F. (1988). *The park bench*. New York: Kane/Miller.

Wright, C. (1994). *Jumping the broom*. New York: Holiday House.

Xiong, B. (1989). *Nine-in-one grr! grr! A folktale from the Hmong people of Laos*. San Francisco: Children's Book Press.

Yashima, R. (1958). *Umbrella*. New York: Viking.

Young, E. (1989). *Lon po po*. New York: Putnam.

Zhensun, A., & Low, A. (1991). *A young painter*. New York: Scholastic.

Information Books

Burton, J. (1989). *Animals keeping safe*. New York: Random House.

Canizares, S., & Chanko, P. (1998). *Water*. New York: Scholastic.

Copeland, C., & Lewis, A. (2002). *Funny faces, wacky wings, and other silly big bird things*. Brookfield, CT: Millbrook Press.

Editions, G. (1994). *A first discovery book: The rain forest*. New York: Scholastic.

Fletcher, N. (1993). *See how they grow: Penguin*. London: Dorling Kindersley.

Fowler, A. (1992). *Rookie read-about science: It could still be water*. Chicago: Children's Press.

George, J. (1999). *Morning, noon, and night*. New York: HarperCollins.

Gibbons, G. (1997). *The honey makers*. New York: Scholastic.

Intrater, R. (1995). *Two eyes, a nose, and a mouth*. New York: Scholastic.

Kottke, J. (2000). *How things grow: From seed to pumpkin*. New York: Scholastic.

Llewellyn, D. (1995). *Mighty machines: Tractor*. London: Dorling Kindersley.

Morris, A. (1989). *Bread, bread, bread*. New York: Scholastic.

Parsons, A. (1990). *Eyewitness juniors: Amazing spiders*. New York: Alfred A. Knopf.

Rehm, K., & Loike, K. (1991). *Left or right?* New York: Scholastic.

Walker-Hodge, J. (1998). *Eyewitness readers: Surprise puppy!* London: Dorling Kindersley.

APPENDIX

B

Preschool and Kindergarten Monitoring Assessments

Upper Case Alphabet Recognition
Child Administration Sheet

(Copy letters as presented on one sheet of paper for older children or copy each line of letters on separate index cards for younger children.)

O	B	S	A	T	M
Q	K	D	U	R	Z
C	F	N	W	Y	G
L	E	H	P	I	X
V	J				

Lower Case Alphabet Recognition
Child Administration Sheet

(Copy letters as presented on one sheet of paper for older children or copy each line of letters on separate index cards for younger children.)

o	a	c	e	g	m
b	s	r	u	t	z
f	n	w	y	d	l
h	p	I	x	v	j
q	k				

Preschool and Kindergarten Monitoring Score Sheet

Name of Child _____ Date of Administration _____

Upper Case Alphabet Recognition Task

(Use child administration sheet provided. Have child identify each letter. Circle letters correctly identified on score sheet.)

O	B	S	A	T	M
Q	K	D	U	R	Z
C	F	N	W	Y	G
L	E	H	P	I	X
V	J				

Lower Case Alphabet Recognition Task

(Use child administration sheet provided. Have child identify each letter. Circle letters correctly identified on score sheet.)

o	a	c	e	g	m
b	s	r	u	t	z
f	n	w	y	d	l
h	p	i	x	v	j
q	k				

Name Writing Task

Give child a sheet of paper and have child write his/her name. Score the signature:

Level 0: Uncontrolled scribble
Level 1: Controlled scribble such as mock cursive
Level 2: Separate marks that do not resemble letters
Level 3: One or two recognizable letters (may have orientation difficulties)
Level 4: Mostly recognizable letters (may have orientation difficulties)
Level 5: Recognizable and correct signature with few orientation difficulties
Level 6: First and last name using mostly correct formation

Writing Alphabet Task

(If child can write a signature at level 3 or higher, ask child to write letters in order presented on upper case alphabet recognition task. Score correct letters that are recognizable even if they have orientation difficulties.)

Concepts about Print Task

(Use a picture book with two pages that have just 2-3 lines of text.)

Bookhandling
(Hand the book to the child and ask child to)
1. show front   2. show back

(Open book and point to right hand page, ask child to)
3. point to top   4. point to bottom

Directionality
(Gesture down right hand page, and ask child "where do I read next?")
5. child must turn to next page

(Ask child on double spread, which page do I read first?)
6. child must point to left page

(Gesture down left hand page, ask child "where do I read after I read this page?")
7. child must point to right page

(Gesture down left page, ask child "where exactly would I begin to read this page?")
8. child must point to first word in first line of text

(Point to first word in first line of text, ask child "after I read this word, where do I read next?")
9. child must point to next word or sweep left to right across first line of text

(Sweep finger across first line of text, ask child "after I read this line, where do I read next?")
10. child must point to first word in second line of text

Letter and Word concepts
(Gesture down right page, ask child to)
11. show one letter   12. show one word

(Ask child to)
13. point to short word (child must point to word with 3 or fewer letters)
14. point to long word (child must point to word with 5 or more letters)

(Sweep finger across the first line of text, ask the child to
15. count words in line of text (child must count words accurately)

Phonological Awareness Task: Generating Rhyming Words

1. "Let's see how many rhyming words you can name for bat. I know one. Hat. Now you tell me words that rhyme with BAT." Count number of rhyming words generated for BAT (may count nonsense words)

2. "Now you tell me words that rhyme with LAKE." Count number of rhyming words generated for LAKE (may count nonsense words)

Phonemic Awareness Task: Isolating Beginning Sounds

("Today we are going to listen to sounds in the beginning of words. My word is boat. Boat begins with /b/, you say /b/. Let's try another one. My word is feet. Feet begins with /f/, you say /f/. Remember say the beginning sound of the word." If child gives the letter name, say, "that is the letter name. Say the sound." Only score the beginning sound correct, not the letter or portion of word.)

1. /r/ rain	2. /b/ bed	3. /k/ kite	4. /h/ horse
5. /b/ bunny	6. /w/ wig	7. /h/ house	8. /d/ duck
9. /t/ tire	10. /s/ sun		

Oral Comprehension and Vocabulary Task: Retelling Checklist for *Laney's Lost Momma* (Hamm, 1991)

"Here is the book we have been reading (show front cover only of book). Now you tell me everything you remember that happened in this story." Put a check beside each statement child makes in retelling (use gist of child's statement). Circle words in italics child uses in retelling. If child make statements not included in checklist, write statements on the checklist.

Laney and her Momma went shopping (shown in illustration only)
Laney is lost (inferred, but not stated)

> She peeked out from skirts *in the department store*
>
> She did not see Momma
>
> She looked around a *rack of* belts
>
> She looked in the *dressing rooms*
>
> The shoes were not her mother's

Laney feels scared

> She thinks Momma is lost
>
> She searches the *main aisle*
>
> She sees lots of women (summary)
>
> She does not see Momma

Laney did not go outside the store (inferred)

  Laney gets to the *large, glass* doors to leave the store

  Laney thinks Momma left without her

  She wants to run to the car

  She remembers what her mother told her

  Never leave the store without me

Momma discovers Laney is gone/lost (inferred, but not stated)

  Momma searches in the *women's department*

  She *peers* under the skirts and belts

  She asks *saleswoman* if she's seen Laney

Momma looks all over the store for Laney (summary, not stated)

  She *raced* down aisle in men's and boy's areas

  She goes to the outside door

  She is *worried* that Laney has left the store

  She remembers what she told Laney

  Never leave the store without me

  Momma did not leave the store

Meanwhile, Laney gets help (summary, inferred, but not stated)

  Laney's stomach hurts because she is worried

  She remembers something else her mother told her

  If you need help, go to someone who works behind a *counter*

  She tells the man in the *shoe department* she can't find her mother

  Laney says her mother's name is Momma

  Salesman tells Laney to sit over by the boots

  Loud voice in the ceiling says, Will Laney's Lost Momma please come to the shoe department

Laney and Momma find each other and go home (summary, not stated)

  Momma hears the announcement and runs to the shoe department

  Momma and Laney *race* to each other

  Momma sweeps up Laney and gives her a hug

  Laney and her mother go to get a treat

  They stay TOGETHER

  They get ice cream (shown in illustrations only)

Ideas _____/44

Vocabulary _____/12

Class Profile Preschool and Kindergarten Monitoring Assessments

Name	ABC	abc	name	Write abc	CAP	rhyme	Begin pho	Retell ideas	Retell vocab

APPENDIX

C

Preschool and Kindergarten Monitoring Assessments

ADVANCED ASSESSMENTS

Letter-Sound Association Child Administration Sheet

(Copy letters as presented on one sheet of paper.)

B	S	T	M		
K	D	R	Z		
C	F	N	W	Y	G
L	H	P			
V	J				

Finger-Point Reading Child Administration Sheet

(Make a booklet with four pages. Put the title on the first page. Pages:

2. I'm a little teapot,
   short and stout

3. Here is my handle.
   Here is my spout.

4. When I get all steamed up,
   then I shout.

5. Tip me over,
   and pour me out.

I'm a Little Teapot

I'm a little teapot,

short and stout.

Here is my handle.

Here is my spout.

When I get all steamed up,

Then I shout.

Tip me over,

and pour me out.

Preschool and Kindergarten Monitoring Score Sheet: Four Advanced Assessment

Name of Child _____ Date of Administration _____

Letter-Sound Association Task

(Use child administration sheet provided. Have child identify the sound of each letter. Circle on this score sheet letters for which child correctly identified sounds.)

B	S	T	M		
K	D	R	Z		
C	F	N	W	Y	G
L	H	P			
V	J				

Invented Spelling:

(Give the child a piece of paper. Say, "We're going to listen to sounds in words and then spell them. Like the word *tea*. I like hot tea in the winter and iced tea in the summer. I'm going to listen to the sounds in the word *tea*. /t/ I know that sound is spelled T. Let me listen again /t/ /E/ I hear E. " **Write Te on the child's paper.** "Now it's your turn. I'll say some words and you spell them by listening to the sounds."

1. man
2. bug
3. fit
4. trade

Scoring:

1. one sound represented with logical letter
2. beginning consonants represented with correct letter
3. beginning and ending consonants are represented
4. blends, long vowels, and short vowels are represented but some may not be spelled conventionally
5. conventional spelling of blends, long vowels, and short vowels

Finger-Point Reading

Prepare "I'm a Little Teapot" booklet with large font and extra large word spaces. Sing the nursery rhyme until child can say it verbatim from memory. Say, "Here is a book with the teapot rhyme in it. Watch as I say it and point to each word." Say the rhyme and point to each word. Invite the child to read along. Say, "This time I'll point to the words and you say the rhyme." Prompt children so that they successfully say each word as the you point to that word. Say, "Now you can point to the words and we'll say the rhyme together." Correct child's pointing as needed. Say, "Now you point at the words and say the rhyme." Teachers score one point for each line of text in which the child correctly points to each word while saying that exact word. No score is given if any word is incorrectly matched.

_____ I'm a little teapot

_____ short and stout.

_____ Here is my handle.

_____ Here is my spout.

_____ When I get all steamed up

_____ Then I shout.

_____ Tip me over

_____ and pour me out.

Locate Words in Finger-Point Reading Text

Say, "This poem has the word teapot. Let me show you." Reread the first line of text. Point to the word *teapot* and Say, "Here is the word *teapot*." "Now you show me the word *short*." Continue with all words. Score one point for each word correctly located.

1. short
2. here
3. spout
4. I
5. up
6. shout
7. tip
8. me

Reading Familiar Rhyming Words

Write the word *bat* on a small white board. Say, "This is the word *bat*. Now I am going to wipe off the letter *b* and make another word. I'll put on an *f*. Now the word is *fat*. Now let me wipe off the letter *f* and make another word. I'll put on an *r*. Now the word is *rat*. Now it's your turn. I'll put on some new letters and you read the words." Add the letters and have children read the word. Score 1 point for each word read correctly.

1. h   hat
2. m   mat
3. s   sat
4. v   vat
5. c   cat

Writing Familiar Rhyming Words

Write the word *big* on the white board. Say, "I wrote the word *big*. Now I am going to change it to the word *pig*. That word starts with /p/, I need a *p*." Erase the *b* and put on a *p*. "Now you are going to write some words. Write the word:" Score one point for each word correctly spelled.

1. fig
2. jig
3. mig
4. wig
5. zig

Class Profile Preschool and Kindergarten Monitoring Assessments: Advanced Assessments

Name	Letter-sound	Invented spelling	Finger-point reading	Locating words	Reading rhyming words	Writing rhyming words

Glossary

Additive Approaches Instructional methods that build on students' home languages and cultures. These contrast with subtractive approaches that attempt to replace children's home languages and cultures with English and mainstream culture. See *Subtractive Approaches.*

Affix A bound morpheme attached either at the beginning of a base word, in which case, it is a prefix, or at the end of a base word, in which case, it is a suffix. See *Bound Morpheme, Prefix,* and *Suffix.*

Alliteration Use of the same sound at the beginning of two or more words. For example, the sentence *Moldy macaroons make Michael mad* is alliterative.

Alphabet Recognition Looking at a letter of the alphabet and immediately saying its name. Also called *Letter Naming.*

Alphabetic Principle A guiding rule for reading and writing whereby both processes depend on the systematic use of sound-letter correspondences.

Alphabetic Reading and Writing Decoding and encoding text by systematically using sound-letter correspondences.

Analytic Talk Discussion that goes beyond the literal meaning presented in a text or in illustrations; children infer character traits and motivations, infer problems, connect events across parts of a book, infer cause-and-effect relationships, and construct explanations for why characters act as they do. For example, a child is engaged in analytic talk when he or she says, "I think Goldilocks should have known that that chair would break. It looks pretty flimsy to me." In contrast, a child who says, "Goldilocks sat on Baby Bear's chair, and it broke" is not engaged in analytic talk. See *Implied Meaning* and *Level of Cognitive Engagement.*

Anecdotal Notes Short written descriptions of events of brief duration, making note of participants' speech, reading, writing, or other actions, without judgment of quality.

Approximations The not fully realized products of children's incomplete literacy knowledge and ability. For example, their invented spellings are approximations of conventional spellings, their finger-point readings are approximations of correct word identification, and their mock letters are approximations of accurate alphabet writing.

Assessment See *Written Language Assessment.*

Assessment Notebook A record book in which a teacher keeps all of the anecdotal notes and analyses of those notes made for a class.

At-Risk Learners Children who struggle to learn even within literacy-rich classrooms and with a wide variety of instructional experiences.

Authentic Materials Materials that, although used for instructional purposes in school, also serve real-world purposes outside of school, for example, telephone books, catalogs, newspapers, magazines, maps, calendars, video tapes, and DVDs.

Authentic Text A text composed and read to serve readers' and writers' own communication needs rather than only to be a vehicle for instruction. For example, a birthday party invitation tells recipients that they are being invited to a birthday party, whose birthday is being celebrated, and when and where it will be held. A poem expresses the poet's feelings, creates an image, or expresses a personally significant idea. It allows the reader to share those feelings, images, and ideas or to create related, personal interpretations. See *Functional Text*.

Automatic Sight Vocabulary All the words that one can read immediately, on sight, without having to use decoding strategies. A reader looks at a sight word and recognizes it in less than one-tenth of a second. Efficient reading depends on readers' having most high-frequency words, especially those that are undecodable, in their automatic sight vocabularies. See *High-Frequency Words* and *Decodable Word*.

Balance of Rights The recognition that both students and their teacher have input in what is learned and how it is learned, in particular, that during instruction they share control of who speaks, what they speak about, and with whom they speak.

Basic Interpersonal Communication Skills (BICS) Language competence needed to interact with and communicate with friends and others in social and play situations. Basic Interpersonal Communication Skills include use of context and of concrete vocabulary. This is one way that they differ from Cognitive Academic Language Proficiency (CALP), which uses more abstract vocabulary. See *Cognitive Academic Language Proficiency (CALP)*.

Beginners Children in the first of the four broad phases of literacy development described in this book (see Chapter 2). Beginners are dependent on others for their reading and writing experiences. See *Novices, Experimenters,* and *Conventional Readers and Writers*.

Being Precise A child's taking care about how he or she matches saying particular words with seeing particular parts of text. Being precise, while not an act of word identification, does involve reading a text the same way across multiple readings because of using the exact words of the author and correctly matching the saying of those words with given parts of text. For example, a child cannot say "House" whenever shown a word card with the written word *house*. However, suppose his or her favorite storybook tells the story of the three little pigs and that one page's text is *The big, bad wolf huffed and puffed and blew their house down. The three little pigs ran into the forest.* A child who always says,

"Huffed and puffed and blew their house down" when coming to that page is being precise. A more advanced form of being precise, but which still is not accurate word identification, is finger-point reading. See *Finger-Point Reading*.

Big Book A large, display edition of a children's book.

Block Center A play space in a preschool or kindergarten classroom with a bin and shelf space for large cardboard blocks, large wooden blocks, smaller wooden blocks, durable cars and trucks, and related toys and displays.

Book Club A small group of children who decide to read a particular book or set of books together. They read the books independently or with partners but discuss the books and engage in response activities as a group.

Book Orientation Concepts Understandings of top and bottom with regard to a book's cover and its pages and of one-by-one and front-to-back page turning. Book Orientation Concepts are a subcategory of Concepts About Print. See *Concepts about Print*.

Bookhandling Skills Ways of looking at, holding, turning pages, and otherwise manipulating books in order for their texts and illustrations to be accessible for accurate meaning making. See *Concepts about Print*.

Booksharing Routines Familiar, expected actions and language that accompany book reading.

Bound Morpheme A morpheme that must be attached to another morpheme, cannot stand alone. See *Morpheme* and *Free Morpheme*.

Caregiver Interactive Responsiveness The degree to which parents and others who care for young children engage the children in give-and-take to which both parties contribute. Infants' contributions may not be intended as communication, but by responding as if they were so intended, adults establish interactive patterns that eventually become truly communicative, that is, intended as meaningful by both parties.

Centers Small partitioned spaces in classrooms, created by an arrangement of bookshelves and other dividers, such as a library center, a computer center, an art center, a writing center, a center for housekeeping and other dramatic play, a block center, and a center for puzzles and other manipulatives. See *Literacy Workstation*.

Children with Special Needs Children with challenging social and emotional behaviors, pronounced differences in learning styles or rates, or deficits in hearing, vision, or mobility.

Classroom Displays Materials placed on walls, shelves, or bulletin boards for children to see.

Classroom Environment The physical layout, schedule of instruction, and patterns of teacher-student and student-student interaction in a classroom.

Cognitive Academic Language Proficiency (CALP) Language competence needed to learn science, social studies, mathematics, and other school subjects. Cognitive Academic Language Proficiency includes abstract vocabulary. This is one way that it differs from Basic Interpersonal Communication Skills (BICS), which uses more concrete vocabulary. See *Basic Interpersonal Communication Skills (BICS)*.

Complex Sentence A sentence with at least one independent clause and one dependent clause (e.g., *I bought a jacket when I went to the mall*). An independent clause has its own subject and predicate and could stand alone if not part of the complex sentence (e.g., *I bought a jacket*). A dependent clause can not be a free-standing sentence (e.g., *when I went to the mall*). See *Compound Sentence, Simple Sentence,* and *Syntax.*

Compound Sentence A sentence with two or more independent clauses, joined by a conjunction, e.g., *I went to the mall and I bought a jacket.* An independent clause has its own subject and predicate and could stand alone if not part of the compound sentence. See *Complex Sentence, Compound Sentence,* and *Syntax.*

Comprehensible Input Speech to English language learners characterized by fewer words in an utterance, a slower rate of speaking, and greater use of very familiar words. This simplified language is supported by pointing and using other gestures, repetition, pictures, and dramatic movements.

Comprehensive Reading Program An approach to teaching reading to all children in an elementary school, including a scope and sequence of skills that will be taught at each grade level, materials that are to be read at each grade level, assessments to determine what children need to learn and to check whether they have learned what they have been taught, materials useful for reteaching when chil-

dren demonstrate a need for it, and provisions for reading intervention.

Concept of Story A person's schema for story. A child's concept of story develops from very simple notions, such as that a story has a beginning, a middle, and an end, to the more complex notions embodied in story grammar. See *Story Grammar.*

Concept of Word Boundaries An aspect of Concept of Written Word. Children's knowledge that words in written text are bounded by the spaces between them. See *Concept of Written Word.*

Concept of Written Word Knowledge that words are composed of combinations of letters, that words in written text are bounded by the spaces between them, and that the sounds within them are related to alphabet letters. See *Metalinguistic Awareness* and *Phonemic Awareness.*

Concepts about Print (CAP) Understandings about how texts work, how they are configured, and how a reader approaches them, including that alphabet letters are a special category of visual symbols and that one reads the print rather than the pictures in a picture book. See *Bookhandling Skills, Book Orientation Concepts,* and *Directionality Concepts.*

Confusable Letters Alphabet letters that beginners easily mistake for one another. For example, *N* is easily mistaken for *Z*; they are alike except for orientation in space (*N* is a rotated *Z*).

Consonant Blend See *Consonant Cluster.*

Consonant Cluster Two or three consonants together in a word, for example, *cl* and *st* in *cluster, fr* and *nt* in *front,* and *str* in *street.* Also called a *consonant blend.*

Consonant Digraph A two-letter spelling of a consonant phoneme. In English, consonant digraphs include *ch* for /ch/, *ph* and *gh* for /f/, *mb* for /m/, *ng* for /ng/, *sh* for /sh/, *th* for /th/ and /TH/ (see Table 1.2). They also include double consonant spellings, such as *ff* for /f/. See *Consonant Phonemes.*

Consonant Phonemes One of the two major categories of sounds in a language. The other is *vowel phonemes.* Consonant sounds involve a more restricted flow of sound than do vowel sounds, and so they are sometimes described as having friction. Vowels involve a more open, unrestricted flow of sound and are sometimes described as lacking friction. Consonant phonemes are more numerous than vowels. They are usually spelled with only one letter, but sometimes with two letters. Two-letter consonant spellings (for example, *sh* for /sh/ or *ph* for /f/) are called *consonant digraphs*. In English, consonant phonemes include /b/, /ch/, /d/, /f/, /g/, /h/, /j/, /k/, /l/, /m/, /n/, /ng/, p/, /r/, /s/, /sh/, /t/, /th/, /TH/, /v/, /w/, /y/, /z/, and /zh/ (see Table 1.2). See *Vowel Phonemes* and *Consonant Digraph.*

Content-Specific Vocabulary Words that are unique to science, social studies, or another content area, or have meanings when used in those areas that are different from their meanings in everyday conversation.

Contextual Dependency A text's reliance on the situation of its composition for the conveying of its meaning. A mock cursive text, for example, cannot be read on its own. If, however, one was present when a child composed the text, then it is meaningful. For example, if during children's restaurant play, a teacher hears a child in the role of waiter repeat a customer's order for coffee and a donut, then the teacher can read the waiter's wavy lines on a pad of paper as "'Coffee' and 'donut.'" Another name for *Contextual Dependency* is the *Sign Concept*.

Contextualization Clues Elements of a situation that contribute to understanding a message. Contextualization clues include gestures, facial expressions, and intonation, but can also include shared knowledge. A child and her mother use contextualization clues when they enter a McDonald's restaurant for the hundredth or even tenth time in the young child's life. When the mother asks, "What do you want?" the child knows that the mother means "What do you want *to eat?*" and that the options include a hamburger and French fries, but not turkey with dressing and gravy.

Contextualized Language Language that occurs amid people, objects, actions, and events, and along with facial expression, gesture, and other forms of body language (e.g., head nodding, head shaking, and body leaning). Spoken language is almost always contextualized in this way, so in addition to information conveyed by words, information is also available from these sources in the context. In contrast, written language usually lacks these sources, and so the written words must do more of work of conveying meaning. See *Decontextualized Language.*

Continuants Consonant phonemes whose pronunciations can be prolonged or stretched out. For example, one can say /s/ for as long as one has enough breath. In contrast, non-continuants can be spoken only in an instant; one cannot, for example, stretch out the pronunciation of /b/. It is difficult to pronounce non-continuants in isolation; one almost always adds a vowel sound, usually /uh/. This sometimes causes teachers mistakenly to pronounce non-continuants as continuants by adding the phoneme /uh/. They say, for example, that the sound of the letter *B* is /buh/, and they stretch out the /uh/ part of /buh/. This can confuse students; what they are hearing and paying attention to is not the phoneme /b/, but the teacher's prolonged pronunciation of the phoneme /uh/.

Continuous Text A text of a sufficient number of words to require building meaning across words, as in a poem, a storybook, or an information book. Words do not stand in isolation, but instead work together, as in a line or a stanza of a poem or a sentence or paragraph of a story or an essay. For example, the five words of the phrase *under a twisted, old tree* convey a single image; the five words of that phrase work together, they have coherence, such that the meaning of the phrase accrues as a reader processes the string of words. The words have meaning together that they lack in isolation. *Under* by itself is an abstract notion, a way of dividing space in general, but *under a tree* denotes a particular kind of space, a very specific place. *A twisted, old tree* conveys an expected image; trees often become twisted as they adjust to their environments over long periods of time. If the phrase had been *under a twisted sapling,* readers would be forced to create an unusual, unexpected image, one that might cause them to wonder how a sapling became twisted (in strong wind? as a victim of vandalism?). Furthermore, the space described by *under a sapling* is different, much smaller, than the space described by *under an old tree.* Similar but more complex processes of coherence building and accruing of meaning happen with texts longer than phrases when writers and readers use syntax to compose and understand sentences, and story grammar and expository text structures to compose and understand stories and informational texts.

Conventional Readers and Writers Children in the fourth of the four broad phases of literacy development described in this book (see Chapter 5). Their reading and writing increasingly resembles what adults in their language community would call "really reading and writing." See *Beginners, Novices,* and *Experimenters.*

Conventions of Written Language The characteristics of texts and the practices and processes for understanding and producing it that are accepted, expected, and used by accomplished readers and writers in a written language community. All writers and readers of English, for example, accept, expect, and use the convention of associating the letters *ph* with the phoneme /f/. Writers and readers of fairy tales accept, expect, and often use the convention of beginning a fairy tale with the phrase *Once upon a time*. Writers and readers of newspaper reporting accept, expect, and often use the convention of an opening paragraph that tells who, what, when, and where.

Core Reading Programs Commercial products promoted as having all that teachers and students need for the students to achieve grade-level expectations through daily instruction and practice in phonics and phonemic awareness, vocabulary, comprehension, and fluency.

Critical Interpretation A reader's appreciation of how literary forces interact with nonliterary (e.g., political, economical) forces in society and culture, especially of how a story might affect a reader's position in society and culture.

Cultural Discontinuity A mismatch between the texts that are written and read, purposes for reading and writing, and ways of reading and writing of the home and those of the school.

Culturally Authentic Literature Fiction and nonfiction that portray the people and the values, customs, and beliefs of a cultural group in ways recognized by members of that group as valid and truthful. See *Multicultural Literature.*

Culturally Responsive Instruction Instruction that is "consistent with the values of students' own cultures and aimed at improving academic learning."*

Curriculum What teachers plan to teach and expect that children will learn.

Curriculum Integration Involving students in learning from more than one subject area at a time. See *Integrated Language Arts Activity* and *Integrated Content Unit.*

Daily Oral Language A whole-class word work and punctuation activity in which children look for and correct errors deliberately included in a teacher-written text, usually as part of a class's opening-of-the-day routine. The text's topic is often related to a current unit of study or to a special occasion or planned school event.

Decodable Word A word that a reader can identify by applying phonics generalizations. For example, *pin* is decodable as /pin/, using the phonics generalization that the vowel in a CVC word is short, and *pine* is decodable as /pīn/, using the phonics generalization that in a CVCe word, the final *e* is silent and the first vowel is long. Not all words are decodable, for example, *put*, which is an exception to the CVC generalization (it is pronounced /poot/, not the predicted /puht/), and *love*, which is an exception to the CVCe generalization (it is pronounced /luhv/, not the predicted /lōv/). See *Phonics.*

Decoding The ability to look at an unknown word—that is, a word that is not a sight word, that the reader cannot identify automatically, on sight—and to produce a pronunciation that is accurate—that is, a pronunciation that identifies the word as one that the reader knows from his or her spoken vocabulary. See *Phonics, Fully Phonemic Decoding* and *Decoding by Analogy.*

Decoding an Unfamiliar Word Identifying an unknown, decodable word using phonics and—if the word occurs in continuous text—grapho-syntax and grapho-semantics. See *Phonics, Grapho-Syntax,* and *Grapho-Semantics.*

Decoding Analysis An examination of a child's reading miscues in order to determine what strategies he or she uses, overuses, or underuses when attempting to identify unknown, decodable words. See *Miscue Analysis, Running Record,* and *Decodable Word.*

Decoding by Analogy Identifying an unknown word by using familiar word parts and knowledge of orthographic patterns, such as phonograms, suffixes, and affixes. Also called *Orthographic Decoding.* For example, familiarity with the phonogram *-it* and the prefix *un-* helps a reader to identify the word *unfit* by recognizing in it the base word *fit*

*Quoted from *Literacy Instruction in Multicultural Settings* (p. 13) by K. Au, 1993, New York: Harcourt Brace Jovanovich.

(from the *-it* word family with the consonant *f* added) and the prefix *-un* (a morpheme meaning *not*). This is decoding by analogy because it involves seeing that *unfit* is like other words in the *-it* word family and other words with the prefix *un-*. See *Phonogram, Orthography, Morpheme,* and *Derivational Words.*

Decoding Coaching All that a teacher might do or say during embedded instruction to support a child in successfully applying phonics generalizations. See *Embedded Phonics Instruction.*

Decontextualized Language Language that greatly depends on itself for meaning. Spoken language usually occurs amid people, objects, actions, and events, and along with facial expression, gesture, and other forms of body language, and so it is contextualized by those co-occurences. Written language, however, lacks those means of reinforcing its message, and so, compared to spoken language, it is relatively decontextualized. When making meaning, readers' only resources are the text's words and the related understandings that the readers had before beginning to read. See *Contextualized Language.*

Derivational Words Words composed by adding prefixes, suffixes, or both to base words. For example, *unhappily* is composed of the base word *happy,* the prefix *un-* (meaning not), and the suffix *-ly* (meaning that *unhappily* functions as an adverb; without *-ly,* it functions as an adjective). See *Morpheme.*

Developmental Spelling Inventory A list of words that children are asked to spell. Their spellings are then analyzed to determine which spelling patterns and spelling strategies—characteristic of various stages of spelling development—they use.

Dictation A child's slowly speaking a message or telling a story as a teacher or other adult writes it, usually for later reading by the adult and child.

Direct Instruction Teaching by modeling how to perform a task and thinking aloud during performance of the task in order to provide explicit explanations of mental activities. Outcomes, that is, what children show they know and can do, are determined ahead of time by the teacher's choices of a task and criteria for children's successful completion of that task. See *Indirect Instruction, Embedded Instruction,* and *Explicit Instruction.*

Directionality Concepts Understandings that print is read from top to bottom and from left to right. Directionality Concepts are a subcategory of Concepts about Print. See *Concepts about Print* (CAP).

Drafting A writing process in which a writer first commits ideas to paper in a first draft. The purpose of a first draft is to begin preserving thoughts in print, without concern for structure, coherence, or correctness of punctuation or spelling. Later in the writing process, revising will result in better structured, more coherent drafts and editing will produce a final draft that meets a writer's current standards for punctuation and spelling (less stringent standards for beginners and higher standards for accomplished writers). See *Prewriting, Revising, Editing,* and *Publishing.*

Dramatic-Play-with-Print Centers Dramatic play centers that contain reading and writing materials relevant to the theme of the dramatic play (e.g., an appointment book and pen next to a telephone in a doctor's office play center). Availability of such materials and teacher modeling promote children's reading and writing as part of their dramatic play.

Dynamic Ability Grouping Forming small groups for reading and writing instruction based on students' similar abilities and needs and using texts carefully matched to those abilities and needs.

Early Production The second of four phases of children's second language acquisition, notable for children's attempting to speak, but still using very limited language, drawing on the words and gestures learned in vocabulary games or other interactions during the first, mostly silent phase. See *Pre-production, Speech Emergence,* and *Intermediate Fluency.*

Early Readers and Writers The first of three phases of conventional reading and writing (see Chapter 5). Early readers and writers can produce simple texts that others can read. They can read with accuracy their own compositions and other simple texts, such as storybooks. See *Conventional Readers and Writers, Transitional Readers and Writers,* and *Self-Generative Readers and Writers.*

Editing A writing process in which a writer produces a final draft that meets his or her current standards for punctuation and spelling. Those standards depend on what a writer has already learned about punctuation and spelling. They are less stringent for beginners, who know fewer correct spellings and know less about punctuation, and higher for accomplished writers, who have learned more from reading and writing experience, mini-lessons, and other instruction in writing workshop. See *Prewriting, Drafting, Revising, Publishing,* and *Editing Checklist.*

Editing Checklist A list of punctuation and spelling expectations for a writer or group of writers to use when preparing a final draft of a piece. These expectations depend on what writers have already learned about punctuation and spelling. They are less stringent for beginners, because beginners know fewer correct spellings and know less about punctuation. They are higher for accomplished writers who have learned more from reading and writing experience, mini-lessons, and other instruction in writing workshop. See *Editing* and *Mini-Lesson.*

Elements of Informational Texts The components of a well-crafted exposition. One way to characterize a well-crafted exposition is in terms of its topic presentation, description of attributes, characteristic events, category comparison, and final summary. Another way is in terms of its consistency, ordered relationships, and hierarchical relationships. See *Exposition.*

Elkonin Boxes See *Say-It and Move-It Activity.*

ELL Interactive Read-Aloud Procedure A technique that teaches vocabulary and comprehension to English language learners, using longer, more complex picture books, both narrative and informational, than they can read on their own. Students read only a third or a fourth of a book each day for three or four successive days, with rereadings and with concentrated instruction about selected vocabulary.

Embedded Instruction Teaching by providing a meaningful reading and writing experience for a whole class or small group of children that includes opportunities for individual children to participate at levels appropriate to their unique needs and phases of development.

Embedded Phonics Instruction Phonics instruction that occurs while children are reading continuous, authentic, and functional texts, such as in guided reading instruction or writing in journals.

English Language Learner (ELL) One whose home language is other than English and who is learning English in a school setting. English language learners are expected also to learn all the usual subjects taught in school and often with most of the teaching of those subjects being in English.

Environmental Print Text found in everyday settings, such as print on signs, clothing, and storefronts, and in logos.

Environmental Print Puzzle A food box-front or other environmental print item cut into puzzle pieces and stored with an identical, uncut item. Children's attention to print is stimulated as they place the puzzle pieces onto the uncut item until it is covered by the fully reassembled puzzle. See *Environmental Print.*

Experimenters Children in the third of the four broad phases of literacy development described in this book (see Chapter 4). Experimenters understand the alphabetic principle; with their reading and writing, they investigate the power and the implications of sound-letter correspondences. See *Alphabetic Principle, Beginners, Novices,* and *Conventional Readers and Writers.*

Explicit Instruction Teaching that includes specifying of learning outcomes, modeling of processes, thinking aloud, and explaining. Deliberately and clearly stating what students are to learn. Explicit instruction has much in common with *Direct Instruction* and is usually part of an instructional sequence called *Gradual Release of Responsibility.*

Exposition Non-narrative, nonfictional text. Expositions serve such purposes as making arguments, persuading, explaining, describing, and instructing. The forms they take include essay, article, how-to text, thesis, biography, textbook, documentary, and exposé. Also called *Expository Text.*

Expository Text. See *Exposition.*

Extended Discourse Sustained conversation or lengthy writing for a variety of purposes and with a variety of partners or audiences.

Feature A component of a schema. A schema for the concept of *house* contains such features as *walls, windows, doors, roof, chimney.*

Finger-Point Reading Putting a finger or other pointer such as a ruler onto a discrete part of a text for each spoken part of a reading, using left-to-right directionality, but without necessarily correctly matching spoken and written words and without being able to correctly identify the same written words in other contexts. For example, a child may point one-by-one, from left to right to the words of the written text *Old Mother Hubbard went to the cupboard* while saying "Old Moth -er Hub -bard went to" and perhaps stop there or perhaps continue with "the cup -board" while pointing to the first three words of the next line of text. Finger-point reading is developmental. Eventually the child will correctly match saying the seven words of that line of the nursery rhyme with pointing to the seven written words. And finger-point can lead to "real reading." The child who can correctly match his or her spoken words with the words of the text may eventually use what he or she notices about that matching to identify those words in print even outside of the context of the memorized nursery rhyme.

Fluent Reading Reading with quick and accurate word recognition and appropriate prosody (voicing and phrasing). Fluent reading includes a component of comprehension because readers cannot read with appropriate phrasing if they do not understand what they are reading.

Forms See *Written Language Forms.*

Formulaic Speech Words or phrases that occur repeatedly and predictably in routine social situations. Their meanings are usually nonliteral; they serve instead to indicate the nature or boundaries of the situation. For example, *How are you?* is not usually intended as a request for information about a person's health. Instead it is a ritual greeting and often marks the beginning of a conversation, equivalent to *Hi* or *Hello.* When formulaic speech occurs as a phrase rather than a single word, for example, *What's up?* instead of *Hello,* that phrase nonetheless conveys meaning as a single unit rather than as a combination of the usual meanings of the words. As such, it works as if it were a single word and the rules of syntax (which is about building meanings from combinations of individually meaningful words) are irrelevant. This is especially apparent when, as often happens, the phrase is contracted to a single word, as, for example, when *What's up?* becomes *'Tsup?* Another example of a formulaic expression is *So long,* which functions as an expression of good will on the occasion of a departure. The meanings of *so* and *long,* even if relevant to the expression long ago when it originated, no longer have in this expression either their usual meanings or any syntactic roles; *so long* works as a single semantic unit. Formulaic expressions in children's

speech almost always work in this way. For example, a child can use *Give me* (usually pronounced "Gimme") as a formulaic request for an object without necessarily knowing the individual meanings of *Give* and *me* or being able to use those separate words meaningfully in other contexts. (It is likely a child will know the meaning of *me* and use it in other situations long before doing so with *give.*) See *Implied Meaning, Literal Meaning, Vocabulary, Semantics,* and *Syntax.*

Free Morpheme A morpheme that can stand alone, is not required to be attached to another morpheme. See *Morpheme* and *Bound Morpheme.*

Frustrational Reading Level The level of text that a child reads with below 70 percent comprehension and below 90 percent word accuracy. See *Instructional Reading Level* and *Independent Reading Level.*

Fully Phonemic Decoding Pronouncing all the phonemes of a printed word by making use of all its letters and letter combinations.

Functional Text A text that serves authentic purposes in people's everyday home and classroom lives. Functional texts can be used for instruction, but their primary function is to help people get things done in their everyday lives that they would not as easily accomplish without the texts. For example, a company directory helps people determine employees' positions and roles and how to contact them; a donors list helps people to know who gave gifts, who should be thanked, and who might respond favorably to solicitations for additional donations; and an owner's manual helps people to operate a newly acquired appliance, electronic device, or vehicle. See *Authentic Text.*

Functions of Written Language Purposes served by reading and writing. These include the functions of spoken language (instrumental, regulatory, interactional, personal, heuristic, imaginative, and representational) and additional writing-specific functions, such as recording and reminding.

Gradual Release of Responsibility An instructional sequence that begins with the teacher's explicit instruction about a single concept or strategy, one that can be expressed in the performance of a discrete task, and then proceeds with the teacher's gradually facilitating students' performance of that task, until students can perform it independently. See *Explicit Instruction.*

Grand Conversation A book discussion prompted by a teacher's open-ended question, such as "What do you think?' but guided by children's comments and questions rather than by the teacher's continued questioning.

Grapho-Phonics See *Phonics.*

Grapho-Semantics One of three interrelated systems for linking the forms of written language to its meanings. Grapho-semantics is the use of meanings of words and word parts (morphemes) to make effective use of written forms. Consider, for example, the written sentence *The artist is sculpting a statue.* And suppose a reader does not recognize the word *sculpting.* Knowing the meanings of *artist* and *statue* predisposes the reader to expect the written word *sculpting* to name something having to do with artists and statues, that some artists make statues through the process of *sculpting.* Efficient readers will use grapho-semantics in conjunction with the other two systems for linking forms and meanings. For example, they will use phonics to determine the sounds in the initial consonant blend (*sc*) and the final consonant blend (*lpt*) of *sculpt*, and will use grapho-syntax to determine that *sculpt* is part of this sentence's verb. In fact, they will see that it is part of the present progressive verb form *is sculpting*, and so it names a continuing action that is taking place in the present. See *Morpheme, Semantics, Phonics,* and *Grapho-Syntax.*

Grapho-Syntax One of three interrelated systems for linking the forms of written language to its meanings. Grapho-syntax is the use of sentence structure knowledge to make effective use of written forms. Consider, for example, the written sentence *The artist is sculpting a statue.* And suppose a reader does not recognize the word *sculpting.* The syntactic knowledge of the present progressive verb tense—that in English it takes that the form *is _____ing*—predisposes the reader to expect a verb after the word *is* and before the suffix *ing.* Efficient readers will use grapho-syntax in conjunction with the other two systems for linking forms and meanings. For example, they will use phonics to determine the sounds in the initial consonant blend (*sc*) and the final consonant blend (*lpt*) of *sculpt*, and will use grapho-semantics to determine that the action named by the verb form *sculpt* is something that artists do to statues. See *Syntax, Phonics,* and *Grapho-Semantics.*

Guided Drawing The teacher's demonstrating basic strokes and shapes used in drawing and writing, such as vertical, horizontal, and slanting lines and circles, squares, triangles, and dots.

Guided Reading Instruction in which the teacher selects a particular text for children to read and then directs and supports children as they read that text.

Guided Reading Approach A method of teaching reading and writing emphasizing strategic reading and using leveled texts and dynamic ability grouping. See *Strategic Readers, Leveled Texts,* and *Dynamic Ability Grouping.*

Guided Spelling Spelling instruction for small groups of children with similar abilities. Instruction is about spelling patterns the members of a group are just beginning to recognize and use.

High-Frequency Words Words that appear often in just about any text that is longer than a few sentences. High-frequency words usually are grammatical words, that is, words that create sentence structure and coherence, such as articles (*the, a, an*), prepositions (e.g., *of, from, with*), conjunctions (*and, or, but*), pronouns (e.g., *I, she, us*), auxiliary verbs (e.g., *have, been*), and all forms of the verb *to be* (e.g., *am, were, is*) rather than content words that name objects, actions, and qualities (e.g., *house, run, big*). Experts have compiled lists of high-frequency words (e.g., The Dolch word list), which if learned as sight words, enable a reader to read a large proportion of words in almost any text automatically, thus freeing him or her to devote conscious attention to other reading processes, such as identifying unfamiliar words and comprehending the text. See *Sight Words* and *Orchestration.*

Home Center See *Housekeeping Center.*

Homographs Words that are spelled the same but do not sound alike, such as *bow* in *bow and arrow* and *bow* in *bow to the king.* See *Homophones.*

Homophones Words that sound alike but are not spelled the same, such as *bare* and *bear.* See *Homographs.*

Housekeeping Center A play space in a preschool or kindergarten classroom with toy kitchen and other household furnishings and supplies and related toys and displays, including dress-up costumes. Also called a *Home Center.*

"I Can Hear" Talk Teachers' demonstrating that they notice sounds and sound patterns in words they read during a storybook read-aloud or write during a shared writing activity. For example, after reading a page containing the words *stumble* and *fumble,* the teacher might say, "Oh, listen! Those words rhyme: *Stumble* and *fumble.* I can hear *-umble* in both of them: *st-umble* and *f-umble.*" Interspersing just a few instances of "I can hear" talk in a storybook read-aloud or a shared writing activity can heighten children's phonological awareness. See *Interactive Read-Aloud, Shared Writing,* and *Phonological Awareness.*

"I Can Read" Bag A paper bag with a child's name and the label *I can read,* in which the child keeps coupons, food wrappers, food box-fronts, and other environmental print items that he or she has learned to read. During choice time, children can read items from their "I can read" bags to one another. See *Environmental Print.*

Implied Meaning Messages or information inferable from but not explicitly stated in the words of a text nor shown in an illustration. Also called *Inferential Meaning.* The opposite of implied meaning is literal meaning or that which is explicitly stated in a text or shown in an illustration. For example, a possible implied meaning of the text *Samantha never failed to take her dog Rex for a walk before school, and she couldn't wait to give him a big hug when she got home* is that Samatha loved her dog Rex. For that to be a text's literal meaning, the text would have to be *Samantha loved her dog Rex.* See *Literal Meaning.*

Independent Reading Level The level of text that a child can read on his or her own, without a teacher's support, determined from 96–100 percent word reading accuracy and 91–100 percent correct responses to comprehension questions. See *Individualized Reading Inventory* and *Instructional Reading Level.*

Indirect Instruction Teaching by providing materials and opportunities for children to learn from doing and from watching others. The teacher plans activities to allow children to respond in their own ways, with multiple acceptable responses. See *Direct Instruction* and *Embedded Instruction.*

Individualized Reading Inventory A commercially published collection of grade leveled texts (from pre-primer to middle school, or even high school), used to determine a child's instructional and independent reading levels. See *Instructional Reading Level, Independent Reading Level,* and *Running Record.*

Inferential Meaning See *Implied Meaning.*

Inquiry Unit Study of a particular topic for which children observe, participate in experiments or other hands-on experiences, read from a variety of texts, and communicate their findings often through writing.

Instructional Reading Level The level of text that a child can read with a teacher's support, determined from 90-95 percent word reading accuracy and 70-90 percent correct responses to comprehension questions. See *Individualized Reading Inventory* and *Independent Reading Level.*

Integrated Content Unit A unit of study planned around a broad theme that includes concepts from more than one content area. Instructional activities provide for active inquiry and incorporate all the language arts.

Integrated Language Arts Activity A single activity involving students in more than one of the processes of reading, writing, listening, and speaking. See *Curriculum Integration.*

Interactive Bookreading A book-sharing experience by a child and a more knowledgeable other person, usually an adult, to which both contribute. During interactive bookreading, for example, the adult invites the child to participate in the making of meanings from the book's texts and illustrations and responds to the child's gestures, facial expressions, statements, questions, and reading attempts by validating, elaborating, and clarifying.

Interactive Pocket Chart Activities Game-like activities placed in a pocket chart. In preschool, for example, teachers may display cards with alphabet letters for children to use in spelling their own names and names of classmates. In kindergarten, cards with pictures of objects may be displayed for sorting by the beginning sounds of the objects' names. In third grade, phrases that are subjects and predicates may be displayed for children to use to build sentences.

Interactive Read-Aloud Reading aloud a storybook or information book to a group of children, allowing them, during the reading, to ask and answer questions, predict outcomes, and make other comments. Interactive read-alouds have many of the features of interactive bookreading, but they are done with groups rather than individual children. See *Interactive Bookreading.*

Interactive Writing Instruction in which the teacher and students write on chart paper. The teacher helps the children to determine what will be written and then selects children to step up to the chart and write words or parts of words. During interactive writing, teachers model for children how to write texts that serve a variety of purposes. See *Shared Writing.*

Intermediate Fluency The fourth of four phases of children's second language acquisition, noteable for children's having acquired sufficient vocabulary and fluency with a variety of sentence structures that they are ready to acquire academic concepts in reading, writing, math, and science. See *Preproduction, Early Production,* and *Speech Emergence.*

Internet Workshop An approach to teaching about the internet that includes regularly scheduled time for children to work online ("workshop time"). Teachers teach mini-lessons about using the internet, students and teachers hold conferences to review and plan internet research around a topic of inquiry, and students share results of internet research. See *Inquiry Unit.*

Invented Spelling Children's systematic but not conventional matching of sounds in words (phonemes) with letters. Invented spelling is developmental, that is, it moves from less to more sophisticated representations. Early invented spellings may be single letters for beginning sounds of words (for example, *M* for *mouse*) and often rely on children's knowledge of letter names and attention to sounds in those names (for example, /m/ in *em,* the name of the letter *M,* which is also the sound at the beginning of the word *mouse*). Later invented spellings, though still not conventional, combine visual and auditory strategies. The visual strategies come from what children have seen in books and environmental print. For example, in the spelling MOSS for *mouse,* the choices of the letters *M, O,* and *S* show awareness of the phonemes /m/, /ow/, and /s/ in beginning, middle, and final positions of *mouse* and awareness of the same or similar phonemes in the names of those letters, but the use of the double *SS* shows also the inventive speller's familiarity with final double consonants in English—from seeing such words as *grass* and *kiss.* See *Phoneme, Phonemic Awareness, Meaning-Form Links,* and *Orthography.*

Journal Writing Children's daily independent writing about personal topics.

Kid Watching Informal observation of children as they use reading and writing independently in play or in groups that have been assigned a literacy task.

Kid Writing A teacher-supported activity in which children decide on a short message, make lines to indicate each word that will be needed to write that message, listen to the sounds in each word, and write the sounds they hear.

Language- and Print-Rich Classrooms Classrooms that accelerate children's language and literacy development through abundant exposure to and opportunity to use spoken and written language.

Language Play Books Books that feature rhyme and alliteration, inviting children's attention to the sounds of a language.

Language Scaffold A teacher's intentional sustaining of conversation to provide children with models of new vocabulary and sentence structures, for example, by repeating but expanding on a child's utterance. When a child says, "Milk!" an adult might say, "Oh, would you like some milk? Just a minute. I'll get you some milk. . . . Here's your milk. Drink up!" Scaffolding of talk supports children's understanding even when they know very little of the vocabulary included in the talk. The term *scaffolding* implies not just support, but also that the support is removable. As children show greater competence, their need for language scaffolding decreases.

Learning The process of acquiring knowledge. One way to characterize learning is in terms of schemas: Learning involves adding to or changing schemas through the processes of assimilation and accommodation. See *Schema.*

Letter Features The lines from which letters of the alphabet are composed. These include straight lines and curves, horizontals, verticals, and diagonals.

Letter Game A sorting activity in which pairs of children put laminated letter shapes cut from construction paper into pasteboard boxes labeled with those letters, usually no more than three boxes and letters for one play session. Teachers model talking about the letters as part of the play. As a player places a *K*-shaped cut-out into the *K* box, for example, the player might identify the letter and remind his or her partner of a classmate's name that starts with that letter.

Letter Naming Looking at a letter of the alphabet and immediately identifying it. Also called *Alphabet Recognition.*

Letter Strings Lines of letters that do not include words and are not invented spellings. See *Invented Spelling.*

Letter-Like Forms Symbols that look like conventional letters of the alphabet because they are composed of letter features, but are not conventional letters. These are also called *Mock Letters.*

Level of Cognitive Engagement The degree to which children's talking and acting demonstrate that they are thinking and learning in response to what a teacher or caregiver presents to or shares with them. For example, when listening to a storybook reading, children show a high level of cognitive engagement when they ask relevant questions, make predictions, or share related experiences. Teachers promote a high level of cognitive engagement when their reading is interspersed with reminders of what children already know about a book's topic, relevant comments about texts and illustrations, and questions that demand more than literal meanings from what was read. See *Thinking* and *Learning.*

Leveled Books See *Leveled Texts.*

Leveled Texts A series of books used for reading instruction that are calibrated and labeled by degree of difficulty. Low-level texts, which are repetitive and use few words, are easier than high-level texts, which use more words, convey more information, and use more complex and more literary language.

Linear Scribble Writing Horizontally arranged wavy lines. These are also called *Mock Cursive.*

Listening Level The level of text for which a child can answer correctly at least 75 percent of questions and which teachers use to choose books for read-alouds. See *Instructional Reading Level, Independent Reading Level,* and *Frustrational Reading Level.*

Literacy Workstation A classroom space—often an already existing center—designated for children's individual use of materials previously used for group instruction. These materials serve children's meaningful practice of reading and writing independent of the teacher. See *Centers.*

Literal Meaning Messages or information explicitly stated in the words of a text or shown in an illustration. The opposite of literal meaning is implied meaning or that which must be inferred from the text or illustrations because it is not explicitly stated or illustrated. For example, the literal meaning of the text *Samantha loved her dog Rex* is that Samantha loved her dog Rex. The same meaning is only implied by the text *Samantha never failed to take her dog Rex for a walk before school, and she couldn't wait to give him a big hug when she got home.* See *Implied Meaning.*

Literary Elements of Narratives The components of a well-crafted story: setting, character, plot, point of view, style, mood, and theme.

Literary Interpretation An understanding of a story at a personal, often abstract, level. Literary interpretations often result in understanding one's self and the world, not just the events of the story.

Literary Language Phrases that are encountered in written language, but usually not in spoken language, such as *Once upon a time* and *In the previous section.*

Literature Text Set A selection of books with a common theme (e.g., that friends are often found in unusual places), author or illustrator (e.g., books illustrated by Jerry Pinkney), literary element (e.g., tricksters or dynamic characters), or genre (e.g., poetry or animal fantasy).

Literature Theme Unit A series of lessons and other instructional activities organized around books selected for something they have in common, such as an author, an illustrator, a genre, a narrative plot point, an expository structure, or an expository topic.

Making Big Words An approach to advanced word study in which teachers help students to build and discuss meanings of words composed from the letters of a multisyllable target word. First they build one-syllable words using subsets of the letters, then multisyllable words other than the target word, and finally the target word using all of the letters. See *Making Words.*

Making Words A word-work activity, using alphabet cards to construct new words from old words by changing or adding just one letter in a word at a time. For example, children begin with *slip* and exchange the *l* for a *k* to make *skip;* then they may change *skip* to *skin* by exchanging the *p* for an *n.*

Mean Length of Utterance See *Utterance Length.*

Meaning-Form Links Connections between understanding of language and the processing of visual characteristics of text. Children use meaning-form links, for example, when they write with invented spelling (connecting what they know about the sounds of spoken language with what they know about the names and shapes of alphabet letters) or when they connect what they know about the functions of a list (to help you organize and re-member information) with what they know about how a list looks (words or phrases arranged verti-cally, without the punctuation and paragraph struc-ture of a story or a letter from Grandma).

Meanings See *Written Langauge Meanings.*

Message Concept The idea that writing can pre-serve exactly the meanings that a writer wants to convey. Marie Clay identified the discovery of this concept as a significant achievement in emergent lit-eracy. Without it, children must see writing as ran-dom and purposeless and so have little reason to write or to read others' writing. Of course, in reali-ty no writer can exactly convey an intended mes-sage; all writing is open to interpretation by readers, sometimes interpretations quite divergent from what writers intend. Fortunately, the discovery of writing's subtleties and inexactness comes later, after the message concept has served to ignite chil-dren's writing development.

Metacognitive Awareness Consciousness of men-tal processes, including those for word identifica-tion and reading comprehension. Children who read with metacognitive awareness are conscious of how well or poorly they are understanding a text and choose appropriate strategies for maintaining or improving their understanding as they continue to read.

Metalinguistic Awareness Conscious attention to properties of language. This includes phonological awareness but also awareness of other aspects of language, such as concept of written word, sen-tence structure, and concept of story. Children demonstrate metalinguistic awareness when they can finger-point read a familiar text, when they cor-rectly use such words as *question* and *statement*, and when they can retell a story including important in-formation from the beginning, middle, and end of the story. See *Phonological Awareness, Concept of Written Word, Syntax,* and *Concept of Story.*

Mini-Lesson A component of writing instruction, in which a teacher provides to a whole-class group a short period of focused instruction about some small part of the writing process. The purpose of a mini-lesson is merely to raise students' awareness,

sometimes as a reminder of what they already know and sometimes as an introduction to a new topic. More individualized writing instruction oc-curs in small groups and during individual writing conferences.

Miscue Analysis A profiling of a child's use and misuse of grapho-phonic, grapho-semantic, and grapho-syntactic cuing systems, determined from an examination of mistakes documented on a run-ning record. See *Running Record, Phonics, Grapho-Se-mantics,* and *Grapho-Syntax.*

Mock Cursive Horizontally arranged wavy lines. These are also called *Linear Scribble Writing.*

Mock Letters Symbols that look like conventional letters of the alphabet because they are composed of letter features, but are not conventional letters. These are also called *Letter-Like Forms.*

Modeled Writing Instruction in which teachers compose a text as children watch. The teacher first thinks aloud about what he or she might write, then talks through the composition process. The teacher then thinks aloud while rereading and revising the text.

Monitoring Assessments Assessments to track children's progress and to identify those who need adjustments in instruction, such as placement in a different reading instruction group. These contrast with screening assessments. See *Screening Assess-ments.*

Morning Message A short text written by the teacher, on a topic that is relevant to students' class-room lives, and posted for children's easy access, for example, written on a special part of the chalk board or written on chart paper and hung on an easel.

Morpheme The smallest unit of meaning. *Hose* is one morpheme; it means a flexible tube through which gases or fluids can move. *Toes* is two mor-phemes; it means *toe* plus *plural* or more than one terminal digit on a vertebrate foot. The /z/ at the end of *hose* is just part of the single unit of meaning pronounced /hOz/; the /z/ at the end of *toes* is an extra unit of meaning, a sound added to /tO/ to make it plural, to give it the extra meaning of *more than one.*

Motif A kind of character, event, or other story el-ement recurring across many folk or fairy tales.

Motor Schemes Learned patterns of movement. Motor schemes for drawing and writing include controlled, intentional making of lines and shapes, usually with a hand-held pen, pencil, crayon, or maker.

Multicultural Literature Fiction and nonfiction that, in addition to representing the lives and concerns of a nation's own majority, also represent the lives and concerns of cultural, ethnic, and religious minorities and peoples living beyond its borders. These representations include minority races and members of minority religions within a nation and other national cultures beyond a nation's borders (even those that are the majority in another nation). Among minority ethnic groups in the United States are African Americans, Asian Americans, Hispanic Americans, and Native Americans. None of these groups is homogenous; all contain their own cultural diversity. See *Culturally Authentic Literature*.

Multiliteracy Using and honoring in both print and speech students' home languages and English.

Multiple Literacies Knowledge of and abilities to make meaning from more than one print medium (for example, from print on computer screens as well as from print in books) or from more than one symbol system (for example, from the visual features of paintings as well as from the graphemes used in reading and writing).

Novices Children in the second of the four broad phases of literacy development described in this book (see Chapter 3). Novices write with an intention to communicate, and their pretend reading is based on their understanding that reading must be meaningful. See *Beginners, Experimenters,* and *Conventional Readers and Writers*.

Onset The initial consonant, consonant blend, or consonant digraph of a syllable. For example, the onsets in *pan, plan,* and *than* are *p-, pl-,* and *-th*. See *Rhyming Words* and *Rime*.

Open-Ended Activities Activities that encourage many different correct responses or contributions. For example, providing an alternative ending to a story is an open-ended activity. This does not mean that "anything goes." There are poor responses (endings that are inconsistent with what readers know about the story's setting, characters, and events), but there is more than one possible good response. In contrast, providing some piece of factual information, such as the name of a story's main character or the location of a particular event, is not an open-ended activity.

Oral Comprehension Understanding of speech. In school settings, oral comprehension usually refers to understanding of classroom conversation, spoken directions, story telling, and books read to children.

Orchestration The ability to coordinate many literacy processes at one time. As some literacy processes become automatic and unconscious, readers and writers are able to give their conscious attention to others.

Orthographic Decoding See *Decoding by Analogy*.

Orthographics Advanced word study based on complex spelling principles that go beyond simple sound-letter associations, including study of phonograms and morphemes. See *Orthography, Phonogram,* and *Morpheme*.

Orthography A system for associating word parts (individual sounds or larger chunks of spoken words) with individual letters or combinations of letters. Orthography is always systematic and often abstract. It is systematic in that it is not random. A writer can't use any string of letters he or she wants when spelling a particular word; there are sound-based and meaning-based reasons for the letter combinations used in a particular written language. For example, in English associating the letter *t* with the sound /t/ enables us to spell the final sound of the word *pit* but also the sound /t/ in literally thousands of other words in which it occurs, sometimes in the final position, but also at the beginning or middle of a word. That is being systematic based on sounds. It is equally important that the /t/ sound be allowed to be associated with the *-ed* at the end of the word *walked*, even though *-ed* looks nothing like *t*. We always associate *-ed* at the end of a verb with the meaning *past tense* even though that *-ed* is sometimes pronounced /d/ (as in *played*), sometimes /uhd/ (as in *wanted*), and, yes, sometimes /t/ (as in *walked*). That is being systematic based on meaning. Orthography is abstract when it ignores some sounds in favor of others (for example, ignoring the /ch/ sound between the /t/ and /r/ sounds in *train*). *Orthography* is synonymous with *Spelling*.

Participation Structures Ways of speaking, listening, and taking turns in conversation. These differ from culture to culture. For example, some cultures require eye contact between all participants in a conversation; in others, eye contact between participants of different social status is considered rude. In some cultures, speaking turns in conversation are exchanged very rapidly; in others, more slowly. When members of different cultures, with differing expectations about speed of turn-taking, converse, the faster turn-takers seem to the slower turn-takers often to be interrupting and giving them little opportunity to speak.

Pattern Innovation Composing a new text based on manipulation of salient features of an existing text. For example, a teacher and students in a shared writing activity may write an extension of the story of the Gingerbread Boy by using the story's frequently repeated language about the boy's running away and his saying "You can't catch me. I'm the Gingerbread Boy," but creating a new character for him to run from.

Phoneme Repertoire The collection of sounds that a language uses in meaningful ways. In each language, approximately forty sounds are phonemic, that is, they are combined and contrasted in meaningful ways in that language's words. However, one language's repertoire of forty or so phonemes seldom exactly matches another language's repertoire of forty or so phonemes. For example, some languages have phonemes not found in English (e.g., the rolled *r* sound in Spanish that is absent in English), and English has phonemes not found in some other languages (e.g., the /ng/ sound in English that is absent in Spanish). See *Phonemes*.

Phonemes The smallest units of sound that are combined and contrasted in meaningful ways in a language's words. For example, in English, the phonemes /p/, /i/, and /t/ are combined to make the word *pit,* and the phonemes /p/ and /b/ are contrasted when distinguishing the words *pit* and *bit* (thus the difference between /p/ and /b/ is meaningful; it allows us to distinguish between the large seed in the middle of a peach and what you did when you sunk your teeth into a peach). But the difference between the phoneme /p/ in *pit* and the phoneme /p/ in *spit* (the /p/ in *pit* is breathy or pronounced with a burst of air, enough to move a piece of paper held before the mouth; the /p/ in *spit* isn't breathy) is not a difference between phonemes (both pronunciations fall within the category of sounds we call the phoneme /p/). That's because the breathy /p/ versus the breathless /p/ difference is not by itself meaningful. *Pit* and *spit* convey two different meanings (the large seed in the middle of a peach and what you do if you expel from

your mouth the worm that was in the peach) not by virtue of contrasting breathy /p/ and breathless /p/ but rather by virtue of contrasting /p/ alone and /p/ combined with another phoneme, /s/. English has no pair of words that is different only because one has a breathy /p/ where the other has a breathless /p/. If there were such a pair, then that difference would be meaningful. Then it could not remain a difference within the /p/ category; we would then have to create two different phonemes, and give them different symbols, perhaps /p/ for the breathy one and /ᴘ/ for the breathless one, just as we already have two different symbols, /p/ and /b/, for the different phonemes—that is, the meaningfully different sounds—at the beginnings of *pit* and *bit.*

Phonemic Awareness The aspect of phonological awareness that involves conscious attention to the phonemes of a spoken language. Children demonstrate phonemic awareness, for example, when they can segment phonemes (e.g., separately pronounce /d/, /aw/, and /g/ after hearing and saying the word *dog*), blend phonemes (e.g., hear /d/, /aw/, and /g/ separately pronounced and combine them to say *dog*), or write with invented spelling (e.g., write *chair* as HAR, because they hear the three phonemes in *chair*—/ch/, /A/, and /r/—and represent them with H, A, and R due to hearing those sounds in the letters' names, the /ch/ in *aitch,* the /A/ in *ay,* and the /r/ in *ar*).

Phonics One of three interrelated systems for linking the forms of written language to its meanings. Phonics is the more or less regular linking of letters and combinations of letters with sounds (phonemes) and combinations of sounds. Also called *grapho-phonics.* When particular letters and combinations of letters (phonograms) frequently—even if not always—stand for particular sounds or combinations of sounds, then those relationships merit teaching as part of the academic subject known as phonics. For example, the letter *b* has a very high frequency of association with the phoneme /b/ (as in *bit, rub, alphabet*); the combination of letters *ch* has a very high frequency of association with the phoneme /ch/ (as in *chin, such, teacher*); the phonogram *ine* has a very high frequency of association with the combination of sounds /In/ (as in *fine, twine, vine*). These relationships do not always hold; that is why our definition includes the words *more or less regular.* For example, *b* does not stand for the sound /b/ in the word *comb, ch* does not stand for the sound /ch/ in the word *machine,* and *ine* does not stand for /In/ in *machine.* Nonetheless, they hold frequently enough to warrant teaching them, especially in conjunction with the other two systems for linking the forms of written language to its meanings, grapho-syntax and grapho-semantics. See *Meaning-Form Links, Phoneme, Phonogram, Grapho-Syntax* and *Grapho-Semantics.*

Phonogram A combination of letters that is reliably associated with a particular pronunciation, especially in the middle and final positions of a word. For example, *-an* is pronounced /an/ in the middle and final positions of *ban, can, fan, pan, plan, tan,* and *van.*

Phonological Awareness Conscious attention to the sounds of spoken language. This includes awareness of phonemes, but also awareness of other units of language, such as syllables, onsets, and rimes, and other aspects of the sounds of a language, such as intonation patterns. Children demonstrate phonological awareness, for example, when they can provide a rhyming word (e.g., *dog* when given *log*) or when they can tell the difference between the question *Sandy can skip rope?* (with end-rising intonation) and the statement *Sandy can skip rope* (with end-falling intonation). See *Phonemic Awareness, Onset, Rime* and *Rhyming Words.*

Phonology Of the four linguistic systems, the one that has to do with sounds. This includes a wide range, from phonemes (e.g., that *night* is composed of three phonemes, /n I t/) to inflections (e.g., *SANDY can whistle* vs. *Sandy can WHISTLE,* where the first emphasizes who can whistle, that of Sandy and her friend Patty, only Sandy can; the second emphasizes what Sandy can do, that she can whistle but perhaps not perform a handstand).

Portfolio A large folder in which a teacher keeps samples of a child's work. See *Work Samples.*

Portfolio Conference A meeting of a student and teacher at which the student selects work samples to include in his or her portfolio and tells why each sample should be included.

Portfolio Summary A description of a child's literacy growth and achievement, based on evidence in the child's portfolio, but also on the teacher's anecdotal notes and analyses and the child's performances on any other assessments. See *Portfolio, Anecdotal Notes,* and *Reflections on Anecdotal Notes.*

Pragmatics Of the four linguistic systems, the one that has to do with how language is used in everyday life to get done that which would be difficult or impossible without language. Pragmatics includes, for example, requests for action and forms of politeness, such that a child who says, "May I have a cookie?" or better yet, "Please, may I have a cookie?" is more effective than a child who only points in the general direction of the cookie jar and grunts.

Prefix An affix attached to the beginning of a base word, for example, *-un* in *unbelievable.* See *Affix.*

Preproduction The first of four phases of children's second language acquisition, most notable for children's speaking very little in the second language. While they are silent, English language learners in this phase are actively listening to the sounds of English spoken around them and trying to connect the actions they see with the sounds they hear. They intuitively acquire information about English intonation, speed, pausing, loudness, and pitch. See *Early Production, Speech Emergence,* and *Intermediate Fluency.*

Pretend Reading A telling of the content of a book, rather than an actual reading of the text, but performed as if it were an actual reading (with reading intonation and often with remembered words and phrases), by a child who cannot read conventionally, usually of a very familiar or favorite book, one that the child frequently has heard read to him or her.

Prewriting A writing process in which a writer searches for a topic, identifies his or her audience and purpose, and collects ideas about which to write. See *Drafting, Revising, Editing,* and *Publishing.*

Prior Knowledge What readers know about a topic before reading about it.

Project Approach Children's construction of simulations of real-world settings for literacy activity. For example, they may build a shoe store. They bring shoe boxes, shopping bags, and old shoes from home; collect newspaper and magazine advertising for shoes; make signs; set up shelves, benches, and floor length mirrors; and make a checkout counter with a toy cash register, a pretend credit card machine, and child-made coupons and receipt forms. Once established, these function like dramatic-play-with-print centers. See *Dramatic-Play-with-Print Center.*

Publishing A writing process in which a writer shares his or her work with an audience. See *Prewriting, Drafting, Revising,* and *Editing.*

Readers' Theater A simple form of dramatization in which players read their lines rather than memorize them. Readers' theater scripts can be composed by the performers as they revise the text of a story they wish to perform, selecting important events and dialogue, and creating descriptive lines for a narrator.

Referential Dimension The range of a writer's possible relationship to the subject matter of the text she or he is composing, from the personal and immediate to the abstract and imaginative. A writer of autobiography works at the personal and immediate end of the referential dimension; a writer of science fiction works at the abstract and imaginative end.

Reflections on Anecdotal Notes Written judgments about the quality of speech, reading, writing, or other actions previously recorded in anecdotal notes. These reflections frequently state conclusions—based on the behavior recorded in the anecdotal notes—about what children have learned, what they know, and/or what they can do. As such, they inform future instruction. See *Anecdotal Notes.*

Reliability A test's yielding the same or similar results over several administrations.

Repeated Reading Reading stories or parts of stories over and over again until the reader can read the selection with only three to six errors. The selections are fifty to one hundred words in length, and the reader must first have listened to and understood the story.

Repertoire of Literacy Knowledge A complete list of what one knows about writing and reading. With children, this can cover a range from nonconventional to conventional knowledge. Children will display different knowledges from their repertoires depending on the task demands of a particular literacy event. For example, a four-year-old boy whose repertoire includes scribble writing and conventional alphabet letter writing may use conventional letters to write his or her name on a classroom sign-in sheet and use scribble writing to pretend to take a classmate's restaurant order in the dramatic play center.

Response Journal A journal in which readers record their reactions to and thoughts about books they read.

Retelling Checklist A list of the important events in a story and a story's important and sophisticated vocabulary. Teachers use a retelling checklist to record which of those a child includes in his or her retelling of the story. See *Pretend Reading.*

Revising A writing process in which a writer rereads a current draft of a writing piece, rethinks what he or she has written, and improves word choice, phrasing, sentence structure, sentence order, and the overall structure of the piece. The goal is greater clarity and coherence. The purpose is to make a piece better communicate what the author intends; those intentions can become clearer to the writer himself or herself as a result of the rereading and rethinking that are part of revision. Final corrections of punctuation and spelling do not occur until the editing process. See *Prewriting, Drafting, Editing,* and *Publishing.*

Rhyming Word Family See *Word Family.*

Rhyming Words Words that have the same rime but different onsets, for example, *can, fan, pan, plan, tan,* and *than.* See *Onset, Rime,* and *Word Family.*

Rime The part of a syllable from its vowel though its end. For example, the rimes in *pan, pen,* and *pie* are *-an, -en,* and *-ie.* Rhyming words have identical rimes, for example, *-an* in *can, fan, pan, plan, tan,* and *than.* See *Rhyming Words* and *Onset.*

Romance Representation A drawing that begins as unintentional but is later claimed to represent something. A child romances a representation when, for example, he or she scribbles and then later looks at the scribbling and says, "This is my blanket."

Rubric An assessment tool that identifies required elements of a work sample and provides a range of descriptions of possible achievements of each element. Teachers compare students' work with the rubric to determine what levels of performance the work represents. Some rubrics assign numerical values to the descriptions, yielding a total numerical score for the work sample.

Running Record A real-time documentation of a child's reading performance, made by observing the child read a grade-leveled text and marking a copy of the text or using checks and other symbols on a separate sheet of paper to show accurate readings, substitutions, omissions, insertions, repetitions, self-corrections, and teacher prompts. A running record provides information about the child's instructional and independent reading levels and his or her use of cuing systems during reading. See *Frustrational Reading Level, Instructional Reading Level, Independent Reading Level, Phonics, Grapho-Semantics,* and *Grapho-Syntax.*

Say-It and Move-It Activity Moving a poker chip or other token into a framed space for each sound segment of a word. At first, children might use this activity while attending to syllables, later to phonemes. If they are learning phonemic awareness, for example, they have a pile of poker chips and a laminated sheet of paper at the top of which are drawn three boxes in a horizontal array. Then as they say each phoneme of *mop,* they slide a chip to one of three boxes drawn at the top of the sheet: one chip to the left-most box for /m/, then another chip to the middle box for /ah/, and finally a third chip to the right-most box for /p/. The use of say-it and move-it with phonemes is also called an *Elkonin box activity* for its originator, D. B. Elkonin. When the tokens are letter tiles, say-it-and-move-it can be used to teach spelling. For example, moving *m, o,* and *p* letter tiles into the left, middle, and right boxes would teach associating those letters with the corresponding phonemes in *mop.*

Scaffolding An adult's or an older child's assisting a child to perform within his or her Zone of Proximal Development. See *Zone of Proximal Development.*

Schema A mental structure in which one stores information necessary for the understanding of a concept. A schema for the game of *football* contains such information as how to play football, how a football field is configured, what positions football players play (e.g., quarterback, center, tight end) and how many points are awarded for scoring plays (e.g., a touchdown, a field goal, a touchback).

School Literacy Perspective A view of reading and writing as ends in themselves, skills to be learned, rather than as tools for genuine communication. This view contrasts with a situated literacy perspective. See *Situated Literacy Perspective.*

Scope and Sequence A list of skills students in a particular grade are expected to learn and that their teachers are required to assess and teach. A scope and sequence of skills is usually found in a published basal reading series or in a district or state curriculum guide.

Screening Assessments Assessments given at the beginning of the school year to support teachers' decisions about initial instruction, such as in which reading group to place a student so as to best match what the student knows and is ready to learn with what will be taught to a particular group. These contrast with monitoring assessments. See *Monitoring Assessments.*

Scribbling Marks made on a page without control, that is, without any intention of making a particular representation, neither drawing nor text.

Self-Generative Readers and Writers The third of three phases of conventional reading and writing (see Chapter 5). Self-generative readers and writers are highly skilled, control many reading and writing strategies, and write and read a variety of complex texts. See *Conventional Readers and Writers, Early Readers and Writers,* and *Transitional Readers and Writers.*

Semantics Of the four linguistic systems, the one that has to do with meanings. Semantics includes vocabulary knowledge (a ball is a round object that can be rolled, thrown, caught, and sometimes bounced), knowledge of word parts (*to roll* means to move end over end along a plane, and *rolled* is *roll* plus *ed* and so it means *roll* plus *past tense* or *roll* plus *already happened*), and knowledge of how words work together (*The ball rolled down the _____* can end with *hill* or *hallway,* but not with *toothpick*).

Shared Language Language that English language learners and their teachers use easily when communicating about reading and writing tasks. Repeated use of a few key words or phrases in instructional routines makes them accessible to students when they can as yet speak and understand very little other English.

Shared Reading A form of reading aloud to children in which, in addition to reading for enjoyment and understanding, the teacher and children read for teaching and learning literacy concepts and strategies. The text (for example, a big book) is large enough so that the children can read the text along with the teacher. See *Big Book.*

Shared Writing Instruction in which the teacher writes on chart paper so that students can see and contribute ideas for the content of the piece. During shared writing, teachers model for children how to write texts that serve a variety of purposes. See *Interactive Writing.*

Shared Writing with Write On An instructional activity that combines shared writing and write-on charts. Teachers compose a text on chart paper so that students can see and teachers can explain writing processes, and then the chart-paper text is available for students to write on during choice time. Children may, for example, copy letters, words, or phrases. They write directly on the chart paper above the teacher's writing. See *Shared Writing* and *Write-On Charts*.

Sight Words Words that one can read immediately upon seeing them, automatically, and without sounding them out. Sight-word vocabularies are personal; their composition varies from one learner to another. They depend on the learning of the individual reader. The words that one reader has learned to read on sight may not be the same as those that another reader has learned to read that way. Eventually, as readers become more skilled, their sight-word vocabularies become large and overlapping. That is, all good readers know a great number of sight words, many of them the same words as in other good readers' sight-word vocabularies, including all high-frequency words. See *High-Frequency Words*.

Sign Concept See *Contextual Dependency*.

Sign-In Procedure A classroom routine in which children begin their day by writing their names on a special form, the sign-in sheet. This serves an attendance-taking function and gives children practice writing their names. Variations include, for very young children, finding their name card and depositing it in a special box and, for older children, in addition to writing their names, writing an answer to a question-of-the-day.

Simple Sentence A sentence composed of a subject and its predicate (e.g., *Chris joined Angela at the piano*, in which *Chris* is the subject and *joined Angela at the piano* is the predicate). See *Compound Sentence, Complex Sentence*, and *Syntax*.

Sit and Stay Teachers' remaining in a center for an extended period of time in order to engage children in authentic conversation.

Situated Literacy Perspective A view of reading and writing as activities taking place in the real world for the purpose of achieving real-life goals. This view contrasts with a school literacy perspective. See *School Literacy Perspective*.

Sound Boxes See *Say-It and Move-It Activity*.

Sounding Literate Children's use of literary language, reading intonation, and dialogue markers (such as *he said*) as they compose their own stories, read their compositions, and pretend to read familiar storybooks. See *Literary Language*.

Speech Density The number of words that infants hear in a given period of time. The more words spoken to an infant in a ten-minute period, for example, the greater the speech density. High speech densities, by exposing children to large numbers of words, result in children's acquiring large vocabularies. Using large numbers of words usually means putting those words into longer and more complex sentences than would be the case when using fewer words. As a result, high speech densities also contribute to children's learning more complex syntax.

Speech Emergence The third of four phases of children's second language acquisition, notable for children's continuing to acquire vocabulary and developing a wider range of sentence structures. See **Preproduction, Early Production**, and **Intermediate Fluency**.

Spelling See *Orthography*.

Story Grammar A representation of the structure of a typical narrative, including the required elements of a main character or characters; a setting; a problem-setting action or event; a goal; an attempt or attempts to solve the problem or attain the goal; resolution (solution of the problem or attainment of the goal); and the main character's or characters' reaction to the resolution. *Story Grammar* is also called *Story Structure*.

Story Structure See *Story Grammar*.

Strategic Readers Readers who take initiative in solving their own reading difficulties by recognizing problems and choosing appropriate strategies for solving them.

Strategy Sheet A graphic that readers fill in as they read to help them apply a target comprehension strategy. For example, for the strategy of identifying a story character's traits, they may write a character's name in the center of a character cluster strategy sheet and then in spaces around that, write information as they find it about the character's traits.

Subtractive Approaches Instructional methods that attempt to replace children's home languages and cultures with English and mainstream culture. These contrast with additive approaches that build on students' home languages and cultures. See *Additive Approaches.*

Suffix An affix attached to the end of a base word, for example, *-able* in *unbelievable.* See *Affix.*

Symbol Salad A mixture of letters, numbers, other symbols, and letter-like forms.

Syntax Of the four linguistic systems, the one that has to do with sentence structure. In English, syntax mostly uses word order. For example, noun-verb-noun signifies subject-verb-object: With *The goat kicked the boy,* the goat is the kicker and the boy is the one who was kicked; with *The boy kicked the goat,* the boy is the kicker and the goat is the one who was kicked.

Systematic Observations A means of assessment that involves planned watching of children's activities with a focus on preselected behaviors and resulting in a written record of what was observed.

Systematic Phonics Instruction Teaching of phonics by following a sequence of skills considered necessary for efficient word decoding and spelling. Most sequences are arranged from those skills considered easiest to those considered most difficult.

Tabula Rasa Literally, "blank slate." According to the *Tabula Rasa* theory, a newborn child's mind is a blank slate; it is empty of knowledge or schemas.

Telegraphic speech Two- or three-word combinations that signal such semantic content as *subject-verb, verb-object,* or *subject-verb-object* without the structural morphemes that are found in mature speech. *Mommy pull, Pull wagon,* and *Mommy pull wagon* are examples of subject-verb, verb-object, and subject-verb-object utterances in telegraphic speech. *Mommy is pulling the wagon* is an example of an utterance in mature speech; it contains the structural morphemes (*is, ing,* and *the*) that are missing in the examples of telegraphic speech.

Text and Toy Sets A storybook and related, realistic, small-scale toys and other props. These are used to stimulate dramatic play about books. During free-choice time, for example, children might tell a story they have heard in an earlier read-aloud and dramatize it using the toys and props.

Text Format The configuration of print characteristic of a particular use of print or purpose for writing. For example, a grocery list, with its collection of words, phrases, and product names arranged vertically constitutes a text form quite different in appearance from a letter to Grandma, with its heading, salutation, body (sentences and paragraphs containing a message), closing, and signature.

Text Reconstruction Reassembling a sentence or other short text from word cards, one for each word of the text.

Thinking Mental processing. One way to characterize thinking is in terms of schemas: Thinking involves calling to mind information from schemas and using that information to perform mental actions such as making inferences, predictions, or generalizations, or drawing conclusions.

Timeless Present Tense A verb form that implies an existing, continuous state of affairs, rooted in the past and expected to last into the future. Timeless present tense is often used to tell about the nature of things, for example, *Squirrels are very active creatures.* This contrasts with a time-specific use of the present tense, used for telling about a current, but changeable condition, for example, *The baby is hungry.*

Total Physical Response (TPR) A vocabulary development activity for English language learners in which teachers hold up an object or a picture of an object and say its name, and children respond physically rather than verbally to indicate their understanding.

Transaction A unique interaction between a reader and a text, founded on prior knowledge and resulting in personal understandings and interpretations. See *Prior Knowledge.*

Transitional Readers and Writers The second of three phases of conventional reading and writing (see Chapter 5). Transitional readers and writers use multiple sophisticated decoding and comprehension strategies to read fluently and to understand complicated informational texts and stories, including chapter books. They become conventional spellers and write in several genres. See *Conventional Readers and Writers, Early Readers and Writers,* and *Self-Generative Readers and Writers.*

Transitive Verb A verb that has a direct object. For example, in the sentence *The goat kicked the boy, kicked* is a transitive verb. The sentence not only names an action (*kicked*), but also names a receiver of the action (*the boy*). That receiver of the action is the direct object. Sentences with transitive verbs are sometimes called Subject-Verb-Object sentences, or SVO sentences. (The subject is the doer of the action; in the example sentence, the subject is

The goat.) Not all verbs are transitive. If they do not have direct objects, they are intransitive verbs. In the sentence *Sam laughed, laughed* is an intransitive verb; there is no receiver of the action of laughing.

Utterance Complexity How many and what kinds of phrases and clauses a child uses to make a number of different kinds of sentences.

Utterance Length The number of morphemes a child uses, on average, in a turn at talking. Also called *Mean Length of Utterance.* Utterance length is computed by sampling a child's language, counting the number of morphemes in the whole sample, and dividing by the number of the child's turns at talking in the sample.

Validity A test's measuring what it purports to measure, for example, that a word identification test really measures word identification and not, for example, world knowledge or concept knowledge.

Vocabulary Word knowledge.

Vocabulary Prop Box A box of objects that are mentioned in a storybook or information book. Teachers display and talk about the items in connection with reading the books aloud, in order to enhance children's vocabularies.

Vocabulary Variety The number of different words, especially rare words, that a child understands and uses.

Volume of Reading and Writing The amount of text read or written in a day or the number of minutes in a day spent reading and writing continuous texts (not working with words, filling in work sheets, or answering questions).

Vowel Markers Letters whose function is not to represent their own sounds but instead to indicate the long quality or other non-short quality of a neighboring vowel. Without vowel markers, vowels often have the default, that is, short, quality. For example, the final *e* in *bite* is silent, but it nonetheless has the important role of marking the *i* as long (*i* in *bite* has the sound /I/). In contrast, *bit* does not need a vowel marker; its vowel is short (/i/). Similarly, the *w* in *fawn* marks the *a* as having a non-short quality, in this case /aw/. Without the vowel marker *w*, the *a* would be, by default, short (/a/); the word would be *fan,* pronounced /fan/. Of course, as with most phonics generalizations, this one does not always apply. That is why we said "often" about default short vowels. It's often the case that unmarked vowels are short, but not al-

ways. The greatest number of exceptions is the case of open vowels that are often long without having markers (e.g., the *e* in *be* and the *o* in *so*), but there are many other exceptions (e.g., the *o* in *dog,* which in most dialects is /aw/ not the short /ah/, and the *a* in *car* which is /ah/ not the short /a/).

Vowel Phonemes One of the two major categories of sounds in a language. The other is *consonant phonemes.* Vowel sounds involve a more open, unrestricted flow of sound than do consonant sounds and for that reason are sometimes described as lacking friction. Consonant sounds are more clipped or restricted and are sometimes described as having friction. In any language, there are fewer vowels than consonants. A vowel sound is the most prominent sound in a syllable. In English, vowel phonemes include /a/, /A/, /ah/, /aw/, /e/, /E/, /i/, /I/, /O/, /oi/, /oo/, /OO/, /ow/, /uh/, and /U/ (see Table 1.2). See *Consonant Phonemes.*

"What Can You Show Us? Activity An activity in which a teacher displays a new text and, before reading it, invites children to demonstrate what they know about it. Children with a wide range of reading abilities can participate successfully. For example, some may identify individual letters, some may point out punctuation, some may read sight words, some may show how they decode a decodable word, and some may read whole phrases or sentences. The teacher uses children's demonstrated knowledge when they later read the text together.

Word Family A group of words that rhyme; they have the same onset but different rimes (for example, *band, hand, land, sand, stand*). Also called a *Rhyming Word Family.* See *Onset, Rime,* and *Rhyming Words.*

Word Hunt A word-study activity in which children search for words with particular spelling patterns in books, magazines, and newspapers.

Word Profile The outline of a printed word. Due to the different shapes of the letters from which words are composed, their profiles can differ considerably (compare **slipped** and **sooner**).

Word Sort Activity A word-study activity in which children collect words by making word cards for them, and then, after several days of collecting, arrange the cards according to the words' spelling patterns.

Word Wall A display on a classroom wall or large bulletin board of word cards for children's reference when reading and writing, usually of undecodable and high-frequency words, grouped by initial letter.

Work Samples Artifacts that children produce during learning, practice, and application of knowledge and skills. As inputs for assessment, work samples have a concreteness and immediacy not always found in children's performances on tests or even in teachers' observation notes and anecdotal records.

Write-On Chart A shared writing or interactive writing chart that is hung low on a wall or placed on an easel for individual children to write on during their free time or center time. See *Shared Writing* and *Interactive Writing.*

Writing the Room An activity in which children walk around their classroom in search of print—usually carrying pencils and paper on clipboards—and then copy words that interest them.

Writing Workshop An approach to teaching writing that includes regularly scheduled time for children to work as writers ("workshop time") by using the processes of drafting, revising, editing, and sharing. Teachers teach mini-lessons about writing processes, and students and teachers hold writing conferences and celebrate students' published writing.

Written Language Assessment Any activity to determine a person's state of knowledge of, understanding about, or ability with reading and writing.

Written Language Forms All aspects of how written language looks. These cover a wide range. At the small end of that range are the features of which individual alphabet letters are composed (such as two vertical lines and two diagonal lines for *M* and

a vertical line and part of a circle for *P*). At the large end are the organizational features of whole texts (such as the rows of words and phrases that make a list to the collection of chapters that make a novel). See *Letter Features* and *Text Format.*

Written Language Meanings Messages conveyed by texts. These include implied as well as literal meanings. Children have acquired the most important insight about written language when they understand that texts are not randomly occurring, haphazard marks on a page, but rather represent a writer's encoded message that is decodable by a reader. See *Literal Meaning* and *Implied Meaning.*

Written Language Talk Teachers' explanations of the conventions of writing. In a shared writing activity, teachers talk about how they write. Such talk is about anything to do with the writing process, from features of a letter of the alphabet (e.g., "I'm making an *N* with on up-and-down line, a slanted line, and another up-and-down line") to elements of story grammar ("I know that a story usually has a problem for one of the characters to solve, so in my story Michel is wondering what to do about his dog chewing his grandmother's favorite shoes. I'm going to write, 'Michel wondered . . .'"). See *Shared Writing.*

Zone of Proximal Development Vygotsky's notion of a space between what a child can do on his or her own and what he or she can do with the help of a more knowledgeable other person, usually an adult. A four-year-old girl, who can put on her shoes but can't tie them, operates in the zone of proximal development when she makes the first knot with the help of her mother and then holds down that knot with her finger while her mother forms loops and makes of them the second, finishing knot.

Name Index

Subject Index